THE SOVIET UNION

THE
SOVIET
UNION

Third Edition

Washington, D.C.

Congressional Quarterly

Congressional Quarterly, an editorial research service and publishing company, serves clients in the fields of news, education, business, and government. It combines Congressional Quarterly's specific coverage of Congress, government, and politics with the more general subject range of an affiliated service, Editorial Research Reports.

Congressional Quarterly publishes the *Congressional Quarterly Weekly Report* and a variety of books, including college political science textbooks under the CQ Press imprint and public affairs paperbacks on developing issues and events. CQ also publishes information directories and reference books on the federal government, national elections, and politics, including the *Guide to the Presidency*, the *Guide to Congress*, the *Guide to the U.S. Supreme Court*, the *Guide to U.S. Elections*, *Politics in America*, and *Congress A to Z: CQ's Ready Reference Encyclopedia*. The *CQ Almanac*, a compendium of legislation for one session of Congress, is published each year. *Congress and the Nation*, a record of government for a presidential term, is published every four years.

CQ publishes the *Congressional Monitor*, a daily report on current and future activities of congressional committees, and several newsletters including *Congressional Insight*, a weekly analysis of congressional action, and *Campaign Practices Reports*, a semimonthly update on campaign laws.

An electronic online information system, Washington Alert, provides immediate access to CQ's databases of legislative action, votes, schedules, profiles, and analyses.

Library of Congress Cataloging-in-Publication Data

The Soviet Union.—3rd ed.

    p.   cm.

    Includes bibliographical references and index.

    ISBN 0-87187-574-8

    1. Soviet Union—History—20th century. I. Congressional Quarterly, inc.

DK246.S68 1990   90-35821

947.084--dc20   CIP

Editor: Daniel C. Diller
Associate Editor: Colleen McGuiness
Contributing Editors: John L. Moore, Jerry A. Orvedahl
Contributing Writers: Daniel B. Berg, Joel Nathan Levin, Michael G. Smith, Lauren L. Van Metre, Sharon L. Werning
Research Assistant: Robert J. Henneberg
Cover: Design, Jack Auldridge; photo, Agence France-Press/V. Armand/A. Durand
Photo credits: pp. 11, 12, 22, 23, 29, 33, 38, 41, 234, 237, 239 - Library of Congress; pp. 54, 63, 65, 69, 77, 81, 90, 107, 134, 137, 153, 174, 186, 200, 205, 240 - AP/Wide World Photos; pp. 56, 236 - John F. Kennedy Library; p. 68 - National Archives; p. 75 - UN Photo; pp. 103, 116, 142, 221, 222, 223, 224, 225, 229, 231, 233, 235, 241 - Novosti Press; p. 119 - Joel Nathan Levin; pp. 163, 217 - Congressional Quarterly/Michael Jenkins; p. 165 - Daniel C. Diller; p. 168 - Black Star/Steve Patten; p. 195 - *The Washington Post*/Ray Lustig
Graphics: Jack Auldridge
Indexer: Patricia Ruggiero

Table of Contents

Tables, Figures, and Maps

THE
SOVIET
UNION

Introduction

Since 1985, when Mikhail S. Gorbachev became general secretary of the Soviet Communist party, the Soviet Union has undergone unprecedented change. This change has forced Western observers of the USSR to completely revise their theories about the Soviet Union. Most Western scholars admit that much of their analysis written in the early 1980s has been proven wrong. At that time no one had anticipated that in 1990 the Communist party would renounce its monopoly on power and a multi-party system would begin to develop. Similarly, no one predicted that changes in Moscow's attitude toward foreign policy would dispose it to sit by and watch fraternal communist governments in Eastern Europe collapse. And no Sovietologist maintained in 1980 that ten years later the chief economic debate would be how to most expediently achieve a market economy. The changes in the Soviet Union have been far more fundamental than anyone in the West expected even after Gorbachev had been in power a year.

In 1990 the experiment with communism begun in Russia in 1917 appeared to have failed. The Soviet economy was in shambles, and Marxist-Leninist ideology—the basis of Soviet politics, economics, and historical interpretation—had been abandoned by all but a few die-hard conservatives. Even V. I. Lenin, the revered founder of the Soviet state, was not immune to criticism by Soviet journalists and historians.

Gorbachev and his colleagues seemed willing to try anything politically possible that might mitigate the Soviet Union's economic and social problems, regardless of its consistency with Marxist-Leninist thought. Responding to angry accusations from conservative party members at the Twenty-eighth Party Congress in June 1990, Aleksandr Yakovlev, a close Gorbachev adviser, said: "A decision of this congress . . . cannot change the fact that the volume of labor production in South Korea is ten times that of the North, nor the fact that people in West Germany live far better than people in the East."

Under Gorbachev most Soviets have admitted that communism as it was being practiced in the Soviet Union was not working. There is no consensus, however, about what reform path to follow, and Soviet society is becoming increasingly fragmented along ethnic, religious, and philosophical lines. Gorbachev and his reformist colleagues had hoped to orchestrate a gradual reform of Soviet society from the top, but change has developed an uncertain momentum of its own that the government can influence but cannot stop.

The Soviet Economy

More than any other factor, the declining state of the economy has been the catalyst for reform in the Soviet Union. Economic growth had declined sharply during the late 1970s and early 1980s, and the USSR suffered from chronic agricultural production shortfalls, a lack of technological sophistication in most industries, unacknowledged inflation, growing environmental problems, and labor shortages in regions where most industry was located. Only in military production could the Soviet Union compete with the West, but high rates of defense spending weakened the general state of the economy by siphoning off investment from other areas. Despite these problems, the Soviet economy in 1985 was not close to collapse. It likely could have continued to muddle along at a stagnant pace without producing serious domestic upheaval.

Mikhail Gorbachev took power in 1985 unwilling to accept economic stagnation. Yet despite pronouncements advocating a major economic reconstruction, his initial strategy was cautious and seemed to reflect his need to consolidate his political power. He tried to improve economic performance by enforcing greater labor discipline, giving factory managers more autonomy, and introducing more sophisticated technology into the workplace.

Glasnost and Economic Reform

By launching his policy of *glasnost* (openness) soon after taking power, Gorbachev showed that he was willing to risk his personal position and the power of the Communist party to accomplish a complete *perestroika* (restructuring) of the Soviet economy. Glasnost had many elements, including more open and honest news coverage by the Soviet media and greater freedom of expression and speech for Soviet artists and common citizens. The policy was designed to put pressure on conservative bureaucrats to accept economic change by allowing the Soviet people and press to criticize abuses of power and unimaginative or timid leadership. It also was intended to facilitate a wider dissemination of information throughout the Soviet Union and combat the social malaise that afflicted the USSR by giving the Soviet people a bigger say in how the country was run. Gorbachev apparently believed that economic reforms could not succeed without glasnost.

But the policy contained inherent risks. Once Soviet citizens felt free to chastise corrupt regional officials and party bureaucrats in the central government, criticisms of the Communist party and the Soviet leadership could not be far behind. Moreover, moves to make society more open and less repressive risked encouraging dissidents and igniting the ambitions of Soviet ethnic groups. Dynamic nationalism in the non-Russian republics was not a force the Kremlin could be expected to deal with effectively, given the large number of nationalities, their varying demands, and the costs and risks of putting down domestic protests by force.

Considering these possibilities, Gorbachev's approach was daring. He could have continued to try to improve the Soviet economy at the margins as previous Soviet leaders had done and as he had tried to do during his first year in power. Even if conservative bureaucrats remained capable of blocking serious economic restructuring, he had reason to hope that additional limited reforms, such as cutting Soviet defense spending and foreign aid in conjunction with a détente with the West, opening up the Soviet Union to more foreign investment, and significantly increasing the size of private farming plots, might have provided a boost without jeopardizing the central role of the Communist party or the stability of the country.

Failure of Reforms

Beginning in 1987, Gorbachev and his increasingly radical economic advisers responded to the failure of the Soviet economy to improve by accelerating glasnost, introducing democratic elections into Soviet society, and launching more far-reaching economic reforms. The Soviet leadership sanctioned limited private enterprise activities, sought greater Soviet involvement in the international economy, and demanded that enterprises and farms become self-financing. Yet these moves fell far short of the economic overhaul that most Western observers believed was necessary to turn around the Soviet economy. Liberals, such as Russian republic president Boris Yeltsin, criticized Gorbachev for implementing "half-measures."

Gorbachev's economic reforms were jeopardized by their failure to produce short-term gains. The Soviet people likely would have been tolerant of almost any reform that produced an obvious improvement in the standard of living, and neither conservatives nor liberals would have had much ammunition with which to criticize Gorbachev if his reforms were working. But the Soviet economy not only failed to improve, it also seemed to become worse. Economic indicators fell, lines at stores grew, and many food and consumer items became increasingly scarce.

Some Western analysts speculated that even if Gorbachev's team had been able to implement radical economic restructuring involving the introduction of market forces on a wide scale, the chaos involved in transforming the Soviet Union's planned economy into one driven by the market would have prevented short-term economic gains in any case. Gorbachev, however, may have erred in promoting technological improvements at the outset of his reforms instead of focusing on enhancing the production of food and consumer goods. Even if Soviet economic growth rates remained low, gains for the Soviet consumer could have

solidified support among the people for Gorbachev's reform program.

Thus Gorbachev may have failed to achieve economic results that were impossible. But the Soviet people's rising expectations, to which he has contributed, leave his reforms little time to develop.

Nationalities Question

Ethnic upheaval throughout the Soviet Union has destroyed the myth that the USSR's more than one hundred nationalities were bonded together into a fraternal confederation by communism. The union was imposed on most non-Russian minorities by the Soviet Red Army, just as the tsars had used force to attach neighboring nations in Europe and Asia to the Russian empire.

As of 1990 the Soviet Union consisted of fifteen union republics, each with its own culture and many with their own language. Many other smaller ethnic groups existed within these fifteen republics. Besides reinvigorating the Soviet economy, resolving the nationalities question is the most pressing problem facing the Soviet leadership.

Moscow's task is made more difficult by ethnic strife between non-Russian nationalities and economic disparity between the ethnic groups. It also is complicated by the presence of forty million ethnic Russians in the non-Russian republics. Russians always have been resented because they tended to enjoy a slightly higher standard of living and better jobs than local non-Russians. Concessions to the republics risk alienating local Russian populations, who are afraid of discrimination if the republic in which they live is allowed to be controlled by local authorities. Moreover, attacks against Russians in the non-Russian republics likely will fuel Russian nationalism in the Russian republic, which contains half of the Soviet Union's people and most of its territory.

As of July 1990, the Baltic republics of Lithuania, Latvia, and Estonia posed the biggest immediate problem for Gorbachev. Lithuania declared its independence March 11. Gorbachev responded by imposing an economic embargo against Lithuania to force Lithuanian leaders to renounce their declaration of independence. The embargo has since been lifted, but Lithuanians seem determined to gain their complete independence, while Moscow seems equally determined to prevent Lithuania's secession. Latvia and Estonia have taken a more cautious approach, formally declaring their intention to become independent, but saying they will negotiate the terms of separation with the Soviet government.

The Soviet leadership might prefer to let the Baltic states go if they were the only republics seeking independence, but permitting the Baltics to leave the Soviet Union would set a precedent that could encourage an avalanche of demands from independence movements in other republics. The departure of the Baltic states would be a severe blow to the Soviet Union, especially since they constitute one of the country's most prosperous regions, but the secession of the Ukraine with fifty-five million people and much of the Soviet Union's most fertile land would cripple the Soviet economy and intensify the Soviets' food production problems. Therefore, the outcome of the struggle over Baltic independence may determine the fate of the Soviet Union.

Secessionist sentiments are not the only ethnic problem facing Gorbachev. Violence between ethnic groups has erupted in Central Asia and the Caucasus region. In the Caucasus, Moscow has been forced to interpose troops between Christian Armenians and Moslem Azerbaidzhanis when conflicts between them reached the point of open warfare in early 1990. The motivating force behind the conflict has been a dispute over control of the Nagorno-Karabakh region, which is located within Azerbaidzhan but populated primarily by Armenians. The hostility between these groups, however, is centuries old and does not depend solely on the dispute over Nagorno-Karabakh. Gorbachev was forced to commit thousands of troops to the region after members of both sides broke into armories and stole automatic weapons. In the Azerbaidzhani capital of Baku, Azerbaidzhanis attacked local Armenians in what amounted to a pogrom. The Soviet army evacuated many Armenians from the city.

In 1990, Gorbachev stated his intention to develop a new union treaty between Moscow and the republics. Many options exist between a centrally controlled Soviet state and the breakup of the Soviet Union into numerous ethnically based independent nations. The Baltic states and several other republics most likely will achieve some form of independence in the near future. Other republics may choose to be a part of a loose Soviet confederation that would allow them to control most aspects of their local affairs. Change is the one certainty with regard to the nationalities question. By the end of the century the Soviet Union will not exist in its present form.

Soviet Foreign Policy

Of all the changes that have occurred during Gorbachev's years in power, none has astounded the West as much as the transformation of Soviet foreign policy. Although the Soviet Union remains a rival to the West and its huge nuclear arsenal makes it the greatest threat to Western security, the USSR no longer appears to be the menacing giant it was as recently as 1986. In a drive to extricate itself from costly regional conflicts, cut foreign aid and defense spending, encourage foreign trade and investment, and improve its international image, the Soviet leadership has adopted a policy of "new thinking" that has radically transformed its international behavior.

New Thinking in Practice

In 1987 the Soviets provided the breakthrough on a treaty with the United States banning intermediate-range nuclear missiles by agreeing to intrusive verification procedures that they had long rejected. In 1988 Gorbachev announced that the USSR would unilaterally cut a half million troops from its armed forces. In 1989 Moscow withdrew its forces from Afghanistan and began working with the United States to end regional conflicts. Most dramatically, however, the Soviet leadership allowed revolutions to take place in Eastern Europe that effectively broke up the Warsaw Pact military alliance and deprived Moscow of its Eastern European empire. Poland, Hungary, Czechoslovakia, Bulgaria, and Romania have taken control of their own affairs, and East Germany is on a course toward full reunification with West Germany, with the Soviet Union's assent.

The Soviets had maintained their dominance over Eastern Europe by working through local communist governments dependent on Moscow. The Soviets recognized that Eastern Europe was not a typical empire. Since the 1970s it had been an economic drain on the Soviet Union instead of an asset. Yet the Soviets felt obliged to continue dominating it because of its role as a buffer between the Soviet Union and Western Europe.

Soviet troops served as the guarantors of the power of Eastern European governments. If an Eastern European regime appeared to be losing control of its population, or if the government itself appeared to be moving too far toward a political liberalization, Soviet troops could be expected to intervene as they did in Hungary in 1956 and Czechoslovakia in 1968. Moreover, the mere threat of Soviet intervention discouraged revolutionary activities in these nations.

But in 1988 Gorbachev was encouraging Soviet-style economic and political reforms in Eastern Europe, and by 1989 he had made it clear that the Soviet Union no longer would use force to prop up communist governments. The economic and political aspirations of Eastern Europeans had been raised by exposure to the Western media, the example of reform in the Soviet Union, and a growing intolerance for their governments' corruption and rigidity. After the Soviet guarantee was removed, the Eastern European Communists could not resist the demands of their people. With the exception of Nicolae Ceausescu's regime in Romania, the governments of Eastern Europe gave up their power peacefully when massive protests demonstrated that they could not hold on to it.

Changing International Environment

Outside of Eastern Europe, changes in the Soviet Union's international conduct also have altered the international landscape. As the USSR has turned inward to focus on its domestic troubles, it has de-emphasized the international geopolitical struggle with the West and rejected Marxist-Leninist ideology as a significant factor in foreign policy making. Consequently nations that had looked to the Soviet Union as a source of economic and military aid have been forced to repair relations with neighbors or with the West. One such example is Syria, which, faced with cuts in Soviet aid, has pursued a détente with its Arab rival and former ally Egypt.

The dramatic changes in Soviet foreign policy could be seen in the Soviet response to the Iraqi invasion of Kuwait in August 1990. Previously, almost any nation or group that threatened the interests of the West would receive Soviet support, encouragement, or sympathy. The Soviet Union did not cooperate with the West in combating terrorism and rarely condemned terrorist acts against Western citizens, saying they were regrettable but understandable. Although the West had more to lose than the Soviets from the Iraqi invasion and Moscow was a major Iraqi arms supplier, the Kremlin quickly joined the United States in condemning Baghdad and agreed to impose an arms embargo against the Iraqis.

Twenty-eighth Party Congress

The Twenty-eighth Party Congress took place in Moscow on July 2-14, 1990, and marked a significant milestone in the history of the Communist Party of the Soviet Union

(CPSU). The congress began after months of speculation that Gorbachev might resign or be ousted as general secretary. In the weeks immediately preceding the congress, party conservatives appeared to be resurgent. In May 1990, the new Russian republic branch of the CPSU held its first congress, and conservatives scored a striking victory. Ivan Polozkov was elected first secretary, promising adherence to orthodox communism. Fear of the conservative momentum even inspired a few liberal party members (including Boris Yeltsin) to suggest delaying the CPSU congress a few months.

Outcome of the Congress

The congress was held on schedule, however, and through strenuous efforts and political skill Gorbachev was able to rein in the conservatives and emerge stronger than ever. After Gorbachev had jockeyed for ten days to avoid a vote of confidence on his program, conservatives ultimately rallied behind him and supported his bid to be reelected as general secretary, primarily because they had no viable alternative candidate. In addition, leading conservative Yegor Ligachev was defeated overwhelmingly for the post of deputy general secretary by Gorbachev's candidate Vladimir Ivashko. Delegates warned that Ligachev's election would result in massive defections from the party ranks. After suffering the defeat, Ligachev lost his other party leadership posts. Some observers have speculated that historians will regard the Twenty-eighth Party Congress as the last gasp of the conservative opposition to Gorbachev.

However, Gorbachev was unable to exert his will as successfully on the left. Some liberals chose to quit the party, despite Gorbachev's prevention of a conservative takeover. The leaders of the liberal Democratic Platform bloc had warned that, unless the party adopted broad reforms at the congress, they would leave the party. Near the end of the congress, Boris Yeltsin announced to the assembled delegates that he was resigning from the party because maintaining party discipline would conflict with his responsibilities to the Russian people as their highest elected official. Within hours, about twenty-five delegates aligned with the Democratic Platform announced that they were leaving the party to form an opposition group with Yeltsin as their leader. They claimed to represent as much as 40 percent of the party membership. In the days that followed, many other prominent communists, including Gavriil Popov and Anatolii Sobchak—the mayors of Moscow and Leningrad, respectively, turned in their party cards. From January 1990 until the party congress began in July, more than 130,000 communists in the 19 million-member party resigned, and the number of resignations is expected to grow significantly as opposition parties are organized.

Significance of the Congress

The Twenty-eighth Party Congress was significant primarily for two reasons. First, Gorbachev advanced his efforts to transfer power away from party structures to government institutions. He expanded the size of the Politburo and gave representatives from each of the fifteen republics an automatic seat. Consequently the Politburo, once the dominant decision-making body in the Soviet Union, has become too unwieldy and too diluted by minor figures based far from the center of power in Moscow to function as a policy-making body. This will enhance Gorbachev's power as president and the influence of his presidential council—a government body created in 1990.

Second, the congress opened a new era of politics in the Soviet Union. For the first time since the revolution, the party is split at the rank and file level. Ruthless enforcement of democratic centralism always had kept the party monolithic, but no longer. An organized opposition to the party is developing, and given the unpopularity of the party with most Soviet citizens, the Communists may have difficulty holding on to power.

Fate of Gorbachev

In the West Gorbachev is seen as a skillful and tough politician who has done what seemed impossible before he came to power: overcome conservative Communist party resistance to reforms that include genuine elements of democracy, greater respect for the rule of law, and major unilateral concessions in the areas of foreign policy.

Gorbachev has been cheered wildly in Western Europe and the United States. Before Gorbachev the Soviet Union appeared as a blustering, aggressive, imperial colossus that constantly threatened surrounding nations, ignored human rights, and pursued an unceasing military buildup. Gorbachev came to power and unleashed forces that within five years had dissolved the Soviet empire and transformed the USSR into an increasingly responsible and rational member of the world community willing to negotiate on almost any issue. People in the West see the astounding change and credit Gorbachev.

Yet Gorbachev is far less popular in his own country. His diplomatic successes have not shielded him from criticism over his domestic failures. Liberals see him as too timid, while conservatives see him as someone who is willing to destroy the cherished foundations of Soviet communism. Most Soviet citizens see him as a leader who has opened up society but failed to deliver on his promises, especially in the economic sphere. Polls taken in 1990 indicate that most Soviet citizens believe they were better off in 1985 than after five years of Gorbachev's leadership. He has retained his position partly because of his political skill and popularity abroad, and partly because there is no obvious alternative to his leadership. Conservatives and some liberals fear that if Gorbachev were removed somebody more objectionable to them would replace him.

Nevertheless, Gorbachev's position is not secure. Because few groups in the Soviet Union are satisfied with the pace and direction of change, Gorbachev's continuing hold on power at times appears miraculous. His immediate position is threatened by the small but real possibility of a military coup or a conspiracy by Communist party conservatives. In 1987 and possibly as late as 1988, Gorbachev's ouster might have led to a reversal of the process of reform in the Soviet Union. In 1990, however, turning back the clock did not seem possible. Although a reactionary coalition could come to power through a coup, it is unlikely such a leadership could sustain the support of the Soviet people. The population's recent experience with glasnost and democratization and its awareness of the liberalization process in Eastern Europe would make it unlikely to accept a Soviet system patterned after the Brezhnev years. Moreover, Soviet dissatisfaction with the Communist party seems to be irreversible.

Gorbachev also is threatened by the growing political

power of the left. In the short term he has insulated himself from removal from the presidency. In 1990 he was elected to a five-year term as president by the Soviet legislature, thus avoiding a popular vote. But Gorbachev has hinted that he would resign if the economy did not improve by 1992. If the liberal opposition parties being formed garner overwhelming public support, Gorbachev might resign regardless of the economy's performance. Journalist William Pfaff has noted that Gorbachev's place in the current Soviet revolution might be like Aleksandr Kerensky's role in the Russian revolution of 1917—that of a progressive reformer who unintentionally sets the stage for a truly radical transformation of society when his reform program fails to improve the economy or satisfy the people's expectations.

Entering the 1990s

The future does not seem bright to most Soviets. The economy appears to be in a helpless decline, and the chaos in the country is more widespread than at any time since World War II. Interethnic violence has become commonplace, and many of the republics are building their own militias to support their claims of sovereignty. Both street crime and organized crime are rampant. In a recent public opinion poll conducted in Moscow, 75 percent of respondents indicated that the Soviet Union's environmental problems were "very important." Many people are nervous, recognizing that conditions probably will continue to get worse before they get better.

Party officials in particular are frightened of a future that does not have a place for them. In a situation of growing chaos, some fear for their physical safety. The party slowly is losing its grip on power. If the party loses its role in society, these officials expect blame, not gratitude, for the last seventy years.

But from a different perspective, the Soviet future does not look as grim. The USSR is a heavily industrialized society with an educated population and unmatched reserves of natural resources. Moreover, if reforms continue, the Soviet Union will begin to reap the benefits of membership in the international economic community. Although the Soviet Union is far from becoming a complete democracy, the democratic reforms that have been implemented appear to have taken hold, and the Soviet people have responded enthusiastically to their freedom to participate in the government.

The environment of cooperation between East and West has never seemed so hopeful. Soviet-American relations are better now than perhaps at any time since the two countries were World War II allies. Similarly Soviet-German relations are warm, despite predictable fears in the Soviet Union of a united Germany. Most Soviets are ready for a change, and a growing minority aspires to a social-democratic future as a part of the common European home envisioned by Gorbachev.

Political and social stability depend on economic progress. The Soviet people would be inclined to follow Gorbachev or any other Soviet leader who could deliver a better economy. Without economic improvement, however, strikes throughout the Soviet Union and continued calls for independence from the republics are inevitable. From the vantage point of 1990 the Soviet Union seemed destined to experience even more change in the future than it had in the recent past. The ongoing revolution that had already transformed the Soviet Union appeared to be only in its initial phase.

Russian and Soviet History

Imperial Russia and the Revolution

The early history of Russia—from 1000 B.C. to the mid-fifteenth century A.D.—was a chronicle of foreign invasion and domination. The Slavic agricultural tribes that inhabited the southern Russian steppes lived between East and West and were conquered by peoples from both Asia and Europe.

From about 1000 B.C. to 700 B.C. the Cimmerians (about whose origins little is known) ruled southern Russia. They were replaced by the Scythians, a central Asian nomadic tribe that dominated until the end of the third century B.C. when it gave way to another group of Asian nomads, the Sarmatians. Around 200 A.D. the Goths, a Germanic tribe, replaced the Sarmatians. The Goths in turn were defeated by the Huns around 370 A.D., reinstituting the pattern of Asian domination. The Huns were ousted by yet another Asian tribe, the Avars, in 558 A.D. Avar rule lasted about a hundred years.

The centuries of invasion caused considerable migration among the Slavs, breaking up the original tribe into three groups. These were the West Slavs: Poles, Czechs, Slovaks, and Lusatians; the South Slavs: Serbs, Croats, Macedonians, Slovenes, Montenegrins, and Bulgars; and the East Slavs: the Russians, Ukrainians, and Belorussians.

While suffering invasion, the Slavs became adept at assimilating the ways of their foreign rulers. They benefited from exposure to foreign influences, notably trade with Greek colonies in southern Russia. By the mid-eighth century A.D. the East Slavs had established several independent city-states that were attractive targets for roving bands of Viking and Asian warriors. The need for joint protection led to consolidation of these city-states and the establishment of the first Russian state.

Establishing a Russian State

Scandinavian Vikings, known as Varangians to the Slavs, played an important role in the development of Russian civilization during the ninth and tenth centuries. Varangian merchants used Russia as a trading route to the Byzantine empire centered in Constantinople. They developed contacts with the East Slavs and eventually became rulers of a united Russian state. Historians have offered three explanations of how the Scandinavians came to rule Russia. The Varangians may have been invited by the East

Slavs to be their rulers in return for guaranteeing order, they may have shared power with local Slav leaders in an effort to create a stable state in which trade would flourish, or they may have established their rule over the Slavs by force. Disagreements also surround the word "Rus" from which "Russia" is derived. Some historians and philologists believe "Rus" is of Scandinavian origin, while others have maintained it was the name of a place in southern Russia.

Kievan Period

Around 862 A.D. a Dane named Rurik assumed control over a united Russian state and settled in Novgorod, a trading town about three hundred miles northeast of present-day Moscow. His successor, Oleg, transferred the seat of power south to Kiev, located on the Dnepr River. Oleg established himself as a prince, brought the neighboring eastern Slavic tribes under his sway, and extracted tribute from them. Trade and culture flourished in the relatively liberal Kievan state as subsequent princes expanded the boundaries of their domain until the eleventh century, when the state reached from the Baltic Sea to the Black Sea and from near the Russian town of Gorkii to present-day Romania.

The Scandinavian rulers, instead of imposing a foreign culture upon their subjects, adopted the local language and customs. Kievan Russia witnessed a tremendous growth of culture, art, architecture, language, and law. Cultural and social development was strongly influenced by the state's relations with the Byzantine Empire, although contacts also were developed with western states. Prince Vladimir, who ruled from about 980 to 1015, established friendly relations with the Byzantine Empire to the south and adopted Byzantine Christianity for himself and his pagan subjects around 988.

The establishment of the Russian Orthodox Church turned Russia away from Western Europe and the influence of the Roman Church, a development that would contribute greatly to Russia's sense of isolation. The conversion of the country gave rise to a written language, based on the Cyrillic alphabet developed by St. Cyril and his brother, St. Methodius. Both were holy men from Moravia (now in central Czechoslovakia) who ministered to the Slavs in the second half of the ninth century. The institution of uniform religion, language, and customs and the consolidation of an empire created the idea of a separate Russian state and a sense of national identity that withstood the subsequent years of disintegration and domination.

Appanage Period

The Kievan state survived until the Mongol invasion, which began in 1236. However, the central authority of the grand prince of Kiev was weakened by the division of the state into principalities—a process of inheritance established by Yaroslav, who ruled from 1036 to 1054. Under this system, each principality was headed by one of Yaroslav's sons.

The most important princedom was Kiev, and, according to Yaroslav's awkward system, it was to be ruled by each of his sons on a rotating basis. The system soon created tension and acrimony among the various uncles and nephews and gave rise to Appanage Russia, a period during which princes ruled their individual lands (appanages). Civil war characterized the two hundred years following the death of Yaroslav. Kiev also declined because changing East-West trade routes sapped its commercial strength, while continual foreign aggression—culminating in the Mongol invasion—undermined its tenuous cohesion.

Among the greatest of the appanage princes was Alexander of Novgorod, who warded off attacks on Russia from the West. In 1240 he defeated Swedish invaders on the banks of the Neva River. From this battle he took the name Alexander Nevski. He also fought the Teutonic Knights, Germanic crusaders dedicated to expansion and Roman Catholicism. They were routed by Alexander's troops April 5, 1242, at a battle on the ice of Lake Peipus in Estonia. This defeat of European invaders, long enshrined in Russian folklore, was depicted in Russian director Sergei Eisenstein's famous 1938 film, *Alexander Nevski*.

Mongol Period

The composition of thirteenth-century Russia—consisting of dozens of informally related city-states—contributed to the Mongols' victory. Skilled and experienced soldiers, the invaders overcame the various Russian princes, who failed to fashion a joint defense. By 1242 all of Russia was under Mongol domination. The Mongols (called Tatars by Russian historians) secured the loyalty of the grand prince and through him collected tribute from the other appanage princes.

During the Mongol domination of Russia, Moscow was established as the center of the state. Kiev had been destroyed during the invasion, and by 1315 the grand prince ruled from Tver (now Kalinin), located about a hundred miles northwest of Moscow. In the early fourteenth century, Yuri, the prince of Moscow, undertook a campaign to win the title of grand prince. After several years of battle and intrigue, Ivan Kalita, the younger brother of Yuri (who was killed by a Tver enemy), was named grand prince by the Mongol khan in 1328. Ivan expanded his territory by buying up appanages and villages from bankrupt princes. He also convinced the Metropolitan Theognost, the head of the Russian Church, to live in Moscow, making it the religious capital of the state.

Ivan's grandson, Grand Prince Dmitri, attempted to overthrow the Mongol lords, and on September 8, 1380, his army defeated Mongol forces at the battle of Kulikovo field. From then on the Mongols' authority in Russia

steadily weakened, even though they reestablished military control of Russia in 1382. Finally, in 1480, Ivan III, also known as Ivan the Great, refused to recognize the authority of the Mongols, and, with their empire falling apart, they failed in a half-hearted effort to perpetuate their control over the Russians.

Muscovite Russia

Under Ivan the Great and his son Basil III, the last independent appanages were brought under Moscow's control. Ivan in 1472 married Sophia, a niece of the last Byzantine emperor, and began to refer to himself as tsar (from Caesar).

The power and authority of the Moscow tsar was established definitively under Basil III's son Ivan IV, better known as Ivan the Terrible. Crowned tsar in 1547 at the age of sixteen, Ivan for several years relied on the advice of a group of liberal-minded advisers, the Chosen Council. He also sought the approval of the *zemskii sobor*, an assembly of landholders. As he grew older, however, he began to suspect the boyars—the descendants of the appanage princes, who now formed the hereditary nobility—of plotting against him. Ivan in 1565 established his personal domain, the *oprichnina* (from the Russian word for "apart"), and gave land to trusted followers, the *oprichniki*. The oprichniki, described by some historians as the first political police force, were assigned the task of eliminating anyone who opposed the tsar. In the reign of terror that lasted until 1572, thousands perished and whole towns—Novgorod, for example—were leveled.

Relative calm was restored under Ivan's son Fëdor I, who ruled from 1584 to 1598. Russia again was thrown into turmoil, however, when Fëdor died without an heir and his brother-in-law and close adviser, Boris Godunov, seized power, ushering in a period of dynastic confusion that became known as the "Time of Troubles."

Boris Godunov was elected tsar by a special session of the zemskii sobor. His rule soon was beset with crises. In 1601-1603, drought and famine decimated the population. At the same time, it was rumored that Godunov had had a hand in the death of Prince Dmitri, the younger brother of Tsar Fëdor. Moreover, some suspected that another child had been murdered in Dmitri's place and that the "real" Dmitri would reappear and claim the throne.

A young man claiming to be Prince Dmitri gathered an army, with Polish assistance, and invaded Russia in October 1604. His campaign gained popular support, and, after Godunov died in April 1605 and his wife and son Fëdor II were murdered, the False Dmitri ascended the throne. His disdain for the Russian people and reliance on Polish advisers soon eroded his support among the nobility, and he was overthrown in May 1606. The leader of the coup, Basil Shuiski, a boyar prince, named himself tsar. A second False Dmitri arose during Basil's reign and almost succeeded in gaining the throne. Basil was overthrown in 1610, and during the next three years the country was ruled by a group of seven boyars.

Basil Shuiski's desperation to defend his throne against the second False Dmitri led him to form an alliance with Sweden. In return for some Russian territory along the Baltic and a Russian promise to fight with the Swedish against the Poles, Sweden provided Basil with troops that helped defeat the second False Dmitri. In 1609, however, the king of Poland, Sigismund III, attacked Russia at the request of the supporters of the second False Dmitri. Basil

Shuiski was deposed, and the Poles occupied Moscow. The Muscovites invited the Polish king's son Ladislas to become tsar, but negotiations stalled over the details of the arrangement. Meanwhile the Swedes had invaded Russia from the northwest to oppose the expansion of Polish power and to punish Moscow for its failure to live up to its alliance responsibilities.

The Russian state faced a dire situation. Its capital was occupied, it had no clear leader, and it was forced to contend with two invading powers. In 1612, however, the Russian people rallied behind a nationalist movement led by the Russian Orthodox Church to rid the country of foreign armies and reestablish a national government. Patriarch Hermogen, concerned about the spread of Catholicism in the Polish-occupied territories, rallied disparate segments of Russian society against the Poles. By the end of the year the Russians had driven the Poles from Moscow. A special zemskii sobor elected Michael Romanov as tsar in early 1613. He was crowned, at the age of sixteen, on July 21, 1613. Although civil strife continued until 1618, the administration of Russia was back in Russian hands. Michael, the grand-nephew of Anastasia, Ivan the Terrible's first wife, was the first member of the Romanov line that would rule Russia until the Russian revolution of 1917.

Rise and Fall of the Romanovs

Michael Romanov took the throne of a country in turmoil. As historian Nicholas V. Riasanovsky wrote in *A History of Russia:*

> The treasury was empty, and financial collapse of the state appeared complete. In Astrakhan, Zarutsky [a cossack leader] . . . rallied the cossacks and other malcontents, continuing the story of pretenders and social rebellion so characteristic of the Time of Troubles. Many roaming bands, some of them several thousand strong, continued looting the land. Moreover, Muscovy remained at war with Poland and Sweden, which had seized respectively Smolensk and Novgorod as well as other Russian territory and promoted their own candidates to the Muscovite throne.

Tsar Michael moved quickly to quiet domestic unrest. His armies broke the rebel movement in the countryside. He reached an agreement with the Swedes in 1617 that returned Novgorod to Russian control and made a truce with Poland in 1618. The truce gave the Poles control over the town of Smolensk and other areas in western Russia. After the truce expired in 1632 the war began anew, but it ended in 1634 with a treaty that again recognized Polish authority in western Russia.

To restore Moscow's financial stability, Tsar Michael levied new taxes and arranged loans generating sufficient funds to keep the country from bankruptcy. Nevertheless, financial problems were to plague the tsars for several decades.

Michael's successor, his son Alexis, ruled from 1645 to 1676. He oversaw the Ukraine's unification with Moscow in 1654 after the Ukrainians broke with their Polish rulers. His armies put down a large peasant rebellion, led by Stepan Razin in 1670. Tsar Fëdor III, Alexis's elder son from his first marriage, assumed the throne in 1676 and died six years later at the age of twenty, without leaving an heir.

Peter the Great

Peter I (1672-1725), known as Peter the Great, transformed Russia into a leading European power during the first quarter of the eighteenth century. Peter was the son of Tsar Alexis I and his second wife. The leading boyars named the ten-year-old Peter tsar after the death of his half-brother, Tsar Fëdor III. But a faction backing Fëdor's incompetent older brother Ivan, and led by Ivan's sister Sophia, rebelled and forced the boyars to appoint Ivan and Peter co-tsars. Under this arrangement Sophia became regent. She attempted to claim the throne for herself in 1689, but the church hierarchy and the boyars backed Peter, and Sophia's coup failed. She was sent to a convent, leaving Peter in control of the country, although, technically, Ivan remained co-tsar until he died in 1696. Peter was aided in running the government by his mother, Natalia Narishkina, until her death in 1694.

At this time, Russia was an extremely backward and isolated nation with few diplomatic and commercial links to foreign countries. Peter, who toured Western Europe on a diplomatic mission early in his reign, was impressed with Western culture and its technological advances. Taking Western Europe as his model, Peter launched a campaign to modernize Russian society. He reorganized the army and created a navy, built ports, expanded manufacturing and mining operations, updated the Russian calendar, modified the Cyrillic alphabet, introduced Roman numerals, mandated compulsory education for gentry children, oversaw the publication of Russia's first newspaper, and imported European teachers and technicians to advance Russian education and science.

Peter also restructured Russia's system of government by creating a new system of provinces and establishing a Senate to handle state financial, legal, and administrative matters. Government ministries *(collegia)* were created to administer commerce, income, war, manufacturing, and other activities. Peter, however, remained an absolute

Peter I, "The Great"

ruler, and no proposal from the Senate or collegia could be implemented without his approval.

He also reformed the traditional system of service to the state by introducing the Table of Ranks (the *chin*) under which a member of the gentry entered service in the military or the government at the bottom and worked his way up through a series of levels, instead of receiving a certain rank based on family influence. Nongentry Russians who entered service were made members of the gentry class for life if they reached a certain rank.

Peter pursued an active foreign policy designed to defeat Russia's old enemies and expand its territory. During his reign, Russia was almost constantly at war with either the Swedes, Turks, or Persians. In "The Great Northern War," waged against Sweden from 1700 until 1721, Russia acquired territories bordering the Gulf of Finland, including St. Petersburg (now Leningrad), as well as Estonia and Latvia. After the defeat of the Swedes, the Senate conferred upon Peter the title of emperor (which subsequently was used interchangeably with tsar), and the Russian Empire formally was established. The capital was moved from Moscow to St. Petersburg in 1712.

Although Peter's modernization campaign and activist foreign policy strengthened his nation, they nevertheless were the source of much suffering and discontent in Russia. His foreign wars forced two generations of Russians to endure the hardships of eighteenth-century military service, and the army and navy required large amounts of capital that Peter could obtain only through oppressive taxes. Peasant uprisings against taxes and conscription led to mass executions, and Peter maintained an active secret police organization to guard against subversion.

In addition, some of Peter's reforms were resented by the Russian people as arbitrary attacks on Russian customs in favor of distrusted Western culture. For example, he forced noblemen to pay a tax if they wanted to keep their traditional Russian beards, and he outlawed the manufacture of traditional Russian garments. Peter's reforms also

Catherine II, "The Great"

extended to the Russian Orthodox Church. In 1721 he decreed that the head of the church would be a layman, thus infuriating clergy who felt deprived of control over religious affairs.

Peter died February 8, 1725, without designating a successor. Over the next thirty-seven years, Russia was governed by six monarchs, none of whom was effective. In the absence of a strong tsar, the gentry class was able to advance its interests.

In 1736 the lifetime term of gentry service to the crown, which the gentry hated, was reduced to twenty-five years, and in 1762 service was canceled altogether. At the same time, the peasant serfs who farmed the gentry's fields had many of their rights taken away. Serfs no longer could gain their freedom through service in the military. Moreover they could not buy land or engage in commerce without the permission of their landlord. The serfs had become little more than the personal property of their gentry masters, who could whip them, sell them, or deport them to Siberia.

Catherine the Great

Catherine II (1729-1796), known as Catherine the Great, was a princess from the small German state of Anhalt-Zerbst, who married Peter, a grandson of Peter the Great, in 1745. She spent the next seventeen years carefully forming alliances among members of the imperial court. Her husband ascended to the throne as Tsar Peter III in 1762, but before the year was over she cooperated with conspirators who murdered her husband and placed her on the throne.

Although she was well versed in democratic thought associated with the Enlightenment (she carried on a celebrated correspondence with Voltaire), Catherine remained a staunch supporter of absolute monarchy in Russia. Mindful that as a foreigner and a usurper her place on the Russian throne was not secure, she cultivated the favor of the gentry. She contributed to the continuing degradation of the serfs by giving away to her supporters thousands of acres of state land. The peasants working the lands were included in the gifts.

A rebellion of serfs in 1773-1775, led by Emelyan Pugachev, ultimately was crushed, but it alarmed Catherine and her gentry supporters. In response she divided Russia's twenty provinces into fifty in a scheme designed to bring greater central control over the countryside.

Gentry privilege was broadened by the 1785 Charter of the Nobility, which guaranteed a trial by a jury of noble peers and freed the gentry from taxation, conscription, and corporal punishment. It also reaffirmed the gentry's 1762 exemption from military or civil service to the state.

Catherine's foreign policy was designed to expand Russia's southern and western boundaries. In the south, the empress's army and navy defeated the Turks in 1774 and gained control over part of the Black Sea coastline. By 1783 Russian forces had captured the Crimea.

To the west, Catherine joined with other European powers in partitioning the Polish empire. The acquisitions from Poland brought millions of non-Russians and their lands into the Russian empire.

Weakened by years of internal strife and civil war, Poland was a likely prospect for domination by her powerful neighbors. In 1772 Russia, Prussia, and Austria divided among themselves about one-third of Poland's territory. Russia received part of what is now Belorussia. In 1792 a second partition awarded Russia most of the rest of Belorussia and the western Ukraine. The Poles rose in rebellion against the loss of their territory but were defeated by the Russian and Prussian armies in 1795. To punish the rebels, the remaining parts of their homeland were divided among Russia, Prussia, and Austria. Poland, as a state, no longer existed.

Catherine died in 1796, and her son Paul took control of one of the world's mightiest powers. During his five years on the throne, Paul codified the law of succession to require primogeniture in the male line (Peter the Great had declared that the emperor had the right to name his successor) and displayed a liberal attitude toward the serfs, reducing the number of days each week a serf was required to work his master's lands. Nevertheless, Paul continued to give the gentry state lands along with the peasants who lived on them. In foreign affairs, he made war against revolutionary France and later entered into a Russian-French coalition. His extreme disdain for the gentry, who had supported his mother's claims to a throne he considered rightfully his, led to a coup in 1801. Paul was murdered and his son, the twenty-three-year-old Alexander, was made emperor.

Alexander I

Alexander I (1777-1825), who had received a liberal education, appeared ready early in his reign to apply the principles of the enlightenment to his rule. He increased the powers of the Senate, which had been moribund for several years; tightened and improved the administration of the ministerial departments; and promoted education. He approved a plan to permit the gentry to release serfs from bondage, although few serf owners took advantage of it.

Alexander's reforms, however, were not far-reaching, and domestic policy frequently took a back seat to foreign affairs because of the developments in Europe. Alexander's apprehension over Napoleon Bonaparte's aggressive empire building caused Alexander to break the treaty his father had negotiated with France. A war with France followed in which the French and their Spanish allies defeated a coalition made up of Russia, Great Britain, Sweden, Prussia, and Austria. The Treaty of Tilsit (now known as Sovetsk), signed in 1807, severely weakened Prussia and left France and Russia as the only two major powers on the continent. Tensions between the two simmered for five years, culminating in Napoleon's ill-fated invasion of Russia.

The French emperor assembled an army of seven hundred thousand men, many of whom were conscripts from his European empire. Napoleon hoped to break Russian defenses in a decisive battle, but the Russian strategy was to avoid major confrontation. Instead Russian forces executed a scorched-earth retreat ahead of Napoleon's Grand Army. Napoleon followed deep into Russia, stretching his supply lines beyond their limits. The one major confrontation of the campaign, the September 7, 1812, Battle of Borodino outside Moscow, resulted in tens of thousands of casualties on both sides. The battle weakened the invasion force but did not check its drive on the Russian capital. That month Napoleon reached and occupied Moscow after the Russians had set it on fire.

Napoleon hoped to pressure Alexander into a negotiated settlement, but the Russian tsar declined to make peace. Napoleon's troops remained in Moscow five weeks before the onset of winter and the scarcity of food and supplies forced Napoleon to order a retreat. On its way out of Russia, the Grand Army had to contend with the Russian winter, disease, short rations, and attacks from Russian troops and partisans. Less than a quarter of Napoleon's force survived.

After forming a coalition with Austria, Sweden, and Great Britain, the Russians pursued Napoleon's army into France. The coalition's forces defeated Napoleon at the decisive Battle of Nations, fought near Leipzig in October 1813. They then occupied Paris March 31, 1814, and Napoleon was banished to Elba.

Alexander represented Russia at the 1814-1815 Congress of Vienna, the momentous gathering of European leaders that redrew the map of the continent in the wake of Napoleon's defeat. The decisions of the Congress were implemented despite Napoleon's retaking of the French throne in March 1815. He assembled an army but was defeated by the British and Prussians at the Battle of Waterloo, June 18, 1815, and was banished permanently to the South Atlantic island of St. Helena.

The Congress of Vienna created a smaller Poland with Tsar Alexander as its constitutional monarch. Prussia emerged as a restored major power, Austria received much of northern Italy, Belgium and Holland were joined in a kingdom, and Switzerland and Germany were awarded constitutions. In addition, Norway was taken from Denmark and given to Sweden. The Congress compensated the Danes with German lands.

Although Alexander was preoccupied with Napoleon during the first fifteen years of his reign, he also engaged in wars on his empire's southern and northern frontiers. His response to a request for help from the small nation of Georgia led to the 1804-1813 war against Georgia's neighbor, Persia, and the 1806-1812 Russo-Turkish war. In both, the Russian armies won and Russian rule was extended over Georgia. In the north, a war with Sweden in 1809 resulted in the Russian occupation of Finland, which Alexander ruled as grand duke.

The moves toward domestic liberalism that characterized Alexander's early rule did not extend to his later years. The emperor investigated and, according to some historians, gave his approval to a proposal for a Russian constitutional monarchy, but the plan was never implemented.

Alexander's disavowal of his earlier liberal tendencies provoked animosity among a small group of aristocratic army officers who, familiar with the democratic changes sweeping Europe, established a secret society in St. Petersburg that aimed to establish a constitutional monarchy in their homeland. When Alexander died suddenly in December 1825 without an heir, the country temporarily was left leaderless while the late emperor's brothers, Constantine and Nicholas, each claimed that the other was the rightful heir. Although Constantine was the older brother, he had renounced his claim to the throne when he married a commoner. In the ensuing confusion, the army officers in St. Petersburg attempted to seize power. Their supporters, however, were quickly defeated by government troops. The leaders of the rebellion, thereafter known as the Decembrists, were tried and either executed or exiled to Siberia by the government of the new emperor, Nicholas I. Although there had been many coups and coup attempts in Russian history, the Decembrist revolt was significant because it was the first to be driven by revolutionary principles.

The Decembrist revolt had two results: It ushered in

an era of repression under the new emperor, and it served as an important symbolic event for the generations of Russian revolutionaries who matured during the nineteenth and early twentieth centuries.

Nicholas I

Nicholas I (1796-1855) was determined to preserve the social and political status quo in Russia and reassert complete control over the lives of his subjects. He greatly expanded the censorship apparatus to block the influx of Western ideas, placed restrictions on the curriculum of Russian universities, prohibited foreign travel by most citizens, and was intolerant of liberalism among military officers and civil servants. To enforce his policies, he gave his political police force the responsibility to monitor anything that might be a threat to the established order. The secret police frequently abused their power, and many Russian citizens were killed or sent into exile.

Although Nicholas was wary of the upheaval that could be caused by a continuation of serfdom, he believed revolution was more likely to be stimulated by the granting of concessions to the serfs. He therefore staunchly supported the privileges of the gentry and made no significant moves toward ending serfdom.

Nicholas adopted a similarly conservative outlook toward international affairs. His defense of the status quo reached beyond Russian borders. He ordered his armies to put down revolutions in Poland (1830-1831) and Hungary (1849). Russian troops also intervened in 1848 to curb increasing Romanian nationalist activities. He even considered dispatching his armed forces to restore order during the revolutions in France in 1830 and 1848.

Nicholas's foreign policy led to disaster for Russia in the Crimean War (1853-1856). Ignited by a dispute over religious rights in the Holy Land, war between Russia and Turkey broke out in October 1853. The tsar not only sought to protect the rights of Orthodox Christians in the Holy Land, but he also hoped to enhance Russian power in the Black Sea region and Russian influence over the Ottoman Empire, which he believed was crumbling. Turkey soon was joined by two powerful allies, Great Britain and France, whose troops laid siege to Sevastopol, Russia's naval base in the Crimea. After nearly a year, the Russians were forced to forsake Sevastopol in September 1855 and accept defeat. The Treaty of Paris, signed March 30, 1856, obliged Moscow to withdraw all its forces from the Black Sea and abandon its claim as the protector of the Orthodox peoples in the Ottoman Empire.

Despite the generally repressive atmosphere that prevailed in Russia during Nicholas's reign, the cultural life of the nation flourished. The years 1820 to 1860 are known as Russia's "Golden Age," especially in literature. The early years of this Golden Age were marked by the writings of Aleksander Pushkin and Nikolai Gogol, as well as the work of several lesser poets and novelists. In later years, the leading Russian writers included Ivan Turgenev, Fëdor Dostoevsky, and Leo Tolstoy. *(Box, p. 144)*

Alexander II

Tsar Nicholas I died in March 1855, before the end of the Crimean War. His son Alexander II (1818-1881) presided over the conclusion of the war and the signing of the Treaty of Paris. Alexander attempted, with some success, to improve Russia's tarnished international image.

He took advantage of the Franco-Prussian War of 1870 to unilaterally void the provisions of the Paris Treaty that restricted Russian activities in the Black Sea region. Russia's standing as a military power improved after it won the Russo-Turkish War of 1877-1878. The peace treaty ending the war granted Russia dominion over Bulgaria, but a conference of European powers at Berlin took much of the territory away from Russia.

In the East, Russia's expansion was unhampered by European political considerations. The tsar's armies established Moscow's dominion over the Caucasus and central Asia, and his diplomats received land concessions from the Chinese, including the area around Vladivostok, which was founded in 1858.

Alexander's most pressing concerns, however, were domestic. Although he was not a liberal crusader, he did recognize that certain changes were necessary for the welfare of Russia. Early in his reign he undertook a series of reforms that dramatically altered Russian society.

The primary question that had to be addressed was what to do about serfdom. Few members of the gentry could afford to maintain vast numbers of serfs, and the changing Russian economy required new types of laborers that serfdom could not provide efficiently. For their part, the serfs in the early nineteenth century began to seek freedom. Between 1800 and 1860, there were more than fifteen hundred peasant rebellions. Almost five hundred had occurred between 1854 and 1860. Emancipation was the only remedy likely to quell the unrest. The Crimean War also contributed to the perception that serfdom should be abolished because the ill-educated, docile serf, who lacked a political and economic stake in the country, had fought poorly. Finally, an increasing number of Russians objected to serfdom on moral grounds. *(Development of serfdom, box, p. 15)*

By 1860 there was a growing consensus in favor of emancipation, but substantial disagreement existed over how it should be done. The powerful landholding class would have to be compensated for the loss of their serfs, while the serfs had to be given enough land and resources to make a living. Landowners also functioned as Russia's local political authority. If serfdom were abolished some type of local government would have to be created to fill the administrative vacuum that would be left. With the strong support of Tsar Alexander, gentry committees began to study the issue in 1858.

On March 3, 1861, Alexander signed an imperial order freeing an estimated forty million serfs. Under the terms of the emancipation, the gentry class gave up about half of its land for which it was reimbursed by the government. This land was given to the serfs to work as their own, although legal title to it was held collectively by a system of village communes. The serf household was obligated to accept its land allotment and assume the taxes on the land and a redemption payment to the government that was extended over a forty-nine-year period.

Although emancipation bolstered the self respect of the serfs, its terms were not generous enough to substantially improve the lives of many of them. The redemption payments were high, and the land each serf had been forced to purchase averaged only about six or seven acres. Consequently, the emancipated peasants had little excess income with which to purchase more land. The emancipation order also did not provide the peasants with other crucial resources needed to improve their lot, such as timber and pasture lands and water rights. The financial bur-

The Development of Serfdom

Serfdom in Russia had its roots in the Kievan period, but the institution developed gradually over many centuries. At the dawn of Kievan Russia in the ninth century, most peasants were free farmers of land owned by the nobility. Frequent economic calamities—droughts, poor harvests, famines—compelled peasants to borrow money from their landlords. Many were unable to repay the loans, however, and they became perpetually indebted to their landlords. Peasants who fell into this plight were required to work for their creditors or supply them with a specified amount of goods every year. In the process they were transformed from free peasants into the gentry's serfs.

Over the centuries, landlords' control of the peasants grew. By the fifteenth century, a peasant could become free of his master only on a specified day each year—some time near the feast of St. George, late in the fall—if he had paid off his debts.

The plight of the peasantry deteriorated further during the Muscovite period (fifteenth, sixteenth, and seventeenth centuries). Landlords were empowered to govern and tax their subjects. The peasants also fell victim to the tsars' practice of awarding vast tracts of state lands (pomesties) to the service gentry, the men who performed administrative chores for the ruler and served in his armies. The peasants who occupied the state land granted to the gentry became serfs. When they resisted by escaping to outlying regions, the government outlawed peasant migration.

The legal code of 1649, the *Ulozhenie,* lengthened to an indefinite time the period during which an escaped serf had to be returned to his master (it had been five years) and stiffened penalties for providing refuge to fugitive serfs. By the end of the seventeenth century buying and selling serfs was common.

In the eighteenth century the position of the serfs continued to decline as the power of the gentry grew. Millions of peasants passed into serfdom as the emperors and empresses expanded on the practice of giving state land to their supporters. Decrees prohibited serfs from owning land, signing government contracts, or escaping servitude by joining the army. Landlords, in contrast, were given authority to exile errant serfs to Siberia and to shift serfs from one estate to another. Because the government did not effectively reach past the district level, landlords also functioned as local judges and tax collectors in charge of their serfs. In 1741 serfs were not among the Russians required to pledge loyalty to the tsar, and a criminal code of 1754 designated serfs as gentry property.

Catherine the Great (who ruled from 1762 to 1796) established serfdom in the Ukraine, continued the practice of giving generous grants of land and peasants to her favorites, and prohibited serfs from complaining to the empress or her government about their treatment by landlords. By 1800 landlords had complete control over the lives of their serfs.

den imposed by emancipation led to a short but intense wave of peasant revolts that died down by the following year.

Additional reforms followed the emancipation of the serfs. In 1864 Alexander introduced provincial and district assemblies known as *zemstvos* to administer local affairs. Zemstvo representatives were chosen through a complicated electoral system that divided representatives among the classes. Although the peasants received significant representation, the gentry class dominated the provincial zemstvos and had slightly more representives at the district level. The zemstvos met once a year and selected committees that served continuously. Although the responsibilities of the zemstovs and their committees were limited primarily to local finances, public health, road maintenance, and education, they improved conditions in Russia and gave the Russian people some experience with representative government.

In 1864 Alexander also instituted legal reforms. The administration of justice was made a separate branch of government, jury trials were introduced, freedom of speech was given to courtroom lawyers, and equal treatment before the law was guaranteed for all citizens. Alexander's reforms eventually extended to the military as well. General conscription was expanded to all Russians (it previously had applied only to peasants), and the term of service was lowered from twenty-five years to six. This created a huge military reserve and was an important factor in the improvement of Russian military strength in the post-Crimean War period.

Rise of Radicalism

During the second half of the nineteenth century, radical movements among Russian intellectuals flourished. Although Alexander's reforms addressed some major popular concerns, Russian revolutionary groups sought the overthrow of the tsar and the establishment of various types of governments. Since the failed Decembrist revolt of 1825, the Russian revolutionary movement had developed into several distinct branches, yet it remained an upper-class phenomenon, centered in the universities and the drawing rooms of Moscow and St. Petersburg. Indeed, Tibor Szamuely, in *The Russian Tradition,* has pointed out that the paradox of Russian radicalism was that the Russian people were regarded as too backward and uneducated to make the right choices about their own and their country's welfare. Therefore it was the job of the intellectual to force them in revolutionary directions that would recreate Russian society for the better.

As early as the 1840s two main intellectual movements had appeared, the Slavophiles and the Westerners. The Slavophiles were nationalists who sought a return to the Russian state as it existed before the introduction of Western ideas and structures under Peter the Great and his successors. Their ideal was an isolated nation whose main characteristics were the peasant commune, a purified Orthodox Church, and an autocracy free of bureaucratic interference. The Westerners advocated a secular, rational approach to Russian development based on increased use of Western technology, thought, and social structures (though many Westerners rejected capitalism). They claimed that Russia was like the nations of Western Europe but had failed to keep up with the West's pace of political and economic modernization. Their inspiration was Peter the Great, who had sought to westernize Russia in the eighteenth century.

A third intellectual group that rose to prominence in the 1840s was the Petrashevskists. Named after Mikhail Petrashevskii, at whose home they met secretly, the Petrashevskists followed the teachings of the French utopian socialist Charles Fourier. They were responsible for the spread of socialist literature among the intelligentsia, an activity that, coupled with their general opposition to the government of Nicholas I, led to the arrest and sentencing to death of some of the group's members, including the great novelist Fëdor Dostoevsky. The death sentences were reduced to prison terms at the last minute.

The intellectual movements of the 1840s were superseded in the 1850s by the rise of populism (narodnichestvo). Its most influential advocate was Aleksandr Herzen (1812-1870), a Westerner and moderate revolutionary who adopted some Slavophile elements into his social philosophy. He embraced socialism but adapted it to Russian conditions, arguing that socialism would spring from a peasant revolution and would be based on the traditional Russian communal village. Herzen's views, contained in *Kolokol* (The Bell), a journal he published during his exile in Europe from 1857 until 1867, found an eager audience among the educated class.

Another Westerner, Mikhail Bakunin (1814-1876), advocated a more radical path than Herzen. Bakunin called for a violent revolution that would abolish the Russian Church and state and establish a society in which no class would be allowed to dominate. In place of the Russian centralized state Bakunin envisioned political authority being held by self-governing communes. Like Herzen, Bakunin spent much of his life in exile in the West. He participated in the 1848 revolution in Europe and later became a leader of the anarchists in the early international socialist movement. He helped establish the First International Workingmen's Association in 1864, but his opposition to Karl Marx's concept of state socialism eventually led to his expulsion from the organization. *(Marx, box, p. 26)*

As the tide of revolution rose in Russia, the ideas of Bakunin, Herzen, and other radical intellectuals were adopted by those committed to the immediate overthrow of the state. Herzen's populism was taken up by Nikolai Chernyshevsky (1828-1889), whose novel *What Is to Be Done?* outlined his vision of Russia under a socialist system. In it, he postulated the existence of the "new men," an elite corps of intellectuals who selflessly would strive to improve conditions for the people. Borrowing from Herzen,

Chernyshevsky argued that Russia should forgo capitalist development and step directly into socialism. But unlike Herzen, who expected that the change to socialism would come about peacefully, Chernyshevsky exhorted his followers to pull down the existing system. Chernyshevsky's ideas enjoyed wide popularity among Russian radicals and made a lasting impression on the generations of revolutionaries who followed him. In 1902, when Lenin wrote a pamphlet describing his blueprint for the development of the Bolshevik party, he chose to call it "What Is to Be Done?"

Numerous conspiratorial groups and radical cliques regularly discussed the problems of Russia and ways to resolve them. These groups, however, took little direct action until 1873, when thousands of students decided to work among the peasants in a movement known as "going to the people." Lasting for several years, the exercise was a failure. Most of the students agreed with Bakunin's assessment that the peasants were ready for revolution and could be converted to socialism and radicalism. In most cases, however, the students met with indifference; in others, the student propagandists were handed over to the police. By 1877 the disillusioned students had returned to the cities.

The failure of "going to the people" convinced many radicals that the revolutionary movement required an elite group of leaders to tear down the tsarist system and recreate Russian society in the name of the "people." The leading proponent of this concept was Peter Tkachev (1844-1886), an exiled Russian radical who would have a profound influence on Lenin's approach to revolution.

In the autumn of 1876, several disparate radical groups that included many anarchists and socialists formed a central organization, Land and Liberty (Zemlya i Volya). Among other goals, Land and Liberty was dedicated to the overthrow of the government through any means, the end of private land ownership, the redistribution of land among the peasants, and self-determination for national minorities.

In January 1878 the pace of radical activity quickened. A revolutionary named Vera Zasulich failed in her attempt to assassinate the governor of St. Petersburg. Although she was caught red-handed, the jury at her trial refused to convict her. The stunned government immediately ordered that all political crimes would be tried by special tribunals.

By 1879 Land and Liberty had split into two groups, one that wanted to prepare the people for revolution and another dedicated to an immediate reign of terror. The latter group, The Will of the People (Narodnaya Volya), decided to throw the government into disarray by killing Alexander II. After several unsuccessful attempts on the tsar's life—including a February 5, 1880, bomb blast that killed eleven servants and destroyed the dining room in the Winter Palace—the terrorists achieved their goal March 1, 1881. A revolutionary assassin killed Alexander (and himself) with a homemade hand grenade.

Alexander III

The son of Alexander II, Tsar Alexander III (1845-1894) was determined to reestablish law and order and reassert the complete authority of the autocracy. He initiated a series of measures designed to destroy Russian revolutionary activity. Police were given broad authority to arrest and imprison troublemakers, and some revolutionaries were banished to Siberia. Many intellectuals who avoided arrest went into self-imposed exile in Europe. In addition, student associations were banned and university

── The Romanov Dynasty ──

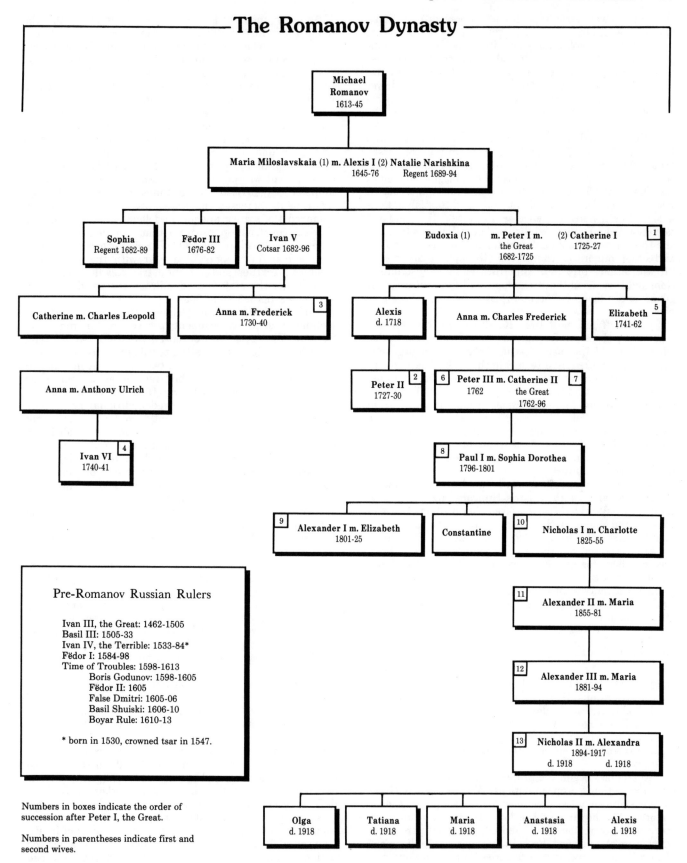

Michael Romanov
1613-45

Maria Miloslavskaia (1) m. Alexis I (2) Natalie Narishkina
1645-76   Regent 1689-94

Sophia
Regent 1682-89

Fëdor III
1676-82

Ivan V
Cotsar 1682-96

Eudoxia (1)   m. Peter I m.   (2) Catherine I [1]
the Great   1725-27
1682-1725

Catherine m. Charles Leopold

Anna m. Frederick [3]
1730-40

Alexis
d. 1718

Anna m. Charles Frederick

Elizabeth [5]
1741-62

Anna m. Anthony Ulrich

Peter II [2]
1727-30

[6] **Peter III m. Catherine II** [7]
1762   the Great
1762-96

Ivan VI [4]
1740-41

[8] **Paul I m. Sophia Dorothea**
1796-1801

[9] **Alexander I m. Elizabeth**
1801-25

Constantine

[10] **Nicholas I m. Charlotte**
1825-55

[11] **Alexander II m. Maria**
1855-81

Pre-Romanov Russian Rulers

Ivan III, the Great: 1462-1505
Basil III: 1505-33
Ivan IV, the Terrible: 1533-84*
Fëdor I: 1584-98
Time of Troubles: 1598-1613
    Boris Godunov: 1598-1605
    Fëdor II: 1605
    False Dmitri: 1605-06
    Basil Shuiski: 1606-10
    Boyar Rule: 1610-13

* born in 1530, crowned tsar in 1547.

[12] **Alexander III m. Maria**
1881-94

[13] **Nicholas II m. Alexandra**
1894-1917
d. 1918   d. 1918

Numbers in boxes indicate the order of succession after Peter I, the Great.

Numbers in parentheses indicate first and second wives.

Olga
d. 1918

Tatiana
d. 1918

Maria
d. 1918

Anastasia
d. 1918

Alexis
d. 1918

Source: Adapted from Nicholas V. Riasanovsky, *A History of Russia*, 3d ed. (New York: Oxford University Press, 1977)

curriculums were strictly controlled to prevent the discussion of liberal ideas. The tsar's government reinforced its efforts against revolutionary activity by increasing its support of the gentry and the Orthodox Church. Among other moves, the government established a bank to extend credit to the nobility, restricted the access of the lower classes to secondary education, and forced many subjects of the Russian empire to convert to Orthodox Christianity.

Alexander III was an ardent Russian nationalist who had been greatly influenced by Konstantin Pobedonostsev (1827-1907), his former tutor. After 1880 Pobedonostsev served as head of the Holy Synod, the managing council of the Orthodox Church. He was a conservative intellectual who preached the virtues of autocracy and Russian nationalism, while criticizing science, secular rationalism, and any deviation from Orthodox religious beliefs. Alexander's desire to advance Russian nationalism and his dislike of Jews and other minorities caused him to support an intense "Russification" program. Minorities endured discrimination, and Russian authorities suppressed local culture, language, and religion in the non-Russian regions of the empire.

Jews suffered most from Russification. Government-organized pogroms in Russian cities resulted in many Jewish deaths and the mass destruction of Jewish property. Most Jews were required to stay in the Pale of Settlement, an area roughly corresponding to the Ukraine and Belorussia, where Jews traditionally had settled. In 1891 the government forcibly removed twenty thousand Jews from Moscow to the Pale. The government also restricted the number of Jews who could be admitted to secondary schools and universities. As a result of this persecution, more than a million Jews emigrated from Russia during the late nineteenth century.

In foreign affairs, Alexander III made one major move. Russia's alliance with Austria-Hungary and Germany, formed in the early 1870s, dissolved over conflicts between Moscow and Vienna in the Balkans. Germany attempted to maintain a secret Berlin-Moscow connection to offset growing French power, but this arrangement fell apart in 1890. Casting about for new European allies, Russia negotiated an alliance with France, which had loaned Russia large sums to advance industrialization. By 1894 Russia and France faced an alliance among Austria-Hungary, Germany, and Italy.

Industrialization

Although the government's reactionary and ethnocentric policies blocked political and social development, the reign of Alexander III saw the beginning of an industrial revolution in Russia. Under the direction of the minister of finance, Count Sergei Witte (1849-1915), the governments of Alexander III and his son Nicholas II created a climate of investment that spurred the development of Russian industry.

Russia had begun the process of industrialization well after most other European nations. When Peter the Great assumed control of the government, Russia had just twenty factories. By the time of his death thirty-six years later, there were more than two hundred, about 40 percent of which were state owned. Peter promoted the establishment of metallurgical and textile factories to furnish guns and clothing to his armed forces.

The progress of industrialization slowed after Peter.

Metallurgy and textile production continued to be the dominant industries. The pace of industrial growth began to accelerate again in the nineteenth century. In 1800 there were about twelve hundred Russian factories; by midcentury, their number had more than doubled. Between 1850 and 1860 the number of factories devoted to machine building increased fivefold.

Russian industrial expansion continued steadily during the early years of the reign of Alexander III. Much of the expansion was fueled by foreign investment, which rose from one hundred million rubles in 1880 to nine hundred million by 1900. In 1892 Russian industrial development was placed in the hands of the new finance minister, Sergei Witte. He continued to encourage foreign investment, increased the state's investment in industry, balanced the state's budget, and launched an ambitious railroad construction program that included the Trans-Siberian Railroad. In the 1890s Russia's growth rate averaged a booming 8 percent a year with the steel, coal, chemical, textile, and oil industries leading the way. Meanwhile, the state-owned railroad system doubled in size between 1895 and 1905.

In the 1880s, a series of labor laws were passed that mandated some government protection for industrial workers. The legislation outlawed the use of women and children for night work in the textile industry, limited to eight hours the working days of twelve- to fifteen-year-old factory hands, and established regulations guaranteeing regular pay for employees. By 1900 the estimated two million Russian workers received additional protection. Factories with more than twenty employees could not require adults to work more than eleven and a half hours daily or ten hours nightly on Saturdays and on the day before holidays. Work was forbidden on Sundays and holidays. Adolescents were permitted to work only ten hours a day, children only nine. In 1903 a law made employers liable for job-related injuries. Despite the improvement of conditions in the workplace, most Russian workers still lived in squalor.

Ironically Witte's success at promoting rapid industrialization contributed to unrest and revolutionary activity. To raise capital for investment and technology, the government imposed severe taxes on the peasants and bought their grain at deflated prices to earn large profits by selling it on the world market. The plight of the peasant during the half century following emancipation in 1861 was complicated by a rural population boom that by 1905 had reduced an average peasant's share of communal land by a third. The deterioration of conditions in the countryside led to famines and frequent peasant revolts.

In the cities, industrialization had created a budding proletarian class that numbered between two million and three million by 1905. Some revolutionary groups, such as the Bolsheviks, targeted their propaganda on the workers, who began to develop a class consciousness. Finally, since the Russian industrial expansion was financed largely by foreign and state capital, no significant entrepreneurial class developed that could pressure the autocracy for liberal reforms, respond to the needs of workers, or at least deflect worker criticism from the state. Under the system of state ownership that developed, discontented workers would blame the government. Although the surge of industrialization had made Russia a stronger, more advanced nation, it had contributed to peasant unhappiness and had created a worker class that was ripe to be influenced by revolutionaries.

Nicholas II

Tsar Alexander III died from a stroke in 1894 and was succeeded by his son, Nicholas II, the last Russian tsar. Nicholas expanded his father's conservative policies, restricting the authority of local zemstvo assemblies and imposing widespread press censorship. Pogroms against Jews and violent harassment of other non-Orthodox denominations intensified as religious persecution and Russification, begun under Alexander III, reached new heights.

Nicholas's conservative policies, the constant threat of famine, and the dreadful living conditions of peasants and workers rallied the disparate liberal and radical movements decimated by the repression of the 1880s. By the early 1900s liberals, many of whom were from the rising professional class, had established the Union of Liberation. In 1905 they created the Constitutional Democratic party. The party's members, who were known as the "Kadets" from the Russian initials for "constitutional democrat," were devoted to the establishment of a constitution, basic civil liberties, and equality for all minorities and classes. The radicals split into two major units, the Marxist-oriented Russian Social Democratic Labor party, which hoped to use the workers as a base of power, and the populist Socialist Revolutionaries, a group that was committed to a peasant revolution that would bring self-determination for minority groups, universal suffrage, civil liberties, and improvement of the peasants' economic conditions.

At its 1903 gathering, the Social Democratic Labor party split into two branches, the "majoritarians" (Bolsheviks) and the "minoritarians" (Mensheviks). The Bolsheviks, led by V. I. Lenin (whose real name was Vladimir Ilich Ulyanov), preferred a concentrated party guided by an elite group of dedicated revolutionaries. The Mensheviks envisioned a more broadly based organization. Yuli Martov, a Menshevik leader, wrote that his group believed that "unlimited democracy [is] the only political form in which the social emancipation of the proletariat can be prepared and realized." The Mensheviks and Bolsheviks also differed on the timing of a socialist revolution. The Mensheviks were loyal to the theories of George Plekhanov (1857-1918), who has been called the "father of Russian Marxism." He maintained that before Russia could achieve socialism, it would have to go through a period of capitalism that would create a large worker class and other conditions necessary to sustain a socialist society. The Bolsheviks, however, claimed that its elite group of revolutionaries could lead Russian society directly to socialism, bypassing the capitalist stage of development that Plekhanov (and Marx) believed was necessary.

Russo-Japanese War

The Russo-Japanese War of 1904-1905 increased domestic opposition to Nicholas's rule. The war resulted from the mutual ambitions of the Russians and Japanese to dominate Manchuria and Korea in an era of waning Chinese strength. To the surprise of the tsar's government and most of the world, the Japanese defeated the Russians. The key event of the war came on May 27, 1904, when the Japanese navy decimated the Russian Baltic fleet, which had sailed to the Pacific, in the battle of the Tsushima Strait. Although Russia was considered a more powerful nation, the Japanese had surpassed the Russians in naval technology and benefited from British support and shorter supply and communication lines. Japan also maintained a high degree of morale and national cohesion, while the war quickly became unpopular with the Russian people. The war ended in September 1905 with the signing of the Treaty of Portsmouth (New Hampshire), which was mediated by President Theodore Roosevelt. Count Sergei Witte served as the Russian negotiator and secured relatively favorable terms given his nation's clear defeat. The treaty, however, obliged Russia to cede southern Sakhalin Island and Port Arthur to Japan, recognize Japan's protectorate over Korea, and remove its forces from Manchuria.

The military humiliation at the hands of what was perceived as an inferior power seriously weakened the prestige of the tsar's government. Moreover, the government's apparent inefficiency in prosecuting the war, the higher taxes necessitated by the war, and the loss of many Russian lives for distant objectives that had little meaning to the average peasant or worker increased the revolutionary activities of the people. Demands mounted for the establishment of a legislative assembly and civil rights as workers went on strike and students demonstrated in the cities.

Revolution of 1905

The series of events known as the Revolution of 1905 began on "Bloody Sunday," January 22, 1905. A large group of nonrevolutionary workers, demonstrating peacefully for moderate reforms in front of the tsar's Winter Palace in St. Petersburg, was fired upon by the police. Hundreds were killed and wounded. Although Nicholas had been away from the palace at the time, the violent police reaction shattered the ideal that a sacred bond existed between the Russian people and a paternalistic tsar who would look after their welfare. Consequently, many traditionally loyal working people who had supported the tsar joined the socialists and other groups calling for radical changes. Bloody Sunday also stunned the Kadets and other moderate liberals who began cooperating more closely with the radical opposition. The anti-tsarist revolution became a broad social movement that included workers, peasants, national minorities, intellectuals, members of the bourgeoisie, and, for the first time, members of the armed forces.

Strikes, disturbances, and mutinies continued until August, when Nicholas announced the creation of an elective *Duma* (representative assembly) to advise the tsar. The proposal satisfied few in the opposition, and the revolutionaries organized a general strike that paralyzed the country from October 20 to October 30. In particular, railroad and communication services were almost totally shut down. The strike forced Tsar Nicholas and his ministers on October 30 to issue a manifesto mandating a Duma empowered to propose and enact legislation and guaranteeing all Russians civil rights, including freedom of the press, speech, and assembly.

This program won the approval of the liberals and the disdain of the radicals, thus splitting the opposition. Disturbances continued, but the government had blunted the momentum of the revolution. In addition, the armies returning from the Far East remained loyal to the tsar. After troops prevailed over dissidents in several days of bloody street fighting in Moscow in December, the revolution was effectively ended.

Duma Period

Although Nicholas had agreed to establish a Duma, he continued to espouse absolutist principles and tried to

Stolypin: Tsarist Minister

As prime minister of Russia from 1906 until 1911, Peter Stolypin built a reputation as an efficient, innovative, and ruthless servant of Tsar Nicholas II. Historians have called him imperial Russia's last effective prime minister.

Although the tsar's creation of a Duma in 1905 had temporarily relieved the threat of a popular revolution, radical intellectual groups and terrorists still operated against the government. Determined to break the radical opposition, Stolypin launched a "pacification" campaign in 1906. He shut down more than two hundred newspapers, backed an aggressive police campaign to infiltrate radical organizations, and established summary courts-martial, under which a suspect could be arrested, tried, and executed on the same day. More than a thousand persons were executed on the order of these courts.

Stolypin's pacification policy achieved its goals by 1908. Many revolutionaries fled the country, several leading revolutionary groups were destroyed, and terrorism was dramatically reduced.

While suppressing the opposition, Stolypin also tried to eliminate the causes of societal discontent, particularly among the peasantry. He aspired to create a free, educated class of peasant land owners that would be economically productive, loyal to the tsar, and immune to revolutionary appeals. To this end, he initiated a program of agrarian reform in the fall of 1906. The Stolypin Land Reforms, also known as the "wager on the strong," provided for the partitioning of commune lands into plots owned by individual commune members. Stolypin's government also allowed peasants to buy state-owned land, created the Peasant Land Bank, and encouraged peasant migration to remote virgin farmland.

The implementation of Stolypin's reform program was cut short by his death and the onset of World War I, but many peasants responded to the program enthusiastically. Given its scope and promising beginning, its full implementation might have changed the course of Russian history.

Stolypin's proclivity to create enemies eventually brought his downfall. Those on the radical left despised him for his ruthless suppression of revolutionary activity, while those on the right feared and resented his power. Even the tsar came to dislike Stolypin, in part because he frustrated the tsarina's unmerited promotions of her favorites to high government positions.

On September 14, 1911, Stolypin was assassinated by a man named Dmitri Bogrov while attending an opera in Kiev with the tsar. Bogrov was apprehended at the scene and labeled a terrorist, but there is evidence that he was a police agent.

avoid relinquishing any power. To this end he and his advisers devised several means through which they could limit the power of the new Duma. The government issued a list of "fundamental laws" that the Duma could not change and announced that the tsar at any time could dissolve the Duma, arrange new elections, and issue legislation in the interval. Under the fundamental laws, the tsar would have sole authority over foreign and military policy, succession to the throne, ministerial appointments, pardons, and internal court affairs. In addition his finance minister would be responsible for currency issues and foreign loans. To further insulate itself, the government secured a large loan from France and allowed the Duma to control only 60 percent of the state budget. Finally the tsar's council of state, an advisory body, was transformed into an upper house with equal power to the Duma so that it could function as a conservative legislative counterweight to the Duma's liberal and radical membership.

The first Duma met May 10, 1906. The tsar and his advisers expected the peasants to vote for conservative representatives who would support the crown, but instead they elected a reform-minded majority. Behind the leadership of the Kadets, the party that won the most seats (38 percent), the Duma demanded land redistribution. The tsar refused, and after a period of bitter debate, he dissolved the Duma in July. Its Kadet members crossed into Finland, where they reconvened and issued a call urging Russian citizens to deny the government tax payments and military service until the Duma was brought back into session. The government declared the Kadets who rebelled ineligible for office in future Dumas and set up new elections.

The second Duma, which opened in March 1907, was even more radical than the first. It was dissolved in July of that year. Nicholas and his advisers realized that the original election laws would not produce a cooperative Duma. They therefore changed the laws to enhance the representation of the wealthier and more conservative groups. As a result the third Duma (1907-1912) served out its full term and was largely supportive of the tsar's government. The fourth Duma (1912-1916) was conservative but displayed greater independence from the tsar. Both Dumas had moderate and radical members who were able to voice their concerns in the assembly, and the bodies advanced some reforms, particularly in the area of improving conditions for workers and peasants.

World War I

Popular dissatisfaction with the imperial government simmered from 1905 until 1914. Radicals continued to agitate, workers struck, and terrorists succeeded in assassinating some government officials. The assassination on September 14, 1911, of Peter Stolypin, prime minister since 1906, was a particularly hard blow to Nicholas's government. Stolypin's land reform policies had substantially improved the lot of the Russian peasantry, thereby complicating the task of radical agitators who sought to convince the peasants to support a revolution. Historians suspect, however, that Stolypin's assassin was actually employed by officials whom the prime minister had alienated. The tsar's agents, meanwhile, sought to infiltrate and disrupt revolutionary societies. *(Stolypin, box, this page)*

The burgeoning political, economic, and cultural transformation of Russia was interrupted when World War I broke out in August 1914. Russia fought with France and

Great Britain against Germany and Austria-Hungary. Its initial goals were to block German and Austrian ambitions in the Balkan states and fulfill its mutual defense obligations to France. However, the tsar's government soon added the acquisition of the Turkish Straits and Constantinople to its list of objectives.

At the beginning of the war the Russian people rushed to support the tsar and his army, believing unprovoked Austro-German aggression necessitated a common effort for national defense. The populace was encouraged by early successes, but a series of military disasters on the German front dashed morale. The government's ineptitude contributed to an excessively high rate of Russian casualties. By 1915 German armies had captured Poland and penetrated into Russia. Arms and munitions were in short supply or completely unavailable. Food was scarce, and the mood of the people toward the government was hostile.

Nicholas had left St. Petersburg in September 1915 to take personal charge of his armies. In his absence, the government was run by Tsarina Alexandra, who for several years had relied heavily on the counsel of Grigorii Rasputin, a strange Siberian monk whom the tsarina credited with relieving her son's hemophilia. Rasputin and the tsarina alienated the members of the Duma, on the left and the right. Rasputin, "the mad monk," was assassinated December 30, 1916, by a group of conservatives in the hope that his elimination would restore confidence in the government. By that time, however, the Russian people had so many grievances with the government, it is unlikely that any reform or change in personalities at court could have slowed the revolution. (Rasputin, box, this page)

The Revolution of 1917

The Russian Revolution began spontaneously in March 1917 in Petrograd, which had been renamed from the Germanic St. Petersburg during the war. A severe shortage of bread led to enforced rationing and long lines at shops. The prospect of hunger and even starvation led to demonstrations and strikes. On March 8 a huge crowd that included many women marched in the streets to demand government action to end the bread shortages. The march was broken up by police, but over the next two days the demonstrations grew.

The government ordered troops to restore order on March 11, but instead of putting down the riots, the soldiers stood by passively or even joined them. The defection of the local army garrisons to the side of the demonstrators caused the government to crumble. Tsar Nicholas II abdicated March 15 in favor of his brother, Michael, who handed power to the "Provisional Government" formed by the Duma two days before. The revolution in Petrograd spread quickly throughout Russia. In most locations tsarist governors and representatives were replaced without bloodshed.

The Provisional Government

The Provisional Government, which initially was led by Prince Georgii Lvov, operated from an inherently weak position. Because it included representatives from several groups that had little in common but their opposition to the tsar, it had difficulty reaching a consensus on policy. The Provisional Government also found it impossible to

Rasputin: Rakish Adviser

Grigorii Rasputin, the strange mystic who wielded enormous influence over Tsarina Alexandra, was a peasant. He was born around 1872 in Pokrovokoe, a village in Siberia, to a family named Novykh. He was given the name Rasputin—in Russian, "dissolute"—by villagers who witnessed his early lecherous behavior. After his marriage to a local woman, Rasputin spent his early adulthood in religious wandering.

During these travels across Russia he fashioned a personal brand of religion, which included his belief that sexual indulgence was part of the process of religious rapture. Most commentators believe that Rasputin's endorsement of uninhibited sexual activity was a convenient justification for indulging his own sexual appetite.

In 1903 Rasputin arrived in St. Petersburg. He persuaded members of the royal circle that he was a clairvoyant and soon became their spiritual adviser. In 1905 he was introduced to the royal family. Presenting himself simply as a holy man, Rasputin won the admiration and respect of the tsarina through his reported ability to improve the health of her son, Alexis, a hemophiliac and heir to the throne.

Over the next several years he became one of the tsarina's favorites, advising her on spiritual and, eventually, political matters. He considered himself the voice of the Russian peasantry; the tsarina, some think, considered him the voice of God.

As Rasputin's influence grew, he was besieged by petitioners seeking the favor of the royal family and the government. The constant flow of visitors to his home in St. Petersburg facilitated his debauchery. He allegedly seduced many of the more attractive female petitioners. Reports of his sexual exploits were circulated widely in St. Petersburg, but the tsarina dismissed them as gossip.

Opposition to Rasputin grew among conservatives at court after Tsar Nicholas II in September 1915 assumed field command of his troops fighting in World War I. Nicholas's departure from St. Petersburg left the tsarina, with Rasputin at her side, in virtual control of the country. As reports of Rasputin's scandalous excesses increased, a group of conspirators hatched a plot to assassinate him in the hope of preserving the monarchy.

According to historical accounts, the group included Vladimir Purishkevich, a conservative Duma member; Prince Feliks Yusupov, a wealthy nobleman; and Grand Duke Dmitri Pavlovich, the tsar's first cousin. On the night of December 30, 1916, during a visit to Yusupov's home, Rasputin was poisoned and, when the poison seemed to have no effect, shot.

Tsar Nicholas II and Tsarina Alexandra with their entourage.

satisfy the great expectations of the Russian people who believed that the revolution would remedy all that was wrong with their nation. In addition the Provisional Government was regarded as a temporary arrangement that would govern Russia until a permanent constituent assembly could be elected. Perhaps the most significant weakness of the Provisional Government's position, however, was that it had to share authority with local assemblies known as *soviets*.

Soviets were grass-roots councils that had been formed throughout the country in neighborhoods, villages, factories, and army posts. They were modeled after the first soviet, which had been formed in St. Petersburg during the October strike of 1905. This soviet had been a committee of elected representatives from various factories that coordinated the strike. After the general strike, the government arrested the members of the St. Petersburg Soviet, including its most famous leader, Leon Trotsky, who was banished to Siberia but escaped to Europe.

On March 12, 1917, revolutionaries reconstituted the St. Petersburg Soviet as the Petrograd Soviet of Workers' and Soldiers' Deputies. In the early days of the revolution thousands of soviets were established across Russia to provide revolutionary forums and administer local affairs. The power of the Petrograd Soviet, however, extended to national affairs because it had influence over soldiers and workers in important industries in Petrograd and other large cities. It quickly became a partner of and competitor to the Provisional Government. The Petrograd Soviet lent support to the Provisional Government in return for some say in the running of the state.

The Provisional Government immediately proclaimed full equality before the law for all Russians and guaranteed freedom of speech, assembly, press, and religion. Unions and strikes were permitted, and new labor laws inaugu-

rated eight-hour days for some workers. The Provisional Government also mandated changes in local government that made it more egalitarian and promised greater autonomy to ethnic minorities.

Although these actions were popular, the Provisional Government failed to assert control over the country or address its two most pressing problems—the economy and the war. The steep decline of the economy was exacerbated by food shortages and the destruction and dislocations caused by the fighting on Russian territory. The government's most fateful decision was to continue the war, despite the dismal state of Russian morale, the lack of supplies, and the decimated transportation system. The Provisional Government had taken modest steps toward establishing a more just society, but the Russian people expected these steps after the revolution. What they wanted was progress toward peace and prosperity.

Peasants formed an overwhelming majority in the armed forces, and with the promise of coming land redistribution, more than one million men simply left the army between March and October to ensure receiving their share of the land. Peasants began to take action against landowners because they felt the Provisional Government was moving too slowly on land reform. Owners who refused to sell their land to peasants at deflated prices were subject to attack. The government was besieged by owners' pleas for help. Little was forthcoming, as the government did not have adequate means to enforce order in the countryside, and it hoped to defer action on land redistribution until a constituent assembly could be elected.

Industrial workers, meanwhile, were rapidly joining the revolutionary ranks. Because they were centered in urban areas and were better organized, these workers had aided the revolution and were among the first to see benefits from it. But things still were not moving fast enough for them, and, as the economic picture rapidly declined, many were forced out of work. With increasing hunger in the cities came increasing violence and protests.

Bolsheviks Seize Power

On April 16, 1917, after ten years of exile in Switzerland, Lenin arrived in Petrograd intending to radicalize the revolution. Lenin's return had been aided by the Germans, who hoped that he would create an intensification of revolutionary activity in Russia that would weaken their opponent. Lenin, however, was not working for the Germans and ultimately expected that the international socialist revolution would engulf Germany as well as Russia.

In Petrograd Lenin issued what came to be known as his "April Theses," a radical Bolshevik strategy that surprised many of his colleagues. Lenin urged his party not to support the Provisional Government or the war effort. He also advocated transferring government power to the soviets (although Lenin did not press for the immediate achievement of this objective, since the Bolsheviks were not well represented in the soviets at this time). Many moderate liberals and socialists denounced Lenin's approach, but the Bolshevik party gradually grew in strength.

Meanwhile, the unpopularity and weakness of the Provisional Government were becoming increasingly apparent. In June, despite the Provisional Government's protests, the Ukraine took action to establish its independence. In early July an offensive against Germany, which the government hoped would turn the tide of the war, stalled. Russian forces were left more exhausted and vulnerable to attack than they had been before. Responding to a sense of impending national calamity, citizens in Petrograd on July 16 and 17 staged massive demonstrations against the government in what became known as the "July Days." Minister of War Aleksandr Kerensky dispersed the two-day riot and arrested some radical leaders. Lenin was forced to flee to Finland. Calm was restored to the capital, but the demonstrations had revealed the vulnerability of the government and the revolutionary mood of the people.

On July 21 Prince Lvov resigned as premier. It took more than two weeks for the disorganized and contentious leaders of the Provisional Government to form a new ruling coalition. On September 7 Kerensky was named premier of a somewhat more leftist government composed primarily of Kadets, Socialist Revolutionaries, and Mensheviks.

In September, the Provisional Government faced its first serious counterrevolutionary challenge. Gen. Lavr Kornilov, the recently appointed commander in chief of the Russian Army, attempted a military coup that became known as the "Kornilov affair." A simple, hard-working man with little capacity for political nuance, Kornilov was convinced the Petrograd Soviet was the source of all Russia's problems. He initiated what most historians now regard as a comedy of errors that contributed to the disintegration of the military and the Provisional Government.

After Prime Minister Kerensky sanctioned the use of troops to put down domestic unrest, Kornilov believed that he had been authorized to take over the government. The general dispatched troops to the capital ostensibly to combat dissent but in reality to ensure military control of the government and the removal of the Petrograd Soviet. After an intermediary urged Kerensky to cede to Kornilov, Kerensky became convinced that Kornilov's efforts were really a conspiracy. He dismissed Kornilov, who refused to give up control of the army, and ordered more troops to the capital.

In the meantime, the Petrograd Soviet and other socialist organizations acted quickly by mobilizing and arming the generally sympathetic workers in Petrograd and the nearby sailors from Kronstadt naval base. It took little effort to disband the arriving Kornilov soldiers once they were convinced their efforts were counterrevolutionary. Kornilov and other officers were arrested, and several government ministers who had cooperated with him were dismissed.

Bystanders scramble for cover as government machine gunners fire at revolutionists in Petrograd, 1917.

Kronstadt Rebellion

The Kronstadt rebellion in early 1921 was a dramatic climax to anti-Bolshevik unrest following the civil war. Terrible conditions in the countryside and strikes and demonstrations in Petrograd over food shortages caused sailors stationed at the nearby Kronstadt naval base to question the leadership of the Bolsheviks. The sailors adopted a platform that called for secret ballot elections, guarantees of civil rights, release of political prisoners, freedom for peasants to use their land however they wished, and an end to the Communist party's monopoly on power.

On March 2 the sailors rebelled by establishing a Provisional Revolutionary Committee to govern the naval base and work for the adoption of their platform. They hoped their rebellion would rally workers and peasants throughout the country to oppose Bolshevik leadership. The nationwide revolution, however, did not materialize.

After the chairman of the Soviet Central Executive Committee, Mikhail I. Kalinin, failed to settle the situation at the Kronstadt base with a personal visit, the government prepared to take the base by force. On March 18 government forces led by Leon Trotsky attacked Kronstadt. The attackers overcame the sailors' resistance, and some fifteen thousand people who surrendered were executed without a trial.

The rebellion had failed, but it succeeded in shaking up Lenin and his colleagues. Although the Bolshevik leaders called the rebellion the work of counterrevolutionary forces, they knew that the Kronstadt sailors were among the staunchest supporters of the revolution and previously had fought bravely against forces threatening the Bolshevik regime. The Kronstadt rebellion, therefore, was a sign that the dictatorship of the proletariat established by the Bolsheviks was being opposed by the class of people it was designed to represent. In response the Bolsheviks passed resolutions strengthening their monopoly on power and outlawing factionalism within the party. They then launched the New Economic Policy, which relaxed economic controls and allowed limited private enterprise.

Although the Provisional Government survived, Kerensky had been forced to appeal to the Bolsheviks for help. He also had released Leon Trotsky and other important radical leaders from prison. Kerensky's reliance on the left cost him the support of the right and many moderates, while strengthening the reputation of the Bolsheviks, who were regarded by many as the defenders of the revolution. This perception was significant since the Bolsheviks' opponents had attempted to portray them as disloyal because of their opposition to the war with Germany. In addition, the Kornilov affair increased support for the Bolsheviks because it seemed to confirm their warnings about the threat of counterrevolutionary activity and the need to expand on the revolution.

The attempted coup also weakened the military. Purges and other moves against men and groups within the army that had supported Kornilov caused the situation at the front to deteriorate further. Desertions increased, and many of the men who remained were embittered, disillusioned, and physically incapable of continuing the war.

The Bolsheviks wasted little time in taking advantage of the disorganized situation. They obtained a majority of the seats in the Petrograd Soviet in September, and by October, Trotsky became its chairman. The Bolsheviks gained popularity largely because they were the only Russian political group that promised the workers, peasants, and soldiers what they wanted—land redistribution, an end to food shortages, and an immediate withdrawal from the war. The Bolsheviks expressed their commitment to these objectives through the simple slogan "land, bread, and peace." They also were popular with the non-Russian minorities because they promised to establish the right of self-determination.

Lenin secretly returned to Petrograd from Finland October 23 and urged his followers to seize power. "History will not forgive us if we do not take power now," he pleaded. His longtime lieutenants Grigorii Zinoviev and Lev Kamenev, however, wanted to postpone the coup to further strengthen support among the masses. After some initial hesitation the Bolsheviks occupied government offices November 7, 1917, as soldiers stood by refusing to defend the Provisional Government. The next day the Bolsheviks took over the Winter Palace after facing weak resistance from troops defending it and placed under arrest those members of the Provisional Government who remained behind after Kerensky and other government leaders escaped the city. The Bolshevik takeover often is called the "Great October Revolution" in the Soviet Union because in 1917 the Julian calendar was still in use in Russia, making the date of the revolution October 25 instead of November 7. The Gregorian, or Western, calendar was adopted January 31, 1918.

The Bolsheviks had accomplished one of the most dramatic political feats in history. At the time of the tsar's overthrow, they were a well-organized, but relatively small party with little influence over the Provisional Government. By November the party had grown more than ten times, acquired substantial support from urban workers and soldiers, and seized power in Petrograd with relatively little bloodshed.

Establishing Bolshevik Rule

The Bolsheviks on November 9, 1917, established the Council of People's Commissars as the highest ruling body in the country. Lenin assumed the chairmanship of the council. Other prominent Bolsheviks in the government included Leon Trotsky, commissar for foreign affairs, and Joseph Stalin, who was assigned responsibility for national minority groups. In March 1918 the party changed its name from the "Russian Social Democratic Labor party, Bolshevik" to the "Communist party, Bolshevik." The Russian Soviet Federated Socialist Republic was created by the first Soviet constitution, which the Fifth All-Russian Congress of Soviets adopted July 10, 1918.

The victory of communism in Russia generally is attributed to the opportunism and organizational brilliance of Lenin and Trotsky and to the Bolsheviks' ability to appeal to the Russian people during a time of national unrest created by a failing economy and Russian military losses in World War I. The Bolsheviks were able to remain in power because they were better organized than their opponents and because they established their own type of totalitarianism that eliminated dissent and challenges to their rule. The Bolsheviks capitalized on the mistakes of their opponents but appropriated popular policies of other parties when it suited their needs. In particular they adopted the agrarian policies of the Socialist Revolutionaries in an effort to increase peasant support for their regime during their first months in power.

In November 1917 the Bolsheviks firmly controlled Petrograd, but they still were struggling to establish their authority over the rest of the country. To achieve this authority, they needed the support, or at least the acquiescence, of the army. Russia's defeats at the hands of the Germans and the Kornilov affair created disarray in the army that aided Bolshevik efforts to gain control of it. The Bolsheviks appealed to the class consciousness of the soldiers who had not already deserted. This propaganda was somewhat successful. Many soldiers, however, threw in their lot with Lenin's government simply out of loyalty to the Russian state or a desire to continue their military careers under whoever happened to be in power. Consequently, although a significant number of soldiers eventually would join units that would fight against the new government in the coming civil war, the Bolsheviks succeeded in co-opting enough of the army to prevent a military coup. On January 28, 1918, Lenin and his colleagues decided to abandon the structure of the old tsarist army and replace it with a new "Red Army" based on socialist principles.

Lenin's efforts to bring all of Russia under Bolshevik authority centered on gaining control of the local soviets. Since the Bolsheviks were not well represented in many city and rural soviets, they resorted to tactics ranging from political campaigning and propaganda to intimidation and the use of armed force. The struggle for control of the soviets in many large cities, including Moscow, was bloody. By the end of the year, the Bolshevik government controlled most major population centers, although many rural areas remained outside their complete authority. Lenin bolstered his government's popularity by reaffirming its intention to redistribute gentry land, establish worker control of industry (which Lenin did within twenty days of taking power), and negotiate a peace settlement with the Germans.

The peace terms eventually accepted by Bolshevik negotiators were harsh. Trotsky and other leaders initially refused to accept the treaty, but they relented after Lenin threatened to resign if it were not approved. The Treaty of Brest-Litovsk, signed on March 3, 1918, obligated Russia to recognize the independence of Estonia, Latvia, Lithuania, Poland, and the Ukraine and to recognize German influence over them. The relinquishment of these lands meant that the Russian empire would lose about one-quarter of its population and arable land, one-third of its manufacturing capacity, and nearly three-quarters of both its iron and coal production. German troops or local non-Russian authorities, however, controlled much of the area given up by Russia, so the treaty primarily recognized political realities that the Bolsheviks were not in a position to change.

Politically, the new government faced a challenge from the Constituent Assembly elected November 25, 1917. Although the Bolsheviks had taken over complete control of the government, they felt obligated to continue paying lip service to democracy. Consequently, they allowed elections to take place for the Constituent Assembly that had been promised by the Provisional Government. The Bolshevik party, however, won only 170 out of 707 seats in the assembly. Behind strong peasant support, the Socialist Revolutionaries won 370 seats, an absolute majority. The Constituent Assembly met for the first time on January 18, 1918, and immediately challenged Bolshevik policies. The next day Lenin ordered the body to dissolve. The Socialist Revolutionaries protested, but the Bolsheviks suffered no major repercussions from their disbandment of the assembly. From then on, opposition to Bolshevik rule would come only from outside the central government.

War Communism

The Bolshevik seizure of power did not end social strife in Russia. From 1918 until early 1921 Lenin and his fellow Bolsheviks faced challenges from several domestic armies seeking their overthrow, non-Russian minorities seeking national liberation, and foreign forces seeking a variety of objectives. The Bolsheviks also had to contend with an economy devastated by World War I and indignation from some segments of society over the harsh terms of the Brest-Litovsk treaty. In this uncertain atmosphere, the Bolsheviks launched a series of policies that came to be known as "War Communism."

War Communism sought to construct a communist society and economic system in the shortest possible time and to mobilize all available resources for the fight against the anti-Bolsheviks. It aimed to achieve these goals by establishing a planned economy based on state ownership of the means of production, eliminating markets, compensating workers according to their needs, and extending egalitarian principles to all aspects of life.

The government, therefore, rapidly took over businesses and factories. By 1920 all production and distribution enterprises employing ten workers or more were controlled by the state. The Bolsheviks also nationalized banks, foreign trade, and all land; repudiated the tsar's foreign debts; outlawed strikes; seized private property; and replaced Russia's inflated currency with a system of barter. To silence domestic critics they dissolved all other political parties and established a political police force—the Extraordinary Commission to Combat Counterrevolution, Sabotage, and Speculation (Cheka). They also initiated compulsory military training and free education and declared a separation of church and state. *(Secret police, box, p. 36)*

War Communism brought about a direct, violent struggle between the new regime and the peasants. To gain peasant loyalty, the Bolsheviks had advocated a general land redistribution. Under War Communism, however, they initiated a plan to transform the peasants into farm workers under a large-scale, centralized system of agricultural production. Peasants resisted this, and the government temporarily acceded to some of their wishes. Meanwhile the food shortages that had contributed to the 1917 revolutionary upheaval in Russia continued under Bolshevik rule. As the food situation grew more desperate (in part because of the ongoing civil war), the government directed

The Philosophy of Karl Marx ...

Karl Marx (1818-1883), the philosopher who gave his name to the system of social, economic, and political thought embraced by Russian revolutionaries, was born in the German Rhineland city of Trier. He studied history and philosophy at the universities of Bonn and Berlin, where he was exposed to the writings of the German philosopher Georg Wilhelm Friedrich Hegel (1770-1831). Throughout his life Marx witnessed the misery and exploitation that accompanied the Industrial Revolution in Europe. These impressions influenced the development of his radical socialist philosophy.

In 1842 Marx began editing a Cologne-based political journal, *Rheinische Zeitung.* The authorities closed the publication in 1843, and Marx moved to Paris to work as an editor of *Deutsch-Franzosische Zeitung.* In 1845 his revolutionary ideas led to his expulsion from France. Marx and his wife, Jenny von Westphalen, took refuge in Brussels. While there he and his colleague and frequent financial supporter, Friedrich Engels (1820-1895), wrote the *Communist Manifesto.* A blueprint for the Communist League, a small group of European radicals, the *Manifesto* called on the oppressed mass of workers, the proletariat, to liberate itself from capitalist enslavement. It ended with the rallying cry:

> The proletarians have nothing to lose but their chains. They have a world to win. Working men of all countries, unite!

Shortly after publication of the *Manifesto* in 1848, Marx returned to Cologne and again published a newspaper, until the German government expelled him the following year. He settled in London, where he spent the rest of his life.

Marxist Theory

The philosophy outlined in the *Manifesto* and Marx's other writings centered on the struggle between social classes. Adapting an idea developed by Hegel, Marx argued that class struggle occurred in cycles: an existing situation (the thesis) inevitably was challenged by a new idea (the antithesis), and the exchange (the dialectic) between thesis and antithesis resulted in something new (the synthesis). According to Marx, throughout history the continuous cycle of thesis, antithesis, and synthesis spurred the evolution of social and economic organization from slavery to feudalism to capitalism.

Marx maintained that labor alone created value. Under capitalism, however, the owners of businesses and factories received profits from the unpaid labor time of those who possessed only their work skills. In Marx's view this inherently exploitive arrangement would become increasingly unendurable for workers as competition forced owners to squeeze greater profits out of them to accumulate more capital. Simultaneously, as capital became concentrated in fewer and fewer hands, small owners would be driven out of business, swelling the ranks of the working class.

Many socialist thinkers had predicted that a peaceful evolution toward socialism (a system where the means of production are owned commonly by society) would occur in industrialized nations. Marx, however, believing that economic conditions more

---

"food requisition detachments" to get food from the countryside any way they could. In theory the peasants were to be compensated for their grain with manufactured goods. But often they were given nothing, and the items that they did receive were likely to be of poor quality or of little use to them. The requisitioned food was transported to the cities, where its distribution was overseen by a growing central bureaucracy.

Lenin's draconian policies in the countryside led to fighting between the peasants and government agents sent to requisition food. The Bolsheviks further enflamed the situation by enlisting the poorer peasants as informers and requisitioners against the wealthier peasants, who were known as *kulaks.* Although the government's use of terror did not approach the magnitude used by Joseph Stalin during the 1930s, some hundred thousand kulaks were killed or sent to labor camps for resisting Bolshevik policies.

The effect of the government's food requisition policies was to alienate much of the peasantry and induce them to either produce less or hide surplus grain, since any food they produced beyond their immediate needs was likely to be requisitioned. Consequently, the food crisis in Russia continued throughout the War Communism period. From 1920 to 1922 the frequent food shortages escalated into an outright famine that killed as many as five million people.

War Communism was almost as unsuccessful in the cities. The Bolsheviks' monetary and industrial policies worsened the deteriorating economy they had inherited. Industrial workers protested economic conditions through absenteeism and illegal strikes. In 1921, with the civil war won, Lenin called a retreat from War Communism and instituted the New Economic Policy (NEP).

Civil War

The most pressing problem facing the new regime during the period of War Communism, however, was the civil war. The war pitted the Bolshevik Red Army against various anti-Bolshevik (White) forces. The White armies were made up of soldiers from the tsar's army, monarchists, conservatives, liberals, Socialist Revolutionaries, Menshe-

... Foundation of a Revolution

than any other factor were responsible for political behavior, reasoned that the pressures created by the exploitation of the working class would inevitably produce a violent upheaval. The unrest would culminate in a proletarian revolution in which workers would overthrow capitalist governments and establish socialist states. Eventually Marx believed that these socialist states would achieve the final (and to Marx the highest) form of society, communism. At this point dialectic tension would end.

Marx envisioned a communist society as one in which all classes would be eliminated and property would be owned commonly by all citizens. Under such a system there would be no exploitation of labor, unemployment would be eliminated, goods would be abundant and fairly distributed according to need, and citizens would be motivated to work hard for the benefit of the whole society. Because Marx thought of political power as a means through which one class oppressed another, he expected state institutions to "wither away." He also expected the bonds between workers in different countries would transcend national identities and loyalties. Consequently, a major cause of war would be eliminated with the establishment of communism.

The radical revolutions that swept Europe in 1848 were not communist inspired, a fact that disappointed Marx. But he continued to promote revolution from London, helping to establish with the radical Russian émigré Mikhail Bakunin the First International Workingmen's Association in 1864 and maintaining a network of revolutionary contacts. Marx also devoted himself to his major scholarly effort, *Das Kapital,* the first volume of which was published in 1867.

Russia's Revolutionary Potential

Marx believed that a society had to pass through the capitalist stage before it could reach socialism. Because Russia had barely entered the industrial age and remained backward and largely agricultural, Marx initially put it low on the list of countries ripe for socialist revolution. He looked instead to the industrialized nations—Germany, France, Great Britain, and the United States—for signs of impending upheaval.

Late in his life, however, Marx became interested in Russia's revolutionary potential. He devoted much time to the study of Russia's language, history, and culture and followed closely the activities of its revolutionary intellectuals. Engels complained to Marx that his preoccupation with conditions in Russia was delaying completion of *Das Kapital.* By the 1870s, the establishment of communism was debated in Russia's radical circles. The revolutionary Populists, members of *Narodnaya Volya,* argued that socialism was uniquely suited to Russia because Russian society was based on the village commune, a primitive communist organization. Under this favorable circumstance, Russia could skip over the capitalist development phase and directly proceed to socialism. In the preface to a new Russian edition of the *Communist Manifesto* published in 1882, Marx and Engels agreed with this analysis of Russia's revolutionary potential.

viks, and most other political and social groups. Many people took up arms against the Bolsheviks in an idealistic attempt to restore democratic principles that the Bolsheviks had rejected in disbanding the Constituent Assembly. Others had been angered by the loss and humiliation of the Treaty of Brest-Litovsk. Still others sought personal power or a restoration of the old tsarist order. Because of their wide political differences, the leaders of the White forces could not agree on a program beyond the overthrow of the Bolshevik government. This factor hampered their ability to recruit soldiers and weakened the morale of their troops.

The war began in the summer of 1918 when a military front was established by White forces under Gen. Aleksandr Kolchak in western Siberia. Soon other White armies formed in the Baltic region, the Caucasus, and the far north near Murmansk. Thus, the White forces challenged Bolshevik rule in central Russia from widely distant bases on the nation's periphery.

Tsar Nicholas II and his family were among the war's early casualties. After the March 1917 revolution, they had been sent into internal exile at Ekaterinburg (renamed Sverdlovsk in 1924). On July 16, 1918, as White forces loyal to the tsar approached the town, local Bolsheviks with the support of Lenin killed the tsar, his wife, and their five children to prevent them from becoming a rallying point for the White armies.

In October 1919 White forces appeared to have the upper hand. Separate White armies reached the outskirts of Petrograd and penetrated to within 250 miles of Moscow (the Bolsheviks had moved the capital to Moscow in March 1918 for greater security). The Bolsheviks, however, stopped the advance of the White armies, and they went on the offensive. By April 1920 the Red Army had routed the White forces and had executed or chased into exile most of the White generals. The last active White army, under the leadership of Gen. Peter Wrangel, had retreated to the Crimea. Wrangel's troops abandoned the fight in November.

Several factors contributed to the Bolsheviks' victory. Foremost among these was their success at creating an army. They used conscription and patriotic appeals to build their Red Army into an effective, unified fighting force of several million troops under the command of Trotsky, who had become minister of war in 1918 after resigning as foreign minister. By 1919 the Red Army was larger than the various White armies arrayed against it. The Bolsheviks also had the advantages of interior lines of communication, control of most of the important railroad lines, and the ability to concentrate their forces against whichever White army was most threatening at the time. The divided White forces suffered from poor coordination caused by the great distances between armies and the personal rivalries of their generals. In addition, the leaders of the White forces refused to back progressive land reform or autonomy for non-Russian states that had been part of the tsar's empire. Had White leaders adopted more enlightened policies in these two areas, they likely would have increased their support among peasants and ethnic minorites—two large societal groups that tended to be dissatisfied with Bolshevik rule.

Foreign Intervention

The civil war between the Red and White armies was accompanied by armed intervention by Russia's erstwhile World War I allies. When the Bolsheviks withdrew Russia from the war against the Central Powers, the Western Allies were alarmed that Germany would be able to transfer hundreds of thousands of troops from the eastern to the western front. They also were concerned that the Germans would seize massive stockpiles of Allied war supplies stored in the northern Russian cities of Archangel and Murmansk. After diplomatic efforts failed to convince the Bolsheviks to reenter the war, the Allies began transporting troops to Russia in March 1918 to protect their supplies from the Germans and explore the opportunities for reestablishing the eastern front. Great Britain, France, Italy, the United States, and Japan landed small contingents in northern Russia or around Vladivostok in the Far East.

At first Lenin did not object to the intervention since it strengthened Russia's bargaining position with the Germans. Soon after the Treaty of Brest-Litovsk was concluded, however, Lenin came to regard the Allied forces as a threat. During 1918 the Allies ignored Bolshevik protests and began building up their garrisons in Russia.

Several generations of Soviet politicians and historians have pointed to the Allied intervention as evidence of the capitalist world's innate hostility toward the socialist experiment in Russia. From the beginning the Allies disliked and feared the Bolshevik government, which had urged workers in industrialized nations to revolt. Western leaders clearly preferred that such a government be replaced. Contrary to Soviet contentions, however, Allied governments initially saw the intervention primarily as a necessary war measure.

In May an incident in Siberia involving a brigade of Czechoslovak soldiers accelerated the movement toward civil war and greater Allied intervention. The forty-five-thousand-man brigade had been formed by Czechoslovaks living in Russia who wanted to fight on the side of the Allies. With Russia's withdrawal from the war, they were no longer needed on the eastern front. The Bolsheviks and Allies agreed on arrangements to transport the Czechoslovaks to the western front by traveling to Vladivostok on Russian trains, and then being transported to France on Allied ships. During their journey east, a fight between the Czechoslovak brigade and a group of Hungarian prisoners, who were being returned to Hungary under the provisions of the Treaty of Brest-Litovsk, led to a Bolshevik order to disarm the Czechoslovaks. The brigade, which was a match for any fighting force of comparable size in Russia at the time, ignored the order, took over the Trans-Siberian Railroad, and began to cooperate with Allied forces who had landed in Vladivostok. The ease with which the Czechoslovaks resisted the Bolsheviks and the growing strength of the Allied forces in Russia encouraged the establishment of White armies. The brigade's success and the spontaneous anti-Bolshevik uprisings that occurred also convinced some Allied leaders that the Bolshevik government was vulnerable.

On November 11, 1918, World War I ended with the Allies victorious. The defeat of Germany removed all justification for the Allies intervention in Russia, but by this time the Bolsheviks' anticapitalist propaganda, ambitions in eastern Europe, repudiation of the tsar's debts, and nationalization of foreign-owned industry had convinced some Allied leaders that they should do what they could to help overthrow the new Bolshevik government. The Allied forces in Russia, therefore, funneled material and financial support to the White armies, although the size of the Allied contingents was reduced. The one intervening nation to go beyond material support of the White armies was Japan, which sent a large contingent of soldiers to occupy parts of Siberia in the hope of permanently expanding its own empire in the Far East.

The Allied intervention, however, never escalated into a large-scale cooperative effort to overthrow the Bolsheviks. The populations of the Allied countries, who had just lived through the most brutal war in history, were in no mood to support large military operations in Russia. Moreover, it was not clear that the White forces could win or that Allied aid would further their cause, since Allied participation in their efforts enabled the Bolsheviks to portray the White armies as puppets of foreign invaders. Finally, several prominent Allied leaders, including President Woodrow Wilson, doubted the legality and wisdom of the intervention. Consequently, when the defeat of the White armies appeared likely in late 1919, the Allies began withdrawing their remaining troops. Except for the Japanese, who remained in Siberia until 1922, all Allied forces had left Russia by the end of 1920.

In 1920 Russia faced a different foreign challenge. Poland had taken advantage of the Red Army's struggle with White forces in 1919 to occupy certain disputed areas to its east that were claimed by Russia. In April 1920 Polish forces under Gen. Joseph Pilsudski attempted to extend these gains by invading the Ukraine. In May, after Pilsudski had reached Kiev, the Red Army counterattacked, driving the Poles all the way back to Warsaw by July. Lenin and Trotsky hoped to establish a communist government in Poland and perhaps touch off a revolution in Germany. The French, however, came to Poland's aid with military supplies and a small contingent of troops. The rejuvenated Poles successfully counterattacked in August and forced the Red Army back into Russia. Both sides agreed to an armistice October 12, 1920. The Treaty of Riga, signed March 1921, gave Poland control of the disputed border regions in the Ukraine and Belorussia, which had been Poland's original objective in 1919.

Creating the USSR

Before coming to power in 1917, the Bolsheviks had supported the concept of national self-determination for the minorities of the Russian empire. On November 15, 1917, a week after seizing power, the Bolsheviks issued "The Declaration of the Rights of the Peoples of Russia," which proclaimed the right of non-Russian ethnic groups to form independent states. For Lenin and his colleagues, however, this was a theoretical statement, not a government policy. They did not intend to allow states that had long been a part of the Russian empire to secede.

When local authorities in the Ukraine and Finland responded to the popular will by moving to establish their countries' independence in December, the Bolsheviks condemned their actions. In January 1918 the Bolsheviks invaded the Ukraine to stop its independence movement. The same month they helped pro-Bolshevik Finns overthrow the Finnish government and establish a new regime based on the Bolshevik model. Latvia and Lithuania, which were occupied by German forces, and Estonia, which came under German occupation early in 1918, also declared their independence despite protests from the Bolshevik government.

The Treaty of Brest-Litovsk of March 1918 temporarily deprived Russia of control over the Baltic states, the Ukraine, and Finland, since it obligated the Bolsheviks to recognize German predominance in these areas. When World War I ended in November 1918 with the defeat of Germany by the Western allies, however, the Bolsheviks immediately repudiated the Brest-Litovsk treaty. As they fought against the White forces in the Russian civil war, they also moved to reestablish control over the non-Russian areas of the tsarist empire. Consequently, the ethnic minorities' fight for independence became entangled in the civil war. Although both the Whites and the Bolsheviks appealed to the minorities for help, neither advocated a program that would guarantee the independence of the non-Russian peoples. As a result members of the various ethnic groups fought on both sides of the civil war, although more sided with the Whites.

After the Bolsheviks defeated the White armies, the Baltic states and Finland remained independent. The Red Army, however, quickly reestablished control over the Ukraine and the Transcaucasia region, which had given much aid to the White forces. The Bolsheviks initiated a program in these areas to suppress local culture and language that resembled the policy of Russification implemented under Alexander III and Nicholas II. By 1920 the Bolsheviks had established theoretically independent "Soviet Socialist Republics" in Belorussia, the Ukraine, Armenia, Azerbaidzhan, and Georgia. These republics, however, did not possess sovereign powers, and during the early 1920s Moscow increasingly deprived them of autonomy over their local affairs.

On December 30, 1922, the Bolshevik government formally established the Union of Soviet Socialist Republics (USSR). It consisted of the Russian, Belorussian, Ukrainian, and Transcaucasian republics. A constitution ratified January 31, 1924, formalized this arrangement. By 1929 the Turkmen, Uzbek, and Tadzhik republics were added to the USSR, and the Transcaucasian republic was split into the Armenian, Azerbaidzhan, and Georgian republics.

New Economic Policy

In 1921 the civil war had ended, and Bolshevik rule no longer was threatened by foreign or domestic armies. Yet the miserable economic conditions in Russia and the restlessness of recently discharged soldiers had led to

Lenin and Stalin confer in 1922

numerous peasant rebellions, urban demonstrations, and strikes. Industrial production continued to decline, goods of all types were in short supply, the Russian currency had lost most of its value, and a thriving black market had developed. An open rebellion in March by the sailors of Kronstadt naval base, who previously had been strong supporters of the Bolsheviks, further emphasized the growing discontent in Russia. Lenin and his colleagues maintained control of the country by force, but they felt vulnerable to the same sort of revolutionary upheaval that had brought them to power. *(Kronstadt rebellion, box, p. 24)*

In this atmosphere, Lenin proclaimed the New Economic Policy as a way to ease the nation's financial woes. The NEP, launched in March 1921, was a dose of free enterprise, designed to rebuild the Russian economy after years of revolution, war, and famine by replacing coercion with market incentives. In announcing it, Lenin said, "We are in a condition of such poverty, ruin, and exhaustion of the productive powers of the workers and the peasants, that everything must be set aside to increase production."

Under the NEP, compulsory surrender of agricultural produce was replaced by a tax, leaving farmers free to sell their surplus on the open market. Peasants also were allowed to lease land and hire farm laborers. In the cities, control of small factories reverted to private owners, and individuals were allowed to engage in retail trade. The government, meanwhile, tried to induce foreign companies to invest in the country's industrialization process. Despite the NEP's permissiveness, Lenin was careful to maintain party control of the country's economic "commanding heights": heavy industry, transportation, foreign trade, wholesale commerce, and banking.

The NEP succeeded in stabilizing the country and revitalizing the economy. By 1928 production in most industries had recovered to pre-World War I levels. This revitalization was accompanied by an increase in prosperous peasants and small business owners.

The Bolsheviks and World Revolution

The men who led the Russian Revolution considered themselves to be the vanguard of an international socialist movement that would sweep through the rest of the industrialized world. George Vernadsky noted in his *History of Russia* that

Uprisings did actually occur in a few nations, but their achievements were short-lived: the Communist government of Bela Kun in Hungary lasted from March 21 until August 1, 1919, and a Bavarian Soviet government, founded on April 7, 1919, held power for an even shorter period. Revolutions were also planned for England and the United States, though in these countries the "plans" could hardly have been more than vague hopes.

In March 1919 the Soviet leadership had brought together the First Congress of the Third International in Moscow, a meeting of communist parties and groups from the international community. The organization of these parties and groups, which was dominated by the Russians, became known as the "Comintern." The goal of the Comintern was "the overthrow of capitalism, the establishment of the dictatorship of the proletariat and of the International Soviet Republic for the complete abolition of classes, and the realization of socialism."

Despite the Comintern's encouragement of international revolution and its dissemination of communist propaganda, it was clear to the Soviet leaders by 1922 that widespread revolution in the capitalist states was not likely to occur. Moscow therefore sought recognition from and commercial relations with the capitalist world as a means of establishing Soviet legitimacy and improving the Soviet economy.

On April 16, 1922, the Soviet Union and Germany signed the Treaty of Rapallo establishing commercial ties.

In 1924 diplomatic recognition was extended to the Soviet state by several nations—Great Britain, France, China, Mexico, Greece, Austria, Denmark, Sweden, Norway, and Italy. The United States, however, did not offer diplomatic recognition to the Soviet regime until November 1933.

The Soviets established relations with their southern and eastern neighbors as well, negotiating treaties with Afghanistan, Persia, and Turkey. In China, the Soviets urged the local Communists to support Chiang Kai-shek's nationalist forces. Once Chiang had the upper hand, however, he purged the Chinese Communists and sent the Russian advisers back to Moscow.

Lenin's Death

Unlike his successors, Lenin never held the official title of party leader, governing instead from the post of chairman of the Council of People's Commissars. Nevertheless, from 1917 to 1922 he was the unchallenged head of the Communist party and the Soviet state.

On May 26, 1922, Lenin suffered a paralytic stroke. He partially recovered and resumed some of his duties, but he had a second stroke on December 16 that greatly reduced his ability to function as the leader of his nation and party. He suffered a third and final stroke on March 9, 1923. As Lenin deteriorated he remained the nation's revered figurehead, but Joseph Stalin, Leon Trotsky, and other leading Bolsheviks took over the tasks of running the country.

After Lenin's death on January 21, 1924, the state honored him by building a mausoleum in Red Square to house his embalmed remains and by changing the name of the former Russian capital from Petrograd to Leningrad. His death opened a succession battle that would take several years to settle.

Stalin Era

When Lenin died no rules existed on how his successor as preeminent leader of the Soviet Union should be chosen. Lenin had hoped that his colleagues would forswear power struggles and institute a system of collective rule, but he realized that this was unlikely to happen. Strokes that impaired his health in 1922 already had precipitated competition for power among his lieutenants, especially Leon Trotsky and Joseph Stalin. In letters unsealed after Lenin's death in 1924, he cautioned the party against factionalism and recommended that Stalin be removed as general secretary of the party. Lenin's warnings, however, failed to prevent a power struggle or block the accumulation of power in Stalin's hands. *(Lenin's "Testament," box, p. 32)*

Trotsky had been Lenin's right-hand man during the revolution and had organized the victorious Red Army in the civil war. Trotsky, however, also had clashed bitterly with Lenin at times and was a Jew—two factors that became weapons against him. In fact, Stalin alone among the contenders for power had never had a major public conflict with Lenin. Stalin also occupied the strongest institutional position of any of the contenders for power. He had been named general secretary in 1922 and from this position had built a power base as he ran the daily affairs of the party. Stalin's development of innumerable contacts in the non-Russian republics during his tenure as commissar for nationalities also contributed to his power.

Grigorii Zinoviev and Lev Kamenev, the influential party leaders in Petrograd and Moscow, respectively, were the other top Bolsheviks in contention for party leadership after Lenin died. Both had clashed with Lenin but retained their standing in the party. Lenin had mentioned one other man, Nikolai Bukharin, as a possible successor. Bukharin, one of the party's leading theoreticians and the editor of *Pravda*, however, was never seriously considered by the other leaders.

To fill the vacuum after Lenin's death, Stalin, Zinoviev, and Kamenev, all members of the Politburo, formed a triumvirate, although Stalin was clearly the most powerful of the three. This group occupied the political center and was challenged by groups on the left and right. The "left" faction was led by Leon Trotsky, who charged that the New Economic Policy (NEP), which was launched in 1921, was a retreat from socialism because it allowed limited free enterprise and foreign investment. Trotsky also maintained that a socialist society could not be constructed in the Soviet Union unless socialist revolutions occurred in other countries that would provide each other with economic and political support. The "right" faction, led by Bukharin, supported the NEP as a way to gain the trust of the peasantry and achieve economic recovery. Bukharin also asserted that socialism could be achieved in the Soviet Union without further international revolution. He urged cooperation with noncommunist groups abroad, including western European Social Democratic parties. In the center Stalin and his followers backed the NEP as a repugnant but necessary tool to further socialism in the Soviet Union. They also adopted the middle position that while socialism could be built in the Soviet Union alone, its final victory could not be achieved without socialist revolutions in foreign countries.

In the power struggle of the 1920s, Stalin, a master of the political switch, maneuvered to extend his personal control over the party membership and eliminate his rivals. Stalin used his alliance with Zinoviev and Kamenev to weaken the position of Trotsky and other powerful party leaders on the left. In 1926 Zinoviev and Kamenev, who long had been wary of Stalin's growing power, formed an anti-Stalin alliance with Trotsky. Stalin countered by joining with the right to discredit Zinoviev and Kamenev. Finally, when the left was defeated, Stalin attacked Bukharin and the right wing. By 1927 Stalin had achieved clear preeminence and had engineered the expulsion of most of his rivals from the party. In 1929, after Trotsky was banished from the Soviet Union, Stalin's power over the country was unchallenged.

Although Lenin and other early Soviet leaders had endorsed terror as a political weapon and believed that an iron-fisted rule was necessary for the establishment and development of the Soviet state, Stalin exercized power with a ruthlessness that far surpassed that of his fellow Bolsheviks. He established dictatorial authority over every aspect of Soviet society and instituted policies that resulted in the execution or imprisonment of millions of Soviet citizens.

In foreign affairs, the Stalin era saw the German invasion of the Soviet Union during World War II, the eventual defeat of Germany and Japan by the Soviet-British-American alliance, the creation of Soviet satellites in Eastern Europe after the war, and the onset of hostile relations between the Soviet Union and its former allies in the West.

Lenin's 'Testament'

In December 1922 and January 1923, Lenin wrote to the Twelfth Soviet Party Congress scheduled to be held in the spring. In his letters the ailing father of the Bolshevik Revolution proposed organizational changes (including an expansion of the Central Committee from fifty to one hundred members) to preserve a unified collective leadership, and he offered judgments of his potential successors. The letters, particularly two written on December 24 and January 4, became known as his "Testament."

In the December 24 letter he warned against a split in the party and cited the strengths and weaknesses of the prospective candidates for succession without making clear who he favored to hold the top leadership posts. He wrote that Joseph Stalin "has boundless power . . . and I am not sure whether he will always be capable of using that power with sufficient caution." The January 4 letter, however, recommended that Stalin be removed as general secretary of the Communist party. Lenin wrote:

> Stalin is too coarse, and this fault, though quite tolerable in relations among us communists, becomes intolerable in the office of General Secretary. Therefore I suggest to the comrades that they think of a way of transferring Stalin from this position and assigning another man to it who differs from Comrade Stalin only in one superiority: more tolerant, more loyal, more polite and more considerate of his comrades, less capricious, and so on.

The letters, however, were not read at the congress. Lenin had sealed them and stipulated that only he could open them unless he had died, in which case only his wife, Nadezhda Krupskaya, could open them. During the congress, Lenin remained alive but too ill to function—a situation he had not anticipated when he gave instructions for disposition of the letters. Consequently, the delegates to the congress did not learn of Lenin's objections to Stalin.

Lenin died in January 1924. The following May, Krupskaya carried out her husband's wishes and gave the letters to the Central Committee so that they could be read by the delegates to the upcoming Thirteenth Soviet Party Congress. Party leaders thus learned of Lenin's appraisal of Stalin, and the general secretary's removal became a topic of discussion among the delegates. By this time, however, Stalin had further solidified his position as party leader by cultivating supporters throughout the party. With the aid of his powerful allies, Grigorii Zinoviev and Lev Kamenev, he was able to minimize the damage of Lenin's criticism and hold on to power.

Prewar Foreign Policy

The foreign policy trend begun after the civil war—developing Soviet contacts with foreign governments—continued under Stalin's one-man rule. Originally intended to lend legitimacy to the regime, this policy in the late 1920s and 1930s was designed to preserve peace and enhance Soviet security while Moscow achieved an economic and social transformation of the Soviet Union.

In 1928 Stalin had fully endorsed Bukharin's concept of "socialism in one country." By this Bukharin and Stalin meant that world revolution was not so essential to the construction of socialism in Russia as Lenin and many other Bolshevik leaders had believed. Stalin and Bukharin maintained that the Soviet Union could build a socialist society regardless of the progress of the revolutionary movement elsewhere. Moreover, because Stalin saw the Soviet Union as surrounded by capitalist enemies that would exploit opportunities to overthrow the Soviet Communist regime, resources had to be devoted to strengthening the Soviet Union instead of financing revolutionary movements abroad. The theory of "socialism in one country" provided a theoretical basis for expanding relations with capitalist countries, which no longer were regarded as being threatened by imminent revolution.

Nevertheless, this did not mean that Stalin and his colleagues had abandoned the concept of world revolution or Soviet support for it. The Comintern, established in 1919 to foment world revolution, continued to receive the enthusiastic backing of the Soviet Union until 1943, when Stalin dissolved it as a concession to his World War II allies, the United States and Great Britain.

Soviet foreign policy during the 1920s and 1930s, therefore, was full of contradiction. Moscow expanded its contacts with capitalist nations, even while Soviet leaders remained wary of an anti-Soviet capitalist alliance and worked for the eventual demise of the capitalist structure. In *Expansion and Coexistence*, Adam B. Ulam noted an additional contradiction in the Soviets' position: By 1933 the increasing instability in the capitalist world, which Moscow had hoped would lead to an era of revolution, threatened Soviet security.

> The historical irony of the situation facing Soviet policymakers at the end of 1933 consisted in the fact that the fulfillment of many long-standing Soviet hopes in international politics promised not successes but a terrible danger to the Soviet Union. The League of Nations and the Versailles settlement had been the object of unremitting Soviet propaganda attacks ever since 1919. Now the League had been rendered even more ineffective since Japan and Germany were turning their backs on it. The Versailles settlement was crumbling, with Germany openly rearming and advancing far-reaching claims in other directions. The great crisis of the world economy had come to pass, but its political consequences were seen in the growth and successes of fascist movements rather than communist ones. The rising level of international tension threatened new wars, but the targets of Japanese and German militarism might become not the other capitalist powers but the Soviet Union. Seldom has an ideology played a comparable trick on its devotees as did communism in 1933: all the major desiderata of its philosophy of international relations were fulfilled, and their sum total promised disaster for the Soviet Union.

In the Far East, Japan embarked on a program of expansion, occupying southern Manchuria in 1929. China could do little more than protest to the powerless League of Nations. Emboldened, the Japanese in 1932 seized northern Manchuria, threatening the Soviet-controlled Chinese Eastern Railway. Moscow, preoccupied with collectivization and industrialization, had no desire for a war with the Japanese and, in 1935, sold the railroad to the Tokyo-controlled Manchurian government. To prevent Japanese expansion into Mongolia and Siberia, however, the Soviets patched up their differences with China's nationalist leader, Chiang Kai-shek, and supplied his armies with materiel and advisers. Soviet-Japanese tensions continued to build through the 1930s, resulting in clashes in 1938 and 1939 on the Manchurian-Mongolian border.

In Europe, the Soviet Union faced the prospect of a rearmed Germany led by a virulently anticommunist Nazi dictator, Adolf Hitler, who publicly proclaimed his desire to expand German borders. To meet the threat Stalin sought improved relations with the West and his eastern European neighbors. Responding to growing German and Japanese power, the United States recognized the Soviet Union in 1933. In 1934 the Soviet Union joined the League of Nations. The following year, Moscow concluded military alliances with France and Czechoslovakia. The Soviets' fears of fascist animosity were confirmed in November 1936 when Germany and Japan signed an "Anti-Comintern Pact" that stated the signatories' opposition to international communism. Italy and Spain signed the pact in 1937 and 1939, respectively.

Moscow's alliance with Czechoslovakia required the Soviet Union to aid the Czechs, provided France also offered assistance. French acquiescence in Hitler's seizure of the Sudetenland, a section of Czechoslovakia densely populated by Germans, relieved the Soviets of any responsibility to defend their Czech allies. However, the French and British capitulation to Hitler—the Soviets had not been invited to participate at the September 1938 Munich conference that sealed Czechoslovakia's fate—made Stalin and his colleagues question the value of the Soviet-French alliance. Stalin had felt similar disillusionment with the West in 1936, when he had tried unsuccessfully to obtain Western cooperation in aiding the Republican forces in Spain against the fascists, who were supported by Germany and Italy.

After appeasing German ambitions in Czechoslovakia, Great Britain and France were determined to take a stand against potential Nazi aggression toward Poland. The two Western allies guaranteed Polish independence but excluded the Soviet Union from participating in their declaration of support for Poland. During 1939 the Soviets continued negotiations with Great Britain and France on forming a united front against Hitler, but Stalin let it be known that he was open to the possibility of concluding an agreement of mutual neutrality with Germany.

On August 23, 1939, while Hitler's armies secretly prepared to invade Poland, Germany and the Soviet Union signed a ten-year nonaggression pact—sometimes called the Molotov-Ribbentrop Pact after the Soviet and German foreign ministers who negotiated it. The agreement included a promise that each partner would remain neutral toward the other and a secret protocol that carved up Poland between them and designated spheres of influence in the Baltic region.

In signing the pact, the Soviet leadership almost certainly understood that Hitler would invade Poland. Stalin may have calculated, however, that the agreement was the only way to avoid war between his nation and Nazi Germany. He also may have believed that the pact would allow the Soviet Union to sit on the sidelines while Germany and the Western allies waged a devastating war that would leave the Soviet Union as the dominant power in Europe. In case Germany did have ambitions to attack the Soviet Union, the pact at least would provide Stalin time to bolster Soviet defenses. Finally, the agreement offered the obvious dividend of giving the Soviets control of lands in eastern Poland and securing German acquiescence for Soviet domination of Finland and the Baltic region.

Joseph Stalin and German foreign minister Joachim von Ribbentrop look on as Soviet foreign minister Viacheslav Molotov signs the nonaggression pact in August 1939.

The treaty assured Hitler and his generals that they could invade Poland without fear that the Soviet Union would declare war. German armies launched a blitzkrieg into Poland on September 1, prompting Great Britain and France to declare war on Germany September 3. Within three weeks the German army had captured Warsaw. The Soviet Army, meanwhile, occupied eastern Poland.

The Soviet Union remained neutral during 1940 and early 1941, a period that saw virtually all of Europe, including France, come under the occupation of Germany and its allies. Great Britain struggled for survival as the only major power that continued to oppose Nazi Germany.

Meanwhile Moscow pursued its ambitions in the Baltic region. Soviet forces invaded Finland in November 1939. To the surprise of the Soviets and most Western observers the Finnish army fought effectively against the Soviet invaders. The Soviets did not subdue their small neighbor until March 1940. The Red Army's poor showing in Finland may have helped convince German generals that the Soviet Union could be defeated quickly. In the summer of 1940 Soviet forces occupied the independent Baltic states of Latvia, Lithuania, and Estonia with little resistance. Moscow set up puppet governments that facilitated the annexation of these nations into the Soviet Union in August.

Domestic Policy

Stalin's reign in the years leading up to World War II was dominated by three programs—forced collectivization of agriculture, rapid industrialization of the economy, and the great purges. This period was a dark time in Soviet history when millions of people were imprisoned in labor camps or killed in pursuit of greater social discipline, the achievement of a socialist economy, and the elimination of all real or imagined opponents of Stalin's totalitarian rule.

During the 1920s the successes of the NEP raised fears among the Communist party leadership that private enterprise was gaining a foothold in Soviet society. In addition, Soviet leaders believed that the development of heavy industry had received inadequate attention and resources under the NEP. In response, the government in 1928 announced the First Five-Year Plan, calling for industrial projects to be financed by the production of agricultural collectives. The plan represented the first attempt by a society to use large-scale, centralized planning and social ownership of the means of production as a basis for national economic advancement.

Collectivization

During the 1920s agricultural production had increased at a rate too slow to supply the rapidly growing needs of the Soviet Union. By encouraging peasants to produce more, the NEP had helped Soviet agricultural production to recover to pre-World War I levels by 1925. Yet Soviet agriculture remained inefficient because the land was broken into millions of small, poorly equipped farms. Production also was held below its potential by peasant dissatisfaction with the artificially low prices at which the state offered to buy surplus grain. It appeared that if Moscow wanted further increases in production it would have to offer the peasants greater material incentives. Devoting more resources to agricultural production,

however, would deprive the industrial sector of the economy of the funds required for the rapid advancement envisioned by Stalin and many of his colleagues. The Soviet leadership, therefore, hoped to increase production at a low cost by collectivizing peasants into larger, more efficient farms under state control that could better take advantage of emerging technology.

Collectivization, however, was not popular in the countryside, especially among the *kulaks*, the wealthier peasants who had taken advantage of conditions under the NEP to increase their land holdings and incomes. The kulaks, who had been targets of oppression during the period of War Communism, staunchly opposed collectivization, high taxes, and any government interference in their affairs. To break the kulaks, Moscow enlisted the support of the poorest peasants, who were promised a share of the kulaks' land and assets once agriculture was collectivized. This led to violence in the countryside between rich and poor peasants.

In December 1929 Stalin declared a new policy of "eliminating the kulaks as a class." Party workers, police, and army units were sent into rural areas to aid in the fight against the kulaks, but this campaign quickly turned into a broader push toward collectivization that engulfed the entire peasantry. Peasants who fought back (and many who did not) were shot, sent to labor camps, or forced to resettle in remote areas. As many as five million peasants were sent to Siberia during the drive for collectivization.

The chaos in the countryside, however, was too much even for Stalin. On March 2, 1930, he published an article in *Pravda* entitled "Dizziness with Success," in which he denounced the excesses of collectivization and blamed them on overzealous local party officials. The article temporarily stalled the collectivization drive, but later in the year it began anew. By 1932 more than 60 percent of peasant households had been collectivized, and by 1938 the number exceeded 90 percent.

Many peasants had resisted collectivization by destroying their assets before they could be confiscated for collective farms. They butchered and ate their livestock, burned their crops, and broke their farm implements. By 1934 Soviet livestock had been reduced to less than half the number that existed in 1928. The lack of implements and draft animals and the chaos in rural society caused agricultural production to decline sharply. This decline created a devastating famine centered in the Ukraine, the northern Caucasus, and parts of Russia. The government denied the existence of the famine and stood by while an estimated five million to ten million peasants died.

Industrialization

In tandem with the radical reconstruction of agriculture, Stalin sought to greatly expand the Soviet Union's industrial capacity. This effort was outlined in the first three five-year plans. These plans were highly ambitious blueprints of economic activity that devoted a large percentage of resources to industrial investment. They were formulated by Gosplan, the Soviet state planning commission, under the supervision of Stalin and other Soviet leaders. The First Five-Year Plan was launched in 1928 and was declared completed December 31, 1932, nine months ahead of schedule. The second ran from 1932 to 1937, and the third ran from 1937 until it was interrupted in 1941 by the German invasion of the Soviet Union.

By concentrating Soviet resources on the development

of heavy industry, Stalin intended to end his nation's economic backwardness and reduce its military vulnerability. The success of his agricultural program also depended on industrialization, since boosting agricultural productivity would require large-scale production of mechanized farm implements and the gasoline to run them. He also hoped rapid industrialization would achieve dramatic successes that would demonstrate to the world the superiority of socialism.

The First Five-Year Plan did not produce economic miracles, but it was a partial success. Industrial growth rates averaged a strong 12 percent annually. Industries created or greatly expanded during this period included machine building, electric power, automobiles, chemicals, agricultural machines, and aviation. Despite the high growth rates, the output of many key products, including iron, steel, coal, and grain, failed to reach their targets. In addition, the plan was frequently out of balance. For example, the production of certain raw materials could not keep up with some industries, and often the lack of technicians needed to repair or install equipment slowed the pace of whole enterprises.

The second and third five-year plans continued the push toward expansion of heavy industry, but they lowered output targets slightly and put more emphasis on the qualitative improvement of goods. Like the First Five-Year Plan, they failed to achieve many of the optimistic goals set by the planners, while dramatically advancing Soviet industry beyond where it had been. The Soviets also greatly expanded their production of electricity and improved the national infrastructure by building new roads, bridges, and rail lines. In the thirteen years of the "era of five-year plans" the Soviet Union succeeded in catching up to the industrialized capitalist nations in most areas of industry. This progress was crucial to the Soviet Union's survival in World War II.

Nevertheless, rapid industrialization was accomplished at great cost to the Soviet people. Most consumer goods were scarce, and many products were rationed. Housing, sanitation, and water projects also received inadequate attention to meet the nation's growing needs during the era of five-year plans. These problems were made particularly acute by the growth of the Soviet urban population. In 1926 only 18 percent of Soviet citizens lived in the cities. By 1940 this figure had risen to 33 percent, as peasants were recruited or forced to take jobs in industry.

While the peasants in the countryside were enduring forced collectivization, workers in the cities lost their freedom to choose their jobs and faced miserable and often dangerous working conditions. Stalin attempted to motivate workers by publicizing the exploits of Stakhanovites, workers with incredibly high outputs who got their name from a coal miner who set production records. The production levels of Stakhanovites in every industry increased the expectations of factory managers, planners, and Soviet leaders, who set higher production targets for all workers. Under this system, many average laborers were punished for not meeting their quotas. Soviet workers had little chance to improve their lot. They had been deprived of the right to strike, and their trade unions were not allowed to challenge industry managers.

To increase industrial production, Stalin also provided economic rewards and incentives to party leaders, bureaucrats, skilled laborers, and factory managers. Citizens with special talents, such as athletes, musicians, writers, and artists, also were rewarded. Stalin thus subverted the old Bolshevik notion that all Soviet citizens should receive equal economic and social benefits. He created an elite class that owed its success to the Soviet state and the Communist party, and therefore could be counted on to support the regime's programs.

The Purges

While his government was extending its control over the Soviet economy and the lives of Soviet citizens, Stalin moved against his political enemies, real and imagined. The purge of the Communist party began in the late 1920s and early 1930s with several trials of groups of minor officials who were accused of sabotage, counterrevolutionary activities, and plotting with foreign agents. These trials were accompanied by partywide purges designed to expel party members who were inefficient in their work or unenthusiastic about party policies.

These purges, however, were merely a preliminary to the bloodbath that was to follow. On December 1, 1934, Sergei Kirov, the party leader in Leningrad, was assassinated. Kirov's murder was used by Stalin as a pretext for mass arrests and executions that marked the beginning of what became known as the "Great Purge." During the rest of the decade, an estimated eight million citizens were arrested on suspicion of disloyalty to the state and other political charges. Most of those arrested were sent to labor camps. *(Secret police, box, p. 36)*

The main events of the purge era were the so-called "show trials" held to disgrace former high-ranking government and party officials. The first show trial, begun on August 19, 1936, resulted in the conviction of sixteen Bolshevik leaders for treasonous activities. The defendants included Grigorii Zinoviev and Lev Kamenev, Stalin's former allies on the Politburo. All sixteen were executed. The accused were not given any rights to due process of law, and confessions and testimony that implicated other high-ranking officials were extracted by coercion and torture.

A second show trial was held in January 1937, at which seventeen other Soviet leaders were found guilty. In March 1938 a third show trial convicted an additional twenty-one former leaders, including Nikolai Bukharin. Of the fifty-four men tried in the show trials, fifty received death sentences and were executed.

The purge extended to every area of Soviet society. It was carried out by the People's Commissariat of Internal Affairs (NKVD), the political police, headed by Nikolai Yezhov. Yezhov himself disappeared in 1938 and was replaced by Lavrentii Beria. The purge hit the military particularly hard. Three of the five Soviet marshals, including Mikhail Tukhachevskii, a Civil War hero, were removed, as well as 13 of the army's 15 commanders, 57 of its 85 corps commanders, 110 of its 195 division commanders, and 70 percent of all officers holding the rank of colonel or above.

The effects of the purge also were severe at the top levels of government. Only 37 percent of the members of the 1934 Central Committee survived the purges. Among Lenin's original Politburo, only Stalin and Leon Trotsky remained alive in 1939. Trotsky, who had been exiled from the Soviet Union in 1929, was assassinated in 1940 in Mexico, presumably on Stalin's orders.

Although there is no historical consensus about what motivated Stalin to conduct the purges of the 1930s, many historians believe that the Soviet leader's paranoid personality disposed him to attempt to eliminate anyone who conceivably could challenge his leadership or threaten his

Secret Police under Stalin . . .

The Bolsheviks who seized power in November 1917 declared themselves eager to erase all remnants of the tsarist era. But they retained one leftover from the monarchy—the secret police. The early Bolshevik secret police organs, like the tsar's police, ruthlessly suppressed dissent to ensure that the regime remained in power. The use of terror was legitimized by Lenin, who wrote in a letter on the Soviet criminal code: "The law should not abolish terror. . . . The paragraph on terror should be formulated as widely as possible, since only revolutionary consciousness of justice and revolutionary conscience can determine the conditions of its application in practice."

Dzerzhinskii and the Cheka

Feliks Dzerzhinskii, the first head of the Soviet security police, was born in Vilnius (now in Lithuania) in 1877. The son of Polish aristocracy, he became a terrorist and revolutionary at an early age. He established his revolutionary credentials by leading a series of unsuccessful raids against the tsar's security forces, the Okhrana. He was arrested for the first time in 1897, two months before he turned twenty, for these raids and for distributing pamphlets demanding release of political prisoners. Sentenced to five years' hard labor in Siberia, he escaped before two years had passed.

As William Corson and Robert Crowley describe in *The New KGB: Engine of Soviet Power,* Dzerzhinskii became a "convict celebrity" by the time he was recaptured. He escaped several more times from the Okhrana, until his final release before the 1917 revolution. In 1906, during one period of freedom, he had a fateful meeting in Stockholm with two other revolutionaries—Lenin and Stalin. Dzerzhinskii lived to serve both men as head of the Soviet security service. (Dzerzhinskii's statue still stands in front of the KGB headquarters building in Moscow in the well-known square that bears his name.) It was Dzerzhinskii, in fact, who urged the Bolsheviks to establish the "Extraordinary Commission to Combat Counterrevolution, Sabotage, and Speculation." The Bolsheviks' Council of People's Commissars established the security service on December 20, 1917, just six weeks after taking over the state. Its acronym, VChK, was soon shortened to ChK, or "Cheka," which means "linchpin" in Russian. Dzerzhinskii celebrated the Cheka's birth with two Americans, Louise Bryant and John Reed.

To combat tsarists and rival revolutionary factions, the Bolsheviks gave the Cheka immense powers. During the Russian civil war the Chekists were free to arrest, imprison, torture, and execute those they judged to be enemies of the revolution. By 1921 the Cheka was thirty thousand strong, had its own armed force, was responsible for protecting Soviet borders and maintaining domestic peace, and had begun to set up an international spy network.

After the civil war ended, Lenin and his colleagues wished to create a less repressive security service that would focus its efforts on counterrevolution and espionage. Toward this end the Cheka was replaced February 7, 1922, by the Main Political Administration (GPU), part of the People's Commissariat of Internal Affairs (NKVD). Unlike the Cheka, the GPU was not granted the legal authority to judge and punish those it arrested. Dzerzhinskii headed the GPU, retaining his place as security chief. In 1924 Stalin also gave him responsibility for the Soviet economic program. Dzerzhinskii became a candidate member of the Politburo and backed Stalin in his succession fight with Trotsky.

Stalin and the NKVD

Despite Lenin's willingness to use terror, Joseph Stalin oversaw the most brutal application of secret police activity in Soviet history. In 1990, the Soviet government released a report that said 786,098 people were shot by state authorities between 1930 and 1953. The total did not include millions of people who died in labor camps, starved during artificial famines, or were executed by other means.

During the 1930s Politburo members and common Soviet citizens alike feared a visit from the secret police that could end in arrest, torture, internal exile, or execution. Many of the victims seemed to be chosen arbitrarily. The dictator's paranoid personality disposed him to order the arrest of individuals for slight provocations or suspicious behavior. Moreover, the general climate of terror and distrust and the existence of a huge police apparatus created conditions that inevitably led to widespread abuses. In *Russia's Failed Revolutions,* however, Adam B. Ulam asserts that terror should not be ascribed entirely to Stalin's derangement:

> To look for an explanation of the terror of the 1930s in just Stalin's irrational characteristics is to postulate that he was entirely mad, an assumption that his ability to retain absolute power for twenty-five years renders quite absurd. . . . It is more reasonable to assume that terror on such a scale was the product of a deliberate design. . . . Terror was part of the educational campaign to convince the nation that all horrors which attended forced collectivization, such as the famine which claimed five million lives, that all the privations and sufferings consequent upon hurried industrialization resulted not from the government's policies, but from sabotage from the people's enemies. Terror, in brief, was necessary not only to make the people obey but, even more so, also to make them believe.

... Feared Tool of Repression

Dzerzhinskii died in 1926 and was succeeded by Viacheslav Menzhinskii, another Pole. During Menzhinskii's tenure the GPU adopted increasingly repressive techniques and oversaw the brutal drive to collectivize the peasantry. Menzhinskii, however, was frequently ill, and the day-to-day administration of the GPU was handled by his chief assistant, Genrikh Yagoda, a close ally of Stalin. In 1932 the GPU became a separate organization, the United State Political Administration (OGPU). Soon after, the OGPU was absorbed by the NKVD. When Menzhinskii died in office in 1934, he was replaced as head of the NKVD by Yagoda.

In *KGB: Inside the World's Largest Intelligence Organization,* Brian Freemantle asserts that Yagoda, a trained pharmacist, first developed the security service's facilities and research on "methods of extermination." Stalin apparently directed Yagoda to arrange the murder of Sergei Kirov, a potential rival of Stalin's. After Kirov's assassination in 1934, which Stalin passed off to the public as a conspiracy, Yagoda was charged with finding the culprits. Dozens of men were charged with the crime and executed. The killing of Kirov's "murderers" marked the opening of the Stalinist purges. Yagoda eventually became a victim. He was dismissed in 1936, charged with "abusing his office," and shot in 1938.

Yagoda's successor, Nikolai Yezhov, directed the bloodiest phase of the Great Purge. While publicly charged with curbing the NKVD's "excesses," he reigned over the greatest period of terror in Soviet history. The period bears his name—the *Yezhovshchina.* Most top-ranking Soviet political and military leaders were killed, and millions of citizens were sent to labor camps in Siberia. Less than five feet tall, Yezhov became known as the "bloody dwarf." Accounts of his fate differ. Stalin removed him from office in 1938. Freemantle claims he was shot. Others say he was first sent to a mental hospital where he either committed suicide or was murdered.

Beria Era

Yezhov was succeeded by Lavrentii Beria, an ally of Stalin and a fellow Georgian. An early Chekist, he entered intelligence work in 1921. During the late 1920s he developed a notorious reputation while serving in the GPU in Georgia. Stalin appointed him party leader in Transcaucasia in 1931 despite the objections of local officials. In 1938 Stalin named Beria to replace Yezhov as head of the NKVD. Soviet dissident historian Roy Medvedev wrote in *Let History Judge*:

> Letters and reports about Beria's crimes and moral corruption reached Stalin from many Party members in Transcaucasia. But Stalin, for all his

suspiciousness, favored Beria, and put the punitive organs of the entire country under a man who had long ago lost any trace of conscience or honor.

However, in 1938-1939 not many people knew Beria for what he really was, so the replacement of Ezhov [Yezhov] by Beria was received as a hopeful sign. And in fact, right after Ezhov's replacement, mass repression was discontinued for a while. Hundreds of thousands of cases then being prepared by the NKVD were temporarily put aside. A special commission was even appointed to investigate NKVD activity.... Soon Beria and his men resumed the repression. Admittedly, the mass scale of 1937-38 was not approached. But Stalin had begun to use terror, and he could not stop; arrests and shooting accompanied him to the last days of his life.

Yezhov had terrorized his NKVD officers and decimated their ranks. Beria tempered the internal purges, though he did not stop them, and reinitiated intelligence work abroad. During World War II Beria's secret police were assigned additional responsibilities, including deportation and destruction of ethnic groups living in the Soviet Union, and guarding the front-line Russian troops to prevent retreat and desertion. Beria became a candidate Politburo member in 1939, deputy premier in charge of security in 1941, and a full Politburo member in 1946.

By the time Stalin died in 1953, Beria controlled Soviet espionage activities, the labor camps, the militia, and more than a quarter-million troops. A candidate to succeed Stalin until other Politburo members turned on him, Beria was convicted of "criminal antiparty and antistate activities" and shot in 1953. Over the next three years at least eighteen of his secret police associates suffered a similar fate.

During Beria's tenure, the security service underwent additional name changes. The People's Commissariat of State Security (NKGB) was established in February 1941 but was dismantled that June, after the German invasion. It was reestablished in April 1943, and in 1946 it became the Ministry of State Security (MGB).

An associate of Beria, Viktor Abakumov, was named head of the MGB. He was succeeded by Semen Ignatiev in 1951. Beria replaced Ignatiev when the MGB and Ministry of Internal Affairs (MVD) merged in 1953. The present-day Committee for State Security (KGB) was established in March 1954.

After Beria's execution, the security organs became directly responsible to the Politburo. The Communist party wished to ensure that its security organs would not be used against members of the regime in the future. The party's efforts to control the KGB were largely successful. It functioned as the regime's instrument of repression against dissidents, spies, and other enemies of the party.

own safety. In addition Stalin may have seen the purges as a way of providing scapegoats for his own mistakes and of enhancing his own reputation. As he disgraced and killed his prominent Bolshevik rivals, Stalin portrayed himself in the mass media as the infallible protector of the communist movement and the Soviet people. He also oversaw the rewriting of Soviet history to further reinforce his preeminent position.

In 1936, under Stalin's direction, the government formulated a new constitution to replace the document adopted in 1924. It purported to guarantee civil rights for all Soviet citizens, including the rights to work, rest, vote, and receive medical care and education. It also declared that women and members of minority groups would enjoy equal rights. The constitution stipulated, however, that only one political organization, the Communist party, was allowed to exist.

World War II

On June 22, 1941, Hitler renounced the Soviet-German nonaggression pact signed less than two years before and turned the fury of his armies on the Soviet Union. Stalin reportedly was stunned by the German surprise attack, which pressed into the Soviet Union along a wide front. Instead of rallying the people against the invaders, he went into seclusion for several days. He also had ignored reports from Western and Soviet intelligence sources that indicated Germany might be preparing for a massive assault.

Hitler had held ambitions of invading Russia for many years. He believed its vast lands and abundant natural resources made it ideal for German colonization and exploitation. Moreover, the defeat of the Soviet Union would be a mortal blow to the ideology of communism, which the Nazis hated, and it would eliminate the only rival to German power on the European continent. *(Nazi invasion plan, box, p. 39)*

In 1941 Hitler and his generals temporarily had abandoned plans for invading Great Britain because of the difficulty that a large invasion force would have crossing the English Channel, particularly given the strength of the British navy. They also believed that Great Britain would be easier to deal with diplomatically and militarily if they first conquered the Soviet Union. Some Nazis even believed that since the British also opposed the international communist movement, they might be persuaded to join Germany in its fight against the Soviet Union.

With most of the continent securely under German domination, Hitler was able to concentrate 175 divisions along the Soviet border. German generals hoped that So-

Soviet Soldiers defend the ruins of downtown Stalingrad. At the height of the battle, German troops controlled 90 percent of the city.

viet defenses would crumble under the pressure of a massive blitzkrieg spearheaded by tanks and air support. The German campaign was designed to defeat the Soviets before late 1941, when the Russian winter would bring mud, snows, and cold that favored the defenders. Many British and American military observers privately estimated after the attack that the Germans' chances of defeating the Russians in a single campaign were good. The German high command was so confident of a swift victory that it made no preparations to supply its troops with cold-weather gear, assuming the fighting would not last into winter.

The Germans made rapid progress throughout the summer. They surrounded Leningrad (which would endure a two-and-a-half-year siege costing the lives of more than a million Russians), pushed Soviet armies back toward Moscow, and captured Kiev. Despite achieving these objectives, the German army could not defeat the Soviet Union before winter. The expanse of Soviet territory not only forced German tanks and troops to cover vast distances, it also stretched German supply lines to their limits. More important, the Soviet people in the unconquered regions rallied to the defense of their nation. Directed by Stalin, who had recovered from his initial indecisiveness, they managed to mobilize millions of troops, convert domestic industries to military production, and transfer many manufacturing plants to the safety of the remote Ural Mountain region. In addition an April 1941 nonaggression treaty with Japan enabled Moscow to shift some army units protecting the Soviet Far East to the European theater after the attack. Nevertheless the German offensive reached the suburbs of Moscow before it stalled, and the Soviets prepared to move the seat of government east in the event the Germans captured the city. *(World War II, map, p. 40)*

In December 1941, with the German army effectively halted by the onset of winter, the Red Army launched its first major counteroffensive. Both sides suffered heavy casualties, but the Soviets dislodged the Germans from some of their advance positions and forced the Germans to concentrate on the fight at hand instead of preparations for a new spring offensive.

The Tide Turns

In the summer of 1942 Hitler ordered an attack designed to capture the industrial regions of the South and eventually the oil-rich Caucasus. By August the Germans had driven beyond the Don River to the city of Stalingrad (now Volgograd). The Soviets' determination to hold the city at all costs led to an epic battle that was the turning point in the war between Germany and the Soviet Union.

To reach Stalingrad, German forces had extended their already stretched supply and reinforcement lines to the limit and expended massive amounts of fuel, ammunition, and human energy. During the fall of 1942, as the Germans engaged the Soviets in a desperate house-to-house battle for the city, the Soviets reinforced units in the region and prepared to take advantage of the overextended German lines. On November 19, 1942, the Soviets launched a counterattack that broke through German lines to the north and south of Stalingrad. The two pincers of the Soviet attack quickly linked up west of the city, trapping Gen. Friedrich Paulus's Sixth Army—nearly three hundred thousand troops—in Stalingrad. Hitler, unwilling to accept his army's dire position, ordered Paulus to stay in Stalingrad and fight instead of attempting to break out of the Soviet encirclement. Totally surrounded, capable of receiv-

Nazi Invasion Plan

The German army may have been more successful in its 1941 campaign had Nazi leaders developed a plan to exploit the anti-Russian and anticommunist sentiments of the Soviet people. In some areas of the western Soviet Union, especially the non-Russian republics, the German armies were greeted initially as liberators. Many members of minority groups hoped that the Germans would break Moscow's hold on their regions and allow them to establish their own independent nations. Similarly, some Russian peasants hoped that the Germans would sanction the division of the fields, livestock, and assets of collective farms, thereby allowing them to fulfill their ambitions of farming their own land.

The Nazis, however, sure that their invasion force quickly would smash all resistance and intending not just to defeat the Soviet Union, but also to strip conquered areas of anything of value and eventually resettle them, largely ignored the grievances of Soviet minorities and peasants. More important, the Nazi assault and occupation were brutal.

Hitler had told his generals three months before the invasion that "The war against Russia will be such that it cannot be conducted in a knightly fashion. This struggle is one of ideologies and racial differences and will have to be conducted with unprecedented, unmerciful, and unrelenting harshness. . . . The commissars are the bearers of ideologies directly opposed to National Socialism [Nazism]. Therefore the commissars will be liquidated. German soldiers guilty of breaking international law . . . will be excused. Russia has not participated in the Hague Convention and therefore has no rights under it." Although some of Hitler's generals objected to this directive, which became known as the "Commissar Order," it was widely implemented.

The Germans' inhumane treatment of prisoners of war and the civilian population, their failure to address the political aspirations of Soviet minorities, and their exploitation of the peasantry hardened Soviet resistance against them and fueled a Soviet partisan movement behind German lines that harassed the occupiers. The lightly armed partisans attacked German supply columns and rear units with surprising effectiveness.

Meanwhile, Joseph Stalin shrewdly had chosen to rally the Soviet people behind the cause of defending Mother Russia and other Slavic lands—a cause dearer to the hearts of most Russians than the defense of the socialist movement and the Soviet state. The fight against Germany became known in the Soviet Union as the "Great Patriotic War."

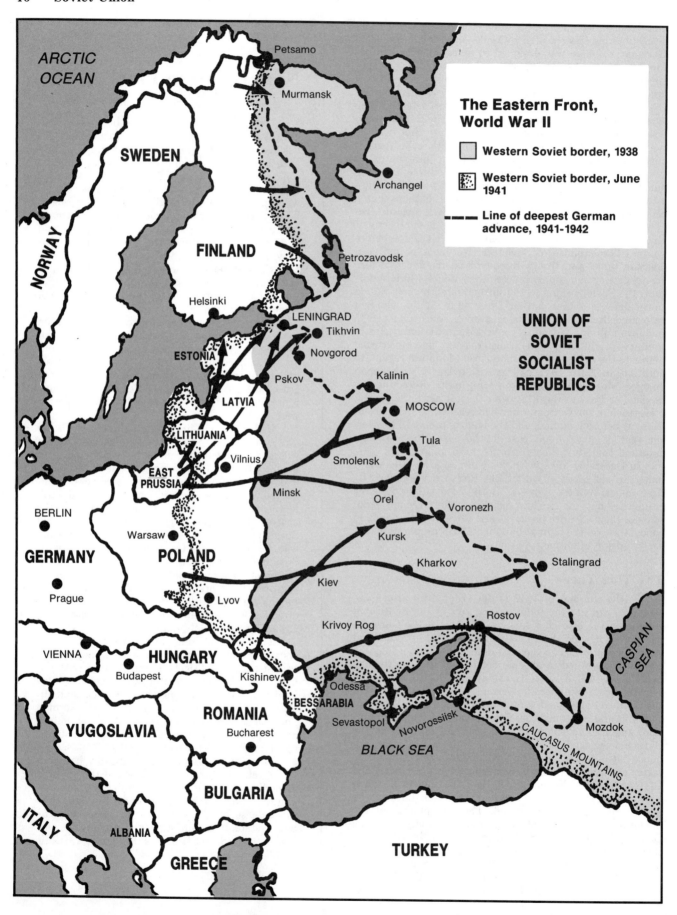

The Eastern Front, World War II

ing only minimal supplies by air drop, and still fighting against pockets of Soviet soldiers within Stalingrad, the German Sixth Army was doomed. The battle at Stalingrad lasted until February 1943, when the exhausted remnants of Paulus's force surrendered.

The defeat at Stalingrad placed the Germans on the defensive for the rest of the war. Although hundreds of thousands of Soviet soldiers were killed or wounded as the Red Army slowly drove back its enemy during 1943 and 1944, the Soviets were better able to replace their losses than the Germans. By January 1945 Soviet troops had recaptured all Soviet territory and secured most of Eastern Europe. Meanwhile American, British, and French forces had successfully invaded France and were driving on Germany from the West. The Germans could not withstand this two-front assault and were pushed relentlessly back toward Berlin. Great Britain and the United States agreed to allow Soviet troops to capture the German capital. In late April 1945 the Soviets carried the fight into Berlin, and Hitler committed suicide. On May 8 the Allies declared that German resistance had ended.

Grand Alliance

German and Japanese aggression led to the Grand Alliance among the Soviet Union, Great Britain, and the United States. However, the three allies did not enter the war simultaneously. Hitler's invasion of the Soviet Union in June 1941 ended Soviet neutrality and led to a practical alliance between Moscow and London. The United States joined the Allies after the December 7, 1941, Japanese attack on Pearl Harbor, Hawaii. During the war the United States and Great Britain shipped 11 billion dollars in aid to the Soviet war effort.

Joseph Stalin, President Franklin D. Roosevelt of the United States, and Prime Minister Winston Churchill of Great Britain met twice to discuss alliance strategy—at Tehran in December 1943 and at Yalta in February 1945.

For Stalin the most important issue at the first meeting was the establishment of a second front in France by Great Britain and the United States, a proposal he had urged on his allies at every opportunity after the German invasion of the Soviet Union. Although British and American troops had captured Sicily and invaded the Italian mainland earlier in 1943, Stalin believed that only a major landing in France could relieve pressure on the Red Army, which had born the brunt of the fighting against Germany since 1941. Stalin got his wish June 6, 1944, when Allied forces invaded Normandy on the French coast.

The Yalta summit dealt with the joint war effort and the administration of a liberated Europe. When the "Big Three" met at Yalta, Germany was almost defeated. Churchill and Roosevelt sought Soviet participation in the war against Japan, an agreement on the occupation of Germany, and Soviet guarantees that the nations of Eastern Europe would be able to decide their own future through popular elections. Stalin agreed to a provisional plan for the partition of Germany into four occupation zones, with the Soviet Union, the United States, Great Britain, and France each administering one zone. Stalin also pledged to enter the war against Japan and gave his Western allies ambiguous assurances that elections would be held in Eastern Europe. In return, Stalin received Roosevelt and Churchill's reluctant approval for Soviet annexation of parts of eastern Poland, for which Poland was to be compensated with German lands to its west.

In the late 1940s', after the Soviet Union had set up communist dictatorships in Eastern Europe, Western politicians and scholars began criticizing the Yalta agreement and Roosevelt in particular for failing to ensure democratic governments in Eastern Europe. Stalin, however, was in a strong bargaining position at Yalta. He argued that the Soviet Union had fought Germany for three years before the allies established a second front in France and that the devastation inflicted upon the Soviet Union by the Germans justified a dominant Soviet role in postwar Eastern

British prime minister Winston Churchill, U.S. president Franklin D. Roosevelt, and Soviet premier Joseph Stalin meet at the 1945 summit conference at Yalta, in the Soviet Crimea.

Europe. Stalin's most potent card, however, was the simple fact that the Red Army occupied Eastern Europe. Unless the Western allies were willing to go to war against the Soviet Union to liberate the countries of the region, there was little they could do to force the Soviets to grant free elections. Roosevelt and Churchill therefore endorsed the vague agreement on Eastern Europe and hoped that the Soviets would wish to maintain good will with the West by allowing pluralistic governments in the region.

Alliance leaders met once more, at Potsdam in late July and early August 1945. This time the summit's participants were Stalin, President Harry S. Truman, and Churchill (halfway through the summit Churchill was replaced by a new prime minister, Clement R. Attlee). As the conference began, Truman was informed that the planned test of an atomic bomb in New Mexico had been successful. Armed with this powerful new weapon, Truman reasoned, the United States had less need to be conciliatory toward Moscow. The leaders discussed the Soviet Union's planned entry into the war against Japan and the arrangements for convening war crime trials in Europe. The Potsdam conference, however, focused on Germany. Truman informed Stalin that, contrary to understandings reached at Yalta, the Americans favored an arrangement under which German war reparations would be extracted by the Allies from their individual zones of occupation. Stalin objected that the Soviet zone in eastern Germany, which was largely agricultural, could not support reparations as large as the industrialized areas of western Germany. The American position on reparations also indicated to Stalin that the Americans were willing to exclude Moscow from participating in the administration of the three western zones. After the Potsdam conference the wartime Allies seemed to move inevitably toward the partition of Germany.

After the fighting in Europe ended in May 1945, the focus of the Allied war effort switched to the Far East. Although at Yalta Roosevelt had secured a promise from the Soviets to declare war on Japan once Germany was defeated, by the time of the Potsdam conference, U.S. leaders saw Soviet involvement against Japan as a mixed blessing. Truman and his advisers wanted to end the war quickly, in part to prevent the Soviet Union from being part of an Asian peace settlement. On August 6, two days before the Soviets were to enter the war, U.S. forces dropped an atomic bomb on Hiroshima with devastating effects. Three days later a second bomb was dropped on Nagasaki.

Truman claimed that the atomic attacks were necessary to bring an end to the war so American lives would not be lost in an invasion of Japan. However, historical evidence suggests that the Japanese, economically and militarily broken, soon would have surrendered even if the atomic bombs were not dropped. Documents and the memoirs of American policy makers indicate that in addition to securing a quick end to the war, Truman's decision to order the atomic attacks was motivated in part by a desire to demonstrate the power of the atomic bomb to the Soviets. The American leadership hoped that the bomb would make Stalin more compliant on other issues, including the fate of Eastern Europe.

As agreed, the Soviet Union entered the war against Japan August 8 and its forces proceeded to occupy parts of Manchuria, the Kuril Islands, and the Japanese section of Sakhalin Island, prizes the Soviets had been promised at Yalta if they joined the fight against Japan. The Japanese formally surrendered to the United States September 2,

1945. The Soviets maintained control of the territories they captured, but the United States refused to accede to Moscow's post-Yalta demand that it have a role in the postwar administration of Japan.

Effects of the War

Estimates of the casualties suffered by the Soviet Union during World War II range as high as twenty million to twenty-five million. In addition to lives lost, the war caused widespread destruction. The Red Army practiced a scorched-earth policy during its retreats; the German forces followed similar practices when they quit Soviet territory. In *A History of Russia*, Nicholas Riasanovsky described the devastation:

> Much of the Soviet Union became an utter wasteland. According to official figures—probably somewhat exaggerated as all such Soviet figures tend to be—Soviet material losses in the war included the total or partial destruction of 1,700 towns, 70,000 villages, 6,000,000 buildings, 84,000 schools, 43,000 libraries, 31,000 factories and 1,300 bridges. Also demolished were 98,000 kolkhozes [collective farms] and 1,876 sovkhozes [agricultural factories]. The Soviet economy lost 137,000 tractors and 49,000 combine-harvesters as well as 7,000,000 horses, 17,000,000 head of cattle, 20,000,000 hogs and 27,000,000 sheep and goats.

The war evoked a strong wave of nationalist feeling in Russia. Stalin came to be directly associated with the war effort, and he portrayed himself as leading the Red Army to victory over the invaders. As a result Stalin and the Communist party emerged from the war more powerful than ever.

Many Soviet experts in the West believe that World War II also profoundly affected Soviet foreign policy during the postwar era. According to this theory, the devastating effects of the war on the Soviet homeland disposed the Kremlin to adopt a conception of security that emphasized the achievement of Soviet military superiority and Soviet domination (or at least the neutralization) of contingent states. The war also probably contributed to the Soviets' adoption of an offensive military doctrine designed to take any fight to enemy soil. Although other factors were involved in the Soviet Union's military buildup during the postwar era and its struggle to control Eastern Europe, it is likely that the experience of World War II did contribute to the push for these objectives.

Cold War

When World War II ended in Europe, the Red Army occupied Albania, Czechoslovakia, Poland, Yugoslavia, Bulgaria, Romania, and Hungary. By 1948 all these countries had established communist regimes (although a rift with the Soviets caused the Yugoslav Communists to adopt an independent course in 1948). East European governments were not governed directly by the Soviet Union. Instead, indigenous communists with close ties to Moscow took power. Soviet military might remained in the background as the ultimate guarantor of the new communist regimes in Eastern Europe. The Red Army also occupied eastern Germany and Austria. The Soviets in 1949 set up the communist-ruled German Democratic Republic (East Germany). In 1955 the Kremlin withdrew its troops from

Austria in return for a pledge by the Austrian government to remain neutral.

The Soviet domination of Eastern Europe—in violation of Stalin's pledges at Yalta to allow free elections—was accomplished with relative ease. Although British and American leaders were alarmed by the rise of communist states in Eastern Europe, there was little they could do to convince or pressure the Soviets to allow free elections. For Moscow, there was no higher foreign policy priority after World War II than establishing Soviet control over Eastern Europe and ensuring that Germany would remain either weak or divided. The Soviets believed their intense suffering during the war at the hands of German invaders justified the creation of sympathetic communist governments on their borders that would provide a long-desired buffer zone between the Soviet Union and the West.

The Soviet expansion of influence in Eastern Europe and elsewhere; the West's interpretation of this expansion as an attempt to achieve domination over as much of the world as possible; and disagreements over specific postwar issues such as German reparations and reconstruction, international custody of atomic weapons, and Poland's borders brought on an era of Allied-USSR animosity, the so-called Cold War.

The question of who or what was responsible for the Cold War has been one of the most debated topics among scholars of postwar politics and history. It is likely, however, that nothing could have prevented the Cold War given that the Soviet Union and the Western allies interpreted their interests so differently, espoused competing ideologies, saw each other correctly as the main threat to their security, and were rivals for influence and power in many parts of the world.

Even during the war the Soviet Union and the Western allies had never completely trusted each other. Although they fought a common enemy, they continued to be suspicious of each other's motives and philosophies. Many leaders in both the West and the Soviet Union regarded their ally as only slightly less malevolent than their common enemy.

There also were many differences over strategy between Moscow and the West, most notably Moscow's anger with what it perceived as unnecessary delays in the opening of a second front in France. In May 1942 Churchill had promised the Soviets in a memorandum that Great Britain was "making preparations for a landing on the continent in August or September 1942." However, in November the Allies landed forces in North Africa, intending eventually to attack Italy through Sicily. Instead of relieving the Soviets, the North African campaign actually may have made their task more difficult. Fewer than fifteen German divisions were occupied in North Africa, while Soviet troops faced nearly two hundred divisions. The commitment of Allied troops and supplies to North Africa negated the possibility of an Allied landing in France, thereby allowing the Nazis to send troops that had been stationed in France to the eastern front. Many Soviet leaders suspected Great Britain and the United States of intentionally holding back an invasion while the massive armies of Germany and the Soviet Union destroyed each other. Meanwhile Stalin insinuated that he might be open to a separate peace with Germany to pressure the Western allies to establish a second front and send larger amounts of war materiel to the Soviet Union.

Nevertheless, during the war the Soviet-British-American alliance endured. After the war, however, relations between the Western allies and the Soviet Union chilled rapidly. The Soviets refused to join the newly established United Nations Atomic Energy Commission and only reluctantly agreed to remove their forces from northern Iran after the United States issued veiled threats of military intervention. Churchill warned of the hazards of growing Soviet domination of Europe in a historic March 5, 1946, speech at Westminster College in Fulton, Missouri. In the speech, Churchill popularized the term "iron curtain," which he said had "descended across the continent." *(Churchill speech excerpts, Appendix, p. 295)*

Expansion and Containment

After the war Moscow's foreign policy appeared to be designed to consolidate its control over regions within its sphere of influence while using diplomatic, economic, subversive, and military means to make inroads into areas outside its sphere. The United States under President Truman initiated a policy of opposing Soviet expansion. As a result a contest of resources, ideologies, and wills developed between the two camps for influence in numerous nations around the world.

The Truman administration's views on Soviet behavior and its corresponding policy prescriptions were set forth in an article in the July 1947 issue of *Foreign Affairs*. Signed "X," the article was written by George F. Kennan, a State Department Soviet expert who became U.S. ambassador to Moscow in 1952. Kennan declared that "we are going to continue for a long time to find the Russians difficult to deal with" and argued that "the main element of any United States policy toward the Soviet Union must be that of a long-term, patient but firm and vigilant containment of Russian expansive tendencies." The term "containment" came to describe longstanding U.S. policy toward the Soviet Union.

Several months before Kennan's article appeared, President Truman and his advisers had taken action to block communist expansion in Greece and Turkey. He proposed March 12, 1947, that the United States assume responsibility for aiding the democratic governments in those countries from an impoverished Great Britain. At the time, the Greeks were engaged in a civil war that pitted government troops against Communist forces, and the Turks were facing mounting pressure from the Soviet Union. In proposing the aid plan, the president outlined to Congress what became known as the Truman Doctrine. He said:

> I believe that it must be the policy of the United States to support free peoples who are resisting attempted subjugation by armed minorities or by outside pressures.... The seeds of totalitarian regimes are nurtured by misery and want.... The free peoples of the world look to us for support in maintaining their freedoms. If we falter in our leadership, we may endanger the peace of the world—and we shall surely endanger the welfare of this Nation.

Despite fears in Congress that direct U.S. aid would undercut the United Nations and worsen relations with the Soviet Union, a four hundred million dollar assistance program was approved. The Truman Doctrine had become U.S. policy.

To bolster European economies, the United States in June 1947 proposed the European Recovery Program, known as the Marshall Plan after its chief architect, Secretary of State George C. Marshall. The original plan included 17 billion dollars in grants and loans to rebuild industry and agriculture in war-torn Europe; aid totaled 10.25 billion dollars over three years. The purpose of this aid was not primarily humanitarian. The Truman administration sought to create strong democracies in Western Europe that would resist communism and become economic and security partners of the United States.

Although Marshall Plan assistance was offered to all European states, including the Soviet Union and its satellites, the United States attached conditions to the offer that made it impossible for Moscow to accept. Instead, the Soviet-bloc countries in October 1947 formed the Communist Information Bureau (Cominform), the successor to Comintern, the propaganda organization abolished in 1943. Dominated by Moscow, Cominform was designed to orchestrate communist policy in Europe. Its early cohesion was damaged in 1948, when Marshal Josip Broz Tito, the Yugoslav leader, broke with the Soviet Union to follow a communist line independent of Moscow's direction.

Western opposition to the Soviet Union was consolidated by the April 4, 1949, signing of the North Atlantic Treaty, establishing a mutual defense pact among the United States and its Western allies: Belgium, Canada, Denmark, France, Great Britain, Iceland, Italy, Luxembourg, the Netherlands, Norway, and Portugal. In 1955 the Soviets would counter the Western alliance by establishing the Warsaw Pact, a Soviet-led alliance of Eastern European nations.

East-West tensions increased in June 1948 when the Soviets blocked land transport of Allied supplies into West Berlin, the Allied-administered section of the former German capital deep inside the Soviet zone in eastern Germany. Stalin hoped that the blockade would cause the West to abandon the city, or at least to make concessions on the political and economic status of the divided Germany. Instead, the Allies mounted an airlift to supply the estimated 2.5 million West Berliners under their jurisdiction, while the United States moved sixty nuclear-capable B-29 bombers to Europe. The tense situation threatened war, but the Soviets were unwilling to risk a confrontation with a nuclear-armed United States by attempting to stop the airlift. Thwarted, the Soviets ended the blockade in May 1949. The same month the Western Allies established the Federal Republic of Germany, with the seat of the new government in Bonn. The Soviets responded in October 1949 with the establishment of the German Democratic Republic in their occupation zone.

The previous month, on September 23, 1949, Moscow announced that its scientists had successfully exploded an atomic bomb. Although it would take the Soviets several years to develop a significant operational nuclear capability and it would not be until the 1960s that they achieved nuclear parity with the United States, the end of the American nuclear monopoly increased the self-confidence of the Soviets, gave them a claim to the status of superpower, and contributed to the atmosphere of confrontation that existed between the two countries.

Also in September 1949, the victory of Chinese Communist forces, led by Mao Zedong, over the nationalist followers of Chiang Kai-shek seemed to confirm the fears of many Western leaders that Soviet-inspired communist subversion was a grave and pervasive international threat. In actuality, although Moscow had given moral support to Mao's forces, it had provided them with little material aid and had continued to recognize Chiang as the legitimate

ruler of China during the civil war. There also were indications that Stalin saw Mao as a rival and was uncomfortable with the idea of a strong, unified China on the Soviet Union's southern border, even if it were led by a communist regime. Nevertheless, after Mao's victory, the Soviets hailed the creation of a communist state and signed a thirty-year Sino-Soviet mutual aid pact on February 14, 1950. The displays of affection between Chinese and Soviet leaders and their close cooperation on many issues greatly disturbed Western leaders, who feared the Sino-Soviet alliance was the beginning of a communist monolith that would challenge and threaten the West. The United States refused to recognize Communist China and instead established ties with the nationalist government established by Chiang on Formosa (now Taiwan).

Korean War

The Cold War turned hot in Korea in 1950. The Asian nation had been divided between occupying forces at the end of World War II, the Red Army in the North and U.S. forces in the South. As in Germany, reunification efforts failed and separate governments were established.

On June 24 (June 25 Korean time), 1950, the Soviet-backed Communist North Koreans attacked South Korea. The following day, President Truman, seeking to aid South Korea and discourage further communist aggression, called an emergency session of the UN Security Council to consider the Korean crisis. By coincidence the Soviets were boycotting the Security Council to protest the exclusion of Communist China from the United Nations. Consequently, their representative was not present to veto a resolution passed by the council condemning the invasion and asking UN members to "render every assistance" to South Korea. President Truman ordered U.S. troops into Korea June 27, the same day that the Security Council passed a second resolution specifically requesting military assistance from UN members to halt North Korean aggression.

The Soviet role in the invasion beyond supplying North Korea with its military equipment is unclear. Although the Soviets likely knew the attack would take place and perhaps hoped to reap benefits from it, it is not certain that they ordered, or even directed, the invasion. North Korean leader Kim Il-Sung had displayed aggressive intentions toward the South and was capable of acting on his own. Moreover, Moscow had reduced sharply the number of Soviet military advisers in North Korea between 1948 and 1950. It was probable that Stalin believed the Americans would do little to defend South Korea, since they had not sent troops to prevent a Communist victory in China, an infinitely larger strategic prize. In addition, in a January 12, 1950, speech, Secretary of State Dean Acheson had outlined an anticommunist defensive perimeter in Asia that excluded South Korea. The speech and subsequent administration actions supporting it may have helped convince Stalin that the North Koreans could attack South Korea without risking U.S. intervention.

The American-led UN forces drove the North Koreans back into their own territory during the fall of 1950. The entry of China into the conflict in November, however, forced the UN army to retreat. Fighting eventually bogged down near the border between North and South Korea. The war continued until the signing of an armistice July 27, 1953.

Soviet Postwar Economy

While directing Soviet foreign policy in the postwar years, Stalin also had overseen the reconstruction of his damaged country. In 1946 the government revealed the terms of the Fourth Five-Year Plan, a blueprint for the rebuilding of Soviet industry, particularly the production of farm machinery and trucks, iron and steel, coal, electrical power, timber, and cement. The plan also devoted a high percentage of resources to defense. Moscow declared the plan fulfilled in four years and three months. The concentrated investment in heavy industry, however, was accomplished at the expense of agriculture, housing, and consumer goods.

Peasants suffered the most under Stalin's reconstruction plan. Collective farms were forced to pay increasingly heavy taxes, while the prices they received from the government for grain remained low. Consequently, as before the war, many peasants left their farms to resettle in urban areas during this period.

The living standard of the average Soviet citizen improved under the Fifth Five-Year Plan, which ran from 1951 to 1955. Although the plan again emphasized heavy industry, wages increased and more consumer goods became available. Economic conditions in the countryside, however, still lagged behind those in the cities, and housing space remained a problem.

Stalin would not live to see the completion of this plan or the end of the Korean War. On the night of March 1, 1953, he reportedly suffered a large brain hemorrhage. He died at the age of seventy-three on March 5, without leaving a clear plan of succession.

Khrushchev Era

When Joseph Stalin died on March 5, 1953, no Soviet leader was in a position to assume the role of preeminent leader of the USSR. Stalin's lieutenants announced that they would institute a collective leadership. Behind the scenes, however, a struggle for power already had begun.

Georgii Malenkov appeared to be Stalin's most likely successor. Stalin had endorsed Malenkov by naming him the main speaker at the Nineteenth Soviet Party Congress in 1952. After Stalin's death Malenkov emerged as both chairman of the Council of Ministers (prime minister) and first secretary of the Central Committee Secretariat. These strong institutional positions could have made him first among equals in a collective leadership or perhaps even could have enabled him to eliminate his rivals. Only a few weeks later, however, Malenkov resigned his Secretariat duties after his colleagues protested the publication in *Pravda* of a picture of Stalin, Malenkov, and Mao in which the images of other Soviet and Chinese leaders had been removed. This weakened Malenkov's position and opened the way for Nikita S. Khrushchev to become de facto first secretary because he was the only Presidium (Politburo) member also in the Central Committee Secretariat.

Another key figure in the succession struggle was Lavrentii Beria, the powerful head of the Soviet secret police, who, after Malenkov, was considered Stalin's next most likely successor. Malenkov, Khrushchev, and their colleagues on the Presidium feared Beria and believed that his control of the vast secret police network gave him a weapon that could threaten not only their positions but also their lives. The Soviet leadership therefore conspired against Beria. He was arrested in July 1953 and charged with "criminal antiparty and antistate work" and with being a British agent. After a short trial on December 17, he was found guilty and executed.

Beria's demise left Malenkov and Khrushchev as the main rivals for leadership. Their power struggle centered on the question of how to allocate industrial resources. On August 8, 1953, Malenkov had announced a moderate shift in resources away from heavy industry and toward consumer goods. This shift was not a radical departure from Stalin's economic policies, because heavy industry would remain the leading component of the Soviet economy. The Soviet leadership, fearful that public impatience with food shortages and with the seemingly endless subordination of consumer needs to rapid industrialization would lead to unrest, endorsed Malenkov's program, which aimed at pro- ducing more and better food, housing, medical care, and household items.

By late 1954, however, the Soviet leadership began to have doubts about the redistribution of resources. Khrushchev became the leader of a growing faction that favored a reconcentration on heavy industry and the military, while Malenkov remained a proponent of increasing the quality and quantity of consumer goods. The debate over industrial priorities came to a climax in early 1955 when Khrushchev had garnered enough support for his position not only to reverse the shift of resources to consumer goods, but also to use the issue as a lever to demote Malenkov. After Khrushchev castigated Malenkov's views at a Central Committee meeting, Malenkov was accused of administrative inexperience and forced to resign as chairman of the Council of Ministers. He was replaced by Khrushchev ally Nikolai Bulganin. Malenkov's demotion left Khrushchev in control of the government and the party. Although Khrushchev was not an unchallenged leader as Stalin had been, he dominated Soviet foreign and domestic policy until his ouster in 1964.

De-Stalinization

After Stalin's death the Soviet collective leadership had cautiously begun dismantling some of the more oppressive manifestations of Stalin's rule. This process came to be known as "de-Stalinization." During this time Soviet political activity gradually returned to more normal operation, and daily life for the citizenry became less repressive. Khrushchev declared that government organizations must operate during traditional business hours, a departure from the secretive midnight meetings common during Stalin's regime. The Soviet leadership allowed greater freedom of movement within the Soviet Union, moderately eased controls on artistic expression, relaxed labor discipline, and rehabilitated some of the victims of Stalin's purges.

The most important aspect of this thawing process, however, was the regime's repudiation of terror. Khrushchev and his colleagues recognized that Stalin's terror tactics had stifled initiative in Soviet society because scientists, artists, educators, party workers, enterprise managers, military officers, and other leaders were afraid of the consequences of being judged wrong or disloyal by Stalin.

The Soviet leadership also realized that because terror had been used widely against top leaders in the government and party, their own lives would constantly be in danger if the system were not changed. The party signaled its repudiation of terror on April 4, 1953, by exonerating the physicians implicated in the "Doctors' Plot," a fictitious conspiracy by nine prominent Moscow doctors who allegedly sought to murder certain Soviet leaders. After their arrest in 1952, the doctors had been tortured on Stalin's orders to obtain their confessions. Two of them had died during their ordeal. Historians have speculated that the nine doctors' arrest was part of a plan by Stalin to launch another purge. The new regime subsequently announced that "strict Leninist legality" would be observed and that arbitrary arrests would end. Soon thousands of prisoners held in Stalin's forced labor camps—the Gulag—were released and officially rehabilitated.

The arrest of Beria and many of his top aides resulted in the enhancement of party control over the secret police. This did not eliminate secret police abuses of power, but it did reduce the arbitrary nature of their activities. After Beria's execution, Soviet leaders also took action to protect themselves from the terror that had prevailed during the Stalin era. Under Stalin an ousted leader was likely to be killed to eliminate any possibility that he might one day make a comeback that could threaten his rivals. Khrushchev and his colleagues instituted an unwritten rule that leaders who came into disfavor or lost a power struggle simply would be demoted or retired.

Kremlin leaders initially, however, were careful not to go too far with de-Stalinization because they all had held powerful posts under Stalin and could implicate themselves with a harsh attack on the abuses of the late dictator. In addition, they did not want to risk weakening the Communist party's preeminent position in society by instituting widespread reforms too fast.

Foreign Affairs

De-Stalinization also extended to foreign affairs as the Soviet leadership abandoned Stalin's unequivocally hostile attitude toward the West and demonstrated a willingness to explore possibilities for cooperation. In 1954 Khrushchev had shown his determination to pursue friendlier international relations by joining the United Nations International Labor Organization (ILO) and the United Nations Educational, Scientific, and Cultural Organization (UNESCO). The following year, the Soviets agreed to remove their forces occupying Austria, thus recognizing Austria's neutrality and independence. Lenin and Stalin had not recognized neutrality as an ideological option. A nation could not be neutral; it was either friendly or an enemy, socialist or imperialist. In return for these moves by the Kremlin, leaders of the United States, France, and Great Britain agreed to participate in a week-long summit with the Soviets at Lake Geneva, Switzerland. Khrushchev and Bulganin attended, meeting President Dwight D. Eisenhower of the United States. It was the first trip to the West by a top Soviet leader.

The Geneva summit began July 18, 1955. Four items were on the agenda: the reunification of Germany, European security, disarmament, and improvement of East-West relations. An overriding external objective of Khrushchev's was to rid West Berlin of the continued Allied military presence.

During the meeting, President Eisenhower proposed an "open skies" arrangement to the Soviets. Under such a system the two nations would "give to each other a complete blueprint of our military establishments" and "provide within our countries facilities for aerial photography to the other country." Although the Soviets refused to rise to Eisenhower's bait, the meeting did result in the "spirit of Geneva," generally equated with a desire on both sides to seek accommodation and avoid confrontation. The four powers directed their foreign ministers to continue the talks in October, though the ministers' talks made little progress on key issues.

Khrushchev took his next step in revising Stalinist foreign policy at the July 1955 Central Committee session. Khrushchev made known his intent to seek a reconciliation with Yugoslavia's leader Josip Broz Tito. This was in marked opposition to Stalin's foreign minister Viacheslav Molotov, a powerful member of the post-Stalin leadership who believed concessions to Tito would undermine East-bloc unity. Molotov's views on Yugoslavia found little support in the Central Committee and his influence began declining.

Also in 1955, the Soviets formed the Warsaw Pact to offset the North Atlantic Treaty Organization (NATO) and the rearming of West Germany. While Yugoslavia did not join the pact, relations between the countries did improve, with past animosity between the two blamed on Stalin.

'Secret Speech'

At the Twentieth Soviet Party Congress in February 1956 Khrushchev dramatically transformed de-Stalinization from a cautious, incremental policy into a vigorous campaign of denunciation against Stalin's methods and the dictator himself. By focusing his attack directly on Stalin, Khrushchev hoped to avoid any responsibility for events such as the Great Purge, in which he had played a role.

Khrushchev had the honored responsibility of delivering the main Central Committee report at the congress. In his speech, delivered on February 14, Khrushchev boldly challenged the world view of many party members. He renounced bedrock Marxist-Leninist doctrines such as the inevitability of war among capitalist states and the eventual revolutionary overthrow of those systems. He declared that the danger of nuclear war dictated the prudent strategy of peaceful coexistence, and that international socialist goals could be achieved peaceably.

The most striking aspect of Khrushchev's performance at the congress, however, was his so-called Secret Speech of February 24, which attacked Stalin and began the process of unrestrained de-Stalinization. In the speech, Khrushchev portrayed Stalin as a ruthless tyrant responsible for the deaths of thousands of loyal high-ranking Communist party members and innumerable innocent Soviet citizens. Khrushchev charged that Stalin used violence "not only toward everything which opposed him, but also toward that which seemed to his capricious and despotic character contrary to his concepts." The party leader accused Stalin of being not only ruthless, but also irresponsible in his failure to prepare the nation for the devastating 1941 Nazi invasion. Khrushchev said that unlike Lenin, who "had always stressed the role of the people as the creator of history," Stalin had systematically constructed his own personality cult—a pervasive, self-glorifying portrayal of himself in the mass media as the unrivaled and perfect hero-leader of the Soviet Union.

Khrushchev Reminisces on War and Arms Race

...World War III *is* possible. There are more than enough crazy people around who would like to start one. I know that *our* government doesn't want war.... But anything is possible....

I remember President Kennedy once stated ... that the United States had the nuclear missile capacity to wipe out the Soviet Union two times over, while the Soviet Union [could] wipe out the U. S. only once.... When journalists asked me to comment, ... I said jokingly, "Yes, I know what Kennedy claims, and he's quite right. But I'm not complaining.... We're satisfied to be able to finish off the U.S. the first time around.... We're not a bloodthirsty people." These remarks of mine drew some smiles....

[T]he capitalist powers are unlikely to risk a world war, [but] they will never miss an opportunity to conduct subversive ideological policies against us. I consider that normal and legitimate.... [But] to speak of ideological compromise would be to betray our Party's first principles.... It was with this conviction in mind that I allowed myself ... to use the expression "We will bury the enemies of the Revolution." I was referring, of course, to America. Enemy propagandists ... blew it all out of proportion: "Khrushchev says the Soviet people want to bury the people of the United States of America!" I said no such thing. Our enemies were purposely distorting a few words I'd just let drop....

The case of the ABMs is a perfect example of how idiotic the arms race is. The spiraling competition is an unending waste of human intellectual and material resources.... Naturally, the updating of defenses is necessary, but it can go to absurd extremes.... The reactionary forces in the West know it's expedient for them to force us to exhaust our economic resources in a huge military budget, thus diverting funds which could otherwise be spent on the ... needs of our peoples....

When I was the leader of the Party and the government, ... I think, at the time at least, I was right to concentrate on military spending.... If I hadn't put such a high priority on our military needs, we couldn't have survived.... [But] once we ... had what it took to defend ourselves and deter our enemy ... we began to economize on our military expenditures.... I can't help noticing ... that now money is being wasted....

Meanwhile, we should keep in mind that it's the size of our nuclear missile arsenal, and not the size of our army, that counts. The infantry has become ... not the muscle but the fat of the armed forces....

We must also press for arms control.... During my political career we reached a partial agreement on nuclear testing.... It was a good beginning, but ... I must also say that the Americans proposed certain arms control measures to which we could not agree.

I'm thinking now about their insistence [on] ... a provision for on-site inspection anywhere in our country.... I agreed in principle to on-site inspection ... but we couldn't allow ... their inspectors crisscrossing around the Soviet Union. They would have discovered that we were in a relatively weak position, [which] ... might have encouraged them to attack us. However, all that has changed.... [W]e no longer lag behind to any significant degree....

Therefore, I think there is no longer any reason for us to resist the idea of international control. If I had any influence ... I would urge that we sign a mutual agreement providing for more extensive inspection.... I would like to see us sign a mutual treaty of nonaggression and inspection.... Naturally, we don't want to undress all the way and stand before NATO inspectors as naked as Adam. Perhaps ... [a] temporary [accord could] give us time to work out other, more far-reaching agreements.... [E]ven if a Soviet-American agreement ... were impossible, we should go ahead and sharply reduce our own expenditures—unilaterally....

Any leadership which conducts a policy of arms control and disarmament must be courageous and wise ... and not let others intimidate them. Who, in our own country, are the "others"...? They are the military. I don't reproach the military for that— they're only doing their job.... However, leaders must be careful not to look at the world through the eyeglasses of the military. Otherwise, ... the government will start spending all its money and the best energies of its people on armaments—[and] ... pretty soon the country will have lost its pants in the arms race.... [T]he government must always keep a bit between the teeth of the military....

A government leader should keep in mind exactly what sort of destruction we're capable of today.... Can you picture what would be left after a few hydrogen bombs fell on Moscow? Forget about "a few"—imagine just one. Or Washington? Or New York? Or Bonn? It staggers the mind....

I know people will say, "Khrushchev is in a panic over the possibility of war." I am not. I've always been against war, but at the same time I've always realized full well that fear of nuclear war on the part of a country's leader can paralyze that country's defenses. And if a country's defenses are paralyzed, then war really is inevitable: the enemy is sure to sense your fright and try to take advantage of it....

Besides, what kind of panic would you expect from a man my age? I'm nearly seventy-seven years old. As they say, I'm no longer on my way to the fair—I started my journey home a long time ago....

—*Khrushchev Remembers: The Last Testament,* ed. and trans. Strobe Talbott. Copyright © 1974 by Little, Brown & Co. (Inc.). Reprinted by permission.

Khrushchev claimed that by doing this Stalin had distorted history, set himself above the party and the principle of collective leadership, and deviated from Leninist precepts. Khrushchev's Secret Speech was not published in the Soviet Union, but it was distributed to party members in the Soviet Union and abroad. A copy was leaked to the West, and on June 4, 1956, the U.S. State Department published the complete text. (Excerpts from "Secret Speech," Appendix, p. 297)

Although the Secret Speech marked the first time a Soviet leader had publicly and explicitly condemned Stalin's abuses of power, Khrushchev's presentation of the facts was neither complete nor perfectly objective. He made no mention of the role he had played in building Stalin's personality cult and executing his orders. In addition, the speech portrayed Lenin as a saintly and judicious father figure while failing to acknowledge that he also had gained near dictatorial power and had advocated the use of terror as a necessary tool in the fight for socialism.

Khrushchev was able to take such a bold step because he had developed a strong contingent of allies among the delegates to the congress, primarily through numerous party personnel replacements in the republics and regions since Stalin's death. Scholars still debate Khrushchev's motives for making these sensational revelations at the congress. Khrushchev said years later that he was trying to preclude recurrence of "such phenomena in the future" and to reinvigorate Leninist "norms" in the party. It is likely, however, that the speech was intended partly to strengthen Khrushchev's hand against rivals in the Soviet leadership.

1956 Foreign Policy Crises

Khrushchev's Secret Speech had unintended consequences in Eastern Europe, where Soviet domination generally was resented. Eastern Europeans took his denunciation of Stalin as a signal that they would have greater freedom over their affairs. In 1956 Communist party control broke down in Poland and Hungary. In late June, Polish workers in Poznan, emboldened by Khrushchev's speech and a growing anticommunist attitude among the Polish people, rioted. They demanded improved living and working conditions, more consumer goods, and government reform. The rioters took over the city, freeing prisoners in police stations and shouting anti-Soviet slogans. Only the arrival of Polish army units reestablished order.

The riot split the Polish Communist party between those who wanted to pursue reforms and those who wanted to maintain a Stalinist hard line. The apparent victory in October of the reformers under Wladyslaw Gomulka caused concern in the Kremlin. A delegation including Molotov, Lazar Kaganovich, Khrushchev, and Anastas Mikoian went hurriedly to Warsaw on October 19 to confer with Polish leaders. Simultaneously, Soviet troops in Poland were put on alert. Gomulka and his colleagues, however, persuaded the Soviets that they did not plan a split with the Soviet Union, and the Soviet delegation returned to Moscow the following day. Further negotiations produced concessions on both sides, including a Polish promise to support Soviet foreign policy and the Soviet cancellation of more than two billion rubles of Polish debt.

Soviet Invasion of Hungary

The upheaval in Poland encouraged reformers in Hungary, where the brutality of the Hungarian regime had created a revolutionary mood among the public and divisions within the Communist party. Hungarian students began mass demonstrations in Budapest on October 20, demanding formation of a new government by former premier Imre Nagy, a liberal Communist party member. The protests turned violent October 23 as the Hungarian people rose in a genuine popular revolt driven by local revolutionary committees. Soviet tanks helped restore order in Budapest, but the Soviets acceded to the replacement of the hard-line communist regime with one headed by Nagy. Soviet forces began withdrawing from Budapest on October 30. That day Nagy inflamed the uprising by appealing for the support of Hungary's "fighters for freedom," by pledging an end to the one-party system, and by calling for Hungary's withdrawal from the Warsaw Pact. This demonstrated to the Soviets that the Hungarian revolt was going far beyond the limited change that they had decided to permit in Poland.

On November 4, eight Soviet military divisions struck at Budapest and other Hungarian cities in an effort to suppress the rebellion. Hungarian resistance fighters fought fiercely but were overwhelmed by superior Soviet firepower. About three thousand Hungarians were killed and another two hundred thousand fled to Austria. Nagy took refuge in the Yugoslav embassy. After receiving a guarantee from newly installed Communist party leader Janos Kadar that he could leave the country, Nagy was arrested on November 22 and executed by Soviet authorities.

Kadar accepted Soviet direction in forming a new government that closely followed the Soviet line. He was faced with the task of rebuilding a country crippled by violence and strikes that continued through the winter. Meanwhile, the Soviets came under worldwide condemnation. The United States, while declining to intervene directly in Hungary, mounted a propaganda campaign in the United Nations and elsewhere against the Soviet action.

After the Hungarian revolt was crushed, Tito again broke with Moscow. This further discredited Khrushchev and his attempts to reconcile with Yugoslavia. It also kept the opposition led by Molotov in a better position from which to maintain support.

Suez Crisis

International condemnation of the Soviet invasion of Hungary would have been more severe had not the world's attention been focused on events in the Middle East. Egyptian president Gamal Abdel Nasser had advocated a nonaligned stance for his country since coming to power in 1952. His opposition to imperialism, however, had brought him into conflict with the Western alliance, particularly Great Britain and France. In 1955 his purchase of Soviet weapons through Czechoslovakia alarmed U.S. leaders and solidified his reputation as an anti-Western maverick. In July 1956 after the United States withdrew funding for the Aswan High Dam, the centerpiece of Nasser's economic development program, he nationalized the Suez Canal.

The move led the British and French to begin planning a military action against Egypt. Not only was the Suez Canal Company a British- and French-owned enterprise, but also Egyptian control of the canal threatened Europe's

Western Schools of Thought On Khrushchev's Power Structure

Nikita S. Khrushchev's tenure as Communist party first secretary was characterized by policy inconsistency and ambiguity. The frequent shifting of priorities between competing programs such as agrarian reform and building military strength made coherent policy impossible. While Khrushchev vocally supported agricultural reform, capital investments for farming lagged far behind those for heavy industry. In cultural areas, official leniency one day was offset by suppression of dissidents the next.

On defense and foreign policy issues, Khrushchev's statements were less inconsistent with his actions than they were in some other areas. They often changed, however, from steps toward détente with the West to steps certain to provoke confrontation, which made Soviet international conduct volatile and unpredictable.

Pressure Factor

Did changes in Khrushchev's individual priorities adequately explain these reversals and inconsistencies? Were the decisions Khrushchev's alone to make, or was he forced to bend to pressures applied by his colleagues and influential institutions? There are two broad schools of thought among Western analysts with regard to these questions, though in recent years distinctions between the two have blurred somewhat.

The first school is generally referred to as the "conflict school." Carl Linden and certain other early Kremlinologists believed Khrushchev was a reformer who fought an uphill battle against powerful bureaucrats opposed to major reforms or concessions to the citizenry that might unleash uncontrollable consequences. Policy decisions, according to this school, resulted either from Khrushchev's defeat on certain issues or his attempts to outmaneuver or compromise with his opponents to ward off defeat. Accordingly, inconsistent, ambivalent policy flowed from Khrushchev's battles to implement at least parts of his reforms.

Scholars subscribing to this view have argued that the events of 1960—particularly his harsh response to the U-2 spy incident—were evidence of Khrushchev's weakening position. The conflict school also has cited the removal of several Khrushchev allies in 1960-1961 from their posts on the Presidium (Politburo) and Central Committee as evidence that serious divisions existed among the top leaders.

The opposing school of thought maintained that Khrushchev was not inherently a reformer. According to Merle Fainsod, Khrushchev was an "essentially conservative transitional figure," willing to experiment with reforms but without necessarily calculating their consequences. Fainsod viewed Khrushchev as a typical national leader who avoided hard policy choices by reacting to events as they occurred instead of developing and promoting a coherent policy course.

This school viewed Khrushchev's inconsistency as being similar to Lenin's. Policy ambivalence was not the result of political battles within the top party leadership; instead it was largely attributed to Khrushchev's changing perceptions of his own policies and the needs of the Soviet Union. Accordingly, this school did not see the 1960-1961 Presidium and Central Committee personnel changes as a political move against Khrushchev engineered by his rivals. Khrushchev himself may have had a hand in removing his own Presidium allies. According to Jerry Hough, this school of thought interprets the "reduction in the number of Central Committee secretaries on the Presidium ... as an attempt to prevent the Secretariat from dominating the Presidium and thereby to strengthen the position of the one individual (Nikita Khrushchev) who headed the three major collective institutions below the level of the Presidium—the Central Committee Secretariat, the Council of Ministers, and the Bureau of the Central Committee for the RSFSR [Russian Soviet Federated Socialist Republic]."

Role of the Majority

In synthesizing the views of the two schools, Hough asserts that the real issue was whether Khrushchev had to have a majority in the Presidium to push through his policies. The abrupt changes in those policies may have indicated that Khrushchev was not always forced to act according to the wishes of a collective leadership. In *How the Soviet Union Is Governed,* Hough said:

> In judging the structure of power in the Khrushchev period, we must ultimately rely upon our sense of the nature of committee politics and the meaning of different patterns of policy outcomes that emerge.... The natural outcome of a divided collective committee is deference to the key individual interests of most of the respective members (logrolling, if you will), compromise on the major issues dividing the committee, and (except in rare cases) gradualism and even conservatism in the change of major policy.

The leadership was not divided in 1964 when it engineered a major policy shift: Khrushchev's removal.

oil supply. In late October, Israeli, French, and British forces attacked Egypt and captured the canal. Eisenhower, however, condemned the action of his allies and applied economic and diplomatic pressure to force them to end their intervention. On November 7 Great Britain and France announced that they would withdraw; Israel did the same the following day. The crisis had bolstered Nasser's standing in the Middle East, confirmed Egyptian control of the Suez Canal, temporarily fractured the Western alliance, and provided Moscow (which pledged financial support for the Aswan High Dam) with an opportunity to increase its influence in Egypt and the Middle East.

Domestic Difficulties

Many of Khrushchev's domestic programs were begun not because of their soundness but because of his hard lobbying work and an outwardly jovial personality that masked what some have called a violent cleverness. Western observers have said Khrushchev was the last "true believer." He took Marxism-Leninism seriously and was convinced of the likelihood of rapid industrial, technological, and societal advancement. He believed in the possibility of perfecting a "new Soviet man" and of the Soviet Union's ability to overtake the West economically in a matter of decades.

Virgin Lands and Decentralization

Khrushchev addressed the Soviet Union's longstanding agricultural troubles by initiating his celebrated Virgin Lands program in 1954. He chose Leonid I. Brezhnev to carry out the risky venture of cultivating for grain millions of acres of previously unplanted (virgin) land in Central Asia and Siberia. By 1960 more than one hundred million acres had been opened for planting. After several years of famines and poor harvests, the program succeeded in temporarily relieving the agrarian crisis, but it failed to solve the underlying problem of low agriculture productivity. The Soviets were forced in the early 1960s to begin buying large quantities of grain from Canada, Australia, and the United States.

Industrial difficulties led, at the December 1956 Central Committee meeting, to a decision to further centralize the country's economic planning machinery. Khrushchev objected, but the Supreme Soviet nonetheless approved the move February 12, 1957. The next day, Khrushchev counterattacked with a plan to decentralize economic power.

Western analysts have questioned why, if Khrushchev controlled the leadership and opposed the changes, he waited until February to move against his opponents. Three possible reasons stand out: the satellite countries were, by February, under control; the Virgin Lands program had brought in a good harvest; and Khrushchev had developed a plan behind which he believed the Central Committee would rally. In short, Khrushchev was in a much better political position in February to launch his attack.

Khrushchev's counterprogram was designed to weaken the power of the highly centralized economic ministries that had flourished under Stalin by abolishing most of them and placing much of their industrial responsibilities in the hands of new regional economic councils—or *sovnarkhozes*. Khrushchev employed the Supreme Soviet

in his effort to line up support among regional officials. It was not a difficult task because decentralization would directly benefit these officials at the expense of entrenched urban industrial administrators. Khrushchev, however, apparently did not fully comprehend the power of these bureaucrats. They supported Khrushchev's opponents on the Presidium in an effort to overthrow him.

Antiparty Group

Since besting Malenkov, Khrushchev had maneuvered to strengthen his position by undermining the authority of weaker rivals. In 1955 he succeeded in demoting Lazar Kaganovich, one of Stalin's top aides, from deputy prime minister to a minor governmental position, although he remained a Presidium member. Khrushchev also had continuously lobbied against Molotov.

At the Twentieth Party Congress Khrushchev's control was greatly strengthened—and his opponents' guard raised further—when 133 new members of the Central Committee were named. Many of these could trace their elevation to earlier associations with Khrushchev. Full Presidium membership did not change, though five new candidate members were chosen who appeared also to owe their promotions to Khrushchev.

After Khrushchev's Secret Speech he stepped up attacks on Stalin's "Old Guard." Molotov, Kaganovich, Malenkov, and Kliment Voroshilov were accused of attempting to thwart Khrushchev's proposal to disclose Stalin's crimes. Dmitri Shepilov replaced Molotov as foreign affairs minister. Kaganovich was relieved from his minor post as chairman of the State Committee on Labor and Wages and named to a still lower ministerial job. Molotov and Kaganovich remained, however, on the Presidium.

In June 1957 Khrushchev's growing circle of powerful enemies, which would come to be known as the "antiparty group," decided to oust him. When it came time for the showdown, Mikoian, Mikhail Suslov, and Aleksei Kirichenko were the only full Presidium members openly supporting Khrushchev. The other members opposed Khrushchev either because of his policies or his efforts to have them demoted. Spearheaded by Malenkov, Molotov, Shepilov, and to a lesser degree Bulganin (in whose office the group met), the antiparty group called for Khrushchev's resignation. The group tried to announce the resignation immediately, so as to present the Central Committee, which was dominated by Khrushchev's supporters, with a fait accompli. Khrushchev, however, refused to resign. He astutely demanded that his fate be decided by the Central Committee, a body that did have the formal authority to rule on such matters, though it had become a rubber stamp for the decisions of the Presidium. The Presidium met in almost continuous session for several days, hoping to forestall a Central Committee meeting, but regional officials swarmed upon Moscow, rallied behind Khrushchev, and demanded a plenum.

Firm support for Khrushchev among both the Central Committee and candidate Presidium members blocked the "resignation." The rising young Central Committee members from the republics likely saw themselves as beneficiaries if Khrushchev retained his position and as direct losers if he did not.

After the situation settled, Khrushchev took aim at his opponents. Malenkov, Kaganovich, Molotov, and Shepilov were accused of "antiparty, factional methods in an attempt to change the composition of the party's leading bodies." All four lost their Presidium and Central Committee memberships and their governmental posts. Other conspirators also were demoted or removed immediately, although Bulganin was not ousted from the Presidium until 1958 and Voroshilov did not resign his posts until 1960.

Khrushchev promoted those officials who had supported him in his fight against the antiparty group, and the Presidium swelled to fifteen members. He rewarded not only numerous lower-level supporters, but also Marshal Georgii Zhukov, who was promoted to full membership in the Presidium from candidate status. Zhukov, however, lasted only four months. The strong-willed World War II hero was removed both from the Presidium and as defense minister amidst accusations of political deficiency and of "surrounding himself with sycophants and flatterers." Khrushchev and other party leaders had objected to several Zhukov moves that appeared to limit party control of the military. His ouster marked yet another instance of a Soviet leader eliminating a perceived source of competition for power. In 1958 Khrushchev replaced Bulganin as chairman of the Council of Ministers. The man who had been a party worker all his career now was head of the government as well.

Khrushchev did not slow down his efforts to bring about a thoroughly industrialized, equally competitive superpower after his 1957 successes. In fact, after 1957 Khrushchev was able to pursue his policies more freely. For the most part, however, his domestic initiatives failed; and, as with many of his foreign adventures, they became known as Khrushchev's "hare-brained schemes."

U.S.-Soviet Relations

The Soviet invasion of Hungary and the Suez crisis had damaged the good will built up between the superpowers at the Geneva conference in 1955. During 1957 tense relations continued as Moscow announced a series of scientific accomplishments that caused alarm in the United States. On August 26, 1957, the Soviets disclosed that they had tested successfully an intercontinental ballistic missile (ICBM). On October 4 they announced that they had placed into orbit *Sputnik I*, a 184-pound satellite. *Sputnik II*, weighing more than eleven hundred pounds and carrying a dog named Laika, was launched November 3. Not until January 31, 1958, did the United States launch its first satellite, a thirty-pound cylinder. The Soviet space shots lent credence to Moscow's claims that it had developed ICBMs capable of carrying nuclear warheads. Although the United States had clear nuclear superiority during this period, the notion that a "missile gap" had developed in favor of the Soviet Union became a popular American concern. Proponents of a U.S. weapons buildup used the fictitious gap to lobby for greater defense spending. Khrushchev, aware of his country's continuing strategic vulnerability, played up the idea that Soviet scientists were making great strides in military technology.

Meanwhile, Khrushchev's political intrigues had enabled him to assume complete control over Soviet foreign affairs. He attempted to walk the line between two conflicting policies: peaceful coexistence with the United States and the West and the militant expansion of communist influence and power around the world. The Eisenhower administration responded by continuing U.S. efforts to contain communist expansion, while exploring opportunities for improved relations.

Middle East Rivalry

The withdrawal of the British and French after the Suez crisis created a power vacuum in the Middle East. The administration in Washington concluded that the U.S. commitment to resist communism in the region had to be fortified. Accordingly, on January 5, 1957, President Eisenhower went before a joint session of Congress to urge support for a declaration that was dubbed the Eisenhower Doctrine.

The Joint Resolution to Promote Peace and Stability in the Middle East (H J Res 117) declared that "if the President determines the necessity . . . [the United States] is prepared to use armed forces to assist . . . any nation or groups of nations requesting assistance against armed aggression *from any country controlled by international communism.*" [Emphasis supplied.]

The resolution did not draw a precise geographical line around the area to which it applied. The Senate and House committee reports on the resolution accepted the administration's view and defined the Middle East as the area bounded by Libya on the west, Pakistan on the east, Turkey in the north, and the Sudan in the south. The Senate report said that no precise listing of nations was contained in the resolution because this "would restrict the freedom of action of the United States in carrying out the purposes of the resolution."

The first test of the Eisenhower Doctrine came in 1958 following a coup in Iraq in which the pro-Western government of King Faisal II was overthrown and replaced with a regime favorable to the Soviet Union and the United Arab Republic (UAR). The new Iraqi government immediately withdrew from the Baghdad Pact—the 1955 mutual defense treaty among Great Britain, Iran, Iraq, Pakistan, and Turkey.

When the government of Lebanon came under similar pressures and its president requested U.S. assistance, Eisenhower ordered U.S. Marines from the Sixth Fleet in the Mediterranean to land in Lebanon to protect the government. Citing the Eisenhower Doctrine, the president said July 15, 1958, that Lebanon's territorial integrity and independence were "vital to United States national interests and world peace." The Soviet Union and the UAR, Eisenhower charged, were trying to overthrow the constitutional government of Lebanon and "install by violence a government which subordinates the independence of Lebanon to . . . the United Arab Republic."

Iraq's withdrawal from the Baghdad Pact persuaded the Eisenhower administration that the three remaining "northern tier" members of the organization needed an additional pledge of U.S. support in resisting communism. Using the Middle East resolution as a basis for talks, the United States initiated negotiations with Turkey, Iran, and Pakistan on defense arrangements, bringing the United States into closer cooperation with the Baghdad Pact, which was renamed the Central Treaty Organization (CENTO). Three identically worded executive agreements were signed in March 1959 between the United States and each of the three nations. Washington pledged to come to the defense of the three countries in the event of communist aggression or subversion.

Superpower Summitry and the U-2 Incident

In 1959 superpower relations warmed considerably. Vice President Richard Nixon visited the Soviet Union

The Nixon-Khrushchev 'Kitchen Debate'

An unlikely public give-and-take session between Soviet premier Nikita S. Khrushchev and U.S. vice president Richard Nixon made worldwide headlines when Nixon visited Moscow from July 22 to August 2, 1959.

The trip was a follow-up to a visit to the United States earlier in the summer by Nixon's Soviet counterpart, First Deputy Premier Frol R. Kozlov. After arriving in the Soviet capital, Nixon quickly found himself defending actions of his government at home. The previous week Congress had passed a "captive nations" resolution, and President Dwight D. Eisenhower had issued a declaration calling on Americans to "study the plight of the Soviet-dominated nations and to recommit themselves to the support of the just aspirations of those captive nations." Khrushchev condemned the resolution as "rude" interference in "our internal affairs" and added that "the camp of the socialist countries has never before been so solid and powerful as now."

The most publicized event of Nixon's visit, however, was his informal discussion with Khrushchev, which took place on July 24 before reporters and videotape cameras at a U.S. trade exhibition. It was soon dubbed the "Kitchen Debate" because part of the colloquy occurred near a display of an American home, complete with a kitchen. Viewing the model home, Khrushchev said, "You think the Russian people will be dumbfounded to see this? But I tell you all our modern homes have equipment of this sort, and to get a flat you have only to be a Soviet visitor, not a citizen."

To which Nixon replied: "We do not claim to astonish the Russian people. We hope to show our diversity and our right to choose. We do not wish to have decisions made at the top by government officials who say that all homes should be built in the same way. Would it not be better to compete in the relative merits of washing machines than in the strength of rockets? Is this the kind of competition you want?" Khrushchev: "Yes, that's the kind of competition we want, but your generals say we must compete in rockets." *(Kitchen Debate excerpts, Appendix, p. 306)*

Premier Khrushchev and Vice President Nixon visit a U.S. trade exhibition in Moscow, July 1959. Leonid I. Brezhnev, who would succeed Khrushchev as party leader five years later, looks on.

from July 22 to August 2. He and Khrushchev discussed superpower relations, West Berlin, and the status of the Eastern-bloc nations. They also held an unlikely public debate on the quality of life in their respective nations that captured the world's attention. *(Kitchen Debate, box, this page)*

In September Khrushchev became the first top Soviet leader to visit the United States. He and President Eisenhower conferred cordially at the Camp David presidential retreat in Maryland. Khrushchev also visited rural Iowa and Eisenhower's farm at Gettysburg, Pennsylvania, all the while projecting an image of a benign, grandfatherly leader who wanted to end the hostility between East and West. The summit visit did not produce significant agreements, but it created expectations on both sides that further summit diplomacy could resolve the major issues of contention between the United States and the Soviet Union. This optimism came to be known as the "spirit of Camp David."

The two leaders agreed to participate in a multilateral summit meeting scheduled for May 1960, to be followed by an Eisenhower visit to the Soviet Union.

The summit meeting was torpedoed, however, by the May 5, 1960, disclosure that the Soviets had shot down an American U-2 spy plane over their territory. The United States had been making the routine flights since 1956, with the planes flying at seventy thousand feet to elude Soviet air defenses. But in May a recently developed Soviet ground-to-air missile reportedly hit the U-2, forcing the pilot, Francis Gary Powers, to bail out. Powers, an ex-Air Force flyer employed by the Central Intelligence Agency, was captured, and the Soviets retrieved the wreckage of the spy plane. After some initial denials of responsibility, Eisenhower admitted May 9 that the flights occurred with his full knowledge and support.

The reaction from Moscow was threatening. Khrushchev warned Turkey, Pakistan, and Norway that "if they allow others to fly from their bases to our territory we shall hit at those bases." He added May 11 that Powers would be tried "severely as a spy" for his "gangster and bandit raid." In regards to Eisenhower's scheduled June 10 visit to the USSR, Khrushchev withdrew the invitation, saying, "The Russian people would say I was mad to welcome a man who sends spy planes over here like that."

The summit meeting in Paris, attended by Eisenhower, Khrushchev, British prime minister Harold Macmillan, and French president Charles de Gaulle, opened May 16 and quickly broke down into mutual recrimination. Khrushchev condemned the U-2 surveillance missions, while Eisenhower defended the overflights as an essential precaution against surprise attack. Nevertheless, Eisenhower claimed, "These flights were suspended after the recent incident and are not to be resumed."

The conference ended in deadlock. The Soviets tried Powers and, on August 9, sentenced him to ten years in prison. He was released February 10, 1962, in exchange for the Soviet "master spy" Rudolph Abel, who was apprehended by U.S. authorities in 1957 and sentenced to a thirty-year prison term. Several strange circumstances surrounding the U-2 incident have led a few observers to speculate that the United States may have intentionally used it to subvert the developing superpower diplomacy. These circumstances include the survival of the plane, which was expected to disintegrate if struck by a Soviet missile; the treatment of Powers (who had willingly confessed the nature and details of his operation to the Soviets) as a hero by the CIA upon his return; and the muted questioning of Powers by the Senate Armed Services Committee after CIA chief John McCone secretly briefed the committee.

Khrushchev returned to the United States in September 1960 to attend a meeting of the heads of government of the eighty-two members of the United Nations. Ostensibly there to help reopen disarmament negotiations, Khrushchev used the gathering to promote a plan to replace UN General Secretary Dag Hammarskjöld of Sweden, whom the Soviets charged was a "willing tool" of the Western powers. The Soviet plan called for replacing Hammarskjöld with a three-member executive committee representing three UN groups: the Western powers, the socialist states, and the neutralist countries. The Soviet proposal garnered little support among world leaders. The heated debate was punctuated by Khrushchev's shouted interruptions and desk-pounding (with his fists and, in a celebrated incident, his shoe). His plan a failure, Khrushchev returned to Moscow October 13.

Germany and Berlin

Despite the failure of the summit meeting the previous year, Khrushchev was eager to meet and size up the new U.S. president, John F. Kennedy, elected in November 1960. A Kennedy-Khrushchev meeting was arranged for June 3-4, 1961, in Vienna. President Kennedy said afterward on June 6 that their "most somber talks" mainly dealt with Germany and Berlin. Khrushchev had made plain his determination to sign a peace treaty with East Germany, a move long interpreted in Washington as part of the Soviet effort to force Western powers out of West Berlin. Kennedy, in press conferences in June and July, stressed the "real intent" of the Soviets to dislodge the Western powers and on July 25 called for an immediate buildup of U.S. and NATO forces. Khrushchev replied, in speeches August 7, 9, and 11, with threats of Soviet mobilization and boasts that Moscow could build a hundred-megaton nuclear bomb.

Then, with no advance warning, the East German regime August 13 began sealing off the sector border between East and West Berlin to stem the flow of East Germans to the West. (Nearly three million East German citizens had emigrated to the West since the end of World War II.) The Soviets and East Germans ignored the protests of the Western allies. Within a few months, the East Germans had built a mortar and barbed-wire wall running along the entire sector border, effectively stopping the transit of refugees from East to West. But Khrushchev's hopes for Western concessions in response to his actions failed, and the Berlin Wall came to symbolize communist oppression.

Cuban Missile Crisis

Another serious confrontation between Washington and Moscow developed in 1962 over a Soviet move to deploy missiles carrying nuclear warheads in Cuba. Since the successful revolution in 1959, Cuban leader Fidel Castro had moved his government solidly into the Soviet sphere of influence. In January 1962, at Washington's urging, Cuba was expelled from the Organization of American States. Cuba's economic isolation in the Western Hemisphere led to increased Soviet shipments of arms and goods to the island nation, a development that was viewed with increasing alarm in Washington.

On October 22, 1962, President Kennedy stunned the nation by announcing that aerial reconnaissance photos revealed that the Soviets secretly were building launching sites in Cuba for medium- and intermediate-range ballistic missiles capable of reaching many U.S. cities. The "secret, swift and extraordinary buildup" of a nuclear capability in Cuba, the president said, "is a deliberately provocative and unjustified change in the status quo which cannot be accepted by this country."

Kennedy announced the imposition of "a strict quarantine of all offensive military equipment under shipment to Cuba," adding that "ships of any kind bound for Cuba, from whatever nation or port, will, if found to contain cargoes of offensive weapons, be turned back." Kennedy said, "Any nuclear missile launched from Cuba against any nation in the Western Hemisphere" would be regarded "as an attack by the Soviet Union on the United States requiring a full retaliatory response upon the Soviet Union." The president called on Khrushchev "to halt and eliminate this clandestine, reckless and provocative threat to world peace."

An estimated twenty-five Soviet-bloc vessels were

moving toward Cuba as the U.S. Navy quarantine officially began October 24. The Soviets recalled several ships that might have been challenged and on October 27 Kennedy received two letters from Khrushchev broaching a compromise. The first letter was conciliatory, offering to remove the weapons from Cuba. The second letter proposed in return the removal of U.S. intermediate-range ballistic missiles from bases in Turkey. The missiles in Turkey were obsolete and had already been scheduled for removal, but Kennedy refused to consider removing them in return for Moscow's removal of the missiles in Cuba. Khrushchev wrote again October 28, agreeing to dismantle the Cuban missiles without demanding any reciprocal U.S. move in Turkey. President Kennedy announced November 20 that "all known offensive missile sites in Cuba have been removed." He declared the quarantine lifted. *(Cuban missile crisis documents, Appendix, p. 307)*

What Kennedy saw as Khrushchev's "statesmanlike decision" to remove the Cuban missiles appeared differently to many hard-line communists. They viewed it as the leader of the world's socialists backing down to the leader of the capitalist camp. The Chinese in particular lost whatever faith they had retained in Moscow's ability to lead the struggle against imperialism. At home the Cuban missile crisis eroded Khrushchev's support in the party. Some members considered his decision to back down a betrayal, while others questioned the party leader's judgment in initiating such a risky scheme.

After the crisis, U.S.-Soviet relations did improve slightly as Moscow and Washington cooperated on several arms control measures. Most notably the two superpowers along with Great Britain signed the 1963 Partial Nuclear Test Ban Treaty, which banned nuclear weapons tests in the atmosphere, in outer space, and under water. That year the superpowers also established a "hot line" between their two capitals to facilitate communication during international crises. Nevertheless, the U.S.-Soviet nuclear arms race continued throughout the decade.

Sino-Soviet Relations

Soviet aid to the Chinese Communists prior to their victory over the nationalists was inconsistent and often came with strings attached. But in 1950, when Chinese Communist leader Mao Zedong went to Moscow and signed a treaty of friendship and alliance with the Soviet Union, old Sino-Soviet animosities appeared to be buried. Western observers saw the new relationship as a logical union of two communist powers. In fact, the similarities in ideologies obscured fundamental differences and did nothing to halt numerous Soviet efforts to interfere in internal Chinese politics.

President Kennedy greets Premier Khrushchev in Vienna, June 1961, as Andrei Gromyko steps from the car.

Strategic Differences

After 1950 Chinese leaders perceived the United States as attempting to surround China, cut it off from the world, and replace its communist regime with the government of Chiang Kai-shek on Taiwan. There were U.S. troops all around China: on Taiwan, in Japan, in the Philippines, and in South Korea. There were U.S. advisers in South Vietnam and British troops in Burma and Malaysia. Mao and his colleagues saw the Sino-Soviet alliance and Soviet atomic weapons as the ultimate guarantors of Chinese security against the West.

Khrushchev, eager to maintain the image of a monolithic Communist bloc led by the Soviet Union, pacified his radical Asian allies with aid and promises of nuclear protection in the event of an attack on China. The Chinese, however, preferred the prospect of relying on their own power and pressed Moscow to supply them with the technology to produce atomic weapons. The Soviets complied in a secret agreement signed in 1957. But the Kremlin's refusal to risk a nuclear confrontation with the United States during the Quemoy crisis of 1958 and its repudiation of the secret nuclear weapons technology agreement in 1959 led Beijing to believe that it could not depend on Moscow. The Chinese continued with their own nuclear program, which, ironically, would produce a bomb tested October 16, 1964, a day after Khrushchev's ouster was announced.

Ideological Differences

Khrushchev's performance at the Twentieth Soviet Party Congress in 1956 sent shock waves through China. While some communist governments embraced the concepts of peaceful coexistence and de-Stalinization, China considered Khrushchev's movement to be heretical. The Chinese had endorsed a never-ending struggle against the imperialist camp, and they found much to criticize in the unthinkable notion of peaceful coexistence. Moreover, Khrushchev's Secret Speech was a condemnation of one-man, totalitarian rule that many Chinese Communists viewed as an attack on Mao. The Chinese at first responded to Khrushchev's actions by moderately relaxing censorship. The intensity of the resulting criticism of the government and party caught the regime unawares, however, and the lid on free expression was quickly slammed shut. The Chinese then challenged Soviet ideological preeminence by asserting that Moscow was revisionist, that peaceful coexistence with the West was impossible, and that Khrushchev had violated the basic tenets of Leninist orthodoxy.

Some of the trouble between the countries stemmed from the personal animosity that developed between Khrushchev and Mao. After Stalin's death, Mao saw himself as the successor to the ideological throne of communism. It soon became obvious that Khrushchev and the other Soviet leaders were not interested in relinquishing the crown. The Soviets also viewed the Chinese as too backward to represent the cutting edge of international communism.

In 1958 with the decision to launch the Great Leap Forward—"a great revolutionary leap toward the building of socialism"—the Chinese tried to solve all their problems at once. They claimed that Beijing, not Moscow, was the true center of the world communist movement. They asserted that, faced with U.S. encirclement and Soviet abandonment, they would modernize on their own. Announcing that Mao had discovered a shortcut to achieving a communist society, the Chinese espoused the principle of "self-reliance." Mao explained that no longer would the Chinese "lean to one side" (rely on Moscow) but would "walk on two legs."

The Soviets heaped scorn on the Great Leap Forward (which soon stumbled) and chided the Chinese for claiming to understand Lenin better than his own countrymen. As the 1960s began, the war of words was confined to ideology and attacks were indirect. The Soviets criticized China's ally Albania, instead of China itself, as "adventurist" and "infantile" for its insistence on direct confrontation with the West. In turn, China castigated Yugoslavia, in place of the Soviet Union, for its "revisionist" views toward peaceful coexistence.

In July 1960 the Soviets retaliated against the Chinese verbal abuse by recalling all their technicians in China and suspending their cooperative scientific and technical ventures. The Chinese continued to accuse Khrushchev of being soft on imperialism.

In 1962 the Soviets refused to help China in its war with India, and Khrushchev responded to U.S. pressure to withdraw the missiles the Soviets had placed in Cuba. Beijing denounced both moves as "retreats" and said they had made no contribution to peace. During the last years of Khrushchev's reign, Chinese and Soviet polemics became increasingly direct and accusatory. Khrushchev himself became the primary focus of Chinese attacks. Nevertheless, Western observers finally began to acknowledge that the Sino-Soviet dispute was more than a temporary rift or a personality conflict between Khrushchev and Mao.

The Fall of Khrushchev

The men surrounding Khrushchev in the Kremlin tired of his inconsistent and overly optimistic plans. Amidst plan reversals, perceived foreign policy humiliations, and fears for personal power, party leaders soon joined in an effort to remove Nikita Khrushchev.

The Soviet Communist party goals of the Seven-Year Plan (so called because the Sixth Five-Year Plan, 1956-1960, was scuttled in 1958) proved impossible to achieve. The goals included an 83 percent jump in housing investment, a 70 percent increase in agricultural production, and a 100 percent hike in productivity on collective farms. Certain areas of the Soviet economy performed well. The heavy industry sector continued to grow, and the Soviets achieved more scientific firsts, including the April 12, 1961, spaceflight of Yuri Gagarin, the first human to be launched into space. Yet in most areas the Soviet economy achieved only modest gains that failed to meet the ambitious targets of Soviet planners.

In addition, Kremlin leaders feared that aspects of de-Stalinization at home—particularly reductions in censorship and restrictions on the flow of information—would provoke unrest. State control over the arts eased after Khrushchev's 1956 Secret Speech, although the thaw never resulted in more than a modicum of artistic freedom. Moreover, in early 1957 Khrushchev had backed off somewhat from his aggressive denunciation of Stalin. The official Soviet position had become that Stalin was guilty of making mistakes and violating legal norms, but that he was a devoted Communist party member who strove faithfully for the cause of socialism. Relaxed censorship was applied selectively. For example, in 1958 Khrushchev prevented the publication in the Soviet Union of Boris Pasternak's *Doctor Zhivago.*

At the Twenty-second Soviet Party Congress in October 1961, however, Khrushchev renewed his assault on Stalin. On October 30, following Khrushchev's lead, the delegates unanimously voted to remove Stalin's remains from Lenin's mausoleum on Red Square to a less prominent spot near the Kremlin wall. Thereafter the Soviet regime attempted to remove all traces of Stalin's influence from Soviet society. Schoolbooks containing nearly thirty years of Stalin-dominated Soviet history were rewritten. Towns and streets bearing Stalin's name were renamed, including Stalingrad, which became Volgograd. Khrushchev personally oversaw the publication in 1962 of Alexander Solzhenitsyn's harsh portrait of Stalin's labor camps, *One Day in the Life of Ivan Denisovich.* This reinvigorated assault on Stalin made Khrushchev's colleagues nervous.

Khrushchev's attempt to reorganize the party and government in 1962 was probably the domestic initiative that most damaged his standing. This reorganization was a bifurcation, or split, of most of the lower party and governmental organs into two independent structures. One was industrial (or urban), the other agricultural (or rural). Important regions of the country were given sections of both. The industrial regional party committees and soviets, which had subordinate units in areas roughly equivalent to U.S. cities or counties, supervised nearly all the population in the cities and those involved with industry and construction efforts. The agricultural counterpart supervised rural citizenry and institutions, as well as institutions in cities that were closely related to agriculture. The bifurcation failed largely because it created needless confusion and threatened or diminished the jobs of many powerful bureaucrats and administrators.

For several years prior to 1964, Khrushchev's supporters as well as opponents became increasingly alarmed over the loss of Soviet international prestige, a loss they attributed to Khrushchev. In relations with the noncommunist world, Khrushchev pursued policies, such as placing missiles in Cuba, that resulted in Soviet humiliation. Within the socialist world, his opponents charged, he presided over and promoted the Sino-Soviet split, thereby relinquishing Moscow's position as unqualified leader of the communist movement and turning an important ally into a hostile, ideological rival.

Khrushchev Removed

Khrushchev was forced to surrender leadership of the state and the party at the October 14, 1964, session of the Central Committee. His actual ouster presumably occurred the day before at a meeting of the Presidium. It was announced October 15 that the Central Committee granted Khrushchev's "request to be relieved of his duties ... in view of his advanced age and deterioration of his health."

In fact, Khrushchev's health was fine. His ouster was the result of a carefully planned plot by his fellow members on the Presidium. Khrushchev, political scientist Adam Ulam has written, "was too unpredictable and too arbitrary to be tolerated as head of the regime. He had ceased to be respected and trusted and was not feared enough—a fatal combination for the head of a totalitarian state."

Unlike 1957 when Khrushchev was able to outflank his opponents by taking his case to the Central Committee, in 1964 the Presidium members prevented him from making a similar appeal. It is not known who was the driving force behind the coup, which occurred without warning. Leonid Brezhnev, a close associate of Khrushchev, was named first secretary of the Communist party, and Alexei Kosygin assumed the premiership.

The seventy-year-old Khrushchev, who was vacationing at his dacha on the Black Sea coast when he was summoned back to Moscow October 13, dropped from sight. Supported by a government pension, he lived in enforced obscurity outside Moscow until he died September 11, 1971. During this period he wrote his memoirs, which were smuggled out of the Soviet Union. They were published in the West in two volumes—*Khrushchev Remembers* in 1970 and *The Last Testament* in 1974. (*Excerpts from* The Last Testament, *p. 51*)

American and Chinese Reaction

American president Lyndon B. Johnson broadcast a message October 18, 1964, in which he said, "We do not know exactly what happened to Nikita Khrushchev. ... We do know that he has been forced out of power by his former friends and colleagues. Five days ago he had only praise in Moscow. Today we learn only of his faults." Johnson added that the Soviet leader had "learned from his mistakes" in the Berlin and Cuban crises and that "in the last two years, his government has shown itself aware of the need for sanity in the nuclear age." As examples of Soviet willingness to cooperate, Johnson cited the 1963 nuclear test ban treaty, the Moscow-Washington hot line, and the agreement to bar deployment of nuclear or other mass-destructive weapons in outer space.

The president disclosed that at an October 16 White House meeting the Soviet ambassador, Anatolii Dobrynin, assured Johnson that the new regime planned "no change in basic foreign policy." Johnson said he pointed out to Dobrynin that "we intend to bury no one, and we do not intend to be buried," referring to Khrushchev's widely reported remark toward the capitalist world in 1956 that "History is on our side. We will bury you!"

In China, the news of Khrushchev's demise was greeted with delight. Chinese leaders sent the new regime a congratulatory note October 16 wishing it success "in all fields and in the struggle for the defense of world peace." China's ally, Albania, welcomed the change in command, saying it was "a heavy blow" to the United States and to "the modern revisionists."

Brezhnev Era

An oligarchy took control of the Soviet Union after ousting party leader Nikita S. Khrushchev in October 1964. In contrast to Khrushchev's unpredictable and gregarious approach to governing, the oligarchy emphasized stability and collective decision making. During the second half of the 1960s the new leadership would preside over a chronically troubled economy, an acceleration of the Soviet military buildup, unrest in Czechoslovakia, an increasingly bitter dispute with the People's Republic of China, and the first tentative steps toward détente with the West. Relations between the United States and the Soviet Union became an increasingly important barometer of the climate of international affairs worldwide. Little was left outside the reach of superpower involvement.

The men who replaced Khrushchev moved quickly to do away with domestic programs instituted during their predecessor's years at the top. They dismantled Khrushchev's regional economic councils, designed to decentralize state authority by allowing local jurisdictions some say over regional matters. In addition they ended Khrushchev's confusing bifurcation of the party and government bureaucracies into industrial and agricultural units. Within two years they also had reversed Khrushchev's program of de-Stalinization. Among other actions, the new leadership curbed public criticism of Stalin. At a November 3, 1967, ceremony marking the fiftieth anniversary of the Bolshevik Revolution, Brezhnev referred to Stalin's reign of terror as "temporary setbacks and errors."

While the new leaders de-emphasized the kind of individual dominance that Khrushchev personified, one of them—Leonid I. Brezhnev—gradually emerged as the leading figure in fact as well as title. During Brezhnev's eighteen-year regime (1964-1982) the Soviet Union built itself into a military superpower with client states around the world. But the USSR's success in the military sphere was not matched in other areas of Soviet society. The living standard of Soviet citizens fell and internal dissent grew as the aging Brezhnev leadership resisted change into the 1980s.

Internal Politics

Brezhnev did not dominate the regime immediately after Khrushchev's ouster. The Presidium was a heteroge-neous group, and Brezhnev had only one close ally, Andrei Kirilenko. Brezhnev had limited influence within the Council of Ministers because Premier Aleksei Kosygin ran the government apparatus. Brezhnev's public role as foreign policy spokesman also was limited by Kosygin, who was primarily responsible for relations with noncommunist countries. Mikhail Suslov was another independent and influential figure who had the potential to erode or supersede Brezhnev's authority. Suslov was seen by his colleagues as the defender of the rights of the oligarchy against individual leadership, something uppermost in the leaders' minds. Nikolai Podgornyi, who was widely regarded in the West as the third-ranking leader in the Kremlin, was primarily responsible for party organization. In December 1965 he succeeded Anastas Mikoian as chairman of the Presidium of the Supreme Soviet (president). If Brezhnev faltered, Podgornyi would have been a logical alternative to assume the general secretaryship.

Other Politburo members were allies of Brezhnev rivals, were vulnerable party elders (such as Mikoian), or were personal protégés of Khrushchev who were on the way out. Less important candidate Politburo members also were waiting to gravitate toward the leader who proved the strongest.

In the wake of Khrushchev's ouster, Petr Shelest was promoted to the Politburo, a move that benefited his associate Podgornyi. Aleksandr Shelepin, who had provided the "muscle" for the Khrushchev ouster through his contacts in the Committee for State Security (KGB), also was rewarded with a Politburo seat.

Shelepin initially was the main threat to Brezhnev. He was young and ambitious and had a foothold in both the Council of Ministers (as deputy premier) and the Secretariat. Shelepin was chairman of the Party-State Control Commission, and he had well-placed personal associates below him.

Despite all these rivals for power, during the first eighteen months after Khrushchev's ouster Brezhnev managed to extend his power base in a number of ways. It was inevitable that some of Khrushchev's cronies would be replaced. These removals opened slots that Brezhnev filled to his advantage, although he sometimes was forced to compromise. One change that benefited Brezhnev was the promotion of his close associate, Konstantin U. Chernenko, to the post of secretary of the General Department of the Central Committee in 1965.

Twenty-third Party Congress

At the Twenty-third Party Congress, convened in March 1966, Brezhnev and Kosygin demonstrated that they were the leading policy makers in the regime. Nikolai Podgornyi's power was diluted when the congress replaced him on the Secretariat with Andrei Kirilenko. As head of the party, Brezhnev was responsible for party matters and relations with other communist countries and parties. He delivered the opening speech at the congress on March 29. Kosygin oversaw economic planning and relations with the noncommunist world. He presented the government's new five-year plan covering the years 1966 to 1970. It included ambitious targets for growth of national income, but Kosygin declared that, because of "mistakes and miscalculations" under Khrushchev's seven-year plan (1959-1965), the growth targets for some industries were set "lower than had formerly been envisioned."

The Twenty-third Party Congress gave its blessing to the moderate course backed by Brezhnev and Kosygin. Although the needs of consumers were not ignored, the economic program adopted at the congress clearly emphasized defense production and heavy industry. The congress also endorsed the new leadership's promotion of stricter artistic and ideological controls. The end of Khrushchev's "thaw" was marked by the trial in February 1966 of two dissident writers, Andrei Siniavskii and Yuli Daniel. The two were convicted of writing articles critical of the Soviet regime and sentenced to several years of internal exile. The congress approved of the treatment of Siniavskii and Daniel and attacked the somewhat relaxed censorship of the Khrushchev years as harmful to the state and the party.

The congress halted the process of de-Stalinization. The Soviet leadership agreed that discussions of Stalinist crimes must end. Since the current leaders had derived their power from Stalin, attacking him would raise questions about the legitimacy of their own rule. Still, Brezhnev was cautious not to completely rehabilitate or associate himself with Stalin, and the Soviet leadership generally discouraged any kind of discussion about Stalin, good or bad. The new regime's desire to curtail de-Stalinization was symbolized by its readoption of the Stalin-era titles for the top policy-making group in the party and the party leader. The policy-making Presidium reverted to its former name, the Politburo, and the designation of the party chief was changed from first secretary to general secretary (both titles had been changed at the Nineteenth Party Congress in 1952).

Brezhnev Consolidates Power

Brezhnev's power increased as the positions of Shelepin and Podgornyi were weakened. Shelepin's downfall came about after rumors surfaced in 1965 that Brezhnev might be replaced. Shelepin's associates were believed to have started the rumors, and the other Politburo members resented this type of "inspired leak" as Sovietologist Harry Gelman has termed it. Brezhnev rivals and allies joined to form a coalition against Shelepin. He was stripped of his deputy-premiership in December 1965 and over the next ten years gradually lost the rest of his power as his associates were demoted. Despite this erosion, Shelepin retained enough influence for some time to help instigate anti-Brezhnev confrontations whenever Brezhnev was vulnerable on an issue. He was not removed from the Politburo until 1975.

Brezhnev's other top rival, Podgornyi, also was neutralized in stages. Opportunistic fence-sitters deserted Podgornyi as Brezhnev's strength became more apparent. Podgornyi's stand on several important issues also had hurt his image among many colleagues. In particular, he had offended the military by urging cuts in defense spending and arguing for increased investment in consumer goods industries. During the 1970s Podgornyi remained an influential figure, but he was no longer a serious threat to Brezhnev's authority. In 1977 he was removed from the Politburo, and Brezhnev replaced him as president.

By the April 1973 session of the Central Committee of the Communist party, Brezhnev was firmly in control. Brezhnev's power had eclipsed Kosygin's, and the party boss was clearly first among equals. At this meeting, two men thought to be hard-line conservatives critical of Brezhnev's opening to the West—Petr Shelest, former first secretary of the Ukrainian Communist Party, and Gennadii Voronov, former president of the Russian Soviet Federated Socialist Republic—were dropped from the Politburo. The Central Committee on April 27 endorsed "entirely and without reservation" the policy of détente with the West that bore Brezhnev's personal imprint. The Central Committee also cited the "important role played personally by Leonid Brezhnev."

The meeting's most important result, however, was the selection of new full members of the Politburo: Yuri V. Andropov, head of the KGB (the first secret police chief in the Politburo since Lavrentii Beria's ouster in 1953), Foreign Minister Andrei Gromyko, and Defense Minister Andrei Grechko. That all three new Politburo members were responsible for some part of the Kremlin's foreign policy apparatus pointed toward a greater emphasis on international affairs within the Soviet leadership.

Evidence suggests that, during most of his years in power, Brezhnev was the only member of the Secretariat who was also a member of the Defense Council (renamed from Khrushchev's Supreme Military Council). This dual membership gave him significant power. The Politburo tacitly agreed to let the Defense Council, a small Politburo subcommittee, dominate military policy. This arrangement created a subelite that other Politburo members were unable to challenge because they lacked information and expertise on most defense issues that did not have to do with broad questions of foreign policy or resource allocation. One important political disadvantage for Brezhnev in the Defense Council arrangement was that a small number of members (perhaps as few as three) could block a Brezhnev policy within the council. He had to reach an accommodation with these colleagues before a defense issue was brought to the Politburo.

Rules of the Oligarchy

The Brezhnev oligarchy was self-contained, self-renewing, and conscious of the barriers between itself and the rest of the party. Even Politburo members based outside Moscow such as Vladimir Shcherbitskii, Grigorii Romanov, and Dinmukhamed Kunaev, the party bosses in the Ukraine, Leningrad, and Kazakhstan, respectively, were generally less influential and excluded from some important matters because they were not always able to attend weekly meetings or receive routine information about impending decisions. The simple circumstance of being based outside of Moscow was a disadvantage.

The Politburo also was divided informally between a

changing group of four or five superelite members and the remainder. The top echelon always included the general secretary, the premier, the president, and the leaders of the Secretariat, which included at various times Andropov, Brezhnev, Chernenko, Kirilenko, Kosygin, Podgornyi, Suslov, and Nikolai Tikhonov.

Brezhnev and the post-Khrushchev oligarchs strove for stability, order, routine, and predictability. Their internal sense of political decorum made it unacceptable to publicly air any internal Politburo disputes, as had happened occasionally under Khrushchev. The leaders wanted to protect the exclusivity of the Politburo and Secretariat's decision-making prerogatives and to limit influence and pressure from below. The Politburo leaders usually punished violators of these unwritten rules, such as apparently occurred with Shelepin's removal. The leadership was suspicious and resentful of members who tried to use public opinion for personal advantage. Even Brezhnev was not immune to criticism when he took independent actions that his colleagues believed sidestepped collective rule.

In Brezhnev's quest for scientific decision-making processes, he employed social science experts and other specialists to a greater degree than any previous Soviet leader. The power and influence of these experts on the policy-making process, however, was circumscribed. They provided information and analyses to decision makers but rarely were included in policy-making discussions.

Although the top Soviet leadership carefully guarded its power, some institutional groups did gain enough access to the central leadership to affect domestic policy making. The influence of interest groups usually depended on the prestige of their patrons on the Politburo or Secretariat. Groups within the Academy of Sciences, for example, developed influence because of their ability to help set Central Committee agendas, but in keeping with the principle of centralism, their power did not extend beyond the discussion stage to the decision-making stage. With the exception of the military, interest groups had almost no effect on foreign policy matters.

Economic Policy

Whether because he truly believed it best or because he found it politically expedient, Brezhnev advocated two "first priorities" in resource allocation: the military and agriculture. Brezhnev "threw money" at the chronic Soviet agriculture problem. Because the leadership feared the implications of food shortfalls created by bad weather and poor management, Brezhnev's spending continued despite unspectacular results.

Similarly, the established 3 to 4 percent growth rate for defense spending remained sacrosanct. Despite the changes in Politburo personnel over time, the Politburo consensus on military issues and priorities did not change much during the Brezhnev era. Brezhnev's political credentials and military contacts enabled him to benefit from a shift of priorities to the military. He knew many military leaders, most of whom disliked Khrushchev; he never uselessly criticized the military and publicly always appeared supportive of it.

Although the Soviet Union had spent a large percentage of its resources on the military during the Khrushchev years, the premier had made moves during the late 1950s and early 1960s to increase consumer production (particu-

larly in the agricultural sector) at the expense of defense. After Khrushchev's ouster, the Soviet leadership reaffirmed the military's priority over national resources. This readjustment pleased conservative leaders who believed Khrushchev had been too liberal. In addition to meeting the perceived military threats from the United States, Western Europe, and China, Soviet military power brought the nation superpower status and influence in foreign relations. Military strength, therefore, became indispensable to the prestige of the Soviet nation and its leadership.

In the Eighth Five-Year Plan (1966-1970), the Soviet leadership tried to satisfy everyone. Through the late 1960s, it largely succeeded. The standard of living rose, and most industries experienced healthy growth. Good weather and the continued expansion of land under cultivation aided agricultural production.

In the 1970s, however, inefficiency and bad weather combined to reduce agricultural production, creating the need to import more food. Adverse demographic trends (a low birthrate in European Russia and high rates of alcoholism and infant mortality) slowed the increase in the labor force, especially in areas where most industry was located. Raw materials, including oil, became more difficult and expensive to extract. As a result of these developments, economic growth rates began to decline. The Soviets were no longer able to depend on extensive growth (wider exploitation of natural and human resources) to achieve economic expansion.

Faced with a tight budget, the Soviet leaders made small cuts in industrial investment and more severe cuts in consumer investment. As the economy continued to decline in the late 1970s, the regime was forced to make even larger cuts in industrial investment. More alarming for the Soviets, they were falling farther behind the West in the development of industrial and agricultural technology. Between 1976 and 1980 the Soviet economy grew by just 2.3 percent per year, according to CIA estimates. *(Economy under Brezhnev, p. 112)*

Foreign Policy

The newly installed Brezhnev leadership endorsed the Khrushchev-era policy of peaceful coexistence. The twin legacies of Khrushchev's foreign policy were a slowly improving relationship with the United States and an increasingly bitter quarrel with the People's Republic of China. Moscow's dealings with both nations would be colored by the growing conflict in Vietnam.

Khrushchev's successors continued the improvement of superpower relations that had begun in 1962 after the Cuban missile crisis. The United States and Soviet Union had agreed in June 1963 to the installation of a hot line between Washington and Moscow to provide immediate communication that would lessen the chance of an accidental nuclear war. On June 10, Kennedy had introduced a new and friendlier tone in U.S. policy toward the Soviets in a speech at American University. This in turn had elicited an amicable response from Moscow.

Kennedy had announced in his American University speech that the United States, the Soviet Union, and Great Britain would begin talks on a partial nuclear test ban treaty. The treaty, which banned nuclear weapons tests in the atmosphere, outer space, and under water, was initialed in Moscow July 25 and ratified by the Senate September

24. Negotiations begun in 1963 resulted in a large American wheat sale to the Soviets in 1964. Other 1964 symbols of comity included efforts to enlarge East-West trade; cutbacks in the production of fissionable uranium by the United States and the Soviet Union; a slight easing of the requirements for passage between East and West Berlin; and a U.S.-Soviet accord signed February 22 that modestly expanded educational, cultural, scientific, and technical exchanges. By 1965, however, superpower relations were once again strained, largely because of the escalating conflict in Vietnam.

Vietnam Dilemma

American involvement in Vietnam in the mid-1960s posed a dual problem for Soviet leaders. Their hopes for a continuing rapprochement with the United States were jeopardized by Washington's increasing role in a war against their socialist ally, North Vietnam. Too much aid to the North Vietnamese and Communist guerrilla forces in South Vietnam could set back bilateral relations with the United States or even cause a superpower confrontation; too little support for the Vietnamese Communists would bring condemnation from China and offer evidence that Moscow had surrendered leadership of the socialist movement.

The optimal solution to the Soviets' Vietnam problem would have been a negotiated peace settlement limiting the U.S. presence in Indochina, while enhancing Soviet influence in North Vietnam. To obtain such a settlement, however, Moscow needed to convince the independent-minded North Vietnamese to accept major concessions that likely would halt, or at least delay, progress toward their goal of a united Vietnam. Soviet representatives, indeed, had urged Hanoi to go to the bargaining table. But in the wake of U.S. air attacks against North Vietnamese targets on February 7, 1965, Soviet hopes for concessions were reduced. The bombing raids, a response to an assault by Communist guerrillas on the U.S. base at Pleiku, South Vietnam, came while Premier Kosygin was on a state visit to Hanoi, the North Vietnamese capital.

On his way home from Hanoi, Kosygin stopped at Beijing and requested access to Chinese air bases to facilitate shipment of Soviet supplies to North Vietnam. Beijing declined. The *Beijing Review* said in a November 1965 article that "if we were to take united action on the question of Vietnam with the new leaders of the CPSU [Communist Party of the Soviet Union] who are pursuing the Khrushchev revisionist line, wouldn't we be helping them to bring the question of Vietnam within the orbit of Soviet-U.S. collaboration?" The verbal fireworks continued into 1966.

These untimely air attacks and the subsequent bombing campaign against North Vietnam that began later in February reduced Soviet flexibility. An attempt by Moscow to pressure Hanoi into a negotiated settlement at that time would have rewarded what was seen as U.S. aggression, would have opened up the USSR to further Chinese accusations of a Soviet-American conspiracy, and probably would have failed, given North Vietnamese resolve. As the war progressed, the Soviets increased their aid to North Vietnam and intensified their condemnations of U.S. behavior in Southeast Asia.

Relations between the USSR and North Vietnam were stable and pragmatic during this period. Hanoi maneuvered to obtain as much aid as possible from Moscow, and

Kremlin leaders were forthcoming. Their investment in Vietnam was considerable, yet Southeast Asia was not an area of vital interest for the Soviets in the mid-1960s. Building Soviet influence in Indochina was less important to Moscow than using the situation in Vietnam against the United States and China.

By supplying aid to the North Vietnamese, the USSR enhanced the military capabilities of the Communist forces in Vietnam, thereby deepening the quagmire in which the United States found itself. The Soviet Union was careful not to offer weapons or assistance that could have produced a confrontation with the United States. But because U.S.-Soviet relations had cooled considerably since 1964, Moscow did not stand to lose much by supporting Hanoi. U.S. involvement in Vietnam also enabled the Soviet Union to portray the United States to the Third World as an aggressive power willing to use massive force against a small nation to protect its neocolonialist interests.

The Vietnamese conflict also gave the Soviet Union an opportunity to outcompete China in a Third World arena. The North Vietnamese primarily were interested in obtaining material aid, and the USSR's capacity for delivering economic assistance and quality arms was far greater than China's. Also, Beijing's rejection of the Soviets' plan for a united effort against the United States in Vietnam made Chinese accusations that Soviet leaders were not selflessly concerned with Vietnam's struggle sound hypocritical. Finally, Moscow hoped its support of Vietnam would not only solidify its reputation as a defender of Third World national liberation movements, but also produce a cooperative relationship with North Vietnam that would limit Chinese influence in the entire region.

Split in NATO

Throughout the 1960s, the Soviet objective in Europe was to gain worldwide recognition of the status quo as it had been established after World War II—the existence of two German nations and Soviet domination of Eastern Europe. The Soviets began to curry favor with the maverick of Europe, President Charles de Gaulle of France. Reluctant to follow Washington's lead in European affairs, de Gaulle announced in February 1966 that France intended to withdraw from the integrated military command of the North Atlantic Treaty Organization (NATO). De Gaulle subsequently expelled all foreign forces, including Americans, from French soil.

France's withdrawal from the NATO military structure officially occurred in April 1968. (As of 1990 France participated informally as an observer in many NATO meetings and cooperated as an active, but not formal, partner in the alliance.) The hearty welcome extended to de Gaulle on a state visit to the Soviet Union in June 1966 demonstrated Moscow's pleasure at the weakening of the Western alliance. Soviet ambassador to France Valerian Zorin said on March 17 that any reduction in the strength or "aggressive character" of NATO probably would be matched by a similar reduction in the Warsaw Pact alliance. He also said Moscow was ready to conclude a treaty of alliance of nonaggression with France.

India-Pakistan Conflict

The outbreak of major hostilities between India and Pakistan in August 1965 gave Premier Kosygin a chance to play the statesman and increase Soviet prestige and good-will in the subcontinent. The dispute between India, which had established ties with Moscow, and Pakistan, a friend of Beijing, was mediated by Kosygin in January 1966. Meeting at Tashkent in Soviet Central Asia, the two sides agreed to withdraw their forces to positions held before August 5, 1965. Kosygin's diplomatic intervention blocked Chinese participation in the resolution of a conflict in which Beijing had a strong regional interest.

The dispute between India and Pakistan over Kashmir had flared intermittently since the partition of the state in 1947, following India's and Pakistan's independence from Great Britain. Fighting in Kashmir continued for more than a year before a cease-fire agreement was negotiated to go into effect January 1, 1949. India was left in control of about two-thirds of the area of Kashmir, while Pakistan was given control of the other one-third.

In August 1965 India broke the cease-fire line with Pakistan, and full-scale Indian-Pakistani hostilities followed. As fighting continued, the United States and Great Britain halted all military aid shipments to both nations. In September, India and Pakistan accepted a UN Security Council resolution demanding a cease-fire. The USSR then stepped in and arranged the January negotiating session.

War between India and Pakistan again broke out December 3, 1971, but the Indians, fortified by Soviet military aid and a new twenty-year friendship treaty, easily defeated the Pakistanis, who were backed by the Chinese.

Six-Day War

On June 5, 1967, Israel began the third major Arab-Israeli war by invading its Arab neighbors. During the conflict, referred to as the Six-Day War, Israel destroyed a substantial part of the armed forces of Egypt, Jordan, and Syria. In addition, large amounts of Arab territory were captured—land that Israel did not relinquish after the

fighting stopped. The UN Security Council June 6 unanimously adopted a resolution calling for a cease-fire. A truce went into effect June 10.

Israel's decisive victory stunned the Arabs and their Soviet backers and left Israel in a position of strength in the Middle East. Despite Soviet and American pressure, Israel announced that it would remain in the newly occupied territories until decisive progress toward a permanent settlement had been made.

The Six-Day War was an important event for Soviet influence in the region. Before the war, the Soviets had worked to create an anti-Western alliance among the Arabs and deter an Israeli attack through arms sales and encouragement of Arab defense cooperation. The Soviets thought they were partially successful when in November 1966 Syria and Egypt signed a joint defense agreement. The Soviets, however, lost prestige by not providing the Arabs with much assistance during the Six-Day War. In fact, the Soviet decision to back a cease-fire while Israel was in Arab territories angered the Arabs. The only significant measure that Moscow and its East European allies took was severance of diplomatic ties with Israel.

Despite the Arabs' disappointment with the weak backing provided by Moscow during the fighting, in the long run the Six-Day War boosted Soviet influence among the Arabs. Egypt, charging that U.S. aircraft had contributed to its defeat, severed diplomatic relations with Washington, as did six other Arab states. While U.S. support for Israel soured U.S. relations with the Arab states, the Soviets solidified their position as the chief benefactor and arms supplier of the Arabs. Partially to make up for its inaction during the war, Moscow rebuilt the armed forces of Egypt, Syria, and Jordan.

Glassboro Summit

Premier Kosygin traveled to New York in 1967 to join the UN debate on the Middle East. While in the United

Soviet premier Aleksei Kosygin and President Lyndon B. Johnson meet at the June 1967 Glassboro, New Jersey, summit with, from left, U.S. secretary of state Dean Rusk, Soviet foreign minister Andrei Gromyko, and Soviet ambassador Anatolii Dobrynin.

States, Kosygin met with President Johnson on June 23 and 25 in Glassboro, New Jersey. Both the nature of the meeting and the site of the impromptu summit conference were in dispute (Kosygin officially was visiting the United Nations, not the United States). The meeting site at Glassboro State College was selected because it allowed Johnson and Kosygin to meet halfway between UN headquarters and the White House.

Neither side claimed major gains as a result of the ten hours of meetings, but the sessions produced a new, although short-lived, feeling of international good will—christened the "spirit of Glassboro." The first session at Glassboro lasted more than five hours and dealt with the Middle East, Vietnam, and the nonproliferation of nuclear arms. After the second meeting it was announced that progress had been made on the nonproliferation issue but that vast differences still existed over the Middle East and Vietnam. The two world leaders termed the meetings "useful," agreed to meet again sometime, and instructed their foreign policy personnel to continue the talks.

Non-Proliferation Treaty

The Non-Proliferation Treaty, signed July 1, 1968, was the culmination of more than four years of negotiations at the eighteen-nation Disarmament Conference in Geneva and at the United Nations. The treaty called upon the nuclear powers not to disseminate nuclear devices to nonnuclear nations for at least twenty-five years and to engage in discussions aimed at halting the arms race. It also pledged nonnuclear nations not to seek to acquire such devices and encouraged cooperation in the peaceful use of nuclear energy. France and the People's Republic of China, both of which possessed nuclear weapons, refused to sign the treaty. India, which detonated a nuclear device in May 1974, also refused to sign, as did at least six nations possessing advanced nuclear facilities: Israel, Spain, Argentina, Brazil, Pakistan, and South Africa.

President Johnson submitted the treaty to the Senate for ratification July 9, and, in the short-lived spirit of good will prevailing after the Glassboro summit, the Senate Foreign Relations Committee took the unprecedented step of beginning consideration of the treaty within twenty-four hours of its submission. After the Soviet invasion of Czechoslovakia in August 1968, however, calls arose to postpone ratification to signal U.S. condemnation of the Soviet move. The Senate decided to hold off consideration until the next session. Presidential candidate Richard Nixon stated during the 1968 presidential race that he strongly opposed ratification at that time for fear of condoning the Czechoslovakian invasion. But in January he called on the Senate to approve the treaty, promising to "implement it in my new administration." The Senate ratified the treaty March 13.

Invasion of Czechoslovakia

Soviet troops, accompanied by forces from four Warsaw Pact nations—Poland, Hungary, East Germany, and Bulgaria—invaded Czechoslovakia August 20-21, 1968, to stem a liberal democratic movement that, according to Moscow, threatened Czechoslovak socialism. The Soviets reported that the intervention was requested by the "party and government leaders of the Czechoslovak Socialist Re-

public." In their statement, however, Czechoslovak leaders asserted that the invasion occurred "without the knowledge of the President of the Republic, the Chairman of the National Assembly, the Premier or the First Secretary of the Czechoslovak Communist Party Central Committee." The invasion, the Czechoslovak statement continued, was "contrary not only to the fundamental principles of relations between Socialist states," but also "contrary to the principles of international law." The statement appealed to the Czechoslovaks "to maintain calm and not to offer resistance to the troops on the march. Our army, security corps and people's militia have not received the command to defend the country."

The Czechoslovak drama began to unfold in December 1962, when the Twelfth Congress of the Czechoslovak Communist Party decided to "correct" the excesses of the Stalin era, the last of the Eastern-bloc nations to do so. The December 1962 decision led to calls for increased personal freedom and to a liberalized economic policy. Although some reforms were implemented, they produced disappointing results.

In June 1967 the Fourth Congress of Czechoslovak Writers adopted a vigorous denunciation of government censorship in literature, culture, and politics. The government expelled from the Communist party the leaders of the anticensorship movement. Afterwards, however, it exhibited a more liberal attitude in foreign relations by signing August 4, 1967, a two-year trade pact with West Germany, despite objections from the Soviets and the East Germans.

The most important development, however, occurred in January 1968 when Alexander Dubcek, a reform-minded Slovak, took over the post of party first secretary from the more orthodox Antonin Novotny. During the "Prague Spring" of 1968, Dubcek and other Czechoslovak leaders repeatedly affirmed their intention of moving the country toward "democratic socialism," as contrasted with the party-controlled socialism of the Soviet Union. The Central Committee of the Czechoslovak Communist party April 15 adopted a program, "Czechoslovakia's Road to Socialism," designed to ensure freedom of speech, the press, assembly, and religion, as well as greater freedom for the country's four noncommunist political parties. Gen. Ludvik Svoboda, who was elected president March 30 following the forced resignation of Novotny from that office, said in May, "We are starting out to create a new type of socialist democracy, a democracy which will lend support to the full development of the human personality."

The first threat of Soviet military intervention developed when Soviet troops, which had moved into Czechoslovakia in June to engage in Warsaw Pact maneuvers, stayed behind when the exercises were completed.

Moscow July 19 summoned the Czech leadership to the Soviet Union to discuss Czechoslovakia's "democratic socialism." The Czechs declined but agreed to meet with the Soviet Politburo July 29-August 1 at the Czechoslovak border town of Cierna. The Soviet delegation consisted of party chief Brezhnev, Premier Kosygin, President Podgornyi, and eleven other Politburo members. Czechoslovakia's representatives included sixteen officials of the party and the government, led by Dubcek. Faced with Czechoslovak determination, the Soviets appeared to back down and agreed to remove their troops from Czechoslovakia. The troop withdrawal was announced and an apparent compromise was confirmed at an August 3 meeting in

Soviet tanks line a street off Old Town Square in Prague following the August 1968 invasion of Czechoslovakia.

Bratislava attended by representatives of the Communist parties of the Soviet Union, Czechoslovakia, Bulgaria, East Germany, Hungary, and Poland.

Yet the relaxation of tension did not last. After three weeks, the Soviet Union August 16 resumed criticism of the Czechoslovak press. Also on August 16, Dubcek pleaded with the Czechoslovak people not to push liberalization too far or too fast. "We need order in our country," he said, "so that we can be given freedom of action in our democratization process." Four days later, an estimated 400,000 troops, three-fourths of whom were Soviet soldiers, entered Czechoslovakia to put down the "counter-revolution."

The invaders promptly arrested Dubcek and other members of the government. They were flown to Moscow, where, under pressure, they agreed to crack down on liberalization. Dubcek remained in power until April 1969, when he was replaced as first secretary by Gustav Husak, a pro-Soviet hard-liner, who dismantled what remained of the liberalization movement.

Widespread Condemnation

World reaction to the invasion of Czechoslovakia was severe. Though most of Moscow's satellites supported the move, the two mavericks of Eastern Europe, Romania and Yugoslavia, were critical. Romanian strongman Nicolae Ceausescu charged that the invasion was "a great mistake and a grave danger to peace in Europe, to the fate of socialism in the world" and warned that "the entire Romanian people will not allow anybody to violate our land."

The Communist parties of France and Italy condemned the Soviet action, as did the governments of France, Britain, Italy, India, Canada, and other nations. The Chinese said the invasion was a "shameless act" comparable to Hitler's occupation of the Sudetenland and U.S. involvement in Vietnam. President Johnson said the invasion "shocks the conscience of the world. The Soviet Union and its allies have invaded a defenseless country to stamp out a resurgence of ordinary human freedom."

The Brezhnev Doctrine

In the wake of the international furor over the invasion of Czechoslovakia, the Kremlin formulated a theory, quickly termed the Brezhnev Doctrine, to justify Soviet interference in the affairs of other communist states. The Brezhnev Doctrine was outlined in an article, "Sovereignty and the International Duties of Socialist Countries," published in *Pravda* September 26, 1968:

> The weakening of any of the links in the world socialist system directly affects all the socialist countries. Thus, with talk about the right of nations to self-determination the anti-socialist elements in Czechoslovakia actually covered up a demand for so-called neutrality and Czechoslovakia's withdrawal from the socialist community. However, the implementation of "self-determination" of that kind or, in other words, the detaching of Czechoslovakia from the socialist community would have come into conflict with Czechoslovakia's vital interests and would have been detrimental to the other socialist states. Such "self-determination," as a result of which NATO troops would have been able to come up to the Soviet borders, while the community of European socialist countries would have been rent, would have encroached, in actual fact, upon the vital interests of the peoples of these countries and would be in fundamental conflict with the right of these peoples to socialist self-determination.

Brezhnev reiterated the argument in a speech to the Fifth Congress of the Polish Communist party, November 13, 1968, and in a speech in Moscow made October 28, 1969, to a delegation of Czechoslovak officials. He told his Polish audience that "when the internal and external forces hostile to socialism seek to revert the development of any socialist country toward the restoration of the capitalist order, when a threat to the cause of socialism in that country, a threat to the security of the socialist community as a whole emerges, this is no longer a problem of the people of that country but also a common problem, a concern of all socialist countries." *(Brezhnev Doctrine, documents, p. 312)*

Rise and Fall of Détente

The invasion of Czechoslovakia in August 1968 was a setback to East-West relations. Nevertheless, in the months that followed leaders in the West made moves to improve relations with Moscow. A new administration in Washington, headed by Richard Nixon, a famous cold warrior, embarked on a course that led to a dramatic series of U.S.-Soviet summit meetings and several agreements on the limitation of nuclear weapons.

After its initial successes, however, the Nixon administration's policy of détente came under increasing attack in the United States, with critics charging that the Soviets got the best of the bargain and demanding that in return for Western cooperation on trade and arms control Moscow should ease its tight emigration restrictions and improve human rights in the USSR. The succeeding administrations of Gerald R. Ford and Jimmy Carter tried to build on the successes of Nixon's détente, particularly in the area of arms control. But by the late 1970s, relations between the superpowers had become increasingly strained. The Soviet invasion of Afghanistan in December 1979 ended détente and ushered in a period of U.S.-Soviet animosity and confrontation.

Détente's Accomplishments

Détente sought to limit tensions between the superpowers and create a stable international atmosphere that would reduce the risk of war and allow for cooperative actions that were in the interest of both the Soviet Union and the West. In the early 1970s détente focused on stabilizing the situation in Europe and concluding arms control agreements.

In 1970 West Germany signed agreements with the Soviet Union and Poland that recognized existing post-World War II borders. This agreement was followed in 1971 by an agreement between the four powers responsible for Berlin (the Soviet Union, the United States, France, and Great Britain) regarding the administration of the divided city. The Soviet Union pledged to refrain from interfering with communication and transportation to West Berlin, and all the parties vowed not to attempt to change the status of the city. In addition, the treaty allowed West Berliners to travel with West German passports and receive West German consular protection abroad, although the four powers did not recognize West Berlin as part of West Germany. In December 1972, the two Germanies signed a treaty that recognized their postwar separation.

In arms control the United States and the Soviet Union concluded several agreements limiting the growth of nuclear weapons. Strategic Arms Limitation Talks (SALT) began in November 1969. By 1972 the superpowers had reached agreement on limiting defensive antiballistic missile (ABM) systems. In May President Nixon became the first president ever to visit Moscow when he traveled there for a summit that included the signing of the SALT I treaty. The treaty provided for limitations on the deployment of ABMs. An accompanying executive agreement restricted each side's offensive weapons to the number already under construction or deployed when the agreement was signed. The executive agreement also placed limitations on the number of missile-carrying submarines that could be constructed.

Nixon on 1972 Summit

"Surprise is another favorite technique of Communist negotiators. After the ceremony on Wednesday afternoon [May 24] when we signed an agreement on cooperation in space exploration, Brezhnev and I walked out of the room together. He began talking about the dinner planned for us at one of the government dachas outside Moscow that evening. As we neared the end of the corridor, he ... said, 'Why don't we go to the country right now so you can see it in the daylight?' ...

"We climbed into the limousine and were on our way while the Secret Service and the others rushed about trying to find cars and drivers.... As soon as we arrived at the dacha, Brezhnev suggested that we go for a boat ride on the Moskva River.... Everyone was in a good humor when we got back to the dacha, and Brezhnev suggested that we have a meeting before the dinner.... For the next three hours the Soviet leaders pounded me bitterly and emotionally about Vietnam.

"I momentarily thought of Dr. Jekyll and Mr. Hyde when Brezhnev, who had just been laughing and slapping me on the back, started shouting angrily that instead of honestly working to end the war, I was trying to use the Chinese as a means of bringing pressure on the Soviets to intervene with the North Vietnamese. He said that they wondered whether on May 8 [the day increased bombing raids and the mining of North Vietnamese harbors were announced] I had acted out of thoughtless irritation, because they had no doubt that if I really wanted peace I could get a settlement without any outside assistance....

"When Brezhnev finally seemed to run out of steam, Kosygin took up the cudgel.... When Kosygin concluded, Podgorny came to bat....

"After about twenty minutes, Podgorny suddenly stopped and Brezhnev said a few more words. Then there was silence in the room. By this time it was almost eleven o'clock. I felt that before I could let this conversation end, I had to let them know exactly where I stood.

"I pointed out that I had withdrawn over 500,000 men from Vietnam. I had shown the greatest restraint when the North Vietnamese began their massive buildup in March, because I did not want anything to affect the summit. But when the North Vietnamese actually invaded South Vietnam, I had no choice but to react strongly....

"With that we went upstairs, where a lavish dinner was waiting for us.... There was much laughing and joking and storytelling—as if the acrimonious session downstairs had never happened."

—Reprinted by permission of Warner Books/New York from *RN: The Memoirs of Richard Nixon* (New York: Grosset & Dunlap, 1978), 612-614, copyright © 1978 by Richard Nixon.

There was speculation immediately preceding Nixon's trip that the Soviets might withdraw their invitation as a result of his decision to thwart a North Vietnamese offensive by increasing air attacks on supply lines in North Vietnam and mining Haiphong harbor and six other ports in the north. That the Kremlin, North Vietnam's main arms supplier, went through with the summit was taken as a sign in the West that Moscow was as eager as Washington to conclude the arms pact and improve relations. Soviet leaders were motivated to hold the summit in part because of the warming relationship between the United States and China (Nixon had visited Beijing earlier in the year). The Soviets feared a Sino-American détente would result in anti-Soviet cooperation between its two rivals.

Superpower relations continued to improve during 1973 and 1974, despite President Nixon's preoccupation with the Watergate scandal that led to his resignation in August 1974. Brezhnev visited the United States in June 1973, and Nixon returned to Moscow in June 1974. These summits produced scientific, cultural, and commercial agreements and pledges to accelerate the pace of arms control.

Waning of Détente

Throughout the early period of détente, arms control had overshadowed progress made by the United States and Soviet Union on establishing better trade relations. As a result of the 1972 summit, the two countries established a Joint United States-USSR Commercial Commission, and Moscow bought millions of tons of American grain in a purchase financed by U.S. credits. On October 18, 1972, the United States and Soviet Union signed a three-year trade pact that would greatly expand commercial relations between the two countries and provide for the Soviets' repayment of their World War II lend-lease debts to the United States. Implementation of the trade agreement hinged on congressional approval of most-favored-nation (MFN) status (nondiscrimination in customs matters) for Soviet production. If MFN status was not granted, the pact would not enter into force, and the Soviet Union, in accordance with the second agreement, would not have to repay the balance of its lend-lease debt of 722 million dollars.

The granting of MFN status to the Soviet Union ran into strong resistance in Congress. Many members objected to the Soviet's backing of the Arabs in the 1973 Arab-Israeli war and Moscow's levying of an exit fee—reportedly up to thirty thousand dollars—on Jews wishing to emigrate from the Soviet Union who held advanced academic degrees. Moscow justified the fees as reimbursement for the state's investment in education, the benefits of which would be lost through emigration. But the effect of the fee was to block the emigration of most Soviet Jews to Israel.

In December 1974, Congress passed the Jackson-Vanik amendment. This legislation made extension of MFN status to the Soviet Union conditional on the liberalization of Soviet emigration policies. The Jackson-Vanik amendment disillusioned Brezhnev and the Soviet leadership. Détente was not paying off so well in their view that they would permit what they considered to be interference in their internal affairs. On January 14, 1975, the Soviets informed the United States that they were rejecting the terms of trade contained in the Jackson-Vanik amendment and accordingly would not put into force the 1972 trade agreement.

The demise of the trade accord did not end détente, but thereafter the U.S.-Soviet relationship gradually deteriorated. Continued harsh treatment of dissidents in the Soviet Union, the USSR's ongoing military buildup, North Vietnam's conquest of South Vietnam in 1975, and Moscow's backing of a Marxist faction in Angola that came to power in 1976 with the help of tens of thousands of Cuban troops discredited détente in the eyes of many American policy makers. Nevertheless the United States and Soviet Union continued to negotiate on arms control. In 1979 Carter and Brezhnev signed the SALT II treaty at a summit in Vienna. The treaty placed limits on the growth of the strategic nuclear arsenals of the superpowers.

The treaty immediately ran into opposition in the U.S. Senate. Opponents claimed that it gave the Soviets unfair advantages and rewarded Moscow despite continued Soviet-backed communist aggression in the Third World and human rights abuses in the Soviet Union. Carter countered that the treaty placed few limits on weapons the United States was planning to build, while restricting the Soviets in some important areas. He also said that he would continue pressuring the Soviet Union to improve its human rights record. In a major defeat for the policy of détente, the Senate Armed Services Committee on December 20, 1979, voted 10-0 to recommend rejection of the SALT II treaty. Within a week the treaty's demise became inevitable when Soviet forces invaded Afghanistan to prop up a pro-Soviet government there. The invasion destroyed what support was left for détente in the United States. (*Afghanistan invasion, p. 171*)

Assessment of Détente

At the heart of détente's demise were the divergent Soviet and American conceptions of what détente meant and what it was supposed to accomplish. The principal American architects of détente, President Nixon and his national security adviser and eventual secretary of state, Henry A. Kissinger, have stated that they saw détente as a way to complement containment of the Soviet Union by slowing the arms race and reducing the risk of confrontation. Most members of Congress and the American public, however, saw détente in more ambitious terms. They hoped that it would lead to an end to superpower arms competition, Soviet adventurism in the Third World, and human rights abuses in the USSR. As a result, American attitudes concerning cooperating with the Soviet Union in areas such as trade and cultural exchanges became linked with assessments of the Soviet regime's domestic and international behavior.

These expectations were bound to produce disillusionment in the United States. For while the Soviet Union welcomed the relaxation of tensions and the increase in trade with the West, it had no intention of allowing the West to make demands that affected its internal affairs or its recruitment of and support for allies and clients.

The Soviets saw no contradiction between détente and the continuation of their worldwide struggle against capitalism. A Soviet publication on foreign policy published during the height of détente declared:

It may be asked whether peaceful coexistence signifies a certain conciliation between socialism and capitalism? Does it mean recognition of the capitalist order? Does it represent the curtailment of the struggle against

President Richard Nixon and General Secretary Leonid I. Brezhnev shake hands after signing the SALT I agreement at the 1972 summit in Moscow.

imperialism?

On no account!

Peaceful coexistence is one of the principal forms of the struggle against imperialism.

Consequently, détente with the West did not dissuade the Soviets from supporting wars of national liberation in such places as Angola and Ethiopia or helping allies such as the Vietnamese and the Cubans to carry out aggressive military operations in the Third World.

As Ronald Reagan took office as president in January 1981, the policy of détente had been thoroughly discredited in the United States and had little appeal for the Soviet leadership. Most Americans, including Reagan, believed that the United States could not engage in a détente with a partner that was perceived as internally corrupt, openly aggressive, and obsessed with its own security. For their part, the Soviets believed that the United States was uncommitted to détente (as demonstrated by the Senate's refusal to ratify the SALT II treaty), bent on interfering in Soviet internal affairs, and unwilling to grant them room to pursue legitimate Soviet national security objectives. Reagan's subsequent anti-Soviet rhetoric ended any faint Soviet hopes that the United States would resume détente and made the Soviet leadership increasingly pessimistic about the usefulness and likelihood of improving U.S.-Soviet relations.

Crisis in Poland

Both sides saw the events surrounding the imposition of martial law in Poland in December 1981 as confirming their opinion of their former partner in détente.

A political crisis was triggered in Poland July 1, 1980, when the government removed subsidies from the price of meat. Scattered strikes erupted throughout Poland to pro-test the price hikes. Workers at the Lenin shipyard in Gdansk, Poland's largest, took over the yard August 14. On August 17 the strikers formed an Interfactory Strike Committee, and its leader, thirty-seven-year-old unemployed electrician Lech Walesa, announced the group's terms for negotiations. In addition to demands for increased wages and reduced meat prices, the committee called for the formation of independent labor unions, relaxed government censorship, and the right to strike.

After some reluctance, the Polish Communist party, led by First Secretary Edward Gierek, agreed to negotiate with the strikers. The settlement reached August 30 permitted workers to form unions free of government interference, reduced official censorship, allowed churches and other groups access to the government-controlled news media, and freed imprisoned dissidents who had supported the strike. In addition, the government vowed to increase wages, upgrade medical services, and improve supplies of basic foods.

After strikers returned to work, the party announced September 6 that Gierek had been ousted. Ironically, Gierek had been named first secretary in 1970 after labor unrest caused the downfall of his predecessor, Wladyslaw Gomulka. The new Polish leader, Stanislaw Kania, formerly the head of the country's security forces, pledged to honor the strike settlement and vowed to retain Poland's close ties with the Soviet Union.

The situation remained tense for the remainder of 1980 as the strike committee, which took the name Solidarity, accused the Kania regime of failing to fulfill the terms of the settlement. Speculation arose that the Soviet military might intervene in Poland to strengthen Warsaw's control. President Carter on December 3 warned the Soviets that any intervention in Poland's affairs would have "most negative consequences" and that U.S.-Soviet relations would be "directly and adversely affected."

The problem facing the Kremlin was considerable. If Soviet forces were not sent into Poland, Moscow feared that the momentum of liberalization would threaten the Warsaw government and perhaps spread to other Soviet satellites and into the Soviet Union itself. Faced with similar situations in Hungary in 1956 and Czechoslovakia in 1968, Soviet armies invaded and occupied these countries. In late December, during the last weeks of the Carter administration, the White House reported that Soviet "preparation for possible intervention in Poland appears to have been completed." Meanwhile the Soviet and Eastern-bloc news media kept up a campaign against the "renewal" in Poland and the Solidarity group.

In his Twenty-sixth Party Congress speech February 23, 1981, Brezhnev, discussing Poland, reiterated the Brezhnev Doctrine. He said the Soviet Union would always stand up for Poland and would "not leave her in the lurch." In Brezhnev's words: "Let no one have any doubt about our common determination to secure our interests and defend the people's socialist gains."

Tension increased after Warsaw Pact military maneuvers in and near Poland were scheduled for March. Moscow stepped up the pressure on the Polish leadership with a June 5 letter stressing measures to block counterrevolution and a July 21 message calling on the Polish Communist party "to resolutely rebuff anarchy and counterrevolution." Further Warsaw Pact maneuvers were held in early September in the Soviet Union near the Polish border.

In the midst of the tense fall of 1981, Polish Communist party leader Kania was purged and replaced by the prime minister, Gen. Wojciech Jaruzelski. Under Jaruzelski's leadership, the Polish Politburo November 28 ordered the legislature to enact a law banning strikes, thus reversing one of the key elements of the government-Solidarity agreement of August 1980. On December 12 Solidarity leaders met in Gdansk to discuss proposals calling for free elections and the establishment of a new government. After the meeting, most top Solidarity officials, including Walesa, were arrested and detained. The government declared martial law, closed the border, and cut off all communications to and from Poland and within Poland itself.

Reaction from Washington was immediate. Secretary of State Alexander M. Haig, Jr., said the United States was "seriously concerned" about events in Poland and repeated Washington's warning to Moscow not to interfere. The Soviets on December 14 said officially that martial law in Poland was "an internal matter." A Tass report December 15 charged the United States with meddling in Polish affairs.

Imposition of martial law provided the first major test of President Reagan's handling of U.S.-Soviet relations. In an address televised from the White House, Reagan announced December 23 that the United States would take "concrete political and economic measures" against Moscow if the Polish crackdown continued. The president said, "I want to state tonight that, if the outrages in Poland do not cease, we cannot and will not conduct 'business as usual' with the perpetrators and those who aid and abet them." Reagan added, "The Soviet Union, through its threats and pressures, deserves a major share of blame for the developments in Poland."

Reagan suspended U.S. government shipments of food to Poland, withdrew its line of export credit insurance with the Export-Import Bank, halted Polish airline service in the United States, and withdrew Poland's permission to fish in U.S. waters. Reagan said, "These actions are not

Joint Venture in Space

A gesture of international comity occurred 140 miles above the Atlantic Ocean July 17, 1975, when a U.S. Apollo spacecraft docked with a Soviet Soyuz craft. The joint venture in space had been arranged at the 1972 Moscow summit. The link-up, telecast live around the world, featured the Apollo commander, Brig. Gen. Thomas P. Stafford of the Air Force, shaking hands with his Soviet counterpart, Col. Aleksei Leonov. The astronauts exchanged gifts, listened to messages from the leaders of their two countries, and ate lunch together. The spacecraft remained linked during two days of joint experiments.

In a prepared message read by mission control in Moscow, Soviet party chief Leonid I. Brezhnev said that "The successful docking proved the correctness of the positions which we carried out in joint cooperation and friendship between Soviet and American designers, scientists and cosmonauts."

President Gerald R. Ford, in a telephone conversation with the U.S. and Soviet crews, said, "Your flight is a momentous event and a very great achievement, not only for the five of you but also for the thousands of American and Soviet scientists and technicians who have worked together for three years to ensure the success of this very historic and very successful experiment in international cooperation. It has taken us many years to open this door to useful cooperation in space between our two countries, and I am confident that the day is not far off when space missions made possible by this first joint effort will be more or less commonplace."

Astronaut Thomas P. Stafford and Cosmonaut Aleksei Leonov work together in space during the Apollo-Soyuz link-up.

directed against the Polish people. They are a warning to the government of Poland that free men cannot and will not stand idly by in the face of brutal repression."

On December 29 Reagan announced sanctions aimed directly at the Soviet Union. Charging that the "Soviet Union bears a heavy and direct responsibility for the repression in Poland," the president suspended new export licenses for high-technology items, including oil and gas equipment; postponed talks on a maritime pact and a grain agreement; restricted Soviet access to U.S. ports; and withdrew Soviet air service privileges. The president, however, declined to cancel either U.S.-Soviet talks on limiting nuclear weapons in Europe or Secretary Haig's January 26, 1982, meeting with Soviet foreign minister Gromyko.

In response to Reagan's sanctions, Tass December 30 said the president was trying "to hurl the world back to the dark times of the cold war." The Tass statement added that Washington wished "to undermine the foundations of Soviet-American relations worked out as a result of huge efforts, and curtail them to a minimum."

Stagnation under Gerontocracy

The Soviet Union under Brezhnev was characterized by its domestic stability. Although dissidence grew and the Soviet people became increasingly disgruntled with economic conditions, Soviet society remained calm due to several factors.

First, the KGB aggressively repressed dissident individuals and groups. This repression had little in common with the systematic mass arrests under Joseph Stalin that sent hundreds of thousands of Soviets to labor camps. Instead it was directed almost exclusively against dissidents who openly criticized or challenged the regime. Dissidents risked being harassed, losing privileges, having their access to education or career advancement blocked, and in extreme cases, being arrested or deported. Second, the Communist party remained in total control of the nation's political, military, and economic institutions. Party members pervaded all institutions of Soviet government and society. They promoted the party's interests and guarded against activities that could undermine the party's authority (and by extension their own privileges). Third, Soviet authorities maintained strict censorship rules. Soviets could voice complaints with specific problems, such as local corruption or defects in a particular consumer item, but the censors did not allow Soviet journalists, artists, and citizens to express dissatisfaction with the ruling regime or the Soviet system. Finally, the Soviet people had become used to the conditions in their country. Although citizens routinely complained and joked to one another about the hassles of life, most had witnessed a very gradual improvement in the standard of living since World War II. As long as conditions appeared to be improving over the long run, few Soviets were willing to risk the consequences of dissent. Moreover, their tolerance for the Communist party's dictatorial rule was reinforced by Russia's long tradition of autocracy.

Brezhnev and his colleagues had succeeded in pacifying Soviet society and protecting their own power and the privileges of Communist party members. The late 1970s and early 1980s witnessed a virtual cessation of turnover in the Soviet leadership. With few exceptions, only leaders who died or became seriously ill were replaced. As a result,

---

Brezhnev Politburo

Below is a list of the full members of the Politburo as of January 1, 1982. The age of each member is in parentheses following his name.

Arvid Pel'she (82)
Mikhail Suslov (79)
Nikolai Tikhonov (76)
Andrei Kirilenko (75)
Leonid Brezhnev (75)
Dmitri Ustinov (73)
Andrei Gromyko (72)
Konstantin Chernenko (70)
Dinmukhamed Kunaev (69)
Yuri Andropov (67)
Viktor Grishin (67)
Vladimir Shcherbitskii (63)
Grigorii Romanov (58)
Mikhail Gorbachev (50)

---

the average age of Soviet leaders rose dramatically. At the beginning of 1982, eleven of the fourteen full Politburo members were at least sixty-seven years old. The average age of Politburo members was seventy (almost seventy-two if the fifty-year-old Mikhail S. Gorbachev were excluded from the calculation). The Soviet Union had become a gerontocracy—a nation governed by old men. Brezhnev, who was frequently ill, had turned over the daily management of the party and state to other leaders, but he still possessed the authority and the energy to block initiatives that he opposed and advance the general outlines of policies that he preferred. (*Brezhnev Politburo, box, above*)

This political stagnation at the top contributed to a stagnation of the Soviet economy and society as the job security and advancing age of prominent Soviet leaders sapped their ability and will to address the Soviet Union's problems. The conservative leadership refused to consider meaningful changes, especially those that held the risk of causing public dissatisfaction, such as price reforms.

The developing malaise in Soviet society manifested itself in numerous ways. A high rate of alcoholism had led to widespread absenteeism from work and drunkenness on the job. Soviet laborers, who did not have access to quality consumer goods and were not rewarded for hard work with higher wages, displayed little enthusiasm for their jobs. Meanwhile the Soviet black market flourished. As much as 18 percent of consumer expenditures went to the "second economy," where Soviets could find scarce items if they were willing to pay high prices. Black market entrepreneurs stole items subject to frequent shortages, such as gasoline and medical supplies, and sold them at inflated profits. Standing in line for coveted consumer items that one did not need, then selling them on the street for a large profit became a common practice. Many service industry workers such as plumbers, cab drivers, and doctors engaged in "moonlighting"—selling their services in their off hours for black market prices. Because services provided by the state were so poor and undependable, moonlighters rarely had to look hard to find extra work.

During the Brezhnev period evidence also existed of growing alienation among Soviet youth. Many young people, starved for entertainment and witnessing the apathy and corruption in adult society, turned to petty crime, black market activities, alcohol, and drugs. Few youths embraced higher socialist ethics, preferring nonconformist diversions such as Western fashions and rock music, which developed a huge following in the Soviet Union, despite the leadership's efforts to discourage their popularity.

Most troublesome, however, was the general decline of the Soviet economy. During the Khrushchev and early Brezhnev years, the Soviet leadership had depended on extensive growth to propel economic expansion. As resources became more difficult to extract and environmental problems became more acute the Soviets could no longer rely on a wider exploitation of their natural riches. The economy had to be made more efficient. But the Brezhnev leadership continued to hope that minor adjustments in central planning could get the economy moving without recourse to significant decentralization, price reforms, increases in worker incentives, and other radical measures.

Hampered by a string of bad harvests in the early 1980s (despite continued high investment in agriculture), Soviet economic growth fell below 2 percent per year for the years 1981 to 1985. The Soviet Union's international trade position also suffered as the growth of oil revenues slowed in the early 1980s and nations imposed sanctions against the USSR in response to the invasion of Afghanistan and the suppression of unrest in Poland. The continuing restrictions on exports of high technology to the Soviet Union by the United States and other Western nations were particularly damaging to Moscow.

Consequently, in the early 1980s, an unusual and ironic situation had developed in the Soviet Union. Despite the USSR's abundant natural resources, well-educated population, huge industrial base and land mass, and unsur-

passed military power, the Soviet people had to endure an intractable housing shortage, shoddy consumer goods, inadequate food supplies, the lowest life expectancy in Eastern Europe, and a standard of living that in many areas of the country approached Third World levels.

On November 10, 1982, Brezhnev died of a heart attack at the age of seventy-five. Two days after Brezhnev's death the Communist party announced the selection of Yuri V. Andropov as the new general secretary.

Brezhnev had held the post of general secretary for eighteen years, a term exceeded only by Joseph Stalin's twenty-nine years. Although Brezhnev's "cult of personality" did not reach the extent of Stalin's or even Khrushchev's, he did systematically promote himself during the latter years of his regime. His writings were widely published, he was frequently quoted in the Soviet media, and his picture appeared on billboards and at official events. In 1976 he was named a marshal of the Soviet Union and his military service during World War II was glorified. In 1977 he pushed weakened rival Nikolai Podgornyi out of the presidency and assumed the ceremonial position himself. Brezhnev was buried in front of the Kremlin Wall in a distinguished spot behind the Lenin mausoleum.

After Mikhail Gorbachev came to power in 1985, however, Brezhnev's official reputation came under attack. At first the criticism was indirect and suggestive, but by 1987 Brezhnev and his cronies were being blamed by name for much of what was wrong with Soviet society. After watching a film on Bolshevik history with a Soviet audience in 1988, *Washington Post* reporter David Remnick observed, "When the film showed Brezhnev in action, the snide laughter in the theater was reminiscent of the way college audiences after Watergate would chortle at films of Richard Nixon's 'Checkers speech,' in which the 1952 vice presidential candidate defended himself against charges of a secret political fund." Whether this appraisal of Brezhnev was fair or not, he had become a symbol in the Soviet Union of inefficient, unimaginative, and corrupt leadership.

Gorbachev Comes to Power

Leonid I. Brezhnev's death in 1982 ended years of stagnant leadership and precipitated a long-delayed succession crisis. Would the Kremlin opt for another aging leader who would continue muddling through? Or would it choose a younger man prepared to institute change? Sixty-eight-year-old Yuri V. Andropov was selected to succeed Brezhnev as general secretary. Although he displayed reformist tendencies, his policies produced only minor results before he died in February 1984. Andropov was succeeded by seventy-three-year-old Konstantin U. Chernenko, a close associate of Brezhnev. Chernenko, who was in ill health, was widely perceived to be a transitional leader who did little to advance reforms during his thirteen months in power. Upon Chernenko's death in March 1985, Mikhail S. Gorbachev and a younger generation claimed the helm.

Andropov's Rule

On November 12, 1982, two days after Leonid Brezhnev's death, Yuri Andropov was chosen to succeed him as general secretary of the Soviet Communist party. Within two months, Andropov appeared to be firmly in control of the Soviet Union. From 1967 to 1982 Andropov had headed the country's intelligence and internal security agency, the Committee for State Security (KGB). As head of the KGB, Andropov had overseen a systematic and effective campaign to suppress Soviet dissidents. He became a candidate member of the Politburo in 1967 and a full member six years later. In May 1982, Andropov had resigned as KGB head to become a member of the Secretariat, a better position from which to succeed to the general secretaryship. On the Secretariat he succeeded his patron Mikhail Suslov as the top party ideologist. Nevertheless, he retained close ties to the KGB, and it was a major institutional force behind his rise to power.

Andropov became chairman of the important Defense Council after becoming general secretary, but he did not assume the presidency (chairman of the Presidium of the Supreme Soviet) until June 16, 1983. Western observers speculated the lengthy presidential vacancy indicated the post's relative unimportance. Other Kremlin watchers suggested the vacancy meant Andropov had less support than met the eye; still others, however, said the choice was his—that he did not want to burden himself with a time-con-

suming ceremonial job, especially after his illness became more pronounced.

Western analysts were impressed with Andropov's apparent intelligence and sophistication. They suggested that he was selected over Brezhnev's personal favorite, Konstantin Chernenko, because Andropov had the support of the military, the KGB, and leading party technocrats who believed Chernenko was incapable of the vigorous leadership necessary to deal with the country's severe economic and social problems. Most Western experts believed that the support of Foreign Minister Andrei Gromyko and Defense Minister Dmitri Ustinov was decisive in Andropov's elevation and that the choice of Andropov seemed to indicate the Soviet leadership's preference for tightly controlled reform in both domestic and foreign policy.

When Andropov was selected as general secretary, former U.S. ambassador to the Soviet Union Malcolm Toon said that "Some measure of reform might be palatable to the old guard ... if carried out under the watchful eye of Andropov." He could, "in the view of the conservatives, be relied upon to use the same ruthlessness he applied to his KGB responsibilities in making sure reforms would not seriously damage the role of the party and thus would not get out of hand," Toon wrote in the *Christian Science Monitor* November 17, 1982.

Any economic reform, however, would risk offending many members of the Communist party bureaucracy. Most Soviet leaders recognized the need for changes, but a shake-up of the procedures or structure of the party bureaucracy likely would infringe on the fiefdoms of powerful national and regional party potentates.

Nevertheless, Andropov proposed a limited decentralization of the party apparatus and economic planning system in an effort to invigorate the economy. His proposals drew strong opposition not only from corrupt elements of the party bureaucracy worried about their jobs, but also from many orthodox Communists who feared that even modest changes in the Soviet system could become uncontrollable and eventually threaten the Communist party's authority over Soviet society.

The Soviet Union's position in international affairs complicated Andropov's efforts to improve the economy. A confrontational administration in Washington had launched a military buildup that the Soviets believed they had to match. In addition, the Soviets were spending large amounts of money to support the governments of client states around the world. Meanwhile Soviet oil export revenues—the USSR's main source of hard currency—had peaked, and subsidies and aid to the failing economies of Eastern Europe had become a tremendous economic drain. China remained stridently hostile toward the Soviet Union necessitating, in the Kremlin's view, the deployment of hundreds of thousands of troops along the Chinese border. And the Soviet military was bogged down in an expensive war in Afghanistan that continued to damage Moscow's reputation in the Third World and showed no signs of ending.

If Andropov was going to initiate change he had to act quickly, for the new Soviet leader was in dubious health. Andropov's kidneys failed only four months into his tenure, and after this setback he had to use a dialysis machine at least twice a week. In September 1983 Andropov became seriously ill. He made a partial recovery after doctors removed one of his kidneys in October. From that point, Andropov was confined almost all the time to a specially equipped apartment inside a government hospital.

Despite his poor health, Andropov was able to run the country. He did not govern in the manner of an interim leader willing to follow his predecessor's policies until a new leader was ready to take over. He pressed his moderate reform package with mixed success and placed his stamp on foreign policy and personnel decisions.

Economic Reform

Until his health failed in the fall of 1983, Andropov devoted himself primarily to attempts at revitalizing the sluggish Soviet economy. He openly criticized the party and government bureaucracies for blocking change and encouraged frank debates among economists and national leaders about how to get the economy moving. The centerpiece of his economic plan was his campaign to reduce corruption, inefficiency, and alcoholism. Though significant for its acknowledgment of these problems, the campaign did little to improve low Soviet labor productivity.

Andropov also advocated giving manufacturing and agricultural enterprises more autonomy and introducing incentives for productive workers. In July 1983 he announced a series of economic experiments in selected enterprises designed to test his proposals and reduce central bureaucratic controls. Ministries were to have less control of daily decisions at enterprises, and enterprise managers were given control of funds used to reward employees for hard work. The profitability of the enterprises involved in the experiment was made an important factor in their operation. Managers' salaries were linked to profits, and fulfillment of production quotas was based on the number of items produced by the enterprise that were sold, instead of on how many items the enterprise produced. In 1984 the Soviet leadership labeled the experiment a success and extended it to additional enterprises, but the Kremlin was unwilling to introduce these reforms on a large scale.

Andropov and his colleagues also were unwilling to substantially cut the Soviet defense budget. If Andropov had suggested large-scale reductions in Soviet military spending, he would have risked losing the support of the military. Another factor working against cuts in the military budget was the continuing defense buildup by the United States. President Ronald Reagan's March 1983 call for the development of a space-based anti-missile weapons system (the Strategic Defense Initiative, or SDI) that would render the Soviet strategic nuclear arsenal "impotent and obsolete" also contributed to Soviet unwillingness to spend less on defense, particularly in the area of weapons technology research. The Soviets feared that an aggressive American SDI program would widen the technological gap between the superpowers.

Personnel Changes

After his health setback in the fall of 1983, Andropov shifted his attention to personnel changes. He retired scores of party and government officials because of their age or ineffectiveness. He promoted Mikhail Gorbachev and numerous lower-level officials who supported reforms. These younger men shared Andropov's concern about the Soviet Union's economic weakness, and they set the stage for future general secretary Gorbachev's more rapid, extensive personnel changes and economic initiatives.

At the time of Brezhnev's death, full Politburo membership had dwindled to ten, giving Andropov the opportunity to influence the appointment of as many as five new members. His first top-level change was announced November 22, 1982, when Geidar Aliev was elevated to full member of the Politburo. Aliev was a fifty-nine-year-old KGB career officer whom Andropov had appointed to oversee the drive against corruption in Azerbaidzhan in the late 1960s. Viktor Chebrikov, who succeeded Andropov as KGB head, was named a candidate Politburo member in December 1983. Mikhail Solomentsev and Vitalii Vorotnikov, never close allies of Brezhnev, were promoted to full Politburo membership at a Central Committee plenum in December 1983. The plenum also approved the appointment of Yegor Ligachev to the Central Committee Secretariat.

East-West Relations

In an inaugural-style address before the Central Committee November 22, 1982, Andropov said: "The policy of détente is by no means a past stage. The future belongs to this policy." Few leaders in either the United States or the Soviet Union, however, expected relations to improve quickly. Immediately after Brezhnev's death President Reagan and other administration officials had stressed their desire for better superpower relations. But explicit or implicit in these statements was the caveat that any improvement would require some change in Soviet behavior. "It takes two to tango," President Reagan quipped at a news conference the day after Brezhnev's death. The *Moscow News* replied November 25 that "asking someone to dance is not generally done by a demand that he or she change their hairdo, let alone thinking."

It was likely that Kremlin strategists offered Andropov conflicting advice about dealing with the Reagan administration. One faction probably argued that, despite Reagan's anti-Soviet rhetoric, the United States faced serious economic problems of its own and wanted an arms control agreement. Reagan, after all, had impeccable conservative credentials that would allow him (like Richard Nixon) to conclude an arms limitation treaty or some form of détente without being undermined by opposition from the right. Other advisers likely contended that the Soviet Union should wait for a more accommodating American leader and focus on weakening U.S. links to Europe, Japan, and China.

In a meeting with *Washington Post* editors and reporters November 12, Secretary of State George P. Shultz

The Soviet delegation listens to an address by President Ronald Reagan at the opening of the UN General Assembly on September 20, 1983. Foreign Minister Andrei Gromyko's chair is empty because of the cancellation of his trip to New York in the wake of the KAL disaster. Delegation members from left are Anatolii Dobrynin, ambassador to the United States, and Oleg Troyanovskii, ambassador to the United Nations.

outlined the steps the Soviet Union had to take before better relations could be established: Soviet withdrawal from Afghanistan, Vietnamese withdrawal from Cambodia, relaxation of tensions in Poland, and progress toward arms reductions. Andropov, in his speech to the Central Committee November 22, countered that "statements in which the readiness for normalizing relations is linked with the demand that the Soviet Union pay with preliminary concessions in different fields do not sound serious, to say the least. We shall not agree to this."

The same day Reagan proposed the deployment of a hundred MX intercontinental ballistic missiles in Wyoming. The new missiles, administration officials argued, would enhance the U.S. land-based nuclear deterrent. The administration hoped that the threat of deployment would move Kremlin leaders to engage in meaningful arms reduction talks. But MX opponents argued that announcing the decision to deploy the missiles so soon after a new Soviet leader had taken power was not the way to convince Andropov that the United States wanted better relations. Moscow denounced the MX decision, saying that it violated existing arms agreements and insisting that the USSR would find "an effective way to reply to Washington" if such provocations continued.

The arms issue that dominated Andropov's reign, however, was the North Atlantic Treaty Organization's (NATO) deployment of intermediate-range nuclear missiles in Europe. During the late 1970s the Soviets had deployed about 350 intermediate-range SS-20 missiles. Most of the SS-20s were targeted on Western Europe, and each carried three highly accurate warheads. In December 1979, NATO agreed to deploy 108 intermediate-range Pershing II missiles in Germany and 464 ground-launched cruise missiles (GLCMs) in five West European countries to counter the SS-20s. NATO leaders also adopted a "dual track" policy under which its deployment plan could be waived if U.S.-Soviet negotiations removed the SS-20 mis-

sile threat to Western Europe. Preventing the deployment of the NATO missiles, scheduled for late 1983, became one of Andropov's highest priorities.

Andropov offered on December 21, 1982, to reduce Soviet intermediate-range missiles to the combined number held by Great Britain and France if the United States would not deploy its Pershing II and cruise missiles. The United States, Britain, and France rejected the offer on the grounds that it would leave Moscow with a monopoly of intermediate-range missiles in Europe. The Kremlin continued to pressure and cajole Western European governments to oppose the deployments, while offering various arms control options short of NATO's demand that the USSR remove its SS-20s. The Soviets also conducted a sophisticated propaganda campaign aimed at undermining support for the deployments among the people of Western Europe. The Soviet tactics failed to break the resolve of the NATO nations to go ahead with the deployments, which began on schedule in November 1983.

As they had threatened to do if the deployments took place, the Soviets withdrew their negotiating team from the Intermediate-range Nuclear Forces (INF) talks in Geneva on November 23. The Soviets also refused to continue other major arms control negotiations, including the Strategic Arms Reduction Talks (START) in Geneva. Arms control negotiations between the superpowers would not resume until 1985.

KAL Incident

On September 1, 1983, a Soviet warplane shot down a South Korean Boeing 747 that passed over Soviet territory, killing all 269 people aboard. Korean Air Lines Flight 007, one of thousands of commercial flights that skirt Soviet air space in the North Pacific each year, had deviated three hundred miles from its assigned course on the last leg of its flight from New York to Seoul. The Soviets initially denied that their pilot had destroyed the plane and refused to permit the United States and Japan to search the waters where the plane went down. On September 6 they admitted downing the plane but claimed that the Soviet pilot was forced to fire on the plane (which they accused of being engaged in espionage), after it failed to acknowledge warning signals. The incident undermined Soviet antimilitaristic propaganda and plunged already declining U.S.-Soviet relations to one of their lowest points since the Cuban missile crisis.

A crisis atmosphere surrounded the incident. President Reagan stated on September 5, "There was absolutely no justification, either legal or moral, for what the Soviets did. . . . It was an act of barbarism, born of a society which wantonly disregards individual rights and the value of human life and seeks constantly to expand and dominate other nations." The United States accused the Soviets of knowingly shooting down an unarmed civilian aircraft and then failing to acknowledge or apologize for the act. The Soviets accused the United States of using the plane for a spy mission and of manipulating public opinion in support of militaristic policies.

After extensively reviewing the evidence, including tapes of intercepted voice transmissions of the Soviet pilots, U.S. intelligence experts concluded that the pilots and the Soviet air defense personnel with whom they were in contact during the incident did not know that the plane was a civilian airliner. Moreover, the United States admitted that an RC-135, an American electronic reconnaissance plane that is the military's version of the Boeing 747, was flying a routine mission outside Soviet airspace within seventy-five miles of the path of KAL 007. Nevertheless the investigation by the International Civil Aviation Organization, an affiliate of the United Nations, concluded that the Soviets "did not make exhaustive efforts to identify the aircraft through inflight visual observations."

Despite the Reagan administration's strong condemnation of the downing of KAL 007 and Moscow's refusal to take responsibility for it, the United States imposed only minor sanctions against the USSR. Reagan suspended a bilateral transportation agreement and talks on opening a U.S. consulate in Kiev. Many other nations temporarily restricted civil aviation with the Soviet Union to protest the incident. On September 17 Foreign Minister Gromyko canceled his annual trip to New York to address the United Nations after the governors of New Jersey and New York denied the Soviet delegation permission to land at commercial airports in their states.

Other Foreign Policy Problems

Another priority for Andropov was reconciliation with China. Talks on normalizing relations, which China suspended after the Soviet invasion of Afghanistan, were reconvened a few weeks before Brezhnev's death. During Brezhnev's funeral, the Chinese and Soviet foreign ministers held the highest-level talks between the two countries in thirteen years, and each side pledged to work toward improved relations. China imposed three primary conditions on a Sino-Soviet reconciliation: a pullback of Soviet troops along their common border, the withdrawal of Soviet forces from Afghanistan, and an end to Soviet support for the Vietnamese invasion of Cambodia.

Western observers noted that the Soviets might consider it in their interest to withdraw their half-million troops from the Chinese border and the more than one

hundred thousand soldiers bogged down in bloody skirmishes with rebels in Afghanistan. The real problem for Soviet leaders was making a convincing case that they were not acceding to Chinese demands.

Andropov might not have been able to withdraw Soviet forces from Afghanistan even if a genuinely neutralist government could have been found to replace the Soviet-imposed regime of Babrak Karmal. Despite the economic, political, and propagandistic benefits of withdrawal, at that time a withdrawal was strongly opposed by Soviet party ideologues, who saw it as a retreat.

Andropov perhaps could have relieved the pressure on the Soviet economy somewhat by cutting back on the estimated tens of billions of dollars in aid given to friendly governments and satellites. (It is impossible to determine the extent of Soviet aid because it was given in a variety of ways, including grants, subsidized prices, and low-interest loans.) But any suggestion to reduce or end assistance to Cuba, Angola, Vietnam, Nicaragua, and particularly Eastern Europe would have sparked at least as much opposition as would have proposals for a withdrawal from Afghanistan.

Andropov's Death

Andropov acted quickly to foster change, and if he had had more time he might have achieved more of his goals. His last public appearance was August 18, 1983, when he received a delegation of nine U.S. senators, at which time he declared a unilateral moratorium on the deployment of Soviet antisatellite weapons. Sen. Patrick Leahy, D-Vt., and several other senators said they were impressed with Andropov.

Andropov continued to run the country from his closely guarded hospital apartment. In responding to various arms control proposals and in appointing or removing personnel, Andropov relied on the telephone. He also was visited almost daily by Politburo member Mikhail Gorbachev. But by the end of January 1984 his condition had deteriorated markedly. According to most accounts, at that time the government came to a standstill. He died February 9, 1984, less than fifteen months after he became general secretary.

Chernenko 'Interregnum'

Konstantin Chernenko's selection as Andropov's successor disappointed many Soviets who privately regarded him as an uneducated professional bureaucrat who rose to positions of power solely because of his association with Leonid Brezhnev. This evaluation of the man was truthful in many respects but incomplete.

Chernenko had depended on Brezhnev for advancement. He also was uneducated relative to many of his colleagues and was not experienced in foreign policy or defense matters. Chernenko had other qualities, however, that made his selection less of an aberration. He was a skilled party functionary, a loyal team player, and a leader who knew his limitations. He could be expected to submit to collective leadership and to defer to better informed Politburo members on issues outside his expertise.

Chernenko was not chosen primarily for his personal qualities, however, but because he was likely to function as a transitional leader. The old guard was not yet ready to turn power over to the next generation. They wanted a leader who could be trusted to protect the positions of Brezhnev-era appointees and return stability to a bureaucracy shaken by Andropov's personnel changes. The younger, more reform-minded leaders, however, wanted to avoid promoting anyone who would obstruct change in the party hierarchy for many years. Western scholars have suggested Chernenko was chosen precisely because of his old age and poor health rather than in spite of them. The younger and more progressive leaders promoted by Andropov could accept Chernenko because he would not be around long, while the old guard could cling to their positions and influence a little longer and possibly prepare for retirement. Indeed, not a single member of the Politburo or Secretariat lost his job under Chernenko.

Although Chernenko's selection as general secretary made sense from the perspective of Soviet internal politics, he was not what the ailing Soviet economy and society needed. He did not possess the strength or will to implement the reforms necessary to substantially improve the lives of Soviet citizens.

To his credit, Chernenko endorsed most of the limited reforms Andropov had been able to push through the system during his fifteen-month tenure. Chernenko called for the decentralization of selected areas of the economy and greater labor discipline and productivity. But he did not aggressively promote or build on these reforms as Andropov might have done had he lived longer. In some cases, most notably his reversal of Andropov's order to reduce the bureaucracy by 20 percent, Chernenko actively worked against reform. In addition, Chernenko offered only a few relatively minor domestic initiatives of his own. He backed education reform, a land reclamation project, better representation in constitutional bodies such as the Supreme Soviet, and elimination of some duplication of economic tasks by parallel party and government bodies.

Despite Chernenko's lack of foreign policy experience, his regime succeeded in renewing the arms control dialogue with the United States that had been silenced during Andropov's short tenure. Chernenko's speeches and writings signaled his support for détente, but his health was too uncertain, his expertise too suspect, and anti-Reagan sentiment in Moscow too strong for him to make many significant changes in the relations between the superpowers. Moreover, during 1984 the Soviets had sought to avoid any action that might contribute to a Reagan-Republican landslide in the November national elections. Thus, even if Chernenko had desired to significantly improve U.S.-Soviet relations (which is doubtful), he probably could not have done so.

The body of Yuri V. Andropov is carried to his Red Square grave by Soviet soldiers and Politburo colleagues. Politburo members from left are Konstantin U. Chernenko, Nikolai Tikhonov, Dmitri Ustinov, and Andrei Gromyko.

What he did do was support a return to the Geneva arms control negotiations following Reagan's election. The real architect of this pragmatic shift may have been Foreign Minister Gromyko, who was reported to have taken over foreign policy formulation under Chernenko. But Chernenko's backing was critical to the speed with which the policy was implemented and the support it received in Moscow. Only eight days after Reagan's election, Anatolii Dobrynin, then ambassador to the United States, indicated that the Soviet Union was interested in holding umbrella talks on strategic and intermediate-range nuclear weapons and on weapons in space. The combined talks initially had been proposed by the United States in 1983, but now the Soviets sought to make the proposal their own. On November 22 the superpowers announced that Gromyko and Secretary of State Shultz would meet in Geneva in January to lay the groundwork for the arms control talks. Negotiations began March 12, two days after Chernenko's death.

Other areas of Soviet foreign affairs appeared to be on automatic pilot during Chernenko's administration. Using traditional tools of Soviet foreign policy, the Soviets continued many Brezhnev-era policies. Through arms sales they improved their relationship with nonaligned nations such as India and Kuwait. They also continued to seek an elusive military solution to the war in Afghanistan, launching a major offensive in the spring following Chernenko's rise to power.

The summer of 1984 saw a setback in Sino-Soviet relations brought on by President Reagan's April visit to the People's Republic of China and rising tensions on the Sino-Vietnamese border. Nonetheless, the Soviets continued their policy of seeking better relations with the Chinese without offering major concessions. By the end of the year, First Deputy Premier Ivan Arkhipov had signed extensive economic and technological cooperation accords described by Beijing as "the most substantial agreements since relations between our two countries were strained in the 1960s."

Gorbachev Takes Control

On March 10, 1985, Chernenko died of heart failure at the age of seventy-three. The next day the announcement that Mikhail Gorbachev had been chosen as general secretary came just four hours after Chernenko's death was disclosed to the public. The speed of Gorbachev's selection indicated that the decision had been made before Chernenko's death. In his acceptance speech to the Central Committee, Gorbachev set priorities for his government. Foremost among these were economic revitalization and arms control. Gorbachev announced the Politburo's decision to go ahead with the U.S.-Soviet arms talks scheduled to begin in Geneva on March 12, despite the official mourning period for Chernenko.

Gorbachev would accomplish much during 1985. He met with an American president at the first superpower summit in six years and placed his personal stamp on arms control negotiations. He overhauled the Kremlin leadership, replacing older officials with men of his own generation. And he initiated several bureaucratic and economic reforms aimed at reinvigorating Soviet society.

During Gorbachev's first year in power, however, he distinguished himself from past Soviet leaders more through his style of leadership than through the policies he promoted. From the day he took power he projected an image different from his three aging predecessors. He exploited his relative youth, presenting himself as a vigorous leader capable of improving the Soviet way of life. He frequently appeared in public with his wife and other family members and startled Soviet people with his penchant for wading into crowds of citizens to shake hands and listen to their problems.

There was little hint during Gorbachev's first year of how far his economic, social, political, and foreign policy reforms eventually would go. Gorbachev appeared to be a more energetic and engaging version of Andropov, his former patron. He reemphasized Andropov's anticorruption and anti-alcohol campaigns and continued Andropov's efforts to create a split in the Western alliance. In an interview published in the September 9, 1985, issue of *Time* magazine, Gorbachev's pragmatic comments about the need to improve the economy and social conditions of his country demonstrated his flexibility and realism. Yet he also claimed confidence in the ideology that had pervaded Soviet life for decades, saying that the Soviet Union's rise to the status of "a major world power . . . has attested to the strength and the immense capabilities of socialism."

New Faces in the Kremlin

The most noticeable change made by Gorbachev during 1985 was the replacement of dozens of party and government personnel. The *Washington Post* reported January 26, 1986, that Gorbachev had replaced 45 of 159 regional party first secretaries and 4 of 15 first secretaries of republics. In addition, 19 of 59 government ministers were replaced, while 37 of 113 seats on the Council of Ministers changed hands. By the end of 1985 Gorbachev had retired at least 26 Central Committee members and promoted 30 people to positions that made them eligible for Central Committee membership. (Andropov retired 21 members and named 26 new members, while Chernenko retired just 8 and placed 13 on the Central Committee.)

Many of Gorbachev's targets for retirement were holdovers from the Brezhnev era. The Soviet press increasingly referred to Brezhnev as an unnamed "former leader" who allowed corruption to flourish among party and government officials. Meanwhile, Gorbachev rehabilitated many associates of Nikita Khrushchev. No longer anonymous, Khrushchev is "unambiguously extolled as a major contributor to victory in the Soviet-Nazi war," Sidney I. Ploss noted in the spring 1986 issue of *Foreign Policy*. Ploss also cited the criticism of Joseph Stalin in the Soviet press as another indicator of Gorbachev's bias toward reform.

The most visible evidence of Gorbachev's bloodless purge was the transformation of the Politburo. Just one month after gaining power, Gorbachev added three new members: Yegor Ligachev, party secretary in charge of high-level appointments and ideology; Nikolai Ryzhkov, initially charged with setting economic reform policy and later named premier; and Viktor Chebrikov, head of the KGB. Like Gorbachev, all three to some degree had been protégés of Andropov and had supported his economic reforms and discipline campaign.

Gorbachev also replaced Foreign Minister Andrei Gromyko with Eduard Shevardnadze. Gromyko, who had presided over the postwar course of U.S.-Soviet relations during twenty-eight years as foreign minister, was named president of the Soviet Union at a July 2, 1985, session of the Supreme Soviet. Many analysts saw Gromyko's elevation to this ceremonial post as a way of gracefully retiring him so Gorbachev could personally direct Soviet foreign policy.

Shevardnadze had made a name for himself by weeding out corruption when he served as party secretary in his native republic of Georgia. Although he had no previous foreign policy experience, he quickly impressed Western observers as a capable diplomat whose relaxed demeanor was in keeping with Gorbachev's own style of leadership.

At the same July 1985 session of the Supreme Soviet, Grigorii Romanov, the Leningrad party chief and Brezhnev protégé who is thought to have posed the greatest challenge to Gorbachev's rise to power, was retired from the Politburo. Ryzhkov replaced Nikolai Tikhonov, the eighty-year-old Soviet premier, in October. Moscow party chief Viktor Grishin, another member of the old guard, was replaced in December by Boris Yeltsin. Yeltsin was promoted to candidate Politburo status just one week before the Twenty-seventh Party Congress in February 1986.

Gorbachev's Early Economic Agenda

From the time he came to power, Gorbachev called for fundamental economic change. But the "radical" changes he claimed were necessary to revive the economy, reinvigorate the bureaucracy, and improve worker productivity did not take place with any great speed. Western observers noted that during his first months in power his calls for reform were not accompanied by concrete plans. It appeared that Gorbachev, like his predecessors, was prepared only to tinker with the basic central planning mechanism in the hope of perfecting it. But Gorbachev's cautious economic reforms launched in 1985 would prove to be precursors to much more dramatic attempts to overhaul the economy. (Gorbachev's economic reforms, p. 115)

Gorbachev needed time to consolidate power. Moving too rapidly on economic reform could foster dissatisfaction among many members of the elite and create limitations on Gorbachev's freedom of action. Gorbachev needed to effect a wider turnover in personnel before he could launch more serious economic reforms.

In the meantime, Gorbachev focused on implementing Andropov's program to combat alcoholism and poor labor discipline. On May 16, 1985, the Soviet government announced that alcohol production was being cut, liquor store hours were being shortened, and the legal drinking age was being raised from eighteen to twenty-one. Gorbachev also used moral appeals to encourage workers to improve their job performance and introduced limited monetary incentives to reward productive employees.

The Twelfth Five-Year Plan adopted in 1985 under Gorbachev's supervision set ambitious goals for growth. The plan called for 4 percent growth per year from 1986 through 1990. This growth was to be achieved through improved worker productivity and the introduction of more high technology machines into factories and farms. Toward this goal, the plan greatly expanded investment in high technology research, development, and production.

Foreign Policy

Upon becoming general secretary, Gorbachev took an active interest in foreign policy making. He displayed a pragmatic willingness to advance arms control negotiations with the United States, while simultaneously focusing on improving relations with other countries. He also appeared

---

Five Leaders on a Train

During the last years of the Brezhnev regime, a joke about Leonid Brezhnev and past Soviet leaders circulated in the Soviet Union.

As the story goes, the top Soviet leaders since the Bolshevik revolution are traveling in the same compartment on a train somewhere in the USSR. Suddenly the train stops without explanation in the middle of nowhere.

Vladimir Lenin rises from his seat and declares, "I'll get the train moving." He goes forward to the locomotive, where he lectures the engineer on his duty to the Soviet state and the international communist movement. But the train does not move.

After Lenin returns to his seat, Joseph Stalin sneers, "You people don't know how to deal with the Russian mentality." He then marches to the locomotive, where he shoots the engineer. Naturally the train does not budge.

Stalin returns to his seat, and Nikita Khrushchev takes up the challenge. He argues, "We must not hold the engineer's past mistakes against him." He enters the locomotive, where he rehabilitates the engineer by propping him up at the controls, but still the train does not move.

After Khrushchev returns, Brezhnev says, "I have an easy solution to our troubles. We'll pull the blinds and imagine that the train is moving." The train remains motionless, but everyone remarks how fast it is going.

After Mikhail Gorbachev came to power and began encouraging open discussion of the Soviet Union's problems, the story came to have a new ending: Finally a disgusted Gorbachev climbs to the top of the train and shouts, "Look everybody, the train is not moving." The passengers are so surprised and excited by his honesty that they no longer care about making progress toward their destination. "Finally," they say, "we have a leader who speaks the truth."

---

to be more adept than any of his predecessors at competing with the United States for world public opinion.

Although under Gorbachev the Soviets did not abandon their efforts to extend their international influence, the new general secretary seemed to have adopted a cautious attitude toward foreign adventures. Soviet efforts to gain footholds in sub-Saharan Africa, Latin America, and Asia had proved costly and usually had yielded few benefits. Gorbachev and his colleagues likely decided that needs closer to home were more pressing. Soviet troops in Afghanistan launched a series of offensives against U.S.-supported resistance forces in 1985, but Gorbachev told the Supreme Soviet in November that he was seeking a political settlement of the six-year war there and the eventual withdrawal of Soviet forces. In 1986 he called Afghanistan a "bleeding wound."

The Kremlin launched an ambitious diplomatic offensive to improve its standing around the world. The Soviets worked toward a reconciliation with Japan that culminated in a trip by Foreign Minister Shevardnadze to Tokyo in January 1986. The trip marked the first time a Soviet foreign minister had visited Japan in ten years. Enemies during World War II, the two countries have never signed a peace treaty because of a dispute over four Soviet-occupied islands north of Japan. Although the visit did not produce a resolution of the territorial dispute or a long-term economic cooperation agreement, it opened the way for moderately improved relations between the two countries.

Gorbachev also pursued an expansion of the thaw in relations with China initiated by Andropov. Yet the "three obstacles" identified by China to complete normalization of relations remained: the presence of Soviet troops along the border separating the two nations, the Soviet presence in Afghanistan, and the occupation of Cambodia by Moscow's ally Vietnam. The appearance of Chinese representatives at the Twenty-seventh Soviet Party Congress in February 1986 would have been a sign of reconciliation. But the Chinese chose not to send a delegation, reaffirming their contention that until the Soviets removed the three obstacles, improvements in the Sino-Soviet relationship would be restricted to trade.

On May 22, Gorbachev and Prime Minister Rajiv Gandhi of India signed a major economic agreement. It outlined a new fifteen-year economic and technical cooperation program and provided for 1.2 billion dollars in Soviet credits for construction of industrial and energy projects in India.

The Kremlin's foreign policy in the Middle East had mixed results. To improve its standing among the moderate Arab nations, the Soviet Union established diplomatic relations with the sultanate of Oman and the United Arab Emirates. But a diplomatic setback followed in mid-January 1986, when civil war broke out in Soviet-backed South Yemen. Although the rebellion was settled by early February with the installation of another Moscow-supported leader, the incident clearly caught the Kremlin by surprise and unprepared to control its closest ally in the region.

U.S.-Soviet Summitry

Superpower relations during 1985 centered around the summit scheduled for November in Geneva. President Reagan had proposed the summit to Gorbachev on March 12, 1985, through a letter delivered by Vice President George Bush, who was attending the funeral of Konstantin Chernenko. Gorbachev accepted the invitation July 3. Few previous summit meetings had stirred as much anticipation among politicians, academics, commentators, and the international community. The Geneva summit would be the first meeting between the leaders of the United States and the Soviet Union since June 1979, when President Jimmy Carter met Leonid Brezhnev in Vienna to sign the SALT II treaty setting limits on both countries' strategic arsenals. In agreeing to go to Geneva, Reagan had put aside his earlier distrust of summits. During his first term he adopted a confrontational tone toward the Soviet Union and dismissed summitry, saying that the Soviets had used past meetings to extract arms control agreements that put the United States at a disadvantage. *(U.S.-Soviet summits, box, p. 203)*

In the months before the summit both leaders and their respective advisers demonstrated skill in the business of public relations. Reagan and Gorbachev tirelessly marketed themselves and their arms control proposals with an eye toward winning support at home, among their adversary's population, and among the citizens of Western Europe.

On July 29, 1985, Gorbachev announced that the Soviet Union, "wishing to set a good example," would "stop unilaterally any nuclear explosions starting from August 6 this year." Not coincidentally August 6 was the fortieth anniversary of the day the United States dropped the first atomic bomb on Hiroshima, Japan. Continuation of the moratorium past January 1, 1986, Gorbachev said, would depend on whether the United States also stopped nuclear testing. The White House dismissed the moratorium as propaganda, saying it would not slow Soviet weapons production because the country had accelerated its nuclear testing prior to the announcement and could easily resume tests in January.

In September Gorbachev played to American public opinion in a *Time* magazine interview by saying that he attached "tremendous importance" to the summit. This attempt to elevate expectations was in contrast to Reagan's cautions against raising "false hopes." To Gorbachev's appeal for a breakthrough in arms control, the Reagan administration said that the Soviet Union had not offered any concrete proposals. Reagan dismissed Gorbachev's condemnation of the Strategic Defense Initiative, saying that it would not become a "bargaining chip" in Geneva. SDI, Reagan's controversial program to develop a space-based defense against nuclear attack, was already emerging as the central issue on the summit agenda.

New Soviet foreign minister Eduard Shevardnadze continued the verbal assault against SDI in his speech to the UN General Assembly September 24. He called for an international space research program of "Star Peace" in contrast to "Star Wars" as SDI was commonly called. Addressing the same forum the previous day, Secretary of State Shultz accused the Soviet Union of making "blatantly one-sided" accusations and invited Moscow to "get down to real business, with the seriousness the subject deserves."

Gorbachev took up Shultz's challenge during a widely publicized visit to Paris in October, his first trip to the West since assuming the Kremlin leadership in March. He used the occasion to publicize the centerpiece of his presummit proposals, an arms reduction proposal Shevardnadze had reportedly presented to Reagan in Washington. If Reagan would give up SDI, Gorbachev said, the Soviet Union would agree to a 50 percent cut in both sides' nuclear weapons.

Gorbachev's trip to Paris did not reignite the West European peace movement of the early 1980s, and President François Mitterrand, while highly critical of SDI, refused to issue a joint communiqué with Gorbachev denouncing the program. France also rebuffed Gorbachev's invitation to negotiate a separate arms control agreement, as did Great Britain, the other European nuclear power.

But Gorbachev's failure to win supporters in Western Europe did not translate into unconditional European backing for Reagan's position. Shortly after Reagan's October 24 UN General Assembly speech in which he called for a joint U.S.-Soviet initiative to resolve conflicts in five countries where insurgents were challenging Soviet-supported governments, Reagan met with the leaders of five allies (Britain, West Germany, Japan, Italy, and Canada), who told him that arms control remained the most important item on the summit agenda. British prime minister Margaret Thatcher urged Reagan to respond to Gorbachev's arms control proposal in a manner that would break the "deadlock in Geneva."

After all the media buildup, the summit (November 19-21) produced mixed reviews and ambivalence. The two leaders agreed to further meetings, and both welcomed the beginning of a new dialogue between the superpowers. However, the summit produced no visible progress on major issues. Those who evaluated the summit as positive expressed satisfaction that Reagan and Gorbachev had conversed amiably and planned to continue talking. This in itself, they said, was a great accomplishment. Those who saw the summit as a disappointment pointed out that arms control, regional, and human rights issues remained unresolved.

In a joint communiqué released at the end of the summit, Reagan and Gorbachev described their discussions as "frank and useful" while acknowledging that "serious differences remain on a number of critical issues."

Despite Reagan's last-minute attempt to give high priority to regional conflicts involving the Soviets, arms control issues dominated the meeting. The two leaders pledged to accelerate efforts for an arms reduction agreement in the ongoing Geneva arms talks and singled out two possible areas for early progress: a 50 percent cut in nuclear weapons and a separate agreement to cut intermediate-range forces based in Europe. In both areas, superficial similarities between the U.S. and Soviet positions masked profound disagreements over what weapons the negotiations should cover.

No concrete arms control accords were signed at the summit, but numerous cultural exchange agreements were reached, as were agreements calling for regular high-level meetings, new consulates, air flights, and other cooperative arrangements.

President Reagan came home to a warm reception on Capitol Hill. Members of Congress on both sides of the aisle applauded the tone of his and Gorbachev's summit statements, many commenting that they seemed to have put U.S.-Soviet relations back on a businesslike basis, stripped of the confrontational rhetoric that had characterized the previous five years. Addressing a joint session of Congress on the evening of November 21, Reagan said that the fifteen hours of discussion—five of them involving the two leaders accompanied only by translators—marked "a fresh start" in U.S.-Soviet relations. Tentative plans for a Gorbachev visit to Washington in 1986 and a Reagan trip to Moscow for a third meeting in 1987 met with approval in Congress.

Gorbachev also stepped up his calls for movement in arms control negotiations. In his address to the Twenty-seventh Party Congress in February 1986 he stated that, before he would agree to a date for the 1986 summit in Washington, he wanted assurance that progress on arms control would be made there.

The Road to Reform

When Foreign Minister Gromyko nominated Gorbachev for the post of general secretary, he told his colleagues in the Central Committee, "Comrades, this man has a nice smile, but he has got iron teeth." Indeed Gorbachev was the first Soviet leader since Khrushchev

with a "nice smile." His outgoing style created a more human image of the Soviet Union abroad and reassured many Soviet citizens that the leadership was interested in their welfare. But he also had the "iron teeth" associated with past Soviet leaders. He was a skillful and aggressive politician who sought to increase Soviet advantages abroad and enhance his own power at home.

As 1986 began almost no one anticipated the economic and social upheaval that would engulf the Soviet Union during the next five years. Gorbachev's first steps toward reform had been cautious, even predictable. He had staunchly upheld the validity of Marxist ideology and the necessity of Communist party control of society. Only in the area of personnel had he taken dramatic steps.

Gorbachev, however, apparently recognized that reversing the malaise in Soviet society and the Soviet economy's stagnation required radical change. Through 1986 and 1987 his reform goals became increasingly ambitious and daring. Limited free market characteristics were introduced into the economy, controls on information were loosened, the Soviet press and public were encouraged to debate candidly society's problems, and the Soviet Union made concessions in arms control that led to a treaty with the United States eliminating intermediate-range nuclear weapons. By 1988 Gorbachev's reforms had progressed so

Mikhail S. Gorbachev's outgoing style contributed greatly to his international popularity.

far that many of the "reformers" he had helped to promote in 1985 had been ousted or remained as the more conservative members within the leadership.

Gorbachev had been successful in initiating a reform program that would transform Soviet society. But it appeared that he had lost control of the process and was responding to events instead of directing reform from the top. By 1989 the communist governments in Eastern Europe had fallen with Soviet assent—something no one would have predicted in 1985. The Soviet Union itself experienced widespread strikes, protests, and ethnic riots. In 1990 the unthinkable continued to occur as the Communist party renounced its monopoly on power. Throughout this tumultuous period, Gorbachev remained in power. But as the new decade began, his future and the future of the Soviet Union were impossible to predict.

The Soviet Union Today

Land and State

The Union of Soviet Socialist Republics is the largest country in the world, with an area measuring 8.65 million square miles and stretching across eleven time zones. About two-and-one-half times larger than the United States, the Soviet Union extends from the Baltic Sea to the Bering Strait. Only fifty-three miles across the Bering Strait lies the Alaskan mainland. With approximately 290 million people, the Soviet Union has the third largest population in the world behind China and India. It contains more than 170 ethnic groups, speaking some 130 languages and practicing numerous religions. Ethnic Russians make up just 51 percent of the population. *(Ethnic groups, table, p. 131)*

Geography has played a significant role in Russian and Soviet history. The vast interior of the USSR, combined with numerous foreign invasions and Russia's early embrace of the Orthodox Church instead of the Church of Rome, contributed to the nation's tendency toward isolation and distrust of the outside world, particularly the West.

Foreign invaders found Russian territory unprotected by natural barriers such as large bodies of water or mountain ranges. This factor long has been cited as justification for Russian and Soviet desires to secure the nation's borders. In the search for security, the Russian and Soviet states invaded other territories, making the nation rich in resources yet difficult to manage in its enormity and diversity. The severe climate has helped complicate the efforts of invaders but has hindered economic development and largely has determined population and economic distribution.

Soviet Geography

The Soviet Union shares borders with twelve other nations: Afghanistan, China, Czechoslovakia, Finland, Hungary, Iran, Mongolia, North Korea, Norway, Poland, Romania, and Turkey. It opens to the Arctic Ocean, Pacific Ocean, Baltic Sea, Caspian Sea, Black Sea, and the Sea of Azov. It encompasses Lake Baikal, the largest freshwater basin in Eurasia and the deepest in the world. The principal rivers in the Soviet Union include the Volga, Don, Dnepr, Amu-Darya, Ob, Irtysh, Yenisei, Lena, and Amur. The Yenisei flows north across Siberia, cutting the Soviet

Union in half. The Volga, one of the mightiest rivers in the world, and the Oka, one of its tributaries, are typical of many Soviet rivers—freezing conditions in the winter make them navigable only about eight months a year.

The Ural Mountains, running for 1,500 miles from north to south, form the traditional dividing line between Europe and Asia. West of this mountain range is the broad East European Plain, encompassing all of the so-called European part of the Soviet Union. East of the Urals lies the vastness of Siberia. The Central Siberian Plateau is more elevated than the eastern plain but equally flat.

The Central Asian territory is largely mountainous, including the Caucasus range between the Black and Caspian seas and the Altai range in east Central Asia. There are other, lower, mountain ranges on the Crimean Peninsula and on the borders of Czechoslovakia and Hungary.

Much of the Soviet Union lies above 50 degrees north latitude (the equivalent latitude in North America is some 300 miles north of Montreal). Moscow lies above the fifty-fifth parallel and Leningrad just below the sixtieth. The northernmost part of the Soviet Union is arctic desert and tundra, where moss and low shrubs are the main vegetation. South of the tundra stretch enormous forests, then the steppes (grasslands), and finally the deserts of Central Asia.

The steppes contain the famous black soil of Russia, which is considered among the most fertile in the world. Two-thirds of the Soviet Union's arable land is on the steppes. However, unfavorable weather conditions—insufficient, unreliable rainfall and hot winds—thwart full exploitation of this significant resource. Less than 20 percent of Soviet territory is suitable for agricultural cultivation.

Moscow, the capital of the Soviet Union, is the heart of Soviet economic, political, and cultural life. The city and surrounding suburbs are densely populated and highly industrialized. Numerous rail lines and highways connect Moscow to other major urban areas. The more than twelve million people living in Moscow and its suburbs rely on energy and food supplies brought from other parts of the country.

The northwest region of the Soviet Union contains one of the nation's largest industrial bases. Subsections include Belorussia, the Baltic states, and the Kola Peninsula on the Soviet-Finnish border. Many of the major cities in the northwest are Baltic ports, including Leningrad, the na-

The Soviet Union

Official name—Union of Soviet Socialist Republics; abbreviated USSR.
Area—8.65 million square miles.
Population—288,742,345 (July 1989 estimate).
Population growth rate—0.8 percent.
Life expectancy at birth—Male, sixty-four years; female, seventy-four years (1989).
Work force—151 million (civilian).
Literacy—99 percent.
Capital—Moscow.
Government system—Federal union.
Suffrage—Universal over age eighteen.
GNP—2.5 trillion dollars (1988).
National day—October Revolution Day, November 7.

Source: *The World Fact Book*, CIA (Washington, D.C.: Government Printing Office), 1989.

tion's second-largest city and the largest seaport. There are numerous rivers in the territory, and timber is a main natural resource.

The largest city in the southwestern part of the country is Kiev, the ancient capital of Russia and the present-day capital of the Ukraine. The Ukraine is the second most populous republic after the Russian republic and is a major producer of grain. The Ukraine's Black Sea coast has developed into a summer resort area that resembles the Mediterranean in climate.

Soviet Central Asia lacks major natural waterways and modern transportation routes, deficiencies that have hindered economic growth despite a rapid increase in population during the second half of the twentieth century. The region produces several types of agricultural products, including livestock, cotton, and rice, but the crops depend heavily on irrigation.

The Caucasus region is the area between the Caspian Sea and the Black Sea straddled by the immense Caucasus Mountains, the highest in Europe. The Caucasus has had a turbulent history because of its location between the Persian, Ottoman, and Russian Empires. It has been conquered and reconquered many times. It is home to the Azerbaidzhanis, Armenians, Georgians, and a number of smaller ethnic groups.

The Caucasus region's Black Sea coast is favored with the most temperate weather in the Soviet Union. It is the only region where citrus fruits can be grown. The Caucasus also produces most of the Soviet Union's grapes and tea. The city of Baku on the Caspian Sea historically has been the center of the Soviet oil extraction industry, although the output of the Caucasus has been eclipsed during the 1980s by production in Siberia.

Westerners usually think of Siberia as the vast, arctic territory where Russian and Soviet political malcontents have been sent for centuries. For the Soviets, it is the "giant construction site of the USSR." Yet the economic

development anticipated for the region because of its natural resources has been significantly hindered by its inhospitable climate. There are few roads and only one east-west rail line, the Trans-Siberian Railway. The region's largest cities are along the rail line and include Novosibirsk and Krasnoyarsk. Surveys have uncovered vast mineral supplies in Siberia, but the region is limited agriculturally. Fish are plentiful, and the trapping of fur-bearing animals is extensive.

The Soviet Far East differs in many ways from the rest of Siberia. It is humid, relatively mild, and has several large cities, including Vladivostok. Because the area is so far from Moscow, the economy has become somewhat self-sufficient. The area's climate and location on the Pacific Ocean long have attracted settlers from throughout the Soviet Union. The Soviet government has devoted many resources to the economic development of the region. There also are numerous sensitive military bases in the area, particularly on Sakhalin Island.

Part of the Soviet Union lies above the Arctic Circle. The Far North is primarily a maritime territory. Murmansk is one of the larger urban areas and has a substantial fishing industry. There are other ports providing navigation between Europe and Asia for a few months each year, and, despite the near isolation, population in the Far North is slowly growing. *(Soviet land use, map, p. 122)*

Natural Resources

Within its enormous territory, the Soviet Union contains at least 25 percent of the world's energy resources and hydroelectric power. The Soviet Union is the world's largest producer of petroleum, leading all members of the Organization of Petroleum Exporting Countries and the United States. It also is the largest producer of natural gas and has more than 37 percent of the world's known natural gas reserves. The USSR is third in coal production behind China and the United States.

In the mid-1970s, the Central Intelligence Agency predicted that the Soviets soon would find themselves in an energy squeeze, but oil production levels climbed impressively until the end of the decade. From 1983 to 1985 Soviet oil production declined by about 4 percent—the first sustained production decline since World War II. By the winter of 1984, Moscow canceled some oil shipments to West European customers. After 1985 oil production recovered somewhat, but the long-term trend of rising oil production had leveled off. Most analysts believe that to sustain the production levels of the 1980s the Soviets would have to devote considerable funding to exploration and drilling in inhospitable regions, notably Siberia. The technology required for such operations must be imported from the West. Labor shortages in the rugged Siberian oil regions also threaten Soviet oil production. *(Oil fields and pipelines, map, p. 124)*

Natural gas production in the Soviet Union continues to increase. Moscow has begun exploring ways to substitute natural gas for oil at home so that it can continue earning hard currency by exporting most of its oil to the West.

Besides its energy wealth, the Soviet Union contains great reserves of other natural resources. Its supplies of timber and manganese are the largest in the world, and it has ample reserves of lead, zinc, nickel, mercury, potash, phosphate, cobalt, and platinum metals. Of the major minerals, the USSR lacks sufficient amounts only of tin and uranium.

Years of emphasis on heavy industry have brought the Soviet Union unwelcome environmental problems, just as in other parts of the industrialized world. By most accounts environmental protection in the Soviet Union has not progressed much beyond mitigating past damage. Several significant environmental problems have implications that could continue for years. Lake Baikal's purity and delicate ecological balance have been severely damaged because of hydroelectric power plants, wood pulp mills, and chemical plants. The lake has thousands of species of animal life known nowhere else in the world. The level of the Caspian Sea has fallen more than fifteen feet because of the extensive use of the Volga River for irrigation and hydroelectricity. This has disrupted the ecological chain and threatened several varieties of fish with extinction. Similar problems endanger the Aral Sea, whose Amu and Syr Darya rivers have been tapped for major irrigation projects in Central Asia. Acid rain and irreparable soil erosion due to deforestation plague several industrial areas. And the effects of the 1986 Chernobyl nuclear disaster caused lasting environmental damage.

The Republics

The Soviet Union is divided into fifteen union republics. Each republic has the trappings of sovereignty: a constitution (that conforms to the USSR Constitution), national anthem, flag, supreme court, and government and party hierarchy paralleling the USSR structure. The republics theoretically have the authority to conduct relations with other nations and the right to secede from the USSR. In practice Moscow has retained tight central control over the republics, but as of 1990 this control was weakening. The Lithuanian republic had declared its independence in defiance of the Kremlin, and several other republics had taken significant steps toward independence. In addition, independence movements of varying strength had been established in all of the republics. Two of the republics—the Ukraine and Belorussia—have their own representation in the United Nations, an arrangement worked out at the end of World War II by Western leaders to obtain Soviet backing of the world organization. *(Ethnicity in the USSR, p. 129)*

The largest and most important union republic is the Russian Soviet Federated Socialist Republic (RSFSR). At 6.5 million square miles, it contains about 75 percent of the Soviet land mass and 51 percent of the population (146.45 million, according to 1988 Soviet figures). Its capital is Moscow, which also is the capital of the USSR.

The other union republics (and their 1988 populations according to the USSR State Committee on Statistics) are:

● Armenian Soviet Socialist Republic. Population, 3.46 million; religious heritage, predominantly Armenian Apostolic; capital, Yerevan. Nationalist sentiment among Armenians is strong.

● Azerbaidzhan Soviet Socialist Republic. Population, 6.92 million; religious heritage, predominantly Moslem; capital, Baku. The republic historically has had strong ties to the Shi'ite Moslems of Iran.

● Belorussian Soviet Socialist Republic. Population, 10.14 million; religious heritage, predominantly Russian Orthodox; capital, Minsk.

● Estonian Soviet Socialist Republic. Population, 1.57 million; religious heritage, predominantly Lutheran; capital, Tallinn. Along with Latvia and Lithuania, Estonia is one of the three formerly independent Baltic nations overrun by the Red Army in 1940.

● Georgian Soviet Socialist Republic. Population, 5.30 million; religious heritage, predominantly Orthodox; capital, Tiflis. The homeland of Joseph Stalin, Georgia attempted to establish an independent state after the Bolshevik Revolution in 1917, but the movement was crushed by Moscow. Separatist feelings in Georgia are strong.

● Kazakh Soviet Socialist Republic. Population, 16.47 million; religious heritage, predominantly Moslem; capital, Alma-Ata. Kazakhstan is the second-largest republic and the scene of the largely disappointing Virgin Lands agricultural scheme of the 1950s.

● Kirgiz Soviet Socialist Republic. Population, 4.24 million; religious heritage, predominantly Moslem; capital, Frunze.

● Latvian Soviet Socialist Republic. Population, 2.67 million; religious heritage, predominantly Lutheran; capital, Riga. Latvia was taken over by the Soviets in 1940; it enjoys a standard of living well above that in the RSFSR.

● Lithuanian Soviet Socialist Republic. Population, 3.68 million; religious heritage, predominantly Roman Catholic; capital, Vilnius. Annexed by the Soviets in 1940, Lithuania declared its independence in 1990.

● Moldavian Soviet Socialist Republic. Population, 4.22 million; religious heritage, predominantly Orthodox; capital, Kishinev. It is the smallest republic—13,012 square miles—and formerly was part of Romania.

● Tadzhik Soviet Socialist Republic. Population, 4.97 million; religious heritage, predominantly Moslem; capital, Dushanbe. The capital was renamed Stalinabad to honor Joseph Stalin, but it was changed back to the original name in 1961 as part of the government de-Stalinization effort.

● Turkmen Soviet Socialist Republic. Population, 3.46 million; religious heritage, predominantly Moslem; capital, Ashkhabad.

● Ukrainian Soviet Socialist Republic. Population, 51.38 million; religious heritage, predominantly Russian Orthodox; capital, Kiev. The Ukraine is the second most populous republic and is considered the USSR's "breadbasket."

● Uzbek Soviet Socialist Republic. Population, 19.57 million; religious heritage, predominantly Moslem; capital, Tashkent.

Government Structure

In mid-1988 Mikhail S. Gorbachev convened a special party conference—the first such meeting in nearly fifty years—to discuss sweeping changes in the Soviet governmental structure. At the heart of Gorbachev's program was the revitalization of electoral organs in the USSR. The program focused on the nationwide system of soviets, which is Russian for "councils."

The constitutional amendments and laws adopted as a result of this conference specified that the national legislature (or USSR Supreme Soviet) would be reorganized and that a new legislative organ (the Congress of People's Deputies (CPD)) would be created. In March 1989, the first multi-candidate, secret ballot elections in the Soviet Union since 1917 were held to elect deputies to the new Congress. At its first session, the Congress elected a new Supreme

The Kremlin

The Kremlin—a contemporary symbol of Soviet power—is a walled fortress built on a hill in the center of Moscow. The walls, forty feet high and twelve feet thick, enclose several cathedrals and government buildings, including the mid-nineteenth century Grand Palace. Built as the tsar's residence, the Grand Palace housed the Supreme Soviet until 1961, when that body moved to new quarters within the Kremlin. The Grand Palace is used today for Communist party meetings and other party and state functions.

Moscow's Kremlin (other cities, such as Novgorod and Rostov, also had kremlins) was built in the twelfth century. The original wooden towers and battlements were replaced by oak and earthen fortifications in 1296. In 1367 the first stone walls were built. They enclosed the palaces of the grand duke and the nobility, government offices, churches, and monasteries. The brick walls surrounding the triangular Kremlin were built in the late fifteenth century. The striking cathedrals within the Kremlin were built around a central square in the fifteenth and sixteenth centuries by Italian artisans working for the tsars. Other buildings within the Kremlin are the Moscow Senate building, which today houses the offices of the Council of Ministers, and the Armory Palace, which is used as a museum.

Along the northeastern wall of the Kremlin lies Red Square, the site of military parades and other state celebrations. Red Square also is the site of the tomb of V. I. Lenin and the multicolored Cathedral of St. Basil the Blessed, built by Tsar Ivan the Terrible.

would be elected directly by the population from territorial units and districts only.

The elections resulted in defeat for conservatives and Communist party hard-liners in many districts of the Soviet Union. Moreover, several candidates who ran unopposed were defeated in important races because a majority of voters crossed out their names on the ballots (for example, first secretary of the Leningrad City Party Committee and candidate member of the Politburo, Yuri Solovev). In all, 12.4 percent of the USSR People's Deputies elected in 1989 were not members of the Communist party. Approximately 29 percent of the Communist Party Central Committee won seats in the Congress, as well as all full and candidate members of the Politburo (with the exception of Solovev).

According to the recently amended Soviet Constitution, the CPD is the supreme organ of power in the USSR. It elects the USSR Supreme Soviet from among its members as well as a Supreme Soviet chairman. The CPD meets at least twice a year and is empowered to amend the constitution, define the basic guidelines of foreign and domestic policy, oversee nationalities issues and relations between Moscow and the republics, and confirm top government officials. It may repeal acts adopted by the Supreme Soviet.

The Congress also elects the Committee for Constitutional Oversight. This is a new body authorized to rule on the constitutionality of USSR and union-republic legislation and on discrepancies between the USSR and union-republic constitutions. Previously, this right belonged to the Supreme Soviet Presidium. As such, this is the first attempt to create a quasi-independent constitutional court in the USSR. Its twenty-seven members are elected by the Congress "from the ranks of specialists in the field of politics and law" for ten-year terms. Committee members are prohibited from serving in the legislature and from holding top government positions. Its first chairman is jurist Sergei Alekseev, former chairman of the Supreme Soviet legislation committee.

USSR Supreme Soviet

The USSR Supreme Soviet is the full-time working legislature in the Soviet Union. It passes laws, ratifies international treaties, approves economic plans and the USSR budget, and confirms ministerial appointments. It usually holds two three-to-four-month sessions per year.

Like the old Supreme Soviet, it is a bicameral legislature, but it is much smaller than its predecessor. Instead of 1,500 members, it is composed of 542 members who are elected from the Congress. Half sit in the Council of the Union (headed in 1990 by Ivan Laptev), and half in the Council of Nationalities (headed in 1990 by Rafik Nishanov). Legislation must be adopted by a majority of each chamber. With the exception of the chairman of the USSR Council of Ministers, top government officials are prohibited from serving in the new Supreme Soviet. Although people's deputies were allowed to keep their jobs, persons elected to the Supreme Soviet were urged to give up their previous occupations and devote themselves full time to legislative work.

As in the old Supreme Soviet, there is a committee structure in each chamber, but it has been revised. There are now four standing commissions unique to each house and fifteen joint standing committees. The two Supreme Soviet chambers are equally represented on the commit-

Soviet and chose Mikhail Gorbachev to fill the newly created office of chairman of the Supreme Soviet (president).

Almost a year later, the legislature adopted new constitutional amendments that reorganized the government once again. The Congress created an executive presidency and transferred many of the powers of the collective head of state, the Supreme Soviet Presidium, to the office of the president.

Congress of People's Deputies

The Congress of People's Deputies consists of 2,250 deputies elected by universal suffrage to five-year terms. The first Congress was elected in March 1989, with a third of its seats elected from territorial units (union republics, autonomous republics, autonomous regions); a third from newly created districts (containing about 257,300 voters each); and a third from public organizations (including a hundred from the Communist party). A December 1989 law rescinded this last provision; henceforth, the Congress

tees. Deputies from the CPD who were not elected to the Supreme Soviet are eligible to serve on Supreme Soviet committees. By some estimates, eight hundred deputies participate in committee work. Although the old committees had some influence on legislation—particularly in the preparatory phase of the budgetary process—the new committees are intended to exercise significant influence over the legislative process. Specifically, they are to hold regular hearings on the performance of bodies elected by it and to draft legislation. There are several new committees, the most unique of which is the Committee for Defense and State Security. This committee was the first legislative body ever set up in the USSR to oversee the Committee for State Security (KGB), Ministry of Defense, and USSR Supreme High Command.

As before the government reform, the Supreme Soviet has a presidium—a type of executive committee. The presidium used to function "as the highest organ of state authority" between Supreme Soviet sessions. It included about forty members, and its chairman was the head of state (president) of the USSR, although the post was mainly ceremonial. It was held by Andrei Gromyko from July 2, 1985, to September 30, 1988. The Supreme Soviet confirmed Gorbachev as the new chairman of its Presidium on October 1. He held the post until May 1989, when it was eliminated in favor of a new position with more power—chairman of the Supreme Soviet. The CPD elected Gorbachev to this office by an overwhelming majority. When the executive presidency was created in March 1990, the presidium reverted to being mainly a coordinating body. It coordinates the work of the Supreme Soviet, the Congress, and the Supreme Soviet committees and commissions. Many of its previous responsibilities were transferred to the office of the president, including the right to declare martial law and the power to issue binding decrees. Because Gorbachev had to resign his Supreme Soviet post after his election as executive president, a new chairman of the Supreme Soviet had to be chosen. Anatolii Lukyanov, the previous first deputy chairman of the Supreme Soviet, was elected.

Although the precise power of the new legislature still is undetermined, the Supreme Soviet has demonstrated much more independence than its rubber-stamp predecessor. For example, it rejected nine ministerial nominees during the 1989 confirmation hearings, and it rejected emergency legislation to ban all strikes in October 1989. The old Supreme Soviet, in contrast, had never even recorded a dissenting vote until 1988. As for the Congress, some deputies have argued that it should be abolished, because its large size and infrequent sessions make meaningful debate difficult.

Republican and Local Soviets

The system of elected soviets is replicated beneath the national level. Each republic has its own supreme soviet and presidium, and local soviets exist at the regional, city, and district levels. All deputies are elected for five-year terms and are allowed to serve in soviets on two different levels simultaneously. Traditionally the soviets were elected under party direction and met infrequently. The local soviets actually were run by the executive committees of the soviets. This ensured Communist party control because the chairmen of the executive committees, although technically appointed by the soviets, were approved by Communist party committees at the corresponding level.

The constitutional amendments passed in 1989 allowed each republic to choose whether to duplicate the national structure and elect a congress of people's deputies, which then would elect a supreme soviet, or to elect just a supreme soviet. Only the Russian republic chose to elect a congress of people's deputies.

In late 1989, the process of electing new republican parliaments and local soviets began. These elections came on the heels of increasing nationalist unrest. Results in elections held by mid-1990 indicated decisive victories for noncommunist candidates and for nationalist candidates in republics other than the RSFSR. In Lithuania, for example, the pro-independence nationalist group Sajudis won a decisive victory over the independent Lithuanian Communist party. In the RSFSR, although the new parliament is not unequivocally "liberal," conservative Russian nationalist candidates fared poorly. Also, several key cities in the RSFSR are under the control of liberals who ran on the "Democratic Russia" platform—Moscow under Gavriil Popov and Leningrad under Anatolii Sobchak.

Although republican parliaments and local soviets used to play a marginal role in Soviet political life (because of party control over policy making), it is likely that they will play a much larger one in the near future. Republics and localities are adopting a system of self-financing that will make them more independent from Moscow.

Executive President

The executive presidency of the USSR is a new institution created by constitutional amendments adopted by the CPD in March 1990. These amendments transferred many of the powers that previously belonged to the Presidium of the USSR Supreme Soviet to the president and also granted him new powers.

The president is commander in chief of the armed

forces and has the right to declare war. He can declare a state of emergency subject to a two-thirds approval by the USSR Supreme Soviet and can impose temporary presidential rule. He can propose the dissolution of the USSR Supreme Soviet under certain circumstances and may issue binding decrees that do not require the approval of the Supreme Soviet. He also may veto legislation passed by the Supreme Soviet, but the Supreme Soviet may override his veto by a two-thirds vote.

The president has the power to nominate the chairman of the USSR Council of Ministers, the chairman of the USSR Supreme Court, the USSR procurator-general, the USSR chief state arbiter, and the chairman of the USSR People's Control Committee. All of these appointments are subject to confirmation by the legislature. He also can ask parliament to remove these officials from their positions (with the exception of the chairman of the Supreme Court).

The constitutional amendments created two new consultative bodies: the Council of the Federation (which is to oversee nationalities policy) and the sixteen-member Presidential Council (which is to advise the president on foreign, domestic, and security policy and formulate economic policy). Events in 1990 suggest that the Presidential Council has taken over many of the policy-making functions of the Politburo and Defense Council.

Although Gorbachev was elected by the Congress (on

Red Square, Moscow

March 15, 1990) for a five-year term, in the future the president will be elected by a direct vote of the people. The president "has the right of inviolability" and can only be removed by a two-thirds vote of the Congress in response to a violation of the USSR Constitution or laws.

USSR Council of Ministers

The USSR Council of Ministers is the governing body of the vast Soviet bureaucracy. It supervises ministries and state committees (such as Gosplan, the state economic planning agency). Before the 1989 reforms, the Council of Ministers had more than a hundred members, which made its operations unwieldy. The real business of the Council, therefore, was conducted through its approximately fifteen-member Presidium, or executive council, which met about once a week to deal with questions of the economy and state administration. The Council's work overlapped with that of the Central Committee Secretariat, but the Presidium handled questions just below the level of significance demanded for Politburo consideration. The Council often issued binding resolutions and decrees, usually related to economic activities. The most important of these frequently were issued jointly with the Central Committee.

In keeping with Gorbachev's plan to streamline the bureaucracy, the size of the Council of Ministers has been reduced to fewer than ninety positions (although it is difficult to determine whether any significant reduction in ministerial personnel has occurred). In 1990 the chairman of the Council of Ministers (premier or prime minister) was Nikolai Ryzhkov, who was appointed to the post shortly after Gorbachev came to power in 1985, replacing Nikolai Tikhonov. Under the current system, the prime minister is nominated by the president and confirmed by the Supreme Soviet. The other ministers, committee chairmen, and members of the presidium are nominated by the prime minister, subject to confirmation by the Supreme Soviet. Ryzhkov was reconfirmed by the newly formed legislature in the summer of 1989 after a rigorous confirmation hearing.

In the same manner that legislative organs are replicated at the republic level, so too are executive bodies. In addition to the "all-union" (national) ministries that are run from Moscow, each republic has its own ministries (known as "union-republic" ministries) and its own council of ministers. As the republics become more self-sufficient financially, their councils of ministers likely will operate more independently of Moscow than they have in the past.

Judicial Branch

The Soviet Union has a four-tier court system, consisting of the USSR Supreme Court, republican supreme courts, regional courts, and a broad network of "people's courts." The USSR Supreme Court is the highest judicial organ in the country, and it supervises the administration of justice by the courts of the USSR and republics. It also hears appeals from the republican supreme courts and can issue decrees that are binding on lower courts (although these are mostly of a technical legal nature). It does not rule on constitutional questions. The court system is managed by the Ministry of Justice.

The USSR Supreme Court has thirty-four judges. Some are elected by the USSR Supreme Soviet for ten-

Soviet Publications

Following are brief descriptions of some major Communist party and Soviet government publications.

Newspapers

Argumenti i Facti (Arguments and Facts)—Weekly newspaper noted for its objectivity and reliability; considered to be at the forefront of glasnost.

Izvestiia (News)—Daily organ of the USSR Supreme Soviet; emphasizes news about the government and current events; considered more liberal than *Pravda.*

Komsomolskaya Pravda (Communist Youth League Truth)—Six-day-a-week newspaper for younger readers; has provided progressive reporting on the reform movement.

Krasnaya Zvezda (Red Star)— Daily newspaper of the Ministry of Defense; useful for learning the views of the military establishment; considered to be very conservative.

Literaturnaya Gazeta (Literary Gazette)—Weekly newspaper of the Union of Writers; emphasizes literary and cultural reporting; has promoted public debate in its pages of various issues of glasnost and perestroika.

Moskovskie Novosti (Moscow News)—Daily Moscow newspaper; noted for its daring reporting that has stretched the limits of glasnost.

Pravda (Truth)—Daily newspaper of the Communist Party Central Committee; expresses party's views and focuses on party affairs and general news; often has backed moderately conservative position.

Sovetskaya Rossiya (Soviet Russia)—Daily Communist party newspaper for the Russian Republic; considered a leading voice for conservatives and Russian nationalists.

Magazines and Monthlies

Kommunist (Communist)—Most important monthly journal of ideology published by the Central Committee; moderate-liberal views.

Krokodil (Crocodile)—Weekly popular satirical magazine.

Mirovaya Ekonomika i Mezhdunarodnye Otnosheniia (MEMO, The World Economy and International Relations)—Monthly scholarly journal of IMEMO, the Institute for the World Economy and International Relations.

Molodaya Gvardia (Young Guard)—Monthly magazine of the Central Committee; includes film and play reviews; noted for strongly conservative outlook.

Novy Mir (New World) and *Oktyabr* (October)—the most important of numerous monthly literary reviews.

Ogonyok (Flame or Little Fire)—Popular weekly sociopolitical journal; edited by Vitalii Korotich; has become a leading critical voice against bureaucratism and stagnation; is a frequent target of conservative attacks.

S-Sh-A (USA)—Scholarly monthly journal of the Institute of the USA and Canada; serves as the main source of information for Soviet scholars about politics and society in North America.

---

year terms and some are the presidents of the republic supreme courts. The Supreme Court also includes forty-five people's assessors—ordinary citizens elected to serve as lay judges. The chairman of the USSR Supreme Court in 1990, Yevgenii Smolentsev, was confirmed by the Congress of People's Deputies in 1989, replacing Vladimir Teribilov.

The lowest-level people's courts handle 96 percent of all judicial activity in the USSR. They are presided over by a judge and two people's assessors. These courts hear civil and criminal cases, and they deliver decisions based on majority rule, although the lay judges rarely vote against the professional judge.

To make judges more independent, a judicial reform package was passed by the USSR Supreme Soviet in 1988 and 1989. This stipulated that people's judges and regional judges must be elected by the next highest-level soviet, presumably to remove the electoral process from the influence of local party manipulation. Republic-level judges still will be elected by the republican Supreme Soviets. The law also extended the terms for judges and people's assessors to ten and five years, respectively.

The procuracy is a ministerial-level organ with corresponding lower-level branches, constitutionally subordinate only to the USSR Supreme Soviet. It is headed by the the USSR procurator-general (in 1990, Aleksandr Sukharev).

The procuracy has several functions. First, it acts as the state prosecutor and investigator in civil and criminal cases with a simultaneous mandate to ensure that the accused's procedural rights are protected. Because a non-conviction often was considered a "failure" of the procuracy to investigate the case adequately, the rights of the accused often were violated and the courts have had a bias toward conviction. In 1989, a judicial reform law paved the way for more protection of the rights of the accused—by permitting defense lawyers to participate from the initial stages of the investigation and by introducing the use of jury trials in serious criminal cases. The procuracy's other functions are reviewing court decisions in civil and criminal cases and providing legal supervision to administrative and executive agencies.

The USSR Presidency

Council of the Federation

Composed of heads of the fifteen republics

Headed by president

Devises measures to implement national policy; ensures participation of republics in issues affecting them

President of the USSR

Chief executive and head of state

Beginning in 1995 will be elected by popular vote to a five-year term

Presidential Council

Sixteen members appointed by president

Headed by president

Makes domestic and foreign policy; ensures country's security

Communist Party of the Soviet Union

Party Congress

About five thousand delegates chosen by local party organizations

Meets about every five years

Elects Central Committee

Holds ultimate authority in party

Politburo

Twenty-four members, including general secretary, deputy general secretary, and the first secretaries of the fifteen republics

Members appointed by Central Committee

Meets about once a month; meetings chaired by general secretary

Makes party policy

Central Committee

About 250 members

Usually meets twice each year

Secretariat

Eleven secretaries

Appointed by Central Committee

Headed by general secretary

Central Committee Commissions

Each commission headed by a Central Committee secretary

Supervises work of Central Committee departments

Six commissions are: Party Development and Cadres Policy; Ideology; Socioeconomic Policy; Agriculture; Legal Policy; and International Policy

Central Committee Departments

Manages party apparatus and day-to-day party affairs

Nine departments are: Party Work and Cadres Policy; Ideology; Socioeconomic Policy; Agrarian; Defense; State and Legal Policy; International; General; Administration of Affairs

Soviet Legislative Apparatus

Chairman of the Supreme Soviet

Elected by Supreme Soviet

Heads Supreme Soviet and Presidium of the Supreme Soviet

Presidium of Supreme Soviet

Forty-three members

Elected by Supreme Soviet

Meets frequently

Serves as executive body of Supreme Soviet

Congress of People's Deputies (CPD)

2,250 deputies

Elected by popular vote to five-year terms

Meets twice a year

Holds supreme legislative authority; can overrule Supreme Soviet

Supreme Soviet

Includes two chambers—Council of Nationalities and Council of Union—of 271 deputies each

Elected by CPD

Holds two sessions per year of three to four months each

Each council has four standing committees, plus fifteen joint committees

USSR Council of Ministers

Prime Minister
(chairman of Council of Ministers)

Nominated by president and confirmed by Supreme Soviet

Heads Council of Ministers and Presidium of Council of Ministers

USSR Council of Ministers

Fifty-six ministers and chairmen of state committees

Nominated by prime minister and confirmed by Supreme Soviet

Presidium of Council of Ministers

Fifteen members

Nominated by prime minister and confirmed by Supreme Soviet

Meets frequently

Serves as executive body of Council of Ministers; manages economy on day-to-day basis

Party Structure

Before the recent reforms, political power in the USSR was concentrated in the Communist Party of the Soviet Union (CPSU). The party platform and USSR Constitution (Article 6) guaranteed the party's "leading role" in society. This permitted the party members who pervaded government organs, factories, universities, and nearly all other institutions in Soviet life to prevent the establishment of other parties and to fulfill the decrees of the party committees that paralleled and oversaw every state organ from the all-union (national) to the local level.

The most important instrument of party control was the *nomenklatura* system, whereby appointments to all important political and administrative positions had to be confirmed by Communist party committees. In this way, the party retained control over all social, political, economic, judicial, and cultural institutions.

Gorbachev's political reforms of 1988-1989 began the process of transferring political power away from the party and to the newly elected national legislature. The legitimacy of the Communist party steadily declined during this time. In February 1990, the Central Committee, under pressure to accept greater political pluralism in Soviet society, renounced the Communist party's monopoly of power. Since then, new party structures and organizations have been formed out of the many informal associations that had been developing within the party.

Politburo and Secretariat

The top decision-making organ of the CPSU is the Politburo (Political Bureau), headed by the CPSU general secretary. While theoretically chosen by the Central Committee (CC) to run the country between CC plenary meetings (plenums), in the past, the Politburo functioned as the real cabinet in the Soviet political system. Its members met weekly to decide all important policy and economic questions.

Since Gorbachev became general secretary in 1985, he has engineered important changes in the Politburo. In September 1988, he scored a victory over conservative rivals by retiring five Politburo members and by redistributing key portfolios to his allies. In September 1989 another major personnel change occurred when hard-liners Vladimir Shcherbitskii, Viktor Chebrikov, and Viktor Nikonov were retired (as well as two candidate, or nonvoting, members). At the Twenty-eighth Party Congress the membership of the Politburo was completely overhauled. None of its previous members was retained except for Gorbachev and Vladimir Ivashko, who was elected to the new post of deputy general secretary. The position of candidate member was eliminated. All top government officials were excluded, and all fifteen republican first secretaries were added to the Politburo's membership. Its membership thus was expanded from twelve to twenty-four.

An important appendage to the Politburo has been the Defense Council. The Defense Council, traditionally headed by the general secretary, decided major defense matters in a highly secretive manner. Only in the summer of 1989 did Gorbachev publicly state that (besides himself) it was made up of the ministers of defense and foreign affairs, the chairman of the USSR Council of Ministers, officials supervising defense industries, and top military commanders. In 1990, however, many or all of the functions of the Defense Council have been assumed by the Presidential Council.

Paralleling the Politburo is the CPSU Central Committee Secretariat. Whereas the Politburo has been the policy-making body of the party, the Secretariat has been the administrative or bureaucratic arm. There is some overlap between the memberships of the Politburo and Secretariat. Membership in both bodies has been considered a prerequisite for election as general secretary. Traditionally the Central Committee secretaries were full-time party officials who supervised the Secretariat's departments and sections. These departments and sections supervised every ministry and major nonministerial institution in the USSR. Each secretary was responsible for some large area of life, such as agriculture, ideology, culture, or science and education. In September 1988, Gorbachev vastly reduced the power of the Secretariat by abolishing its economic departments (thereby attempting to diminish party influence in economic matters) and by reorganizing the Secretariat into nine departments under the jurisdiction of six broad commissions. Previously, the Secretariat contained twenty-two departments.

Central Committee

The Central Committee is the body that is officially charged with directing the party's work between party congresses. It is elected at the party congresses and meets approximately every six months at special plenary sessions. Theoretically the Central Committee selects Secretariat members (including the general secretary) and the Politburo. Most Western scholars, however, believe that in reality it had little decision-making authority. Others, such as Jerry Hough of Duke University, have argued that it did have significant influence and that Politburo decisions usually reflect the consensus in the Central Committee. In the past, membership on the CC conferred considerable status on individuals; virtually all major officials in the party and state hierarchy were CC members.

The Central Committee, like the Secretariat and Politburo, has undergone substantial personnel changes during Gorbachev's tenure and also has diminished in influence. In a major cleanup of the Central Committee in April 1989, Gorbachev retired dozens of its most conservative members. These were the so-called dead souls—members who had lost or retired from the jobs that qualified them for CC membership. The Central Committee's membership was overhauled at the Twenty-eighth Party Congress.

Party Congress

The party's highest formal authority is the party congress. It is held about every five years at which time its approximately five thousand delegates elect the Central Committee, a Central Auditing Commission to oversee party finances, and a chairman of the Party Control Committee to oversee party morality and expulsions from membership. The delegates are elected at regional and or republic-level conferences. In the past the central party leadership closely supervised delegate selection, but before the Twenty-eighth Party Congress in July 1990, the process was made more democratic. However, the leadership rejected the demand by radicals that delegates be chosen in direct elections by the entire party membership.

Party congresses have not been decision-making forums. Usually they have been ceremonial occasions in which a "state of the party" address was delivered by the general secretary, followed by a report on the new five-year plan by the chairman of the Council of Ministers. Nevertheless, several party congresses have been significant turning points in Soviet history. The Twentieth Party Congress of 1956, for example, heard Nikita S. Khrushchev's famous "Secret Speech," which marked the beginning of de-Stalinization. The Twenty-seventh Party Congress held in February 1986 revised the party's platform and laid the foundation for a more active reform effort.

In the spirit of glasnost, the boistrous Twenty-eighth Party Congress, held July 2-14, 1990, broke with the tradition of passively endorsing the program of the general secretary. Gorbachev achieved most of what he sought at the Congress, but only with difficulty. He was not always able to maintain control of the meeting and on occasion scolded the delegates like errant children for violating the rules of order. At one point the delegates voted to subject Politburo members to a vote of confidence individually on their past performance. Gorbachev prevented the confidence votes only by taking the floor and explaining to the delegates that they had violated procedure. He then ordered the delegates to recast their votes, and this time the measure was defeated.

At the congress Gorbachev removed the party leadership from the business of making day-to-day policy for the Soviet Union. He kept his positions as general secretary and president, but all other top government leaders were excluded from the Politburo and secretariat. Thus the party will have far less control over the governing of the country.

The change in the structure of the Politburo fundamentally weakened it. For many years, non-Russians had complained bitterly about being underrepresented in the Politburo. Gorbachev proposed to the Congress that the first secretaries of the fifteen republics be added to the Politburo. Naturally, most non-Russian delegates heartily endorsed this idea. As a result the Politburo membership was expanded and the influence of the conservative Russians on the Politburo was diluted. Since the first secretaries do not live in Moscow, the Politburo will be able to meet no more than once a month, further weakening its policy role. In the past, the Politburo had met weekly, although in the first half of 1990, Gorbachev reportedly convened the Politburo only four times. Thus in a single move, Gorbachev weakened the party's policy-making role, limited the power of party conservatives, and placated the demands of the republics.

Some scholars have suggested that the party congress was the last gasp of party conservatives. They made a strong showing at the Congress, continuing their momentum from the Russian party congress in May, where conservatives had been elected to key posts. However, in the end, they had no alternative but to endorse Gorbachev's leadership and strategy. Yegor Ligachev's bid for deputy general secretary was rejected because of fears that he would split the party. Likewise, the conservatives endorsed Gorbachev as general secretary because they had no better option. No prominent conservative could have commanded the support of the party's center.

Other observers, including Boris Yeltsin and the leaders of the Democratic Platform bloc, maintain that the Congress was the party's last chance for reform, and it is now doomed to be swept aside by other forces in Soviet society. Many party members who were dissatisfied with the party were waiting for the congress to decide what to

Soviet Leaders, 1917-1990

Chairmen of the Presidium of the Supreme Soviet (Presidents)

Mikhail I. Kalinin	1923-1946
Nikolai M. Shvernik	1946-1953
Kliment E. Voroshilov	1953-1960
Leonid I. Brezhnev	1960-1964
Anastas I. Mikoian	1964-1965
Nikolai V. Podgornyi	1965-1977
Leonid I. Brezhnev	1977-1982
Yuri V. Andropov	1983-1984
Konstantin U. Chernenko	1984-1985
Andrei A. Gromyko	1985-1988
Mikhail S. Gorbachev	1988-1990[1]

President of the USSR

Mikhail S. Gorbachev	1990-

Chairmen of the Council of Ministers (Prime Ministers)

V. I. Lenin	1917-1924
Aleksei I. Rykov	1924-1930
Viacheslav M. Molotov	1930-1941
Joseph Stalin	1941-1953
Georgii M. Malenkov	1953-1955
Nikolai A. Bulganin	1955-1958
Nikita S. Khrushchev	1958-1964
Aleksei N. Kosygin	1964-1980
Nikolai A. Tikhonov	1980-1985
Nikolai I. Ryzhkov	1985-

Communist Party Heads

V. I. Lenin[2]	1917-1924
Joseph Stalin[2]	1922-1953
Nikita S. Khrushchev	1953-1964
Leonid I. Brezhnev	1964-1982
Yuri V. Andropov	1982-1984
Konstantin U. Chernenko	1984-1985
Mikhail S. Gorbachev	1985-

[1] In 1989 the office of chairman of the Presidium of the Supreme Soviet was strengthened and renamed "chairman of the Supreme Soviet." Gorbachev was elected to this new office and served until the Congress of People's Deputies created the executive presidency in March 1990. The office of chairman of the Supreme Soviet remained, but its executive and ceremonial functions were transferred to the executive presidency.

[2] As chairman of the Council of People's Commissars, Lenin was the de facto head of the party and the government; although Stalin was named general secretary of the party in 1922, he was unable to assert unquestioned control over the party until after Lenin's death in 1924.

do. Reformers had hoped that a restructured party might become a real force for change in Soviet society, but these hopes were dashed at the congress. A number of reformist leaders left the party with Yeltsin, including Vladimir Lysenko, Gavriil Popov, and Anatolii Sobchak. The trickle of people turning in their party cards could turn into a flood.

The party may be able to stumble on for the forseeable future, but it will be less involved in decisions made at the highest levels of the Soviet government. In addition, the party likely will continue to lose members as it loses prestige—even if no serious opposition party develops. According to official party statistics, membership in the CPSU (about nineteen million in 1988) has begun to shrink for the first time since 1954. During 1989 party membership declined by slightly more than 1 percent, and in the first half of 1990, 130,000 members resigned.

At the same time, the party has been splintering regionally. The Lithuanian Communist party seceded from the CPSU. This is significant because traditionally each union republic (except for the RSFSR) had its own party, presidium, secretariat, central committee, and party congress—but each republican communist party operated under the guidelines of democratic centralism and was subordinated to the CPSU. In 1989 Communists party members from the Russian republic began lobbying for some form of autonomous party organization. A founding congress of the RSFSR party was held in May 1990, and conservative Ivan Polozkov was chosen as first scretary. These events seem to signify a further breakup of the CPSU along national lines.

The Communist Youth League (Komsomol), the feeder organization for the CPSU, also has splintered regionally. In Lithuania, for example, the Komsomol has declared itself independent of the all-union organization while the Estonian Komsomol decided to replace itself with another youth organization. The all-union Komsomol was preserved at its twenty-first congress held in spring 1990, but the organization has lost much of its prestige, as students have begun to form alternative youth leagues and clubs.

Other Parties and Organizations

About fifty delegates representing the "Democratic Platform in the CPSU," walked out of the Twenty-eighth Party Congress and declared their intention to start an opposition party, headed by Boris Yeltsin. The Democratic Platform, a reform wing of the CPSU, held its founding congress in January 1990 and had developed its own platform for presentation at the Congress. A myriad of other political parties have formed since the CPSU abandoned its monopoly on power. Some analysts estimate that there are between two thousand and three thousand social and political groups in the Soviet Union. These include national popular fronts, Russian nationalist groups such as Pamiat, independent workers' movements, ecological groups, and parliamentary opposition groups.

Soviet domestic politics has included a network of social and other institutions to encourage citizen participation in public life. Like the ministries, soviets, and judicial organs, these have been under the party's control. They include cultural and professional institutions (such as the USSR Union of Writers, the USSR Union of Artists, and the USSR Union of Cinematographers) and scholarly institutions (such as the USSR Academy of Sciences).

The All-Union Central Council of Trade Unions (AUCCTU) has been an important mass organization, but workers have exhibited increasing restlessness with party and state tutelage over the past two years. The AUCCTU is a national organization overseeing subordinate unions organized by industry or profession. In July 1989, striking coal miners organized strike committees to negotiate with the USSR Council of Ministers on wage and labor conditions. In 1990, the miners, angered by the government's failure to follow through on its promises and disappointed with the AUCCTU, held a congress of their own trade union to declare independence from the official trade union. For its part, the AUCCTU has attempted to improve its tarnished image as the defender of working-class interests by moving forward its congress originally scheduled for 1992 to October 1990. It also replaced its chairman, Stepan Shalaev, with former deputy chairman Gennadii Yanaev in April 1990.

Reforming the Soviet System

Since coming to power in March 1985, Mikhail S. Gorbachev has taken dramatic steps toward the destruction of the totalitarian regime in the USSR. Under his leadership, the Soviet people have explored uncharted territory on their television screens, in their movie houses, and on their stages. The pervasive repression that once haunted Soviet streets is gone. The forces of political pluralism have been unleashed—in the first multi-candidate elections in more than seventy years, in the renunciation of the Communist party's monopoly on power, and in elections that transformed reformers and secessionists into officeholders. Steps, albeit tentative, have been taken toward a market economy. Soviet-American relations have turned from confrontation toward cooperation. The Soviet-bloc in Eastern Europe no longer exists, and the Warsaw Pact military alliance is disintegrating.

What prompted these changes? Did Gorbachev have a strategy from the time he became general secretary in 1985 or has his reform program been a response to changing domestic and international conditions? Do these changes constitute a revolution, if only from above? This chapter examines these questions and traces the development of reforms from Gorbachev's ascension to power in 1985. It also reviews the major threats to the reform movement.

Impetus for Reform

During the last years of the regime of Leonid I. Brezhnev, the defects of the political and economic system that had endured since the rule of Joseph Stalin had become painfully obvious to many top Soviet leaders. Socially, culturally, economically, and even politically, the Soviet Union was stagnating. As former U.S. national security adviser Zbigniew Brzezinski states in his 1989 book, *The Grand Failure: The Birth and Death of Communism in the Twentieth Century*, "though it started as a modernizing regime, attempting to introduce rationality into [Nikita S.] Khrushchev's tempestuous reforms, the Brezhnev regime before too long became tantamount to a quasi-Stalinist restoration."

There were numerous signs of stagnation. First, the impressive growth rates achieved by the Soviet economy during the 1950s and 1960s had dwindled by the late 1970s. In addition, the Soviet Union was lagging far behind the West in scientific-technological development. This was particularly worrisome to the Soviet military command, which realized that military strength in the 1980s would depend on acquiring and adapting the latest technological innovations.

Second, the Stalinist economic system was wasteful and inefficient. As Ed Hewett points out in *Reforming the Soviet Economy*, enterprises had a "hunger" for all inputs—both labor and material—with no incentives to economize. The system had a bias toward imbalances and chronic shortages because the transportation infrastructure was often unreliable. The large central planning bureaucracy also made coordinating supplies and deliveries difficult. This inefficiency contributed to falling growth rates and hampered the Soviet leadership's efforts to allocate resources effectively. Moreover, labor productivity was low. Soviet workers had little incentive to work hard because job security was guaranteed and high-quality performance at work did not bring higher wages. The problem of low labor productivity was compounded by absenteeism and the epidemic of alcoholism in the country.

Third, social conditions and living standards were more like those of a Third World country than those of an industrial superpower, particularly in the rural regions of the Soviet Union. A large percentage of Soviet hospitals had no running water, lacked basic sanitation, and relied on equipment that dated back to World War II. Male life expectancy had declined from sixty-six years to sixty-two years during the Brezhnev era, while the infant mortality rate had increased to almost twice the rate in the United States.

Agriculture (traditionally the bane of the Soviet economy) had failed to improve during the 1970s despite massive investment. Approximately 25 percent of overall food production spoiled before it reached the market because of improper storage and transportation. Private plots that made up only 2 percent of Soviet arable land produced almost 30 percent of Soviet food. Collectivized agriculture, like Soviet industry, was an inefficient and uncoordinated giant. Finally, real per capita consumption, perhaps the best measure of living standards, had steadily declined during the early 1980s, and regional inequalities in goods and services had exacerbated national and ethnic tensions.

Fourth, the USSR's foreign economic relations were problematic. The Soviet economy produced low-quality goods that did not meet world standards. Consequently, the Soviet Union could earn the hard currency needed to trade for food and technology only by exporting raw materials and natural resources. Its inconvertible ruble hindered its participation in the world economy, and the subsidies it provided to its Eastern European allies were a huge drain on its budget.

Fifth, the Soviet population in the early 1980s had become more educated, politically sophisticated, and internationally aware than ever before. It was thus more impatient for economic and social advancement. A "civil society," with all its differing interests and concerns, was developing. In addition, Soviet tourism to Eastern Europe had increased in the 1970s, and the Soviet people observed living standards there that were far better than their own. Televisions and radios conveyed information from abroad that weakened the myth that life in the Soviet Union was better than anywhere else. The rise in popular dissent in the mid-1960s was one indication that people were less inclined to believe the standard ideological fare about the superiority of Soviet socialism.

Finally, the Brezhnevite stagnation encompassed more than economic and social conditions. It was a political problem as well. Under Brezhnev's policy of "respect for cadres" (personnel), party and government figures had become intertwined in a web of personal corruption. In return for unswerving loyalty, Brezhnev had adopted a hands-off policy in the republics and localities. As a result, local political elites wielded unchallenged power. This contributed to rising doubts in Soviet society about the efficacy of socialist leadership, and ultimately, of socialism itself.

Gorbachev came to power in March 1985, not as a radical reformer but as a leader with a mandate from his Politburo colleagues to get the country moving again. He had been promoted by former general secretary Yuri V. Andropov and, after Konstantin U. Chernenko's death, seemed to be the figure most likely to continue Andropov's disciplinarian-style reforms. As political scientist Timothy J. Colton suggests in *The Dilemma of Reform in the Soviet Union*, Gorbachev spoke animatedly of the imperative of economic modernization and for social and economic reinvigoration through more efficient organization and greater discipline.

Gorbachev also was much younger than his competitors in the succession struggle. Presumably both his youthful vigor and proven record in economic and party organizational work had set him apart from the others. As former *New York Times* correspondent Hedrick Smith noted in a 1990 television documentary, Gorbachev was a "child of the Twentieth Party Congress." Born in 1931, he had become a leader in the Komsomol (Communist Youth League) and had begun party work during the era of de-Stalinization launched at the 1956 Twentieth Party Congress by Khrushchev. Gorbachev represented a clean break from the generation of Leonid Brezhnev—a generation that had been shackled by traditional thinking. Gorbachev's approach to internal politics was different from Brezhnev's consensus-building strategy. Colton notes in a 1988 essay that Gorbachev replaced 64 percent of the Council of Ministers, 38 percent of the Politburo, 76 percent of the Central Committee, and 39 percent of the regional first party secretaries during his first two years in office. In this respect, he resembled Khrushchev in his willingness to inject a measure of conflict into elite politics. He also adopted Khrushchev's populist approach by appealing directly to the people in an effort to build advance support for his reforms. Unlike Khrushchev, however, Gorbachev encour-

aged others to take extremist positions while he himself remained squarely in the center. Finally, he was much more skillful than any of his predecessors in using the media to popularize his policies.

Gorbachev's Reforms

With a mandate for change, a knack for flexibility, and a large measure of political savvy, Gorbachev gradually launched his reforms, which have transformed the Soviet Union and Eastern Europe. His reforms, however, have not been a carefully scripted program. Instead, they have been a continual process of adapting to changes at home and abroad. As such, the fundamental concepts of his reform effort have evolved.

Perestroika

Perestroika, or "restructuring," is actually the umbrella concept for Gorbachev's entire reform program, meaning the decentralization of political and economic decision making, increased openness, modernization based on technological restructuring, and a new foreign policy that emphasizes international interdependence. This word, however, is used most often in reference to the restructuring of the Soviet economy.

Perestroika has assumed many forms during Gorbachev's first five years in office. When the concept first was introduced at the April 1985 Central Committee plenum, Gorbachev spoke mainly about economic improvements. Using phraseology employed by Andropov, Gorbachev talked in broad, general terms about "basic restructuring" of the economy and "perfection of the economic mechanism." His watchword was "acceleration" (*uskorenie*) of social and economic development, which would be accomplished in the long run by technological modernization. In the short run, he called for an "activization of the human factor," which meant a return to Andropov's emphasis on tightening labor, technological, and state discipline.

The policies adopted during Gorbachev's first year reflected this limited definition of perestroika. Gorbachev initiated an anti-alcohol campaign to reduce absenteeism and poor job performance. His draft five-year economic plan for 1986-1990 increased targeted rates of GNP growth to an ambitious 3.5 percent per year. Targets for machine-building and metal working industries also were overly optimistic. Furthermore, Gorbachev continued the limited restructuring experiments begun by Andropov by increasing the local decision-making powers of individual enterprises. He also tried to streamline administrative planning by creating "super-ministries," notably in the agricultural sector.

This early gradualist approach can be attributed in part to sharp differences in the party and government elite about the best way to modernize the economy. Gorbachev's careful beginning also could have been due to the hope of the leadership (including Gorbachev) that the economy was suffering primarily from the mismanagement and corruption of the Brezhnev years. If this were true, they reasoned, a little "fine-tuning" might be all that was needed to jump-start the economy. In 1985, most of the political elite still had faith in the basic institutions of Soviet economic and political life. Finally, even if Gorbachev had wanted to

Soviets Reassess Marxism-Leninism

In the Soviet Union, Marxist-Leninist ideology has been treated as an all-embracing, universally applicable social and economic theory based on objective laws. For decades this ideology was the intellectual basis for the Communist party's program. In launching his reforms, Mikhail S. Gorbachev did not repudiate Marxism-Leninism, but he de-emphasized the influence of ideology in policy making and he allowed the press and the public to debate previously sacrosanct ideological and historical topics, including the role of V. I. Lenin. Because Marxist-Leninist ideology was the cornerstone of the Soviet political and economic system and the justification of the power of the Communist party, these debates have called into question the foundations of Soviet socialism.

In the early stages of his political reform, Gorbachev attempted to use "historical glasnost" to reinterpret socialism and restore its legitimacy among the people. New historical interpretations by scholars and the party portrayed Lenin as an idealistic politician, whose altruistic intentions and institutions had been distorted by Joseph Stalin. Evaluations of Lenin focused on his liberal New Economic Policy and the "Last Testament" (the letters he wrote to the party leadership shortly before his death that warned about Stalin's character).

In 1988, however, scholars began to suggest that the deformations of socialism wrought by Stalin actually had their roots in Lenin's own ideas. In May 1988, for example, economic journalist Vasilii Selyunin stated in *Novy Mir* that Stalin's economic policies were a return to Lenin's repressive program of "War Communism." This was the first time that the Soviet media had directly linked Lenin and the Stalinist terror. A two-part article in *Pravda* later that year took this debate even further. In it, two scholars from the Central Committee's Institute of Marxism-Leninism inferred that Stalin's administrative-command economic system had its roots in Lenin's ideas about socialism. In 1989, another taboo was broken. Aleksandr Tsipko of the Institute of the Economics of the World Socialist System argued that the roots of Stalinism could be found in Marx's writings.

Perhaps the most significant reassessment of the ideological and historical underpinnings of the Soviet state began in 1989 with the publication of Alexander Solzhenitsyn's book *The Gulag Archipelago* in *Novy Mir*. In his book, Solzhenitsyn openly condemned Lenin, the October Revolution, and the first Soviet political police, the Cheka. Some members of the Soviet leadership tried to block the publication of *The Gulag Archipelago*; failing that, they sponsored a rebuttal to Solzhenitsyn that was published in *Literaturnaya Gazeta* in January 1990.

In May 1990, the Institute of Marxism-Leninism dealt another blow to Lenin's image by verifying the authenticity of a letter written by Lenin to the Politburo in 1922. In the letter, Lenin instructed the Politburo to confiscate the property of religious groups "with the most furious and ruthless energy" to build up the Red Army. This revelation undercut the traditional Soviet line that Stalin had begun the repression of religion.

This "dismantling" of Lenin has had several repercussions. First, it has weakened the Communist party's claim of being the ideological stewards of Soviet society. For decades, the legitimacy of the party rested on its connections with Lenin and Marxist-Leninist ideology.

Second, the issue of Lenin has contributed to the polarization of the party. Some party members still vigorously defend Lenin's heritage—as Central Committee secretary Ivan Frolov did in March 1990 when he called for reformer Yuri Afanaseyev's resignation from the party after his critical remarks about Lenin. (Afanaseyev subsequently did resign.) Others have completely abandoned Lenin's precepts and policies. The Politburo has taken to equivocating. In its endorsement of the Central Committee theses in celebration of Lenin's birthday in April 1990, the Politburo stated that mistakes will be made if people think they can learn nothing from Lenin; on the other hand, it also is a mistake to presume that everything can be explained with reference to Lenin.

Third, the reassessment of Lenin has become a quandary for history teachers. In 1988, the USSR State Committee for Public Education canceled its once-mandatory graduation examination on the country's history for secondary schools. In late 1989, after much debate and revision, a new history textbook was published. The textbook strongly condemns Stalin's collectivization and purges and hails the October Revolution as a great event in the history of the country. It takes a more cautious view of Lenin, criticizing the period of War Communism but stressing that Lenin was forced into adopting the policy and tried to prevent unjust repression.

But in February 1990, the same committee abolished the mandatory state examination in Marxism-Leninism. Henceforth every higher-education institution will have the right to replace its courses in Marxism-Leninism with courses in twentieth-century sociopolitical history, the theory of modern socialism, philosophy, or political economy. Moreover, a recently published Soviet philosophy textbook for use in university-level courses stated that Marxism did not have the answer to all questions. *Pravda* praised this approach. Marxist-Leninist ideology has ceased to be the official source of wisdom in the Soviet Union. Like the Communist party, it now must compete for influence.

initiate dramatic reforms when he entered office, he first needed to weed out holdovers from the Brezhnev era. By the end of 1985 he had engineered the removal of several top conservatives, including Leningrad party chief Grigorii Romanov, Moscow party chief Viktor Grishin, and Premier Nikolai Tikhonov.

The Twenty-seventh Party Congress in February 1986 was a watershed event in the refinement of the meaning of perestroika. Gorbachev for the first time talked about perestroika with reference to far-reaching institutional changes in the economy. In contrast to his earlier optimism about the economy's ability to modernize itself, he called for a "radical reform." He stressed that the perfection of economic management procedures alone would not be enough to turn the economy around. He spoke approvingly of Lenin's New Economic Policy (NEP) and talked about revitalizing the "political economy" and creating new conceptions of property. From this point on, he referred to perestroika as a "revolutionary" change, implying that he would go beyond Andropov's disciplinarian emphasis and even Khrushchev's reorganization and decentralization of the economic planning apparatus.

At the same time, he acknowledged the political obstacles to economic change, alluding to "functionaries" in the party and state bureaucracies who were resisting change. At the party congress, Gorbachev replaced 41 percent of the full (voting) members of the Central Committee—not as many as he had wanted, but still a significant turnover.

The Twenty-seventh Party Congress therefore opened the way for reformers to challenge long-held assumptions about Soviet socialism. Emboldened by Gorbachev's words, the radicals went to work during late 1986 and early 1987 to give shape to Gorbachev's broad parameters for change.

The culmination of many months of debate and negotiation was the June 1987 Central Committee plenum on the economy. There Gorbachev laid out his plan to decentralize the economy and to experiment with limited market forces. He spoke in favor of legalizing small-scale private and cooperative businesses, and he stated that enterprises must become self-financing. Since then, the perestroika debate has continued in a lively manner, as other central tenets of socialism have been challenged (such as bans on private property and income equality). But the primary questions remain the same: How fast and how far should the Soviet economy decentralize? What constitutes a "socialist market economy"? How can "social justice" for the worker be guaranteed while introducing much-needed economic competition? And perhaps most important, does the repudiation of the administrative-command system represent a return to Leninism and NEP, a new form of socialism, or a departure from socialism altogether?

Glasnost

Glasnost, or "openness," stems from the old Russian word *glas*, meaning "voice" or "vote." Sovietologist Jerry Hough interprets glasnost in his 1988 book, *Russia and the West: Gorbachev and the Politics of Reform*, as a call for a more open society that does not necessarily advocate an undercutting of the authority of the leadership. In his book *Perestroika*, Gorbachev states that the functions of glasnost are twofold: to facilitate an open search for truth and to ensure the accountability of the government to the people.

Gorbachev introduced this concept into the political discourse in early 1985. He maintained that glasnost was inextricably linked with perestroika because economic reforms would not work unless they were supported by broad public participation and enthusiasm. As Gorbachev had noted, public apathy was widespread; a sense of inertia pervaded most economic and social institutions. At the same time, the power of the corrupt and intransigent bureaucracy to block or stall significant changes would have to be broken. Glasnost, by allowing public and media pressure to focus on corruption, inefficiency, and elite privileges, was to serve as the means to overcome the entrenched bureaucracy.

The concept of glasnost has changed in tandem with changes in the meaning of perestroika. In early 1985, when Gorbachev's emphasis was on routing corruption and fostering discipline, glasnost focused mainly on exposing abuses in the state bureaucracy and wastefulness in the economic sector. The glasnost campaign reinforced Gorbachev's emphasis on establishing accountability in government and encouraging individuals to evaluate and criticize their leaders. Televised call-in shows, for example, encouraged public oversight of ministry bureaucrats, while the press was instructed to publish letters from the public condemning abuses of power by officials. Also, glasnost was intended to stimulate public interest in the economy and society—thus encouraging people to work harder and more efficiently.

The Chernobyl nuclear disaster in April 1986 marked a turning point in the glasnost campaign because it illustrated to the Soviet leadership why freer information was important. Defects in the reactor had been allowed to exist without the knowledge of higher-level officials, and the government's tight control on information about the disaster brought severe international condemnation and domestic apprehension. More important, after Chernobyl, Soviet writers began to link the disaster with overall shortcomings in the Soviet economic system. Sweeping historical questions still were off limits, but the scope of discussion broadened to include some critical reappraisal of the past.

By this time, Gorbachev had buttressed his authority among the political elite with his sweeping personnel changes. He realized, however, that he needed additional allies for his reform program, particularly among the intelligentsia. In 1986 Gorbachev moved to take over the leadership of most cultural institutions, including the all-union film maker's union and such publications as *Literaturnaya Gazeta* and *Sovetskaya Kultura*. In January 1987, he named fellow reformer Aleksandr Yakovlev a candidate member of the Politburo and soon afterward gave him responsibility for the social sciences, culture, and the media. In the following year, taboos on what could be discussed in the media disappeared one after another. By early 1989 it was becoming easier to define what was unacceptable under glasnost than what was acceptable.

Concurrently, glasnost was used to accomplish a much deeper de-Stalinization than Khrushchev had ever attempted. In 1986, public discussion began to open up about the defects of Stalin's personality, and by 1988, most Stalinist institutions were under full scrutiny. Gorbachev encouraged the full-scale discrediting of the old system to make room for the new. Although in 1988 and 1989 certain topics were still off limits, such as the meaning of the Bolshevik Revolution and the person of Lenin, by 1990 even those taboos had been broken.

Finally, Gorbachev was counting on glasnost to stimulate public initiative that would advance economic and societal reforms. He hoped people would become more

Reforming the KGB

The Committee for State Security (KGB) long has been associated with repression in the Soviet Union. The Soviet political police (known as the KGB only since 1954) has "protected" the Soviet state against political subversion for more than seventy years. In reality, its main function has been to keep the Soviet regime in power. It has engaged in a variety of activities besides providing intelligence, including border security, political surveillance of the armed forces, and suppression of political dissent.

During Mikhail S. Gorbachev's tenure, the KGB has undergone reform, but these changes reflect an uneasy tension between Gorbachev's need for the KGB as an ally and his professed commitment to build a "socialist law-governed state."

During his first year and a half as general secretary, Gorbachev allowed the KGB to retain the high political status it held during the Brezhnev era. Amy Knight asserts in *The KGB: Police and Politics in the Soviet Union* that in April 1985 Gorbachev appealed to the KGB for help in purging Brezhnev holdovers in the leadership and promoted KGB chief Viktor Chebrikov to full membership on the Politburo. Gorbachev left the existing KGB apparatus relatively intact, directing it to root out corruption in the party and state bureaucracies.

In early 1987, the "Berkhin affair" changed party-KGB relations. KGB officials in the Ukraine had ordered the illegal arrest of journalist Viktor Berkhin, who had been investigating local party corruption. He later died as a result of his arrest. Up to that point, muckraking press accounts had never discussed the KGB, but after the Berkhin affair the Communist party leadership refused to shield the KGB from public criticism. The press began attacking KGB violations of the law and over-zealous protection of secrets. At the Nineteenth Party Conference in June-July 1988, Gorbachev pointedly stated that no aspect of Soviet political life could remain untouched by perestroika and stressed that this applied particularly to the Ministries of Defense and Foreign Affairs and to the KGB.

Another indication that Gorbachev intended to curb KGB powers was the sharp curtailment of the campaign against political dissent in 1987 and 1988. According to Knight, in 1987, more than three hundred political prisoners were released from prisons and camps and sixty-four were released from psychiatric hospitals. Arrests for political crimes virtually ceased, even though arrests of dissidents for lesser violations, such as hooliganism, have continued. One example of this type of arrest was that of journalist Sergei Kuznetsov in late 1989 for slandering local police and resisting arrest. He was freed in January 1990.

In response to this policy shift, the KGB mounted a public relations campaign to humanize its image and portray itself as a champion of glasnost. In 1988, the KGB established a regular column in the newspaper *Argumenti i Facti*, and *Pravda* published an unprecedented front-page interview with Chebrikov. The KGB also has stated its intention to ease its secrecy regulations.

In 1988 the KGB underwent extensive personnel changes in its leadership. The most important was Chebrikov's replacement as head of the KGB by Col. Gen. Vladimir Kryuchkov in September 1988. Chebrikov finally was removed from the Politburo in late 1989. As a consequence of ethnic disturbances or exposures of corruption in the republics, at least seven of the fourteen republic KGB chairmen were replaced between 1988 and 1989.

In 1989 the KGB reorganized the structure of its domestic services. The KGB's Fifth Administration—set up in 1967 to suppress ideological dissidence—was transformed into the Administration for Safeguarding the Constitution. An Administration for Combating Crime has been created, and some 80 percent of the KGB apparatus is now said to be engaged in fighting crime. However, the Fifth Administration has not been reduced in size, and the redirection of the KGB domestically toward safeguarding the constitution and counterintelligence in the economic sphere leaves much leeway for interpretation by local KGB officials.

Regarding international operations, Kryuchkov has stressed the KGB's willingness to cooperate with other foreign secret services in combating terrorism, drug trafficking, and smuggling. At the same time, the counterintelligence services of major Western countries have reported a growth in KGB activities abroad during 1989, particularly in industrial espionage. Indeed, Kryuchkov has stated that foreign intelligence was the most profitable enterprise in the USSR. In early 1990, the head of the KGB's foreign intelligence service, Leonid Shebarshin, stated that information-gathering efforts abroad would be indispensable in helping the USSR overcome its economic crisis.

Perhaps the most important development concerning the KGB is that it has been subjected to legislative oversight. The new Committee for Defense and State Security of the USSR Supreme Soviet hears reports from KGB department heads, and Kryuchkov is required to report annually to the committee (although some have charged that the committee is dominated by military, defense industry, and KGB personnel). Moreover, in 1990 the Supreme Soviet was considering long-awaited legislation on the KGB that would make it accountable to the legislature, the president, and the Council of Ministers.

involved in political and civic activities, thereby accepting responsibility for improving the life of the nation. This strategy, however, posed the Soviet leadership with the problem of determining how much political participation was desirable because a rising tide of political activism could threaten the Communist party's monopoly on power.

Demokratizatsia

By January 1987, it was clear that perestroika faced serious opposition from the bureaucracy. Although Gorbachev had carried out purges in many key party and government institutions and had promoted many of his supporters, the strongest resistance to his reforms was rising from the lower levels of the bureaucracies. Glasnost in the newspapers and freer cultural expression were not capable of removing the "dead wood" from the system. Moreover, public support for perestroika centered more on exposing the ills of the previous system than on creating a new one.

To address these problems, Gorbachev initiated a far-reaching political reform called *demokratizatsia* (democratization). In an important speech at the January 1987 Central Committee plenum, Gorbachev directly linked political reform with economic reform. "The business of restructuring," he stated, "has turned out to be more difficult ... than we had imagined earlier." Party leaders had become immune to public criticism and had participated in the widespread corruption pervading Soviet society. Hence, Gorbachev argued, a "profound democratization" of the political system was needed so that people could once again take charge of their own destinies.

To accomplish this, he proposed sweeping electoral reforms whereby members of all soviets (elected councils ranging from the local to the all-union level) would be elected on multi-candidate ballots. He assured the Central Committee that democratization would activate latent social energies and stimulate public interest in perestroika. As freely elected bodies, the soviets would return to their rightful places as the instruments of the people's power. Gorbachev also proposed that multi-candidate elections be extended to party positions as well, including the first secretaries of the republican central committees. The latter idea was extremely controversial and was not approved by the plenum.

Gorbachev developed the specifics of his political reform at the specially convened Nineteenth Party Conference in June-July 1988 (the first party conference in nearly fifty years). In his opening speech to the conference delegates, Gorbachev stated that during the Brezhnev years ministries and departments had begun to dictate their will in the economy and in politics. It was exceptionally important, he argued, to create a uniform system of public and state control subordinate to elected bodies. Furthermore, Gorbachev observed that the party's role had grown through the years to include economic management and administration, and this had hindered it from fulfilling its vanguard role in society.

Gorbachev's solution was to separate the functions of the party and the state. The party would return to its Leninist origins and be freed from its economic-administrative duties. It would concentrate instead on key areas of domestic and foreign policy.

On the national level, Gorbachev advocated the resurrection of a full-time working parliament to replace the rubber-stamp body of the past. Specifically, Gorbachev proposed the creation of an entirely new legislative body: a 2,250-member Congress of People's Deputies (CPD), which would elect a much smaller, full-time Supreme Soviet. Elections to these bodies would make high-level party and state officials more accountable to the people, and those officials who did not win in the elections would have to, according to Gorbachev, "draw the appropriate conclusions" (step down from their positions). At the conference, Gorbachev also proposed the creation of a powerful new post—the chairman of the Supreme Soviet. This new chairman would assume many of the duties that had been reserved for the Communist party general secretary since the Brezhnev era. Gorbachev's plan for multi-candidate elections extended below the national level. As he stated, the soviets should be rejuvenated "from the bottom to the top."

Another of Gorbachev's themes at the conference was the need to develop a "socialist law-governed state." Too often, he argued, laws were arbitrarily ignored by officials. Ministerial departments and party agencies were accustomed to changing, repealing, and suspending legislation at will. The restoration of the legitimate organs of people's rule—the soviets—was to be accompanied by a new respect for legislation.

Although these proposals represented the most radical political reforms in the Soviet Union since the revolution, they were not intended to undermine party influence in policy making. Instead, they were designed to improve and streamline the policy-making process. How could this be done? First, the elections could weed out the opponents of perestroika. Second, by subjecting party officials to competitive processes, the party could gain an added measure of legitimacy before the people. Third, the newly elected legislators could become a sounding board for the rising tensions in the USSR by debating public issues. Fourth, by separating party and state functions, the policy-making process could become more effective and less cumbersome.

But Gorbachev was adamant about retaining the party's "leading role" in Soviet political life while transferring "all power" to the soviets. He recommended, therefore, that the first secretaries of the appropriate party committees run for the posts of chairmen of the soviets. According to him, this would raise the prestige of the soviets by investing them with the authority of the party. At the same time it would increase the public's control over the party secretaries. Gorbachev probably in part made this suggestion so that he could run for the chairmanship of the Supreme Soviet while remaining general secretary.

Throughout 1988 and 1989, these resolutions and principles were put into action. Gorbachev streamlined the top party structure in September-October 1988. He reorganized the twenty-two Central Committee Secretariat departments into nine departments under the jurisdiction of six commissions—presumably to reduce their involvement in day-to-day affairs. He also eliminated party economic departments on all levels to remove the party from economic decision making. Also in 1988, he retired conservative Politburo members Andrei Gromyko and Mikhail Solomentsev, among others, and reassigned Committee for State Security (KGB) chief Viktor Chebrikov and "second secretary" Yegor Ligachev to less powerful positions as the heads of the Secretariat's legal and agricultural commissions, respectively. The Central Committee apparatus (bureaucracy) was trimmed, and the apparatus at the regional and republican levels was reduced by about 30 percent. Perhaps most significant, in 1988 Gorbachev also assumed

Aleksandr Yakovlev (left), a member of the Politburo and close confidant of Mikhail S. Gorbachev, speaks with academician Svyatoslav Fyodorov at the Second Congress of People's Deputies, December 13, 1989.

Gromyko's position as chairman of the Supreme Soviet Presidium, or de facto head of state, a move that indicated a more complete consolidation of power by the general secretary.

The March 1989 elections to the new Congress of People's Deputies were a turning point in the development of demokratizatsia, although an unexpected one. Communist party members won 87.6 percent of the seats in the CPD. After the elections, Gorbachev skillfully used defeats of Communist party candidates to weed out a number of conservative party officials from the Central Committee and lower-level party organizations. The composition of both the CPD and Supreme Soviet made both bodies relatively pliable for Gorbachev, and he had been elected by an overwhelming margin to the new powerful post of Supreme Soviet chairman. But the elections nevertheless were disturbing for the party, which had expected to dominate the voting. Party officials at all levels had suffered surprising defeats, despite evidence of electoral rigging during both the nomination process and the elections. Gorbachev himself acknowledged in July 1989 that public dissatisfaction was expressed in the defeat of a number of party and state officials who sought seats as people's deputies.

In late 1989, moreover, turnover in lower-level party personnel began to accelerate as a result of grass-roots discontent. Resignations by and dismissals of first secretaries of regional party committees occurred frequently throughout 1989 and into early 1990. In addition, the Bolshevik slogan "all powers to the soviets" assumed new meaning on the national level. The newly elected CPD actively debated the most serious issues of Soviet life in televised sessions, while Soviet citizens, mesmerized, watched members challenge even Gorbachev. In addition, the Supreme Soviet demonstrated its independence in numerous ways. It rejected nine out of seventy-one ministerial nominees in the first real confirmation hearings ever held in the Soviet Union. In October 1989, it blocked emergency legislation proposed by the USSR Council of Ministers that would ban strikes for more than a year. In that same month, the Supreme Soviet voted to abolish the reservation of 750 seats in the CPD for public organizations such as the Communist party. Perhaps most significant, during the fall sessions of the Supreme Soviet and the CPD, the new Inter-regional Group of Deputies (a group of about two hundred reformers in the parliament) called for debates on revoking Article 6 of the USSR Constitution (which guarantees the Communist party's leading role in society).

As 1989 progressed, public opinion polls revealed the sinking prestige of the Communist party. Other events indicated a comparative rise in the influence of the national legislature. Striking coal miners in Vorkuta, for example, declared in the summer that their faith in the Communist party, government ministries, and trade unions was gone; instead they were relying on the Supreme Soviet for assurances on government promises.

Until 1990, Gorbachev continued to insist on the party's indispensable "unifying and inspirational role" in Soviet political life. By January of that year, however, it appeared that his personal position as head of both party and state was in danger. The CPD could remove him as chairman of the Supreme Soviet, and the Central Committee likewise could remove him as general secretary (or, it could force his resignation as Supreme Soviet chairman by recalling him as a representative of the Communist party in the Congress).

In February 1990, Gorbachev made two significant changes: He persuaded the Central Committee to revoke Article 6 of the USSR Constitution guaranteeing the Communist party's leading role in society, and he pushed through a proposal for an executive presidency. The proposal granted to the president many of the powers that had been vested in the Supreme Soviet Presidium—the powers to declare martial law and issue binding decrees, for example. It also granted the president new powers, including the power to request the parliament to dismiss the Council of Ministers and the USSR procurator-general (the highest-ranking state prosecutor)—and under certain circumstances, the right to ask the CPD to call new elections to the Supreme Soviet. In addition, new consultative bodies were to be created. The Council of the Federation was to oversee nationalities policy, and the Presidential Council was to serve as the president's personal "cabinet."

These changes went beyond Gorbachev's early conception of demokratizatsia in several ways. First, they represented the final acknowledgment of a complete separation between the party and the state. The way was clear for a multi-party political system and, with it, genuine parliamentary factions. Second, they represented a tentative move toward a Western-style separation of powers among the executive, judicial, and legislative branches. In December 1989, for example, the CPD passed legislation to create a quasi-independent constitutional court, the Committee for Constitutional Oversight, to rule on the constitutionality of legislation. The executive presidency now has the right to veto Supreme Soviet legislation, but the Supreme Soviet may override his veto. Third, they exhibited an openness to experimenting with other countries' democratic practices. Whereas Soviet ideologists traditionally had condemned Western democracies, now leading Soviet theoreticians were calling for democratic features of foreign governments to be incorporated into the Soviet system. And finally, the 1990 constitutional amendments provided for a popular election of the head of state. Gorbachev was elected by the CPD as president in 1990 for a five-year term, but beginning in 1995 the president would be elected directly by the people. Although the new office of president has many unchecked powers and judicial reform is proceeding slowly, the changes initiated under demokratizatsia do represent significant, if incomplete, moves toward democracy.

New Thinking

Gorbachev introduced "new thinking" (*novoe myshlenie*) in foreign and military policy in 1987 and 1988. This policy rejects the notion that peaceful coexistence was only a breathing spell in the competition between the socialist and capitalist camps, urges the abandonment of exporting revolution, and de-emphasizes the military threat to the Soviet Union from the West. It also seeks to make the USSR a participant in the economic and political affairs of the world community.

Gorbachev believed new thinking, like glasnost, was necessary for perestroika to be successful. While glasnost was required to create an energetic, critical, and motivated domestic population, new thinking was needed to promote a long-term period of peace in foreign policy. This would allow the Soviet Union to redirect spending from military to consumer purposes. It also would permit the USSR to gain entrance into international financial institutions and to be eligible for foreign loans. Finally, it would allow the country to obtain needed technology from the West to boost its sagging economy.

The foundation of new thinking is a redefinition of the concept of national security. This new definition maintains that military power alone is insufficient to guarantee security. In this light, Gorbachev introduced the doctrine of "reasonable sufficiency" at the Twenty-seventh Party Congress in February 1986. This doctrine called for the USSR to avoid matching every U.S. military program. Instead, tough procurement decisions would be made concerning what was absolutely necessary for national security, and offensive military doctrine would be rejected in favor of less expensive and less threatening defensive weapons and tactics. This reorientation was motivated by cost considerations as well as by the realization that offensive doctrine was counterproductive because it pushed opposing nations into defensive alliances and caused them to conduct their own military buildups.

In addition, new thinking emphasizes the existence of common human interests in a complex, interconnected world. It abandons the old antagonism between opposing systems based on class interests and, in its place, suggests that mutual security is in the best interest of all mankind. It presumes that regional problems can be solved through international cooperation and that the Third World no longer has to be a battleground for superpower hegemony.

Finally, new thinking is a commitment to adhere to international legal norms and standards of human rights.

One of the earliest and most tangible signs of Gorbachev's new thinking was his December 1988 UN speech, in which he promised to demobilize five hundred thousand troops. The most dramatic of the changes brought about by new thinking was the collapse of Communist governments in Eastern Europe in 1989. Although one can argue that the changes in Eastern Europe had less to do with Gorbachev than events in that region, Gorbachev avoided responding to the instability in Eastern Europe with force, as Khrushchev had done in Hungary in 1956 and Brezhnev had done in Czechoslovakia in 1968. As early as 1988, Gorbachev's remarks appeared to indicate that the Soviet Union would not stand in the way of revolutionary change in Eastern Europe.

As of 1990, the Soviet Union already has derived benefits from its new thinking policy. The most obvious benefit has been the Soviet Union's partial entry into the world diplomatic and economic community. The USSR is participating in negotiations on the future of Germany and the North Atlantic Treaty Organization. The USSR also has been granted observer status in GATT (General Agreement on Tariffs and Trade) and was promised six billion West German deutschmarks (more than 3.5 billion dollars) in loans after Chancellor Kohl's 1988 visit to Moscow. In addition, the West has eased restrictions on exporting some technologies to the Soviet Union.

Domestically, new thinking has de-emphasized the military-industrial complex, which in the past had a strong influence on allocation decisions in the economy. With the diminished threat abroad, Gorbachev has been able to order defense industries to produce much-needed goods for domestic consumption (a process called defense conver-

May Day 1990

Of the many rituals of Communist party rule in the Soviet Union, perhaps none is more symbolic than the annual parade. The November 7 parade in honor of the 1917 Bolshevik Revolution traditionally features Soviet soldiers marching unflinchingly across Red Square under the watchful gaze of Politburo members perched atop Lenin's Mausoleum. The newest weapons in the Soviet arsenal roll past in a triumphant display of the achievements of socialism.

The May Day (May 1) parade saluting international worker solidarity has been no less celebratory. Orchestrated columns of cheerful Soviet citizens usually march on Red Square with placards bearing official slogans and portraits of Politburo leaders, shouting "Hurrah" at well-timed intervals.

The 1990 May Day parade was astonishingly different. For the first time, the Kremlin made the demonstration voluntary and permitted unofficial groups and parties to join the procession. At the end of the parade (which was dominated by trade unions and workers warning against rapid economic change), throngs of protestors marched onto Red Square. In a stunning display of discontent, protesters carried uncensored placards reading "Down with the KGB!," "Gorbachev, Resign!," and "Socialism? No Thanks!" For twenty-five minutes, they milled underneath the mausoleum, shaking their fists and crying, "Resign!" and "Shame!" Mikhail S. Gorbachev and the rest of the leadership watched in evident amazement until the Soviet leader finally led his colleagues off the mausoleum.

The unofficial demonstration was organized by the Moscow Voters Association, a progressive political group that helped install the radical free-market economist Gavriil Popov (who stood with Gorbachev on the mausoleum) as mayor of Moscow. Moscow Communist party officials had permitted the demonstration as a sign of the new pluralism in the Soviet Union. They also may have wanted to avoid a repeat of the November 7, 1989, parade, in which unofficial demonstrators were not allowed to enter Red Square and upstaged the official parade with a rally at a local stadium.

The implication of the protests escaped no one's notice. An article in the government newspaper, *Izvestiia*, called the unofficial slogans irresponsible. It warned that the protest could have led to an avalanche of "unforeseeable consequences." Gorbachev, for his part, criticized the antigovernment protests and stressed that his proposals soon would lead to an upturn in the country's economic situation. One demonstrator interpreted Gorbachev's departure from the mausoleum as a refusal to acknowledge the "voices of the people." Both sides seemed to understand that the demonstration revealed the plunging legitimacy of the Communist party and the rising influence of alternative political groups.

The mood in other cities in the Soviet Union was similar. In the Ukrainian capital of Kiev, the official columns of workers were joined by demonstrators protesting the 1986 Chernobyl nuclear accident. Crowds in Kishinev, the capital of Moldavia, carried Romanian—not Soviet—flags. Several cities, including Leningrad and the capitals of the Baltic and Caucasus republics, broke with tradition by canceling their May Day festivities altogether.

---

sion). He also has been able to give consumer or "soft" industries a higher priority, as well as to spend hard currency on imported consumer goods to appease the population.

In addition, new thinking has created a more permissive attitude at home. As Foreign Minister Eduard Shevardnadze has asserted, the conduct of foreign policy cannot be separated from the treatment of one's own people. In accordance with this notion, Gorbachev has attempted to reform the state security apparatus to eliminate human rights abuses. *(KGB, box, p. 101)*

Threats to the Reforms

In 1990 Gorbachev seems to be a leader caught in his own devices. By articulating and implementing his program of perestroika, glasnost, demokratizatsia, and new thinking, he has set in motion forces that could block or reverse the process of reform.

Popular Discontent

The Soviet population is growing increasingly disillusioned with Gorbachev's economic reforms. After many years of cradle-to-grave security, most Soviets are unwilling to relinquish their job security, guaranteed wages, and low-cost medical and social security benefits. They are fearful of plunging into a free market economy without socialist guarantees. Yet the cornerstone of perestroika is the pegging of material rewards to performance and the shedding of superfluous labor.

Apprehension toward reform also has affected the reception of Gorbachev's policies in rural areas. Soviet farmers remember the 1930s when peasants who had taken advantage of the regime's sanction of limited free enterprise in the 1920s were stripped of their land and "eliminated as a class" by Joseph Stalin. This memory has made Soviet farmers wary of privatizing reforms. Although they now have permission to lease land for fifty years, few farmers have taken advantage of the opportunity. One factor in this reticence is their distrust of the government's word: How can they be sure that their land will not be taken away from them again?

The Soviet Union also lacks an entrepreneurial foundation, and many Soviet citizens regard with suspicion those who "pull ahead" of their neighbors. This attitude has been evident in the widespread public antipathy to the lucrative cooperative movement, a form of small-group private enterprise encouraged by Gorbachev in which the workers in the business share the profits.

The Soviet people would be more willing to bear the risks and disadvantages inherent in perestroika if immediate economic gains could be achieved. But the economy is in a near-crisis situation. Shelves are bare, and the population is weary of unfulfilled promises of long-term prosperity. As Ed Hewett has stated, Gorbachev's economic reforms mean nothing if the ruble remains inconvertible, and that depends on a full-scale price reform. But the difficulty in introducing controversial reforms such as price reform was demonstrated by the announcement in May 1990 of a proposed hike in the price of bread that would take place in July. Panic buying ensued, and store shelves were quickly cleared of foodstuffs. Ultimately, the plan was rejected overwhelmingly by the Supreme Soviet.

The Soviet leadership finds itself trapped in a paradox. Prosperity is not likely without further reforms, while the population's willingness to accept further reforms depends upon achieving an improvement in the standard of living.

Piecemeal economic reforms so far have not worked, and the Soviet leadership has rejected the Polish strategy of "shock therapy" in which prices and wages are decontrolled virtually overnight. Hence the fear of widespread public unrest in the face of the government's dwindling legitimacy has delayed the transition to market forces—the only measure likely to reverse the slide of the Soviet economy.

Conservative Backlash

A second threat to Gorbachev's reforms is a conservative "backlash," by party hard-liners, the military, or both. This threat has received much attention in the Western media, especially the possibility of a military coup or a right-wing ouster of Gorbachev. Hard-line party officials have been the most resistant to Gorbachev's reforms, as perestroika for them has meant the loss of their privileges, job security, and prestige. As of July 1990, however, the party's influence has greatly diminished, and Gorbachev's ouster by party officials alone is unlikely. Moreover, the elections in the republics earlier in 1990 demonstrated the increasing influence of the democratic-leaning political groups. Hence, the form of a right-wing backlash centered in the party would more likely be one of continued lower-level resistance and sabotage.

The threat from the military (and security apparatus) is perhaps more realistic. The officer corps has experienced some humiliation with the "loss" of Eastern Europe and with the decreasing attention in Soviet society to military matters. It also is concerned about the growing number of deserters and draft evaders, the impending defense budget cuts, the lack of housing for demobilized troops, the ethnic violence among draftees, and the increasing public criticism of the armed forces. Moreover, there is growing dissent in the military about Soviet foreign policy, particularly the Kremlin's apparent willingness to allow German reunification.

At the same time, however, reformist officers have risen through the ranks who are more amenable to Gorbachev's new thinking. Prominent Gorbachev adviser Georgii Arbatov and Politburo member Aleksandr Yakovlev have stressed that the military and Gorbachev are not at odds. But high-ranking military officers, such as Lt. Gen. Boris Gromov, one of the most popular figures in the Soviet military, have issued thinly veiled criticisms of Gorbachev's world view.

Ethnic Upheaval

The threat of ethnic upheaval to the reform process has become a reality. The blockade of Armenia by Azerbaidzhan in late 1989, for example, led to widespread violence and hardship; the unrest in Baku in January 1990 caused stoppages in the oil production facilities located there. Even the peaceful secession drives in the Baltic states have created serious social divisions in the other republics, especially the Russian republic. The Moscow-imposed blockade on Lithuania's oil and gas supplies has caused cuts in Lithuanian food shipments to the Russian republic.

When the forces of political liberalization and economic decentralization were unleashed in Eastern Europe, they did not stop until those countries had achieved a complete break from Moscow and a measure of political pluralism. It appears that in many of the Soviet Union's own republics, the reforms will have a similar result. The dissolution of the Soviet Union has become almost inevitable. Depending on the form and timetable of such a dissolution, however, it could ameliorate ethnic tensions. It also could allow greater Western economic benefits to flow into the Soviet Union because independent or semi-independent republics might serve as a conduit through which such benefits would reach the rest of the Soviet Union.

Other Threats

Several other scenarios could threaten the reform movement. Although liberal groups have advanced the reform cause by pushing for democracy and free market mechanisms, it is possible that such pressure could produce an unstable decentralization of power or result in more radical reform than the Soviet people will support. Liberals in the USSR Supreme Soviet such as Yuri Afanaseyev and Sergei Stankevich have been calling for a rapid transition to a market economy, a lifting of all controls on the press, and a complete decentralization of decision-making authority. This pressure is likely to accelerate now that key cities, such as Moscow and Leningrad, are under the control of reformers and the Russian Republic is under the leadership of Boris Yeltsin.

It also is possible that the reform movement in the Soviet Union could end or be redirected through a return to a centralization of power in the hands of one person, presumably Gorbachev. Institutional structures are in place whereby the president could declare martial law or a state of emergency in local areas (subject to some restrictions). Evidence exists of public support for such a concentration of power. In the debates on the executive presidency in the spring of 1990, for example, several deputies criticized the legislature for its slow, arduous decision-making process. In a series of articles in *Literaturnaya Gazeta* in the fall of 1989, academicians Andranik Migranyan and Igor Klyamkin argued for an "iron hand"

Boris Yeltsin: Maverick Politician

The career of Boris Yeltsin typifies the unpredictability of Soviet domestic politics under Mikhail S. Gorbachev. A pro-reform politician who was sacked as Moscow party boss in November 1987 and shortly thereafter as candidate member of the Politburo, Yeltsin was elected president of the Russian Soviet Federated Socialist Republic (RSFSR) in May 1990. Then, at the Twenty-eighth Party Congress in July, Yeltsin announced his resignation from the party.

Early in his career, Yeltsin was a typical Communist party bureaucrat. Gorbachev made Yeltsin, who hailed from Sverdlovsk, the head of the Central Committee Construction Department in April 1985. Soon after, he became a member of the Central Committee Secretariat and then in December 1985 replaced Viktor Grishin as first secretary of the Moscow City Party Committee. Two months later he was promoted to candidate membership in the Politburo.

At this time, he began his campaign against party privileges and elitism. At the Twenty-seventh Party Congress in February 1986, he denounced the "zone beyond criticism" surrounding the party elite. At the October 1987 Central Committee plenum, he criticized the Politburo, the Secretariat, and conservative Politburo member Yegor Ligachev and charged that Gorbachev was developing a cult of personality. This tirade cost him his job and his party position.

Since then he has been a persistent critic of both the party apparatus and the slow pace of Gorbachev's reform effort. His popularity among the Soviet people has soared as a result. Yeltsin was not selected by the party to run on its slate in the 1989 elections to the Congress of People's Deputies, but he was nominated for the Congress in at least fifty constituencies. He chose to run for Moscow's national-territorial seat. In a dramatic moment during the election campaign in March 1989, Moscow city officials blocked a rally for Yeltsin, only to have nine thousand Muscovites spontaneously demonstrate on his behalf.

Yeltsin was elected to the Congress of People's Deputies with 89 percent of the votes cast. In another move to keep Yeltsin out of the policy-making arena, the party leadership worked to prevent the Congress from electing him to the Supreme Soviet. This drew protests from the radical deputies and the public, and Yeltsin subsequently gained a seat in the higher body when an elected deputy stepped down to give him his place.

Yeltsin was one of the cofounders of the Interregional Group, the opposition bloc in parliament of more than two hundred deputies. He also is a member of the coordinating council of the Democratic Platform, the reform wing of the Communist party that advocates radical changes in the party's platform.

On his highly publicized trip to the United States in September 1989, Yeltsin drew attention for voicing pessimistic views on perestroika and Gorbachev's ability to stay in office. He gained public support in the Soviet Union by promising to spend the proceeds of his speaking tour on disposable hypodermic needles to help fight AIDS (acquired immune deficiency syndrome) in the USSR. He also received support from the Soviet people after *Pravda* reprinted an editorial from an Italian newspaper about his supposedly drunken behavior in the United States.

Yeltsin's election as chairman of the Russian parliament (president of the RSFSR) has reinforced the anti-establishment cast to his career. He won the position only on the third round of voting, after several visible attempts by Gorbachev to influence the elections in favor of his own hand-picked candidate. In his first days as president, Yeltsin laid out a radical plan for Russia's economic sovereignty and for establishing bilateral trading contracts among the fifteen republics.

Yeltsin's appeal is formidable among common Soviet citizens and the liberal intelligentsia. He and Gorbachev have stated their intentions to work together, but their relationship more likely will be one of uneasy coexistence. Gorbachev understands that Yeltsin is a personality to be reckoned with—an unpredictable maverick let loose by Gorbachev's own political reforms.

Boris Yeltsin accused Mikhail S. Gorbachev of having come to represent conservatives in the government in this November 3, 1989, speech.

to guide the country to democracy. Some Western historians suggest that the lack of a democratic tradition in the Soviet Union predisposes the people to prefer the imposition of reforms from above by a strong leader in the tradition of Peter the Great or Alexander II.

Finally, and most unsettling, is the threat of instability. As some have observed, the situation in the USSR is so volatile that one cataclysmic event could provoke widespread unrest and chaos or, as the Soviets are prone to warn, civil war. This event could take the form of wildcat strikes, an ecological disaster, another large earthquake, a localized military rebellion, an assassination attempt against Gorbachev or other prominent figure, or any number of other possibilities.

Yet in any discussion of "threats" to the reforms, one must consider precisely whose reforms are meant. Perhaps the Soviet Union has simply grown out of Gorbachev's definitions of perestroika, glasnost, demokratizatsia, and new thinking. Perhaps the domestic and international conditions have changed so drastically that his reforms cannot keep up. It is possible that the Soviet Union needs a new definition of reform—perhaps one more in line with the platforms of liberal groups that are gaining influence. The Soviet Union does appear to be at the brink of a new era, for it has fundamentally changed and cannot return to the way it was before. The way forward is clouded with risks, but if it attempts to retreat the likely result will be deeper stagnation and perhaps chaos.

Soviet Economy

The Soviet Union has the world's largest land mass, an educated population, and tremendous supplies of natural resources. It also has an economy that is in total disarray. Despite the emphasis that each Soviet leader since Joseph Stalin has given to improving the Soviet economy, it has performed progressively worse during the post-World War II era.

On coming to power in March 1985, Mikhail S. Gorbachev was expected to continue the policies of his former benefactor, Yuri V. Andropov. Few experts believed Gorbachev—or any other Politburo figure—was capable of implementing dramatic economic reforms. Gorbachev's first economic programs were *uskorenie* ("acceleration," meaning more efficient use of economic resources) and a revival of Andropov's anti-alcohol and anticorruption campaigns. This approach seemed to confirm the assertions of Kremlinologists that Gorbachev would seek to improve the Soviet economy by making changes at the edges rather than by launching an economic revolution.

Although Gorbachev, beginning in February 1986, discussed radical economic ideas in public, it was not until the June 1987 Central Committee plenum that a more comprehensive plan of reform was publicized. Acknowledging that the Soviet economy's "crisis state" was eroding the country's international influence and the Communist party's domestic legitimacy, Gorbachev announced an aggressive program, theoretically advancing a complete *perestroika* (restructuring) of the economy. Economic demands also became the impetus for significant political reform, such as *glasnost* (openness) and "new thinking" in foreign policy. The economic reform program's success, Gorbachev admitted, demanded more open discussion of economic problems and new theoretical approaches to once-inviolate Marxist-Leninist dogmas: "As never before, we need no dark corners where mold can reappear and where everything against which we have started a resolute struggle could start accumulating."

Yet despite implementation of major reforms, the Soviet economy continued to deteriorate during the late 1980s. The government newspaper, *Izvestiia*, in its 1989 annual review stated: "Tension in the consumer market has increased. According to many important indicators, plans have not been fulfilled." Consumers complained because government promises were not met, store shelves remained bare, and many goods began to be rationed. The haphazard introduction of reforms produced chaotic results as enterprise managers pondered whether to follow the old or the new rules. Attempts to increase the returns on government investment and lessen technological lags failed. Difficulties in key sectors, such as energy and agriculture, continued to be albatrosses around the government's neck.

One reason often cited for the continuing economic failure in the USSR has been Gorbachev's hesitancy into 1990 to fully implement market-oriented reforms. In 1989, responding to popular discontent, Gorbachev backtracked in several areas. Free market price reforms and cooperative and private enterprises were shackled by major restrictions on price, wage, and production decisions. Yet 1989 was a year when Gorbachev again was forced to choose between moving forward with more radical reforms and stepping backward to safety. He chose to move forward.

Despite Gorbachev's occasional caution, he has launched the most far-reaching economic experiment in Soviet history since Stalin set out in the 1920s and 1930s to collectivize the peasantry and rapidly industrialize the nation. The economy was stagnant when Gorbachev came to power, but the country also was stable. By implementing radical reforms, Gorbachev accepted huge political risks. He did so because he realized that, without reform, deteriorating social and economic trends were sapping the country's strength and eventually would cause the people to lose faith in the Communist party. Therefore, Gorbachev attempted to reinvigorate, with whatever means available, the centralized economy. Radical reforms were bound to be accompanied by many tactical mistakes and challenges from conservative members of the Soviet leadership and bureaucracy. Yet, each time Western observers thought Gorbachev would be forced to end his program, he has instead advanced a new, daring reform proposal.

In mid-1990 it was impossible to judge the success or failure of Mikhail Gorbachev's reforms. They must be allowed to run their course. It is possible, however, to review Gorbachev's reforms to date in the context of Soviet history and ask whether he has started a program capable of turning around the Soviet economy.

History of the Soviet Economy

To understand the Soviet Union's present economic quandary, the historical development of the Soviet economic system first must be examined. Gorbachev is encountering difficulties common to all centralized economies, yet many are unique to the Soviet experience. Past Soviet leaders have tried to overcome these problems, and Gorbachev has looked to their programs for inspiration. For example, various scholars have noted that Gorbachev's reforms borrow from the New Economic Policy (NEP) instituted by Lenin in the 1920s and from policies initiated by the more efficient tsarist ministers (including Peter Stolypin). Gorbachev also has looked abroad for models of economic reform, turning to, among others, Janos Kadar's New Economic Mechanism in Hungary, Deng Xiaoping's Chinese reform attempts, and even Adam Smith's capitalist theories.

The Soviet economy developed over the years into a system in which the state owns all productive resources, excluding small family farm plots. Every aspect of the economy—from the use of natural resources and capital to trade flows—was planned in Moscow. The leadership consistently supported heavy industry at the expense of consumer welfare. Agricultural labor and resources were gathered into communal *kolkhozi* (collective) and *sovkhozi* (state-owned and -managed) farms. In agriculture and industry, Soviet authorities stressed volume of production over quality. Finally, the Soviets attempted to establish a self-sufficient economy, isolated from the world system. Each of these choices continues to have a profound effect on the Soviet economy and the prospects for change.

Tsarist Period

Bolshevik economic plans in 1917 were constrained by the tsarist legacy. Russia had the weakest economy among the European powers. Economist Alec Nove, in *An Economic History of the USSR*, calculated that Russian per capita income in 1913 was less than 25 percent of per capita income in the United Kingdom and less than 50 percent of Austria-Hungary's. Worse, during the two previous decades, per capita income had grown at a slower rate in Russia than in any other European power. Only size made Russia a great power. It had a large population to fill the army's ranks, an abundance of natural resources (including oil and gold), and a massive land base.

The tsars learned lessons slowly and usually only in response to embarrassing military defeats or domestic turmoil. Russian peasants remained under the yoke of serfdom until 1861. Emancipation of the serfs and other political and economic reforms came because Russia's economic backwardness had contributed to its humiliating defeat in the Crimean War. Despite emancipation, rural conservatism remained prevalent in the villages well beyond the 1917 revolution (and continues to manifest itself today). This conservatism reduced productivity. For example, peasants inefficiently utilized the land by rotating it among village commune members.

Tsarist policies—laced with xenophobia and conservatism—also stunted industrial progress. The attempts of Russian leaders to insulate their country from Western influences, especially enlightened liberalism, delayed Russia's participation in the industrial revolution. Because an entrepreneurial class was slow to develop in Russia, all development had to begin with the tsar. Russian infrastructure and technological innovation lagged as a result. Again, military humiliation—in the Russo-Japanese War of 1904-1905—led to some reform, but when World War I began in 1914, the Russian economic system was ready to collapse.

Tsar Nicholas and his advisers failed to see the disastrous consequences of entering World War I. In fact, given Russia's backward economy, limited infrastructure, and urban revolutionary upheaval, it is surprising that the Russian war effort lasted as long as it did. By the November 1917 revolution and the subsequent Russian withdrawal from the war, the economy was completely devastated. Many key industrial regions (which were situated in the north and west) were ceded to Germany in the Brest-Litovsk Treaty. Adding to the confusion, the Bolsheviks could not control their own countryside, where White (anti-Bolshevik) and Green (peasant) militias established control. After Germany's defeat by the Western allies, the Bolsheviks recovered some of the lands lost to Germany. But territorial settlements associated with the civil war and the 1920 Russo-Polish War forced the Bolsheviks to surrender their claims to Finland, the Baltic states, Polish territories, and Bessarabia, all areas that were among Russia's most developed.

War Communism and NEP

After seizing power the Bolsheviks worked to create a socialist society and economy. Although Marxist doctrine addressed international class harmonization, the withering away of the state, and many other economic and social theories, it provided few concrete instructions for establishing an economic system. Trusting in the imminence of a world revolution that would bring Russia assistance from the developed nations of Europe, the first Bolshevik policies were radical. Lenin called for nationalization of all banks and large commercial enterprises, the end of commercial secrecy, and other measures to ensure efficient rationing of resources. To win urban support, the Bolsheviks backed the establishment of workers' soviets (councils) in every enterprise to allow self-management. In the countryside, Lenin allowed the peasants to seize whatever land they could.

When the world revolution failed to occur, the Bolsheviks realized that they would have to cope with their own problems without the aid of an international community of socialist states. In 1918, the urgent needs of the civil war and the urban food crisis caused Lenin and his colleagues to adopt a new, more draconic policy—War Communism. Lenin ordered requisitions of the peasants' grain to prevent hoarding, free trade was outlawed, liberal policies in the cities were abandoned, and single managers replaced workers' control at enterprises. At the height of War Communism, severe penalties were applied to enforce efficiency in the work place. *(War Communism, p. 25)*

Although War Communism did not last long, it established trends that reverberated through seven decades of Soviet economic policy. Worker management was never again established in the Soviet Union. To pay for accelerated wages, the Bolsheviks printed more and more money, and the ruble lost its value. Inflation accelerated, and the government began paying for its deficits by printing more and more money. In their revolutionary zeal, many Bolsheviks were convinced that in the new order money no longer would be used. Finally, because Russia did not have the infrastructure to facilitate foreign trade and because the Western powers were imposing an economic blockade, the Russian economy learned to operate independently from the world system.

War Communism was too harsh to continue indefinitely. Moreover, it was largely unsuccessful—inflation increased, grain production stagnated, and the nation's infrastructure continued to collapse. In early 1921 the government, which still was unable to feed the cities, was alarmed when sailors at the Kronstadt naval base, who had provided key support to the Bolsheviks in November 1917, again rose in revolt—only this time against the Bolsheviks. The revolt was crushed, but Lenin reacted by replacing forced requisitions of grain with a progressive tax. *(Kronstadt rebellion, box, p. 24)*

This was the first step in Lenin's New Economic Policy. Under NEP, the central authorities continued to control the economy's "commanding heights" (heavy industry, banking, foreign trade, wholesale commerce, and transportation), but free enterprise and competition were reintroduced into the agricultural, small business, and retail sectors. Domestic change went hand in hand with greater interest in international trade. Lenin declared that Soviet representatives to the post-World War I Genoa Conference in 1923 would go not as communists, but as merchants. *(New Economic Policy, p. 29)*

There are many parallels between NEP and Gorbachev's program. New forms of ownership—private or cooperative—were permitted in agriculture and industry. The government strove to construct a healthy banking system to replace widespread use of barter. NEP's stress on foreign contacts also parallels Gorbachev's theme of international economic interdependence. Although NEP seemed to improve the economy, it also contradicted Marxist dogma. Stalin used NEP's successes to outmaneuver his opponents on the left who criticized NEP's ideological backtracking. Then he turned against the right, claiming NEP was a betrayal of Marxism. Citing the threat of war from the capitalist countries and calling for rapid industrialization, Stalin brought NEP to its conclusion in 1928.

The Stalinist Economic System

On February 4, 1931, Stalin stated:

> One feature of the history of old Russia was the continual beating she suffered because of her backwardness. She was beaten by the Mongol Khans. She was beaten by the Turkish beys. She was beaten by the Swedish feudal lords. She was beaten by the Polish and Lithuanian gentry. She was beaten by the British and French capitalists. She was beaten by the Japanese barons. All beat her—because of her backwardness.... They beat her because to do so was profitable and could be done with impunity.... Such is the law of the exploiters—to beat the backward and the weak.... That is why we must no longer lag behind.... We are fifty or a hundred years behind the advanced countries. We must make good this distance in ten years. Either we do it, or we shall be crushed.

This famous speech made Stalin's program clear. Since the world was not on the verge of revolution, he called for building "socialism in one country." Stalin cited the alleged threat of attack from the capitalist powers to justify the use of terror and a period of forced austerity during which Russia would devote its energies to industrialization.

The true foundation of the economic system that Gorbachev has attempted to reform was created between 1928, when Stalin consolidated power and completely undermined NEP, and Stalin's death in 1953. This period saw the rapid industrialization of the Soviet Union. In addition, Stalin brutally collectivized the Russian peasantry, instituted complete centralized economic planning, and strove

to make Russia economically self-sufficient.

The first changes occurred in the countryside, where entrepreneurial peasants were using NEP's liberal provisions to profit from private trade. Stalin needed grain at low prices to pay for investment in heavy industry, and he used the Marxist condemnation of profiteering as a justification for squeezing the peasants. Beginning in 1926, he took steps to eliminate private trade. He raised taxes on the peasants by two-thirds between 1926 and 1927. By 1930, private trade virtually had been wiped out. In 1929 Stalin called for full collectivization and a class war against the *kulaks* (better-off peasants). Poorer peasants often participated in the violence against their wealthy counterparts. Severe requisitioning of grain by Soviet authorities and peasant resistance to collectivization (many peasants chose to kill their livestock rather than turn them over to the authorities) led to a famine that killed millions of people. *(Collectivization, p. 34)*

Stalin's vision of development demanded complete state control of every aspect of the economy. Therefore, the First Five-Year Plan (FYP), approved in 1928, allocated all state resources and outputs. This plan was overly optimistic and could not be achieved (although it was declared fulfilled at the end of 1932).

Still convinced of a future conflict with capitalism, Stalin supported heavy industry over consumer-oriented manufacturing. As John Scott, an American who traveled and worked in Russia in the 1930s, concluded in his book, *Behind the Urals*, although excesses may have occurred during the industrialization drive, "ten million tons of steel will make a great many tanks whose military effectiveness bears no relation to the price paid for the steel." Historians have criticized Stalin for being unprepared for World War II, but the Soviet Union did survive and actually emerged from the war as a stronger power. Without Stalin's industrialization program in the late 1920s and 1930s, the Soviet Union could have been defeated by Nazi Germany. Nevertheless, Stalin left an economic legacy that would remain a problem for his successors. *(Industrialization, p. 34)*

Legacy for Stalin's Followers

Central planning—organizing all economic activity to ensure party control and facilitate development—became the common denominator of economic activity in all communist countries. The First Five-Year Plan covered 1928-1932, and authorities are implementing the thirteenth, which is scheduled to cover 1990-1995.

The planning system has resulted in competition between planners, who have tried to force more efficient resource utilization by imposing ambitious quotas, and factory managers, who have lobbied to keep quotas as low as possible. To control factory managers, planners have required them to meet a confusing array of guidelines covering everything from how many workers to employ to how to make use of excess scrap metal. Management, however, has found ways to frustrate planners. When production quotas have been set according to weight, enterprises have produced heavy products. When quotas have been set according to quantity, enterprises have ignored quality. Managers also have hoarded labor and materials so that they could meet their quotas in case planners neglected to provide them with necessary resources. Finally, because plans were based on the "ratchet" mechanism—under which quotas were automatically increased a certain percent above levels achieved the year before—managers have been encouraged to hide the true productivity of their enterprise. This has led to "storming"—speeding production late in the month so that the quota is barely achieved. According to one Soviet economist in the 1970s, "total national income could be increased by 30 to 50 percent if 'storming' could be replaced by efficient use of resources."

The distribution of bank credit also is planned and is controlled through the state bank (Gosbank). Banks, like industries, are not judged according to their financial success, and credit is granted for political, not economic, reasons. Because bankruptcy is not an option—it implies a failure of communism—out-dated and inefficient capital rarely is retired.

Moreover the planners' tendency to construct "taut" plans (plans that do not anticipate shortages of supply, equipment failures, and other problems) contribute to the practice of not retiring capital or maintaining its condition because the plans do not allow for downtime. John Scott, in the 1930s, described an explosion that put a blast furnace out of commission (the incident is reminiscent of the Chernobyl nuclear disaster a half century later): "For two weeks prior to the disaster everybody connected with the furnace had known that the tapping hole was in bad shape.... Nobody realized the dangers ... and no one wanted to take responsibility for shutting down the furnace ... when the country needed pig iron very badly."

The absence of worker initiative and the poor quality of goods produced have been the main failures of the Stalinist economic system. Because collective farm workers have been paid by the hour instead of according to the volume and quality of their output, their productivity has been poor. Labor productivity has remained low in industry as well. With profits guaranteed by the central authorities, producers have not had to respond to market demands for high-quality products. And because producers have not competed on world markets, the quality of Soviet goods has fallen behind international standards. Finally, lack of competition has meant that domestic producers can ignore consumer needs, while the resulting scarcity of goods has forced consumers to accept whatever is produced.

Attempts at Reform

In his seminal work on Soviet reforms, *Reforming the Soviet Economy*, Sovietologist Ed Hewett of the Brookings Institution notes:

> In the post-Stalin era Soviet leaders have never been even close to fully satisfied with the performance of the economic system.... There is no year in which some change in the Soviet system is not introduced, some new experiment not begun.... This constant tinkering with the system has never had the desired effect. As a result, the leadership has gone for a new reform package at fairly regular intervals, taking elements from previous reforms and experiments, but possibly some new ideas also.

Hewett cites five major economic reform initiatives in the post-Stalin era. In 1957, Nikita S. Khrushchev launched his *sovnarkhoz* (economic councils) reforms, in which regional economic councils were granted greater influence vis-à-vis central authorities in economic decision making. Khrushchev's ouster and the failure of his program brought on the second wave of reforms. Prime Minister Aleksei Kosygin and First Secretary Leonid I. Brezhnev in 1965 initiated what has come to be known as the "Kosygin reforms." These reforms sought to fine tune the control

and planning system, increase initiative in the enterprises by linking bonuses more closely to performances, reorganize the pricing system, and improve consumer welfare. After a period of half-hearted implementation, the Soviet leadership accepted that the Kosygin reforms had failed. A third set of reforms was introduced in 1973 that was intended to "reduce the size of administrative hierarchy in industry and increase the efficiency with which industrial enterprises were managed by the center." After the failure of the 1973 reforms, another wave of minor (and unsuccessful) economic reforms was brought on in 1979. Thereafter the leadership muddled along until Brezhnev's death in 1982. Gorbachev's economic program represents the fifth attempt at reform.

Each of the pre-Gorbachev reforms was unable to overcome the deficiencies of the Stalinist system. A common factor doomed them to failure: The Soviet leadership refused to risk tampering with the basic structure of the economy. Because Marxist economic theory abhors capitalist competition—competition means wasted energy—the Soviet leadership consistently steered away from allowing market forces to play a role in the economy. Even since Gorbachev came to power, most Soviet leaders and planners have continued to believe that they can achieve an ideal allocation of resources through a scientifically determined central plan instead of through market mechanisms as in the West. Despite their sincere efforts the Soviets have been unable to find a combination of control mechanisms that will make the economy work efficiently.

Economy under Khrushchev and Brezhnev

During the 1950s and 1960s the Soviet economy was an inspiration to Third World leaders because it posted admirable growth rates while giving central authorities control of resources and production. According to Alec Nove's calculations, GNP grew 14 percent per year between 1950 and 1955, 12 percent per year between 1955 and 1960, and 9 percent per year between 1958 and 1965 (during the life of Khrushchev's Seven-Year Plan). Under Brezhnev, GNP increased an average of 8 percent per year between 1965 and 1970, 5.5 percent between 1970 and 1975, and 4 percent between 1975 and 1980. CIA estimates are somewhat more conservative, showing GNP increasing 5 percent between 1961 and 1965, 5.3 percent between 1966 and 1970, 3.4 percent between 1971 and 1975, 2.3 percent between 1976 and 1980, and 1.9 percent between 1981 and 1985.

The reason for the impressive growth in the 1950s, 1960s, and into the 1970s is that resources previously had not been fully utilized. In other words the Soviets could produce high growth rates by increasing exploitation of their vast natural resources even if their economy remained inefficient. Soviet leaders consistently relied on extensive growth (adding to the resource pool through greater exploitation of natural resources) as they proved unable to achieve intensive growth (qualitatively more efficient use of resources). For example, Khrushchev opened up huge tracts of land for agricultural use under his Virgin Lands program of the 1950s. Brezhnev continued land reclamation programs and turned to Siberia's vast mineral, gas, and oil deposits as another source of unexploited natural resources.

Extensive growth led, however, to declining efficiency as the productivity of labor, capital, and land all plummeted. With extensive growth also came wasted resources—the number of unfinished projects increased dra-

Alcohol Abuse: A Soviet Curse

"It is Russia's joy to drink. We cannot do without it," wrote Kiev's Saint Vladimir in the tenth century. That observation apparently holds true in the 1990s as well. Soviet sources estimate that as many as twenty million Soviets are dependent on alcohol, and alcohol is the nation's third leading cause of death. In 1984 Soviet annual alcohol consumption was measured at 15.5 liters of absolute alcohol per person. This translates into between three and four drinks per person per day. Western experts believe that crowded living conditions, urbanization, boredom, and a host of other factors have contributed to the alcohol problem in the Soviet Union.

Scientists, journalists, scholars, and public health officials in the Soviet Union have all bemoaned the number of deaths, workplace accidents, and related health problems caused by alcohol in their country. Retardation, infant mortality, miscarriages, and other alcohol-related problems have increased with the significant rise in alcoholism among women during the 1970s and 1980s. Labor productivity problems and higher suicide, crime, and divorce rates also have been attributed to alcoholism.

In May 1985 General Secretary Mikhail S. Gorbachev announced several measures to fight alcohol abuse. On June 1 the legal drinking age was raised to twenty-one from eighteen, and the opening of liquor stores was delayed for three hours on work-days. The state also began gradually increasing alcohol prices and cutting alcohol production. Those caught drunk in public or driving while intoxicated faced stiffer penalties.

Early in the anti-alcohol program, the government claimed positive results. State sales of alcohol and public drunkenness declined sharply, and health statistics improved. However, the anti-alcohol program was far from an unqualified success. Production of *samogon*, a homemade vodka-like beverage, increased dramatically, making up for some of the decline in state alcohol sales. Many Soviet citizens, frustrated in their attempts to buy alcohol or unable to pay higher prices, died from consuming tainted homemade brews or surrogate alcohol products such as shoe polish, antifreeze, cleaning fluid, varnish, and shaving lotion. By Gorbachev's estimates, the program also cost the government fifty billion rubles in revenue from alcohol sales. Finally, increased alcohol prices and longer lines at liquor stores had excited more public discontent than any other aspect of Gorbachev's early economic reform program.

Since late 1987, the government has retreated from its aggressive campaign, allowing production to increase in 1988 and 1989. Soviet authorities now are examining "education" campaigns instead of discipline programs. These new programs may be more effective, especially now that authorities are not turning their backs on social problems.

---

matically because they were begun without full cost assessments. As indicated by the growth rates, the Soviet economy was slowing steadily. Despite technological feats, such as the launching of Sputnik in 1957, the Soviets were falling farther behind the West in technology and the quality of goods, while they failed to catch their Western competitors in terms of GNP, per capita income, consumption, or any other major economic indicator. Trade—especially with the West—remained almost nonexistent. Worse, for the first time, the Soviets became dependent on what little trade did occur: Their inability to produce enough grain necessitated costly grain imports that could only be paid for with hard currency earned through oil exports.

Khrushchev and Brezhnev responded to economic problems by rearranging priorities instead of introducing new economic methods. For example, during the post-Stalin era the leadership did give consumer welfare a higher priority. Khrushchev partially backed away from Stalin's blatant support of industry over the consumer, although he did so in Stalinist fashion. The main element of his effort to improve the lot of consumers was to increase expenditures on the chemical and fertilizers industry, which he hoped would increase food production.

During the Brezhnev era the trend toward consumerism was more noticeable. The relative domestic calm of the late 1960s and early 1970s in part could be attributed to Brezhnev's commitment to improving the lot of Soviet consumers. At his first party congress as party chief—the Twenty-third in 1966—Brezhnev pledged "a fuller satisfaction of the material and cultural requirements of the Soviet people." In the years 1965 to 1972, per capita consumption rose 5 percent while per capita income was up 6.9 percent. Ownership of television sets increased from 8 percent of Soviet households in 1960 to 75 percent by 1977. Similar increases in the availability of other consumer goods also occurred. Meat consumption, for example, increased by 25 percent.

Although these gains were substantial, at the Twenty-fifth Party Congress in 1976 Brezhnev honestly assessed the party's failure to improve the economy: "We have not learned to accelerate the development" of consumer goods. As in the past, agriculture was the bane of the Soviet economy—after 1970, the country was transformed from an exporter to the world's largest net importer of grain. At the Twenty-fifth Party Congress, Brezhnev blamed droughts in 1972 and 1975 for this sector's dismal performance. The leadership made the agriculture minister, Dimitri Polianski, a scapegoat, dropping him from the Politburo in 1976. Soviet leaders also were aware of their failure to equal Western efficiency and productivity in industry.

While Brezhnev allowed some further economic freedoms—for example, greater leeway for private plots—he was unprepared to institute effective reforms. Instead, as Soviet specialist Marshall Shulman noted in *Foreign Affairs* in October 1973, the Soviets "opted for a massive effort to overcome its [the Soviet economy's] shortcomings by increasing the flow of trade, advanced technology and capital from abroad." Shulman also made a remark that applies to the situation under Gorbachev: "The realization of these [Brezhnev's] expectations manifestly requires an international climate of reduced tension." For Brezhnev, this meant a détente with the West. Like Brezhnev, Gorbachev has attempted to increase foreign participation in the Soviet economy and to divert resources to consumer needs. Therefore, like Brezhnev, he has needed a reduction in international tension. *(Détente, p. 66)*

Precursors to Reform

As the aging Brezhnev leadership proved unable to institute dynamic policies, economic problems accelerated in the late 1970s and early 1980s. With détente's failure the Soviets continued to spend a large share of their resources on defense. Labor force productivity did not increase. Soviet workers, who had job security but no way to raise their wages through performance, had little incentive to work harder. The agriculture sector experienced a string of poor harvests in 1977, 1979, and 1980. Agricultural productivity remained low: Soviet farmers outnumbered American farmers five-to-one in 1980, but the Soviets produced less than one-third the amount of agricultural products produced in the United States.

The Soviets could not respond to their declining economy with old tactics because further extensive growth had become more difficult. Labor force growth, especially in European regions, slowed noticeably, dropping from 2 percent annually between 1970 and 1975 to about 1 percent by 1980. New agricultural lands could be opened only by risking a further erosion of the environment. Although mineral and energy sources still were abundant, the most plentiful stocks were located in remote locations. Increased extraction required high-technology equipment that the Soviets lacked.

The state of the economy was a major agenda item at the November 27, 1979, Communist party Central Committee plenum. During a speech, Brezhnev criticized by name twenty-seven government ministers for "negligence, irresponsibility, or bungling" in handling economic affairs. Brezhnev also called for energy conservation, despite huge Soviet reserves of oil and natural gas. Due to the uncertain state of the economy, the Twenty-sixth Party Congress in 1981 adopted a conservative five-year plan for 1981-1985, which contained the lowest projected growth rate of any five-year plan in Soviet history. At the time, Brezhnev stated, "Any improvement in the standard of living can be achieved only by hard work on the part of the Soviet people themselves."

Perhaps most alarming was the effect of the defunct economy on Soviet society. Alcoholism in particular had increased dramatically during the Brezhnev years. Soviets drink three times as much distilled spirts as their West European peers and twice as much as East Europeans. Also during Brezhnev's tenure, life expectancy in the Soviet Union fell until, along with Romania, it was the lowest in Eastern Europe. In addition, the Soviet Union was the only country in Eastern Europe with a long-term decline in life

expectancies. *(Stagnation under Brezhnev, p. 70)*

During the slow economic collapse, the stars of two Politburo members rose. Yuri Andropov used his KGB connections and reputation as an efficient administrator to vault to national prominence and, after Brezhnev died, to the position of general secretary. Meanwhile, Mikhail Gorbachev was building his reputation as the secretary in charge of agriculture. He often is cited as the force behind Brezhnev's 1982 Food Program. Gorbachev showed a willingness to reform: The 1982 program incorporated Khrushchev's tactic of allowing more autonomy to workers on collective and state farms and allowed an increase in private plots.

Andropov and Chernenko Interregnum

Although the early deaths of Andropov and Konstantin U. Chernenko prevented the full development of their economic programs, neither Andropov (general secretary, November 1982-February 1984) nor Chernenko (February 1984-March 1985) promoted economic initiatives on the scale of Gorbachev's. Andropov is noted most for his campaigns to improve efficiency and reduce corruption and alcoholism. Chernenko continued Brezhnev's policy of attempting to guard the party's legitimacy through fulfillment of consumer demands. Toward this end he increased spending on food and light industry programs.

Andropov repeatedly stated that his "highest priority" was to revive the economy. Since he admitted, "I do not have ready recipes" for solving the country's economic problems, he encouraged greater debate of economic questions among specialists. Andropov was willing to consider nontraditional suggestions for reinvigorating the economy. For example, he said the Soviet Union should "take account of the experiences of the fraternal countries" (a likely reference to economic reforms in Hungary and possibly China) as well as "world experience." He even was prepared to offer capital incentives in return for more efficiency: "Shoddy work, inactivity, and irresponsibility should have an immediate and unavoidable effect on the earnings, official status, and moral prestige of workers." He also underlined the need "to extend the independence of amalgamations, enterprises, and collective farms." Andropov, at least rhetorically, was not going to allow the same muddling that hamstrung Brezhnev's reforms.

Despite his rhetoric and backing of limited experimentation, Andropov did not introduce the type of decentralizing reforms needed for an efficient economy. Most importantly, he left the bureaucrats and their ministries intact and powerful. Andropov's term in office, however, must be viewed as a positive step forward on the economic front. First, he promoted reform-minded leaders. For example, Nikolai Ryzhkov, previously a deputy chairman of Gosplan, was named Central Committee secretary for economic coordination. Gorbachev's position also was strengthened, and it is believed that he had a major role in creating and coordinating Andropov's reform program. Second, Andropov allowed greater debate of economic issues—a policy Gorbachev has extended. Finally, Andropov realistically examined and criticized the state of the economy, instead of glossing over its weaknesses as the Brezhnev leadership had done. Andropov's attitude toward reform was summed up by his one-time confidant, liberal economist Oleg Bogomolov, who stated in 1989: "Andropov is being idealized now. If he had lived he probably would have changed things some, but he would not have touched overlying structures of society. He was careful, conservative, maybe a bit like [conservative Politburo member] Yegor Ligachev." *(Andropov reforms, p. 74)*

As a long-time Brezhnev devotee, Konstantin Chernenko favored his benefactor's conservative style. Chernenko seems to have considered a popular uprising like the one in Poland in 1980-1981 a real possibility in the Soviet Union. Believing that Poland's trouble arose because the Polish Communist party had not met the workers' needs, he emphasized Brezhnev's policy of greater concern for consumer welfare. But Chernenko also perpetuated many of the changes begun under Andropov. In particular, he allowed debates on the economy to continue and did not impede Gorbachev and his new leadership circle from assuming positions of authority.

While Chernenko floundered through thirteen months in office, the economy continued to deteriorate, especially the agricultural sector. The country suffered its sixth consecutive bad harvest in 1984, due both to poor weather and inefficient farming. In October, at an unexpected session of the Central Committee, Chernenko announced the harvest had suffered "a substantial shortfall," especially in feed grains needed to increase meat production. Yet, aside from increasing grain imports, Chernenko's responses were traditional. Chernenko and Premier Nikolai Tikhonov called for land reclamation, a retreat to the policy of extensive growth. In addition, Chernenko cautiously supported a decades-old plan to divert the Siberian rivers Ob and Irtysh to cultivate additional Central Asian lands. This plan—technically near impossible and environmentally disastrous—was an example of the failures of dogmatic economic centralization. *(Chernenko interregnum, p. 76)*

Gorbachev Takes the Helm

Despite numerous political and societal distractions, Gorbachev's foremost policy concern throughout his reign as general secretary and president has been the economy. In April 1985, at the first Central Committee plenum after he came to power, he stated, "The development of Soviet society will be defined in decisive measure by qualitative shifts in our economy, by the transfer of it onto the rails of intensive growth." Although Gorbachev might have liked to jump quickly into reforms, he realized that day-to-day management tasks—especially negotiating the Twelfth Five-Year Plan—required his immediate attention. After the plan was approved in June 1986, Gorbachev appeared to focus more on long-range goals.

Gorbachev's reforms have come in three stages. Stage one began in 1985 when he became general secretary and lasted until the June 1987 plenum. At that time Gorbachev initiated a second set of reforms and altered investment priorities in response to the first stage's failure. During mid-1989, the Soviet leadership judged this second stage of reforms to have been ineffective as well. Gorbachev then began implementing even more radical changes. Through mid-1990, however, he had not been willing or able to enact certain far-reaching reforms, such as the breakup and privatization of state-owned monopolies, price restructuring, and the privatization of agricultural property, that many foreign economists considered necessary for reinvigorating the Soviet economy.

Stage One: March 1985-June 1987

Most observers consider the period from Gorbachev's ascension to power in March 1985 until the June 1987 Central Committee plenum as a first phase of economic reform. He initially hoped to achieve greater economic growth, reintroduce efficiency and discipline into the economy, and implement limited changes in the economic system. His three-pronged attack was an aggressive version of Andropov's program. Though eager to reinvigorate the economy, Gorbachev, like Andropov, did not have an economic reform blueprint when he launched his program. Instead, as Gorbachev stated in his 1987 book, *Perestroika: New Thinking for Our Country and the World*, he intended to progress "step by step in the chosen direction, rounding out and perfecting the economic mechanism on the basis of acquired experience, getting rid of everything that is obsolete or has not proved itself." Like Andropov, Gorbachev criticized economic malaise, inefficient and low-quality production, the decline in workers' productivity, excessive drinking, and rampant corruption. Although his criticism of the Brezhnev regime was elliptical at first, it soon became more direct and vociferous.

Like Andropov, Gorbachev also supported more open discussion of economic problems. During the Brezhnev era, such discussion was permitted only among specialists, but Gorbachev expanded it to a nationwide scale. He also widened the range of acceptable topics to include previous taboos, such as bankruptcy and unemployment. Perhaps most important, Gorbachev placed supporters of economic reform in key positions throughout the economy.

Gorbachev's plan called for increasing the system's dynamism by switching from extensive growth to intensive improvements. As noted above, labor and capital productivity growth rates had been particularly poor under Brezhnev (for labor, only 1 percent growth in 1982; for capital, a decline of 4 percent in that year). In an effort to reverse this trend, Gorbachev called for increased investment in technological research and development. He also advocated earlier retirement of aging plant and equipment—estimates of the service life of Soviet industrial equipment in the 1970s ranged from fourteen to forty years, compared with the Western average of twelve years. New construction projects, so popular under Brezhnev, were reduced, and greater emphasis was placed on refurbishing existing facilities. In a recent Joint Economic Committee report, economist Stanley Cohn noted that refurbishing can increase labor and capital productivity compared with new plant construction, decrease expenditures on construction by 50 percent or more, and speed technology absorption by three times.

The acceleration encoded in the Twelfth FYP (1986-1990) ambitiously called for reversing the declining growth rates of the previous decade. The original goal was for GNP to increase by 4 percent per year in the Twelfth FYP and 5 percent through the century's final decade.

To achieve Gorbachev's long-term modernization goals, the first two years of the Twelfth FYP were to stress improving performance in the machine-building, computer, and technology sectors. The machine-building sector was to become self-sufficient—improvement would come from domestic initiative instead of imported equipment. Technology standards were to catch up quickly with levels in Western countries. With these goals in mind, investment in 1986 and the beginning of 1987 soared by 7.5 percent over the levels of the previous year. During this FYP, equipment was scheduled to be retired twice as fast, and investment in the civilian machine-building and metalworking (MBMW) ministries was to increase 80 percent over the Eleventh FYP. The Twelfth FYP called for an annual 18 percent increase in the production of computer equipment between 1986 and 1990, an annual 11 percent increase in the production of instrumentation equipment during the same period, and similar increases in the production of robots and high-tech machine tools. These modernization programs were to account for two-thirds of overall GNP growth.

Fulfilling machine-building reconstruction meant that other areas of the economy would have to do with less in the Twelfth FYP. The plan called for only minor improvements in consumer welfare. Investment in agriculture and construction—high priority sectors under Brezhnev and Chernenko—was delayed. Western analysts predicted that defense still would receive priority status, but Gorbachev argued that long-term security could be achieved only through technological improvements and not through continued massive defense spending. The energy sector, however, was to retain its priority status. It received major investment increases over the duration of the plan. Most Sovietologists remained skeptical that the "intensification" called for in the Twelfth FYP could be achieved.

The second area of reform—what Sovietologist Herbert Levine has called the "people program"—was designed to complement "intensification" by increasing worker efficiency. In *Perestroika*, Gorbachev wrote that it was necessary to "wake up those who have fallen asleep." Increased worker productivity and managerial efficiency were to produce the final third of the increase in GNP. Gorbachev urged workers to accept more strict discipline in the workplace. He said that he hoped to end the practice of "workers pretending to work and the government pretending to pay them" by promising future improvements in the

quality and availability of consumer items. Gobachev also worked for the reduction of wage controls. Scientific workers and engineers were to receive wages based on the usefulness, not the quantity, of their new inventions. Managers were given greater control over employees' wages so that they would be able to reward more productive workers. To decrease material damage at work, absenteeism, and personnel injuries, the government drastically reduced state sales of alcohol. To further decrease absenteeism and labor turnover, the authorities used moral appeals to reinvigorate socialist labor discipline. The "people program" also included an expansion of management and technological education. Finally, hoping to limit losses sapped from the system through crime, Gorbachev extended Andropov's anticorruption campaign.

In the program's third area, Gorbachev began changing the operating methods of the economy. He intended to increase local economic autonomy, introduce full cost accounting and "self-financing," and make enterprises and farms operate under the principle of *khozrashchet* (the reduction of costs and expansion of profits in accordance with basic economic laws). The advancement of khozrashchet meant enterprises would have to act efficiently, not a new concept in the Soviet Union, but one that had been forgotten under Stalin, Khrushchev, and Brezhnev. Self-financing meant that enterprises would no longer receive subsidies if they were unable to make a profit.

An Andropov experiment allowing greater local control of selected industries was to be extended across the entire industrial sector by 1987. According to Harvard Sovietologist Joseph Berliner, the goal of this decentralization was for the central planners to avoid "petty tutelage" of ministries and for ministries to do the same in relation to enterprises. The center—for example, Gosplan—was to concentrate on long-range planning instead of management of the economy. In the light industry sector, ministerial

Mikhail S. Gorbachev is the most gregarious Soviet leader since Khrushchev, often wading into crowds to hear workers' and citizens' comments. Here he speaks with oil field workers in 1985.

guidelines given to the enterprises were to be reduced to as few as three and were to be linked to profits. Ministries would finance themselves through a tax on enterprise profits. Obviously, profits would have to play a more active role in enterprise decision making, and, therefore, the new "Law on Light Industry" called for a maximum tax on enterprise profits of 30 percent, leaving the enterprise in control of the remainder. Finally, Gorbachev called for eliminating the "ratchet" effect by introducing "stable" normatives. A limited number of enterprises also gained the right to trade directly with foreign firms.

While these reforms were geared toward decentralization, Gorbachev believed that the Communist party should maintain its leading role in society, and therefore central control over economic reform was to continue. One early program strengthened central organs by creating super-ministries to oversee the agro-industrial complex; the computer industry; and the energy, construction, and machine-building sectors. The super-ministries were to eliminate duplication of labor and facilitate the distribution of research and development to individual industries.

Finally, in the hope of improving product quality, Gorbachev established *Gospriyemka*, a new national committee for quality control. Its mission was to place inspectors in the factories; conduct random quality examinations; and, when appropriate, fine enterprises and ministries that did not meet quality standards. By the end of 1987, 1,500 inspectors had been assigned to more than seven hundred enterprises. Soon after, 30 percent of all industrial production was under surveillance by state inspectors. Yet Gospriyemka later was scrapped because its intrusive inspection often added to overall plan confusion.

During stage one, the Soviet leadership also began sanctioning some private enterprise activities. At the Twenty-seventh Party Congress (February 25 to March 6, 1986), Gorbachev promoted greater freedom for individuals to sell privately produced goods and for enterprises to sell above-plan production for a profit. The Law on Private Enterprise (November 1986) legalized certain small-scale private businesses. For example, taxi drivers—long cited as a prime example of Soviet economic inefficiency—were allowed to operate privately. Though fares rose dramatically, there was a corresponding improvement in service. Small food producers also received further privileges, and independent farmers' markets offered more and better food at higher prices.

Another area of decreased centralization was foreign trade, where certain industries received expanded rights to conduct trade without interference from the Committee on Foreign Economic Relations. Gorbachev also began promoting greater foreign involvement in the economy, especially through joint ventures. However, restrictions on control of the ventures—foreigners could own only 49 percent of the company's assets, and the company director had to be a Soviet citizen—limited foreign interest in joint ventures late into 1987.

Performance in Stage One

The results of the first two years of economic reform were disappointing. The economic program was set back by natural and man-made shocks, including bad weather and strikes. While workers for a time might have been expected to accept increased discipline in the name of modernization, they were bound to become disillusioned with the extra work, increased social inequities, and harsher living conditions demanded by intensification. In addition, the reform program contradicted itself. Ministries and enterprises were supposed to revamp equipment, but high growth targets left little time for reequipping.

Despite these problems, the Soviet economy did improve during 1986. Most workers accepted the hardships called for by Gorbachev's discipline program. Labor productivity increased during the year as a result of decreased absences and drunkenness and more effective management. The weather helped as agricultural production achieved record harvests. The 210 million ton grain harvest allowed the Soviets to cut grain imports and increase livestock production. Overall economic performance was good. The Soviet GNP grew by 3.9 percent, the highest rate in more than a decade, with the industrial sector growing by 3 percent and the agricultural sector growing by 8 percent.

Although the year's results were positive, the reforms' contradictions were evident. Because most enterprises and ministries remained responsible for meeting plan requirements, they were unwilling to slow production to replace equipment. Therefore, the extremely high goals for replacing equipment in the machine-building sector could not be met. Furthermore, the Soviets were unable to bring partially finished projects on line. Although the 1986 plan called for an increase of 14.1 percent in production machinery in operation, only 6.4 percent growth was achieved. The Soviets also were not able to reach their goals in technological progress. The 1986 Soviet year-end economic report stated that a number of ministries "did not raise the technical level and quality of output."

Other ominous trends developed in the agriculture and trade sectors. The impressive growth in agricultural output required an unexpectedly large investment in the agro-industrial complex—a 10 percent increase over 1985. Meanwhile, as oil prices continued to decline, the Soviet trade position suffered. In addition, because Soviet exports are mostly denominated in dollars while imports are denominated in European currencies, the dollar's devaluation during 1986 meant Moscow's real import capacity fell even further.

Given the low priority of consumer investment, it is not surprising that the Soviet consumer experienced little improvement in the availability and quality of goods in 1986. Although consumption of some agricultural products (including meat) had healthy increases, per capita consumption of all goods rose only 1 percent over the previous year. Because wage controls had been loosened, many consumers found themselves with excess cash. The Soviet leadership began to worry that the populace would grow impatient with the lack of consumer goods on which to spend their unused disposable income.

Meanwhile legal sales of alcohol declined by more than one-third. Although this helped labor productivity, it was a blow to the regime in three ways. First, the government deprived itself of tens of billions of rubles in revenues from alcohol sales. Second, Soviet citizens resented the regime for making the purchase of alcohol more difficult. Finally, production of *samogon* (home brew) rose drastically, depleting supplies of sugar and causing many accidental deaths from tainted liquor. *(Alcohol abuse, box, p. 113)*

The nuclear reactor disaster at Chernobyl in April 1986 was another unexpected shock to the Soviet economy. Cleaning up the disaster cost the Soviets an estimated eight billion rubles. The event also slowed the Soviet energy program as nuclear power came under the scrutiny of a number of domestic environmental groups.

Despite these problems, Gorbachev could be pleased with the start of intensification in 1986. However, 1987 saw a return to the low growth rates of 1981-1985. Soviet GNP grew less than 1 percent in 1987, with the industrial sector growing only 1.5 percent. Machine building, the modernization program's centerpiece, saw zero growth. Agricultural output fell 3 percent from the record levels achieved the year before. The consumer suffered most in 1987 as living standards failed to improve. Shortages of consumer products became worse and were a common theme of Soviet press reports. In late 1986, the Soviet leadership promised increased investment in consumer programs, particularly housing construction.

A variety of factors contributed to the Soviets' economic woes in 1987. Record cold temperatures in January and February wreaked havoc on agriculture and transport plans. Bottlenecks in transporting supplies could not be overcome even later in the year. Newly introduced reforms confused managers who were unsure how to use new privileges to negotiate supply or fulfill contracts. Gospriyemka also took a toll on early plans. About 80 percent of the machine-building enterprises worked under supervision of this program, and inspectors were turning down up to 20 percent of production, which led to supply shortages in other industries. Soviet consumers saw less than a 1 percent increase in per capita consumption in 1987, and unsatisfied demand continued to increase—up by 2.6 percent. This was reflected in a 10 percent increase in bank deposits.

At the same time, workers were unhappy with parts of the reform, and strikes became more common in 1987. Wage reforms brought reduced wages to some workers and threatened others with unemployment. Gospriyemka standards often meant harder work with no increased pay. Worker productivity, which had accounted for a large part of 1986's growth, did not show similar increases in 1987.

As 1987 progressed, Gorbachev's concern about consumer discontent grew. He and fellow reformers adopted a "go to the people" approach. Moscow party chief Boris Yeltsin, for example, began haranguing the ministries and enterprises for not fulfilling consumers' needs.

In *Dilemma of Reform in the Soviet Union*, political scientist Timothy J. Colton observed that in 1986 "elite discontent is directed in the main at the performance of the Soviet system and not at its existence.... If would-be Alexander Dubceks [the reformist leader of the 1968 Prague Spring] lurk in the upper or middle echelons of the Soviet Communist Party, they are doing a superlative job of keeping their convictions to themselves." In other words, during the first stage of economic reform, Gorbachev and his colleagues seemed to believe that limited economic adjustments dictated from above could reverse the Soviet economy's slide. Only radical reforms, however, were likely to significantly improve the centralized Soviet economy.

Stage Two: June 1987-Summer 1989

Despite opposition from inside the Communist party, as 1987 progressed Gorbachev began to give consumer complaints greater attention, and economic discussions within the leadership expanded to include more radical proposals. This process culminated at the June 1987 Central Committee plenum. By then, Gorbachev and his advisers had realized that reforms had to go further than they had in 1986 and 1987. Enterprises needed greater independence in deciding how to market goods, where to purchase supplies,

and how to pay workers. Prices needed to reflect production costs more realistically. More effective incentives had to be introduced into the system, both for the worker (through wages) and for the enterprise (through the threat of bankruptcy). Although Gorbachev had not turned into a free market capitalist, he did write in *Perestroika* that there was a "need for radical reforms of the economic mechanism and for restructuring the entire system of economic management."

At the June Central Committee plenary meeting, Gorbachev described his new reform proposals as "including the transfer of enterprises to complete cost accounting, a radical transformation of the centralized management of the economy, fundamental changes in planning, a reform of the price formation system and of the financial and crediting mechanism, and the restructuring of foreign economic ties." A flurry of decrees emerged from the plenum. By the end of June, the "Basic Principles for a Radical Reform of the Economic Management" had been approved, followed closely by the "Law on State Enterprises." The government published numerous decrees on reforming Gosplan, *Gossnab* (Committee for Material and Technical Supply), *Gostekhnika* (Committee for Science and Technology), and *Goskomtrud* (Committee for Labor and Social Problems), as well as statistical practices, price formation, the banking system, and regional and ministerial bodies.

The "Basic Principles" and the "Law on the State Enterprise" claimed that "state subsidies will be an exception," meaning firms that lost money would not be supported by the government and would face bankruptcy. This had implications that went beyond the financial health of individual enterprises. The bankruptcy of important enterprises could threaten Soviet security from import dependence and could create unemployment.

Planning mechanisms were to be reoriented in this second stage of reform. Instead of allowing state authorities to plan what and how much would be produced, enterprises were to produce only a portion of their output according to state orders. The enterprises would be free to make most production decisions. State orders were to be more prevalent at first in priority sectors and would cover 80 percent of all production in 1988. However, state orders were to be reduced to 60 percent in 1989, 50 percent in 1990, 35 percent in 1991, and eventually to 20-25 percent.

The reforms also called for the introduction and increasing use of wholesale trade to ration producer goods in place of the centralized supply system. Beginning in 1988, this new system was to account for 20 percent of industrial sales. By 1992, the plan called for 80 percent of sales to be handled through wholesale trade. However, scarce producer goods would continue to be rationed.

Wage controls were to be lifted further, with a long-range goal of 60-70 percent of the work force employed in enterprises that tied salary increases to worker performance and enterprise profits. By 1988, enterprise autonomy would be widened so that 40 percent of all enterprises—accounting for 60 percent of agricultural and industrial production—were to finance their own activities without government interference. The state would no longer be responsible for losses at these firms.

In December 1988 all enterprises were given access to foreign trade, provided they registered their trade activities and used hard-currency exports to pay for imports. The immediate goal was for 26 percent of imports and 14 percent of exports to be arranged directly by enterprises instead of through the State Committee for Foreign Economic Relations. However, the government backed away from this step in March 1989, when it announced a list of restrictions on eight import sectors and seventy-eight export areas. Exports were restricted on medical equipment, food products, precious metals, and "goods which are in short supply" in the Soviet Union. Import restrictions included military equipment, drugs, and most publishing and video equipment.

Performance in Stage Two

The Soviet Union's GNP continued to grow very slowly—at only 1.5 percent—during this second stage. Industrial growth increased by 2.0 to 2.5 percent in 1988. According to Soviet statistics, the total value of unfinished capital construction increased by 8.7 percent in 1988, despite the regime's efforts to end this waste. Consequently, fourteen billion rubles' worth of new equipment remained idle by the end of the year. Equally frustrating, technical goals were not achieved. Twenty-five percent of newly produced machinery "did not meet world technological standards" according to the 1988 Soviet year-end report. Agricultural output declined in 1987 and 1988, although grain production reached record levels in 1987.

Workers became even more unhappy with the reforms, and labor unrest increased—the most notable example being the coal miners' strike in the Donbass region in the summer of 1988, which threatened to cause a nationwide energy shortage and to cripple the transportation system. The authorities agreed to the strikers' demands, but this only led to more strikes in other sectors of the economy.

Consumers continued to fare poorly, with per capita consumption increasing only 1.5 percent in 1988. Most of this gain was in alcohol sales, which increased after the anti-alcohol campaign was eased in late 1987. Complaints from consumers grew more strident. On a trip to Krasnoyarsk in September 1988, Gorbachev met with people in the street who complained bitterly of inadequate housing, food, education, and health care. This trip seems to have moved Gorbachev to give consumer concerns a higher priority. The leadership increased consumer investment in 1989—that year's revised plan called for consumer production to increase by 7 percent instead of the 5.7 percent increase originally called for in the FYP.

During stage two, Soviet investment priorities began to shift from defense and heavy industry toward consumer concerns. Gorbachev's reductions in military spending probably were used to meet investment needs in the consumer sector as well as in other areas.

Despite taking some relatively radical steps by past Soviet standards, Gorbachev's second-stage reforms still avoided introducing market-oriented changes. The Soviet leadership also failed to anticipate unexpected shocks when setting its goals and allocating resources. The most dramatic shock during stage two was the Armenian earthquake on December 7, 1988, which killed 25,000 people and left 500,000 homeless. The quake damaged the entire region's infrastructure, including railroads and power systems. According to Soviet reports, the government intends to carry out massive housing construction projects in Armenia that will consume up to 5 percent of total state investment in construction for 1990 and 1991. It will be years before Armenian industrial and agricultural capacity recover to pre-1988 levels, and the expenditures on reconstruction in Armenia will divert funds that would have gone to other priorities.

The absence of a storefront or billboard does not disguise this Moscow liquor store. Soviets spend countless hours waiting in lines.

In 1989 the failure of the reform program continued to alarm the Soviet leadership. Although the Soviets reported a GNP growth rate of 5 percent in 1988, the CIA estimated the Soviets actually achieved only a 1.5 percent increase in GNP. The economy's performance seems to have been equally disappointing in agriculture and industry. Consumption improved only slightly (1.5 percent, according to the CIA), despite the government's extensive efforts to satisfy consumers' needs.

Other economic trends were equally alarming. Wages were rising much faster than labor productivity. In October 1988, Prime Minister Nikolai Ryzhkov announced that wages had increased by forty billion rubles, while production of goods went up by only twenty-three billion. As Ed Hewett notes, savings in government-run banks had held steady at about 7 percent for the first half of the 1980s but increased to more than 10 percent between 1986 and 1988 and more than 12 percent in the first half of 1989. Soviet workers were earning more, but because of the shortage of quality goods, they were forced to save a larger share of their income.

In November 1988, Soviet authorities for the first time admitted that inflation was a problem. The government reported that inflation was running between 1.0 and 1.5 percent, but some Soviet and Western observers were predicting (it turned out correctly) actual inflation rates as high as 10 percent for 1989. Enterprises were criticized for contributing to inflation by taking advantage of new price reforms that allowed them to make slight modifications to products and sell them at much higher prices.

The problem of government debt also became more evident at the end of stage two. Before 1985, the debt had averaged 17.5 billion rubles. However, by 1989, Prime Minister Ryzhkov acknowledged a massive expansion in government debt to 120 billion rubles, which totals almost 14 percent of Soviet GNP. Moreover, Valentin Pavlov, the Soviet finance minister, announced in the fall of 1989 that the Soviet Union had "a domestic state debt that will amount to about 400 billion rubles by the end of 1989." Ryzhkov and Gorbachev have cited unexpected losses that have contributed to the debt explosion: thirty billion rubles because of the Soviet Union's declining trade position, more than twenty-five billion rubles for cleanup at Chernobyl and reconstruction in Armenia, thirty billion rubles unexpectedly spent on agriculture and social services, lower receipts from alcohol sales tax (Ed Hewett approximates a loss of fifteen billion rubles), and five billion rubles per year for Afghanistan until the Soviet withdrawal in 1989.

All of these problems were being aired in public, because open discussion of the economy had expanded to include the new Congress of People's Deputies. The deputies sharply criticized the leadership's entire economic program during vigorous televised legislative debates in May 1989 that were watched avidly by the Soviet people.

Stage Three: Radical Experimentation

The summer of 1989 marked a turning point in the Soviet economic reform movement, as Gorbachev and his advisers realized that the reforms they had introduced during the second stage still were not improving economic performance. Moreover, pressures were building up throughout the economy. Citizens were dissatisfied with the continuing lack of quality consumer goods, and workers were resistant to stricter discipline in the absence of greater rewards. The economy was beset by a growing debt problem, the threat of energy shortages, labor unrest (particularly the late summer coal miners' strike), and inflation. The Soviet economy also had failed to attract significant Western participation.

In response to the declining situation, the leadership began a third stage of economic reform that is ongoing. This third stage has been characterized by wide-open debate on the economy that has considered radical (nonsocialist) solutions and by the Soviet leadership's willingness to experiment. Moscow also has been closely observing events in Eastern Europe as those countries convert to market systems.

Gorbachev seemed willing during the third stage to act decisively in response to the economy's problems. His first action was to bolster consumer production and other areas popular with the Soviet public. The 1989 and 1990 budgets included major increases in spending on consumer industries, housing, health care, education, and environmental protection.

In 1989 Leonid Abalkin was appointed to head the State Commission on Economic Reform, which Ed Hewett suggests is "an expanded version of the Commission on the Improvement of Management, Planning and the Economic Mechanism." Representatives of all economic ministries serve on the commission, including the finance minister; the head of Gosplan; and the chairmen or deputy chairmen from the committees on prices, labor, statistics, construction, material-technical supply, science and technology, and the Foreign Economic Commission. Beginning in the summer of 1989 the State Commission on Economic Reform suggested more far-reaching reforms. For example, it sharply attacked state monopolies and instructed the Institute for the Study of the USA and Canada to draft antimonopoly legislation. The committee also pushed for removing restrictions on private ownership and promoted long-term "leases" on land in an attempt to—as Gorbachev has said—"return the peasant to his position as master of the land."

During the third stage, the regime has appeared determined to force enterprises to operate profitably. Abalkin

stated as early as January 1989 that "economic reforms will inevitably lead to the closing down of more and more unprofitable enterprises." He was willing to consider unemployment: "By the year 2000, the state expects it will have had to retrain and find new jobs for fifteen million people." Soviet economic statistics began to include estimates of unemployment. The end of year report listed thirteen million people out of work in 1989 but claimed that most were housewives, part-time or migrant laborers, and army retirees (accounting for four million each).

Finance Minister Pavlov addressed the debt problem in September 1989 by announcing a proposed program to cut the 120 billion ruble deficit to 60 billion rubles in 1990. This was to be accomplished by freezing wages of state sector employees, closing unprofitable enterprises, selling bonds (another Soviet first), cutting investment in heavy industry by 18 percent, and cutting defense spending by 14.5 percent from the original 1990 budget plan.

In 1990 it seems possible that economic gains can be achieved through defense spending reductions. Announced defense cuts include troop reductions of at least 500,000 troops and the retirement of 10,300 tanks, with half of them converted into tractors. Eight hundred aircraft are scheduled to be taken out of service, with savings gained through the use of old planes for spare parts. More important, the defense industry has come under increasing pressure to convert to the production of consumer goods. Prime Minister Ryzhkov announced in 1990 that by 1995 current defense industries would produce up to 60 percent of civilian goods.

Gorbachev and his reforms also reevaluated promises of quick and tangible improvements in the living standard made in the early stages of reform. In January 1990, Abalkin began stating that the economic reform program would not significantly improve the standard of living in the Soviet Union until 1995. Because of popular unrest, certain reforms were put on hold. Perhaps remembering the Polish experience, the Soviets have delayed decontrolling prices on consumer goods, such as milk, meat, and rents. In May 1990, the Congress of People's Deputies rejected a government proposal to increase prices on certain foodstuffs by as much as 300 percent.

In October 1989, Finance Minister Pavlov submitted his proposed 1990 budget, which called for increased prices on cigarettes, beer, and other luxury goods, to raise three billion rubles for social programs. He also announced that diesel fuel, cement, and steel would be sold in market auctions by 1991. However, the Supreme Soviet voted against the "sin taxes" on luxury goods and instead approved a 490 billion ruble budget that included a 60 billion ruble government deficit. Instead of price hikes, the legislature called for bond sales to raise government money.

In December 1989, Gorbachev called for an All-Union Scientific-Practical Conference in which almost every major economic figure took part. While conservative and liberal economists argued over the path to be taken in the future, both sides agreed that the past four-and-a-half years had failed to reinvigorate the economy and that perestroika had pulled down the old structures but failed to erect effective structures in their place.

Many conservative and liberal economists agreed that the government would have to play a powerful role in reorganizing the economy. Ed Hewett describes the government's response as an "Emergency Program for 1990," and it includes delaying price reforms and controlling wage hikes. However, the liberal proposals to emerge from the program are just as decisive. For example, economist Oleg Bogomolov called for a market system of ownership in agriculture, light industry, and food sectors because these are the most responsive to profit incentives.

Following the conference, Leonid Abalkin proposed a wide-ranging reform program that included enterprise bankruptcy in the absense of profitability by 1995, ownership deregulation, fully competitive wages, a stock market and credit system, and anti-trust laws. Most Soviet economists, including Abalkin, however, maintain confidence in some aspects of a socialist economy. For example, Abalkin defends a government role in unemployment programs and government ownership of large enterprises.

In November 1989, Alexander Burkov, chairman of the State Savings Bank, stated, "Our aim is to help every Soviet person, should he desire, to become a businessperson and to grant credits for various projects." In late 1989 Gorbachev went as far as to reassess Marx: "Marx underestimated the capacity for self-development displayed by capitalism, which was able to assimilate the achievements of the scientific and technological revolution, to set up social-economic structures which would ensure its vitality, and to create a relatively high level of prosperity for most of the population."

However, radical changes may not improve the economy fast enough to ensure stability. A late 1989 survey revealed that while only 28 percent of Soviet citizens said they felt a direct financial loss because of the economic situation, 75 percent felt the economy was not functioning well. The government is forced to respond to these sentiments. As part of Gorbachev's emergency package, Premier Ryzhkov predicted an increase in consumer goods production from 27 billion dollars in 1989 to 105 billion dollars by 1996. But responding to popular unrest has distracted the leadership from conducting a true reform, and in 1989 and 1990 it often has seemed that Gorbachev was running from one trouble spot to the next.

Soviet Agriculture

For decades agriculture has been one of the problem areas of the Soviet economy. Lenin and the Bolsheviks came to power in the name of the proletariat, but in 1917 the workers constituted only a small percentage of the population. An early priority of the regime was to reach an accommodation with the peasants to overcome anti-Bolshevik sentiments and ensure a food supply for the cities. Although Lenin ordered forced requisitions of grain during the War Communism period (1918-1921), he attempted to establish good relations with the peasantry during the New Economic Policy of the 1920s. The state promised to provide more consumer goods to the villages and to use a *prodnalog* (tax in kind) instead of requisitions to acquire agricultural goods.

In the late 1920s Stalin returned to the use of requisitions and began mass collectivization of the peasantry into communal farms (*kolkhozi*). Many poorer peasants actively supported collectivization because the program took land from the richer peasants (*kulaks*). The policy escalated out of control, however, and peasants who resisted collectivization were labeled kulaks and deported to labor camps.

Alec Nove described the short-term results of collectivization: "The peasants were demoralized. Collective farms were inefficient, the horses slaughtered or starving

[peasants slaughtered their animals instead of turning them over to the authorities], tractors as yet too few and poorly maintained, transport facilities inadequate, the retail distribution system utterly disorganized by an overprecipitate abolition of private trade." The establishment of collectivized agriculture was brutal, and the system failed to fulfill the Soviet Union's food needs.

Agricultural performance was a much higher priority under Khrushchev and Brezhnev. As Nove states, Khrushchev's Virgin Lands program "between 1953 and 1956 increased cultivated land by 35 million hectares, an area equivalent to the total cultivated land of Canada. World history knows nothing like it." Brezhnev used river diversion and land reclamation schemes to further increase Soviet arable lands. Unfortunately, because of the adverse environmental effects of such programs, the leadership cannot return to the policy of massive land reclamation.

Despite these aggressive investment programs, growth of agricultural output continued to decline, leaving the Soviets, in the 1970s, dependent on grain imports. Each time production failed to improve, the authorities expanded the peasants' privileges regarding private plots and food markets. These private plots—from which peasants can receive profits—are much more productive than the collective farms. Private plots use less than 3 percent of arable land but produce about 30 percent of total agricultural output. The success of private plots has demonstrated that the most serious defect of the Soviet agricultural system is that farmers have no incentive to produce on state-owned land. Collective farmers are paid on a wage basis, not for the output of their land, and therefore have no interest in using the land efficiently.

Upon taking office Gorbachev promoted reforms of agricultural methods. His original speeches extolled independent brigades—an idea revived from Khrushchev—in which ten or twelve collective-farm peasants would work a certain part of the collective's land and receive extra earnings if they achieved above-plan output. While this still would be a collective form of production, Gorbachev believed brigade workers would show greater initiative. The agricultural super-ministry—*Gosagroprom*—was established to coordinate the industrial, research, and economic needs of the agricultural sector. In the meantime, Gorbachev followed the old pattern of increasing investment in agriculture and stressing central planning.

However, agricultural output declined by 2.5 and 2 percent in 1987 and 1988, respectively, and it increased by only 1.9 percent in 1989, though the plan called for growth of more than 6.6 percent. According to 1989 Soviet statistics, 3 percent of all collective farms are failing to break even, but the number of unprofitable collective farms is probably higher. Because farms still are failing to fulfill Soviet needs, the government was forced to purchase 223 thousand tons of wheat at world market prices in 1989.

Gorbachev's agricultural policies have grown increasingly liberal, and proposals in this sector have been among the most progressive of his economic reforms. As Leonid Abalkin noted in 1990, because new methods can be applied to agriculture each year without major capital investments, the agriculture sector can quickly convert to new economic conditions. Therefore he called for it to be switched over to a free market system as quickly as possible. At the Central Committee plenum in February 1990, Gorbachev stated, "All obstacles should be removed in the way of the farmer, he should be given a free hand."

Toward this end the Soviet government is allowing

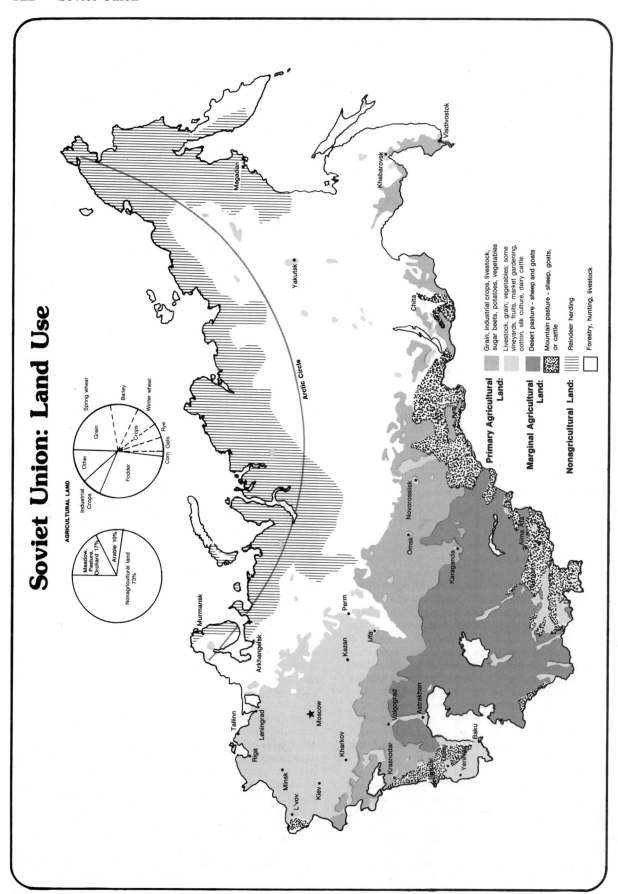

Soviet Union: Land Use

AGRICULTURAL LAND

Spring wheat
Barley
Grain
Winter wheat
Other
Crops
Rye
Industrial
Crops
Corn
Oats
Fodder

Meadow,
Pasture,
Orchard 17%
Arable 10%
Nonagricultural land
73%

Primary Agricultural Land:
Grain, industrial crops, livestock, sugar beets, potatoes, vegetables
Livestock, grain, vegetables; some vineyards, fruits, market gardening, cotton, silk culture, dairy cattle

Marginal Agricultural Land:
Desert pasture - sheep and goats
Mountain pasture - sheep, goats, or cattle

Nonagricultural Land:
Reindeer herding
Forestry, hunting, livestock

Arctic Circle

Magadan
Yakutsk
Chita
Vladivostok
Khabarovsk
Novorossiisk
Omsk
Karaganda
Alma Ata
Perm
Kazan
Ufa
Volgograd
Astrakhan
Baku
Yerevan
Krasnodar
Moscow
Kharkov
Kiev
L'vov
Minsk
Leningrad
Riga
Tallinn
Murmansk
Arkhangelsk

more private farms to be established and is allowing leasing of collective-farm property, steps that should give farmers more interest in using their land efficiently. In early 1990, the government also proposed allowing the inheritance of private land by the owner's children.

Social and technological problems related to agriculture also need to be solved. Gorbachev has called for improved rural living conditions to induce people to return to or stay in the villages. The Soviets have acknowledged the need to upgrade their rural infrastructure, which has deteriorated because the government focused its attention in rural areas almost exclusively on expanding agricultural production. The lack of proper storage and transportation facilities causes the Soviets to lose as much as 30 percent of agricultural output before it can be consumed.

Perhaps the most problematic aspect of reforming Soviet agriculture is that effective reforms must include higher food prices. The government has been hesitant to raise food prices because the Soviet people have come to expect subsidies. Nevertheless, both collective and private farm produce prices have begun to increase. According to Soviet statistics that likely are low, spending on food products in the USSR increased between 5 and 10 percent. In February 1990, consumers were told that because farmers were not selling as much grain to the state, meat production would begin declining. Party conservative Yegor Ligachev announced at that time that industrial centers were suffering "serious difficulties" because producers were not meeting grain delivery orders. Because a food shortage would stir public unrest, improving the food supply remains one of the Soviet leadership's top priorities.

Energy

The Soviet Union remains the only major industrial nation not dependent on some outside source of energy. In fact, the USSR has the largest reserve of oil in the world outside the Persian Gulf. It also has more than 37 percent of the world's proven natural gas reserves. Abundant coal supplies and an effective hydroelectric program also have played major roles in Soviet development. Finally, at least prior to the Chernobyl nuclear disaster in 1986, the nuclear energy program was moving briskly forward.

However, as Leslie Dienes of Radio Liberty has pointed out, "In 1977 and 1984-85, the USSR was confronted with an energy crisis. In both cases, the leadership responded with a crash program involving massive infusions of resources, hasty improvisation, and gigantic waste." Many Western analysts consider 1989 and 1990 to be new crisis years for the Soviet energy complex.

According to statistics printed in *Izvestiia* that likely are optimistic, 1989 oil output declined 2.6 percent from the previous year and coal extraction decreased 4 percent. The effect of these declines was evident in the number of articles printed in the Soviet press on energy shortages and rationing. The worst part of energy production shortfalls for the Soviets, however, was the lost hard-currency income from energy exports. Coal exports fell short of expectations by two million tons, and oil delivery backlogs were reported by the Soviet Union's East and West European trade partners.

Past programs, geared for extensive growth of energy resources, can be blamed for many current Soviet energy problems. In their rush to extract ever-greater quantities of energy, the Soviets failed to develop adequate technology for resource exploitation. Environmental issues also were ignored as demonstrated by Chernobyl and the all-round environmental degradation in the Soviet Union.

One of Gorbachev's first trips after becoming general secretary was to Tyumen in Western Siberia, where he delivered a speech that was critical of past management in the energy sector. He criticized past exploitation techniques, overzealous production that led to inefficiency, and the failure to build an effective infrastructure. He called for an "intensive" energy program that included increased conservation efforts, an emphasis on developing new technology, and increased participation by Western companies. Gorbachev's choices in energy policy are limited, however, because existing resources are less accessible than in the past, hard-currency shortfalls do not allow for decreases in energy exports, and new technologies needed for nuclear energy and more efficient exploitation require large investment at a time when the Soviets have no excess capital.

Gorbachev's energy program has progressed in stages like the rest of perestroika. At first, while talking about greater efficiency, the Soviets continued to pour resources into raw material exploitation. The Soviets announced in 1985 that they would step up oil drilling by 40 percent nationwide through 1986. During the first three years of the Twelfth FYP (1986, 1987, and 1988), average expenditures on oil extraction continued to increase by 10 percent yearly. Meanwhile, conservation schemes had little effect. The price of energy remained low, causing enterprise managers to disregard energy usage among their budgetary considerations.

In 1989 Gorbachev appeared to recognize that further extensive exploitation of energy resources would be difficult and counterproductive. He cut back investment in the oil industry and focused on other energy resources and strategies. He since has tried to turn the energy situation around by holding enterprises accountable for their energy usage, allowing energy sales to more accurately reflect market prices in the domestic and East European markets, and continuing to promote Western involvement in resource exploitation. The Soviets also are hoping to rely more heavily on their abundant reserves of natural gas to meet domestic energy needs.

Environmental concerns will play an important role in decisions regarding further exploitation of hydroelectric and nuclear energy capabilities. River diversion projects have come under severe criticism for their effect on the environment. In the wake of Chernobyl, the Soviet nuclear program has limped on. But, authorities no longer are able to conduct their nuclear policy in secrecy. As Soviet citizens become more involved in political affairs, it is likely that they—like their West and East European neighbors—will call for cutbacks in the nuclear energy program.

Oil production has remained relatively stagnant since 1981, with a production of 609 million tons in that year and 607 million tons in 1989. Production in 1989 was 18.7 million tons below target but still accounted for approximately 12 million barrels of oil per day. This is slightly less than production between 1986 and 1988—which went as high as 12.6 million barrels per day. Two-thirds of proven Soviet oil deposits are located in Western Siberia, and the difficult climate and over-exploitation in this area have led to decreasing oil production.

Natural gas production, in contrast to oil, has grown strongly, accounting for most of the gain in fuel production during the 1980s. In fact, production of natural gas has

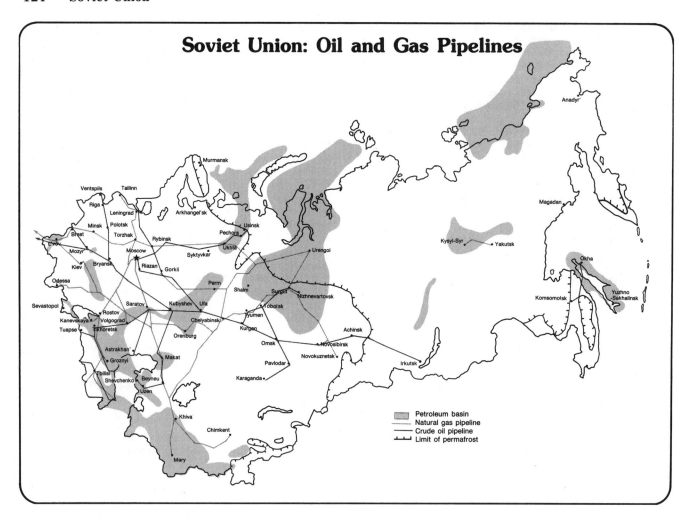

Soviet Union: Oil and Gas Pipelines

Petroleum basin
Natural gas pipeline
Crude oil pipeline
Limit of permafrost

consistently grown beyond planners' expectations. Total natural gas production was 770 billion cubic meters in 1988, and this increased to 796 billion cubic meters in 1989—again slightly above plan targets. Natural gas exports to Western Europe increased dramatically during the second half of the 1980s.

The Soviet Union depends heavily on oil and gas exports to earn foreign currency for vital imports such as machinery and grains. Approximately one-third of oil production is earmarked for export. Fuel, raw materials, and energy-complex equipment account for 80 percent of Soviet trade with Organization for Economic Cooperation and Development (OECD) countries. Economic relations with Western and Eastern Europe have revolved around oil and natural gas exports.

The depressed world oil price through most of the 1980s led to declining Soviet hard-currency reserves, which Gorbachev and other Soviet officials have cited as an excuse for present economic difficulties. The purchasing power of a barrel of Soviet oil is only one-quarter of what it was in 1985. Increasing need for oil in the Soviet Union and declining value of that oil abroad led to a downward trend in Soviet oil and gas exports during the late 1980s, with East European and West European partners noting slowdowns and delays in deliveries throughout 1989. Bulgaria, in January 1990, reported that Soviet oil deliveries were down 50 percent, forcing the Soviets to buy oil from Iran.

This trend not only limited technology imports from the West, it caused the Soviets to lose economic influence in Eastern Europe, which has long been dependent on Soviet energy supplies.

International Trade

The Soviet Union's trade pattern, which like many Third World nations consists of raw material exports and finished product imports, has been criticized by the Soviet leadership. In 1986, machinery, equipment, and consumer goods accounted for only eighteen billion of the Soviet Union's total ninety-seven billion dollars' worth of exports. Soviet exports have consisted mostly of raw materials—especially oil. As oil prices have declined and production has stagnated during the 1980s, the Soviets have found themselves with a deteriorating trade situation. Gorbachev has expressed his unhappiness with Soviet trade, saying that the Soviet Union's "position in international trade is not commensurate with its economic potential and political status." The Soviets hope to reduce their dependence on raw materials for export earnings and instead begin exporting light-industrial and manufactured products. In November 1989, Ivan Ivanov, deputy chairman of the State Commission on Foreign Economic Relations, stated that the

Soviet Union would increase the percent of finished products in exports by 50 percent by the year 2000. He also called for a freezing of exports of raw materials at 1985 levels.

Beginning in the early 1970s Soviet grain imports from the United States and other countries began to increase. Despite the grain embargo imposed by Jimmy Carter in response to the Soviet invasion of Afghanistan in 1979, Soviet imports continued to grow as Moscow turned to other exporters—Argentina, Canada, Australia, and Brazil. In 1981 President Ronald Reagan fulfilled a campaign promise to end the embargo. Subsequently the United States and Soviet Union completed a five-year grain purchase agreement. Soviet agriculture has remained unable to meet the country's food needs, and imports have continued to rise during the 1980s. In 1990 the United States and the Soviet Union completed yet another agricultural agreement, which called for further increases in Soviet grain imports from U.S. suppliers.

Before Gorbachev, the Soviets prided themselves on a balanced budget overall and balanced trade relations with each of their trade partners. The United States was one of the few countries with which the Soviets ran a trade deficit. The Soviets made up for this deficit by having a trade surplus with Western Europe. Until recently, all trade was controlled by the State Committee for Foreign Economic Relations. Gorbachev's reforms have allowed almost any enterprise that produces an exportable good to enter into its own trade relations.

East-West Trade

After World War II political relations between East and West soured and economic ties suffered as a result. After the Soviets defaulted on the remaining payments on their lend-lease loans—estimated, together with unpaid loans to Kerensky's Provisional Government, at 1.54 billion dollars—the United States restricted further economic cooperation with the USSR. The Soviets created the Council for Mutual Economic Assistance (CMEA or Comecon) in 1949 to ensure economic and political coordination with the new East European satellites. The Western nations created CoCom (the Coordinating Committee on Multilateral Export Controls) also in 1949 to prevent the sale of high-tech goods to the East Bloc that might damage Western security interests. As long as Western Europe accepted American leadership, this coordination was relatively successful, yet during the 1970s and 1980s Western Europe became more willing than the United States to pursue economic cooperation with the Soviets.

The improvement in East-West relations in the early 1970s led to increased economic cooperation between the West Europeans and Soviets. The United States, however, continued to believe that economic leverage could force the Soviet government to make policy changes in areas such as foreign affairs and human rights. In December 1974, Congress passed the Jackson-Vanik and Stephenson amendments. The first linked most-favored-nation (MFN) status to human rights performance and the second limited U.S. lending to the Soviets. The Soviets denounced the Jackson-Vanik amendment as interference in their internal affairs and refused to comply with its terms. As a result, U.S.-Soviet trade remained limited.

Despite Western restrictions, Soviet trade with the developed countries increased. By the late 1970s, trade with the United States, Western Europe, and Japan made up more than one-third of all Soviet trade. However, during the 1980s this trend reversed, and by 1985 Soviet trade with the developed countries was less than 30 percent of the total.

The Reagan and Bush administrations and Congress have reacted slowly to the Soviet Union's economic and political reforms. In 1988, the United States voted against Soviet participation in GATT (General Agreement on Tariffs and Trade) international trade negotiations. In October of that year, Sen. Bill Bradley, D-N.J., expressed the popular feeling of caution toward expanding trade ties too quickly: "It would be a tragic mistake if Western capital enables the USSR to put off the hard choice between guns and butter." However, as Gorbachev's reforms have grown more radical, many U.S. policy makers have reconsidered the need for restrictive trade policies. American business leaders have increased pressure on the government to respond positively to Soviet trade overtures. When President Bush met with Gorbachev in Malta, he delivered a list of proposals for economic cooperation that included providing bilateral insurance for investments in the Soviet Union (a prerequisite for many American businesses) and a waiver of Jackson-Vanik on the condition that the Soviet Congress approves a new immigration law. In 1989 and 1990, the administration worked toward streamlining CoCom restrictions (most notably on personal computers), a move that reflected a growing pragmatism toward East-West trade. In December 1989, the Soviets signed a ten-year trade agreement with the European Community, and in February 1990, the United States and the Soviet Union opened trade talks. In 1990 several members of Congress proposed including the Soviet Union in the Support for East European Democracy (SEED) program, which grants economic assistance as an incentive to continue democratic and economic liberalization.

To enhance their ability to work with Western nations, the Soviets have opened branches of the Moscow People's Bank in other countries. In July 1989, the New York office opened. Other branches are located in Great Britain, Singapore, West Germany, France, Luxembourg, Switzerland, and Austria. The first issues of Soviet bonds have been floated on Western European markets and have been popular with investors. Soviet enterprises are even participating in Western-style, high-risk capital ventures.

Soviet foreign trade increased by 4.7 percent in 1989. Overall exports (totaling 68.2 billion rubles) were up 1.7 percent, while imported goods (totaling 70.2 billion rubles) increased 7.9 percent. Twenty-six billion rubles' worth of production were exported to the capitalist states, while imports from these states totaled 26.8 billion rubles (23.6 percent growth over 1988). However, 80 percent of Soviet trade with the OECD countries continues to be in fuels, raw materials, and equipment processing these goods.

The ruble's inconvertibility—it is illegal to transport the currency into and out of the Soviet Union and foreign companies have difficulty repatriating profits made in the country—has been a longstanding obstacle to increased foreign participation in the Soviet economy. In August 1989, Finance Minister Pavlov announced that "in 1960, one ruble bought 1.42 rubles' worth of goods, but in 1989, one ruble buys less than .2 rubles' worth." The government seemed to be moving in the right direction in 1989 when it devalued the ruble by ten times, decreasing its value from 1.0 ruble per 1.6 dollars to 1.0 ruble per .16 dollars. However, this new exchange rate applies only for tourists, forcing foreign companies to continue using counter trade (a form of barter). The Soviets are planning a full currency reform scheduled for the early 1990s. This plan envisions reducing the ruble to three different convertibility rates: one for raw material exports, another for manufactured goods, and, finally, one for travellers. The first currency auction was held in October 1989 at which Soviet enterprises could purchase hard currency for rubles. Buyers purchased 13.5 million "hard-currency rubles" at a price of 15.2 regular rubles for 1 hard-currency ruble, reflecting the true value of the ruble.

One of the most publicized methods for increasing Western and Japanese participation in the Soviet economy has been the joint venture, which usually has combined Soviet labor and resources with foreign management techniques and capital investment. However, the joint venture program got off to a slow start for two reasons. First, Soviet partners were inexperienced in creating joint ventures. Second, few Western partners have been willing to participate because the new Soviet legislation remained restrictive, and they saw little advantage in such ventures given the current economic climate in the Soviet Union.

As of May 1989, only two hundred joint ventures had been agreed upon between Western and Soviet partners. However, the Soviets have continued to modify joint venture regulations, easing them to allow foreign management and more than 50 percent ownership. Later in 1989, the number of joint ventures began to increase so that by year's end there were 1,274 agreements involving sixty foreign countries. According to Soviet statistics, 33 percent of the joint ventures are in food production and another 15 percent are involved in the petroleum sector. Only two hundred of these joint ventures are actually in operation.

Trade with CMEA and the Third World

In 1949, the Soviets founded the Council for Mutual Economic Assistance with the new East European regimes as a mechanism to consolidate control over Eastern Europe. As of 1990 the USSR, Poland, Hungary, Czechoslovakia, Romania, Bulgaria, East Germany, Mongolia, Vietnam, and Cuba remained members. The Soviets first used CMEA to strip Eastern Europe of its industrial strength as a form of reparation. Later, seeing the Marshall Plan's appeal to Eastern Europe, CMEA became more of an "assistance" council. At least until 1973, however, economic ties with the socialist states benefited the Soviet Union because the Soviets forced disadvantageous terms of trade upon their partners. However, the Soviets also wanted to ensure the loyalty and stability of Eastern Europe and, therefore, subsidized trade with those countries, especially after the Hungarian Revolution in 1956. Beginning in 1975, prices between Comecon members were set according to the "Bucharest Formula," which is a five-year moving average of the world price on each good. This allowed the Soviets to further subsidize their East European partners by accepting higher prices for their manufactured goods than they could get on the world market. The system also insulated Soviet and East European economic decision making from world fluctuations. When the price of oil skyrocketed in the 1970s, the Soviets opted to supply their partners with low-cost energy. The Soviets also picked up the defense burden for their allies. Therefore, in the 1970s, the Soviet Union's East European empire became more of a burden than an asset. Sovietologist Dina R. Spechler—who makes one of the most conservative calculations of the burden of the Soviets' East European empire—argues that

funds flowed from the empire to the Soviets until 1973, reversed and peaked in 1980 when the Soviets were spending 1.5 percent of their GNP subsidizing their empire, and by 1988, had decreased to between .75 and 1 percent of GNP.

Among CMEA members, Soviet raw materials have been exchanged for East European manufactured products. All transactions have taken place in nonconvertible, accounting units known as transferable rubles. East European nations have built up surpluses that can be used for future purchases. The CMEA nations have found themselves dependent on the Soviet Union because their goods are not of high enough quality to sell on world markets and the Soviets offer the cheapest price for oil.

Eastern Europe's revolutions have made the future of CMEA uncertain. Nikolai Ryzkhov, at a CMEA meeting in early 1990 in Sofia, stated, "Cooperation has become less attractive. Most of the [CMEA] countries have experienced a decrease in their competitiveness on foreign markets, a drop in their share of world trade and an increase in foreign debt."

The developing world makes up a third category of nations trading with the Soviets. These are the only countries that import Soviet manufactured goods. Most Soviet exports to the Third World, however, consist of raw materials and arms, another major source of export earnings. In the past the Soviets have traded arms to Middle Eastern nations in exchange for gas and oil, but the drop in oil prices has limited these types of exchanges. The Soviets also have been under pressure from the West to reduce exports of arms.

Countries that Moscow once considered the tools of capitalists have garnered greater Soviet attention. For example, trade with Brazil, Argentina—the Soviets' largest Latin American trade partner outside of Cuba—South Korea, Thailand, Singapore, and others (including Israel) has been reevaluated. The Soviets have slowly worked toward better political relations with these countries, and economic activity has shown modest increases.

Future of Economic Reform

When Gorbachev came to power, the Soviet economy was in trouble, but it was not in utter collapse. Despite widespread inefficiency, consumer shortages, and economic malaise, the Soviet economy likely could have stumbled along for a number of years. The confusion and upheaval that have accompanied Gorbachev's reforms, however, seem to have caused the Soviet economy to decline. Regardless of whether the overall state of the economy has deteriorated, polls show that the Soviet people believe this to be the case, and more consumer goods are being rationed. The economy's apparent stagnation during Gorbachev's first five years in power does not mean that the reforms will fail. But for the reforms to succeed, the Soviet people have to be willing to withstand the hard times that likely will continue.

Gorbachev's habit of throwing money at problems as they occur, instead of establishing a blueprint for change, has hurt the prospects for successful reform. Although he is responsible for beginning the reform process, and he has pushed reforms faster than most Soviet and Western observers would have predicted, through June 1990 he had continued to work within a socialist framework that opposes many of the reforms necessary to build an effective market economy. He also has taken some steps in the wrong order. For example, introducing the anti-alcohol campaign in 1985 only hurt his popularity and cost the state billions of rubles.

However, in judging Gorbachev's performance, one must remember that no precedent exists for creating an efficient, market-style economy from the ruins of a centralized one. Polish Solidarity leader Lech Walesa observed that this is like putting a scrambled egg back into its shell. Gorbachev's backtracking and ad hoc methods, therefore, are understandable, particularly given the many political pressures that he has faced.

Economic reform has been difficult to implement within the powerful Communist sociopolitical culture that exists in the Soviet Union. Since it took power, the party has had an informal pact with the Soviet people, whereby it provides them with basic needs in return for their acceptance of the party's leadership role. The party, therefore, was expected to ensure full employment, adequate supplies of basic needs such as housing and food, and wage equalization. Gorbachev understands that continuing to fulfill this contract will lead to a further slide of the Soviet economy. However, breaking the contract with the people has cost the party much of its legitimacy. Gorbachev has not been able to forge a new contract with the people, and until he does their disgust with his economic program likely will grow. The people also have become used to the "easy" life of communism. Workers were not threatened with unemployment for their poor work. Enterprises could operate unprofitably but remain in business. Although the Soviet system brought less improvement in long-term consumer welfare, most Soviet citizens were not willing to risk the economic guarantees that they enjoyed to improve the system. The popular rejection of reform may be Gorbachev's greatest opponent. During a break in the Twenty-eighth Party Congress in July 1990, Gorbachev sought to ease popular impatience with the economy by stating: "I think that in two years, if there are no changes [economic improvements], this leadership must go."

It is difficult to predict exactly which combination of policies will turn the Soviet economy around, but most Western analysts believe that the Soviet Union must increase its economic efficiency through market mechanisms. This will require further decentralization of economic decision making combined with assurances to entrepreneurs that the system will remain stable. Profits must act as the incentive for economic activity. Enterprises and workers must be able to make a profit for their labor and retain it. If they fail to make a profit, they must be faced with full financial responsibility. Finally, government interference— price controls and subsidies—must not be the norm of economic activity. Factors of productivity—labor, land,

rents—if they are not at their market price, will continue to be used inefficiently.

Under Mikhail Gorbachev the Soviet economy has started down this path, though Gorbachev has been hesitant to allow changes that diminish Communist party control. Nevertheless, each time it seemed that the party had been pushed as far as it would go, that some ideological restriction would make the next step impossible, Gorbachev has surprised the world and accepted that step. As recently as 1988, it seemed implausible that the 1990 Communist party platform could include the statement, "The CPSU believes the existence of individual property, including ownership of the means of production, does not contradict the modern stage of the country's economy development." After all this, it is difficult to doubt Gorbachev's willingness to try any experiment to reinvigorate the economy.

Some conservatives in the Soviet Union will fight this progress, but as of 1990, the only group that still favors stopping the reform process are the Russian nationalists. If they were to take control of this multi-ethnic country, they would be in for a civil war, throwing the economy into a worse predicament than it is in now. And, as Sovietologist Dimitri Simes has stated, conservatives and neo-nationalists have "not offered attractive leaders or a credible alternative program" to Gorbachev and perestroika.

What then can be expected in the short term? First, decentralization of economic mechanisms will continue, with markets operating in most areas, including the currency. At the same time, the Communist-led government, which cannot completely drop its socialist ideology, will defend social programs at least as encompassing as Sweden's.

The Baltic republics will continue to seek some form of independence. Their economic and social links with Russia and small size, however, will demand at least a temporary economic collaboration with the Soviet Union. They probably will join the more progressive CMEA countries in establishing a market-oriented economic community. The Soviet Union will need to continue cutting back on defense spending, pursuing arms control, and negotiating settlements of regional conflicts.

As of 1990, the prospects for Gorbachev's economic reforms were mixed. On the one hand, new economic mechanisms had begun to take hold, and new forms of economic activity had become widespread, including leases, cooperatives, and joint ventures. On the other hand, popular unrest had grown, and the leadership had delayed painful reforms—such as freeing prices—that were necessary to make the economy more efficient. However, if Gorbachev manages to stay in power and surprises the world once again by moving the reform program ahead, the Soviet economy may improve dramatically.

Ethnicity and Culture

For decades the Soviet people (*sovetskii narod*) have had to reconcile the stated ideals of the Bolshevik revolution with the realities of life in the Soviet Union. Since 1917, the Soviet people have been living under the banners of socialist internationalism, the collegiality of member republics of the USSR, and socialist labor and equality. Yet the facts of Soviet life have matched poorly with these high values. This disparity is not new. Since the end of World War II, many Western scholars have used it as a tool to understand Soviet politics and society. Nor is this disparity between social ideals and realities unique to the Soviet Union. As Soviet commentators have been quick to point out, both developing and developed states around the world have their own ethnic tensions and social inequalities.

The discrepancy proves useful in drawing attention to the ideals of Soviet life and in focusing on the way in which Soviet institutions really function. Indeed, under Mikhail S. Gorbachev's administration, the process has begun to remake Soviet ideals so that they might conform better to the demands of modern life. The Soviet people, after decades of censorship and misinformation, have begun to focus on the inconsistencies of their living conditions. Under Gorbachev's policy of *glasnost* (openness), the entire Soviet population has been invited for the first time since the 1920s to participate in the life of the state by identifying and offering solutions to the problems in their lives. "There is no democracy, nor can there be, without glasnost," wrote Gorbachev in his 1987 book, *Perestroika: New Thinking for Our Country and the World.* For the Soviet citizen, glasnost means being able to criticize the state as a first step in making it accountable to the people it is charged to serve, with the ultimate aim of making the ideals of the Bolshevik revolution more a part of reality.

One of Gorbachev's most impressive achievements has been to mobilize the various institutions of cultural life (literature, journalism, theater, television) behind reform. The ethnicity or nationality question has been more troublesome and less open to control from above. This lack of success partly is due to the characteristics of Soviet history—that very history that now is being reevaluated and rewritten in the context of glasnost. Both ethnic and cultural leaders have begun to construct, in effect, a historical balance sheet of promises made, of promises kept, and of promises broken. The settling of these accounts holds different consequences for the future of the Soviet state.

Ethnicity in the USSR

The USSR has the third largest population in the world (almost 290 million people according to 1989 figures) behind China and India. The Soviet Union, however, is unrivaled in the number of native ethnic groups it contains. It brings together Slavic, Turkic, Caucasian, Baltic, Finno-Ugric, Iranian, Mongolic, and Siberian peoples, each of which share the ties of language, folklore, customs, and lifestyles. Within these ethnic groups also exist separate nationalities that enjoy certain rights of political autonomy and territorial integrity.

This mosaic is made even more complicated by geographic, language, and religious factors. An estimated sixty million Soviets live outside of their home republics or regions. Tens of thousands of Christian Armenians live within the borders of Moslem Azerbaidzhan, and hundreds of thousands of Moslem Tatars live within the borders of the Russian Republic, which is predominantly Orthodox Christian. Approximately twenty-four million Soviet Russians live outside the Russian Republic, mostly in urban centers. For example, two-thirds of the population of Alma Ata, the capital of Kazakhstan, is Russian. The populations of Tashkent (capital of Uzbekistan) and Kiev (capital of the Ukraine) are approximately one-quarter Russian.

Speakers of the same language group in the Soviet Union sometimes live far removed from each other. Estonians speak a Finno-Ugric language but live in the Baltic region of the Soviet Union, sharing the values of neighboring Latvians and Lithuanians, who speak variants of the Indo-European language group. The Iakuts are a Turkic-speaking people but live in Siberia, sharing the lifestyles and values of their Mongolic and Siberian neighbors, far away from their Turkic kin of Central Asia. Although this ethnic mixing is a remarkable characteristic of Soviet life, most nationality groups (as members of the same linguistic group) speak languages that are, to a degree, mutually intelligible.

Beyond the traditional factors of ethnic separation and mixing, Soviet nationality groups are subject to contemporary strains on their cohesiveness. Urbanization, education, military service, the media, bilingualism, intermarriage, and social mobility are among the most important processes that are at work in integrating these diverse peoples. The Ukrainians, Belorussians, Karelians, Mordvinians,

Germans, and Jews have been most susceptible to integration, particularly in their acceptance of Russian values and the Russian language as native or near native. So far, however, most ethnic groups have resisted integrating pressures.

Fifteen ethnic groups of the Soviet Union enjoy the special status of having their own Soviet Socialist Republic (SSR). These "union" republics (Russia, the Ukraine, Belorussia, Estonia, Latvia, Lithuania, Moldavia, Georgia, Armenia, Azerbaidzhan, Kazakhstan, Uzbekistan, Turkmenistan, Tadzhikistan, and Kirgizia) are "nation-states" of a kind, possessing separate republic governments, legislatures, court systems, academic and scientific institutions, and the formal legal right to secede from the Union. Each of the union republics is granted thirty-two delegates within the new Congress of People's Deputies.

The remaining territorial units within the USSR exist within the confines of and are subject to the authority of the union republics. These units (thirty-eight in all) are the autonomous republics, the autonomous regions, and the national districts. Most of them either lie within or adjoin the Russian Republic. They have certain linguistic and cultural rights and are entitled to representation within the Congress of People's Deputies (eleven representatives from each autonomous republic, five from each autonomous region, and one from each national district).

This federal system, since its first foundations in 1922, has been qualified by the central control of the Communist party (which always has been predominantly Slavic, staffed by Russians, Ukrainians, and Belorussians). The party has ruled the Soviet Union with an executive power guaranteed to it by historical events and by the Constitutions of the USSR (1924, 1936, 1977). Since this central monopoly of power was renounced in February 1990 by the Communist party the question arises: What new shape might the federal structure take? Part of the answer to this question lies in history, part in the flow of contemporary events. How did the peoples of the Soviet Union secure recognition of their rights as nationality groups within the union, yet lose the power to exercise them fully? What are their prospects for regaining full rights? These questions are the subject of the following review.

Early Soviet Nationality Policy

As Gail Lapidus, professor at the University of California, has noted in a 1989 article in *Foreign Affairs,* the conflict between economic integration and national self-determination is at the heart of Communist party policy toward the Soviet state. This conflict was evident in Lenin's own writings and those of his party comrades, and it can be found in contemporary party platforms and discussions such as a recent debate in the controversial party theoretical journal *Kommunist.*

The Soviet ideal, predominant in Communist party writings from Lenin to Gorbachev, places a high value not on national self-determination, but on a central, unified state. Marx assumed that economic unification—through modernization, industrialization, and urbanization—would compel social and ethnic unification as well. Early in his revolutionary career, Lenin subscribed to this view. Beginning with the years just before World War I, however, he began to qualify his demands for an integrated state, recognizing that, for the Bolshevik party to achieve power in "imperial" Russia, a compromise that would consider the desires of the non-Russian ethnic groups was necessary.

His choice of compromise was a federated state structure, one in which the ethnic and nationality groups within the empire would realize cultural autonomy and formal state powers—both nevertheless set in the political context of the central monopoly control of the Communist party. This right to national self-determination, promulgated in the pre-World War I platforms of the Bolshevik party, became a reality with the war and revolution of 1914-1917. The peoples of Finland, the Baltic states (Estonia, Latvia, Lithuania), Poland, the Ukraine, the Transcaucasus (Georgia, Armenia, Azerbaidzhan), and Central Asia (Kazakhstan, Kirgizia, Uzbekistan, and Turkmenistan), among others, broke off from the disintegrating Russian empire to form their own fledgling states.

With the reconquest of these territories (except Finland, the Baltic states, and Poland) by the Red Army between 1918 and 1922, Lenin conveniently neglected the very principle that he had been preaching before the war and revolution. His purpose was to keep some semblance of the former Russian state system intact. In constructing the new Russian federation upon the old empire, however, he continued to employ the principle of national self-determination. The new union republics retained governmental structures, the rights of representation within the union, the rights of diplomatic relations with foreign states, the rights of native language and cultural development, and even the right to secede from the USSR. These rights were guaranteed by the treaties and decrees signed between 1920 and 1922 that linked the first eight national republics and eleven national regions with the Russian Soviet Federated Socialist Republic (RSFSR), by the 1922 Declaration and Treaty on the Formation of the USSR, and by the subsequent constitution of 1924. In practice, these privileges were limited by several factors. Between 1920 and 1922 the RSFSR retained executive functions for the whole federation. Moreover, after the formation of the USSR in 1922, the Russian Communist party subordinated all other ethnic communist parties under its authority, thus maintaining its own "leading role" over the whole union. The right to secession also was conditioned by what the Communist party called the "interests of the proletarian revolution"—the defense of which for more than seventy years effectively precluded secession by any union republic from the USSR.

In terms of language development, Lenin himself was an opponent of "russification" (the imposition of the Russian language and Russian values on native cultures). His position can be attributed perhaps to his father's liberal views on the subject and his own upbringing in Simbirsk (now Ulianovsk), a territory heavily populated by non-Russians. During the 1920s, as a result of Lenin's influences, the union and autonomous republics and other national regions were allowed to develop their own cultures and languages through education and the press. "National communist" parties took shape in many of the republics. To emphasize this new compact, Moscow instituted a policy of "rooting" (*korenizatsiia*) local government and party officials in the national territories by emphasizing that they should use the native language. This policy applied to Russian officials working in non-Russian republics as well as to natives of the republics. Though the attempt to create cadres of Russians fluent in native languages failed, the development of native languages and cultures was a great success, as was the growth of literacy, particularly in the Caucasus, Central Asia, and the national regions of the RSFSR.

Population of Soviet Nationalities

Nationality	Population in thousands		1989 population with second language proficiency (in percent)	
	1979	1989	Russian	Other
USSR	262,084	285,688	24.2	5.3
Russian	137,397	145,071	0.1	4.0
Ukrainian	42,347	44,135	56.2	8.5
Uzbek	12,455	16,686	23.8	3.7
Belorussian	9,462	10,030	54.7	11.7
Kazakh	6,566	8,137	60.4	2.9
Azerbaidzhani	5,477	6,791	34.4	2.2
Tatar	6,185	6,645	70.8	5.3
Armenian	4,151	4,627	47.1	5.0
Tadzhik	2,897	4,216	27.7	12.2
Georgian	3,570	3,983	33.1	1.0
Moldavian	2,968	3,355	53.8	4.4
Lithuanian	2,850	3,068	37.9	1.6
Turkmen	2,027	2,718	27.8	2.0
Kirgiz	1,906	2,530	35.2	4.6
German	1,936	2,035	45.0	1.6
Chuvash	1,751	1,839	65.1	5.9
Latvian	1,439	1,459	64.4	2.5
Bashkir	1,371	1,449	71.8	3.6
Jewish	1,761	1,376	10.1	29.2
Mordvinian	1,191	1,153	62.5	8.9
Estonian	1,019	1,027	33.8	2.0
Chechen	755	958	74.0	.9
Udmurty	713	746	61.3	7.1
Mariitsy	621	670	68.8	5.8
Avartsy	482	604	60.6	6.7
Ossetin	541	597	68.9	12.2
Lezgin	382	466	53.4	19.8
Korean	388	437	43.3	3.7
Karakalpak	303	423	20.7	11.4
Buriat	352	421	72.0	2.8
Kabardin	321	394	77.1	.8
Iakut	328	382	64.9	1.5
Bulgarian	361	378	60.3	8.7
Dargin	287	365	68.0	1.8
Greek	344	358	39.5	16.6
Komi	327	345	62.1	6.2
Kumyk	228	282	74.5	1.1
Crimean Tatar	132	296	76.0	8.0
Uigur	211	262	58.3	10.9
Gypsy	209	262	63.3	13.8
Ingush	186	238	80.0	1.0
Turkish	93	207	40.2	30.6
Tuvinian	166	207	59.1	.4
Northern Peoples	158	197	49.5	5.4
Gagauz	173	197	71.1	6.9
Hungarian	171	172	43.3	11.7
Kurdish	116	153	28.8	40.3
Komi-Permiak	151	152	61.2	8.0
Romanian	129	146	50.9	11.6
Lak	100	118	76.4	2.9
Abkhaz	91	103	78.2	3.6

Source: Murray Feshbach, of Georgetown University, provided information from State Committee of the USSR for Statistics, *The National Composition of the Population* (Moscow: 1989).

Russian, however, remained the de facto state language in the 1920s, a practical requirement in such a large multi-ethnic state. Hence compromise was reached: The nationalities retained limited cultural and linguistic rights, as well as formal political rights, but they were subject to the executive power of the Russian-speaking Communist party.

More often than not during Joseph Stalin's long reign (1928-1953), the compromise was breached. Decrees on collectivization and industrialization destroyed traditional forms of life (especially in the Ukraine and Kazakhstan); decrees on Latinization of Arabic scripts between 1928 and 1934 and on Cyrillicization of Latin scripts between 1936 and 1940 created confusion and language divisions throughout the USSR; party purges beginning in the late 1920s, and continuing into the 1930s, targeted "national communists" for their localism, their ties abroad, or their alleged antiparty conspiracies with other Soviet ethnic groups.

The Stalinist violence of the late 1920s and 1930s reached into the 1940s and 1950s as well. As a result of World War II, Stalin confiscated the lands of hundreds of thousands of ethnic Crimean Tatars, Volga Germans, Meshketian Georgians, Chechen-Ingush, Kalmyks, Karachai, and Balkars, deporting them from their homelands to Central Asia and Siberia. They were accused, in most cases unjustly, of joining forces with Nazi Germany during the war. Moreover, as a result of the Hitler-Stalin Pact of 1939 and the westward advance of the Red Army during World War II, the Baltic Republics, Moldavia (Romanian Bessarabia), and parts of Finnish Karelia, Eastern Poland, and the Western Ukraine were annexed to the Soviet Union. The peoples of these territories also were subject to arrest, deportation eastward, and even execution.

One of the most important social developments during the Stalin era was the urbanization of the Soviet Union. Between 1929 and 1959 the urban population roughly doubled as the USSR was transformed from a predominantly rural-based society and economy into a modern, industrializing, and urbanizing superpower. Thirty-two million workers left the countryside for the cities during these three decades. Many peasants were compelled to take jobs in the cities as part of Stalin's drive for industrialization; others moved there seeking a better life.

This urbanization trend was most prevalent in European Russia. Overall, according to 1989 figures, 66 percent of the people of the USSR live in urban areas and 34 percent live in rural areas. In the Slavic and Baltic republics of the USSR, the percentage of urban dwellers ranges from 65 percent to 75 percent. In the less developed regions of the Caucasus and Central Asia the percentages of urban population are: Georgia, 56 percent; Armenia, 68 percent; Azerbaidzhan, 54 percent; Kazakhstan, 57 percent; Uzbekistan, 41 percent; Turkmenistan, 45 percent; Kirgizia, 38 percent; Tadzhikistan, 33 percent.

Soviet Nationality Policy after Stalin

During the regimes of Nikita S. Khrushchev and Leonid I. Brezhnev, social and economic progress within the national republics and regions was mixed. Great strides were made in the fields of economic development, literacy, and cultural affairs, especially in the Caucasus, Central Asia, and the RSFSR.

In the post-World War II era, particularly under Khrushchev and Brezhnev, a tacit deal was made between Moscow and the republics, especially those of the Caucasus and Central Asia. The republics were allowed to direct their own local party and administrative matters in exchange for ethnic peace. In support of this arrangement, an affirmative action program was put in place that was designed to increase the number of natives in party and government posts. By the late 1970s, corruption had become rampant in the republics. Bribery, nepotism, and clan politics dominated the affairs of many republic party and government bodies. The new political bosses included: Sharaf Rashidov in Uzbekistan, Dinmukhamed Kunaev in Kazakhstan, Vladimir Shcherbitskii and Petr Shelest in the Ukraine, Vasilii Mzhavanadze in Georgia, Antanas Snieckus in Lithuania, and Turdakun Usubaliev in Kirgizia.

Moscow glossed over many of these problems, pronouncing in exaggerated tones that a process of "mixing" of peoples and even "uniting" of peoples was well under way. Both Khrushchev and Brezhnev declared that the nationality problem in the USSR was fully "solved."

But during Brezhnev's last years, Moscow launched anticorruption drives against the party bosses in Azerbaidzhan and Georgia. During the regime of Yuri V. Andropov, this campaign was intensified and extended into Central Asia (Uzbekistan, Tadzhikistan, Turkmenistan, and Kirgizia), where party leaders were replaced with more reliable and efficient native Communists. When Gorbachev replaced the Kazakh party boss Dinmukhamed Kunaev in 1986 with an ethnic Russian, Gennadii Kolbin (a progressive-minded technocrat in Gorbachev's own mold), student riots resulted. The riots were partly a reaction against the violation of the traditional Moscow-republic contract of appointing only native Communists to top party posts, and partly a reaction against years of Russian migration into Kazakhstan.

Soviet Nationalities under Gorbachev

The degree of independence sought and achieved by the various nationality groups in the Soviet Union has depended, and likely will continue to depend, on a combination of political and social factors. Popular fronts for national self-determination have risen first in those republics of the USSR that were annexed during World War II, specifically the Baltic Republics and Moldavia. The Ukraine, in turn, has been slow in developing a popular front movement, partly because earlier attempts to construct nationality movements were crushed as recently as the late 1960s and early 1970s. In addition, russification policies have been intense there ever since.

The Caucasus has been one of the most volatile regions of the USSR because of the complex ethnic mix of peoples and their age-old antagonisms. The Soviet newspaper *Nedelya* has reported that between 1988 and 1990 ethnic violence (primarily in the Caucasus and Central Asian regions) claimed the lives of three hundred civilians and resulted in five thousand more being wounded. The ardent nationalism of the Georgians, Armenians, and Azerbaidzhanis, which compares with the nationalism found in the Baltic states, has fueled their drive toward a more independent status.

Demands for independence are less pronounced in the republics of Central Asia, which owe their high standards of living and progress in the fields of literacy and education (relative to neighboring Moslem states such as Afghanistan and Pakistan) to their relationship with Moscow. These republics have been less inclined to unite to pursue nationalist demands, partly because they are new on the international scene and have less of a national consciousness. Nevertheless, popular front organizations seeking greater autonomy and even independence have been established in these republics.

Nationalist demands for independence and ethnic violence do not mean the end of the Soviet state but point instead to the end of the old system of rule. The 1990s will be a decade of transition, as Moscow and the Soviet nationalities come to agreements about their new relationships. These relationships will depend on many complex factors, including the balance of power in Europe and Asia, the balance of power between ethnic groups within the Soviet Union, the economic success of Gorbachev's reforms, and Moscow's willingness to use economic coercion to keep the union together. Paul Goble, former adviser to the State Department on Soviet nationality affairs, has predicted that a revised Union Treaty soon will be negotiated between Moscow and the nationalities that will formalize their new relationships and will become part of the Soviet Constitution (the 1922 Union Treaty was included in the 1924 constitution, but not in the constitutions of 1936 and 1977). In June 1990, Gorbachev announced that he favors rewriting the Union Treaty. In April 1990, the USSR Supreme Soviet passed a language law giving the union and autonomous republics the right to determine the legal status of the languages of their territories and making Russian the official language of the USSR.

As Gail Lapidus has noted in her *Foreign Affairs* article, while the demands of some republics threaten the integrity of the state, the demands of lesser nationalities for redress of interethnic and boundary problems and for greater status within the union amounts to a "constitutional crisis." These kinds of demands open up "a Pandora's box from which redress of the grievances of one national group can be achieved only at the expense of another." It is a Pandora's box that Gorbachev has so far been unwilling to open.

What kind of new system will replace the old? Zbigniew Brzezinski, national security adviser under Jimmy Carter, has predicted that the Soviet Union will become a "Eurasian commonwealth," or "decentralized Eurasian confederation," whereby Moscow would retain ultimate authority in foreign policy and security affairs but allow ever-increasing political and economic autonomy to Soviet nationality groups. This type of loose confederation likely would include most or all the nations of the Caucasus, Central Asia, and Siberia, which generally see their economic ties to Russia as advantageous. The Baltic states and Moldavia, with their stronger ties to Europe, presumably would choose not to participate in such a political system and would seek to secede. This scenario roughly corresponds to the suggestion of Alexander Motyl of Columbia University, that the union republics of the USSR will undergo "Bulgarization," meaning "the possession of limited autonomy and genuine national identity under the rule of an outside hegemony."

Gorbachev's focus on efficiency and fighting corruption have sometimes hurt his relations with the nationalities. They have objected to his replacement of corrupt ethnic leaders with Russians, his elimination of affirmative action, and his emphasis on making all republics (including the poorer ones) self-supporting. That Gorbachev has never worked outside the Russian republic led to charges that he was ignorant of the needs of the nationalities. As Gorbachev has allowed the republics to become more autonomous, however, these complaints have diminished.

As of 1990 Gorbachev was approaching the nationality problem according to a formula that included respect for national autonomy and national forms of communism within a Soviet federation of nations, controlled in practice by the Communist party, the traditional guardian of the ideal of economic integration. Although Gorbachev has strongly opposed the immediate secession of union republics, he has shown a willingness to accommodate nationalist demands in limited ways. Clearly he has broken with the whitewashings of the Khrushchev and Brezhnev years.

Slavic Republics

The Slavic Republics of the Soviet Union comprise the RSFSR, the Ukrainian SSR, and the Belorussian SSR. Like all Eastern European Slavic peoples (which include the Poles, Czechs, Slovaks, Slovenes, Croats, Serbs, and Bulgarians), the Russians, Ukrainians, and Belorussians share ethnic and linguistic traits stemming from a common Slavic culture. This culture was dispersed as a result of migrations, foreign conquests, ethnic mixing, and the development of separate nations between the twelfth and the twentieth centuries.

The Ukraine and Belorussia both contain sizeable Russian minorities. Ever since the 1930s, both republics have endured severe Communist party russification policies, most notably the advancement of Russian language and culture over Ukrainian and Belorussian language and culture in secondary schools, universities, and publishing. Yet the Ukrainians (and to a lesser extent the Belorussians) have played significant roles in the leadership positions of the Communist Party of the Soviet Union (CPSU). According to statistics from the early 1980s, membership in the CPSU is dominated by Russians (60 percent), Ukrainians (16 percent), and Belorussians (3.8 percent). These three Slavic nationalities hold an even greater percentage of government leadership posts, with the Russians occupying 70 percent, the Ukrainians 15 percent, and the Belorussians 5.2 percent. This dominance has been reinforced under Gorbachev, who has replaced unreliable non-Russian party and government leaders with Russians of his own outlook and experience. Millions of Ukrainians and Belorussians also have joined the Russian migration into Central Asia and the Far East.

Popular front movements have been slow to flourish in the Ukraine and Belorussia, due to the pressures of russification and the strength of the Communist party there. *Rukh*, the Ukrainian popular front for national resurgence, is strongest in the western part of the republic, which was annexed after World War II, and weakest in the eastern part, which is heavily populated by ethnic Russians. The Belorussian cultural and ecological front, *Adrazhenne* (Rebirth), has won more supporters during 1989 and 1990, but it remains relatively weak.

The RSFSR is the largest republic of the Soviet Union (just over 75 percent of the total land mass), enjoys a special status within the union (its capital, Moscow, is also capital of the USSR), and contains the largest number of ethnic and national groups within its borders.

As the 1990s began Russian nationalism was on the rise. This was attributable partly to a backlash against years of official party condemnation of it and partly to a reaction against rising nationalisms in other parts of the

Soviet Union. Like other Soviet nationalist movements, Russian nationalism is neither monolithic nor inherently evil, and it is characterized by both moderate and extremist factions.

The Russian nationalist organization *Pamiat* (Memory), for example, began as a group organized to protect Russian literary artifacts and cultural monuments. It has degenerated, however, into an association of vocal extremists known to wear blackshirts, admire the tactics and methods of Naziism and Fascism, and espouse a virulent anti-Zionism (which they distinguish from anti-Semitism). The Writers' Union of the Russian Republic, the Association of Russian Artists, the Foundation for Slavic Writing and Culture, and the association *Rodina* (Homeland) all have adopted stances that *The Economist* magazine has described as "equally anti-western, anti-democratic, and pro-tsarist." Although these groups receive much attention and have ties to similar movements and prejudices in Russian history, they are not representative of the views of most Russian citizens. In the elections to the Congress of People's Deputies in 1989, for example, all of the fifteen announced *Pamiat* candidates lost their races.

The resentments voiced by Russian nationalists are as legitimate as resentments voiced by other nationalist groups within the USSR. Russian nationalists take note, for example, of the sacrifices that the Russian population has endured over the years as a result of collectivization, the purges of the 1930s, and World War II. They also point out that the RSFSR has given generous subsidies to its Baltic, Caucasian, and Central Asian neighbor republics for economic and cultural advancement. The RSFSR, they maintain, endured the worst effects of Stalinist central control of the economy, with the result that a tradition of entrepreneurship is lacking most in the RSFSR, while the republic endures the worst shortages and one of the lowest standards of living in the Soviet Union.

In elections to the Congress of People's Deputies and in republic legislative elections, clear divisions have appeared between the voting of Russians and non-Russians. In the national republics with sizeable Russian ethnic minorities, for example, Russian ethnics have been supporting either their own ethnic Russian candidates or local ethnic candidates who are running on platforms of "socialist internationalism" (meaning Gorbachev's platform of economic integration under Russian tutelage). Many non-Russians, however, have been supporting local candidates running on platforms of anti-Russian nationalism. In the Lithuanian elections to the Congress of People's Deputies in 1989, for example, the Lithuanian popular front *Sajudis* won thirty-one out of the forty-one contested seats.

Baltic Region and Moldavia

The Baltic peoples of the Soviet Union are the Estonians, Latvians, and Lithuanians. They traditionally have enjoyed a higher standard of living than the rest of the USSR. Popular fronts for national regeneration first came together here in mid-1988.

Each of the Baltic republics has declared its native language to be the official state language and has restored its traditional native flag and holidays. In August 1988, hundreds of thousands of Estonians, Latvians, and Lithuanians participated in rallies protesting the 1940 incorporation of their countries into the Soviet Union. By 1989, each of the Baltic republics had declared these pacts to be invalid.

In Lithuania, the most ethnically homogeneous of the Baltic republics, the local Communist party declared its independence from Moscow in 1989 and allied itself with the popular front movement *Sajudis*. This alliance has worked to achieve complete Lithuanian independence. On

Lithuanian citizens confront a Soviet army officer whose troops occupied Communist party headquarters in Vilnius, March 27, 1990.

March 11, 1990, the Lithuanian SSR unilaterally declared its independence from the USSR, prompting a struggle of wills with Moscow. Several days later, the USSR Supreme Soviet passed a secession law that allows union republics to secede, but only after a six-year transition period and with possible loss of territory and financial reparations. Gorbachev demanded that Lithuania rescind its declaration of independence before any negotiations on the scope of and timetable for independence take place, and he imposed economic sanctions on the Lithuanians to coerce a settlement. After several weeks, however, Moscow began informal negotiations with the Lithuanians on a settlement of the crisis. On May 16, the Lithuanian parliament agreed to suspend laws passed to implement its declaration of independence. The next day Gorbachev met with Lithuanian prime minister Kazimiera Prunskiene, a move that signaled the Kremlin's desire for some type of negotiated settlement of the crisis.

Estonia and Latvia have taken a more cautious approach. Mindful of the Lithuanian stalemate and of Moscow's economic blockade of the republic, the Estonians and Latvians declared in April and May of 1990, respectively, that they were moving toward independence. Their declarations of independence, however, were not to take effect for five years, so as to allow for equitable agreements on the issue to be concluded with Moscow.

Like the Baltic republics, Moldavia (formerly Bessarabia) was annexed to the Soviet Union in 1940 under the terms of the Hitler-Stalin pact of 1939 (it was joined to an already-existing Moldavian territory in the USSR) and is now bordered on its east by the Ukrainian SSR. Moldavians share their history, language, and ethnicity with their Romanian kin to the West and since the late 1980s have voiced their irredentism (appeals for unification with their former homeland). In 1989, the Moldavian SSR converted its Cyrillic script, imposed shortly after incorporation into the USSR, to its traditional Latin alphabet. Still heavily populated by ethnic Russians and Turkic Gagauz peoples, Moldavia as a whole generally opposes reunification with Romania.

The Caucasus

The Caucasus region comprises the diverse peoples of Georgia, Armenia, Azerbaidzhan, Daghestan, and the mountain areas of the Northern Caucasus. The republics of Georgia, Armenia (with highly educated populations), and Azerbaidzhan (a Turkic people, with an industrialized capital, Baku) have been the scenes of the most violent episodes in the general upheaval of Soviet nationalities during Gorbachev's rule. Nationalist demonstrations in Armenia in February 1988 against Azerbaidzhan resulted in twenty dead and about two hundred injured. The Armenian National Movement in 1989 boycotted elections to the Soviet Congress of Deputies, and as of mid-1990 it also was calling for a boycott of local republic elections. Most Armenians, however, do not want complete independence from Moscow. An independent Armenia would be a small state forced to contend with its historical enemies—the Azerbaidzhanis and the Turks—without Soviet troops to protect it.

Armenia and Azerbaidzhan have been in conflict over the status of the Nagorno-Karabakh autonomous region, which was made a part of Azerbaidzhan in 1921 even though it is ethnically Armenian. In January 1990 violent Azerbaidzhani popular front demonstrations in Baku, first directed against Armenians, turned against the CPSU itself. Government troops suppressed the uprising, leaving forty dead. Thousands of Armenians fled from Azerbaidzhan during 1988 and 1989, and the U.S. Department of State reported that in 1988, 9,564 Armenians emigrated from the USSR. Along their border with Iran, Azerbaidzhanis have been pressing for greater freedom of travel and communication between themselves and their fellow Shi'ite Moslem kin in Iran and have engaged in violence that has forced the evacuation of ethnic Armenians from these border regions. In 1990, a continuing Azerbaidzhani railroad blockade of Armenia was hampering normal lines of transport. However, negotiations were being conducted between the disputing peoples, with the Georgians as mediators.

Meanwhile in Georgia, ethnic Ossetians and ethnic Abkhazians (both of which have autonomous territories of their own but are subject to Georgian authority) have been protesting for greater independence from Georgia. In the spring and summer of 1989, ethnic violence between Abkhazians and Georgians caused more than forty fatalities. On April 9, 1989, in Tbilisi, the capital of Georgia, Soviet Internal Ministry troops fired poison gas at a crowd of ten thousand Georgian nationalists demonstrating in favor of Georgian independence. Twenty demonstrators were killed and thousands were wounded. The Georgians are perhaps the most cohesive ethnic group in the Caucasus and have the best organized (and armed) popular front movement in the region. Following the Baltic example, Georgian legislators began serious discussions in April 1990 about declaring Georgia's independence from the USSR and have already declared illegal the pact that united Georgia to the USSR.

Elsewhere in the northern Caucasus, popular fronts in the Abkhaz, Kabardin-Balkar, and Chechen-Ingush autonomous republics and in the Karachai-Cherkess autonomous region are calling for the establishment of a new union republic to unite their peoples.

Central Asia and Siberia

The Central Asian republics of the Soviet Union are Uzbekistan, Kazakhstan, Kirgizia, Turkmenistan (predominantly Turkic), and Tadzhikistan (predominantly Iranian). Popular front movements and informal civic associations have been organized in the urban areas of Uzbekistan (the *Birlik* or Unity movement), Kazakhstan (the Nevada-Semipalatinsk antinuclear and pro-environment movement), Kirgizia, and Tadzhikistan. In Uzbekistan, the *Erk* (Free) movement broke from the Birlik popular front in early 1990, forming its own Erk Democratic party and calling for independence from the USSR. The Tadzhiks began agitating in 1990 not only for greater autonomy, but also for recovery of what they saw as traditionally Tadzhik cities, Bukhara and Samarkand, now located in Uzbekistan.

These "Moslem" republics of the USSR are characterized by high birth rates, sedentary populations, and predominantly agricultural economies. The issues unifying the Central Asian popular fronts have been language rights and the environment. Environmental issues are particularly important in Uzbekistan, where, in some areas, more than 80 percent of children suffer from a serious chronic disease (often typhoid, hepatitis, or cancer of the esophagus). Two-thirds of the population of the Karakalpak autonomous republic are said to suffer from these diseases, partly as a result of pollution and poor management of the cotton industry there.

The major incidences of violence in Central Asia in the late 1980s have occurred in Kazakhstan and Tadzhikistan—in the former as a result of the dismissal of Kunaev, in the latter as a result of rumors that Armenian refugees were being resettled, with preferential treatment, in Tadzhikistan. Yet the discontent goes deeper. The Kazakhs resent the high proportion of Russian settlers, while the Tadzhiks are unhappy with their economic difficulties.

In the summer of 1989, violence erupted in Uzbekistan when Meshketian (Moslem) Georgians rioted against Russians and Uzbeks, leaving seventy dead, most of them Meshketians. As of 1990, 160,000 Meshketians live in Uzbekistan, deported there by Stalin after World War II (thirty thousand to forty thousand died en route). The Meshketians have been protesting against their substandard living conditions and for the right to return to their homeland.

Thirty-nine national groups, including Turkic Iakuts, Mongols, Buriats, and Eskimos, live in Siberia along with Slavic settlers. The region is sparsely populated, and many local cultures remain tied to nomadic, tribal, and clan traditions. In early 1990, leaders of Siberian national groups began calling for the establishment of an independent Far Eastern republic, and demonstrations were held against the many ecological disasters that have plagued the region during the 1980s.

Other notable national groups include the Germans and the Tatars. Both of these groups were deported from their homelands after World War II, ostensibly because of their disloyalty to the Soviet Union during the war. Two hundred thousand Crimean Tatars were sent eastward after World War II, half of them dying on the way. Although they have been officially rehabilitated since the 1960s, they have not been allowed to return to their original homelands in central Russia and the Crimea in great numbers, as such a move would uproot those peoples who settled on these lands in their absence. The government's position drew vocal protests in 1987 from Crimean and Volga Tatar groups especially. Germans recently have been allowed to emigrate to Germany in greater numbers. According to the U.S. State Department, 30,136 emigrated in 1988.

Church and State

Although Soviet sources in the past have estimated that some form of religious belief was shared by only 15 to 20 percent of the population (10 to 15 percent in the cities, 20 to 30 percent in the countryside), Western studies have maintained that up to 45 percent of the population are believers of large religious faiths: Christianity, Islam, Judaism, Buddhism. Soviet public opinion surveys conducted in the late 1980s confirm that up to 50 percent of the population believes in a god. On the basis of the latter figure, and given the recent resurgence of religious activity in the USSR, the official party and state policy of atheism, often violently imposed over the last seventy years, must be judged a failure.

Although the constitutions of 1924, 1936, and 1977 provided for the right to believe and the right to worship, both rights were limited by official state policy as well as by complementary constitutional provisions. Article 52 of the 1977 Constitution granted Soviets the right "not to believe" and the right to "conduct atheistic propaganda." After 1917, church and state officially were separated, but in reality the first was subjugated to the second. The charity, missionary, and educational activities of religious organizations, in particular those of the Russian Orthodox Church, were limited severely. Church lands were nationalized. Especially during the years of civil war (1918-1921) and cultural revolution (1928-1932), religious persons and the organized church itself suffered physical persecution at the hands of the party and its fronts. (*Soviet Constitution, Appendix, p. 316*)

Russian Orthodox Church

Between 1925 and World War II, the Russian Orthodox Church was forbidden by the government to select a patriarch, its spiritual leader. In 1929, the Law on Religious Associations gave legal force to many of the ad hoc Communist party actions taken in the years before. Between 1914 and 1941, the number of Russian Orthodox Church buildings decreased from an estimated 54,400 to 4,200; its priests decreased from 57,000 to 5,600; its monasteries decreased from 1,498 to 38; its seminaries decreased from 57 to 0; and its bishops decreased from 130 to 4.

During World War II, Stalin allowed a renewal and reinvigoration of the Russian Orthodox Church because he needed to inspire nationalism in the Russian people in defense of the motherland. Eighteen thousand parishes were reopened and enjoyed a revival into the late 1950s. This policy, however, extended neither to the Ukrainian and Belorussian autocephalous (independent) Orthodox Churches nor to the Ukrainian Uniate Church (allied to Rome), which was persecuted after World War II and subjected to the authority of the Moscow Russian Orthodox patriarch (who was subject to Communist party controls).

The most concerted and violent persecution of religious groups after World War II occurred between 1959 and 1964 during Nikita Khrushchev's antireligion offensive. During this period many of the parishes and monasteries reopened during the war were closed. Of the twenty thousand church buildings in existence by 1959, eleven thousand were shut by Khrushchev's campaign. Although the official antireligious program ended with Khrushchev's ouster in 1964, its effects and militant spirit continued into the Brezhnev period. By 1966, only seven thousand church buildings remained open. Another effect of Khrushchev's campaign was to split the Russian Orthodox and the Baptists (the two main targets of the campaign) into official (party-sanctioned) and nonofficial (dissident) groups.

Only in the late 1980s have official antireligion policies begun to lose their force. Liberal intellectuals and party reformists, including Gorbachev, have come to believe that religious and moral values must be a part of perestroika, especially in the fight against alcoholism and social apathy. At his December 1989 meeting with Pope John Paul II (which resulted in negotiations for the establishment of diplomatic ties between the USSR and the Vatican), Gorbachev declared his support for "respect for the national, state, and spiritual and cultural identity of all peoples." Religious institutions in the Soviet Union are being allowed to revive physically. Soviet medieval historian Dmitri S. Likachev, with the aid of Raisa Gorbachev, has established a Soviet Cultural Fund for the protection and rebuilding of historic and religious monuments of the Soviet Union.

In 1988, the Russian Orthodox Church, the largest Eastern Orthodox Church in the world, celebrated the

Despite seven decades of atheist propaganda, religious belief remains widespread in the Soviet Union. Here priests of the Russian Orthodox Church celebrate Easter, April 1990.

millennium of Christianity in Russia, marking the A.D. 988 conversion of Kievan Russia to the Christian faith under Grand Prince Vladimir of Kiev. Counting 96.7 million nominal believers as its own, the Russian Orthodox Church is the largest and best organized church in the USSR. In October 1989, after thirty years of prohibition, an Orthodox seminary was allowed to resume teaching. Church schools have been revived without harassment. Priests and church authorities have gained access to television and the press. The bells of St. Basil's Cathedral in Red Square rang in January 1990 for the first time in seventy years. And on January 7, 1990, for the first time in Soviet history, Soviet television broadcast Russian Orthodox Christmas services.

Other Religious Groups

Islam (mostly Sunni Moslem) is the second largest religious faith in the USSR. About 20 percent of the Soviet people practice Islam, a tie that binds its Soviet adherents to the Turkic, Arabic, and Persian cultures of the Middle East and Asia. Moslems live throughout the USSR, with concentrations in the Crimea, the Tatar regions, Bashkiria, North Caucasia, Daghestan, and particularly in the republics of Azerbaidzhan (mostly Shi'ite Moslem), Kazakhstan, Uzbekistan, Kirgizia, Turkmenistan, and Tadzhikistan.

Until 1928, the Moslem clergy maintained a strong hold on the courts, schools, and landholding in these regions. Twenty-six thousand mosques and forty-five thousand mullahs served Moslems at the time of the Bolshevik revolution. As of 1990 only four hundred fifty mosques and some two thousand mullahs were allowed to function. But underground and unofficial congregations, including Sufi Brotherhoods (conservative Moslems), were widespread.

The Roman Catholic Church has up to 3.5 million believers in the USSR, with 2.5 million of them concentrated in Lithuania. Lithuanian Catholics have been especially active in religious dissent, publishing an underground

journal, *The Chronicle of the Catholic Church in Lithuania*, since 1972. Crowds of Belorussian and Eastern Polish (Poles who remained in the USSR after Polish-Soviet borders were redrawn after World War II) Catholics welcomed Josef Cardinal Glemp, primate of Poland, on his trip to their homeland in September 1988.

Eastern Rite Catholics (Uniates) are concentrated in the Ukraine, comprising people whose ancestors accepted the authority of the pope in the late 1500s, in exchange for being allowed to practice what are essentially Eastern Orthodox doctrines and rituals. Uniates have suffered some of the worst persecution and repression at the hands of the Soviet government, largely because of their Ukrainian homogeneity and allegiance to Rome. After World War II, the Uniate Church was officially disbanded in the USSR and made a part of the Russian Orthodox Church, although it has displayed its vitality in 1989 with peaceful demonstrations. Its standing has improved as Vatican-Kremlin relations have warmed, and Ukrainian Catholic parishes now are being allowed to officially register with the state. In April 1990, despite protests from Orthodox believers, the Cathedral of St. George in Lvov was transferred from Orthodox control to the control of the Ukrainian Catholic Church.

Protestants number almost four million in the Soviet Union. Up to 850,000 Lutherans are concentrated in Latvia and Estonia and are among the German settlers of Central Asia and Siberia. The remaining Protestant believers include Baptists, Evangelicals and Pentecostals, Adventists, and Jehovah's Witnesses. These groups have endured particularly harsh persecution because of their unofficial status, their missionary zeal, and their ties abroad.

Judaism occupies a unique and difficult place in Soviet society. Living mostly in the cities of European Russia and speaking Russian as a native or second language, Jews belong to both a religious and a nationality group. The Jewish Autonomous Region of the Far East, established in

1928 as a homeland for the USSR's Jewish population, borders China and has Yiddish, used in many schools, as its official language. At first, the homeland was to be located in the Crimea, north of the Black Sea, but the Far East was eventually chosen to contribute to the development of the region.

Russian and Slavic peoples long have experienced strained relations with the Jewish communities and individuals living among them (diaspora Jews found refuge in Eastern Europe after migrations from the West in the fifteenth and sixteenth centuries). Open anti-Semitism became a harsh reality in late imperial Russia as reactionary groups, with the tsar's approval, imposed pogroms, or repressive policies (from deportation to murder), on the Jews of Eastern Europe.

In recent years, anti-Semitism has reappeared in extremist corners of the Soviet press. The magazines *Nash Sovremennik* (Our Contemporary) and *Molodaya Gvardia* (Young Guard), for example, have directed attacks against "Jewish cosmopolitanism" and "Jewish anti-Russianness," using Soviet Jews as convenient scapegoats for Soviet problems. Liberal and reformist groups in the USSR have denounced such prejudices.

After the 1967 Arab-Israeli war, the USSR severed relations with Israel. "Anti-Zionism" increased in the Soviet press, as did nationalism among Jews, whose dissidents began to emigrate to the United States and Israel in 1971. The 1973 Arab-Israeli war intensified anti-Zionist and anti-Semitic propaganda in the USSR, prompting the U.S. Congress in 1974 to pass the Jackson-Vanik amendment. This legislation offered favorable trading policies to the USSR, only if Moscow implemented more liberal emigration policies for Soviet Jews.

As a result of Jackson-Vanik, the USSR released a record 51,230 Jews in 1979 (about 225,000 Jews left the USSR between 1971 and 1979). However, strained relations between the Soviet Union and the United States in the early 1980s ended the liberal emigration policies. From 1982 to 1986 only 6,952 Jews were allowed to emigrate. *(Jewish emigration, graph, p. 177)*

Glasnost has completely altered the situation. In 1988 more than 19,000 Jews emigrated from the Soviet Union. The number of Jews emigrating skyrocketed in 1989 to more than 79,000. This pace has continued in 1990. According to the National Conference on Soviet Jewry in Washington, D.C., 7,300 Jews emigrated from the USSR in March of that year, all but twenty of them settling in Israel. The Israeli government estimates that between 1990 and 1993 as many as 250,000 more Soviet Jews will emigrate. Given strict limits on the numbers of Soviet Jews allowed into the United States, most of them will go to Israel. In May 1988 the Soviet government also allowed the first rabbinical school to hold classes in the USSR in more than fifty years.

In the Caucasus, the Georgian Orthodox Church and Armenian Apostolic Church have survived and prospered as national Christian churches and are the most cohesive and well-organized churches in the USSR. Faring less well have been several Russian religious sects that broke off from the Orthodox Church and are dispersed mainly within the RSFSR: the Old Believers (numbering two million), the Molokans, and Dukhobors. Approximately fifty thousand Buddhists, mostly among the Buriat ethnic groups, are in the Soviet Far East. In 1988, Hare Krishnas were recognized as an official religious group.

Lastly, according to Soviet estimates, between six mil-

lion and ten million confirmed atheists are in the USSR, for whom the Soviet ideologies of socialist equality and scientific atheism have become a secular religion. These atheists trace their roots to the League of the Militant Godless of the 1920s and 1930s, the Knowledge Societies of the 1950s, 1960s, and 1970s (both of which spread atheistic propaganda), and the "god-creating" movement, organized by several early Bolshevik leaders: Maxim Gorky, Anatolii Lunacharskii, and Aleksandr Bogdanov. These leaders believed that Soviet society should create a new god, not of heaven, but of the earthly collective community of workers and peasants. Although Lenin disbanded the movement, its influence was felt after his death in subtle ways—primarily in the creation of the pseudo-religious cult of Lenin himself.

Lenin did favor the creation of a new communist morality and new communist rituals, as reflected in the establishment of secular national holidays (including celebration of the October Revolution, November 7; Workers' Day, May 1; Lenin's Birthday, April 22; and International Women's Day, March 8) and the "Red" marriages, which have become a common part of Soviet life. These marriages are simple secular ceremonies, often followed by a visit to the local World War II monument by the wedding party.

Glasnost and Soviet Culture

Gorbachev's perestroika has three main concepts: *uskorenie* (acceleration of economic progress), *demokratizatsia* (reform of the political system to make it more participatory), and *glasnost* (the limited granting of free expression). Glasnost opened debate within Soviet society about the pace and scope of economic and political reform. In both imperial and Soviet Russia the word described critical discussion within the ranks of bureaucrats and administrators intended to correct abuses and weaknesses of the system. In the first years after Gorbachev took power, glasnost was used by most top party leaders in this limited sense.

But in the late 1980s, glasnost came to mean not simply critical discussion, but the actual creation of well-defined and real civil and political rights for Soviet citizens—in challenge to the central monopoly of power of the Communist party. Gorbachev has called his new form of communism, which is rooted in the policies of Lenin's New Economic Policy (NEP) of the 1920s, "socialist pluralism." The most recent forebearers of this concept were the open Eurocommunism of the Italian Communist party and the humanist socialisms associated with the reform movements in Hungary (1956), Czechoslovakia (1968), and Poland (1979).

At Gorbachev's side in the creation of this new civil society and political system has been Aleksandr Yakovlev, who was rapidly promoted between 1985 and 1987 to become full member of the Politburo in charge of ideology, culture, the mass media, and scientific and academic life. Gorbachev and Yakovlev have been successful in securing the support of the liberal intelligentsia for their policies in these areas. Through the last years of the 1980s, Yakovlev engineered the filling of several important editorial posts with supporters of perestroika, including Vitalii Korotich at *Ogonyok* (Flame), Yegor Yakovlev at the *Moscow News*, Sergei Zalygin at *Novy Mir* (New World), and Grigorii Baklanov at *Znamia* (Banner). Allied with Gorbachev and

Yakovlev in this process are several top academic leaders, including Vladimir Kudriavtsev, director of the Institute of State and Law; and Tatiana Zaslavskaia, a leading sociologist and founder of the Center for Public Opinion Research on Social and Economic Issues, whose articles have appeared in progressive press organs such as *Argumenti i Facti* (Arguments and Facts) and *Kommunist. (Soviet publications, box, p. 91)*

These and other mouthpieces for reform often have stepped beyond the formal and informal limits of official censorship. They have launched unmerciful criticisms of the Stalin and Brezhnev years and proposed candid and bold renovations of civil and political society. The following review of cultural life gives an indication of how both cultural and political leaders are changing Soviet society.

Human Rights

Dissent in the Soviet Union has changed radically since Gorbachev's ascension to power in 1985. The new situation has its precedents not only in the open NEP period of the 1920s, but also in the "thaw" of the early Khrushchev years. During the early 1920s political rights were circumscribed by the Communist party, and many cultural and academic leaders were persecuted for their backgrounds and beliefs. But the Soviet state adopted a liberal stance toward cultural practices and customs. Moreover, under the party's policy of democratic centralism, debate and disagreement were allowed within the party on vital issues until the party policy was defined.

Stalin, however, squelched all forms of dissent (including internal Communist party debates) and attempted to standardize cultural and artistic life. The Khrushchev years brought more freedom of expression, especially in literature and the arts. Suppression of cultural and political freedoms again was heightened under Brezhnev.

Beginning in 1966, laws were decreed that criminalized "anti-Soviet propaganda" or smears against Soviet life and formalized the state's authority to declare dissidents mental incompetents needing psychiatric evaluation. Dissident groups were organized to protest these and other violations of human rights. Unofficial publications, called *samizdat* (native dissident publications) and *tamizdat* (publications from abroad), were widely distributed to avoid the censors. In the late 1960s Andrei Sakharov and others founded the Democratic Movement, whose unofficial journal, *The Chronicle of Current Events,* reported human rights violations. In the mid-1970s Yuri Orlov established the Helsinki Watch Group to monitor human rights abuses in the USSR from posts in Moscow, Kiev, Vilnius, Yerevan, and Tbilisi. In 1976 the Working Commission against the Use of Psychiatry for Political Purposes was established. Andrei Amalrik, author of *Will the Soviet Union Survive until 1984?* and *Notes of a Revolutionary,* employed the tactic of demanding that Soviet state actions correspond to the civil and political rights written into Soviet law.

Gorbachev's policy of glasnost is, in effect, legalizing such traditions of dissent in the Soviet Union, answering Amalrik's demand, and creating institutions to protect the basic human rights of Soviet citizens. Censorship has been relaxed, as has access to archives and libraries. The use of computers, word processors, and photocopying equipment is much more widespread—making for the beginnings of an information revolution within the USSR. One of Gorbachev's goals, for example, is to double the telephone system during the 1990s. Currently the Soviet Union has only ten phones for every hundred people, while other industrialized nations have between sixty to one hundred phones for every hundred people.

Soviet television also has come alive under glasnost (90 percent of Soviet homes have televisions). Popular shows include "Vremia," a fast-breaking news and current events program. "Vremia" and other documentary shows report on the pressing conflicts in Soviet society, making accessible to viewers news and information previously censored.

In general, the process of pluralization is taking place in two ways: through specific pieces of legislation protecting peoples' rights and through new associations in which these rights are being realized in action.

Procedures were drawn up in 1987 by the Supreme Soviet on how to proceed with a national referendum, a right that only had been guaranteed vaguely by the Soviet Constitution. New laws in 1988 gave Soviet citizens the right to appeal the decisions and actions of government officials and the right of protection against psychiatric abuses (psychiatric hospitals were removed from the jurisdiction of the Ministry of Internal Affairs and placed under the authority of the Ministry of Health). Serious debate has taken place about either limiting or repealing those articles of the criminal code against anti-Soviet propaganda. Laws on freedom of conscience, on an end to censorship, and on the free movement of peoples both within and across the borders of the USSR now are being debated in the Ministry of Justice and in various legislatures of the Soviet Union and its republics.

Significant progress also has been made in the area of emigration. The State Department estimated in 1990 that 95 percent of all emigration applications from Soviet citizens were being granted. Armenians, Germans, and Pentecostal Christians have been leaving the USSR by the thousands since 1988. Of the eleven thousand names of refuseniks that Reagan gave to Gorbachev at Reykjavik in 1986, fewer than three thousand remain in the USSR. The Conference on Security and Cooperation in Europe reported that the number of political prisoners in the Soviet Union went down from 745 in 1986 to 250 in 1988. As of 1990 up to one hundred of them still were held in psychiatric institutions, but they were slowly being released.

Emerging Pluralism

The Gorbachev years also are witnessing the gradual creation of a civil society in the USSR—that is, the flowering of civic, cultural, religious, professional, and even political associations. For the most part, these groups are independent of the state and have a stake not only in criticizing the abuses and imperfections of government and the Communist party, but also in searching for the means to make Soviet society stronger and more democratic. Civic organizations, which first began to organize behind environmental and linguistic-cultural causes, now have rallied behind political causes.

In March 1988, representatives from thirty-six cities came together to form a nationwide student pro-environment network. In December 1988 an All-Union "Social-Ecological Union" was formed. In May 1988, the Democratic Union was founded on the platform of a multi-party system, legal opposition, free press, and free trade unions—although it has endured repression and surveillance ever since. Sergei Kuznetsov, a member of the Democratic Front, was arrested and severely beaten in December of 1989 and is expected to stand trial for slander against the

Three Famous Soviet Dissidents ...

The careers of dissidents Alexander Solzhenitsyn, Andrei Sakharov, and Natan Shcharanskii—who were active during the Brezhnev years and continued their dissent into the Gorbachev years—speak eloquently about past struggles for cultural freedom and human rights and highlight standards of conduct and challenges for the future.

Solzhenitsyn

Alexander Solzhenitsyn gained international acclaim in 1962, when Nikita S. Khrushchev permitted the literary magazine *Novy Mir* to publish *One Day in the Life of Ivan Denisovich*, a novel portraying the harsh conditions in a Stalinist labor camp. Solzhenitsyn's subsequent novels, including *The First Circle*, *Cancer Ward*, and *The Gulag Archipelago*, also criticized Stalinist-era abuses. Banned in the Soviet Union but published in the West, they became best sellers and established Solzhenitsyn's reputation as a great writer. Although Solzhenitsyn was expelled from the Soviet writers' union in 1969, he won the Nobel Prize in literature the following year, an action that the writers' union said was "deplorable." Solzhenitsyn declined to attend the award ceremonies in Stockholm because he feared that he would not be allowed to return home.

The Soviet regime mounted a press campaign against Solzhenitsyn following the December 1973 publication in France of his novel *The Gulag Archipelago*. The author announced that if he were arrested he would publish abroad five sequels to *The Gulag Archipelago*, accounts purportedly detailing repression under Khrushchev and Leonid I. Brezhnev. Although Soviet authorities were hesitant to imprison an artistic giant such as Solzhenitsyn, they did settle for banishment. Solzhenitsyn was stripped of his citizenship and exiled February 13, 1974, for "performing systematically actions that are incompatible with being a citizen of the USSR."

The most prominent Soviet citizen to be exiled since Leon Trotsky, Solzhenitsyn lived in Switzerland for a year before settling in Cavendish, Vermont, where he continues to criticize the Soviet system. Solzhenitsyn's passionate Orthodoxy and Russian nationalism have led some critics to brand him a reactionary. He is at odds with many promi-

nent supporters of perestroika in the Soviet Union for his assertion that V. I. Lenin founded the brutal labor camp system that Stalin used to imprison and kill millions. Some Soviet liberals have branded him a Slavophile and an anti-Semite.

In truth, Solzhenitsyn writes in the tradition of late nineteenth and early twentieth century Russian theologians and philosophers such as Vladimir Soloviev, Nikolai Berdiaev, and Sergei Bulgakov. His fiction praises moral values, individual dignity, civic virtue, the rule of law, and spiritual salvation.

Under glasnost, Solzhenitsyn's works (including selections from *The Gulag Archipelago*) first were published in small journals in Estonia and the Ukraine but now are being published in leading Soviet literary journals. He has said that he will not return to the Soviet Union until all of his works have been published there.

Sakharov

After Solzhenitsyn's deportation in 1974, Andrei Sakharov became the leading dissident in the USSR. A brilliant nuclear physicist who played a major role in developing the Soviet hydrogen bomb, he first attained international fame with the publication in the West of his essay "Progress, Co-existence and Intellectual Freedom" (1968).

In November 1970 Sakharov and his dissident colleagues founded the Moscow Human Rights Committee to publicize Soviet violations of individual liberties guaranteed by the Soviet Constitution. At a news conference August 21, 1973, Sakharov warned the West that its desire to preserve détente should not foreclose efforts to improve human rights in Soviet society. Sakharov's comments set off a two-week Soviet press campaign designed to discredit him.

By 1975 Sakharov had abandoned his scientific career for a life of political activism. That year he was awarded the Nobel Peace Prize, but the Soviet government denied him a visa to Oslo to accept the award, claiming his role in the hydrogen bomb project made him a security risk. Sakharov's wife, Yelena Bonner, accepted the award in his place.

Despite the threat of arrest, Sakharov continued to draw world attention to repressive conditions in the Soviet Union. In 1977 he wrote to President

state security apparatus—although progressive forces in Soviet society have rallied to his defense, a mark of the success of glasnost. In 1988, the Commission on Humanitarian Cooperation and Human Rights was founded, with Communist party encouragement. Directed by Fëdor Burlatsky, the commission has campaigned for socialist legality and civic and political rights. In October 1989, the

Inter-regional Association of Democratic Organizations held its first meeting, bringing together representatives from more than 170 regional popular fronts, rallying for the rule of law, for labor rights, and for a political opposition—in general for a new regime of pluralism in Soviet life.

In response to the Communist party's February 1990 renunciation of its monopoly on power (though as of June

... Solzhenitsyn, Sakharov, Shcharanskii

Jimmy Carter, asking him to put more pressure on the Soviet government to improve human rights. In 1980 Sakharov opposed the Soviet invasion of Afghanistan and supported an international boycott of the 1980 Moscow Olympics. The Kremlin clamped down on the outspoken critic by sending him into internal exile January 22, 1980, for "conducting subversive activities against the Soviet state." He was sent to Gorkii, about 250 miles east of Moscow, to keep him from speaking to Western reporters.

While in Gorkii, Sakharov and his wife used hunger strikes to obtain permission for their daughter-in-law, Yelizaveta Alekseyeva, to join her husband in the United States. She had been married by proxy in the summer of 1981 to Sakharov's stepson, Aleksei Semyonov. Seventeen days into their hunger strike, Sakharov and Bonner were told that Alekseyeva would be allowed to emigrate.

In the first years of Sakharov's exile, he maintained contacts with supporters through Bonner. This changed in May 1984, when Sakharov began a hunger strike in support of his wife's efforts to go abroad for medical treatment. Five days after his hunger strike began, Sakharov was summoned to the Semashko Hospital; on May 11 the hospital began force feeding him. He abandoned the fast May 27 because he was unable to endure the pain of forced feeding, he later reported.

On August 10 Bonner was sentenced to five years of exile in Gorkii. Sakharov was released from the hospital in September, and for seven months he and Bonner lived in near total isolation under police surveillance. In 1985 Sakharov began another hunger strike to obtain permission for Bonner to travel to the West for medical treatment. Sakharov again was taken to a hospital and force fed. On September 5, 1985, the Soviet government indicated that if Bonner agreed not to give news conferences or interviews she could travel to the West. On October 21 Bonner was called to the Gorkii visa office where she received a three-month travel visa for medical purposes. On December 2, 1985, Bonner arrived in Italy to consult an eye specialist. The following month she had heart bypass surgery in the United States.

Mikhail S. Gorbachev freed Sakharov in 1987, whereupon he joined other dissidents and activists in support of Gorbachev's first cultural and political reforms, which were many of the same changes that Sakharov had advocated for twenty years. In 1989 he was elected to the new Congress of People's Deputies (CPD). A vocal proponent of radical reform, he helped establish the Inter-regional Group, an opposition organization composed of liberal deputies. In December 1989, just before his death, Sakharov was at the lead of a drive in the CPD to repeal Article 6 of the Soviet Constitution, which designates the Communist party as "the leading and guiding force of Soviet society and the nucleus of its political system." The repeal was defeated 1,138 to 839, although in February 1990 the Communist party would renounce Article 6. Sakharov's last speeches before the CPD often were impossible to understand because of his failing health and catcalls made by conservatives in the chamber. He died December 14, 1989.

Shcharanskii

Natan Shcharanskii (formerly Anatolii Shcharanskii), human rights activist and champion of Soviet Jewish emigration, was released to the West February 11, 1985, after eight years in a Soviet prison camp. Shcharanskii's release was part of an East-West prisoner swap—a result of months of secret negotiations spurred by the November 1985 Geneva summit. His release was sudden and dramatic. Only one day after Shcharanskii was told he would be freed, he walked across the Gleinicke Bridge separating East and West Germany. He flew to Israel and landed a few hours later among welcoming crowds.

In 1978 Shcharanskii, a thirty-eight-year-old computer expert, was imprisoned for trumped-up charges of espionage, treason, and anti-Soviet agitation. In reality he was imprisoned for speaking out for the right to emigrate and for his contacts with foreign journalists. He had been campaigning not only for more liberal emigration policies, but also for a renewal in the USSR of Jewish culture, religion, and nationality, which for many years were suppressed by severe russification policies. He was sentenced to thirteen years in prison and labor camps.

Now living in Israel with his wife, Avital, Shcharanskii remains a defiant critic of Gorbachev's reforms. He has referred to glasnost as a "new system of instructions" from above.

1990 this renunciation had yet to be formalized by law), opposition political parties have formed. In April 1990, for example, the Liberal Democratic party of the Soviet Union was established, modeling itself on the moderate Constitutional Democratic (Kadet) party, which enjoyed strong support in Russia before the 1917 revolution. According to reliable Soviet estimates, as of 1990 as many as thirty thousand "independent social and group associations" were in existence. *(Kadet party, p. 19)*

Although Gorbachev retains almost complete power in the party, as well as political control over the electoral processes, political pluralism is beginning to emerge. In a 1990 campaign for a Leningrad city council seat, for example, the main rival to CPSU reformist candidate Alexei

Bolshakov was Rostoslav Yevdokimov, a dedicated anticommunist who served some five years in the labor camps for "anti-Soviet propaganda." Following Amalrik's tactics of the previous decade, Yevdokimov pointed to the hypocrisy of the CPSU. "It is not I who is anti-Soviet," he claimed. "Who do you think has taken power away from the Soviets for the past seventy-two years? Not my party, but the party that's been in power all that time. It's the Communists who are the real anti-Soviets."

Yevdokimov's points have been taken up by less extremist reformists within the party itself. They hope to undercut the Yevdokimov forces, who are leading a revolution from below, by imposing their own limited reforms in a more controlled way, thus leading a revolution from above.

Although these signs of emerging pluralism are promising, the Soviet Union has not yet transformed itself into a democratic nation. The presidential system that Gorbachev has established concentrates power in his hands and his supporters in the Communist party leadership. At the March 1990 session of the newly elected Supreme Soviet, for example, Gorbachev and his colleagues sat for five hours listening to debate, then in about twenty minutes pushed through their reform plans with limited amendments. Boris Yeltsin and the Inter-regional Group, the main radical reformist opposition group in the Congress of Deputies, have branded such high-handed political tactics as totalitarian. Gorbachev's disdain for the Inter-Regional Group is well publicized. The criticisms and taunts that Gorbachev received from the crowds at the May Day parade in 1990 were dramatic proof of the new freedoms. Yet that embarrassing episode has prompted calls for new legislation to suppress such public displays of opposition against the president, making it likely that protests will not be allowed to take place so openly during May Day celebrations in the near future.

As civic, cultural, and political associations have begun to form, so too have extremist dissenting groups. At the fringes of society, for example, are the *liubery,* a group of young men from the Moscow Liubertsy suburb who are obsessed with body building and who declare extremely anti-Western, pro-Soviet values. This "Rambo-style youth cult," as Jim Riordan, author of a study on Soviet youth culture, calls it, has been known to inflict beatings on individuals or groups suspected of pro-Western sentiments or activities, including punk rockers, hippies, heavy metal fans, Jewish refuseniks, and foreign journalists. Akin to the liubery are small groups of pro-Nazis, mostly students who are infatuated with the style and shock value of Hitlerism.

Another nonofficial dissenting group is the *Afgantsy,* made up of veterans of the Afghanistan war (between 1980 and 1987 approximately fifteen thousand to twenty thousand young men were sent each year to fight in Afghanistan). Returning home to a country in the midst of the radical transformations of perestroika, many veterans found the new pro-Western and even pro-American values to be a betrayal of their own sacrifices during the war. They accordingly have organized into patriotic veterans' associations.

The Legacy of the Arts

The Russian literary and visual arts enjoy an esteemed place in the history of world culture, not only for the unique techniques that they have employed, but also for the messages that they have communicated. From the critical essays and novels of the mid-1800s to the memoirs and historical novels of the mid-1900s, Russian and Soviet literature has placed a premium on photographing reality at its harshest as a means of social and political criticism. From Byzantine icons of the Kievan period to the cubist

Delegates to the Second Congress of People's Deputies placed carnations on Andrei Sakharov's chair in memorium to the nuclear physicist-turned-human rights activist. Sakharov died December 14, 1989.

paintings of the Soviet era, Russian art has displayed a remarkable beauty of form and subtlety of expression.

Russians have appreciated the power of the word and the power of the image as means of artistic expression and social communication. The Russian term for literature, for example, is *slovesnost,* which conveys a sense of the power of the word in human culture (the root slovo means word). Artists and writers have valued *obraznost,* the power of imagery in a painting, sculpture, or narrative to communicate meaning (the root obraz means image).

Moscow and Tartu (in Estonia) have been among the leading centers for the modern science of semiotics, the study of sign systems (primarily in language and the arts) and their role in human communication. Following well-established Russian traditions, modern semiotics defines the word as an image, and the image as a type of word, for both share the qualities of pictures and of signs.

Semiotics has a long tradition in Russian history. Icon painters of the Kievan period, for example, often manipulated artistic forms and images (as signs and symbols) to communicate new ideas about God and man. Nineteenth-century writers employed words and phrases in original ways, with a keen grasp of linguistic structure. Maiakovskii's futurist poems and Malevich's cubist paintings experimented with new sounds and shapes as well as envisioned a whole new world of Einsteinian relativity and technological progress. Although these artists and writers shared their techniques and ideas with comparable innovators in other European countries, the Russians and Soviets stand on their own as remarkable achievers.

Russian and Soviet Literature

Literature has been more than just an artistic endeavor for Russian and Soviet writers. They have used it as a means of social and political criticism, and indeed as a means of social construction. In the eighteenth and nineteenth centuries, Aleksandr Radishchev and Peter Chadaev, the first in a long line of alienated intellectuals, were silenced and imprisoned for the radical nature of their narratives and essays, which were directed primarily against tsardom and serfdom. The innovative writers, Mikhail Lomonosov and Denis Fonvizin, helped to create a new literary language for the rising strata of intellectuals of imperial Russia, popularizing as they did new French words in the salons of St. Petersburg or shocking the establishment with their biting satires.

Beginning with the mid-1800s, literature became an even more powerful vehicle for social and political change. The Decembrists (Aleksander Pushkin, Vladimir Odoevskii), the Populists (Vissarion Belinskii, Aleksandr Herzen), and the Nihilists (Nikolai Chernyshevsky, Nikolai Dobroliubov, Dmitri Pisarev) were social activists and poets, literary critics, and essayists. They used the power of the word (by employing new expressions and styles) to create new ways of thinking and acting. Some readers took on the habits and attitudes of characters in novels, or of the novelists themselves, all in protest against the falsity and hypocrisy of established society. Chernyshevsky's stark novel, *What Is to Be Done?,* had this effect, inspiring many members of the young generation, including Lenin, to radical protest of imperial society. Belinskii, the literary critic and populist, coined the term "critical realism" as a new literary genre, which depicted the harsh realities of life as a means of stirring the educated elite toward revolutionary change.

The masters of the "golden age" of Russian literature (mid-nineteenth century), though not revolutionaries themselves, also depicted the sharp tensions and divisions in Russian society. Fëdor Dostoevsky portrayed the pathology of the alienated intellectual trying to make a go of it without God. Ivan Turgenev wrote of the exactions of peasant life and of the frustrated idealism of nihilist radicals. Leo Tolstoy revealed the conflicts in upper-class life, becoming in his later years a moralist and philosopher who condemned violence, wealth, and ecclesiastical hypocrisy.

The first literary trends of the twentieth century were much more experimental, in anticipation of the coming convulsions of war and revolution. The symbolist school (Aleksandr Blok, Andrei Bely) used language in unique ways to create spiritual images through allegory and metaphor. The futurists (Vladimir Maiakovskii, Velemir Khlebnikov, Roman Iakobson) experimented with new forms of grammar and syntax, even creating a nonsense language called zaum, returning people to a world of primitive sound-gestures.

At another extreme, the formalist school of writers and literary theorists (Viktor Shklovskii, Veniamin Kaverin, Yuri Tynianov) experimented with new ideas about the fabric and structure of writing, which they considered to be more important than actual substance or content. Although Lenin had little taste for such innovations, preferring the classical realist texts of the nineteenth century, he allowed writers a great deal of artistic freedom. This was especially the case after the years of revolution and civil war (1917-1921), when deprivations forced some artists, especially those not favored by the regime, either to flee the country or to suffer in isolation at home.

During these years, the literary allies of the Bolshevik government prospered under state patronage. Futurists and formalists worked in relative freedom through the early and mid-1920s, as did other noted writers of the age, including Mikhail Bulgakov (author of a classic parody of Soviet society, *The Master and Margherita*) and Yevgenii Zamiatin (whose science fiction novel, *We,* was the prototype for George Orwell's *1984).* These writers, together with other artists not favored by the CPSU, were able to work thanks to the atmosphere encouraged by the liberal Anatolii Lunacharskii, party leader of cultural affairs.

Beginning with the mid-1920s, however, these authors and other nonofficial artists came under increasing attack from the Communist party, mainly through the Russian Association of Proletarian Writers and like-minded groups. Through these associations, the party attacked nonofficial writers and artists for their "formalism" (or attention to form over content, art over political substance) and for their neutrality in the midst of the pressures of class struggle and socialist construction. Many writers whose work had been tolerated in the 1920s lost their positions and contracts. Zamiatin was one of the few allowed to emigrate. Lunacharskii was sent off to Spain as ambassador; Maiakovskii committed suicide. Other writers perished in the purges of the 1930s, among them Osip Mandelshtam and Anna Akhmatova.

In an ironic reversal of critical realism, which contributed to the revolutionary fervor in prerevolutionary Russia with its harsh depictions of social ills, a new policy of "socialist realism" was put into effect. Writers now were called upon to help build Soviet society not by criticizing its defects, but by portraying socialist society as it ought to be, this as a means of inspiring people to achieve that goal.

After Stalin's death, Khrushchev put into motion a

Russian and Soviet Writers

The following are some of the major Russian and Soviet writers and a sampling of their works.

Nineteenth Century

Sergei Aksakov (1791-1859), novelist: *Family Chronicle, Recollections of Gogol.*

Aleksander Pushkin (1799-1837), father of Russian literature: *Eugene Onegin, A Captain's Daughter, Boris Godunov, Bronze Horseman.*

Nikolai Gogol (1809-1852), playwright, novelist: *Inspector General, The Overcoat, The Nose, Taras Bulba, Dead Souls.*

Mikhail Lermontov (1814-1841), poet, novelist: *Death of a Poet, A Hero of Our Time.*

Ivan Turgenev (1818-1883), novelist: *Rudin, On the Eve, Fathers and Sons, Smoke, Virgin Soil, Sportsman's Sketches.*

Nikolai Nekrasov (1821-1878), poet: *Who Lives Well in Russia, Peasant Children.*

Fëdor Dostoevsky (1822-1881), novelist: *Notes from the Underground, Crime and Punishment, The Gambler, The Idiot, The Possessed, The Brothers Karamazov.*

Aleksandr Ostrovskii (1823-1886), first major Russian playwright: *The Storm.*

Mikhail Saltykov-Shchedrin (1826-1889), satirist: *Contradictions, A Confused Case, Gentlemen of Tashkent, Provincial Sketches.*

Leo (Lev) Tolstoy (1828-1910), novelist and moral philosopher: *War and Peace, Anna Karenina, The Resurrection, Kreutzer Sonata.*

Nikolai Leskov (1831-1895), novelist: *Cathedral Folk, The Enchanted Wanderer.*

Anton Chekhov (1860-1904), playwright: *Ivanov, Uncle Vanya, The Sea Gull, Three Sisters, The Cherry Orchard.*

Twentieth Century

Maxim Gorky (Aleksei Peshkov) (1868-1936), first major Marxist writer; founded socialist realism: *Mother, The Artamonov Business, Klim Samgin.*

Ivan Bunin (1870-1954), novelist, 1933 Nobel Prize winner: *The Village, The Well of Days, Dark Alleys.*

Leonid Andreev (1871-1919), symbolist: *Darkness, Days of Our Life, He Who Gets Slapped.*

Aleksandr Blok (1873-1924), symbolist poet: *The Twelve, Scythians.*

Andrei Bely (1880-1934), symbolist: *Petersburg, Kotik Letaev.*

Aleksei Tolstoy (1883-1945), novelist: *The Road to Calvary, Peter I, Bread.*

Yevgenii Zamiatin (1884-1937), novelist, short story writer: *We, The Islanders, The Dragon.*

Anna Akhmatova (Gorenko) (1889-1960), poet: *Poem without a Hero, Courage, Requiem.*

Mikhail Bulgakov (1891-1940), playwright, novelist: *Heart of a Dog, The Master and Margherita.*

Osip Mandelshtam (1892-1938), poet: *The Age, Meganom, The Twilight of Freedom.*

Marina Tsvetaeva (1892-1941), poet: *An Ancient Song, After Russia, An Attempt at Jealousy, The Horn of Roland.*

Vladimir Maiakovskii (1893-1930), poet: *Cloud in Trousers, 150,000,000, The Bathhouse.*

Isaac Babel (1894-1941), short story writer: *Red Cavalry, Odessa Tales.*

Sergei Yesenin (1895-1925), poet: *Autumn, I am the last village poet, Last Lines.*

Boris Pasternak (1896-1960), novelist, poet, 1958 Nobel Prize winner: *Doctor Zhivago.*

Valentin Kataev (1897-1986), novelist, playwright: *The Embezzlers, Squaring the Circle, Time Forward.*

Mikhail Sholokov (1905-), novelist, 1965 Nobel Prize winner: *Quiet Flows the Don, Virgin Soil Upturned.*

Alexander Solzhenitsyn (1918-), novelist, 1970 Nobel Prize winner: *One Day in the Life of Ivan Denisovich; Cancer Ward; The First Circle; The Gulag Archipelago; August, 1914.*

Andrei Siniavskii (1925-), novelist: *The Trial Begins, The Icicle, The Makepeace Experiment.*

Yuli Daniel (1925-), short story writer: *This Is Moscow Speaking, The Flight, Atonement.*

Yuri Trifonov (1927-), novelist: *The Exchange, The House on the Embankment, Students.*

Chingiz Aitmatov (1928-), novelist: *The Day Lasts More Than a Hundred Years, Executioner's Block, The Place of the Skull.*

Fazil Iskander (1929-), novelist, short story writer: *Sandro of Chegem, The Gospel According to Chegem, Small Giant of the Big Sex.*

Robert Rozhdestvenskii (1932-), poet: *Winter of Thirty Eight, Nostalgia, They Killed the Lad.*

Vasilii Aksenov (1932-), short story writer, novelist: *Halfway to the Moon, A Ticket to the Stars, Oranges from Moscow, The Island of Crimea.*

Vladimir Voinovich (1932-), novelist: *I Want to Be Honest, The Extraordinary Adventures of Private Ivan Chonkin, In Plain Russian.*

Yevgenii Yevtushenko (1933-), poet, novelist: *Babi Yar, Dwarf Birches, A Hundred Miles from the Capital City of Hope, Wild Berries, Precocious Autobiography, Kindergarten.*

Bella Akhmadulina (1937-), poet: *String, A Fairytale about Rain, My Genealogy.*

Joseph Brodsky (1940-), poet, essayist: *A Stop in the Wilderness, To a Certain Tyrant, Candelmas, A Part of Speech, Less Than One.*

period of cultural renewal known as the "thaw," after Il'ia Ehrenburg's novel of the same name (1953) and its metaphor of a frozen stream (the Stalinist state and society) melting with springtime (Khrushchev's de-Stalinization program). Yevgenii Yevtushenko was able to publish his offbeat and critical poems, among them *Babi Yar* (about World War II and anti-Semitism) and *Nasledniki Stalina* (The Heirs of Stalin, about the purges and terrors of Stalinism). By the late 1950s, however, relaxed censorship standards had been tightened. For example, Boris Pasternak's 1958 novel *Doctor Zhivago* was prohibited, while Alexander Solzhenitsyn's study of everyday life in the Gulag, *One Day in the Life of Ivan Denisovich*, was published in 1962.

The early Brezhnev years saw examples of both repression and liberal openness. In 1964 poet Joseph Brodsky was tried on charges of "social parasitism." Yuli Daniel and Andrei Siniavskii were arrested in 1965 for their attempt to publish their uncensored works in the West. They were convicted in 1966 on charges of "anti-Soviet propaganda."

Yet there also were bright spots. Mikhail Bulgakov's *The Master and Margherita* was published in censored form, as were selections of Osip Mandelshtam's and Marina Tsvetaeva's poems. Yevgenii Zamiatin's *We* was distributed via tamizdat. Critical novels (far outside the mainstream of socialist realism) also appeared in the 1970s by Yuri Trifonov, Valentin Rasputin, and Fëdor Abramov. Yet in 1979 the attempt to publish in the West the uncensored anthology *Metropol* was repressed, and its main organizer, Vasilii Aksenov, was forced to emigrate.

Glasnost and the Revival of Literature

Since 1985, the policy of glasnost has supported a return to the nineteenth-century genre of critical realism. Socialist realism has been abandoned as an official party policy, though remnants of its style remain in the works of many second-rate writers. In the spirit of the Decembrists and Populists of old, contemporary Russian and Soviet writers are attempting to use literature and poetry as the primary vehicles for a renewal and cleansing of Soviet society, by way of criticism of old values and inspiration of new ones.

Anatolii Rybakov's *Children of the Arbat,* Vasilii Grossman's *Life and Fate,* and Daniil Granin's *Aurochs* reveal the abuses and terrors of Stalinism. Valentin Rasputin's *The Fire* and Viktor Asafev's *The Sad Detective* reveal the crime and corruption in everyday Soviet life. Pasternak's *Doctor Zhivago* has been published, as has Anna Akhmatova's *Requiem*.

A new official literary establishment has come into shape, staffed by liberal gorbachevtsy (Gorbachevians), including Vitalii Korotich and Yegor Ligachev in journalism, Yevgenii Yevtushenko and Andrei Voznesenskii in literature, and Sergei Zalygin and Grigorii Baklanov in literary journalism. Another key liberal supporter of Gorbachev's reforms is Vladimir Karpov, a former prisoner in the Gulag, who was elected first secretary of the Union of Writers in June 1986.

Not all is peaceful on the literary front, however. Although many journals and newspapers have taken a progressive stance toward reform, including *Novy Mir* (New World), *Druzhba Narodov* (Friendship of Peoples), *Znamia* (Banner), *Literaturnaya Gazeta,* (Literary Gazette), *Sovetskaya Kultura* (Soviet Culture), *Ogonyok* (Flame), and *Moskovskie Novosti* (Moscow News), several

others have defended in strident tones the old values of socialist realism and have been linked by Western observers to the reactionary and Russian nationalist movements. These publications include *Molodaya Gvardia* (Young Guard), *Nash Sovremennik* (Our Contemporary), and *Moskva* (Moscow).

Theater and Film

Theater traditionally has been one of the more experimental and open art forms in Russia and the Soviet Union, and this has continued under glasnost. Theaters in Moscow and Leningrad regularly perform avant-garde productions, critical of the state and established Soviet society. Most Soviet theaters in the smaller cities, however, have been less open to innovation, preferring to follow party directives and perform plays dealing with sanctioned themes in the manner of socialist realism.

The modern theatrical tradition in Russia began with the collaboration between playwright Anton Chekhov and director Konstantin Stanislavsky, who laid the foundations of modern realistic drama. The theater that they founded in 1898, the Moscow Art Academic Theater, has been one of the world's leading stages.

During the years of revolution and civil war, the Bolsheviks first recognized the value of the theater as an instrument of mass education and agitation. They nationalized all theaters, which were placed under the supervision of the innovative director Vsevolod Meierhold and subsumed under the authority of the Peoples' Commissariat for Education. Under Meierhold's direction, and with the participation of a mass movement for proletarian culture (called Proletkult), theater became an experimental medium for proletarian and avant-garde art. Scenery changes took place in front of the audience to heighten audience participation in the production and to break through the barrier between the stage and seats. Mass revolutionary productions were staged involving thousands of participants. Directors studied the semiotics of the pronunciations and body movements of actors to better communicate their dramas to the audience.

Soviet theater has been an important medium for social and political criticism (a characteristic in evidence during the Brezhnev years). In the 1960s and 1970s, Yuri Liubimov was at the forefront of such a critical theater. Founder of the famed Taganka Theater in 1963, he staged modernistic productions of Shakespeare and Molière (replete with anti-Stalinist undertones), as well as highly interpretive productions of modern works (such as Bulgakov's *The Master and Margherita*). Alternately acclaimed and suppressed by the Brezhnev regime, Liubimov was exiled from the USSR in 1984.

The theater remains a very popular form of entertainment in contemporary Soviet society. It is accessible and inexpensive, and performances attract large audiences. Professional theatrical companies number about six hundred. Under Gorbachev, Liubimov has returned to the USSR to direct the Taganka again, though not permanently. Indeed, Gorbachev has several of his own allies in the theater, notably playwrights Kiril Lavrov, Mikhail Shatrov, and Fëdor Burlatsky. Shatrov's plays *Forward, Forward, Forward!; The Brest Peace;* and *Dictators of Conscience* and Burlatsky's *Political Testament* have portrayed the more open and liberal-minded Bolshevism of the 1920s in a favorable light, this in service to Gorbachev's own emerging model of communism. Vladimir Gubaryev's

Remaking Soviet History

The science of history has been reinvigorated in the age of glasnost, which requires not only criticism of the present but also a rediscovery and reevaluation of the past. Under Mikhail S. Gorbachev, Soviet historians and citizens have been encouraged to sort through the past as a means of self-discovery.

During the tenure of Leonid I. Brezhnev, the historical profession was used by the regime to glorify the state and the leading role of the party. Joseph Stalin's violence against society received little criticism (a backlash against the de-Stalinization campaigns launched by Nikita S. Khrushchev). History remained official, glossing over or denying embarrassing moments in the past.

Glasnost has been accompanied by a full historical repudiation of the Stalinist system and the less brutal Brezhnev regime. Only under Gorbachev has the complete truth been told about the violence and abuses of the Stalin era. In 1988, the USSR Supreme Court officially rehabilitated the "right" and "left" opposition parties that had opposed Stalin. The Communist party's Control Committee has restored party membership to several liberal-minded leaders who became victims of Stalin's purges, including Nikolai Bukharin, Mikhail Tomskii, and Aleksei Rykov. A Soviet-Polish committee of historians has been at work since 1988, exploring the evidence of the murder of thousands of Polish officers by Soviet forces in the Katyn Forest in 1939. The protocols of the Hitler-Stalin pact of 1939 were published and denounced in the Soviet press in 1988 (although in 1989 the Congress of People's Deputies failed to pass a resolution renouncing the Hitler-Stalin Pact).

In the arts, film makers, writers, and dramatists have begun to confront the Stalinist past in their works. Tengiz Abuladze's much acclaimed film *Repentance* examines the legacy of Stalinism. Anatolii Rybakov's novel *Children of the Arbat* recounts the experiences of a group of Soviet youth at the beginning of the purges. Mikhail Shatrov's play *Forward, Forward, Forward!* reproduces on stage the personal and professional conflicts between Lenin, Leon Trotsky, Bukharin, Stalin, and other leaders from the revolutionary period, leaving Stalin lingering on stage at the end of the play, against Lenin's wishes. Indeed, a whole new genre of literature has been created in journals called *publitsistika*: past and present denunciations of Stalinism.

Under glasnost Soviet historians have worked to develop alternative models to Stalinist politics and economics. A group of Soviet historians focusing on the period between 1917 and 1945 are publishing new studies of the era. The main professional historical journals, *Problems of History* and *History of the USSR*, have opened their pages to revisionist articles about the Soviet past, including interviews with American historians specializing in the Soviet Union. The government has permitted Stephen Cohen, professor at Princeton University, to translate and publish in the USSR his classic biography of Bukharin. In 1988, final examinations at secondary schools in Russian and Soviet history were canceled because of the lack of reliable textbooks. Students instead were given oral examinations on their knowledge of the history of perestroika.

Leading the reevaluation of history has been Yuri Afanaseyev, who was appointed rector of the Moscow State Institute of Historical Archives in 1987. He has been a vocal proponent of freeing history from ideology and making it an objective science and profession. In 1985, as editor of the history section of the party theoretical journal, *Kommunist*, Afanaseyev advocated a full and free confrontation by the Soviet people of their past history. He also has called for the opening of all archives of the Soviet government and the Communist party to historical researchers. In 1987, he helped to organize meetings that publicized statistics and details of the party and army purges of the 1930s. Afanaseyev also is one of the leading advocates of radical reform in the USSR. In 1989, he was elected to the Congress of People's Deputies, where he has attacked conservatives and denounced the slow pace of reform. The "falsified history" of the Stalin and Brezhnev years must be overcome, he says, so that the Soviet people might confront the totalitarian model and its crimes. As Afanaseyev wrote in his essay, "Historical Knowledge and Perestroika," "only an open competition of the most differentiated ideas can permit a free, democratic choice of the path to take in strengthening perestroika. It is precisely in this that history and politics, the past and the present merge."

play, *Sarcophagus,* has presented the 1986 Chernobyl nuclear power plant disaster as critical drama. In 1986, the Congress of the All-Russian Theater Society joined perestroika by disbanding itself and forming into a new Union of Theater Workers of the RSFSR, with a new program and new leadership loyal to Gorbachev.

The Bolsheviks recognized the usefulness of the cinema as early on as they recognized the value of the theater.

In a largely illiterate society as Soviet Russia, they knew that the theater and cinema were more powerful means of political communication than the written word. Early Soviet films were not only successful in communicating such political messages—portraying the power of mass movements and revolution—but also did so using new and innovative techniques of film making. Following similar trends in literature and the arts, the great early Soviet directors studied the semiotics of film making, using innovative angles and montage shots to accentuate images. Among the film classics of the period are Sergei Eisenstein's *The Strike* and *The Battleship Potemkin;* Vsevolod Pudovkin's *Mechanics of the Brain, The End of St. Petersburg,* and *Mother;* and Aleksandr Dovzhenko's *Arsenal* and *The Land.*

Soviet traditions of great film making continued into the 1950s and 1960s, with the release of such classics as *Othello* (1955), *Three Men on a Raft* (1954), *The Cranes Are Flying* (1956), and *Ballad of a Soldier* (1956). As with films produced during the Brezhnev era (*Moscow Does Not Believe in Tears, My Friend Ivan Lapshin*), these films dealt with themes of history and problems of daily life left untouched during the Stalin period.

Soviet film makers continued to produce high quality films during the 1960s and 1970s, but their work was not fully appreciated by the Brezhnev regime. Andrei Tarkovsky's films (*Andrei Rublev, Stalker, Nostalgia*) were shown intermittently in the USSR but mostly were exported abroad. Sergei Paradzhanov's *Shadows of Forgotten Ancestors* was shown abroad, but not in the USSR because of its alleged Ukrainian nationalism. Elem Klimov's *Agony* also was prohibited from most Soviet screens under Brezhnev, allegedly for its sympathetic treatment of Tsar Nicholas II.

In the age of glasnost, Gorbachev has found allies in the cinema (Elem Klimov and Vadim Abdrashitov are the two most prominent), who have used their medium to deal with pressing problems of Soviet life. In 1986, three-quarters of the leadership of the Union of Cinematographers were replaced and Elem Klimov elected its first secretary, in a move to join perestroika as well as boost attendance at movie theaters, which had dropped off during the Brezhnev era. Of special note, for example, is Tengiz Abuladze's surreal and allegorical *Repentance,* a Georgian production from 1984, but released only after 1987, which confronts all of the lingering tensions and divisions in Soviet society about Stalinism.

Musical Arts

Russia's musical contribution to world culture is first-rate, especially in the field of classical music. Mikhail Glinka (1804-1857) combined Russian folk melodies and traditional church music to create a unique Russian style. This movement away from European classical standards was continued by Alexander Borodin (1833-1887), Modest Mussorgskii (1839-1881), and Nikolai Rimsky-Korsakov (1844-1908). Piotr Tchaikovsky (1840-1893) composed music in this emerging tradition but combined it with European styles as well.

Igor Stravinsky (1882-1971), who composed *Firebird, Petrushka,* and the *Rite of Spring,* is perhaps the most important Soviet composer of the twentieth century. Sergei Prokofiev (1891-1953) and Dmitri Shostakovich (1906-1975) also are among the most famous of the Soviet composers, together with Aram Kachaturian, Isaac Dunaevskii, and Dmitri Kabalevskii.

Prokofiev, whose famous works include the opera *War and Peace,* the ballets *Romeo and Juliet, The Stone Flower,* and *Peter and the Wolf,* and the orchestral work *Scythian Suite,* was censored by Stalin but never officially disgraced, partly because of his universal fame. Harassed under Stalin and condemned in 1936, Shostakovich was rehabilitated in 1956 and became secretary of the Union of Composers of the RSFSR in 1960. Shostakovich's well-known works include the operas *The Nose* and *Lady Macbeth of Mtsensk,* the ballet *The Golden Age,* and eleven symphonies.

Stalin's successors established cultural contacts with the noncommunist world, among the most spectacular being violinist David Oistrakh's tour of the United States and Europe and the Bolshoi Ballet's European tour, both in 1956. More recently, émigré Soviet musicians have been able to return to the USSR for performances, notably pianist Vladimir Horowitz's triumphant 1986 return to the USSR after sixty-one years in exile, and conductor Mstislav Rostropovich's National Symphony (Washington, D.C.) concerts in the USSR in early 1990.

The large cities of the USSR have their own symphony orchestras, opera and ballet houses, and musical comedy theaters. Opera houses have their own ballet companies, the best known being the Moscow Bolshoi Theater and the Leningrad Kirov Theater. In Moscow, the Tchaikovsky Conservatory and the Gnessin State Musical Pedagogical Institute are the two main centers of musical culture.

Modern music and dance (like modern literature) have been criticized for expressing formalism instead of realism or traditional styles, not only by the party establishment but also by the Russian public, which has traditionally opposed innovation in the fine arts. Consequently, although ballet companies and symphony orchestras are impressive technically, they generally perform nineteenth-century repertoires. However, avant-gard composers are at work in the USSR today, most notable of whom is Alfred Schnittke, whose compositions have been well-received both in the USSR and in the West.

Authorities tried throughout the 1970s and early 1980s, without success, to undermine the popular music culture in the USSR by banning performances, limiting recording opportunities, jamming foreign radio broadcasts, arresting musicians, censoring lyrics, and impeding access to musical instruments and equipment. Denied official status, the musical underground thrived during this time on *magnitizdat,* or self-recorded music. Magnitizdat includes all types of unofficial music, but folk, rock, and jazz are the most widely distributed.

Bulat Okudzhava (1924-) and Vladimir Vysotskii (1938-1980) are the most popular folk poet-musicians. Both gained their fame through magnitizdat. Okudzhava's most popular songs are "Burn, Fire, Burn" and "A Paper Soldier." Vysotskii is considered the most popular of the magnitizdat musicians. Although not officially sanctioned, Vysotskii was tolerated by the Brezhnev regime. His poems were never published, but he remained a leading actor at the Taganka Theater in Moscow and was allowed to perform before small groups. By 1990 he had been rehabilitated and honored in the spirit of glasnost.

Both American and Soviet jazz, permitted even under Stalin, are widely popular. The Ganelin Trio is the best known Soviet jazz group and was one of the first jazz groups to perform in Europe and the United States beginning in the 1980s. In turn, American jazz musicians have been performing in the USSR with official permission for several years.

Modern rock music was considered decadent throughout the Brezhnev period and was not available except on the black market and through magnitizdat. To limit and control such activity, Soviet authorities did allow limited releases of rock music and several concert tours of both Soviet and Western rock groups in the late 1970s and early

Women in Soviet Society

The claim of equality for women in Soviet society (Article 35 of the Soviet Constitution) is a source of pride for the Soviets. This legal equality, however, is undermined by social customs and a deeply rooted sexism in Soviet culture. Soviet women routinely endure hardships created by male chauvinism in their daily lives and in the division of labor.

Traditional Russian society, heavily influenced by Mongol and Turkic customs, by Orthodox church practices, and by the chauvinism of a clan society, placed women in an inferior social position. Despite a few powerful women such as Catherine the Great, most Russian women were subservient to their husbands and fathers. Peasant women, at the bottom of the social scale, not only attended to household duties, they also worked in the fields while the men cared for the livestock.

Women's roles changed dramatically when the Bolsheviks came to power in 1917. The new government granted women full legal rights. Marriage, divorce, and abortion became subject to their choice and request under the law. A special department—the *Zhenotdel*—was organized to help fulfill (through education and participation in party work) Lenin's goal of freeing women from the drudgery of domestic chores.

Beginning in the late 1920s, Stalin overturned many liberal family laws to create stable family units, which he believed were necessary for industrialization and modernization. Divorce became harder to obtain, and marriage and childbirth were encouraged. In 1936 the government outlawed abortion, which remained illegal until 1955.

Although women previously had a large role in the labor force, beginning in the late 1920s with the industrialization drive, women went to work in industry in mass numbers. Between 1932 and 1937, four million new workers were put to work in industry, 82 percent of them women. World War II, which cost as many as twenty million Soviet lives (most of them male, at the front), led to an even larger role for women in labor.

In 1990 women made up approximately 51 percent of the work force. Nine out of ten women between the ages of twenty and forty-nine were employed outside the home—a figure higher than in any other industrialized nation. The large numbers of women in the labor force have been a mixed blessing. As Francine du Plessix Gray, an expert on Soviet women, has written in a 1989 essay, "the Bolshevik rhetoric of equal rights has been a camouflage for the hardships of a double shift life." Most Soviet women have a full-time job and are expected to do the housework and care for their children with little help from their husbands. The strains created by this situation have contributed to a nearly 50 percent Soviet divorce rate.

Although the medical profession has been dominated by women, and other professions such as teaching, engineering, and economics have seen large numbers of women achieve distinguished careers, most Soviet women are employed in menial, low-paying jobs. Moreover, they earn on average only between 60 percent and 75 percent of men's pay for the same work, and they do not enjoy the same access to promotion.

Women spend much free time waiting in lines at stores or tending to life at home. These burdens leave women with less time to spend in continuing education and party and government work—traditional roads to advancement in the Soviet Union. Women account for only 10 percent of leaders in industry and business, and women have been excluded almost entirely from top party and government positions.

Women receive up to three months of maternity leave with full pay and up to another year with 30-40 percent of their salary, but few women are able to afford the loss of salary after three months. Child care and health care for women and children are widely available but are generally of poor quality. Infant mortality is three times higher in the Soviet Union than in the United States.

The absence of dependable birth control techniques (including the pill) has caused most Soviet women to rely on abortion as a method of contraception. According to a 1988 report in the Soviet weekly *Ogonyok*, only 10 percent of Soviet women use contraceptives, more than 80 percent have had at least one abortion, almost 80 percent of all pregnancies in the Soviet Union end in abortion, the average Soviet woman will have three abortions during her lifetime, and 25 percent of the world's abortions are performed in the Soviet Union.

The feminist movement has, in the 1970s and 1980s, been almost nonexistent. One of the few documented signposts of feminist activity appeared in 1979 with the samizdat publication *Almanac: Women and Russia*, an anthology critical of women's work, child care, and health care in the USSR (only two issues were published). Several of the *Almanac*'s leading organizers were deported.

Under glasnost, women's issues and problems often are discussed, but the feminist movement remains weak and unpopular. Male chauvinist values surface regularly in the media, relegating women to their traditional roles as wives and mothers. Mikhail S. Gorbachev himself broached the issue of the "double shift life," calling, however, not for improvements at work, but for the return of women to the home. In effect, perestroika so far has encouraged women to choose the single burden life of the family.

1980s. By the mid-1980s, two of the USSR's most popular rock bands, Aquarium (led by Boris Grebenshchikov) and Time Machine (led by lyricist Andrei Makarevich), attained superstar status. New officially sanctioned outlets, such as the Leningrad Rock Club (established in 1981)—made into a nationwide network in 1986—have given these and other bands (Kino, Popular Mechanics, DDT, Black Coffee) a forum for performance, much to the dismay of many sophisticated Russian rock fans who regard the sanctioned bands as watered-down and official. Heavy metal and punk rock bands enjoy wide popularity among the young.

In the Baltic states, rock music was more accessible during the 1970s because of Western and Finnish television and radio. Youth discontent with official suppression of rock reared itself most powerfully in the Baltic states in 1980. When a performance by the punk rock band Propeller was cancelled at a halftime soccer game, youths rampaged the city of Tallinn, causing Soviet authorities to disband the group. Rock groups in the Baltics also have helped to inspire and unite the peoples of Estonia, Latvia, and Lithuania to national consciousness. By 1988, the words from Alo Mattiisen's popular rock refrain, "Estonian I shall remain," were drowning the local airwaves.

Visual Arts

Like Russian and Soviet musicians, Russian and Soviet artists have contributed major trends and styles to world culture. Along with Russian and Soviet literature, the visual arts have followed the critical realist, revolutionary, and social realist trends. At the turn of the century, for example, the *peredvizhniki* artists (the "travelers") were known for their realistic portrayals of Russian rural life.

During the years of war and revolution, Russian and Soviet artists experimented with new artistic trends evident elsewhere in Europe—Surrealism, Cubism, and Constructivism, all of which were linked to similar trends in literature (Futurism and Formalism). The Surrealists aimed to distort reality through new color and shape schemes. The Cubists sought to display a new geometry of art with squares and rectangles, in celebration of modernization. The Constructivists attempted to make art socially useful and technologically advanced. Avant-garde artists from these trends were at the forefront of modern art worldwide, among them were Kazimir Malevich, Vasilii Kandinsky, Marc Chagall, Vladimir Tatlin, Liubov Popova, Ivan Kyun, Kliment Rutko, and Aleksandr Rodchenko. Kandinsky and Chagall fled to the West as the avant-garde fell out of favor in the mid-1920s. Through the 1970s, only selective rehabilitations and exhibitions of the avant-garde artists and trends from the 1920s were allowed.

By the 1980s, the best known "official" artists continued with the sanctioned styles: Aleksandr Gerassimov (portraits, heroic scenes), Vera Mukhina (sculptures and monuments), and Isaac Brodskii (portraits, heroic themes, historic scenes).

Under glasnost, art and sculpture have been slow to respond to the new climate, although several unofficial artists have made names for themselves, for example, Il'ia Kabakov and Erik Bulatov. Beginning in the late 1980s these and other avant-garde artists have been able to freely exhibit and sell their works, as well as express their ideas by way of religious and abstract themes. Art from the avant-garde period of the early 1900s now is on display in a new wing of Moscow's Tretiakov Gallery of Russian Art. The Soviet art scene is on the verge of self-discovery.

Perestroika and Society

The term perestroika leaves powerful impressions on the Russian and Soviet psyche. It takes its meaning from the Russian root *stroi*, denoting a structure or construct, and from the Russian word *stroitel'stvo*, denoting construction in the physical sense. Throughout Soviet history, the Communist party set as its task to build, using the proper engineering metaphors, a whole new society. The aim was to thrust Russia and her sister republics into the twentieth century by way of various processes of "socialist," or "cultural," or even of "language" construction.

Cultural and language construction have indeed been very successful. The Russian language and its literature, like art in general, are as powerful and vibrant as ever. The peoples of the Caucasus and Central Asia, in particular, have initiated and have continued to develop their languages and cultures through the Soviet period and have in some cases even thrived. But the matter of "socialist construction" is more problematic. This process refers to the building of a fully employed, fully egalitarian economy and society, as well as the construction of a state system in which all national groups are allowed the full rights of national self-determination. In this latter respect, the Soviet government faces the task of making real what has always been written into its laws and propagated by its pronouncements. The continuing process of perestroika demands, in effect, not only a rebuilding of the Soviet economy, but also a rebuilding of that that has been assumed to have been finished: the federal state system.

Foreign Policy

Almost since the October Revolution, Western observers have debated the role of ideology in Soviet foreign policy. The Bolsheviks who carried out the revolution were unshakable in their belief in communism. It is unclear, however, how much of Soviet foreign policy since then can be ascribed to ideology and how much has been based on cold calculations of Soviet national interest.

In accordance with Marx's writings, the Bolsheviks expected that, following the revolution in Russia, other revolutions would occur throughout Europe, and as a result, traditional foreign policy would become unnecessary. After a world socialist revolution, the Bolsheviks believed that national boundaries would cease to have any meaning.

The prospect of revolution hung heavily over Europe immediately following the conclusion of World War I. In Germany, the Kaiser had abdicated, and for a time the country seemed on the edge of a revolution. Hungarian Socialist leader Bela Kun had established a short-lived Soviet-style regime in Budapest. Italy was divided between communists and fascists. Throughout the rest of Europe, and even in the United States, communists and socialists were making strong political gains.

The Bolsheviks not only expected other revolutions, they depended on them. They believed that without the benefit of fraternal socialist nations in Western Europe, a single backward Socialist Russia would not be able to survive. So at first the Bolsheviks devoted themselves to fomenting revolution abroad and ignored most of the traditional niceties of diplomacy. In a famous episode, Leon Trotsky, upon being named commissar for foreign affairs, declared that he would simply issue a few proclamations and then close down the ministry.

The expected revolutions, however, did not materialize. The Bolsheviks promoted the collapse of the tsar's army, believing that a socialist country would not need such an archaic institution. Meanwhile, during late 1917 and early 1918, German troops were advancing deep into Russian territory virtually unhindered. Instead of fighting them, the Bolsheviks tried to convince the German soldiers that serving in the army went against their class interests and that they should revolt. This failed to stop the advance, and the Bolsheviks were forced to accept harsh peace terms in the Treaty of Brest-Litovsk, under which they relinquished territory containing about a quarter of the Russian empire's population.

Since the early 1920s, when it became obvious that a wider European socialist revolution was unlikely to occur soon, Soviet leaders usually have subordinated ideology to pragmatic assessments of national interest when formulating foreign policy. Nevertheless, up until Mikhail S. Gorbachev became general secretary in 1985, the Soviets continued to insist that their foreign policy (like their domestic policy) was scientifically determined, and that it sprang directly from the writings of Marx and Lenin.

Soviet ideology has made subtle twists and turns over the years, keeping pace with changes in policy. In 1928, Stalin turned away from the notion that world revolution was essential for building socialism, proclaiming the doctrine of "socialism in one country." Marx had suggested that the surrounding capitalist powers would be totally hostile to the first socialist state, sensing in it their own doom. Because the other revolutions were not forthcoming, Stalin proposed that the best way to advance socialism was to strengthen the Soviet Union, the world's only socialist state, against expected capitalist attacks. Stalin may have believed in the wisdom of this appoach, but it also was a maneuver to get foreign communists to de-emphasize their local interests and work for the benefit of the Soviet Union.

Citing the USSR's vulnerability and the hostility of the capitalist states, Stalin created a war hysteria. In the late 1920s and early 1930s, the Soviet Union was in no danger of attack, but Stalin needed to create the illusion of impending war to justify his rapid industrialization program. If the Soviet Union did not industrialize swiftly, Stalin warned, it would be defeated militarily, as Russia repeatedly had been during the previous century.

Protecting the motherland also was the justification for the 1939 Molotov-Ribbentrop Pact with Nazi Germany. In 1939, Nazi Germany was the leading threat to peace and to socialism. Thus, the accommodation with Germany came as a great shock, particularly to foreign communists. It was justified, however, as the best way to keep the Soviet Union out of the war, and thus to protect the gains of socialism. Later Stalin's supporters claimed that the two years of peace between the pact and the 1941 German invasion had allowed the Soviet Union to better prepare for the war.

"Peaceful coexistence" was Khrushchev's contribution to Soviet foreign policy doctrine. The phrase had been coined by Lenin, but Khrushchev gave it new meaning for the nuclear age. He argued that the advent of nuclear weapons made it exceedingly dangerous to blindly insist that eventual armed conflict with the West was unavoidable (as Stalin had done). Khrushchev said that because of the new weapons, military conflict with the capitalist nations of the West was no longer inevitable, and that competition would move to the economic arena, where he was confident that socialism, with its superior economic system, would "catch-up and surpass" capitalism.

The socialist-capitalist competition continued during the tenure of Leonid I. Brezhnev, but under the conditions of détente. Beginning in 1968, the Soviet Union signed a series of treaties with the United States, and relations became warmer than at any time since World War II. According to Dimitri Simes, a specialist in Soviet affairs at the Carnegie Endowment for International Peace, the Soviets saw themselves moving into a qualitatively different stage of relations with the United States. The Soviets believed the United States had entered a period of relative decline and inactivity in international affairs following the debacle of Vietnam.

In Marxist-Leninist theory, the sum of all factors that affect political influence and dynamism—economic, political, and military strength; national confidence; ideology; alliance relationships; and so on—is known as the correlation of forces. Under Brezhnev, Moscow believed that the correlation of forces was finally beginning to turn in the direction of socialism. The Soviets had achieved rough strategic parity with the United States in the late 1960s, had shown the political will to use their new muscle (in Czechoslovakia, for example), and were aggressively pursuing their interests around the globe. Many different factors are included in the correlation of forces model, but Brezhnev regarded the massive Soviet military buildup as key.

The Soviets saw détente as a codification of their new relationship with the United States. They believed that the United States had been forced to the negotiating table by the new strength of the Soviet Union. The Americans could not dictate terms from a position of strength and thus were forced to seek accommodation through negotiation. According to an old axiom of tsarist policy, resorting to diplomacy is a demonstration of the failure of policy.

The United States saw détente in a totally different light. President Richard Nixon believed that détente could be used to complement containment of the Soviet Union and reduce international tensions. His administration and the administrations of Gerald R. Ford and Jimmy Carter sought to limit Soviet actions through a web of treaties and superpower interdependence that would make Moscow a less disruptive force in world politics.

Simes has asserted that Brezhnev saw détente as a green light from the United States to proceed as he wished. The rapid growth of Soviet defense expenditures continued. Meanwhile, the Soviet Union became involved in one Third World country after another in an attempt to expand its influence beyond Europe's deadlocked borders and to further shift the correlation of forces in its favor. This aggressive posture was reinforced by the reluctance of the United States to directly meet Soviet global challenges. In the years following the end of the Vietnam War, American defense spending declined, and Americans were loath to become involved in limited regional conflicts.

This was not the first time that the Soviet Union had actively supported governments and movements in the Third World. Khrushchev also had backed newly emerging countries in their struggles against colonial powers. The difference under Brezhnev was that for the first time the Soviet Union was not just sending aid, it was committing

ground troops—and the troops of its proxies, such as Cuba, East Germany, and Vietnam. During the second half of the Brezhnev period, the Soviet Union and its proxies introduced troops into Afghanistan, Angola, Cambodia, Ethiopia, Grenada, and South Yemen.

The New Thinking

Although it took a long time to become apparent, the growth of Soviet power did not achieve any of its expected goals. The correlation of forces model assumed that other nations would seek accommodation with the Soviet Union when it was clear that socialism was gaining ground globally. But this assumption proved to be incorrect. Relations with the other major powers worsened significantly during the late seventies and early eighties.

The Soviets had expected that the United States would be forced to continue détente despite Soviet activism in the Third World. But the United States never felt so compelled. The U.S. Senate refused to ratify the SALT II treaty, signed by President Carter and President Brezhnev in 1979, largely because of American displeasure with Soviet actions around the world, including the Soviet invasion of Afghanistan. American defense spending began to increase under Carter and accelerated rapidly under President Ronald Reagan in the early 1980s. Relations became further strained with the declaration of martial law in Poland in 1981 and the Soviets' downing of Korean Airlines flight 007 in 1983. Western Europe permitted the installation of Pershing II intermediate-range missiles in 1983, despite heavy Soviet pressure. While Sino-Soviet relations remained cool during the 1970s and 1980s, Sino-American relations improved dramatically following President Nixon's 1973 trip to China and President Carter's 1979 recognition of the People's Republic of China.

In the Third World, the Soviet Union once had been seen as the superpower most sympathetic to national liberation movements and to the concerns of lesser developed countries. It was regarded as an alternative model of development worthy of consideration. Soviets, however, lost much good will with the invasion of Afghanistan. The Third World, particularly the Islamic countries, reacted very strongly to the invasion, criticizing it as great power imperialism. China also condemned the invasion, pointing to it as a serious roadblock to improved Sino-Soviet relations.

Thus, by 1985 when Gorbachev came to power, the Soviets' perceived success at improving the correlation of forces had not led to foreign policy gains. Their search for absolute security through military means had led to a high level of global tension and to the active hostility of China, Japan, Western Europe, and the United States. The development of the Soviet military ironically had led to the creation of new threats and to a higher level of insecurity than before. Instead of bringing new influence, involvement in the Third World had merely left the Soviet Union bogged down in a series of costly ventures in relatively unimportant countries.

Simes suggests that the leadership was blind to abundant evidence of the failure of its policy because of its staunch belief in the model. Suggestions from policy institutes that foreign policy was not working were rejected out of hand.

When Gorbachev came to power, he inherited a situation in which foreign policy corresponded less and less to

Speaking before the UN General Assembly on December 7, 1988, Mikhail S. Gorbachev dramatically announces unilateral troop reductions in Europe and along the Soviet-Chinese border.

real international conditions. This incongruity was one of the prime motivations for launching a fundamental reevaluation of foreign policy that Gorbachev labeled the "new thinking." The serious domestic problems faced by the Soviet Union also were an important factor in the development of the new thinking. Soviet internal problems had become so severe that the leadership no longer was willing to devote the energy or resources necessary to continue the old style of foreign policy. Supporters of President Reagan's military buildup maintained that the need to keep up with the massive growth of American defense spending increased the pressure on the Soviet economy and may have contributed to Moscow's decision to reevaluate its foreign policy stance.

The new thinking has been developing gradually since 1985, appearing in many areas of foreign policy, while leaving others relatively untouched. Despite the Soviet Union's genuine progress toward implementing the new thinking, it is a paradigm for a new foreign policy, not a precise description of Soviet policy as it currently stands. Columbia University Soviet scholar Robert Legvold has characterized the new thinking as a genuine revolution of thought. He believes that it has "altered the assumptions by which Soviets explain the functioning of international politics and from which they derive the concepts underlying the deeper pattern of their actions." Three concepts constitute the essence of the new thinking: the new interpretation of national security, the doctrine of reasonable sufficiency, and the de-ideologization of foreign policy.

The New Thinking and National Security

Since the signing of the humiliating Treaty of Brest-Litovsk in 1918, the Soviets have been firm believers in the

value of military strength for achieving foreign policy goals. Under Brezhnev in particular, military might was seen as the means to security. The stronger the military, the more secure the country would be. Gorbachev, however, developed a much broader definition of security. He maintained that because no military means exists to repel a nuclear attack once launched, the strongest military could not absolutely ensure a nation's security. In his 1987 book *Perestroika: New Thinking for Our Country and the World*, Gorbachev wrote, "Security can no longer be secured through military means.... The only way to security is through political decisions and disarmament."

Under Gorbachev the military has played a much smaller role in the policy-making process. Gorbachev and most of his Politburo appointees have had minimal military experience. This contrasts with the Brezhnev Politburo, in which many of the top posts were held by career military men.

Gorbachev still sees a role for the military but does not view military power as an end in itself. It can no longer bring security, as it might have a century ago. The military buildup of the seventies made the Soviet Union less secure because it led to the American buildup of the eighties, and it hurt relations with other countries.

In a historic speech before the United Nations on December 7, 1988, Gorbachev noted that "one-sided reliance on military power ultimately weakens other components of national security." Accordingly he announced a unilateral reduction of the Soviet armed forces by five hundred thousand troops. This de-emphasis of military power has done far more for Soviet security (defined as security from the threat of attack) than a military buildup might have done. The unilateral troop cuts and the revolutions in Eastern Europe in 1989 that brought noncommunist governments to power have caused North Atlantic Treaty Organization (NATO) leaders to rethink the future of the alliance. The U.S. Congress is considering proposals to unilaterally reduce American forces in Europe, plans to upgrade short-range Lance missiles have been canceled, and every member of NATO has reduced defense spending. Many Western observers seriously doubt that NATO can continue to play a military role much longer, in light of the shrinking threat from the East. No level of Soviet military muscle could have led to this hesitancy and loss of purpose in the West. *(Gorbachev's UN speech, Appendix, p. 320)*

In a speech to the Twenty-eighth Party Congress in July 1990, Foreign Minister Eduard Shevardnadze observed: "One can arm oneself to the teeth and still be afraid of attack. But it is also possible to be sure that you will not be attacked because your policy creates conditions where the country will have no enemies or opponents.... Clearly, if we continue the way we have done it before, ... that is to spend one fourth of our budget on military expenditures ... we will ruin the country.... We simply would need no defense because a ruined country and a poor people do not need an army."

Gorbachev also has noted that many modern political goals cannot be achieved by military force. The Soviet Union hopes to join the International Monetary Fund and the General Agreement on Tariffs and Trade as steps in its economic reform. A continuing emphasis on military might is a hindrance to membership, since Western democracies have indicated that a less threatening Soviet defense posture is a prerequisite to improvements in political and economic relations. In his speech at the United Nations,

Gorbachev said, "It is obvious . . . that the use or threat of force no longer can or must be an instrument of policy."

A large part of Gorbachev's unilateral troop reduction has come from the heavily militarized Sino-Soviet border. This has led to a dramatic improvement in relations with the Chinese from a few years ago, when tensions were high and military incidents at the border were not uncommon.

Gorbachev has stated the importance of "mutual security"—the conception that no nation's security can be achieved at the expense of another country. If the United States feels insecure, the Soviet Union is placed in a position of insecurity as a result. If the United States feels its position to be secure then it will be far more amenable to arms control and peaceful cooperation with the USSR. In the spirit of mutual security, the Soviets have launched simultaneous drives to improve relations virtually everywhere. This is in contrast with past Soviet attempts to improve relations with Western Europe to weaken NATO, and to strengthen ties with China to limit Sino-American cooperation.

Reasonable Sufficiency

The military doctrine of reasonable sufficiency was announced by Gorbachev at the Twenty-seventh Party Congress in 1986. Legvold describes the doctrine as setting the goal of "coping with rather than keeping up with the Joneses." Instead of attempting to match the United States weapon for weapon, it prescribes "the simpler and cheaper route of developing the means of foiling the weapons the Americans field." It is a far more flexible doctrine than trying to maintain parity with the United States.

Reasonable sufficiency accepts the American concept of stability. Conventional forces should be strong enough to deter an attack from any realistic combination of forces, but they should not be able to sustain an offensive. Gorbachev made a step in this direction in 1989 with the withdrawal of many tank and river-crossing units from Eastern Europe.

De-emphasizing Ideology

Since Marx's time, communists have seen international politics as an epic struggle between socialism and capitalism. Marx wrote that the capitalist countries would find in the nascent socialist movement the seeds of their own destruction and would seek to crush the movement at any cost. Socialism would fight back using its inherently more powerful system of production and the loyalties it could call upon among the proletariat of the capitalist countries. The world would divide along class lines. Thus, according to Soviet ideology, the formation of every left-wing guerrilla movement was a step forward for socialism. Every new American weapons system, and every U.S. dollar spent on foreign aid, was an attempt by dying capitalism to save itself. While this ideology has not been formally discarded, it now plays little role in policy. No longer heard is rhetoric about "a mighty wave of national liberation revolutions sweeping away the colonial system and undermining the foundations of imperialism," as was included in the 1961 Party Program.

In his speech before the United Nations Gorbachev said that the new thinking includes "de-ideologizing the relations between states. We are not abandoning our convictions, our philosophy, or our traditions, but neither do we have any intention to be hemmed in by our values."

Gorbachev has said that the common dangers faced by mankind—nuclear holocaust, environmental destruction, terrorism, growing poverty, drug abuse, and others—unite humanity in an interdependence that outweighs the class struggle. The Soviets' new focus is on the resolution of regional issues and global problems, not on ideology (which in the past often has been a cover for more immediate national interests). Gorbachev also has recognized the durability of capitalism. Vadim Medvedev, the party secretary for ideology, has noted that the Soviet Union has a lot to learn from the West, in such areas as economic production and the creation of legal and political institutions.

Gorbachev has encouraged the Soviet Union's Third World clients to follow its lead in seeking less ideological policies. He recognizes that the rigid application of Marxism-Leninism has left Soviet clients such as Nicaragua, Mozambique, South Yemen, and Ethiopia impoverished and politically unstable, even by Third World standards. The Soviets also are tired of bankrolling their Third World clients. The cost of propping up stagnant economies has become particularly odious as Gorbachev seeks ways to bolster domestic living standards. The 1985 Party Program encouraged the "socialist-oriented states" to develop their economies "mainly through their own efforts." The Soviet Union, the program said, will provide aid "to the extent of its abilities." The effect of tighter Soviet purse strings is apparent virtually everywhere, as Soviet clients have become more flexible in resolving their economic problems and political conflicts. Former clients from Poland to Nicaragua have aggressively courted Western donors for new sources of foreign aid.

A corollary to the new focus on interdependence is greater Soviet interest in international institutions, particularly the United Nations. The Soviets want to give the United Nations a larger role in resolving regional conflicts in such places as Angola, Namibia, Cambodia, and Afghanistan. Increased use of international bodies in conflict resolution would give the Soviet Union a greater political role in many regions even as its military presence is being cut back.

With the new thinking, the overriding concern of Soviet foreign policy has become the construction of a stable and peaceful world order with the Soviet Union as an active participant. The unending wars in the Third World no longer are seen as valiant struggles against imperialism, but as bloody and often senseless conflicts, best ended by quick political compromises. Gorbachev has said, "The bell of every regional conflict tolls for all of us."

The Soviet Union has become a strong advocate of unqualified nonintervention in the affairs of other countries. Under the Brezhnev Doctrine, enunciated after the 1968 Soviet invasion of Czechoslovakia to put down a liberalizing political movement, the Soviet Union reserved for itself the right to intervene in socialist countries to preserve the status quo. The Soviets, however, now maintain that international relations between socialist countries are no different from relations between other countries. The Soviets have said that they have no more right to intervene in Eastern Europe than they do anywhere else. The Soviet Union took an almost completely hands-off approach to the 1989 revolutions in Eastern Europe, and Soviet leaders made it clear that they expected no less from the United States. When the United States invaded Panama in December 1989, the Soviet Foreign Ministry noted that it was a violation of international law, as would be any use of armed force against another nation.

Dr. Andrei Zagorski of the Moscow State Institute for International Affairs characterizes the new thinking as a new methodology of foreign policy. It is an attempt by the Soviets to join the international system by adopting international norms in areas such as human rights and trade. It also highlights the use of diplomacy, relies less on military means, and implies a less secretive approach to policy making.

Progress of the New Thinking

Skeptics in the West have challenged the Soviets' commitment to the new thinking. These skeptics point out that it still does not govern many areas of foreign policy. Despite significant cuts in overall military spending, the Soviets are continuing to build new generations of intercontinental ballistic missiles, submarine-launched ballistic missiles, and manned strategic bombers. Tanks are produced at a rate far above that of NATO. Moreover, although Soviet troops have left Afghanistan, aid to the Kabul government continues to flow at a rate of almost two hundred million dollars per month. The Soviets also sold Su-24 Fencer long-range bombers to Libya in 1989. It is reasonable, therefore, to argue that the new thinking is not as ubiquitous as Soviet statements would suggest.

The Soviet response to these complaints is that the new thinking barely has begun. The Soviets argue that the Cold War approach to foreign policy, which has been practiced since World War II, cannot be changed overnight. They also say that new thinking must develop in Washington, too. In the Soviet view, the United States and the Soviet Union must learn to cooperate if they are to jointly solve world problems. Merely changing Soviet attitudes is not enough.

Moreover, the new thinking still is being debated by the Soviet leadership and foreign affairs apparatus. It is not universally accepted. Many Soviet conservatives believe that Gorbachev is giving away the store. Why, they ask, should the Soviet Union stop aiding the governments of Afghanistan and Angola and leftist guerrillas in El Salvador, when the United States is still aiding the Afghan mujahideen, anticommunist guerrillas in Angola, and the El Salvador government?

Domestic Sources of the New Thinking

Because Soviet domestic problems have become so menacing, Gorbachev has had to give domestic concerns priority over foreign policy interests. The Soviet economy is in a state of crisis. Growth has all but ceased, and living standards are sliding backward. Because of the new openness in society, public discontent with the situation has been clear. The widespread strikes of the summer of 1989 are likely to be repeated on an even larger scale if there is no improvement in the consumer economy. Gorbachev told President Bush at Malta that getting more and better consumer goods into shops was his single greatest challenge.

There is nationalist ferment in every republic, from the Baltic to the Ukraine, from the Caucasus to Central Asia. Nearly unanimous agreement exists among Lithuanians on the goal of independence. Meanwhile Armenia and Azerbaidzhan are in a virtual state of civil war.

Gorbachev recognizes the seriousness of his country's domestic problems. He needs an international environment that does not get in the way of their resolution. For example, he wants to participate more fully in the "international division of labor." He wants to increase trade and strengthen economic cooperation and technology transfer with the West. The Soviets are actively pursuing membership in international economic organizations and are making plans for a convertible ruble. To devote more resources to the consumer sector, Gorbachev needs to continue drawing them away from the defense sector and foreign aid. He is willing to be flexible in international negotiations because he needs immediate results. He cannot afford to wait years for an arms control treaty and thus has been willing to make key concessions to the United States.

The Soviets are concerned about the possibility of foreign countries exploiting the unrest in the republics. Gorbachev has made it clear that American encouragement to separatists would be both unwelcome and dangerous to perestroika. The Bush administration has respected Gorbachev's appeal. Despite continuing its policy of recognizing an independent Latvia, Lithuania, and Estonia, the United States has decided that encouraging perestroika is more important than Baltic independence. It has not discouraged these movements, but neither has it promoted them. When a protest in Georgia was violently crushed, the United States criticized the loss of life, but in surprisingly mild terms. Without the improvement of U.S.-Soviet ties, Moscow would not have reaped this benefit.

Domination of Eastern Europe

In the latter stages of World War II, Stalin ordered Soviet troops to capture as much European territory as possible—a goal that resulted in far more Soviet casualties than was necessary. Stalin intended his armies to establish the basis for a large Soviet sphere of influence in Eastern Europe and to limit the area that would come under the control of his American and British allies. Once the land was occupied, however, the actual consolidation of communist rule in most of Eastern Europe was a slow process, lasting several years. Most of these countries experienced a pattern of consolidation similar to the one that occurred in Poland, where domestic Communists, backed by the Soviet military, used both terror and reforms to establish their control.

In Poland the Red Army destroyed what was left of the underground nationalist resistance and established the Committee of National Liberation, controlled by the Communists, to rule the country. The committee then initiated a series of popular reforms. Land was redistributed to the peasantry, and large factories (which were mainly German-owned) were nationalized. The redistribution of farms, homesteads, and factories located on expropriated German land across the Oder and Neisse rivers gave the Polish Communists a unique opportunity for massive patronage.

At the same time, Poles wishing to distance Poland from the Soviet Union, including those sympathetic to the London-based government-in-exile, found themselves subject to arrest.

As a result of these measures, the Communist party, which held a slim minority in Poland, gradually gained in strength and consolidated its power. The free elections that Stalin had promised at the Yalta conference never took place. In each Eastern European country, marginal Communist party electoral strength ultimately was parlayed into complete power through reforms, patronage, selected

EASTERN EUROPE

Barents Sea

White Sea

Miles

0   100   200   300

UNION OF SOVIET SOCIALIST REPUBLICS

FINLAND

Helsinki

• Leningrad

NORWAY

Oslo

SWEDEN

Tallinn

ESTONIA

Gulf of Finland

• Moscow

Stockholm

LATVIA

Riga

LITHUANIA

Minsk

DENMARK

Baltic Sea

Vilnius •

BELORUSSIA

RSFSR

Copenhagen

Warsaw

• Kiev

Berlin

POLAND

UKRAINE

Sea of Azov

EAST GERMANY

MOLDAVIA

Kishinev

WEST GERMANY

Prague

CZECHOSLOVAKIA

Budapest

Black Sea

Vienna

RUMANIA

Bucharest

AUSTRIA   **HUNGARY**

use of terror, and support from the Red Army. However, the complete overturning of society, including massive collectivization and nationalization with indiscriminate use of terror, did not begin in earnest in Eastern Europe until 1948.

In Czechoslovakia the Communist party had particularly strong local roots. It came to power as part of a freely elected coalition government. Soviet prestige was high in Czechoslovakia because only the Soviet Union had protested the dismemberment of that country by the 1938 Munich Conference. In free elections in 1946, the Communist party polled 38 percent, and their leader, Klement Gottwald, was asked to be the premier by President Eduard Benes. Gradually the Communist party increased its hold on the army, police, and other key ministries. It seized absolute control in a 1948 coup.

Yugoslav Communists also came to power on their own, but the pattern was unlike that in Czechoslovakia. One important difference was that no Soviet troops remained stationed in Yugoslavia. Also, the leaders of the Yugoslav Communist party, particularly Josep Broz Tito, enjoyed genuine popular support because of their role in fighting the Nazis during the war. The Yugoslav Communist party was not merely a creation of Moscow, as in the other "people's democracies" of Eastern Europe.

Nevertheless, the Yugoslav Communists were slavishly loyal to Moscow and were committed to a radical social agenda that included nationalizing industry and collectivizing agriculture. Stalin, however, did not trust them because unlike communists in other countries, the Yugoslav Communists were not dependent on him. Tito also had sought a much more activist foreign policy, which Stalin feared would lead to conflict with the United States. In particular, Stalin and Tito disagreed over Yugoslav support for Greek partisans.

Consequently, Stalin wanted Tito replaced and accused him of a variety of ideological errors. An increasingly public war of words ensued, beginning in June 1948, that marked the first major division in the monolithic Communist bloc—one that foreshadowed the far more critical break with China in the 1960s.

Fearing that Titoism would spread to the rest of Eastern Europe and feeling American pressure from the Truman Doctrine and Marshall Plan, Stalin sped up the pace of change. Beginning in 1948, Eastern Europe was rapidly rebuilt on the Soviet model. Nationalization and collectivization were quickly completed and widespread purges of suspected Titoists were carried out. The Soviets ruthlessly enforced absolute conformity, suppressing the national identities in their new client states. Even the constitutions of East European nations were rewritten to match the Soviet constitution. During this period, the Eastern Europe Communists came to base their rule almost entirely on Soviet support. For more than four decades the regimes in Eastern Europe struggled unsuccessfully for legitimacy and popular support. Their failure was evidenced by the rapid tumbling of one communist government after another in 1989 when the Soviet guarantees were withdrawn.

Finland's experience with the Soviet Union was completely different. During World War II it had hosted Soviet troops, but they were later removed peacefully. Finland was allowed to develop as a capitalist country, although one with a sharp awareness of Soviet security interests. Analysts speculate that several factors motivated the Soviets to allow a different path in Finland. In 1940, Finland inflicted heavy losses on the USSR in the Winter War. The danger

of a repetition of this fiasco presumably was in the back of Stalin's mind. Also, no great threat existed of an anti-Soviet government appearing in Finland, since the Finns understood their delicate position. Finally, Finland bordered only neutral Sweden, not a Western ally. The Kremlin may have reasoned that no anti-Soviet threat was likely to come through a neutral Sweden, but if Finland were forced into the Soviet bloc, the Swedes might be driven into the Western alliance.

The steady consolidation of communist power in Eastern Europe led to increasing apprehension in the West. On April 4, 1949, the North Atlantic Treaty was signed by twelve countries, including the United States, Great Britain, and France. The rapid development of NATO into an anti-Soviet alliance was seen by Moscow as a clear threat to its empire. In 1954, West Germany was admitted as a full member of NATO. In retaliation for the rearming of West Germany, Moscow and its Eastern European allies signed the Warsaw Pact the next year.

De-Stalinization

After Khrushchev's famous Secret Speech condemning Stalin before the Twentieth Congress of the Soviet Communist party in 1956, controls were relaxed on political and cultural conformity throughout the Soviet Union and Eastern Europe. Tito was welcomed back into the Soviet bloc, which undermined the leaders of Eastern Europe who had made careers out of following Stalin and purging alleged Titoists.

In Poland and Hungary, Stalinist leaders were deposed with Soviet approval in favor of more moderate nationalist Communist party members. In Warsaw, Wladislaw Gomulka oversaw continued de-Stalinization while maintaining the party's authority—although just barely. In Hungary, relaxation triggered more demands. On November 1, 1956, the new government of Imre Nagy announced Hungary's withdrawal from the Warsaw Pact and the creation of a multi-party system. This was an infringement of what Western analysts considered the Soviet Union's two minimum security requirements for Eastern Europe in the Cold War era: membership in the Warsaw Pact and control by the Communist party. The result was a swift and bloody invasion of Hungary by Soviet troops a few days later.

Brezhnev Doctrine

Such measures were not used again by the Soviets until the 1968 "Prague Spring" reforms in Czechoslovakia. Under Leonid Brezhnev, diversity was allowed to grow gradually in Eastern Europe. The rigid conformity that had been abandoned in 1956 was not reintroduced, but definite limits were placed on freedom of Eastern European governments to diverge from the Soviet example. In the case of Czechoslovakia, liberal Communist leaders had agreed to democratization and an open press, seriously threatening the Communist party's monopoly on power. Once again, the Soviets felt compelled to invade. The invasion was justified after the fact by the Brezhnev Doctrine. This doctrine was outlined by Brezhnev in a November 13, 1968, speech in Poland (*Brezhnev speech, Appendix, p. 312*):

> When the internal and external forces hostile to socialism seek to revert the development of any socialist country towards the restoration of the capitalist order, when a threat to the cause of socialism in that country, a threat to the security of the socialist community as a

whole emerges, this is no longer only a problem of the people of that country but also a common problem, concern of all socialist countries.

It goes without saying that such an action as military aid to a fraternal country to cut short the theat to the socialist order is an extraordinary, enforced step, it can be sparked off only by direct actions of the enemies of socialism inside the country and beyond its boundaries, actions creating a threat to the common interests of the camp of socialism.

The Brezhnev Doctrine became the basis for Soviet policy in Eastern Europe until Gorbachev came to power. The doctrine explained socialist international relations as being qualitatively different from those between nonsocialist states. Western observers have been fascinated by the Brezhnev Doctrine. As changes occurred in Eastern Europe, beginning with the instability in Poland in 1980, analysts debated whether the doctrine still was being applied by the Kremlin. Even during the extraordinary events of 1989, debate continued as to whether, under certain circumstances, it might still have been applicable.

Economic Policy

From the invasion of Czechoslovakia to the new thinking, Soviet economic policy toward Eastern Europe has had two basic planks: to integrate these economies within the framework of the Council for Mutual Economic Assistance (CMEA) and to "buy" political stability. Both have failed impressively.

When Eastern Europe first came under Soviet hegemony after World War II, the Soviets transferred a tremendous amount of capital, including whole factories, east to the Soviet Union. After years of protest and unrest in Eastern Europe, this policy was reversed. Soviet leaders concluded that the strategic goal of creating a tranquil Eastern Europe was more important than exploiting Eastern Europe's resources. They determined that subsidizing the standards of living there could buy off unrest and ultimately would be far cheaper than repeated military interventions.

None of the countries of Eastern Europe was given direct subsidies. Instead, subsidies were built into the trade flows. The Soviets sold raw materials and energy to Eastern Europe at prices substantially below world market levels. These were goods that otherwise could have been traded to the West for hard currency. In return, the Soviets received various low-quality manufactured goods that would not be marketable in the West. If not for this advantageous trade with the Soviet Union, Eastern Europe would have found it difficult to finance hard-currency purchases of raw materials and energy. In addition, Moscow gave Eastern European countries cheap trade credits and permitted them to run huge trade deficits with the Soviet Union. As these deficits grew over time, they effectively became subsidies. According to Western estimates, during the 1970s and early 1980s Soviet subsidies to Eastern Europe ranged between five billion dollars and ten billion dollars a year.

CMEA was created in 1949 to facilitate trade among the communist nations, as a response to the Marshall Plan. Particularly since 1971, the Soviets have tried to integrate these economies without success. This failure has been caused by both institutional factors and deliberate Eastern European resistance. Under central planning it is difficult to make production enterprises in different countries co-ordinate their planning, investment, and production, particularly for the duration of a five-year plan. Managers have no incentive to seek out lower-priced imported inputs. Moreover, with arbitrary pricing and exchange rates, it is often impossible to determine which product is cheapest. The Eastern European countries also are reluctant to integrate because genuine integration would position their economies as mere appendages to the much larger Soviet economy, catering to its particular needs and shortages.

Failures in Eastern Europe

The invasion of Czechoslovakia ushered in a period of relative calm in Eastern Europe. However, fundamental problems were present in the region, which Brezhnev managed to ignore for a long time. These reemerged in the late seventies when dissenters began to speak out more forcefully. After the signing of the Helsinki Final Act in 1975, human rights proponents became more active both in Eastern Europe and in the USSR. The new period of unrest also was triggered by a sustained decline in economic growth in Eastern Europe, which continued through the 1980s.

The economic problems faced in Eastern Europe parallel those faced in the USSR, and in all centrally planned economies, although they vary in severity from country to country. These problems included inefficient use of resources, low labor productivity, technological backwardness, poor planning and shortages, aging infrastructure, and lack of foreign exchange. Except for Romania and Albania, Eastern Europeans enjoy a higher standard of living than Soviets. However, their expectations also are higher than Soviets'. Because of the proximity of Western Europe, Eastern Europeans tend to compare themselves with their neighbors to the west, not to the east. Thus, as economic problems worsened, instability grew more rapidly in Eastern Europe than in the Soviet Union. East European instability was stimulated by other factors as well, including communism's shorter history in the region and its imposition by foreign troops.

Eastern European countries also became heavily indebted in the seventies. Most Western analysts and bankers had regarded Eastern Europe as politically stable and a good credit risk. They believed that the Soviet Union would act as an economic and political umbrella in case of severe problems. Consequently, the West lent Eastern Europe billions of dollars. Instead of using the influx of Western credits to modernize their economies, the Eastern European governments generally used them to expand industrial capacity (primarily through older energy-intensive technologies) and to increase supplies of consumer goods. In some places, notably Hungary, advanced technologies were imported, but their usefulness was limited by the lack of planning and management innovations and incentives to increase labor productivity and efficiency. As a result, the Eastern Europeans backed themselves into a corner. Poland and Hungary in particular became so indebted that Western bankers began to compare them to debt-ridden Latin American countries that struggled to pay even the interest on their loans. In 1989, the total hard-currency indebtedness of the six Soviet satellites exceeded eighty-one billion dollars. The oil shocks of 1973 and 1979 exacerbated their economic problems, although as their chief energy supplier, the Soviet Union sheltered them from some of the price increases. However, in the 1980s the Soviet Union began reducing its oil shipments to Eastern Europe and charging more for what it does send.

When detailing the economic woes of Eastern Europe, the devastating environmental damage must be mentioned. Particularly in Poland, East Germany, and Czechoslovakia, the use of high-sulfur coal, and other environmentally unsound practices related to heavy reliance on smokestack industries, has led to entire forests being destroyed by acid rain, the contamination of water supplies, and air pollution so severe that some areas are virtually uninhabitable. The ultimate costs of correcting these problems will be astronomical.

The New Thinking in Eastern Europe

Late in the 1980s, Moscow was faced with the breakdown of communist control in Eastern Europe. Protests were seen in every country except Bulgaria. Poland seemed on the verge of a collapse. Under the Brezhnev Doctrine the Soviets would have intervened in some manner to prevent the defeat of communism in their satellite states. However, several factors caused the Soviet leadership to reject this approach. A Soviet military intervention would have been the death knell for the improvement of economic and political relations with Western Europe and the United States that Gorbachev sought. It also could have led to an explosion of already restless segments of Soviet society. The old approach to Eastern Europe was interfering with Gorbachev's program. To achieve his goals, Gorbachev required a completely new approach to the region.

Additionally, Stalin's original reasoning for controlling Eastern Europe had become less compelling by 1985. A Western invasion of the Soviet Union through Eastern Europe was not plausible. Moreover, any economic benefits the Soviets derived from Eastern Europe were outweighed by the economic disadvantages of materially supporting unpopular Eastern European Communist governments. This was especially true at a time when oil prices were down and Moscow desperately needed hard currency. Ideologically, Gorbachev received nothing from Eastern Europe, since he had already discarded the Marxist-Leninist tenets still held by most Eastern European leaders. In short, the Soviets' Eastern European empire was providing them with few benefits, while they continued paying a steep economic and diplomatic cost to maintain it.

At the end of Gorbachev's 1988 visit to Yugoslavia, a joint communiqué was issued affirming the principles of "mutual respect for independence, sovereignty, and territorial integrity, equality and impermissibility of interference in internal matters under any pretext whatsoever." The communiqué continued: "Proceeding on the basis of the conviction that no one has a monopoly on truth, the sides declare their lack of any claim to impose their own ideas about social development upon anyone else whomsoever. The success of each of their paths to socialism is tested by sociopolitical practice and confirmed by concrete results."

This was the clearest indication up to that time that Gorbachev had rejected the Brezhnev Doctrine. He has done so repeatedly since then, insisting that the principle of nonintervention applies as much in Eastern Europe as it does anywhere else. Gennadii Gerasimov has quipped that the "Sinatra Doctrine" is now in force in Eastern Europe. Those countries are free to "do it their way."

Despite all of these declarations, most Western observers believed that if Eastern European nations attempted a complete break from Moscow, Gorbachev still would take steps, be they military, economic, or diplomatic, to keep communists in power and the Warsaw Pact intact. Only when the Solidarity government headed by Prime Minister Tadeusz Mazowiecki came to power in Poland in August 1989 did it become evident how serious Gorbachev was. Gorbachev also displayed his willingness to tolerate the dissolution of the Warsaw Pact. He has accepted German reunification, and Hungary has declared its intention to press for neutrality. The remarkable changes that have been permitted in Eastern Europe in such a short time are an indicator of the seriousness of the problems Gorbachev is facing at home.

Consider the benefits Gorbachev is receiving or expects to receive from the "Sinatra Doctrine." Relations with Western Europe, particularly with West Germany, are at their highest point ever. On his last trip to Bonn, Gorbachev was cheered in the streets like a war hero. This has brought him credits, investment, and the opportunity to make massive defense cuts. Western countries are lining up to offer investment and loan packages to Eastern Europe, freeing up Soviet resources for other goals. As Eastern Europe embarks on economic reforms, it will provide models for the Soviet Union to either emulate or avoid in its own reform. The Eastern Europeans also will continue to trade with their neighbor to the east, providing the Soviet Union with benefits from their reformist economies and contacts with the West. Finally, reform in Eastern Europe creates momentum for reform in the Soviet Union, strengthening Gorbachev's hand against domestic conservatives. The need to learn from the changes in Eastern Europe (and avoid the fate of the Communist party in Romania) was a key factor in the discussions on repealing the Soviet Constitution's Article Six (which designates the Communist Party as the guiding force in Soviet society) at the February 1990 Central Committee plenum.

Revolutions of 1989

At the time of Stalin's death, Soviet leaders claimed that there was only one path to socialism: absolute emulation of the Soviet model. Any deviation was labeled Titoism and treason. However, since then, the socialist countries have been allowed to follow widely disparate paths, although within certain boundaries.

With the new thinking, Gorbachev has abolished those boundaries. He has encouraged the Eastern European countries to follow his program of glasnost and perestroika, but beyond this encouragement he has adopted a strict policy of nonintervention. The changes that occurred in Eastern Europe followed two very different paths, although they headed toward the same goals. Poland and Hungary have struggled to implement reforms for years. Consequently, both countries became early supporters of Gorbachev and perestroika. In Bulgaria, Czechoslovakia, East Germany, and Romania, however, perestroika and glasnost were given a cool reception. The hard-line leaders of these countries did whatever was necessary to maintain their power as long as possible, giving in to demands for change only after hundreds of thousands of citizens had taken to the streets to demand it.

Change Comes to Poland

Throughout much of the post-World War II period, Poland was the most explosive country in Eastern Europe, erupting into protests and strikes at regular intervals. In both 1956 and 1981, upheavals brought Poland to the verge of chaos, causing fears that Soviet troops would be used to restore order. Strikes in 1970 brought down the government of Wladyslaw Gomulka. Many of these protests were sparked by the Polish government's repeated attempts to reduce food subsidies as a step toward economic reform. Since the mid-seventies, the Polish dissent movement has received broad support from workers, students, intellectuals, and the Catholic Church. This contrasted with Czechoslovakia, the Soviet Union, and other East-bloc countries where dissent was for a long time confined to a lonely group of intellectuals.

Poland also was distinguished from the rest of Eastern Europe because the powerful Catholic Church remained outside of state control. The Church served as a rallying point for Poles alienated from communism, particularly since the election of Pope John Paul II, a Pole.

Since the late seventies, the Polish economy has been in a state of continuing crisis. In September 1980, in response to a series of devastating strikes, the Polish government permitted the formation of Solidarity, the first independent trade union in Eastern Europe. After a stormy fifteen months, punctuated by Solidarity's increasingly political demands against the government, General Wojciech Jaruzelski declared martial law on December 13, 1981. Polish army tanks rolled into the streets of Warsaw, and Solidarity was declared illegal. Its leaders went into hiding or were arrested. However, Solidarity continued to operate underground throughout the eighties, printing a newspaper and organizing strikes.

After Gorbachev came to power, Jaruzelski became his most devoted ally in Eastern Europe. Jaruzelski had been trying unsuccessfully for years to reform the Polish economy, but it continued to fall deeper into crisis. By January 1989, the Polish hard-currency debt had reached thirty-nine billion dollars, and Poland had the lowest per capita export earnings in Europe. Meanwhile, inflation was raging out of control, slowed only by occasional price freezes. Shortages of consumer goods and food were becoming chronic. The bleak economic conditions caused popular unrest to mount and wildcat strikes to become more frequent.

Jaruzelski opened negotiations with Solidarity activists in September 1988 despite the objections of Communist party hard-liners. He hoped to negotiate a legalization of Solidarity in exchange for its support of his economic program. Solidarity, however, was unwilling to share responsibility for programs over which it would have no control.

Against a background of paralyzing strikes, an agreement was reached to hold new elections. Solidarity promised not to run candidates for 65 percent of the seats in the 460-seat Sejm (Polish Assembly), guaranteeing those spots to the Communists or their allies in the Peasant and Democratic parties. A one hundred-seat Senate would be created, with all of its members freely elected. These two bodies together would elect someone to fill the powerful new post of president. By agreement, the first president would be Jaruzelski. He would appoint a prime minister and government that would be confirmed by the two houses. The Communists had expected that they would capture a large number of rural seats, since Solidarity's organization was limited to the large cities. They, however, had not counted on the organizational skill of the local clergy, who rallied rural voters to support Solidarity. The Communists suffered an unparalleled defeat as Solidarity won virtually every seat it contested.

After the devastating loss, many Peasant and Democratic party deputies, and even some Communists, expressed their hesitation about voting for a Communist president. A breakdown of the round-table agreement appeared to be imminent.

In the past, such chaos in an East European nation would not have been tolerated in Moscow, but Gorbachev expressed support for the process and hope that the governmental crisis could be solved as quickly as possible to limit damage to the Polish economy. He reaffirmed the Soviet commitment to nonintervention, saying: "How the Polish People will decide to structure their society and lives will be their own affair." Gorbachev then predicted that "the process of democratization" would ultimately transform all of Eastern Europe.

Jaruzelski was elected, but with exactly the minimum number of votes necessary. The Parliament, however, refused to support a Communist government. After protracted negotiation, Tadeusz Mazowiecki of Solidarity on August 25, 1989, became the first noncommunist prime minister in postwar Eastern Europe. His government had four Communist cabinet ministers, including the vital posts of defense and interior. Gorbachev's only intervention into this process appears to have been a phone call to the Polish Communists encouraging them to participate in the Solidarity-led government. However, as revealed later, in the first days of the Mazowiecki government, the Soviet Union quietly sought and received assurances that Poland would respect its obligations under the Warsaw Pact, and that the West would not try to interfere in Poland for strategic advantages. Beyond that, Gorbachev assured Poland that he expected continued close relations with the Mazowiecki government.

Mazowiecki and his administration interpreted the overwhelming electoral support for Solidarity as a mandate for drastic change. Beginning January 1, 1990, they implemented an economic reform program designed to transform the system of central planning into a market economy within months. The government cut price subsidies on consumer goods, allowed most prices to float freely, froze wages, and eliminated subsidies and loose credit to unprofitable industries. These measures caused inflation to fall from its January rate of 78 percent to just 4 percent by the end of May. In addition, formerly empty store shelves now were filled with goods.

However, slamming the brakes on inflation threw the economy into an unprecedented recession. In the first five months of 1990, output dropped by 27 percent and personal income fell by about 40 percent. The foreign investment that the government counted on to take up the slack was slow in coming. Foreign investors were frightened by the chaos in Poland.

That the already impoverished Polish population was willing to tolerate these austerity measures was an indication of the overwhelming support that the Solidarity government brought into office. However, by mid-1990 that support was showing signs of weakening. Coal miners and railway workers threatened to strike for wage increases, and the Solidarity ministers who had used such tactics in the past found themselves on the other side of the table pleading with workers to give the reforms more time to work.

The Process of Reform in Hungary

Hungary in many ways has been a model for Gorbachev's program of perestroika. In 1968, Janos Kadar implemented the New Economic Mechanism (NEM), to the benefit of Hungarian consumers. Among other NEM reforms, agricultural prices were raised to encourage production and small private enterprise was legalized. The results have been reflected in the Hungarian standard of living. The economy did well in the seventies, and a sizeable middle class developed. However, by the eighties the economy was suffering many of the same problems found elsewhere in Eastern Europe. For example, the 1990 Hungarian hard-currency indebtedness of twenty billion dollars was even heavier per capita than Poland's debt.

Gorbachev's policy of glasnost also might have been based partly on Hungarian policies. During the 1970s and 1980s Hungary had the best human rights record in Eastern Europe. The Kadar government allowed a relatively open society to develop. Travel to the West, a rare privilege in Eastern Europe, was permitted for most Hungarians, although until recently they were limited to one trip every three years.

Like Poland, Hungary has a long history of experimenting with reforms. The essential political difference between the two is that Polish reforms have been driven by demands from below—from Solidarity protests and popular dissent. The impetus for change in Hungary has consistently come from within the Communist party. In the 1970s, Kadar had been considered among the most progressive leaders in Eastern Europe, but by 1988 he was holding back the pace of reform sought by a new generation in the party. In May 1988, he was replaced as party leader after twenty-eight years by Karoly Grosz.

Grosz immediately announced his full support for perestroika and promised radical economic and political reforms, but only within the framework of a single party system. These promised reforms were slow in coming, and it became clear that Grosz, like Kadar, was lagging behind the changes taking place in Hungary. In January 1989, the Parliament established the freedoms of assembly and association. In February, opposition political parties were legalized. In June, Imre Nagy, the leader of the 1956 revolution, was taken from his anonymous grave and reburied as a national hero.

In October, the Communist party split, and its liberal wing reconstituted itself as the Hungarian Socialist party. In an indication of his support for the process of gradual political reform in Hungary, Gorbachev called to congratulate Reszo Nyers, the new president of the Hungarian Socialist party, within an hour of his selection. To enhance their popularity, the new Socialists tried to distance themselves as much as possible from the Communist party's past. The Hungarian Socialist party characterizes itself as a Western European-style social-democratic party, without any hint of Marxist-Leninist ideology.

Nevertheless, the Socialists and all parties of the left were decisively beaten in elections held in March 1990. The Hungarian Democratic Forum received the most votes, but not enough to gain a majority in parliament. It established a coalition government with the Alliance of Free Democrats (which received the second most votes) and the Smallholders party. Jozsef Antall, the head of the Democratic Forum, was elected president. The Democratic Forum is more conservative and nationalistic than the Free Democrats and advocates a gradual transition to a market economy. The Free Democrats seek a fast shift to a market economy.

The new Hungarian government wants to integrate Hungary into Europe as a neutral country. Moscow and Budapest have signed a treaty providing for the withdrawal of all Soviet troops from Hungary by the end of 1991. Antall also has stated his intention to pull Hungary out of the Warsaw Pact as soon as possible.

An Explosion in East Germany

The most dramatic events of 1989 took place in East Germany. Erich Honecker, the Communist leader of the German Democratic Republic (GDR), had long rejected the idea that perestroika was applicable to East Germany. He said it was a solution to Soviet problems, not German ones. If a neighbor paints his house, he reasoned, does that mean that you should paint your house also? East Germany had been the Eastern European economic pacesetter in the sixties and seventies, but its performance had weakened in the eighties. The seriousness of its economic problems has only become apparent since the fall of the Honecker government. Many of its problems, including the burden of a heavy foreign debt, were offset by extensive West German trade and credits that allowed East Germany to get around the tariff barriers of the European Community.

The Honecker government had its own problems with unrest, which, although not as widespread as Poland's, were dealt with ruthlessly by Stasis, the East German secret police. Travel to the West was tightly restricted after the Berlin Wall was built in 1962, although the GDR has been exposed to Western influences through West German television, which reaches almost the entire country.

The revolutionary events in East Germany were catalyzed by Hungary's announcement that it was tearing down its border fences with Austria as part of its liberalization process. During the summer of 1989, East German tourists in Hungary began trickling across the open border to Austria. From there they went on to West Germany. In accordance with West Germany's constitution, East Germans are automatically granted West German citizenship, a luxury not enjoyed by other refugees. Initially, Budapest reacted to East German complaints that its border policy was in violation of a 1968 treaty by tightening its border security. According to the treaty, Hungary could not allow East Germans to travel to third countries without explicit GDR permission. However, by September, thousands of East German tourists were refusing to go home and were beginning to pile up as refugees in Hungary. Sending them back to East Germany would have violated a thirty-five nation agreement on free travel that Hungary had just signed in January and would have severely damaged the good relations that Hungary was trying to build with the West, particularly with West Germany. So on September 10, Hungarian borders were formally thrown open to the East Germans, and tens of thousands crossed to the West in the first few days. The number then slowed to a trickle as East Germany restricted travel to Hungary. Hungary's move posed a challenge to East German legitimacy and Eric Honecker's rule. According to Gyula Horn, the Hungarian foreign minister, the options before Hungary were raised with Soviet authorities in advance, but they pointedly insisted that it was not their place to intervene.

When the Hungarian escape valve was shut, thousands of East Germans began seeking refuge in the West German embassy in Prague, because Czechoslovakia was the only country to which East Germans could freely travel without a visa. Many East Germans believed that the door to the West was closing, and that this would be the final opportunity to leave East Germany. The rush was a major embar-

When the Wall Came Down

When East Germany lifted restrictions on emigration and travel to the West on November 9, 1989, tens of thousands of East and West Berliners swarmed across the Berlin Wall within hours for a boisterous celebration. East German border guards at Bornholmer Strasse crossing, Checkpoint Charlie, and other crossings gave up trying to check credentials, even though the new regulations said East Germans still would need permission to leave the country. Some guards smiled and took snapshots, assuring passers-by that they were just recording a historic event.

The mass crossings began about two hours after Gunter Schabowski, a member of the East German politburo, announced at a press conference that permission to travel or emigrate would be granted quickly and without preconditions, and that East Germans would be allowed to use any crossing into West Germany or West Berlin. "We know the need of citizens to travel or leave the country," Schabowski said. "Today the decision was taken that makes it possible for all citizens to leave the country through East German crossing points."

Once Schabowski's announcement was read on radio and television, a tentative trickle of East Germans tested the new regulations. When it became obvious that the announcement was for real, the trickle quickly turned into a jubilant horde that was joined at the border crossings by crowds of celebrating West Germans. Thousands of Berliners clambered across the wall at the Brandenberg Gate, passing through the historic arch that long had been inaccessible to Berliners of either side.

By 3:00 a.m., West Berlin resembled a gigantic block party. East Germans were crossing at Checkpoint Charlie at a rate of about 450 an hour. They were greeted at the border by a crowd of about five hundred West Berliners. Onlookers stood at the border barricades on the western side of Checkpoint Charlie, drinking and cheering as groups of waving, smiling East Berliners arrived and nervous East German border guards looked on. Some Germans chipped away at concrete sections of the wall with picks and hammers. The streets of West Berlin were filled with pedestrians and lines of East German autos, honking and flashing their lights.

All through the night and through the next day, East Berliners continued to flood into West Berlin. They formed long lines to pick up the hundred marks in "welcome money" that West Germany traditionally has given East Germans on their first trip to the West, gaped at shop windows, and drank in the feeling of freedom.

rassment to Honecker, who was preparing festivities to welcome Gorbachev to East Berlin on October 7 for the fortieth anniversary of the GDR. Yet Honecker still refused to back down from his hard-line position. He tried to resolve the problem by blocking further travel to Czechoslovakia and then allowing those already in the embassy to travel freely to the West.

This move caused the situation in East Germany to explode. Thousands began marching for democracy in Leipzig in weekly demonstrations that grew steadily larger. The Leipzig police refused to fire on the demonstrators despite orders from Berlin to use any means necessary to stop them. The fortieth anniversary celebration was marked by protests and the worst violence in the country since 1953. The central government was unprepared to cope with the hundreds of thousands of people in the streets. On October 18, Honecker resigned and was replaced by Egon Krenz, the former chief of security.

Krenz promised to follow a more moderate path, recognizing the need for serious reforms. He went to Moscow and on his return proclaimed himself a disciple of perestroika. In a dramatic change from Honecker, he met with representatives of New Forum, an umbrella opposition group. Nevertheless, the protests continued and intensified. Krenz re-opened the border to Czechoslovakia, and within hours the population was again streaming out of the country. Recognizing that only radical steps would have a chance to keep the people in the country, he and his Communist colleagues opened the Berlin Wall on November 9, 1989. Extensive economic and political changes also were promised, but protests continued. Within a month, Krenz, all of his cabinet ministers, and the entire party leadership had been forced to resign, leaving the government adrift. Hans Modrow, a moderate Communist leader from Dresden, formed an interim government in coalition with several opposition groups to prepare for elections.

Meanwhile the economy was crippled as the population seeped out at a continuing rate of more than two thousand per day. Protests within East Germany grew so large and frequent that they set the political agenda. In November, neither the Communists nor any of the opposition groups advocated German reunification. It was considered a less pressing question than the creation of a viable East German state. But the marchers in the streets made it known that they sought reunification above all else, and both the Communists and the opposition were forced to reverse themselves and call for reunification.

As elections scheduled for March 18 approached, the major West German political parties moved into East Germany and bolstered their sister parties with funds and political advice. Some observers charged that the West Germans commandeered the whole process, shutting out any parties that did not have access to Western money.

As in Hungary, the left-wing parties were defeated. The Christian Democratic Union (the party of conservative West German chancellor Helmut Kohl) gained the most seats in the parliament. It formed a coalition with the centrist Liberals and the leftist Social Democrats. The three parties hold the two-thirds majority necessary to amend the constitution for unification with West Germany. The party of Democratic Socialism—the renamed Communist party, not to be confused with the Social Democrats—fared poorly in the voting and was shut out of the coalition.

Parliament approved a new government, headed by Lothar de Maiziere of the Christian Democrats, on April 12. De Maiziere declared that his government's primary goal was to expedite union with West Germany and to ensure that East Germany's interests were satisfied.

The first step toward unification was a monetary union that would replace the virtually worthless East German currency (ostmark) with the West German deutschemark. Negotiations on an exchange rate lasted several months. The East Germans insisted on a one-for-one exchange, while the West Germans called for an exchange of two or more ostmarks for every deutschemark, saying that a one-for-one exchange would fuel inflation by forcing them to print tremendous quantities of money. The East and West Germans compromised by applying the one-for-one rate to private savings up to four thousand ostmarks and a two-for-one exchange to everything else. The swap took place on July 2 amid champagne and celebrations in East Germany. West Germany effectively took over management of the East German economy. Retail stores quickly were filled with Western goods. East Germans proved surprisingly frugal with their new deutschemarks, allaying fears of a massive inflationary spending binge. Unemployment is expected to skyrocket in East Germany, as East German goods go unsold and factories find they cannot compete with the West.

However, the Kohl government has indicated that it understands the heavy costs of modernizing East Germany and unifying the two countries, and it is willing to pay the bill. A seventy billion dollar fund (mostly borrowed) has been established by the West German government to pay for unification.

The next stage in unification is the reestablishment of the five prewar states that made up what is now East Germany. (After the war, East Germany was divided along different political lines.) Then, according to the constitution of West Germany, each of these states could apply for admission to West Germany. Finally, elections would be held for an all-German parliament. These elections are scheduled for December 2, 1990—assuming that talks on reunification between the World War II occupying powers (France, Great Britain, the Soviet Union, and the United States) and the two Germanies have resulted in an agreement on reunification. *(German reunification and Soviet security, p. 165)*

Velvet Revolution in Czechoslovakia

With the upheaval that had developed in East Germany, pressure for change also began building in Czechoslovakia, but protests were met with violence, and the government of Communist party leader Milos Jakes refused to make any kind of concessions. Since the 1968 invasion, Czechoslovakia had been among the most vigilant of the Eastern European countries in suppressing dissent. The Charter 77 human rights movement had been a long running thorn in the side of the government, but the movement was made up of a relatively small group of intellectuals without the active support of the whole population. The hard-line Jakes leadership, which was installed in 1968, managed to keep the population relatively content through steady improvements in the standard of living. Before World War II, Czechoslovakia had been among the most highly industrialized countries of Europe and the only genuine democracy among the states that make up contemporary Eastern Europe. With its industrial base and disciplined work force, the Czech economy had performed well, but the events taking place across Eastern Europe galvanized its citizens into action.

Vaclav Havel—playwright, dissident, and now president of Czechoslovakia—addresses a joint session of Congress, February 21, 1990.

Nonviolent protests in Prague led by student groups and the umbrella opposition group Civic Forum brought the government to its knees within weeks. The Soviets also had quietly informed the Czech government that they expected change to remain peaceful. They hinted that any use of the military might be blocked by Soviet troops. On November 24, Jakes resigned, and on December 10, President Gustav Husak resigned. Vaclav Havel, a dissident playwright and leader of the Charter 77 movement, was sworn in as interim president, along with a noncommunist majority government. Because of the nonviolent character of the uprising in Czechoslovakia, it became known as the "velvet revolution."

In June 1990 elections, Civic Forum won large majorities in the parliament. The Communists received 13 percent of the vote, and Havel was reaffirmed in the post of president.

Upheaval in Bulgaria

At the same time that dramatic events were unfolding around the Berlin Wall, a startled world learned that Todor Zhivkov of Bulgaria had resigned after thirty-five years as head of the ruling Communist party. He was replaced by Foreign Minister Petar Mladenov in a palace coup, which many analysts speculate was done in consultation with Moscow. As in East Germany, the rigid limits on political life were lifted, and free elections were promised.

Unlike the rest of Eastern Europe, little anti-Russian feeling exists in Bulgaria. Among other close historical and cultural connections between the two countries, the Russians were the saviors that rescued Bulgaria from the Ottoman Turks in 1878. Under Zhivkov, Bulgaria had been the

Soviet Union's closest and most loyal ally. Zhivkov carefully followed every change in Moscow's official line. When Gorbachev came to power, Zhivkov declared himself a great proponent of perestroika, although his attempts to implement it were halting and unenthusiastic. Bulgaria also has little history of popular dissent. When waves of unrest were sweeping other Eastern European countries, Bulgaria was quiet. Only after Zhivkov resigned did Bulgaria begin to be racked by the mass protests seen in Germany.

The parliament November 10, 1989, appointed Mladenov as interim president and Andrei Lukanov, a liberal Communist, as prime minister. Lukanov aggressively punished officials who had committed abuses under Zhivkov and soon was more popular than any of the noncommunist politicians in the country.

In elections held June 10, 1990, Bulgaria became the only Eastern European country to return the Communist party (renamed the Socialist party) to power. The Socialists, together with several small left-wing parties, gained enough seats in the parliament to form a slim majority. They offered to establish a broad coalition government with the opposition Union of Democratic Forces, but the Union declined the offer.

Despite scattered complaints of irregularities, observers agreed that the election was fair. The result can be explained by two factors. First, for years a vote against the Communists was extremely dangerous. The climate of fear had been changed only months before, and many people were unwilling to risk voting against the Communists. Second, many Bulgarians were fearful that movement to a free market system would bring unknown economic calamities, such as severe unemployment and inflation.

Violence in Romania

Since 1968, Romania has been set apart from the rest of the Warsaw Pact by its independent foreign policy. Under its Communist dictator, Nicolae Ceausescu, it has frequently taken positions at odds with Soviet policy. Ceausescu so infuriated the Brezhnev leadership that many Western analysts considered a Soviet invasion of Romania in the 1970s a serious possibility. Romania was the only Warsaw Pact nation that did not participate in the invasion of Czechoslovakia. During the 1970s Romania sought closer ties with China and the West at the expense of its relations with the Soviet Union. It refused to condemn the Camp David agreement and was the only Soviet ally that refused to explicitly support the invasion of Afghanistan.

In the past, the United States maintained good relations with Romania. However, as Romania's human rights record worsened, relations cooled dramatically. During the 1980s, Romania was among the most oppressive countries in the world. Ceausescu carried out a campaign of "systematization"—leveling villages and building monolithic apartment blocks—aided by the dreaded Securitate secret police. This campaign was particularly directed against Romania's large Hungarian minority. At the same time, Ceausescu built a cult of personality around himself, much like Stalin's.

During the 1970s, Romania borrowed heavily from abroad to finance industrial development. Then in 1981, Ceausescu announced a plan to rapidly pay off the entire sum, and in fact the entire twenty billion dollars was paid off by 1989, but at a cost of terrible suffering to the Romanian people. By some estimates, 80 percent of the country's abundant agricultural produce and the bulk of its energy were exported.

Ceausescu's relations with Gorbachev were very cool, even at the beginning of Gorbachev's tenure. Ceausescu saw perestroika and glasnost as threats to his dictatorship, and he completely rejected them. Because of his iron grip on Romania, most observers expected that Ceausescu would be able to insulate his country from the upheaval in the other Warsaw Pact countries. However, on December 14, crowds gathered in the city of Timisoara to protect a dissident Lutheran minister who was being deported. The crowds were dispersed by violence, and estimates of the dead ranged into the thousands. When workers marched again the following week, the army refused to fire and instead joined the crowds. Subsequently it was reported that the defense minister had deliberately failed to give ammunition to the soldiers and was then executed for this breach by Ceausescu. The protests spread to Bucharest and turned into a battle between the army and the Securitate, which had remained loyal to Ceausescu. After several days of violence, Ceausescu was captured and executed by the army, and the Securitate was mostly defeated.

Ion Iliescu, a former Communist party secretary who had fallen into disfavor with Ceausescu in the mid-eighties, took power as the head of the National Liberation Front, relying heavily on the support of the army. The Front was composed largely of former Communists like Iliescu. It promised to guarantee civil rights and to hold free elections in May 1990. The Front initially relaxed Ceausescu's rigid control over society. However, within months, reports surfaced of the Front using strong-arm tactics against its opponents.

The two main opposition parties, the National Liberal party and the National Peasant party, were overwhelmingly defeated in the May election by the National Liberation Front, which received 73 percent of the votes cast. Iliescu was elected president with 89 percent of the vote. Western observers noted significant irregularities and harassment of voters and claimed that, because of a lack of opposition resources in some remote areas, many rural voters were unaware that anyone other than the Front was competing. Nevertheless, the election generally was considered fair. Voters apparently believed Iliescu was a dramatic improvement over Ceausescu but were frightened by the opposition's call for swift movement toward privatization and a market economy. Iliescu has advocated a more gradual transition and a steady integration back into the European mainstream. However, Western observers are skeptical about the future of democracy in Romania because of the long history of oppression there.

Creating a New Europe

From the end of World War II until the rise of the new thinking, Soviet policy in Western Europe had three primary goals: to seek Western recognition for the German Democratic Republic and for Soviet hegemony in Eastern Europe in general, to weaken the Western alliance, and to prevent any future threat to the Soviet Union from arising on German soil.

The Soviets' first breakthrough on recognition of East Germany came in 1970. An agreement was signed with West Germany to "respect without restriction the integrity of all of the States of Europe within their present borders."

This amounted to a de facto West German recognition of East Germany. The document was a precursor to the Helsinki Final Act, signed five years later. The Final Act, which was signed by the heads of state of thirty-five countries (including the United States and Canada) on August 1, 1975, was a political settlement of World War II. It recognized all established borders in Europe. It also pledged the signatories to act in accordance with a number of human rights principles that the Western countries subsequently pressured the Soviet Union and its allies to observe.

In pursuit of the goal of weakening the Western alliance, every Soviet leader since Stalin has tried to strengthen Soviet relations with the major Western European powers at the expense of the United States. The Soviets believed that if the Western alliance could be split, they would enjoy greater security and influence over Europe.

In the era of new thinking, the Soviets' approach to Europe has changed significantly. They no longer seek hegemony in Eastern Europe or exclusion of the United States from European affairs. They have recognized that the United States has become a stabilizing influence in Europe. However, preventing a united Germany from becoming a threat to Soviet national security remains extremely important to the Soviets, especially now that it is unifying.

Gorbachev has admitted that the division of Europe has not benefited the Soviet Union in the long run. At the Twenty-eighth Party Congress in July 1990, he was sharply criticized by party conservatives for allowing socialism to be defeated in Eastern Europe. He responded to his critics by noting that there was no socialism in Eastern Europe left to be saved. Those regimes were merely "a variety of the Stalinist authoritarian and bureaucratic system that we ourselves have abandoned." Foreign Minister Shevardnadze responded to the criticisms of conservatives by commenting: "Is the collapse of socialism in Eastern Europe a failure of Soviet diplomacy? It would have been so if our diplomacy had tried to prevent changes in the neighboring countries. Soviet diplomacy did not and could not set out to resist the liquidation of those imposed, alien and totalitarian regimes."

Gorbachev and his advisers have not discarded traditional Soviet security concerns about Germany, but they now approach these concerns from the framework of the new thinking. In his speech to the party congress, Shevardnadze continued: "The concern over the process of German unification is understandable. We all have pain deep inside bearing in mind our past experience. . . . Yes, we have been used to certain German realities. We viewed them as a guarantee of our security. Let us think: can such a guarantee that is based on the artificial and unnatural division of a great nation be reliable? Could it last forever?. . . The fact is that the army of the future united Germany will be smaller than the West German Bundeswehr. Which is better for us: to have a million strong West German Bundeswehr against us, or an army of united Germany half this size?" Kohl had agreed in talks with Gorbachev that the army of a united Germany would not exceed 370,000 troops.

Gorbachev's new strategy in Europe seeks to create what he has called a "common European home." When Gorbachev first started talking about this concept, Western analysts dismissed it as another attempt to woo Western Europe. Although Gorbachev has been vague about its specific features, his common European home would be less confrontational and would contain fewer armaments. While NATO and the Warsaw Pact might not disappear, their activities would become more politically oriented. Some countries might opt out of the alliance system and choose to become neutral. Hungary, for example, has chosen this option. Soviet hegemony in Eastern Europe would disappear, but Soviet access to Western European markets and capital would increase. In essence, Gorbachev wants to create a new Europe, one over which the Soviets would have less control, but one which would better fulfill Soviet needs.

Influential Soviet political scientist Fëdor Burlatsky has said that the common European home concept implies a return to a single European civilization. It is not a geographic concept that would exclude the United States; instead, it is a Western cultural ideal.

There has been some discussion in the Soviet press of creating an all-European security arrangement, which would be based on the Conference on Security and Cooperation in Europe (CSCE) and ultimately would supplant the two alliances. It is unclear exactly how this would operate. So far it has received a skeptical response in the West.

German Reunification and Soviet Security

The biggest question to be resolved in Europe has been the fate of Germany. On May 5, 1990, the foreign ministers of East and West Germany and leaders of the four occupying powers from World War II (France, Great Britain, the United States, and the Soviet Union, which still retain legal rights over Germany) met in Bonn for the opening of the Two Plus Four talks. These talks were intended to resolve the issues that arise from German unification by negotiating a security arrangement agreeable to all parties.

The Bonn government and the three Western powers insisted that a unified Germany should remain in NATO. But the Soviets at first demanded that a unified Germany be neutral. Gradually their position modified. On July 16, 1990, after two days of meetings with Chancellor Kohl, Gorbachev agreed that a unified Germany could be completely sovereign and could join any alliance it chose. Soviet troops would be withdrawn from East Germany within four years. In exchange Kohl agreed to limits on the size of

Checkpoint Charlie, a major crossing point between East and West Berlin, was removed in June 1990.

the future German military and a large package of economic aid for the Soviet Union, including paying the expenses of the Soviet withdrawal from East Germany.

The Bush administration has emphasized that a Germany in NATO would be less threatening to the Soviet Union than a neutral Germany. Germany is too large and powerful to be politically neutral (like a giant Switzerland). It inevitably would become an independent power. Germany would be more secure and less aggressive if it were tied to NATO. Poland and Hungary also have opposed the idea of a neutral Germany.

The Military Balance in Europe

Several processes are occurring simultaneously that will affect the future balance of military forces on the European continent. These processes are negotiated arms reductions, unilateral arms reductions, and nationalist pressures for withdrawal of U.S. and Soviet troops.

The Conventional Forces in Europe (CFE) talks between the Soviet Union and the United States seek to lower American and Soviet conventional force levels in Europe (from the Atlantic to the Urals) and to make the two sides' forces about equal. The talks have been proceeding slowly. Because the makeup of conventional forces is more complex than that of nuclear forces, verification is a problem.

While CFE is moving forward, the other processes threaten to render it irrelevant. In bilateral agreements, the Soviets have agreed to withdraw all of their forces from Hungary and Czechoslovakia by mid-1991 and from East Germany from 1994. These unilateral withdrawals put pressure on the United States to follow suit in Western Europe. The U.S. Congress has considered proposals for unilaterally withdrawing troops from West Germany. The Bush administration claims that such actions by Congress make it more difficult to negotiate a treaty.

Another concern is that if German unification is completed before CFE, the German government will pressure the United States to withdraw its forces from Germany. The United States will be hard pressed to explain the continued presence of hundreds of thousands of occupying troops on the soil of a unified sovereign state. If progress is not made on CFE, the Bonn government may feel pressure to ask the United States to unilaterally withdraw some of its troops.

If American troops do remain in Europe, they no longer will be there to protect Europe from a Soviet invasion. Instead, their mission will be to provide stability to the new European order and to smooth the historically explosive relationship between Germany and Russia. Because of Soviet uneasiness about a reunified Germany, American troops in Europe will ease Soviet fears about unification. Such an arrangement likely will be the best guarantee for the Soviets against a resurgent German military threat.

Sino-Soviet Relations

When the People's Republic of China was proclaimed on October 3, 1949, it was the beginning of the end of absolute Soviet domination of the Socialist bloc. Chinese Communist leader Mao Zedong was slavishly obedient to Stalin's political line, despite the restrained Soviet reception of Mao's triumph in China. Stalin had maintained ties with the Kuomintang (Chinese Nationalists) until their final defeat by the Communists and, according to some sources, hoped that China would be left divided and weak.

Nevertheless, Sino-Soviet relations continued on a steady footing until Khrushchev began his opening to the West in 1955. Mao resented Khrushchev's attempt to improve relations with the United States and feared that it would come at China's expense. Mao began to take a more shrill line on the dangers of cooperating with the capitalist world. The Chinese boasted that the socialist movement had nothing to fear from a nuclear war, since it could certainly live through it, while capitalism would be destroyed. This line horrified the Soviets as they were trying to reduce tensions with the West. The Chinese and Soviets also sparred ideologically about China's attempt to build communism rapidly through small-scale labor-intensive industry.

The Soviets denied as long as possible their disagreements with the Chinese to present the West with a unified Socialist bloc. The split, however, came into the open in 1960 with the increasingly public Chinese attacks on Soviet "revisionism."

While on the surface the split was couched in terms of an ideological dispute, in reality it ran far deeper. Fundamental differences in the histories, cultures, levels of economic development, geographic realities, and goals of the two communist giants made them unnatural allies, linked only by a common ideology and a common enemy. They shared centuries of mistrust. As the two great competing Asian land powers, it was improbable that their previous close relationship could continue. Thus they were never able to reconstruct the alliance, even after the ideological disputes long had become irrelevant.

And contrary to Western expectations, Sino-Soviet relations did not improve after Khrushchev's departure. The Chinese applauded his demise, and Brezhnev and his colleagues communicated their desire to improve relations by ending anti-Chinese propaganda and delaying an international communist conference so the two powers would have a chance to reconcile their differences beforehand. But in spite of the new Soviet regime's goodwill gestures and the economic and political concessions it offered, the differences between Beijing and Moscow were too deep to permit a reconciliation. The lull in Sino-Soviet polemics began to erode by the spring of 1965, and relations became increasingly hostile during the five-year period that followed.

Developing Hostility

The focus of Sino-Soviet differences in the mid-sixties was the Vietnam War. The key issue dividing China and the Soviet Union was whether they should engage in "united action" to get maximum impact from their material support for their Vietnamese allies. Moscow and Hanoi pressed Beijing to agree to united action. In April 1965, the Soviets asked for an agreement that would allow them to ship aid to North Vietnam through China, fly over China, and use Chinese airfields and ports near North Vietnam. Mao and his supporters rejected all Soviet proposals for united action. They feared that such cooperation could lead to Soviet interference in Chinese internal affairs, a Soviet military presence in China, the growth of Soviet influence in North Vietnam, and a possible extension of U.S. air strikes to Chinese territory.

Instead of uniting behind the North Vietnamese war effort, Moscow and Beijing competed for influence in Hanoi through separate aid programs. The North Vietnamese leaders skillfully played their two supporters off each other to maximize the benefits they could squeeze out of Sino-Soviet competition.

Two major developments further exacerbated Sino-Soviet relations in the years following the ouster of Khrushchev. The first was the Chinese Cultural Revolution, launched in August 1966. The second was the Soviet military buildup along the Sino-Soviet border.

The chaos within China and its militant attitude toward the outside world during the period of the Cultural Revolution diminished its diplomatic, military, and economic capabilities. The resulting international isolation of the Chinese strengthened Moscow's hand against Beijing among socialist nations. China's advocacy of a relentlessly militant posture toward the perceived enemies of communism weakened its standing with more pragmatic Communist parties. By the end of 1966, only the Albanian Communist party described itself as pro-Chinese. The Cultural Revolution also reduced China's capacity to compete with Soviet material support of North Vietnam.

The Cultural Revolution was accompanied by escalating propaganda exchanges and the disintegration of meaningful cultural and diplomatic relations between the two nations. In January 1967, student demonstrations at the Soviet embassy in Beijing became so violent and abusive that the families of Soviet diplomats were evacuated from China, and Soviet diplomats became virtual prisoners in their own compound. During this period, the Chinese also harassed the crews of Soviet ships and expelled a number of Soviet journalists and diplomats. The Soviets responded with similar expulsions and constant radio broadcasts denouncing the Cultural Revolution and urging the Chinese people (especially the ethnic Moslem minorities) to resist Mao's rule.

In 1965, Khrushchev's successors were faced with an "ally" who refused to cooperate with them in the Socialist bloc and the Third World and who brushed aside all attempts to improve relations. In addition, since 1963, Beijing openly had denounced nineteenth-century border treaties between Russia and China as being "unequal." Mao claimed that nearly a million square miles of Soviet territory rightfully belonged to China. Finally, China's emergence as a nuclear power a year earlier added a new dimension to the Chinese threat.

Consequently, the Soviets began to increase substantially their military strength along the Chinese border during the second half of 1965. In January 1966, the Soviet Union signed a treaty of friendship, cooperation, and mutual aid with Mongolia, which led within a year to the deployment there of a hundred thousand Soviet troops. The Soviets also took measures to add to their firepower and troop strength in the Soviet Far East.

Beginning in 1967, a number of confrontations took place between Soviet and Chinese troops patrolling in disputed border areas. These incidents intensified following the Soviet invasion of Czechoslovakia, but until the spring of 1969 both sides had refrained from firing upon the other. On March 2, the situation exploded into armed conflict when Chinese forces ambushed a Soviet patrol on Damanskii (Zhenbao) Island in the Ussuri River, which forms part of the border between Manchuria and the Soviet Union. The Soviets responded by returning in force to the island thirteen days later. They attacked a numerically inferior force of Chinese and inflicted many casualties. Yet in spite of Soviet conventional and nuclear superiority, the Chinese resisted curtailing their patrols in and near disputed territory.

The March exchange set off a series of border clashes that lasted throughout the spring and summer. In August and September the Soviets began hinting about a possible nuclear strike against Chinese nuclear facilities. In the face of this threat, the Chinese backed down and agreed to border negotiations. Those negotiations produced no significant progress toward a resolution of the border issue, and the decade came to an end with China regarding the Soviet Union as its greatest enemy and painfully aware of its diplomatic isolation and vulnerability to a Soviet nuclear attack.

Triangular Diplomacy

In the Chinese civil war, the United States had sided with the Kuomintang against the Communists, although at times it had been less than generous with aid, out of frustration with the Nationalists' corruption and lack of popular support. When the Nationalists were forced to flee to Taiwan, a wave of recriminations swept Washington, with all sides trying to fix blame for the "loss" of China. Out of the resulting sense of obligation, military guarantees were given to Taiwan, and official recognition was withheld from the People's Republic of China.

President Nixon, however, saw normal relations with Beijing as central to his goals of hastening the end of the Vietnam War and encouraging Moscow to moderate its relations with the West. As early as 1968, Nixon, as a presidential candidate, indicated his intention to seek improved relations with China: "We simply cannot afford to leave China forever outside the family of nations, there to nurture its fantasies, cherish its hates and threaten its neighbors. There is no place on this small planet for a billion of its potentially most able people to live in angry isolation."

China's emergence from the Cultural Revolution, its experience of vulnerability during the Sino-Soviet border crisis of 1969, the beginning of U.S. troop withdrawals from Vietnam, and the continuing Soviet military buildup on the Chinese border created the conditions under which a détente with the United States could begin. China needed to seek an accommodation with its less threatening enemy—the United States—to enhance its security against the Soviet Union.

Nixon Visits China

The thaw in U.S.-Chinese relations took a dramatic step on July 15, 1971, when President Nixon announced that he would visit Beijing in early 1972 "to seek the normalization of relations between the two countries." The initial Soviet reaction was restrained, but Kremlin leaders privately displayed renewed interest in a summit meeting between Brezhnev and Nixon, a topic that had been under discussion for several months. In the wake of the China breakthrough, American and Soviet officials made significant progress on a comprehensive accord concerning the status of Berlin and agreed to a May 1972 summit meeting.

Soviet leaders had a variety of reasons for pursuing détente with the West, including the fear of being left on the wrong side of the American-Soviet-Chinese triangle.

Moscow sought to convince American and West European leaders that it had more to offer than Beijing. Indeed, there were areas of cooperation such as arms control and resolution of the Berlin problem where the Chinese had nothing to offer. But the Soviet Union's growing détente with the West did not stop the United States from engaging in a simultaneous détente with China. Meanwhile the Soviet Union continued its efforts to ensure its own security, further building up its forces facing China throughout the decade.

The Soviets had hoped that when Mao passed from the scene his successors might seek to put Sino-Soviet relations back on agreeable terms. Accordingly, the Soviet Union signaled its desire to repair Sino-Soviet differences when Mao died in September 1976. But Mao's death brought no more improvement in relations between Beijing and Moscow than Khrushchev's ouster had produced twelve years earlier. The new leaders in Beijing ignored the Soviet curtailment of anti-Chinese propaganda and even rejected Brezhnev's note of congratulations to Hua Guofeng for his election to the post of chairman of the Chinese Communist party.

Meanwhile U.S.-Chinese relations were developing steadily. On December 15, 1978, President Carter announced, "The United States recognizes the government of the People's Republic of China as the sole legal government of China." Full diplomatic relations officially began January 1, 1979. This development substantially improved the capability and willingness of China and the United States to cooperate with each other in new ways, including arms sales and technology transfers from the United States.

While not condemning the move, Moscow warned against using the continuing Chinese-American détente against the Soviet Union. Washington insisted that the establishment of relations with Beijing would not affect U.S.-Soviet relations. The Chinese, however, did not hesitate to call for U.S.-Chinese-Japanese cooperation against the Soviet Union. Although a formal anti-Soviet Asian alliance was not forthcoming, Soviet interests in Asia now were opposed by three powerful nations with a shared interest in containing the Soviet Union and a growing potential for cooperation.

American and Japanese trade and business ties with China grew steadily until the 1989 Chinese crackdown on student protesters in Tiananmen Square. It is too early to predict the effect this will have on U.S.-Chinese ties in the long run, but the Bush administration appears eager to limit the damage to the strategic relationship with China.

Cambodia and Vietnam

In 1975 the fanatical Khmer Rouge Communists swept the Lon Nol government from power in Cambodia. Lon Nol himself had come to power in a military coup against Prince Sihanouk in 1970. China's massive support for the Khmer Rouge greatly alarmed Vietnam. Based on its radical ideology, the Khmer Rouge immediately set about reshaping Cambodia. All cities were immediately emptied, and the entire population was sent out to the countryside to engage in agricultural labor. Anyone considered an intellectual or connected with the previous regime was executed. During the three-year reign of the Khmer Rouge, about one-sixth of the population of seven million was killed.

When Saigon fell in 1975, Hanoi still enjoyed friendly relations with the Chinese, even though the Soviet Union had become the dominant supplier of military and economic assistance to North Vietnam during the last years of the war. From 1975 to 1977 Hanoi tried to maintain its

The Soviet-backed Vietnamese invasion of Cambodia in 1978-1979 swept the bloody Khmer Rouge from power. These Khmer Rouge guerrillas, supported by China, are trying to overthrow the Cambodian regime installed by Vietnam.

relationship with the Chinese in spite of its opposition to Beijing's support of the Khmer Rouge. By the beginning of 1978, however, large-scale hostilities had broken out between Vietnam and Cambodia along their border. Hanoi, in need of increased military and economic assistance, leaned more heavily on an obliging Moscow, while China threw its full support behind the Khmer Rouge. China also terminated its aid projects in Vietnam and withdrew its advisers and technicians.

On November 3, 1978, Hanoi and Moscow further solidified their relationship by signing the Soviet-Vietnamese Treaty of Friendship and Cooperation. It did not require the Soviet Union to intervene militarily on the side of Vietnam if it came under attack, but it formally stated the Soviets' commitment to Vietnam, thereby increasing the likelihood of a strong Soviet response in the event Vietnam's security was threatened.

On December 25, 1978, Vietnamese forces invaded Cambodia, ostensibly in support of Cambodian opponents to the Khmer Rouge. By January 9, 1979, Phnom Penh had fallen, though forces loyal to the Khmer Rouge and supported by China continued to battle the Vietnamese in the countryside. The Soviet leadership applauded the defeat of the Khmer Rouge regime. Leonid Brezhnev denounced it as "a political system of the Chinese model." The Vietnamese blitzkrieg into Cambodia made apparent Hanoi's primary motivation for formalizing its close relationship with the Soviet Union. It hoped the agreement would deter China from intervening militarily on behalf of the Khmer Rouge.

However, on February 17, 1979, Chinese leaders made good on their threats to teach Hanoi some "necessary lessons." They launched a multipronged armored invasion into northern Vietnam. The Chinese announced that the invasion was a limited punitive action in response to the Vietnamese invasion of Cambodia and alleged aggression along the Sino-Vietnamese border.

Brezhnev and his colleagues reacted cautiously to the invasion. They issued vague warnings to the Chinese to get out of Vietnam, but Soviet support for Hanoi was limited to propaganda, resupply efforts, and intelligence assistance. Soviet forces in the Asian military districts were not even put on alert. The Brezhnev Politburo appeared unwilling to risk a confrontation with China over Vietnam, in spite of the recently signed Soviet-Vietnamese treaty.

The Chinese began their withdrawal on March 5, declaring that they had achieved their objectives. In the wake of the Chinese invasion, Soviet access to Vietnam, including the naval facilities at Cam Ranh Bay, became more extensive.

Soviet and Chinese ambitions in Southeast Asia reflected their anxieties in dealing with each other. The Soviets sought a firm ally in Vietnam to enhance their security at the expense of China. The Chinese accurately viewed this as a Soviet attempt at encirclement. They tried to deflect it by increasing their influence in Cambodia, and by strengthening their ties with Japan and the United States.

The New Thinking in East Asia

During the first half of the 1980s, the Soviets had poor relations with most East Asian nations. Moscow heavily subsidized Vietnam's efforts to maintain its domination over Cambodia. Relations with China were improved over the previous decade, but they still were far from warm.

The Pacific Rim was fast becoming the world's most economically dynamic region, yet the Soviet Union was almost completely shut out of it because of its Cambodian involvement, its invasion of Afghanistan, and its heavy-handed military buildup. Not only was the region dominated by the Japanese-American alliance, but virtually every other country in the region stood opposed to Soviet power. The Soviet Union had minimal relations with noncommunist countries in the region and few tools of influence besides its military power. The result was a classic situation in which the "old thinking" had left the Soviet Union simultaneously entangled and isolated, but at a huge cost in defense expenditures and foreign aid. During the late 1980s Gorbachev appeared determined to reverse this situation.

Gorbachev has shown great flexibility in East Asia, as in other regions of the world, and a willingness to reach out to other countries while reining in his allies. Gorbachev has attempted to improve relations with China in particular, but also with Japan, South Korea, Taiwan, Australia, New Zealand, and the ASEAN countries (Association of Southeast Asian Nations: Brunei, Indonesia, Malaysia, the Philippines, Singapore, and Thailand). He has sought to reduce military tensions, while expanding diplomatic ties and tapping into East Asia's rapid economic development. Moscow has shown interest in joining regional economic organizations such as the Asian Development Bank and the Pacific Economic Cooperation Council.

Nevertheless, after years of coping with Soviet expansion, East Asians have greeted Gorbachev with considerably more skepticism than Europeans. Japan especially seems in no rush to cash in on perestroika.

China's Three Conditions

In 1988, when the Soviets first indicated their desire to seek a rapprochement with China through a summit meeting with Deng Xiaoping, Beijing reminded the Soviets that no summit would be held until they met three longstanding Chinese conditions for improved relations: withdrawal of their forces from Afghanistan, an end to their support for Vietnam's occupation of Cambodia, and a reversal of their arms buildup along the Chinese border.

The ASEAN countries also made the end of the Vietnamese occupation of Cambodia a litmus test for improving relations with the Soviet Union. They have taken a leading role in resolving the Cambodian issue and regard a political settlement as central to their own security.

To the surprise of Western analysts, all three conditions were addressed in 1989, clearing the way for a summit meeting with China and improving Moscow's standing in the region in general. The last Soviet troops left Afghanistan in February 1989. As part of the unilateral troop cuts announced by Gorbachev at the United Nations in December 1988, "the major portion" of Soviet troops were to be removed from Mongolia. The last Vietnamese troops (presumably under heavy Soviet pressure) left Cambodia in September 1989, although allegations have been made by Cambodian and foreign sources that as many as five thousand Vietnamese have remained behind, wearing Cambodian uniforms.

The Continuing Cambodian Dispute

As of 1990 the various parties involved in Cambodia had not reached a consensus, so the bloodshed in that country has continued despite the Vietnamese withdrawal.

When the Khmer Rouge was forced from power in 1978, it fled with thousands of other Cambodians to refugee camps just across the Thai border. From these camps it has continued to carry out a guerrilla war. Two other opposition groups, the Khmer People's Liberation Front, led by Son Sann, and a group loyal to Prince Sihanouk, also operate from the camps. Both groups are noncommunist and receive aid from the United States. The three groups have united in a coalition that is recognized by many countries as the government of Cambodia and holds Cambodia's seat in the United Nations. Because of continued Chinese military backing, the Khmer Rouge is by far the strongest of the three opposition groups. Since the Vietnamese withdrawal, they have gained ground against the troops of Hun Sen (the leader installed by Vietnam) and could conceivably return to power by military force.

Settlement talks were stalled for a long time by Soviet unwillingness to allow the Khmer Rouge to participate in an interim government. Other countries also were hesitant to allow the return to power of a faction that had presided over the slaughter of more than a million people. However, on January 16, 1990, the five permanent members of the UN Security Council agreed on a plan proposed by Australia for resolving the conflict. Its key features included a verified withdrawal of all foreign (Vietnamese) forces from Cambodia, a cease-fire and cessation of all foreign military assistance, UN-supervised elections, "an effective UN presence during the transition period ... to assure internal security," and a "Supreme National Council" to retain sovereignty during the transition period.

The statement was vague enough to gloss over the many differences that remain, but it nevertheless represented a real compromise between China and the Soviet Union—both of whom appear to want the conflict to end. The Hun Sen government is under pressure to accept the terms from its Vietnamese backers and its precarious military position will likely cause it to work for a negotiated settlement. The Khmer Rouge has so far rejected any settlement. It is well armed and could continue the civil war for some time, even if Chinese aid were cut off.

Gorbachev in Beijing

With the three Chinese conditions met, the path was cleared for Gorbachev's historic trip to Beijing in May 1989. The trip represented a tremendous foreign policy success for Gorbachev. Since the mid-1960s the Soviets had tried unsuccessfully to mend their relations with China. Gorbachev had made Soviet-Chinese rapprochement one of the highest goals of the new thinking.

On May 15 Gorbachev became the first Soviet leader to meet with his Chinese counterpart since Khrushchev held a summit with Mao in 1959. By meeting with Deng, Gorbachev hoped to reduce the strategic advantages the United States reaped from the Sino-Soviet rivalry. The trip also marked the formal normalization of Sino-Soviet relations after a thirty-year rift. Nevertheless, serious problems remained in the relationship, and the trip highlighted the new ideological division that runs through the Socialist bloc.

Gorbachev's domestic reforms had sent shock waves across China. Chinese students who had taken over Tiananmen Square to protest for democracy in the weeks before Gorbachev's trip to China had been galvanized by events in the Soviet Union, and they invoked Gorbachev's name as a symbol of hope. Although the protests coincided with Gorbachev's trip largely by accident, his presence was fully exploited by the demonstrators. While Gorbachev was in Beijing, the crowds swelled at one point to more than a million people, and the Chinese government was greatly embarrassed by the massive outpouring of support for Gorbachev's reforms. On May 20, a few days after Gorbachev had left, the protests were violently crushed with tanks, and thousands were killed or imprisoned.

More than anything, the Chinese value stability. But the reforms emanating from Moscow have created pressure from below for changes the Chinese leadership is unwilling to make. Perestroika has caused a new ideological split in the Socialist bloc between those nations committed to political and economic reforms and those trying to avoid them. China is at the top of a short list of rejectionists: Albania, Cuba, Ethiopia, North Korea, and Vietnam.

Diplomats and journalists have reported that privately Chinese officials have criticized perestroika, claiming that Gorbachev has turned his back on the ideals of socialism. The Chinese, however, have declined to attack him publicly. Officially, China insists that Soviet internal affairs are its own business, and that they will have no effect on the normalization of relations between the two countries.

Soviet-Japanese Relations

Achieving improved ties with Japan is probably Gorbachev's biggest remaining challenge in East Asia. Bet-

ter relations with Tokyo are an essential precondition for Soviet participation in the East Asian economy and for Soviet access to Japanese capital and technology.

Before the Soviet Union can hope to benefit from Japanese investment, however, it must find a solution to the dispute over four Soviet-occupied Kuril islands, known in Japan as the Northern Territories. These four islands were seized by the Soviet Union in the closing days of World War II. They are strategically important because they straddle the entrance to the Sea of Okhotsk, where many Soviet submarines hide, and they are home to some thirty thousand Soviet soldiers and civilians.

Since 1945, Japan has insisted uncompromisingly on the return of all four islands and has yet to sign a treaty ending World War II with the Soviet Union because of this issue. While Gorbachev has not shown a willingness to give up the islands, the Soviet position has moderated. Foreign Minister Shevardnadze has recognized publicly that a dispute exists, contrary to the Soviet position in the past that possession of the islands was a closed question.

Despite deep-rooted Japanese mistrust of the Soviet Union (Japan and Russia have gone to war four times), relations have warmed under Gorbachev. Shevardnadze has resumed regular exchanges with his Japanese counterpart after a ten-year lapse. The Soviets now recognize Japan's growing international importance, after years of treating it merely as a vehicle for American imperialism.

Gorbachev has stated his desire to visit Tokyo, and it appears that such a trip could take place in early 1991 and would become the first visit ever to Japan by a Soviet leader. Gorbachev may issue a bold stroke before the visit, such as a further cut in Soviet military forces in the Far East or an offer to return some or all of the four islands in exchange for Japanese credits and investment. As the Soviet economy weakens, the pressure on Gorbachev to make a deal on the islands will grow.

Nevertheless, Soviet rapprochement with Japan has its limits. Primary among them is Japan's alliance with the United States. Despite disputes over trade, this alliance has been the cornerstone of prosperity in East Asia. America is Japan's closest trading partner, and Japan thus is unlikely to do anything to put the alliance at risk. The Soviet Union also has little to offer Japan. Reduced military tensions would be beneficial, but Japan is not straining under its defense burden. The opportunity to open up the Soviet Far East is provocative, but investing in the underdeveloped and unpredictable Soviet Union is far riskier and more costly for the Japanese than concentrating investments in other more hospitable countries of East Asia. Therefore, the Japanese have continued to respond coolly to Soviet gestures, while waiting for Gorbachev to make major concessions.

The USSR in Afghanistan

On April 14, 1988, in Geneva, representatives of the governments of Pakistan and Afghanistan signed a package of agreements known as the Geneva accords, intended to end the war in Afghanistan. An additional "Declaration on International Guarantees" was signed by the United States and the Soviet Union as states-guarantors. The Soviet Union also pledged in an agreement with the Afghan government to begin withdrawing its troops from Afghanistan by May 15, 1988, and to complete the withdrawal by February 15, 1989. The Soviets' nine-year military intervention in Afghanistan began moving toward its conclusion.

Background of the Invasion

Afghanistan was demarcated in the early twentieth century as a buffer state between British colonies in south Asia and Russia. It was inhabited by a mosaic of different peoples and had little national integration. Although the country was ruled by a king, most areas within Afghanistan retained their local systems of self-government and their hostility to foreign invaders, built up over centuries. By pursuing a policy of careful neutrality, Prime Minister Muhammad Daoud created a modern state during the 1950s, funded by aid from both the United States and the Soviet Union.

In 1973, King Zaher Shah was removed in a military coup, and Daoud took power as president. Pro-Soviet military officers, disappointed with Daoud, staged another coup in April 1978, killing him. Power was turned over to the People's Democratic party of Afghanistan, a Marxist-Leninist party that embarked on a radical agenda and began relying heavily on Soviet backing. According to Barnett Rubin, an expert on Afghan affairs with the U.S. Institute of Peace, the new leaders' "brutality and ill-considered radicalism drove much of the population into its traditional pattern of revolt against overweening central government." The Afghan leaders "also defied Soviet advice to moderate their policies."

By the end of 1979, the regime was on the verge of collapse. Revolt based on Islamic fundamentalism had spread throughout much of the country. Hafizullah Amin, the Afghan president, seemed unable to consolidate his grip on the reins of power. The Soviets were faced with the likelihood of a second Islamic state being established on their southern border (a revolutionary Islamic government had come to power in Iran earlier in the year). Moscow was concerned about the effect this would have on the large Moslem population in bordering areas of the Soviet Union. The danger of religious fundamentalism spreading through the sizeable Soviet Moslem minority was not one the Kremlin took lightly. One indication of the Soviets' concern with the phenomenon was the development of a large body of literature trying to explain why religious fundamentalism could never take hold in Soviet Central Asia.

The Soviets also believed that they had a legitimate security interest in ensuring a stable regime in Afghanistan. Because they expected the United States would recognize this, and because a limited Soviet military presence already existed in Afghanistan, they presumed that criticism from the West would be minimal.

On December 24, 1979, the Soviets began airlifting troops and supplies into Afghanistan. Three days later about twenty thousand troops crossed into Afghanistan from Soviet border towns, and by early January, the Soviets had moved an army of eighty thousand troops into the country. Soviet troops quickly captured all major towns and highways, but opposition continued in the mountainous countryside from the Afghan guerrillas who had been at war with the Kabul government since the April 1978 takeover. Tens of thousands of troops defected to the guerrillas from the Afghan army. President Amin was replaced with Babrak Karmal, whom the Soviets found easier to control. The Soviets had hoped that the campaign would be completed swiftly, but the guerrillas, calling themselves mujahideen (holy warriors), followed the centuries-old pattern of resisting invaders from the mountainous Afghan terrain and proved impossible to dislodge.

The reaction from the United States and other countries was swift and harsh. The Soviet Union was severely criticized by the Third World. The Islamic countries were especially angered and frightened by the invasion. The invasion was condemned by the UN General Assembly 104 to 18, on January 14, although a similar resolution in the Security Council was vetoed by the Soviets. President Carter, among other measures, called for a boycott of the 1980 Moscow Olympics, which was joined by fifty-six countries.

During the fifteen years prior to the invasion, the Soviets had been making a concerted effort to develop their relations with the Islamic world. Moscow attempted to put on a "Moslem face," reminding the world that it had the fifth largest Moslem population. Delegations of Islamic officials and scholars from the Soviet Union were sent to conservative Islamic regimes. The Soviets also allowed Islamic conferences to be held and relaxed controls on other Islamic activities. Leninism was promoted abroad as being completely compatible with Islam. This policy, however, collapsed with the invasion of Afghanistan. Fierce Moslem criticism of the invasion quickly isolated the Soviet Union from the Islamic countries.

The first troops sent into Afghanistan included about 40 percent Central Asians. Moscow hoped that the sight of Moslems fighting for socialism might make it more palatable to the Afghans. What happened was quite the reverse. Soviet Moslems fraternized extensively with the Afghans. One defector described the following scene:

> I was waiting in front of the Pul-i Charkhi prison in early 1980 for information about several family members who were being held by the revolutionary government. Along came six Soviet armored personnel carriers full of Soviet Uzbeks and Tadzhiks. When the APCs [armored personnel carriers] stopped in front of the prison, these Soviet Muslims swarmed out and began buying Korans, swapping weapons, and generally fraternizing with the local Afghans. This was soon stopped by the Russian officers who forced the Soviet Muslim soldiers back into the APCs at gunpoint and then shut and locked the lids.

The Central Asians also made poor soldiers because they were reluctant to fire on the mujahideen. There were reports of guns being smuggled to them, along with information on Soviet troop movements—and even some defections. Three months after the invasion, the Central Asians were pulled out en masse and replaced with other troops.

Détente Destroyed

Preoccupied with the hostage crisis in Iran, the United States was caught off guard by the invasion. Many American policy makers had not thought such an inflammatory Soviet move was possible at a time when the recently signed SALT II treaty was being debated in the U.S. Senate and Moscow was preparing to receive thousands of international visitors at the 1980 Summer Olympics. After the invasion, Carter asked Congress to delay action on the treaty, pulled the United States out of the 1980 Summer Olympics, and halted shipments of grain and high technology goods to the Soviet Union. *(Sanctions, box, p. 172)*

Although Afghanistan had been in the Soviet orbit since 1978, the Soviet invasion represented the first time Moscow had intervened with its own troops outside the area the Red Army had occupied in 1945. The invasion

Sanctions against USSR

President Carter imposed numerous sanctions against the Soviet Union following the 1979 Afghanistan invasion. An embargo on grain sales to the USSR, imposed January 4, 1980, affected all transactions above the eight million metric tons provided by the 1975 U.S.-Soviet grain agreement. This blocked a previously approved sale of 14.7 million metric tons of corn, wheat, and soybeans. The president also placed an embargo on the sale of items incorporating high technology, such as large computers, advanced machine tools, and certain oil and gas production equipment.

The International Longshoremen's Union, on January 9, 1980, said its workers would not handle Soviet-bound cargo. The United States also suspended a range of economic and cultural contacts with the Soviet Union. Formal contacts with Moscow by any U.S. official at or above the rank of assistant secretary could be made only with the personal approval of President Carter. The immediate results of this policy included:

• Suspension of plans for a U.S. consulate-general in Kiev and a Soviet consulate-general in New York City.

• A reduction in flights of Aeroflot, the Soviet airline, to the United States from three to two a week.

• Cancellation of a scheduled U.S.-Soviet conference on marine pollution control and on marine navigation systems.

• Deferral of negotiations to renew the U.S.-Soviet cultural exchange agreements that expired December 31.

When Ronald Reagan became president in 1981, he lifted the Soviet grain embargo imposed by Carter. Reagan had criticized the embargo as hurting American farmers more than the Soviets. Other restrictions imposed on the USSR because of the invasion gradually were eased or lifted during Reagan's first term. The Central Intelligence Agency began covert assistance to the mujahideen, working through Pakistan. The scope of the assistance grew rapidly and soon became the largest U.S. covert operation since the end of the Vietnam War. American aid to the guerrillas through 1988 totaled more than two billion dollars, with approximately six hundred million dollars more being given in 1989.

Saudi Arabia has roughly matched the American financial commitment to the Afghan rebels. Other Arab countries have taken a role in training and aiding the mujahideen. China "worked hand in glove with the United States" in supplying the rebels with weapons, according to State Department officials. Iran, surprisingly, provided only modest amounts of aid to the guerrillas.

raised fears in the West that the Soviet Union would make further political and military advances toward the Persian Gulf. Some also feared that the Soviets planned to use Afghanistan as a steppingstone to Pakistan, fulfilling the longtime Russian goal of gaining access to a warm-water port.

In his January 23, 1980, State of the Union address, President Carter lambasted the Soviets for their "radical and aggressive" invasion of Afghanistan. Enunciating what came to be known as the Carter Doctrine, he bluntly warned the Kremlin to stay out of the oil-producing nations along the Persian Gulf: "An attempt by any outside force to gain control of the Persian Gulf region will be regarded as an assault on the vital interests of the United States, and such an assault will be repelled by any means necessary, including military force."

On December 30, National Security Adviser Zbigniew Brzezinski stated that the Carter administration was prepared to respond with military force if Pakistan were invaded. Several days later, Carter asked Congress to lift a ban on arms sales to Pakistan, which it soon did.

Soviet Quagmire

Throughout the eighties, the Soviet Union became increasingly bogged down in Afghanistan, unable to secure a decisive victory, but unwilling to pull out. After Gorbachev came to power in 1985, Soviet attacks on the guerrillas increased in number and intensity. Nonetheless, despite the presence of an estimated 110,000 to 130,000 Soviet troops, the Afghan government was able to control only the country's largest cities.

The war also had an increasingly negative effect on Soviet society. In the beginning little media information was given to Soviet citizens beyond the official line that a "limited contingent" of soldiers was performing an "internationalist duty" after the Afghan government asked the Soviet Union to help defend it against attacks by imperialist forces. But as thousands of Soviet casualties returned from Afghanistan, the size of the conflict became more evident. More than a million Soviet troops ultimately served in Afghanistan. The State Department has estimated that about fifteen thousand Soviets were killed and another twenty thousand wounded. Returning soldiers, many disabled in the war, became a dissonant element in Soviet society, much like the American soldiers who returned from Vietnam unsure of why they had been sent to fight in the first place.

In 1986, the United States first supplied the mujahideen with Stinger missiles—hand-held anti-aircraft weapons. Before then, the guerrillas had no defense against Soviet planes attacking their bases. In March 1986, President Reagan approved delivery of Stinger missiles to the mujahideen, despite strenuous opposition from within his administration. The missiles had an immediate effect on the war. During the first two years of their use, they shot down 270 Soviet aircraft. This greatly increased the cost of the war to the Soviets and seriously hampered their ability to support their ground troops. Western analysts have cited the Stingers as playing an important role in the Soviet decision to withdraw from Afghanistan.

In 1986, Gorbachev first began to hint that he might be willing to withdraw Soviet forces, making his famous reference to the Afghan war as a "bleeding wound." Regardless of how Gorbachev dealt with the Afghanistan problem, there would be costs. A withdrawal would be a humiliating retreat that would leave the de-legitimized Afghan government seemingly doomed to overthrow by forces hostile to the Soviet Union. Continuing the war, however, appeared worse. The war had left the Soviet Union diplomatically isolated. China and the Islamic countries said that any improvement in relations hinged on a Soviet withdrawal from Afghanistan. While Soviet forces were still battling in Afghanistan, Gorbachev would find it difficult to fully implement his new thinking. Finally, the costs of the war, while not unbearable, constituted a drain on Soviet resources during a time when rebuilding the failing Soviet economy was the Kremlin's top priority. In 1987 Gorbachev began hinting diplomatically to the United States that he would be willing to negotiate a withdrawal of Soviet forces from Afghanistan.

Talks on the Afghan conflict in Geneva had been ongoing since 1982, conducted by the UN undersecretary for special political affairs, Diego Cordovez. The talks were between the governments of Pakistan and Afghanistan, although conducted indirectly through Cordovez, since Pakistan did not recognize the Afghan regime. The United States and Soviet Union, however, were closely involved.

The Geneva accords signed on April 14, 1988, committed the Soviet Union to withdraw all its troops by February 15, 1989. No mention was made of Soviet advisers and military aid. The United States adopted a policy of "symmetry" toward Soviet involvement in Afghanistan—continuing to supply the mujahideen at whatever level the Soviets choose to supply the Afghan government. Gorbachev initially rejected a mutual cut-off of aid and then later accepted it. But by this time, the United States had decided that a mutual cessation was no longer acceptable, saying the Afghan government had stockpiled massive amounts of Soviet weapons.

The Geneva accords were enacted as signed. The last Soviet troops left Afghanistan as scheduled, although not without repeated accusations from Moscow that Pakistan was violating the terms of the agreement.

Afghanistan after the Withdrawal

As the last Soviet troops were leaving Afghanistan, the United States and Pakistan pressured the fractured Afghan opposition to convene a shura (council) to form an interim government. Afghan political leaders in exile met in Rawalpindi, Pakistan, on February 10, 1989, but the government they produced was narrowly based and exacerbated the conflicts among the mujahideen. Iran pressed for representation at the shura for the smaller Afghan Shi'ite opposition groups based in Tehran, but Saudi Arabian influence ensured that only Saudi-endorsed candidates were selected. Supporters of King Zaher Shah also were refused representation, and the seats supposedly reserved for "good Moslems" from Kabul were left empty. Finally, according to Barnett Rubin, "the political leaders in exile hardly consulted the commanders [fighting in Afghanistan].... In essence, they were asking the commanders to fight in order to put them—the exiled leaders—in power in Kabul.... The entire shura was thus composed of delegates representing only the seven leaders of the Pakistan-based alliance."

A broad consensus was held among Western analysts that the Afghan regime of Najibullah (who had replaced Babrak Karmal in 1986) could survive for no more than a few months once the Soviets withdrew. The immediate collapse of the Afghan government, however, did not occur.

The mujahideen's feuds made coordination of their attacks difficult and occasionally led to fighting among themselves. The largest battle since the departure of the Soviets was the attack on Jalalabad. The interim government had hoped to capture a major city and establish itself on Afghan territory, but the mujahideen sustained heavy losses and proved unable to translate their success in conducting guerrilla warfare into the ability to capture a large city. For the first time, government morale grew, as it seemed that the Najibullah regime would be able to hold its own against the mujahideen.

In 1990 the war in Afghanistan continued to be a stalemate despite the departure of Soviet troops. Virtually none of the five million to six million refugees straining the resources of neighboring Pakistan and Iran have returned. The Soviet Union still maintains a presence in the country of several hundred advisers. Soviet aid is estimated to be continuing at the extremely high level of two hundred million dollars per month. American deliveries of aid to the mujahideen for 1989 were estimated at six hundred million dollars. The Soviets are trying to set up a "government of national reconciliation," but negotiations have been stalled by the resistance's demand that the ruling People's Democratic Party of Afghanistan (PDPA) not be allowed to participate.

Iran has been more willing to accommodate the Najibullah regime and the Soviets, because of the exclusion of its Shi'ite client groups from the interim government. Iran advocates a political solution that could include noncommunists in the current regime.

Meanwhile, the Najibullah government has begun a campaign to reach out to the resistance. Large parts of the countryside are controlled by local mujahideen who have established shuras. According to Rubin,

> These representative (although not democratic) bodies have the potential to serve as the basis of a new form of organization for the Afghan state. Najibullah has offered to recognize them as local authorities, permit them to keep their weapons (not that he has much choice in the matter), and provide them with aid, without even requiring them to recognize his authority formally. It is a testimony to the strength of the Islamic ideology and the hatred inspired by the PDPA's record of terror and subservience to the Soviet Union that so few have accepted his offers, even though they are more generous than anything the interim government has proposed to them.

Afghanistan, Pakistan, and India

The war in Afghanistan has greatly increased the geopolitical importance of Pakistan, and greatly complicated international relations in South Asia. Before the Soviet invasion, Pakistan was prohibited from receiving U.S. military aid because of its nuclear program. Since the invasion, Washington has signed a 3.2 billion dollar military and economic aid package and agreed to deliver sophisticated F-16 aircraft to Pakistan, to bolster its decision to act as a conduit for aid to the mujahideen.

These developments have made India very uncomfortable. Because of historical animosity and unresolved border disputes, India long has considered Pakistan to be the primary threat to its security. Consequently, it was concerned with Washington's decision to provide military aid to Pakistan. However, in arming Pakistan, the United States was reacting to a situation caused by the Soviet Union, a nation with whom India has had a long and fruitful relationship.

Despite the withdrawal of Soviet troops from Afghanistan in February 1989, the war between the Soviet-backed regime and mujahideen continues, driving refugees such as these to Pakistan.

Soviet-Indian ties go back to 1955, when Nikita Khrushchev and Jawaharlal Nehru exchanged visits and the Soviets provided India with a one hundred million dollar development loan. The two countries have shared similar views on many issues. Both have had border disputes with China and thus seek to limit Chinese influence in South Asia. Both also aim to keep the region free from superpower competition, which translates into keeping the United States out. India has been among the leading voices of the nonaligned movement. Thus, by close relations with India, the Soviet Union gains credibility as a supporter of this movement.

Within a month after the invasion of Afghanistan was launched, Soviet foreign minister Andrei Gromyko was sent to New Delhi to seek Indian approval of the action. India declined to endorse it but refrained from the loud condemnations seen elsewhere in the Third World. The Indians instead pressed Moscow for a timetable on withdrawals.

Indian apprehensions about the American arming of Pakistan were so great that it sought a rapprochement with China, despite Beijing's occasional support for Pakistan and a continuing Indian-Chinese border dispute. This move added to the isolation Moscow was experiencing as a result of the invasion, and no doubt contributed to the general pressure from all sides for a withdrawal.

USSR in the Middle East

Unlike the United States, which has been involved in the Middle East since the breakup of the Ottoman Empire at the end of World War I, the Soviet Union did not have a significant role in the region until the 1950s. Historically, to the extent that it was concerned with the Middle East, tsarist Russia had been most interested in the adjacent northern tier of countries, which includes Iran, Afghanistan, and Turkey.

In 1955, Egypt became the first Soviet client state in the region and the first Arab country to purchase Soviet-made arms. Since then, Moscow has taken an active interest in the Middle East. Despite Soviet influence over several client states, Moscow has remained an outsider in Middle Eastern affairs. Like the United States, the Soviet Union has had little success imposing its own views on Middle Eastern nations. But in contrast to the Soviet Union, the United States has remained a central figure in the continuing peace process between Israel and its neighbors. Through American efforts, the Soviet Union has been largely frozen out of this process. Nevertheless, most Middle East nations have not become clients of either the United States or the Soviet Union. American support of Israel has hindered U.S.-Arab relations, while many Mideast states harbor deep concerns about the ultimate goals of the Soviet Union in the region. The Soviet invasion of Afghanistan also did serious damage to Soviet credibility, which has yet to be fully repaired.

Origins of Soviet Involvement

In the 1940s the Soviet Union's policy in the Middle East was designed to weaken British influence, while expanding its own. Moscow welcomed the creation of Israel in 1948 from territory that had been a part of the British mandate. The Yeshuv, the Jewish settlement in Palestine, actively opposed the British mandate and seemed more likely than the Arabs to push out the British. Moreover, most of the Yeshuv leadership was socialist in orientation, which the Soviets hoped would make it inclined to cooperate with the Soviet Union. The Soviets also were a main source of arms for the Yeshuv during its fight for Israeli statehood.

With the rise of American involvement in the region, Soviet policy was directed toward U.S. influence instead. With their first weapons sale to Gamal Abdel Nasser of Egypt in 1955, the Soviets discovered that arms could be their key to the Arab world. The Soviet Union actively encouraged Egyptian opposition to the American-led Baghdad Pact signed that year and in general encouraged Arabs to resist American influence in the region. The Suez crisis in 1956 helped the Soviets to expand their foothold in the Middle East. In that year, Egypt seized the Suez Canal from European control. Britain, France, and Israel united in a military attack to regain the waterway. This gave the Soviet Union an opportunity to identify with Arab nationalists against the Western imperial powers.

Nevertheless, Soviet opportunities to gain influence were limited by several factors. Many Arab nationalists were unwilling to surrender their independence to the USSR. They also were not attracted to the atheistic ideology of communism. Most Arab nationalists were secular in their orientation, but they were not atheists. Moreover, they depended on the support of many Arabs who were devout Moslems. At times, Moscow found Communist parties in Arab countries attacked by regimes it supported. In Egypt, for example, Nasser considered the Communists a threat and clamped down vigorously, eventually banning them. Syria and Iraq also dealt severely with their domestic Communist parties.

The 1967 Six-Day War was a turning point for Soviet influence in the area. On June 5, 1967, Israel, provoked by the Egyptian blockade of a vital waterway—the strait of Tiran—attacked neighboring Arab countries, destroying much of the armed forces of Egypt, Syria, and Jordan and capturing large amounts of Arab territory.

The Soviet Union's prestige among the Arabs plummeted when it provided little actual aid and backed a cease-fire while Israel occupied Arab territories. The only significant measure that the Soviets took was to sever diplomatic ties with Israel, although they resisted Arab demands that the Soviet Union revoke its recognition of the Jewish state. Partially to atone for inaction during the war, the Soviet Union rebuilt the armed forces of Egypt, Syria, and Jordan. Militarily defeated and politically humiliated, Nasser moved closer to Moscow as a result of the conflict.

Sadat Takes Power in Egypt

President Nasser died suddenly on September 28, 1970, bringing Anwar Sadat to office, a relatively inexperienced man whose views on foreign affairs were unknown. Sadat, however, quickly moved to put his stamp on Egyptian foreign affairs and came into conflict with the Soviet Union while doing so. The Soviets did not want Sadat to go to war to regain the territories lost to Israel in 1967, and they would not sell him the offensive weapons that he believed he needed. To Sadat it seemed that the Soviet Union was more interested in promoting détente with the United States than in supporting Egyptian interests.

Sadat gradually concluded that Egyptian and Soviet goals were incompatible. His increasingly hostile statements reflected anger over the Soviet Union's lack of support in the conflict with Israel, despite its large presence in Egypt. Finally on July 18, 1972, Sadat ordered twenty thousand Soviet military advisers out of the country. Since Egypt was the primary Soviet client in the Middle East, Sadat's action severely damaged the Soviet Union's position in the region. The Soviet Union was forced to look elsewhere in the Arab world for clients.

Relations with Iraq, which had improved sufficiently to allow a treaty of friendship in 1972, continued to get better. The Soviets also courted Syria, although that country, unlike Iraq and Egypt, refused to sign a treaty of friendship. Nevertheless, Syria's President Hafez Assad obtained some of the Soviet military equipment he believed was necessary to counter Israel. In addition, Moscow's relations with the Palestinian groups began to warm, and Soviet arms for the first time went directly to the Palestine Liberation Organization (PLO) instead of through Arab governments.

The fourth Arab-Israeli war, in October 1973, diminished Soviet influence in the area. In joining with the United States to halt the war, the Soviet Union initially was part of the peacemaking process. The two superpowers presented a joint resolution to the UN Security Council calling for a cease-fire and implementing the 1967 Security Council Resolution 242, which required Israeli withdrawal from Arab lands occupied in the 1967 war. The United States and the Soviet Union also cosponsored a conference in Geneva in late 1973 to resolve the war issues. This marked the last time the Soviet Union was a direct participant in the Middle East peace process. The conference lasted two days, ended without success, and was never reconvened.

Secretary of State Henry A. Kissinger in early 1974 began a protracted effort in personal diplomacy, which came to be called "shuttle diplomacy" because of the many trips he made to Middle East nations. His effort largely excluded the Soviet Union from a role in the peacemaking process. Despite its close ties to Israel, the United States positioned itself as a mediator and improved its standing in the Arab world as a result. Because its diplomatic relations were never reestablished with Israel, the Soviet Union has been unable to play such a role, seriously limiting its policy options in the Middle East. It has had to content itself with building ties with the Arab "rejectionist" states and the PLO.

Camp David

In 1977, Sadat visited Jerusalem in a historic step toward a peace with Israel. Personal negotiations followed with Israeli leader Menachem Begin and President Jimmy Carter at Camp David, Maryland. The talks led to the Camp David accords, which established peace between the two countries and provided for Israel's return of lands captured from Egypt in 1967. Having been excluded from any role in the Middle East peacemaking process, the Soviets reacted negatively to the Camp David peace treaty. They accused Sadat of betraying the Arab—particularly the Palestinian—cause and of allying himself with the "reactionary" forces of Zionism and imperialism.

Although the Soviets were frustrated by their exclusion, they saw the American-engineered Egyptian-Israeli settlement as an opportunity to improve their own ties with Arab opponents of Camp David. There was, on the surface at least, greater amiability between Moscow and Syria, Iraq, Libya, and the other hard-liners. Contacts between the Soviet Union and Jordan expanded, and the Jordanian media began supporting a strong Soviet Middle East peacemaking role.

During the late seventies and early eighties the focus of Soviet efforts to be included in the peace process was a resumption of the Geneva Conference or the establishment of another international forum. Israel, however, strongly opposed Soviet participation in an international conference because the two nations had no relations. Moscow's harsh denunciation of the Camp David accords had angered Israel, and Israeli leaders were wary of the international pressure that such a conference might place on Israel to give up occupied territory.

Soviet Policy in the 1980s

In December 1979, the Soviets seriously damaged their standing in the Moslem world by invading Afghanistan. The Arabs resented the Soviets' use of modern weapons and more than a hundred thousand troops against their Moslem brethren. Moderate Arab governments saw the invasion as an indication of Moscow's willingness to use force in the Third World, a tool that could one day be directed against them. Saudi Arabia and Iran sent financial aid to the rebels, while other states helped to train them.

The Soviets also continued to have both ideological and practical problems with their Arab clients. The Libyans, for example, were a major benefactor of Soviet arms and received Soviet diplomatic support, but the two countries continued to differ on a number of issues. Libyan leader Muammar Qaddafi rejected the possibility of making peace with Israel, while the Soviets accepted the permanent existence of the Jewish state. On the practical side, Moscow regarded Libya's aggression against its neighbors in North Africa as undermining the Soviet position there. Soviet leaders also were hesitant to expand relations with Libya because Qaddafi's unpredictable behavior and rhetoric made him a potential target of Western enmity. After the April 1986 U.S. bombing of Libya, Moscow canceled a trip to Washington by the Soviet foreign minister but did little else to support Qaddafi.

The Soviets clashed with Syria over objectives for Lebanon. Both agreed that a pro-Western government in Lebanon friendly to Israel was undesirable, but their agreement ended there. The Syrians wanted to become the dominant power in Lebanon, while the Soviets were cool toward any moves that might lead to a Syrian-Israeli military clash as had occurred in 1982. The Kremlin also had little patience for the longstanding enmity between Syria's Assad and PLO chairman Yasir Arafat. It saw this feud as counterproductive to Soviet goals of diminishing Western influence in the region and to Arab goals of recovering lands lost to Israel in 1967.

The New Thinking in the Middle East

Under Gorbachev, Soviet diplomacy in the Middle East has been more creative and flexible than it had been under his predecessors. He has sought to broaden Soviet ties in the region instead of relying exclusively on hard-line Arab states such as Libya, Syria, and Iraq to promote Soviet interests. The Soviets have tried to improve relations with moderate Arab nations and Israel and have pushed their allies to be more conciliatory. According to Galia Golan, an expert on Soviet-Middle Eastern affairs at Hebrew University, the primary objective of limiting American political and military influence has not changed under Gorbachev. The difference is that now "both in the Gulf and in the Arab-Israeli conflict this policy now dictates a policy of conflict avoidance, possibly even of conflict resolution, to eliminate pretexts for American military engagement." In pursuit of this goal, Moscow reportedly pressured PLO leader Yasir Arafat in December 1988 to explicitly recognize Israel's right to exist and renounce terrorism. Since 1988 the Soviet Union also quietly has urged Syria to negotiate with Israel.

Gorbachev's efforts to improve relations with moderate Arab countries were aided by his withdrawal of Soviet forces from Afghanistan. As it became clear in 1987 and 1988 that the Soviets would withdraw, Arab attitudes softened noticeably toward Moscow.

The Soviet Union's acceptance of Kuwait's 1987 request for help in escorting its tankers through the Persian Gulf prompted the U.S. move to provide similar protection against Iranian harassment. Earlier, in October 1985, two other Gulf states, Oman and the United Arab Emirates, had established diplomatic relations with the Soviet Union. Nevertheless, conservative Saudi Arabia still is hesitant to expand relations with the Soviet Union. Atheistic communism is antithetical to its religiously based monarchy, and any revolutionary ideology represents a threat to the traditional Saudi political structure.

In December 1987, King Hussein of Jordan visited Moscow for the first time since 1981. His frustration at the refusal of the U.S. Congress to sanction arms sales to Jordan during the mid-eighties led him to seek Soviet weapons to supplement those Jordan bought from Great Britain.

When the Palestine National Council declared an independent state of Palestine on November 15, 1988, the Soviets recognized it quickly, reaffirming their support for the Palestinian cause. Western observers believe that the Soviets saw the declaration as a new impetus to the convening of an international conference on the Middle East. Nevertheless, into 1990 such a conference remained blocked by Israeli opposition.

Improved Relations with Israel

While working to improve ties with Arab nations, Gorbachev moved to establish a dialogue with Israel that had the potential to lead to a normalization of relations. In August 1986, Soviet and Israeli diplomats met in Helsinki to discuss the establishment of consulates. A month later, Soviet foreign minister Shevardnadze met with Israeli prime minister Shimon Peres at the United Nations. The meetings were the first official contact between the two nations since Moscow broke relations after the 1967 Six-Day War. As a result of these discussions, a Soviet consular delegation set up shop in Israel in July 1987 to look after Soviet property in Israel. Also, regular consultations now are conducted between the two countries.

In April 1987, Gorbachev impressed the Israelis by announcing in the presence of Syria's President Hafez Assad that Soviet lack of relations with Israel was not normal. Since then, there have been many other Soviet-Israeli gestures of good will.

Foremost among these has been Moscow's loosening of controls on Jewish emigration. The Kremlin allowed 71,196 Jews to emigrate in 1989. This figure compares with the 914 Jews who were allowed to emigrate in 1986 and eclipses the previous high of 51,320 in 1979. During the first five months of 1990, Jewish emigration was averaging more than 7,500 per month. Israel's encouragement of new immigration and the sharp limits on the number of Soviet immigrants allowed into the United States have combined to influence many Soviet Jewish emigrants to settle in Israel. Observers have estimated that as many as 750,000 Soviet Jews could settle in Israel by the mid-1990s. *(Jewish emigration, graph, p. 177)*

To facilitate the flow of emigration, Aeroflot signed an agreement with Israel in December 1989 to begin direct

Jewish Emigration from the USSR

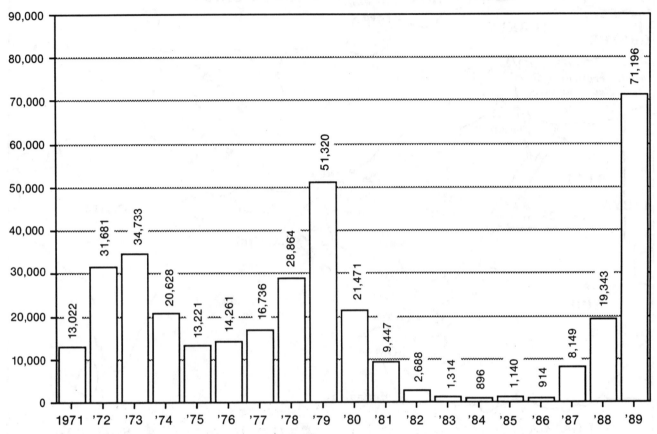

Source: Soviet Jewry Research Bureau/National Conference on Soviet Jewry

flights from Moscow to Tel Aviv. Previously, Soviet Jews wishing to go to Israel first had to fly to a third country. However, the Soviets canceled the flights at the last moment because of intense Arab pressure. Moderate Arab governments had denounced the Soviet decision to allow emigration directly to Israel, fearing that the new immigrants would be settled by the Israeli government in the occupied territories. Blocking the direct flights soothed Soviet-Arab relations by complicating emigration to Israel, while still fulfilling the American demand for free Jewish emigration.

Many observers have speculated that the two nations will reestablish relations in the near future. Soviet spokesmen have said that Gorbachev regards the breaking of ties with Israel as a mistake. In July 1989, a Kuwaiti newspaper quoted Deputy Foreign Minster Gennadii Tarassov as saying "A time will come when normal relations are restored [with Israel]." Nevertheless, the two nations appear to be at an impasse: Israel has demanded that the Soviet Union reestablish ties before it will agree to Soviet participation in a Middle East peace conference, while Moscow insists that it will not restore relations until Israel agrees to such a conference.

Shevardnadze Tour

In February 1989 Foreign Minister Shevardnadze traveled throughout the Middle East to try to establish a role

for the Soviet Union in the Middle East peace process. The visit came as the new Bush administration still was putting together its foreign policy team and developing foreign policy strategies. The visit appeared designed to express the Soviets' desire to expand their role in Middle East peacemaking and their willingness to step into the temporary vacuum created by the Bush administration's slow start. The visit also appeared timed to take advantage of recently improved Arab perceptions of the Soviet Union brought on by the completion of the Soviet withdrawal from Afghanistan earlier in the month.

Shevardnadze met with Egypt's President Hosni Mubarak, Syria's President Assad, Jordan's King Hussein, the PLO's Chairman Arafat, Israel's Foreign Minister Moshe Arens, and Iran's leader Ayatollah Khomeini. Shevardnadze became the first high-level Soviet official to visit Cairo since Anwar Sadat expelled Soviet advisers from Egypt in 1972. Shevardnadze also reportedly tried to heal the rift between the Soviet Union's Syrian and PLO allies that had complicated its peacemaking role.

The Persian Gulf

In 1979, the U.S.-backed government of the shah of Iran was overthrown by a fundamentalist Islamic revolution led by the Ayatollah Khomeini, and the Islamic Republic of Iran was established. Anti-American and anti-Western sentiments in Iran were running high, creating

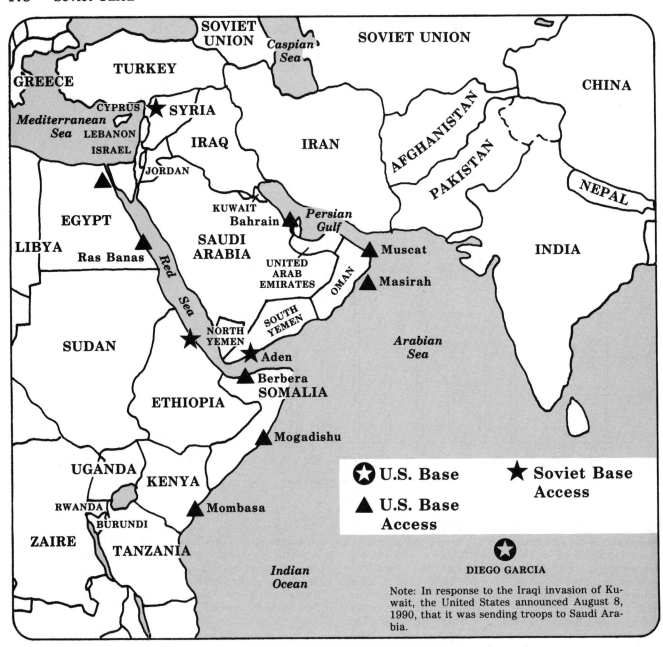

U.S. Base
U.S. Base Access
Soviet Base Access

DIEGO GARCIA

Note: In response to the Iraqi invasion of Kuwait, the United States announced August 8, 1990, that it was sending troops to Saudi Arabia.

opportunities for the Soviets to gain influence. However, the outbreak in 1980 of the Iran-Iraq war created a dilemma for the Soviet Union. Iraq and the Soviet Union had signed a Treaty of Friendship and Cooperation in 1972. The Soviets could not improve relations with Iran without harming relations with Iraq. Although it was officially neutral, the Soviet Union began showing a definite Iranian tilt in its foreign policy.

Iran borders the Soviet Union and physically separates it from the Gulf. In the eyes of the Soviets, Iran is the real strategic prize in the region. The Soviet Union cut off arms sales to Iraq, while at the same time offering Iran major weapons systems and other forms of assistance. The Iranians rejected the Soviet offer, but Soviet arms and military supplies were provided indirectly by Libya, Syria, and Eastern European states. Despite rebuffs, the Soviets continued to woo the Iranians in numerous ways. They

pledged military, technical, and economic assistance. They offered to help the new regime deal with internal security threats. And they blocked UN sanctions against Iran during the American hostage crisis in Tehran. Despite these efforts, the Soviets made little headway with the Iranians.

Following the Iranian offensives into Iraqi territory in 1982, the Soviets concluded new arms agreements with the Iraqis. According to Dennis Ross, executive director of the Berkeley-Stanford Program on Soviet International Behavior, this change in policy came for a variety of reasons. First, the Soviets had been rejected by the Iranians and were frustrated by Iranian hostility. Second, it was not necessarily in the Soviet Union's best interests to further the tide of Islamic fundamentalism and the image of an invincible Iran. The threat of a row of Iran-dominated Shi'ite states bordering the Soviet Union's heavily Moslem regions must have affected the Soviet outlook. Third, the defeat of Iraq, which depended on Soviet weapons, would have embarrassed the Soviets. Additionally, the Soviets seemed to believe that until Khomeini died little chance existed to increase significantly their influence in Iran. They also seemed aware that a decisive victory by either side would not serve Soviet interests. Both Iran and Iraq had demonstrated that they were not very receptive to Soviet overtures, and a significant strengthening of either nation's position would not create an opening for Moscow.

Despite improved relations with the Iraqis, the Soviets probably wanted to see the war end in some sort of political compromise at the earliest date possible. The continuation of the war hurt the Soviet Union in several ways. The war increased the influence of moderate anti-Soviet Arab nations in the region, such as Saudi Arabia. And Syria, a Soviet ally and longtime rival of Iraq, was alienated because of Moscow's support for Iran. Finally, the war reduced some of the Arab states' reluctance to allow an American military presence in the region.

Since the end of hostilities in the Gulf war, Iranian support for the mujahideen in Afghanistan has been a contentious issue in Soviet-Iranian relations. In addition to the seven Sunni groups based in Pakistan, eight Shi'ite mujahideen groups are based in Iran. These Shi'ite groups are ideologically very close to Iran and would like to see an Iranian-style Islamic state established in Afghanistan.

Nationalist and religious upheaval in Soviet Azerbaidzhan also has created a potentially explosive issue for Soviet-Iranian relations. However, Iran has in recent years made little effort to export its revolution, declaring that Soviet Azerbaidzhani demands for autonomy are an internal Soviet matter. Iran has its own population of Azerbaidzhanis and appears hesitant to do anything that would encourage a renewal of calls for an independent Azerbaidzhan, carved out of both Soviet and Iranian territory.

USSR in Africa

Soviet involvement in Africa dates from the fifties, when Moscow first became an actor in the Third World. The Soviet Union's interest in Africa was motivated mainly by the Kremlin's desire to expand its international influence. The Soviets never have considered any part of Africa to be a vital interest. Many African leaders have skillfully played off both superpowers to maximize the potential for aid, while avoiding, as far as possible, joining either camp. The Soviets have most often offered military aid, primarily because it could not match the West's ability to provide economic support. Soviet involvement in Africa has been opportunistic. The Soviets have moved in when power vacuums appeared, for example, when the Portuguese empire in southern Africa broke up in the 1970s.

The East-West competition in Africa largely has been a contest to provide aid. Few African regimes are strongly pro-East or pro-West. Most are simply nationalist. More than a few have switched sides when they felt that their interests were not being adequately addressed by their patron.

In general, the Soviets have provided aid to governments and movements that claimed to be struggling against imperialism, even when they were not formally Marxist-Leninist. Communism has developed a sizeable popular following in only a handful of African countries.

Despite gains in the 1970s, Soviet influence in Africa has remained limited because of a number of factors. Many African countries are unstable, often with serious tribal rivalries and ongoing power struggles. This has restricted the possibilities for consolidating secure Soviet-oriented governments. Also, when a regime close to Moscow is overthrown, the new one often has shifted its allegiance away from the Soviets. Africans have been fearful of moving too close to the Soviet Union because the West could choke off its substantial packages of aid. Economic aid to Africa from the West dwarfs that which Moscow gives, even to its closest allies. Many countries also continue to retain close cultural and trade ties with the colonial power that formerly dominated their country. Finally, Marxism-Leninism has been overshadowed by African nationalism and has not gained wide popularity in Africa.

The Soviet role in Africa cannot be assessed fully without taking into account the role of Cuba. Since the 1970s, Cuba has become deeply involved in African affairs, working hand in hand with the Soviet Union, and often with East Germany. Even in the conflicts where the Soviet Union was considered to be most deeply involved (such as Angola and Ethiopia), it was the Cubans who provided the ground troops, while the Soviets paid the bills and provided advisers and technicians. Since the mid-1970s, Cuba has provided troops, military advisers, and technical personnel to seventeen African countries and three insurgencies.

The new thinking has had an effect in Africa much as it has elsewhere. The new focus of policy in the region is on resolving conflicts through cooperation and avoiding dangers to the wider peace. Soviet clients in Africa are feeling the new pressure both diplomatically and financially, and they have accordingly exhibited a new flexibility in resolving their problems. Discussing the situation in Angola, one Soviet commentator wrote in *Pravda*:

> The world has become so fragile and dependent that playing with fire in any one part of it threatens great disaster. The necessary components of the de-ideologization of foreign policy—the categorical demand of our era—are not only to stop sending armies to other countries but to stop inflaming conflicts indirectly—by sending weapons, advisors, and money.

Southern Africa

The Soviet Union first became involved in southern Africa with the collapse of the Portuguese empire in Angola in 1975. Early in that year, an independence agreement was signed between Portugal and Angola, scheduling elections for October. Before the elections could be held, however, civil war broke out between Angola's three main factions. The MPLA (Popular Movement for the Liberation of Angola) was a European-oriented, Marxist-Leninist group that placed the goal of national liberation above traditional tribal loyalties. It was based in central and western Angola. The MPLA received early support from Cuba, some Western European governments, and Algeria. Holden Roberto's FNLA (National Front for the Liberation of Angola) based its power largely on tribal allegiances in the north. Roberto, related to the U.S.-backed president of neighboring Zaire, relied heavily on Zairian military support. Jonas Savimbi had been a member of the FNLA until 1963, when he split over tribal questions and organized UNITA (National Union for the Total Independence of Angola).

Shortly after the independence accord was reached, the Ford administration authorized the CIA to provide both Savimbi and Roberto armaments to hold off the MPLA until the October elections. The Soviet Union resumed its military assistance to the MPLA, which it had cut off two years before. Cuba sent a first contingent of 230 military advisers, which ultimately grew to about fifty thousand troops.

By July 1975, the MPLA had repelled both the FNLA and UNITA. It declared the People's Republic of Angola in November. The FNLA dissolved, but UNITA set up a rival government in the south. Also in July the Ford administration asked Congress for an additional twenty-eight million dollars in covert CIA funding for UNITA. News of the request leaked to the press, prompting critics to warn against U.S. involvement in a distant conflict that could turn out to be another Vietnam War. With that Southeast Asian defeat still fresh in mind, Congress banned all further American assistance for Angola, although the ban was lifted in 1986. Since then, according to Raymond Garthoff, a specialist on Soviet foreign affairs, the policy of the Angolan government has been "general political alignment with the Soviet Union . . . but has included encouragement for diplomatic and trade ties with the West." For example, Gulf Oil Company operates the offshore oil fields that provide Angola's chief source of foreign exchange.

Despite the presence of tens of thousands of Cuban troops, the MPLA was unable to dislodge Savimbi, who received substantial South African financial and military support. In addition, the South African Defense Forces stationed across the border in Namibia supported Savimbi with occasional attacks against the MPLA.

Namibia was a territory controlled by South Africa, bordering Angola, and generally considered to be the last colony in Africa. The Angolan government allowed SWAPO (Southwest African People's Organization) guerrillas to stage raids on Namibia from Angolan territory to pressure South Africa into permitting Namibian independence. South Africa supported Savimbi in an effort to limit raids by SWAPO guerrillas and to pressure the Angolan government to end its support for SWAPO.

By the mid-1980s, the situation was at a stalemate. Negotiations had been conducted on and off since 1981, mediated by Chester Crocker, the U.S. assistant secretary for African affairs. In December 1988, an agreement was reached among Angola, Cuba, and South Africa. It reflected several new political realities. Primary among these was the new thinking in Moscow, and the resulting Soviet pressure on Havana and Luanda. The conflict also was becoming costly for the Soviet Union. Soviet arms deliveries to Angola were estimated to average about one billion dollars annually during most of the 1980s. Additionally, South Africa was displaying more flexibility to improve its image abroad and to strengthen its poor relations with its neighbors. The agreement provided for a withdrawal of all South African forces from Angola and Namibia and independence for Namibia. It also stipulated that a phased withdrawal would take place of Cuban troops and Soviet advisers from Angola, and South Africa would end its military support for UNITA. The accord was implemented as signed. Cuban troops have been withdrawing on schedule, and Namibia became independent on March 21, 1990.

The fighting between the Angolan government and UNITA, however, has continued unabated. The cease-fire agreed to in June 1989 broke down within days. Both sides believed that without outside support the other would be fatally weakened, and that a quick offensive could bring quick victory. Both sides were wrong. The superpowers talk about having established peace in the region, but the conflict merely has been indigenized.

Angola was not the only country from the Portuguese empire in which the Soviets sought influence. Although Moscow had little to do with the rise to power of the leftist Front for the Liberation of Mozambique (FRELIMO), the regime was strengthened by Soviet support and Cuban troops in fighting a war against antigovernment RENAMO (Mozambique National Resistance) guerrillas supported by South Africa. The Soviet Union signed a friendship treaty with the new government of Mozambique in March 1977. However, Soviet backing for FRELIMO was limited. The Soviets warned that they would not support Mozambique in any direct confrontation with South Africa. The Soviets also failed to provide significant economic aid to Mozambique.

Beginning in 1989, the South African government has cut its aid to RENAMO and has encouraged a settlement in the Mozambique conflict. The FRELIMO government has begun to relax its hard-line Marxist economic policies and has changed its constitution to allow for open presidential and national assembly elections. It also has improved relations with the United States and the West as it has reduced its reliance on the Socialist bloc.

The Horn of Africa

The Soviet Union first became involved in Ethiopia when Ethiopian leader Haile Mengistu Mariam flew to Moscow in May 1977 to sign a deal for arms needed in his war with Somalia. The Soviets already had close ties to Somalia, which gave them access to Somalian Red Sea ports. Soviet leaders, however, regarded Ethiopia as a larger prize, with two deep water ports on the Red Sea. They were willing to risk angering Somalia to establish close relations with Ethiopia. Within months, large numbers of Soviet weapons and Cuban troops were arriving in Ethiopia. In response, Somalia expelled all Cuban and Soviet advisers, abrogated its 1974 friendship treaty with the Soviet Union, and sought aid from the United States. But by March 1978, the war had been won by Ethiopia.

Under Soviet pressure, Mengistu established the WPE (Working Party of Ethiopia) in 1984 as a Marxist-Leninist vanguard party to rule the country. Many Western scholars have questioned the depth of Mengistu's commitment to Marxism-Leninism and note that the party lacks a popular base and bears many characteristics of a military regime.

In recent years the combination of Mengistu's policies and the ongoing civil war with nationalists in Eritrea and Tigre (two Ethiopian provinces) have led Ethiopia to economic disaster. Mengistu has followed a line of doctrinaire Marxism-Leninism, collectivizing his country's faltering agriculture while famine threatens. The bulk of Ethiopian resources have been poured into the military, leaving little for economic development or social services. These policies contributed to the creation of severe famines that swept Ethiopia in 1984-1985 and again in 1990. Additionally, the beleaguered and demoralized Ethiopian army has suffered a number of serious setbacks. At the start of 1990, it controlled only a few cities in Eritrea and had been pushed completely out of Tigre.

In September 1989, the Ethiopian government held talks with the Eritreans, mediated by former U.S. president Jimmy Carter. Considered a major step, these were the first publicly announced talks in almost three decades of fighting. Mengistu's new flexibility was inspired in part by pressure from the Soviet Union. Not coincidentally, it also was announced in 1989 that the last of the Cuban troops were pulling out of Ethiopia. Their numbers had gradually been diminishing from about eleven thousand in 1984.

In March 1990, Mengistu announced that the tight controls on the Ethiopian economy were being relaxed. Small private ownership of businesses and land would be permitted, and trade would be expanded. Despite the Soviet pressure on Ethiopia to pragmatically address its problems, the Soviet Union does not appear to be abandoning its ally. In 1989, Moscow supplied eight hundred million dollars in military equipment—a significant increase from 1988.

Latin America

Soviet involvement in Latin America and the Caribbean was virtually nonexistent before the Cuban revolution in 1959. Since then Moscow has attempted to increase its influence in the region through military and economic aid and commercial relations. Nevertheless, Soviet leaders have been cautious in their approach to Latin America, partly because they recognize that the United States considers the area to be a vital interest.

Anti-American sentiments in Latin American nations aided the USSR's efforts in the Western Hemisphere. The United States traditionally supported governments that allowed American businesses to operate profitably in their countries. Many of those governments, however, did not extend the benefits of U.S. investment and trade to the majority of their people. The governments' frequent abuse of human rights and failure to reduce unequal distribution of wealth made these nations ripe for revolution.

In his book *Soviet Strategy in Latin America*, Robert Leiken wrote that U.S. backing of these regimes "lent socialism prestige and cast Cuba and the Soviet Union in a favorable light. . . . U.S. backing of oppressive regimes in the Third World persuaded many Latin Americans that the United States was the enemy of self-determination and the Soviet Union their natural ally." Soviet leaders have tried to develop this image as the superpower on the side of oppressed peoples.

Soviet involvement in the Western Hemisphere also is rooted in superpower rivalry. Both nations realize the strategic value to the Soviet Union of access to land in the region. For the United States, the region is both economically and strategically vital. Nearly two-thirds of U.S. trade, movement of U.S. oil and strategic minerals, and shipment of NATO defense supplies to Europe depend on uninhibited use of Caribbean sea lanes by commercial and naval vessels. Nevertheless, the Soviet Union has remained cautious in the Western Hemisphere because of fear of conflict with the United States and because of the region's geographic distance from the USSR.

Soviet Policy toward Cuba

The Soviet Union was slow to respond to the Cuban revolution. The Soviet press hailed the 1959 revolution as a blow to "Yankee imperialism" but denied that it was a victory for communism. Moscow publicly did not recognize

Cuba as socialist until April 1962. The Soviets were wary of a repetition of the 1954 U.S. overthrow of the regime of Jocobo Arbenz in Guatemala. In that affair, a leftist regime came to power through free elections but was overthrown soon after by a CIA-engineered coup.

Despite Moscow's restrained rhetoric on Cuba, the Soviet Union, beginning in 1960, provided substantial economic aid to Havana and directed all Latin American Communists to support the Cuban revolution as their first priority. At the same time, the speed of the Cuban revolution alarmed the Soviets. Fidel Castro nationalized private businesses throughout the country and began calling for armed struggle everywhere in Latin America. The Soviet Union did not endorse this aggressive approach, advocating instead that Latin American nations take the "peaceful road to socialism"—a course adopted by the Twentieth Soviet Party Congress in February 1956. Moscow discouraged Latin American Communist parties from joining guerrilla movements and encouraged them to back broad electoral fronts. Meanwhile the Soviets sought diplomatic and commercial relations with established governments.

Moscow tolerated Cuba's lack of discipline because the addition of a new member to the Socialist bloc was a testament to the dynamism of the Soviet Union and to Khrushchev's leadership. The Cuban revolution reaffirmed the success of Marxism-Leninism and was central to the spread of Soviet influence into the traditionally U.S.-dominated Western Hemisphere. Cuba also could be used as a base for forward deployment of Soviet medium-range missiles that would offset the large American lead in long-range missiles. Soviet efforts to use Cuba as a missile base led to the Cuban missile crisis in 1962. *(Cuban missile crisis, p. 55)*

The Soviets saw the Cuban revolution as a model for Latin America, although they played down Castro's call for continentwide armed struggle, fearing to alienate the non-Marxist Latin American governments that still were sympathetic to Cuba. Cuba also became an instrument for carrying out Soviet foreign policy. During the 1970s, Cuban aid and Cuban "soldier-internationalists" began to support insurgencies and leftist governments in Latin America and Africa. Castro became the point man for Soviet efforts to dominate the Non-Aligned Movement (NAM). Castro's offer to send troops to fight Israel during the 1973 Arab-Israeli War and his implacable hostility toward South Africa and the Portuguese empire bolstered the Cuban leader's reputation among Arab, African, and socialist states. This enabled him to play a key role in the NAM and secure greater support for the USSR in the UN General Assembly and other international forums. Castro's role as a leader of the NAM and his willingness to use Cuban troops to support Soviet foreign policy goals in the Third World made Cuba one of the USSR's most important allies. As a result Castro received concessions from the USSR not granted to other socialist countries.

During the 1970s Soviet aid to Cuba was between four billion dollars and six billion dollars annually, which was about 20-30 percent of the entire Cuban GNP. This aid was primarily in the form of oil—sold to Cuba significantly below world prices and which Cuba then resold—and Soviet purchases of Cuban sugar at prices several times greater than its value on the world market.

However, Cuba's importance for the Soviet Union has declined with Gorbachev's new focus on resolving conflicts, and not on expanding Soviet international influence. Instead of seeing Cuba as a force for altering the correlation of forces, Moscow now sees Castro as the "culprit" behind Brezhnev's disastrous Third World adventures.

The Soviet Union and Cuba have been following increasingly disparate paths since 1985. Moscow has tried to integrate itself into the rest of the world and "to adopt international norms." Cuba, meanwhile, continues to challenge the world order. For example, Cuba has called for all Latin American debtors to unilaterally renounce their debt obligations—an action that would threaten the world banking system. The Soviet Union, seeking membership in the International Monetary Fund, has called only for a moratorium on interest payments. Castro also has expressed alarm about the deepening détente between the superpowers, fearing that Cuba will be abandoned by Moscow economically and militarily.

Cuba has become increasingly critical of perestroika. When Gorbachev visited Cuba in 1989, Castro declared in his presence that "If a socialist country wants to build capitalism, we must respect their right." Like ousted East German leader Erich Honecker, Castro does not feel that perestroika has anything to offer his country.

During 1989 and early 1990, while communist governments around the world were making concessions or giving up power, Castro tightened his Stalinist system of rule. As a result, he found himself increasingly isolated. His closest allies, the Nicaraguan Sandinistas, accepted their defeat at the ballot box in February 1990. Cuban troops have left Ethiopia and are scheduled to leave Angola. Massive Soviet support no longer is assured.

Moreover, Gorbachev and Castro have not gotten along well personally. Castro has been attacked on occasion in the Soviet press for his dictatorial policies. Perhaps most disconcerting for the Cubans, the Soviets no longer are willing to underwrite the Cuban economy at the same level they have been and have begun to trim their subsidies. In January 1990, Soviet ships carrying wheat to Cuba were delayed, and bread disappeared from the stores in Havana causing panic. The Soviets blamed the incident on a scheduling problem, but the delay may have been a deliberate warning to Castro to reduce his reliance on Soviet aid.

Officials in Moscow have hinted that Castro would be wise to seek an accommodation with the United States to end the American economic boycott of Cuba. But, as of 1990 Castro had not made any moves in that direction.

It is too early to write off Castro. He will continue to receive Soviet support despite the disagreements between the two countries. Cuba supports the largest Soviet military base outside of the Warsaw Pact. The base is also an irreplaceable listening post directed at the United States that will become even more important in an era of arms control verification. The Soviets would not give it up casually. Castro also probably will not go too far in displeasing the Soviets since he has nowhere else to turn.

Soviet Policy toward Nicaragua

When the Sandinistas came to power through a revolution against the dictator Anastasio Somoza in 1979, they quickly became Castro's closest ally in the hemisphere. Along with extensive aid from the Soviet Union and Eastern Europe, Cuban military backing (including advisers) helped Nicaragua build the largest army in Central America. But Nicaragua soon became embroiled in a protracted civil war with the contras, an American-backed guerrilla army, operating out of Honduras and Costa Rica. The contra opposition was a politically heterogeneous group composed of disillusioned Sandinistas, former members of Somoza's feared National Guard, and other Nicaraguans who had developed a grudge against the revolutionary government.

The Reagan administration made the overthrow of the Sandinista regime of Daniel Ortega a top priority. The United States declared a trade embargo against Nicaragua in the spring of 1985 and for most of the 1980s provided the contras with military aid, although Congress cut off or limited this aid during several intervals. Meanwhile, the Sandinistas seized every opportunity to attack the United States in international forums, welcomed Cuban military advisers, established closer political and economic relations with the Soviet Union, supplied arms to Marxist guerrillas in El Salvador, and rapidly established control over most institutions in Nicaraguan society.

Over the course of ten years, the contra war along with the American economic blockade ravished the Nicaraguan economy. At the end of 1989, inflation had reached 1,700 percent, with at least 25 percent unemployment. Living standards were estimated to have dropped by 90 percent under the Sandinistas.

Ortega promised to hold free and fair elections in 1990 as a means of getting the United States to cut off aid to the contras. Sandinista leaders hoped that once they had won a popular mandate, international pressure would force the United States to stop seeking the overthrow of a freely elected government. Nicaragua also would be brought out of its international isolation.

Gorbachev likely played a role in convincing the Sandinistas to hold genuinely free elections. The war in Nicaragua long had been a sore point in Soviet-American relations. An election that was internationally recognized as fair would eliminate the problem for the Soviets one way or the other. The Sandinistas allowed more than three thousand observers from the United Nations, the Organization of American States, and other international organizations into the country to monitor the elections. The observers, led by former U.S. president Jimmy Carter, agreed that except for minor violations, the campaign and election had been fair—the first such election in Nicaraguan history.

In a spectacular upset, Violeta Barrios de Chamorro of the United Nicaraguan Opposition defeated Ortega for the presidency on February 25, 1990, by a vote of 55 percent to 40 percent. Most analysts believe that the election result was less a vote for Chamorro, who is considered a figurehead for a fractious alliance of fourteen parties ranging from the far right to the far left, than a rejection of the Sandinistas. The once popular Sandinistas had alienated the population by their economic mismanagement and constant efforts to dominate every aspect of society.

The Sandinista defeat changed the political landscape of Central America. Ortega admitted that he had been defeated and handed over the presidency to Chamorro on April 25 in accordance with the law. The Sandinistas, however, remained the largest party in Nicaragua. Within weeks of the transfer of power, the United States lifted its economic embargo of Nicaragua, and Congress appropriated three hundred million dollars in aid for it.

Contrary to the demands of the more conservative members of her coalition, Chamorro retained Humberto Ortega (the brother of Daniel Ortega) as the head of the army. This move caused some of the more conservative parties in her fragile coalition in the assembly to express their reservations about her government. Many contras vowed that they would not put down their arms while

Ortega headed the army. The Bush administration also expressed its concern over continued Sandinista control of the military.

Other observers lauded the move as a brilliant political maneuver that would aid national reconciliation. They pointed out that Chamorro would need firm control of the military while reducing Sandinista influence over other areas of society and while disbanding the far more threatening security police controlled by Tomas Borge.

In negotiations with the new government, the contras had first agreed to move from their camps in Honduras to zones supervised by UN troops inside Nicaragua, where they would be disarmed by June 11. After the announcement that Ortega would continue to head the armed forces, many contras began returning to their camps in Honduras. However, under heavy American pressure and with promises of free land in Nicaragua, the remainder of the contras grudgingly disarmed by mid-June, only a few weeks behind schedule.

As she had promised in her campaign, Chamorro ended conscription and reduced the size of the armed forces. By late July 1990, she had reduced the eighty thousand-troop military by half. This cut freed up funds for development and other pressing needs.

Exactly how much material support the Sandinistas provided for the other leftist movements in Central America, particularly the FMLN (Farabundo Marti National Liberation Front) in El Salvador, remains undetermined. But the Sandinista loss was a huge setback for them. The FMLN has shown impressive resilience and has had some success fighting against the government of El Salvador. However, many observers now believe that continuing the war without the Sandinistas will be difficult. The FMLN has shown more flexibility since the Nicaraguan elections, calling for a cease-fire and negotiations with the government.

Soviet Military

Throughout Soviet history, military power has been one of the most important instruments of foreign policy. The Bolsheviks used the newly created Red Army to defeat the White forces that challenged the revolution between 1918 and 1920. After the civil war, the Red Army consolidated the Communist regime's hold over non-Russian regions of the tsarist empire. During World War II the Soviet military fought a desperate battle to defend the motherland from the Nazi invasion, then pushed the Germans back to Berlin. In the process, the Soviet military established control over the nations of Eastern Europe.

Military modernization efforts focusing on the construction of a huge nuclear arsenal began in the 1950s and expanded in the 1960s and 1970s. Soviet military might allowed the Kremlin to increase significantly the use of the armed forces for diplomatic purposes. The Soviet military was called upon to preserve and expand the Kremlin's authority in Eastern Europe and in Afghanistan, for example, as well as to influence other communist regimes and counteractions by the West and China. In *Diplomacy of Power*, Stephen S. Kaplan wrote:

> The Soviet nuclear arsenal, which affords the USSR superpower status, is the principal foundation of the Soviet Union's international position. Without nuclear armaments, Moscow could not orchestrate conventional armed forces with confidence, and Moscow's diplomacy would not be taken as seriously as it is by the United States, China, Western Europe, Japan and other nations.

By the late 1960s the Soviets had achieved rough strategic nuclear parity with the United States. Their headlong rush to reach this status was accomplished by devoting vast amounts of resources to defense, usually at the expense of domestic needs. The capabilities of the other components of the Soviet military also improved. Naval forces, in particular, came to symbolize the USSR's new ability to project power throughout the world.

In the late 1970s, however, the Soviet military began to downgrade the importance of nuclear weapons and consider the option of a protracted conventional war. Many Soviet military leaders considered the limited use of nuclear weapons to be an obsolete tactic, given their enormous destructive capabilities. At the same time, new technologies were improving the accuracy and range of conventional weapons. Advances in automated weaponry, command-and-control, reconnaissance, and radioelectronic

warfare were changing the manner in which warfare was conducted. Since these innovations increased the pace of battle, the modern military had to be able to respond more quickly and employ more flexible war-fighting techniques. This led to radical changes in Soviet military doctrine and a new emphasis on conventional warfare.

The North Atlantic Treaty Organization (NATO) allies recognized these same trends and began adopting their strategy to incorporate the latest advances in weapons technology. NATO's rapid military buildup in the early and mid-eighties and its ability to develop and deploy advanced weapons caused great concern among Soviet military and civilian leaders. As a nation, the Soviet Union was increasingly unable to respond to this technological revolution and was falling behind in critical military technologies. The Soviets' reaction to the Strategic Defense Initiative (SDI), a U.S. space-based antiballistic missile program, exemplified their apprehension about the West's ability to outpace them in the area of military research and development. After President Ronald Reagan proposed SDI in March 1983, superpower arms control negotiations became stymied when the Soviets refused to negotiate on most arms control issues unless limits on SDI were included.

Many years of sacrificing consumer needs to build up the Soviet military had weakened the civilian economy and contributed to public dissatisfaction without eliminating the nuclear threat to the Soviet Union. Moreover, because the Soviet military buildup and Third World adventures were perceived as aggressive by the Western alliance, China, and many other nations, the Soviets found themselves confronted by an array of enemies and often isolated diplomatically and economically.

Mikhail S. Gorbachev, who was chosen general secretary of the Communist party in March 1985, became the leader of a nation in a severe economic crisis. His policy of *perestroika* has been adopted to restructure the failing economy so that it can meet the needs of both the civilian and military sectors. This restructuring has altered the role of the military in Soviet society. Once the recipient of the best personnel and resources, the Soviet military has lost its priority status. The military budget has been slashed, troop levels have been cut, and military industries have begun to convert to civilian production.

Other reforms initiated by Gorbachev also have affected the military. *Glasnost* (openness) has given Soviet citizens the opportunity to participate in elections and has ended most censorship in the Soviet press. As a result, the military no longer is exempt from public scrutiny and criticism. Meanwhile, Gorbachev's "new thinking" has de-emphasized military force in favor of diplomatic solutions. Like the shifting of resources away from defense production, this new emphasis on diplomacy has reduced the prestige and influence of the Soviet military.

Command Structure

Three bodies are at the top of the Soviet military command structure: the USSR Defense Council, the Defense Ministry Collegium, and the General Staff. These organizations constitute the Soviet High Command. Other important military leadership organizations include the command and staff of the Warsaw Pact forces and the Military-Industrial Commission (which is outside the Ministry of Defense).

In *Armed Forces of the USSR*, Harriet Fast Scott and William F. Scott noted that as a group these bodies, especially the Defense Council, have almost "complete control over the military-economic direction of the Soviet Union." Since the advent of Gorbachev's reforms, however, other government institutions, such as the Ministry of Foreign Affairs, the Presidential Council, and the Congress of People's Deputies, are acquiring significant influence in military affairs. The Presidential Council may have superseded the power of the Defense Council.

The High Command

The Soviet High Command is the group of the highest-ranking officers who direct military affairs. While the Communist party has had the final word on most military matters, these officers have substantial control over the daily affairs of the services. As the Scotts noted, the members of the Soviet High Command

> have proved themselves over the course of many years in positions of great responsibility.... Many of the senior members of the Soviet high command have been popularized as military leaders.... The top Soviet military leadership is much more visible than its counterpart in the United States.... [T]hey are closely integrated with the rest of the party, with those at the top wearing two hats: one, that of their military position, and the other, that of their membership on the Central Committee.

The High Command military offices include the minister of defense, the chief of the General Staff, the commander in chief of the Joint Armed Forces of the Warsaw Pact Nations, and several deputy ministers of defense (the commanders in chief of each of the five services and commanders of several supporting branches, such as rear services and armaments). The High Command also includes

Light snowfall has not discouraged these jubilant Soviet soldiers—among the last to leave Afghanistan—as they wave from atop their tanks on the Salang Highway, February 2, 1989.

the chief of the Main Political Administration of the Soviet Army and Navy, several commanders of important military districts (including Belorussia, Transbaikal, and Moscow), and a few other high-ranking deputy chiefs.

Defense Council

During the 1970s and 1980s the most important Soviet political-military organization was the USSR Defense Council. Its structure illustrates the interconnecting nature of political-military organization and decision making and the supremacy of the top civilian leadership in that process.

In peacetime the Defense Council operated as an elite subgroup of the Politburo. It determined the country's overall defense posture and ensured that the country was prepared for war; that is, it was responsible for strategic and military-economic planning. It examined programs to develop and procure new weapons systems and formulated plans to mobilize industry, transportation, and manpower. The Defense Council defined the missions of each of the five services and could create new military districts or change the entire structure of the armed forces.

The Defense Council was responsible for examining proposals from the Ministry of Defense Collegium and the General Staff for both military development and armed forces development. The council made judgments on those plans and issued decrees for the plans to be implemented. According to the Pentagon, in wartime the Defense Council "would function similarly to the World War II State Defense Committee, ensuring centralized political and economic direction of the entire war effort." The party's general secretary, like the president of the United States, acted as the commander in chief of the armed forces. His directives were to be channeled to the field commanders through the Stavka (headquarters) of the Supreme High Command.

Until recently, the composition of the Defense Council was unknown to the West. Its existence and responsibilities were gleaned piecemeal through arduous efforts at Kremlinology. However, during the July 1989 USSR Supreme Soviet confirmation hearings for Defense Minister Dmitrii Yazov, Gorbachev divulged both the membership of the Defense Council and its duties. In early 1990 the Defense Council consisted of the chairman (Mikhail Gorbachev), the defense minister (Dmitrii Yazov), the chairman of the Council of Ministers (Nikolai Ryzhkov), the foreign minister (Eduard Shevardnadze), officials who supervise the defense ministry, and principal members of the command staff of the armed forces (Aleksei Lizichev, Mikhail Moiseev, and the first deputy and deputy defense ministers).

According to Stephen Foye, of Radio Liberty Research, Gorbachev also revealed that the Defense Council under Leonid I. Brezhnev had failed to fulfill its responsibilities. During Brezhnev's tenure, the uniformed military, not the Defense Council, drafted military policy. At that time, Defense Council authority was concentrated in the hands of Brezhnev, who only accepted policy formulated primarily by military officers.

Under Gorbachev many of the duties of the Defense Council appear to have been shifted to the Presidential Council created by constitutional amendments passed in March 1990. This shift is in keeping with the general transfer of power under Gorbachev from party institutions to government institutions. The Presidential Council's pre-

cise functions and methods of operation regarding military policy are not known and as of mid-1990 probably still were developing. However, the constitutional amendments did state that the president is the commander in chief of the Soviet military.

Ministry of Defense Collegium

The highest body in the Ministry of Defense is the Collegium. The minister of defense chairs this advisory group. The defense minister has powers roughly comparable to those of the chairman of the U.S. Joint Chiefs of Staff and the secretary of defense combined. Other Collegium members include the four first deputy ministers of defense, the chief of the Main Political Administration of the Soviet Army and Navy (MPA), the five service commanders, and various other deputy ministers and branch chiefs.

Since a 1985 reorganization, the Collegium has acted purely as an administrative organ during peacetime. The Collegium is responsible for such tasks as logistics support, training, and manpower management. It also oversees and manages the development and acquisition of weapons and equipment.

According to the Pentagon, members of the Collegium probably will serve on the Stavka of the Supreme High Command. The Stavka will include—along with the president—the minister of defense, the chief of the General Staff and other first deputy defense ministers, the chief of the Main Political Directorate, and the service commanders. The Stavka is instituted in wartime to plan strategic operations and to oversee the wartime development of the armed forces. The General Staff would work with the main staffs of the other five services to provide operational plans for the approval of the Stavka. Upon orders from the Stavka, operational commanders would execute these battle plans.

General Staff

The General Staff is the largest body in the Soviet High Command. The Soviets have stated that in a future war the "General Staff will be the main agency of the Stavka of the Supreme High Command." The General Staff is immediately subordinate to the defense minister.

In the 1970s and 1980s the General Staff has been responsible for basic strategic planning. It determines roles for each of the services, probably in draft form sent to the Defense Council for approval. According to Soviet publications, one of the General Staff's major tasks is to ensure "the coordinated actions of the main staffs of the services." This includes the staffs of the rear services, civil defense, Ministry of Defense administrations, staffs of military districts, groups abroad, air defense districts, and naval fleets. Because of this coordination responsibility, the services and branches of the armed forces are subordinate to the Ministry of Defense through the General Staff.

Some compare the General Staff to the Pentagon's Joint Staff, but the General Staff's functions are much broader. The General Staff's activities encompass "the work of the entire Department of Defense in the Pentagon, some of the work of the National Security Council, plus a great many of the activities of the departments of the army, navy, and air force," according to the Scotts.

The General Staff has eleven directorates, according to experts Jeffrey Richelson and Viktor Suvarov: Operations,

Intelligence (GRU), Organization-Mobilization, Military Science, Communications, Topography, Armaments, Cryptography, Strategic Deception, Military Assistance (abroad), and Warsaw Pact. The three most important are Operations, Intelligence, and Organization-Mobilization. Although General Staff members come from different services, their promotions depend on work done on the staff and attention to party duties, not on how well they represent service interests.

Revelations in the Soviet press in 1989 indicate that the General Staff has resisted the implementation of Gorbachev's policies. Both former chief of the General Staff Akhromeev and Defense Minister Yazov have criticized the General Staff's reluctance to adopt the tenets of perestroika and new thinking to the armed forces. While serving as chief of the General Staff, Akhromeev even called for a reform of the General Staff.

Committee for Defense and State Security

Since 1989 the USSR Supreme Soviet has exercised a military oversight role. This developing responsibility was demonstrated when Dmitrii Yazov had to appear before the Supreme Soviet in July 1989 for confirmation of his reappointment to the post of defense minister. The Supreme Soviet's decision to confirm Yazov was not a rubber stamp of Gorbachev's decision to nominate him. The hearing was contentious, and, in the end, Yazov was approved only because a change in election rules that day allowed a nominee to be approved by a majority of delegates present rather than a majority of the entire Supreme Soviet (272 votes). The rule change allowed Yazov to be confirmed with only 256 votes.

In 1989, the Supreme Soviet announced the formation of commissions that would act as legislative supervisory organs over certain governmental institutions. The Committee for Defense and State Security will be responsible for monitoring the Committee for State Security (KGB) and the Soviet armed forces. Specifically, this Supreme Soviet commission will participate in discussions concerning the defense budget, the use of military force abroad, and other issues. Many civilian leaders in the Soviet Union believe military secrecy has had adverse effects on both Soviet domestic and foreign policy. This commission will oversee future military policy to ensure that it is not conducted in isolation. If the committee establishes itself as a serious institution, military policy will be more likely to conform to the principles of Soviet domestic and foreign policies.

Military Services

The Soviet military is organized unlike any other nation's. It has five services: the Strategic Rocket Forces (RVSN), the Ground Forces, the Troops of Air Defense, the Air Forces, and the Navy. The Ministry of Defense directly controls the troops of the five services. Each commander in chief of the five services is a deputy minister of defense. Special engineer, chemical, signal, and road troops provide support for each service. The Soviet armed forces also contain three units that are not part of any service— Construction and Billeting Troops, Troops of the *Tyl* (rear services), and Troops of Civil Defense. Each of these units is headed by a deputy minister of defense.

Until March 1989, the Border Troops under the KGB, Internal Troops under the Ministry of Internal Affairs (MVD), and Railroad Troops under the Ministry of Defense were part of the Soviet armed forces. At that time, a Presidium of the Supreme Soviet decree made them separate institutions.

Military Districts and Theaters of Operation

In peacetime, Soviet combat forces (other than the Strategic Rocket Forces and certain other air units) are deployed in fourteen military districts, four groups of forces abroad, and four fleets. Each district has its own commander, political administration, and units of various armed services (including ground, air, and air defense units). District commanders report to the General Staff. The districts are not controlled by any of the five services. The districts vary in importance and are maintained at different levels of combat readiness, depending on the threat they face. In wartime, they could operate independently if communications were severely disrupted. In peacetime, the district commander's responsibilities include training, registration and induction of draftees, civil defense, and mobilization.

The Soviets have devised large-scale theaters of war (TVs) that would bring together under a single commander the various services and independent units in a region to make the most effective use of all forces and weapons. The Soviets have established three major TVs: Western, Southern, and Far Eastern. According to the Pentagon, TVs are further broken into several theaters of military operations (TVDs): the Far East, Northwestern, Arctic, Atlantic, Western, Southwestern, and Southern. During wartime, the TVDs could be combined into the three major theaters of war. TVD high commanders, appointed by the Stavka of the Supreme High Command, will act as intermediaries between the Stavka leadership and the TVD operational commanders. On occasion, special High Commands will be created for important operations not already under the geographic jurisdiction of an existing High Command.

Strategic Rocket Forces

Since their creation in 1959, the Strategic Rocket Forces have been referred to by the Soviets as the "primary service." The RVSN commander in chief takes precedence over commanders of other services, and the RVSN personnel represent the elite of the services. These forces "are the youngest and most formidable service of the Armed Forces, and compose the basis of the defensive might of our Motherland and are troops of instant combat readiness," the Soviet *Officer's Handbook* reported. According to *Brassey's Military Balance, 1989-90*, the Strategic Rocket Forces have 287,000 active duty personnel.

The service's mission has never been clearly stated, but, according to a Soviet publication cited by the Scotts, the Strategic Rocket Forces are

> the basis of the defense might of the Soviet army and navy.... Strategic Rocket Forces are designated for performing strategic tasks in nuclear war. They are the main and decisive means of achieving the goals of war since they can solve in the shortest period of time the tasks of demolishing the military economic potential of an aggressor, of destroying his strategic means of nuclear missile attack, and of crushing the main [military] groupings.

Foreign Intelligence Role of the KGB

The Soviet Union's foreign intelligence gathering operations are executed primarily by the Committee for State Security (KGB). The General Staff's Chief Intelligence Directorate (GRU) also is involved in foreign intelligence gathering, focusing on military intelligence. This concentration of most foreign intelligence responsibilities in the KGB is different from the organization of the U.S. intelligence community, where a number of government agencies monitor events in foreign countries.

According to Amy Knight in *The KGB: Police and Politics in the Soviet Union*, the KGB's foreign activities include intelligence collection, espionage, counterintelligence, and sabotage. The KGB also is the primary agency for supplying the Kremlin with intelligence analyses.

Serving in the KGB is considered to be prestigious employment in the Soviet Union. No recruitment problems exist. Personnel receive high salaries, a military rank, and access to foreign currency. Most Soviets, however, regard the opportunity to live abroad as the most desirable benefit offered by KGB employment.

KGB officials involved in the foreign divisions have earned prominent roles in the upper echelons of Soviet leadership. Former KGB head and general secretary Yuri V. Andropov was a top KGB official in Hungary during the Soviet invasion in 1956. Viktor Chebrikov, the last KGB chief, and Vladimir Kryuchkov, the chief as of 1990, were both active in operations abroad.

The KGB is considered one of the chief institutional supporters of Mikhail S. Gorbachev and his reforms. Top KGB officials who have lived abroad have recognized the Soviet Union's increasing economic and technological backwardness. They have acknowledged that reforms are necessary if the USSR is to continue to influence world affairs.

The KGB is divided into five chief directorates, six other directorates, and six departments. These also are subdivided into smaller directorates, services, and departments. Intelligence collection, analysis, offensive counterintelligence, and espionage operations are the responsibility of the First Chief Directorate. Within the First Chief Directorate are three directorates and three services that are responsible for specific types of operations.

Directorate S, the "Illegals Department," trains and oversees agents who live in foreign countries. These agents have assumed fake identities. They collect general information such as bus schedules, street maps, building plans, and birth certificates. Directorate S also is responsible for planning and carrying out assassinations and sabotage.

Directorate T, or the Scientific and Technical Directorate, is the second largest division in the First Chief Directorate, according to John Barron in *KGB Today: The Hidden Hand*. Directorate T is responsible for the collection of scientific intelligence. When thefts of high technology occur, as in the Richard Mueller affair, Directorate T agents are involved. Richard Mueller, a West German, arranged illegal exports of computer equipment to the USSR. It is believed Mueller was involved in this activity from the early 1970s until his disappearance in 1983.

The primary responsibility of Directorate K is the penetration of foreign intelligence services, according to Jeffrey T. Richelson in *Sword and Shield: Soviet Intelligence and Security Apparatus*. This is usually done by recruiting employees of these foreign organizations. In addition, Directorate K monitors the activities of Soviet citizens abroad.

All the raw intelligence information gathered by these directorates is sent to Service I, the KGB's information service. It analyzes and disseminates all intelligence, although Knight asserts that Service I lacks the manpower to perform this function adequately. As a result, the KGB often overlooks important intelligence information in its possession.

All espionage operations are planned and overseen by Service A. Personnel in this division work closely with the International Department, the Defense Department, and other departments of the Central Committee Secretariat. According to Barron, Service A is one of the most important KGB divisions. Among other planning activities, it has developed propaganda campaigns designed to influence events in other countries. One of the most significant campaigns undertaken by this service was its effort to influence European public opinion against NATO's deployment of Pershing II missiles in Western Europe. The KGB was actively involved in distributing propaganda and inciting Western Europeans to rally against these nuclear missiles.

The last service that falls under the First Chief Directorate is Service R. Its mission is to monitor and analyze the performance of KGB operators and operations abroad. In general, Service R is responsible for improving the efficiency of KGB operations.

The operational core of the KGB, however, is divided into eleven geographic departments. These departments target specific countries and regions around the world. For example, the First Department operates in the United States; the Fourth Department focuses on Germany and Austria; the Sixth Department has responsibility for China, Vietnam, Korea, and Cambodia; and the Eighth Department is devoted to the Middle East.

According to Knight, 30 to 40 percent of the Soviet officials stationed in the United States are involved in intelligence gathering. In Third World countries, this number can be as high as 50 percent.

All land-based missiles with ranges exceeding one thousand kilometers are maintained by the Strategic Rocket Forces. Until recently, this included intercontinental ballistic missiles (ICBMs) as well as intermediate-range nuclear forces (INF). However, the INF treaty signed in 1987 by the United States and the Soviet Union provided for the elimination all intermediate-range nuclear missiles.

Ground Forces

Until the nuclear age, the Ground Forces were the most important of the Soviet military's services. Now they are considered by the Soviets to be the second most important. The Ground Forces remain the largest service, however, with approximately 1.5 million personnel in 1989. Many ground forces officers are in the upper echelons of the High Command.

According to the Pentagon, all Ground Forces are subordinate to the fourteen military districts as well as the groups of forces abroad. The Ground Forces are composed of motorized rifle troops, tank troops, airborne troops, missile troops and artillery, troops of troop air defense (service branches), army aviation, and units and subunits of special troops (engineering, chemical, communications, radiotechnical, and others).

Following reorganizations in the early 1980s, troop air defense and army aviation, which were once part of the Ground Forces, became part of the Air Defense Forces and Air Forces. The 1986 Soviet *Military Encyclopedic Dictionary* states that the

> Ground Forces are able, independently or in cooperation with other branches of the Armed Forces, to conduct an offensive with the aim of both defeating enemy troop groupings and seizing his territory, to launch strikes against the deep rear, to repel major enemy air and amphibious invasions, and to resolutely retain territory, regions and boundaries.

Because of ongoing troop reductions and the new emphasis on a defensive military doctrine, the composition, organization, and missions of the Ground Forces were being reviewed as of 1990.

Troops of Air Defense

Since World War II, the USSR has devoted more attention than the United States to developing defenses against aircraft, missile, and satellite attacks. By 1949 the MiG 15 jet fighter was considered a formidable threat to advanced American aircraft, and by the mid-1950s the Soviets had deployed SA-1 ground-to-air missiles around Moscow. Throughout the 1960s, Soviet ground-to-air missiles (SA-2s) proved themselves in Southeast Asia.

More recent efforts to defend against satellites and ballistic missiles also have been significant. The Moscow antiballistic missile system has been substantially upgraded and as of 1989 provides the area with a two-layered defense.

The controversial Krasnoyarsk radar station in Siberia, however, has been permanently deactivated. In 1989, after the United States had pressured the Soviets to remove the radar for several years, the Soviets acknowledged that this additional antiballistic missile (ABM) component violated the conditions of the ABM treaty.

All these air defenses are under the direction of the Troops of Air Defense (VPVO), as the service has been called since 1981, when the name Troops of National Air Defense was dropped. As part of the reorganization, the service gained most, if not all, of the Ground Forces' air defense troops and lost its interceptor aircraft to the Air Forces. As of 1990 the components of Air Defense are aviation, the zenith rocket troops (which operate surface-to-air missiles), and radiotechnical troops.

Air Forces

The Air Forces are not equivalent to the U.S. Air Force, largely because the USSR has assigned strategic missiles to other services. The Soviet Air Forces have an estimated 448,000 troops according to *Brassey's Military Balance, 1988-89*. Traditionally, the Air Forces were composed of long-range aviation, frontal aviation, and military transport aviation. However, to improve coordination, the Air Forces, as part of the 1980s reorganization, received interceptors from the Air Defense Forces. This has allowed military district air commanders to control all the air assets in their district.

The main job of long-range aviation is to destroy the "nuclear means" of the enemy, which indicates that ICBMs and nuclear arsenals would be top bomber-targeting priorities. The Air Forces' strategic bomber fleet is made up of Bears; Backfires; Badgers; Blinders; and Blackjacks, the newest intercontinental bombers, which entered the force in 1988. According to the Pentagon, the number of long-range bombers in the Soviet arsenal has remained constant for many years. However, the bombers' capabilities have been upgraded significantly.

According to the Scotts, Soviet frontal aviation is "roughly equal to tactical aviation in the United States." Its primary mission is to "achieve air superiority and to provide air defense over the battle area within the TVD." Air transport supports military operations beyond Soviet borders.

Navy

The Soviet Navy has become one of the Kremlin's foremost tools of power projection. Largely through the efforts of Commander in Chief and Admiral of the Fleet Sergei Gorshkov, who headed the branch from 1955 until late 1985, the Navy expanded from a limited coastal force into a service that supports Soviet interests internationally. As of 1990 the Navy had approximately 437,000 personnel. In 1988 a Soviet publication said that "in addition to the traditional force arms (submarines and surface combatants) inherent only to them, navies have marines, aviation, and missile artillery troops in their makeup."

According to Soviet military literature, submarines are the principal striking force against enemy submarines and surface ships. Surface forces perform such important missions as antisubmarine and anti-aircraft warfare, support of landing operations, mine warfare, protection of naval sea lines of communication, and strikes against enemy territory. Naval aviation aircraft have four main missions according to the Scotts: reconnaissance and surveillance, antiship strike, antisubmarine warfare, and aviation support. Most of the Navy's aircraft are land based and are likely to remain so. The naval infantry's main job, according to the Pentagon, is to "spearhead amphibious landing for other ground forces—sometimes in concert with airborne troops."

The Navy also deploys between sixty and seventy strategic nuclear-powered ballistic missile submarines (SSBNs). The Soviets' newest and largest SSBN class, the Typhoon, carries twenty SS-N-20 missiles, each equipped with up to ten warheads. As of early 1990 six Typhoon submarines were deployed. The Soviets maintain a relatively small percentage (15 to 20 percent) of their SSBNs on operational patrol within range of their targets in the United States. In the event of a crisis, Soviet strategy calls for "surging" most of the rest of the submarines out to sea for a limited period. The Typhoon- and Delta-class SSBNs carry missiles with ranges great enough to strike U.S. targets even if launched from Soviet home waters.

There are four naval fleets: Northern, based at Severomorsk; Baltic, based at Kaliningrad; Black Sea, based at Sevastopol; and Pacific, based at Vladivostok. According to the Pentagon, the fleet commanders control the operations of all ships, planes, and other military assets within their fleets and are subordinate to the chief of the Main Navy Staff. During hostilities, the fleet commanders report to their TVD commanders. Naval forces contribute to the combined arms operations administered within the TVD structure. However, the activities of nuclear missile submarines are controlled at the national level.

Conscription

The Soviet military draws its personnel through universal conscription. Only a small permanent cadre of officers is maintained. The draft provides a steady flow of noncareer personnel for the cadre to train and lead. Soviet conscription in the past has been successful in instilling the notion among the Soviet people that military service is a part of life. Besides being useful for political socialization, conscription has provided abundant cheap and adaptable labor for priority projects such as the Baikal-Amur railroad.

Gorbachev's efforts to reform Soviet society, however, have caused the organization of the military based on conscription and the length of mandatory military service to be questioned. In part, Soviet citizens are concerned with the military's isolation policy and incidents of ethnic violence within the armed services.

Isolation Policy

The Soviet military has a policy of "isolation," which calls for conscripts to be stationed outside their home republics. Soviet draftees usually are sent far from home, both out of necessity and because isolation makes their control easier. This is particularly important during episodes of civil unrest. A soldier stationed near home may refuse orders to use force against his own ethnic group.

Isolation has made it possible for military commanders to keep troops unaware of or misinformed about their missions or even their whereabouts. In Afghanistan, for example, soldiers were told they would be fighting American and Chinese agents. Some participants in the 1968 invasion of Czechoslovakia thought they were in West Germany.

Ethnic Diversity

Ethnic diversity makes managing the armed forces difficult. Moslems made up about 18 percent of the draft

Soviet Space Program

The Soviet Union opened the space age in 1957 with the launching of *Sputnik*—the first man-made satellite. Since then the Soviets have trumpeted their space program as a symbol of their scientific achievement. The USSR has had its most notable successes in the area of manned space flight. Its record in planetary exploration and with weather, communications, military, and scientific satellites has been spottier.

Military needs dominate the Soviet space program. According to the Pentagon, only about five percent of all Soviet satellites are dedicated entirely to civilian or scientific purposes. The rest support military operations with reconnaissance and surveillance, provide missile launch detection and attack warning information, or have dual military-civilian use.

In the past, the short life span of Soviet satellites required that the Soviets perform more launches than the United States. However, *Soviet Aerospace*, an American journal that follows the activities of the Soviet space program, noted a drop in Soviet launch rates during 1989. The lower rate is a result of many factors: improved satellites, economic constraints on the space program, and "the Soviets just not needing as many military satellites."

The centerpiece of the Soviet manned space program is the *Mir* space station launched in February 1986. The *Mir* space station enabled the Soviets to compile twenty-seven months of a continuous manned presence in space that ended in April 1989. The Soviets plan to attach several modules to the original *Mir* core, where cosmonauts will perform both scientific experiments and military missions. In November 1988 the Soviets conducted the first successful unmanned shuttle mission using their new *Buran* shuttle. It will be used to maintain *Mir* and future space stations.

The manned space program also is being used to generate hard currency for the Soviet economy. For a price of 11.3 million dollars, a Japanese journalist will visit the *Mir* space station in 1991. According to *Soviet Aerospace*, Western firms will be able to advertise on the sides of rockets, space suits, and even billboards on the space station.

The Soviets experienced a setback in planetary exploration in 1988-1989. Plans to explore Mars were frustrated when two *Phobos* spacecraft failed to reach the planet. In September 1988, the Soviets lost *Phobos I* due to computer and operator errors. The Soviets lost contact with *Phobos II* in March 1989 when the onboard computer stopped functioning. These failures have damaged the prospects of further unmanned and manned missions to Mars in the near future.

pool in the mid-1970s. Because of the high birthrates in the Central Asian republics, 37 percent of the total draft intake in 1989 was Moslem.

According to Soviet sources, the increasing number of minorities serving in the military has lowered the combat capability of the armed forces. Generally, minorities enter the services with little or no knowledge of Russian, the military's official language, and they are less educated than their Slav counterparts. These factors complicate military training and operations. For example, in 1987 an East German train hit a Soviet tank stalled on the tracks because the tank-driving trainee was unable to get out of the train's path when he did not understand commands given to him in Russian.

The varied ethnic composition of the Soviet armed forces also has resulted in incidents of ethnic violence. Military companies often are composed of soldiers representing more than ten different nationalities. Soldiers commonly must mix with members of hostile ethnic groups, increasing the chances of beatings and fights that can turn deadly. The Soviet press has reported attacks on conscripts from the Baltic states in 1990. Russian officers, irritated by the attempts of the Baltic republics to gain independence, have abused subordinates from that region. In addition, conscripts serving in regions of the country that are becoming increasingly antimilitary or anti-Soviet have been subject to harassment by local citizens.

The Conscription Debate

Increasing incidents of ethnic violence and problems related to the isolation of conscripts are being reported in the Soviet press. This has mobilized leaders of the Soviet republics, who are lobbying for military restructuring and a reduced service period for draftees. The growing Soviet economic crisis also has prompted calls for military restructuring—universal conscription deprives the national economy of needed engineers and scientists while they fulfill their military obligations.

Until 1982, all full-time students could defer military service until graduation. The law was changed at that time to require all students to serve three years in the navy or two years in any other service. Only those students attending higher education institutions specified on a special list were exempt from service until graduation. Through the eighties this list became shorter until few deferments were granted.

However, on April 12, 1989, the Supreme Soviet responded to citizen pressure for military reform by decreeing that mandatory service for graduates of higher education institutions would be reduced from eighteen months to one year. Also the decree allowed full-time university students to defer service until completion of their studies or until they reached the age of twenty-seven.

Many Soviet citizens and some military officers are demanding that the military leadership consider broader military reforms. Proponents of military reform have advocated a professional military or a military based on a territorial militia system. A professional military, like that in the United States, would allow the services to recruit the "best and brightest" and therefore increase efficiency and combat readiness. In addition, the military could decrease ethnic diversity by concentrating recruitment efforts on the Slavs. The territorial-militia system is being promoted primarily by republican organizations. If the military were to reorganize along territorial lines, each republic would be responsible for manning and equipping its own army. If either of these plans were adopted, universal conscription would be eliminated. Military opponents to these reforms cite the high cost of a professional army and the difficulties associated with organizing and controlling a system of decentralized territorial-militias.

Gorbachev's Reforms

President Gorbachev's efforts to restructure the economy and his "new thinking" in foreign policy have led the Soviets to reevaluate the role of the Soviet armed forces. Soviet military adventures in the Third World launched under Brezhnev caused the world community to isolate the Soviet Union by denying it access to trade, advanced technologies, and certain international organizations. This isolation and the high rates of Soviet military spending contributed to the Soviet economic crisis. Soviet foreign policy since 1987 has been designed to improve the USSR's international reputation, decrease international tensions, and enable the USSR to participate more fully in the world economy. According to Gorbachev, diplomacy, not military power, is the basic tool for achieving international goals. New thinking has affected military strategy and doctrine, the military budget, and the status of the military in society and in national security decision making. It also is the basis for the Soviets' aggressive pursuit of arms reductions.

Arms Control

In 1987, the United States and the Soviet Union signed the INF agreement, which provided for the elimination of all intermediate-range nuclear missiles in Europe. By agreeing not to link the United States' SDI space-based ballistic missile defense development program to the INF negotiations and by agreeing to intrusive verification measures (U.S. representatives would be able to monitor the destruction of these missiles on Soviet soil), the Soviets supplied the breakthroughs needed to seal the deal on the INF treaty.

In addition, the Soviet Union has offered to remove all its nuclear missiles from the territories of its allies, if the United States does the same. The Soviets also offered to negotiate with the United States on the elimination of short-range nuclear weapons. In the conventional sphere, Gorbachev announced in a December 1988 speech at the United Nations that the Soviet Union intended to unilaterally reduce the strength of its armed forces by 500,000 troops during 1989 and 1990 (Gorbachev reported in April 1989 that Soviet armed forces numbered 4,258,000 troops). The reduction in forces is being accompanied by substantial cuts in conventional arms. The USSR will withdraw six tank divisions and a number of landing assault units and their equipment from East Germany, Czechoslovakia, and Hungary by 1991. Soviet forces stationed in Warsaw Pact countries will be reduced by a total of 50,000 troops and 5,000 tanks. *(Gorbachev UN speech, Documents, p. 320)*

Reductions in conventional forces and weapons also are scheduled in the Far East. During a 1989 visit to China, Gorbachev announced that Soviet Far Eastern forces would be reduced by 120,000 troops and that twelve army divisions and eleven air force regiments would be disbanded. In addition, many Soviet troops are being withdrawn from Mongolia. According to *Brassey's Military*

Soviet Military Advisers in the Third World

Since Lenin published his thesis *Imperialism: The Highest Stage of Capitalism* (1916), the Communist party has viewed the leaders of national and colonial liberation movements as potential allies against the capitalist countries. Following World War II, many former colonial powers such as Great Britain and France were unable to hold on to their colonies. By providing financial and military support to liberation movements in the Third World, Moscow gained influence with the governments of emerging countries. During the 1970s and 1980s, after most colonies had achieved independence, Moscow continued to aid its Third World allies involved in regional conflicts.

The level of Soviet commitment to its Third World allies is demonstrated by the type and amount of military assistance it provides. Delivery of modern equipment such as advanced fighter planes and battle tanks signifies a serious Soviet commitment. Less important allies generally receive older equipment that is being phased out of the Soviets' military inventory. The number of military advisers assigned to a country is another measure of the importance Moscow attaches to a client state.

When the Soviet Union sells military equipment to foreign countries, it generally provides the buyer with technical advisers. Weapons systems can be very complex, and skilled personnel are needed to assemble them and train local military personnel in their operation. According to Roger Pajak in *The Soviet Union in the Third World: Successes and Failures*, technical assistance involves "the training in the Soviet Union of military personnel from the developing countries and the dispatch of Soviet military technicians and instructors to countries receiving military aid." Pajak maintains that Soviet military advisers and technicians assist "essentially in three functions: the delivery, assembly and maintenance of military equipment; the training of local personnel in the operation and maintenance of equipment; and the instructing of indigenous military officers in staff and operational units." In addition, many Soviet advisers teach at local military academies, and defense industry advisers have helped design and construct arms production facilities in Third World countries.

These advisers allow the Soviet Union to maintain a permanent presence in client countries, a goal as important to the Soviets as the good relations they develop by providing weapons. According to the Pentagon, military assistance is designed specifically for the recipient, but it also is used "to create a dependence [on the Soviet Union] that is militarily, politically, and economically costly to break."

Soviet military advisers sent to the Third World not only provide technical assistance but also gather intelligence valuable to the Soviet Union. Adviser delegations also can provide a cover for stationing Committee for State Security (KGB) officers in a given country. One of the duties of Soviet advisers is to identify potential leaders who can be sent to the Soviet Union for education and training. Military advisers also serve as links between the client country's own military and government. This allows the Soviets to influence the course of internal affairs in these countries.

In keeping with Mikhail S. Gorbachev's foreign policy based on the concepts of "new thinking," the Soviets have reduced their commitments to revolutionary groups in the Third World, as demonstrated by the military withdrawal from Afghanistan. Gorbachev also has encouraged Soviet clients to reduce their activities in other countries, and he has publicly stated that he supports the withdrawal of Vietnamese troops from Cambodia.

An ongoing policy debate in the Soviet Union in 1990 indicates that substantial cuts in military aid are likely. Articles have appeared in the Soviet media criticizing the role and activities of military advisers. Military advisers have been accused of impairing relations with Third World countries because they failed to learn the native languages and could not communicate with their hosts. Furthermore, the articles have claimed that advisers' arrogant attitudes often caused diplomatic "incidents."

Many Soviet leaders believe that military support of and intervention in Third World countries has had a negative effect on Soviet foreign relations in general. In some cases, the Kremlin is considering reducing military aid in favor of economic support, but Soviet domestic economic problems, including a growing budget deficit, have put pressure on Soviet leaders to cut back on all types of foreign aid.

Balance, 1988-89, approximately 2,800 troops accompanied by 200 tanks and 170 artillery pieces had already been removed from Mongolia by June 1989.

Perhaps the best example of the abatement of Soviet military force worldwide was the Soviet withdrawal from Afghanistan. As promised, the last Soviet troops left by February 15, 1989. Soviet sources state that fifteen thousand Soviet soldiers died during the occupation.

Defense Spending

In the past, the Soviets kept the total amount of their defense spending secret. Analysts in the West recognized that the "official" defense spending figure reported by the Soviets did not correspond to the high levels of weaponry and forces employed by the military.

In keeping with the policy of glasnost, the Soviets have

attempted to provide an actual accounting of their defense expenditures. It was revealed that the Soviet authorities formerly had reported expenditures only on manpower. Weapons procurement and research and development were not contained in official Soviet defense spending estimates. In 1989 Gorbachev announced that the defense budget for that year was 77.3 billion rubles. This amounts to between 8 and 9 percent of Soviet GNP. By comparison, the United States spent approximately 5.8 percent of its GNP on defense in 1989. While testifying before the U.S. House Armed Services Committee in July 1989, General Sergei Akhromeev, former chief of the General Staff, admitted that even the new Soviet figures were probably low. However, he said Soviet economists were working to provide a more accurate accounting.

In 1989, Gorbachev announced that overall defense spending would be reduced 14.2 percent and weapons production reduced 19.5 percent by 1991. According to Soviet sources, the military budget would fall from 77.3 billion rubles to 70.9 billion rubles in 1990. This was 12 billion rubles less than the target for that year in the Twelfth Five-Year Plan (covering 1986-1990). Expenditures for operation and maintenance of the Soviet Army and Navy would be reduced from 20.2 billion to 19 billion rubles. In keeping with the plan to cut weapons production, the Soviets have terminated many technical programs related to offensive weapons systems.

The reductions in weapons procurement also will affect defense industries. Those enterprises that no longer are producing for the military will manufacture consumer goods. It is hoped that the conversion of defense enterprises to civilian production will improve economic conditions by providing more goods for the consumer. Because Soviet defense firms are respected for their technical sophistication and the high quality of their products, converted defense industries may produce higher quality consumer goods than current consumer industries.

In December 1988, Gorbachev proposed in his speech to the United Nations that all countries submit plans for national conversion of their defense industries to civilian production. The Soviet Union is in the process of drawing up an internal conversion plan, and three defense enterprises have been converted to civilian production as part of a conversion experiment.

Military Strategy and Doctrine

Soviet military doctrine (theories about how military forces should be used) is divided into two parts: political and military-technical. Traditionally, the political doctrine behind Soviet military policy has been defensive in nature, but the military methods developed for executing the goals of the political leadership have been offensive. Soviet leaders acknowledge that the military-technical side of Soviet military doctrine was allowed to dominate policy, especially during the Brezhnev years. Soviet military and civilian leaders believe this contributed to severe foreign policy mistakes, such as the invasion of Afghanistan and the deployment of SS-20s in Europe. These policies caused the United States and NATO to build up their military capabilities and led to a general international distrust of the Soviet Union and its policies.

The Soviet leadership has called for a reassertion of political defensive doctrine over the offensive military-technical side. Moreover, Soviet leaders are demanding that the military adopt the strategy of "reasonable suffi-

ciency," which calls for a more defensive doctrine and force posture. In the past, the Soviet military was built and organized to carry out offensive missions (such as a conventional attack on Western Europe), even if the probability of actually conducting those missions was low. According to Dale Herspring, an expert on the Soviet military, the Soviet blitzkrieg approach to war fighting is being phased out. In its place, the Soviets are preparing to deter attacks by being able to fight a long-term war of attrition. To conform to this defensive doctrine, Soviet forces left in Europe and in the Far East are to be reorganized so that they will be able to respond to enemy military operations but will be unable to launch large-scale offensive attacks.

Military Prestige

The military traditionally has played a very important role in Soviet society and politics. The armed forces have received the best personnel, the most advanced equipment, and a large portion of the national budget. Military officers also participated in national security decision making at the highest levels. The military enjoyed great prestige primarily because the Soviet Union relied on military power for its superpower status. Therefore, military needs drove most domestic and foreign policy considerations. Under Mikhail Gorbachev, however, the military's role has been diminished. New thinking has advanced the idea that military power no longer is the key to foreign policy success or international prestige.

Many signs have appeared that the status of the military has been downgraded under Gorbachev. No military officer has been appointed to the rank of marshal of the Soviet Union during the late 1980s. Furthermore, the military has been less prominent in official ceremonies such as the Revolution Day Parade, when high-ranking officials appear on top of Lenin's mausoleum.

Evidence also exists that the military no longer participates in national security decision making to the degree that it once did. The Ministry of Foreign Affairs has played a dominant role in developing positions for recent arms control negotiations, a function that previously was dominated by the military. Soviet foreign affairs officials also have been privy to data on the military. Military secrecy had prevented officials outside the military and the highest echelons of the party to see this type of information.

According to Herspring, in the past military officers also "dominated national security analysis in the USSR." Military officers assessed the foreign threat, devised strategies to counter it, and procured weapons to support these strategies. Civilians had little opportunity to participate in the process. Government and party officials in the Ministry of Foreign Affairs, Supreme Soviet, and other bodies are becoming more actively involved in national security and military analysis.

However, the greatest challenge to military dominance over national security planning comes from the *instituchiki*—the civilian analysts who work for Soviet institutes such as the Institute for the World Economy and International Relations and the Institute for the Study of the USA and Canada. These institutes are similar to think tanks in the United States. Their members are challenging the military's position on such issues as the draft, student deferments, harassment of conscripts, and past military assessments of the external threat. Many leading instituchiki are advisers to Gorbachev.

Glasnost, Democratization, and the Military

In the past, the affairs of the military have been considered sacrosanct. The military was above criticism and generally was revered in the press for its role as the protector of the Soviet homeland. However, the military has not been exempt from the new policies of glasnost and democratization. The military has come under increasing public scrutiny, and many Soviets have called for it to adopt more democratic principles. In fact, the military has become a popular target in the Soviet civilian press and has been criticized for a broad range of offenses including hazing of young recruits, promoting aggressive foreign policies, recruiting the best personnel and resources for the defense industries to the detriment of the civilian sector, and general misconduct and corruption. The campaign against the military has been comprehensive and often vitriolic.

In response, the military has denounced these criticisms as prejudicial and harmful to the armed forces. Even top military leaders appointed by Gorbachev have complained that the military's portrayal in the Soviet press is causing "pacifistic" trends that could undermine the military and its ability to ensure national security.

Despite the conflict with the civilian press and its treatment of the military, the military press has addressed certain problems with openness. Military journals have printed many articles on the armed forces' personnel problems, and the coverage of the conflict in Afghanistan during and after the Soviet withdrawal was relatively candid under glasnost. The military also participated in the general Soviet campaign to correct historical inaccuracies, which included a re-assessment of Soviet military performance in World War II. The military views these discussions of history as opportunities to improve its doctrine and performance. (Remaking Soviet history, box, p. 146)

Newly appointed military leaders have appeared receptive to a controlled democratization of the military. This means that criticism of superiors will be accepted, while hazing of subordinates will not. In addition, the new campaign promotes independent thinking and actions, personal initiative, and open discussions between officers and enlisted personnel. The military press has stated that a system for reporting the illegal activities of officers will be developed. Until this procedure has become institutionalized, however, military enlisted personnel are being encouraged to use Communist party and Communist Youth League (Komsomol) meetings to discuss their concerns.

Perestroika and the Soviet Military

Perestroika (restructuring) is the attempt to improve social and economic conditions through reform. While perestroika generally is associated with the economy, it also includes plans for better management-personnel relations, increased individual responsibility, and turnover in personnel. These aspects of perestroika are having the greatest effect on the Soviet military.

One of the basic tenets of perestroika is the importance of the individual. By enhancing the role of the individual, perestroika aims at improving the quality and increasing the quantity of work performed in the Soviet Union. The military, on the other hand, always has relied on a rigid command hierarchy to achieve its goals. Soldiers are instructed to follow all orders and policies. The services do not regard an independent soldier as an asset.

Therefore, an essential conflict exists between perestroika and military discipline. However, the armed services have been told that they must re-orient their personnel policy to comply with perestroika. According to an article in *Parameters* by Natalie Gross, an expert on Soviet political-military affairs, restructuring the military means "decentralization of decision making to the lower levels, reduction of red tape, and a freer exchange of views, especially regarding shortcomings in training and cadre policies." To achieve this the Soviet military leadership has advocated three new management techniques: "closeness to people, exactingness, and personal responsibility," according to Herspring. In other words, the Soviet officer corps is expected to be accessible to subordinates and respect their opinions. Also, officers are expected to be self-motivated and even question illegal or unwise orders.

The military initially responded ambivalently to the concept of perestroika. Military officers and the military press made no attempt to address the issue. In response to

Defense Secretary Frank Carlucci (left) and Soviet chief of the general staff Sergei Akhromeev (middle) enter the Pentagon for discussions, December 9, 1987. Accompanying them are Viktor Karpov, Soviet arms control adviser (right), and Chairman of the Joint Chiefs of Staff Admiral William Crowe (behind Karpov). Moscow's new thinking in foreign and defense policy has led to ongoing talks between the superpowers' military establishments.

the military's stance, Gorbachev initiated a series of personnel changes at the highest levels of the military hierarchy.

In 1985, he replaced the chief of the Main Political Directorate, the commander in chief of the Strategic Rocket Forces, and the commander in chief of the Navy, among others. The next year more high-ranking officers, including the commander in chief of the Ground Forces and the chief of Civil Defense, were replaced. The most important military shake-up occurred in June 1987 when a Cessna aircraft piloted by a young West German civilian landed in Red Square. Gorbachev used this embarrassing incident to remove Defense Minister Sergei Sokolov and Air Defense Commander in Chief Aleksandr Koldunov from office. Other officers of the Moscow Air District also were dismissed.

In general, Gorbachev has replaced these men with officers who have shown support for military restructuring. Army Gen. Dmitrii Yazov, who succeeded Sokolov as Defense Minister in 1987, has been openly critical of the state of the Soviet armed forces. Writing primarily about personnel issues, Yazov has stressed the need for personal responsibility and self-discipline and has encouraged criticism of incompetent officers.

Another common characteristic of military leaders promoted under Gorbachev is their experience before being summoned to Moscow. Many of these newly appointed officers—including Defense Minister Yazov, Commander in Chief of the Air Defense Forces Ivan Tretyak, and Chief of the General Staff Mikhail Moiseev—served in the Far Eastern Military districts. Western analysts believe that officers who lack a close association with the Moscow military elite and who had combat experience in Afghanistan also have been more likely to be promoted.

Despite Gorbachev's efforts to replace hard-line military leaders with leaders who support his reforms, the top military leadership remains conservative. At the Twenty-eighth Party Congress in July 1990, delegates from the armed services were openly supportive of conservative speakers, proposals, and candidates. Michael Dobbs of the *Washington Post* reported, "When Gorbachev declared in his final speech that 'the Cold War has ended' the hall erupted in applause. All but one of the military men sat in grim silence."

U.S.-Soviet Relations

Since World War II the United States and the Soviet Union have been the most important actors in the international arena. The war left the two nations as the world's strongest military powers and the leaders of opposing ideological blocs. Although the Soviet Union could not match the economic strength of the United States, its military strength provided the basis for its claim to superpower status. This claim was solidified after 1949, when the Soviet Union joined the United States as a nuclear power. Thereafter, the Soviets waged a nuclear arms race with the United States as both countries devoted huge amounts of resources to expand and improve their nuclear arsenals.

The superpowers' conflicting geopolitical goals, competing ideologies, and reciprocal military threat caused the foreign policies of both countries to focus on the other. American post-World War II policy aimed at containing Soviet expansionism, building alliance systems to oppose the Soviet military threat, and isolating the Soviet Union diplomatically. The Soviets sought U.S. and Western European recognition of their domination of Eastern Europe and competed aggressively with the United States for influence in the Third World.

In the name of the international socialist revolution, the Soviets funded governments and guerrilla groups throughout the world. Yet a group's anti-Western hostility and willingness to permit Soviet influence in its affairs had more to do with Moscow's decision to extend economic and military aid than the group's ideological commitment to Marxism-Leninism. Similarly the United States backed some anticommunist governments and groups that were not committed to democratic principles. The two superpowers thus engaged in a traditional great power contest for geopolitical influence around the world that only partially was motivated by their ideological differences.

Beginning in the 1960s, the danger of nuclear war led the superpowers, despite their ongoing arms race, to pursue nuclear arms control. The agreements that were concluded did not end the arms race, but they were considered the most important diplomatic achievements of the leaders of both nations. Summit meetings between the Soviet leader and the U.S. president had global implications and became international media events.

The United States, besides being the Soviets' foremost adversary, was the yardstick by which the Soviets measured their own success. Soviet leaders wanted the United States to consider the USSR as its equal. Premier Nikita S.

Khrushchev noted in his memoirs how opposition to the United States was coupled with admiration: "America occupied a special place in our thinking about the world. And why shouldn't it? It was our strongest opponent among the capitalist countries, the leader that called the tune of anti-Sovietism for the rest."

As Sovietologist Dimitri Simes has explained, throughout the 1960s and 1970s there was "fear and competitive impulse" in the U.S. and Soviet images of each other. "But in the American case they were mixed with contempt; in the Russian, with jealousy and respect." The Soviets expected the United States to treat U.S.-Soviet relations as the most important aspect of world relations. They have been sensitive to indications that U.S. policy makers were giving precedence to non-Soviet foreign policy issues.

By the late 1980s the central role played by each superpower in the foreign affairs of the other had begun to diminish. In an effort to help repair the ailing Soviet economy, Soviet leader Mikhail S. Gorbachev had de-emphasized the USSR's quest for international influence and sought to divert funds from military production to the civilian economy. Competition with the United States was subordinated to a new superpower cooperation that would allow the Soviets to focus on their enormous domestic problems. In addition, the development of other power centers based on economic strength, particularly Japan and the European Economic Community, made the world less bipolar. Because the Soviet Union was not a major player in the arena of international economics, its importance to U.S. foreign policy decreased as economic interdependence between the industrialized nations of the West increasingly became a determining factor in U.S. foreign policy calculations.

Nevertheless the relationship between the Soviet Union and the United States remains vital to both nations and to the world. Arms control cooperation holds the possibility of significant economic and national security benefits, and the two nations have an important role to play in European stability. In addition, a deepening U.S.-Soviet rapprochement could be the basis for resolution of many regional conflicts and broader international cooperation in areas such as nuclear nonproliferation, environmental protection, and Third World development. Finally, deeper U.S.-Soviet economic ties could provide a boost to the Soviet economy and further the process of reform in the USSR.

Adversarial Relationship

For most of the Soviet Union's history, it has had an adversarial relationship with the United States. American forces were among the Allied contingent sent to Russia following the Bolshevik withdrawal from World War I in 1918. The Allies sought to protect war supplies sent to Russia before it had concluded its separate peace with Germany and to support White armies that were fighting to overthrow the new Bolshevik regime. By 1920 the Bolsheviks had gained the upper hand in the civil war, and most Allied troops had been withdrawn from Russia. The Red Army defeated the remnants of the White forces by 1921. (Foreign intervention, p. 28)

After the civil war, the Bolsheviks attempted to gain recognition and loans for reconstruction from the United States and other major powers. The United States, however, refused to recognize the Bolshevik government or loan it money, although Washington did aid Russian famine victims through the American Relief Administration. In March 1921 the United States also excluded the Bolsheviks from participating in an international naval conference held in Washington. The Bolsheviks were resented in the United States for their revolutionary propaganda, their withdrawal from World War I, and their refusal to pay tsarist debts.

During 1924 most European countries, believing that the Bolsheviks had consolidated their power, recognized the Bolshevik government. The United States, however, refrained from recognizing the Soviet Union until November 16, 1933. The decision to establish formal ties with the Soviet Union was motivated primarily by Adolf Hitler's rise to power in Germany and the Japanese occupation of Manchuria in 1931-1932. In return for recognition, Moscow promised to stop disseminating propaganda aimed at overthrowing the U.S. government and to protect the rights of U.S. citizens in the Soviet Union. These promises were not kept, however, and U.S.-Soviet political relations remained cool and distant.

The U.S. entry into World War II following Japan's attack on Pearl Harbor, Hawaii, December 7, 1941, transformed the United States and the Soviet Union into active wartime allies. During the war the United States shipped billions of dollars of supplies to the USSR to sustain the Soviet war effort against Nazi Germany. Nevertheless, even during the war, the Soviet Union and the United States were uneasy partners, linked only by a common enemy.

In the closing stages of World War II, President Franklin D. Roosevelt believed that an oligarchy was forming between the great powers that would create a stable postwar order. The wartime partnership between the Soviet Union and the United States, however, quickly broke down when the Axis powers were defeated. Soviet domination of Eastern Europe, disagreements over the future of Germany, and other issues combined to create a cold war between East and West. (Cold war, p. 42)

During the cold war, world affairs became increasingly bipolar, as the United States and the Soviet Union competed for the friendship of peoples around the world. The United States and the nations of Western Europe created the North Atlantic Treaty Organization (NATO) as a response to the military threat from the Soviet Union. The Soviets countered by establishing their own alliance system—the Warsaw Pact—with the nations of Eastern Europe.

The Soviet foreign policy process underwent significant evolution after 1953, with dynamism and pragmatism largely replacing the more irrational posture dictated by Joseph Stalin. During Khrushchev's tenure, the Soviet Union solidified its claims to being a superpower. But this status was primarily one-dimensional because it depended largely on military power. The Soviet domestic economy made gains in the postwar years, but the USSR remained a limited player in the international economy. Moscow viewed America as the principal obstacle to its international ambitions and sought to compete with the United States in areas outside the military realm. The Soviets saw U.S. efforts to "contain" them and deal with them "from a position of strength" as direct challenges to their superpower status and concomitant right to exercise influence internationally.

The wily, gregarious Khrushchev vacillated in his policy toward the United States. The Soviet military was upgraded under his guidance, with emphasis on nuclear forces. Yet Khrushchev advanced the concept of peaceful coexistence with the West, and this idea became a cornerstone of Soviet foreign policy even after his removal from power in 1964. Peaceful coexistence did not end superpower confrontation, however. Soviet attempts to gain a military advantage by deploying nuclear missiles in Cuba led to the Cuban missile crisis in 1962, during which President John F. Kennedy estimated the chances of nuclear war between the superpowers as "one in three." Yet peaceful coexistence was a recognition that because of the destructive power of nuclear weapons, war had to be avoided. (Cuban missile crisis, p. 55)

While less emotional and volatile than Khrushchev, Leonid I. Brezhnev also displayed a need to be reassured of Soviet equality in international affairs. During Brezhnev's tenure as top Soviet leader, the Soviets reached nuclear parity with the United States and became more assertive in their quest for Third World allies and clients. Nevertheless, the cold war was interrupted in the 1970s by the efforts of U.S. and Soviet leaders to pursue a détente—a relaxation of tensions. (Détente, p. 66)

Although the superpowers cooperated on many issues during the era of détente, including arms control, they remained competitors. The fundamental adversarial relationship had not changed. The Soviets continued their military buildup and their aggressive support of anti-Western governments and guerrilla groups. Meanwhile many conservatives in the United States criticized détente for providing benefits to the Soviets while bringing the West little more than a false sense of security.

Gradually during the second half of the 1970s enthusiasm for détente in the United States waned. The Soviets were perceived as using every possible loophole in the arms control treaties concluded under détente to continue their military buildup. Moscow stepped up military aid to the anti-Western governments of Angola, Ethiopia, and Afghanistan and supported the Vietnamese invasion of Cambodia in late 1978. In addition, the Kremlin resisted Western attempts to force it to improve its domestic human rights record, particularly in the area of emigration. Finally, the Soviet invasion of Afghanistan in December 1979 destroyed what was left of détente.

Thus as the 1980s began the U.S.-Soviet relationship had returned to its "normal" state of acrimony and suspicion. President Ronald Reagan denounced the Soviet Union and accelerated a military buildup begun under Jimmy Carter. Reagan said in his first presidential news

The Cold War, McCarthy, and the 'Red Scare'

Soon after World War II, rising tensions between the United States and the Soviet Union, coupled with the disclosure that a communist spy ring had been operating in Canada, prompted a wave of concern over communist espionage and subversion within the United States that became known as the "red scare."

Few movements in U.S. history have so pervaded the fabric of national life as the anticommunist movement of the late 1940s and early 1950s. Not only did states have their own anticommunist statutes and legislatures their own un-American activities committees, but loyalty oaths and investigations became commonplace both in public and private employment. Some veterans organizations became involved in the movement to expose and eliminate alleged communist influence in American life.

There were widespread efforts to weed out communists and communist sympathizers in the legal profession, on college and university faculties, in the mass communications field (especially motion pictures and radio), and in many other industries not directly involved in the nation's security.

Fear of communist infiltration of the federal government first focused on the State Department. The revelations in the *Amerasia* case, involving the discovery of secret U.S. records in that allegedly procommunist magazine's files, began a series of congressional investigations of communist subversion that continued for years. The *Amerasia* case also figured in President Truman's initiation of a comprehensive loyalty program for all government employees in 1947.

The same year, Congress reached out beyond the government in its anticommunist crusade. It moved against communist labor leaders by attaching a noncommunist affidavit requirement to the Taft-Hartley Act, and the House Un-American Activities Committee (HUAC) undertook a controversial probe of the motion picture industry. Ronald Reagan, then the newly elected president of the Screen Actors Guild, testified as a friendly witness before HUAC in October 1947. He supported the blacklist that Hollywood producers created to deny work to actors and writers suspected of having communist ties.

But it was the committee's investigation in 1948 of State Department official Alger Hiss, and Hiss's subsequent conviction for perjury, that established internal communism as a leading political issue and the committee as an important political force. The case against Hiss was based on testimony by Whittaker Chambers and Elizabeth Bentley, members of the Communist party, who alleged that at least seventy-five government officials had been involved in spying during the 1930s. The charges against Hiss, which at one point appeared flimsy to other committee members, were vigorously developed by Richard Nixon, then a young member of the committee. Truman called the investigation a "red herring."

Between 1950 and 1954 Congress enacted a wide variety of restrictive legislation. High priests of the anticommunist movement were congressional investigators—members of HUAC, the Senate Internal Security Subcommittee, and, briefly, the Senate Permanent Investigations Subcommittee headed by Joseph R. McCarthy, R-Wis. Viewed as heroes by their supporters, as witch-hunters and character assassins by opponents, these men were largely responsible for the Internal Security Act of 1950, the Communist Control Act (CCA) of 1954, and other antisubversive laws.

With the return of Congress to Republican control in 1953, McCarthy assumed chairmanship of the Senate Permanent Investigations Subcommittee, and under him that group became a headline forum for anticommunist charges.

On June 19, 1953, Julius and Ethel Rosenberg, a married couple convicted of conspiracy to commit espionage by passing atomic information to the Soviets, died in the electric chair. The Rosenbergs were the first civilians to be executed for spying, and their case aroused considerable controversy.

Before the 1954 midterm elections, Republicans and Democrats traded charges with abandon. McCarthy accused the Democrats of "twenty years of treason," and the Democrats, hoping to embarrass the Eisenhower administration, countered with legislation to outlaw the Communist party. The result was the Communist Control Act, the most controversial of the antisubversive legislation enacted in 1954. The CCA was a patchwork law of doubtful impact.

Anticommunist fervor reached its peak in 1954, but the movement began to wane after the Senate censured McCarthy by a 67 to 22 vote on December 2 of that year for acting contrary to Senate traditions during his investigations of alleged communist activity. In ensuing years the courts and Congress curbed some of the most extreme anticommunist laws and regulations. Some others never were enforced completely or were repealed quietly. The demise in January 1975 of HUAC, renamed the Internal Security Committee in 1969, ended thirty years of controversy over its pursuit of subversives.

A new measure of anticommunist sentiment developed in the early 1960s. The Supreme Court in 1961 upheld an order requiring the Communist party to register under the Internal Security Act. Congress tightened antisubversion acts and tried to curb the flow of communist propaganda into the United States. New anticommunist organizations, notably the John Birch Society, also emerged—to the accompaniment of widespread criticism and with marked lack of political success.

conference in January 1981 that "so far, détente's been a one-way street the Soviet Union has used to pursue its own aims." He also claimed that the Soviets reserve the "right to commit any crime, to lie, to cheat." In 1983 he called the USSR "an evil empire" and "the focus of evil in the modern world."

Reagan's harsh rhetoric came amidst continuing nuclear arms competition, stagnating arms control talks, continuing conflict between superpower clients in the Third World, and similarly harsh rhetoric from Soviet leaders. During the early 1980s the state of arms control negotiations became a measuring stick of the superpower relationship. In late 1983, after West European countries began accepting the deployment of NATO intermediate-range nuclear missiles and ground-launched cruise missiles (GLCMs), the Soviets broke off all major arms control negotiations. Talks did not resume until after Gorbachev had become Soviet general secretary in March 1985. Superpower relations had been further strained by Reagan's 1983 proposal to build a space-based antiballistic missile defense—the Strategic Defense Initiative (SDI). SDI was seen by the Soviets as an attack against their two weakest areas: their economy and their technological capabilities.

Under Gorbachev, U.S.-Soviet relations continued to be based on competition. The new Soviet leader, however, brought a new pragmatism to negotiations and appeared to conduct business with the United States with an eye toward supporting Soviet domestic needs. He also provided a challenge to the U.S. leaders in the area of public relations, as he skillfully lobbied to improve the international image of the Soviet Union.

In 1987, with the conclusion of the Intermediate-range

President-elect George Bush, President Ronald Reagan, and President Mikhail S. Gorbachev take their places for a prearranged photo opportunity on Governors Island in New York harbor, December 7, 1988.

Nuclear Forces (INF) treaty eliminating all intermediate-range nuclear missiles from Europe, superpower relations began to change fundamentally. The Soviets had made several major concessions in agreeing to the treaty, the terms of which were close to a proposal made by Reagan in 1981. Meanwhile, the Reagan administration had ceased its harsh anti-Soviet rhetoric and was exploring new areas for superpower cooperation.

Soviet actions in 1989, including withdrawal of forces from Afghanistan and consent to the establishment of democratically elected governments in Eastern Europe, convinced most U.S. policy makers that the Soviet Union had changed dramatically. Moreover Soviet society was being transformed, as Marxist-Leninist ideology lost its luster, non-Russian minorities clamored for greater autonomy, the Communist party leadership introduced democratic processes, and Soviet society increasingly became subject to the rule of law. In response to these changes, the United States began to take actions designed to aid the domestic transformation of the Soviet Union. Superpower relations appeared to have entered a new stage where cooperation would replace competition.

Arms Control

Throughout the 1960s, 1970s, and 1980s arms control was the central element of negotiations between the United States and the Soviet Union. Both sides stated their desire to conclude agreements that would limit, reduce, or otherwise restrict the construction and deployment of nuclear weapons. Some agreements were concluded, but mutual fear and distrust continued to fuel the arms race.

Test Ban

The difficulties in reaching a strategic arms agreement were evident in the long and arduous negotiations to limit nuclear weapons testing—the first major arms control goal pursued by the superpowers. Prime Minister Jawaharlal Nehru of India had urged a suspension of tests, and the Soviets called for a halt in their disarmament proposals of May 10, 1955. In the years that followed, each superpower temporarily suspended its own testing, but no agreement was reached until 1963. The Soviets were opposed to on-site inspection measures demanded by the United States. In addition, a ban on testing was viewed by some U.S. officials as a backdoor approach to total nuclear disarmament. Henry A. Kissinger, then a Harvard professor and later secretary of state, took note of this connection in an article in the October 1958 *Foreign Affairs*. "If a cessation of nuclear testing is a 'first step' to anything," he wrote, "it is to an increased campaign to outlaw nuclear weapons altogether."

Despite overtures from Soviet premier Khrushchev, President Kennedy ordered a buildup of intercontinental ballistic missiles (ICBMs) soon after taking office in 1961. The buildup was intended to counter what many U.S. defense analysts perceived as a "missile gap" that favored the Soviet Union. In actuality, a gap in missile capabilities did exist, but it favored the United States. Not until after the Cuban missile crisis of October 1962 did the two sides resume serious negotiations on a nuclear testing agreement. A limited treaty ending experimental nuclear weapons tests in the atmosphere, outer space, and under water was signed by the United States, the Soviet Union, and Great Britain in August 1963. More than 110 other countries subsequently signed the test ban treaty.

Buildups Continue

Although the test ban treaty was a positive step, it did not signal a new era of arms control. Both sides proceeded to conduct their testing underground. The United States conducted more nuclear tests (469) in the ten years after the test ban than it had in the previous eighteen years (424). The American strategic buildup, which began two years before the treaty was signed, continued for the rest of the decade. The number of ICBMs was substantially increased, submarine-launched Polaris missiles were developed and deployed, supersonic fighter-bombers were ordered, and, by 1965, contracts had been given to the Boeing Company for work on multiple independently targeted reentry vehicle (MIRV) technology that would allow a single missile to carry several warheads.

Meanwhile the Soviet Union was pursuing its own nuclear weapons buildup. During the early 1960s its arsenal was inferior to the U.S. nuclear arsenal, but it was large enough to provide a credible deterrent to an attack. By the late 1960s the Soviets had achieved rough nuclear parity with the United States. The Soviet buildup focused on ICBMs and antiballistic missile (ABM) systems. In 1966, for example, the Soviet Union had about one-third as many ICBMs (250) as the United States. Two years later, according to U.S. estimates, the Soviets had 900.

Johnson Presidency

A number of factors prevented serious consideration of strategic weapons reduction during the 1960s, including the growing American involvement in Vietnam, the Soviet invasion of Czechoslovakia in August 1968, and the strategic buildups under way in both superpowers. Nevertheless, two important multilateral agreements on nuclear weapons were signed in the late 1960s: a 1967 treaty banning the orbiting of devices equipped with nuclear weapons and the 1968 Nuclear Non-Proliferation Treaty. The treaty established international safeguards to prevent the spread of nuclear weapons to nations not already possessing them.

During his years in office, President Lyndon B. Johnson suggested several plans for nuclear arms limitation. Behind many of these proposals was growing American concern about the Soviet ABM program. A Soviet breakthrough in missile defense technology would, if not matched by the West, overcome Washington's advantage in offensive weaponry. By making its territory less vulnerable to American missiles, the Soviet Union might be tempted during a crisis to attack the United States, hoping to withstand the inevitable U.S. nuclear counterattack. The choice facing Johnson, and later President Richard Nixon, was either to begin building a multibillion-dollar ABM system or to persuade the Kremlin to discard its ABM defenses.

At the summit meeting between Johnson and Soviet premier Aleksei Kosygin in 1967 at Glassboro, New Jersey, Secretary of Defense Robert S. McNamara unsuccessfully urged the Soviet leader to abandon ABM construction and hold back an arms race. McNamara opposed the development of American antiballistic missiles as too costly, possibly ineffective, and certain to provoke escalation of the arms race. But faced with the Kremlin's refusal to limit its system, the Pentagon announced late in 1967 that the

United States would deploy the limited Sentinel ABM system. Soon after taking office in 1969, President Nixon asked Congress for the Safeguard ABM system.

SALT Begins under Nixon

Since June 1969, Nixon had urged talks with the Soviet Union on limiting strategic nuclear weapons. The talks eventually began November 17, 1969, in Helsinki, Finland. After U.S. and Soviet negotiators worked arduously to prepare the documents, Nixon and Soviet leader Brezhnev signed them during a summit in Moscow in May 1972. The strategic arms limitation (SALT) accord signed May 26 was the most important of the documents signed at the summit.

The SALT accords included both a treaty limiting ABM deployments and an executive agreement designed to limit offensive weapons and missile-carrying submarines. Under the ABM treaty, both the United States and the Soviet Union were limited to one ABM site for the defense of their capital cities and one additional site each for the defense of an ICBM installation. (In 1973 Congress prohibited the Defense Department from beginning work on the ABM site to defend Washington; a 1974 protocol between the two nations restricting each to just one site was approved by the Senate November 10.)

The five-year interim agreement limiting offensive missile launchers—land-based silos and submarine missile tubes—left the United States 1,710 launchers, of which 1,054 were ICBMs and the remaining 656 were SLBMs (submarine-launched ballistic missiles). The White House estimated the total Soviet strategic missile launcher strength to be 2,358—1,618 ICBM launchers and 740 SLBM launchers. (The London-based International Institute for Strategic Studies arrived at a lower estimate.) Besides the numerical edge, the Soviets also had the advantage in throw-weight, estimated at several times that of U.S. capacity. (Throw-weight is the measure of a missile's lift potential and ultimately the number and size of warheads a missile can carry.)

The United States, however, had a numerical advantage in warheads, as well as superiority in strategic bombers—460 at the time, compared with a Soviet total of 140—and aircraft that could strike the Soviet Union on one-way missions from European airfields.

The offensive arms agreement required approval by simple majorities in both the House and Senate; the ABM treaty had to be ratified by a two-thirds majority in the Senate. A provision in the 1961 law establishing the U.S. Arms Control and Disarmament Agency specified that any agreement to limit U.S. armed forces or armaments required approval by legislation or treaty. Nixon submitted the two accords to Congress in June together with documents explaining U.S.-Soviet agreements and disagreements on interpretations of the accords.

The Senate ratified the ABM treaty 88-2 on August 3, 1972. But the interim agreement on offensive weapons had some rough moments before it finally was approved, because the Senate attached language demanding a stiff U.S. bargaining stance in future SALT talks.

The hard-line amendment sponsored by Sen. Henry M. Jackson, D-Wash., requested that any future permanent treaty on offensive nuclear arms "not limit the United States to levels of intercontinental strategic forces inferior to" those of the Soviet Union, but instead be based on "the principle of equality." The amendment stipulated that failure to negotiate a permanent treaty limiting offensive arms would be grounds to abrogate the U.S.-Soviet ABM agreement. It also endorsed the maintenance of a vigorous research, development, and modernization program. Controversy over the Jackson proposal threatened to delay the resumption of SALT talks, then scheduled to begin in Geneva in mid-October. The House September 25 accepted the Senate changes rather than risk further delay. The Jackson amendment and others added to the measure emphasized congressional disquiet concerning the interim agreement, although they did not affect the accord itself as signed in Moscow.

1973 and 1974 Summits

When Soviet leader Brezhnev came to the United States to meet with President Nixon in June 1973, the talks were marked by their jovial tenor, not by their substance. The leaders signed a declaration, among several relatively minor agreements, they hoped would guide U.S. and Soviet negotiators in working toward a permanent strategic arms treaty. The declaration did not go into detail.

Nixon and Brezhnev also signed an agreement pledging each side to avoid nuclear war and said they were willing to sign interim agreements until a permanent accord was reached. The details of a permanent strategic arms limitation treaty to replace the earlier interim agreement were left for negotiators to work out.

Only a month before he would resign from the presidency, Nixon went to Moscow amid considerable domestic criticism seeking a breakthrough in permanent limits on offensive nuclear weapons. Instead of broadening and extending the five-year-old SALT treaty, however, Nixon and Brezhnev were able to sign only a treaty placing more limits on underground nuclear tests and a protocol limiting the number of ABM sites each country could maintain. The leaders agreed to seek a new interim SALT accord that would last through 1985. The main stumbling block to progress on SALT had been devising a way to balance the Soviet missile advantage and the U.S. warhead advantage.

The ABM protocol limited to one the number of ABM sites each superpower could have within its territory. The 1972 ABM accord had allowed each country to defend its national capital and maintain one other intercontinental ballistic missile site. But each country had deployed only one system of ABM interceptors by mid-1974; the Americans at Grand Forks, North Dakota, and the Soviets around Moscow.

Vladivostok Accord

After Nixon resigned in August 1974, President Gerald R. Ford went to Vladivostok in the Soviet Far East to meet with Brezhnev. No major agreements were expected from the summit, but Ford and Brezhnev surprised officials and the public by announcing a tentative agreement on limiting strategic offensive nuclear weapons and delivery vehicles. The Ford-Brezhnev talks jump started the stalled SALT negotiations.

The Vladivostok guidelines called for acceptance of the principle of equivalence in strategic forces—as opposed to the 1972 SALT accord that had set different but counterbalancing quotas. Each country was to be accorded latitude to choose land-based strategic missiles, submarine-launched missiles, or strategic bombers for delivery vehicles. Broad limits were set on the deployment of MIRVs. While mentioning restrictions on the total number of MIRV-equipped vehicles, the agreement left open the number of individual MIRVed warheads that could be deployed.

The Vladivostok guidelines for a SALT II agreement contained these main points:

● Each nation was limited to 2,400 strategic nuclear weapons systems and would have the freedom to mix its ICBMs, SLBMs, and heavy bombers within the ceiling. Excluded from the 2,400 limit were tactical aircraft and medium bombers. Strategic nuclear systems belonging to third countries, such as Great Britain, France, and China, were not included.

● Construction or enlargement of new ICBM silos or other fixed-site ICBM launchers was restricted, thus imposing a separate ceiling on larger missiles.

● Within the 2,400 limit on launchers of nuclear weapons, up to 1,320 missiles could be equipped MIRVs.

Secretary of State Kissinger told reporters November 24 that the Soviet Union had made one basic concession to the United States at Vladivostok. It had dropped its earlier insistence that the U.S. total of strategic delivery vehicles include the "forward-based" fighter-bomber systems deployed in Europe.

Differences over the Soviet Backfire bomber and U.S. cruise missiles (small missiles launched from land, sea, or air that fly at subsonic speeds at treetop level toward their targets) stalled SALT progress in 1975 and forced an extended delay in Brezhnev's planned visit to Washington. The Backfire was a new medium-range bomber that U.S. military experts maintained could strike targets in the United States on one-way missions. The Soviets denied that the Backfire had sufficient range for such missions and argued that it should not be included in negotiations on strategic nuclear weapons (those capable of striking the homeland of the other superpower).

Peaceful Explosions Treaty

On May 28, 1976, in the midst of the U.S. presidential election race, President Ford and Soviet leader Brezhnev signed the Peaceful Nuclear Explosions (PNE) treaty. The treaty, which was to be in force for five years, was a companion to the Threshold Test Ban treaty signed by Nixon and Brezhnev in July 1974, which limited underground tests for nuclear weapons. The Ford administration had postponed seeking Senate ratification for the 1974 treaty because it was regarded as incomplete without the PNE treaty.

The 1974 treaty established a nuclear threshold prohibiting tests having a yield exceeding 150 kilotons. The parallel PNE treaty placed the same limit of 150 kilotons on the yield of any nuclear explosion for peaceful purposes, such as might be conducted as part of an engineering project. It also limited any group explosion (consisting of a number of group explosions) to an aggregate yield not exceeding 1,500 kilotons. If either the Soviet Union or the United States planned to exceed the 150-kiloton level, the pact required on-site inspection by the other.

President Ford called the new agreement a "historic milestone in the history of arms control agreements." But critics charged that the 150-kiloton threshold was excessively high and the inspection provisions contained loopholes that limited their effectiveness. The Senate declined to ratify either treaty, but both sides pledged to observe their provisions while awaiting approval. During the 1980s

U.S.-Soviet Summit Meetings, 1945-1990

Participants	Location	Date	Main Issue
President Franklin D. Roosevelt Soviet leader Joseph Stalin British prime minister Winston Churchill	Yalta, USSR	February 1945	Composition of postwar world
President Harry S. Truman Soviet leader Joseph Stalin British prime minister Winston Churchill British prime minister Clement R. Atlee	Potsdam, East Germany	July-August 1945	Partition and control of Germany
President Dwight D. Eisenhower Soviet leader Nikolai Bulganin British prime minister Anthony Eden French premier Edgar Faure	Geneva, Switzerland	July 1955	Reunification of Germany, disarmament, European security
President Dwight D. Eisenhower Soviet leader Nikita S. Khrushchev	Camp David, Md.	September 1959	Berlin problem
President Dwight D. Eisenhower Soviet leader Nikita S. Khrushchev French president Charles de Gaulle British prime minister Harold Macmillan	Paris, France	May 1960	U-2 incident
President John F. Kennedy Soviet leader Nikita S. Khrushchev	Vienna, Austria	June 1961	Berlin problem
President Lyndon B. Johnson Soviet leader Aleksei N. Kosygin	Glassboro, N.J.	June 1967	Middle East, Vietnam War
President Richard Nixon Soviet leader Leonid I. Brezhnev	Moscow, USSR	May 1972	SALT I, trade
President Richard Nixon Soviet leader Leonid I. Brezhnev	Washington, D.C.	June 1973	Détente
President Richard Nixon Soviet leader Leonid I. Brezhnev	Moscow and Yalta, USSR	June-July 1974	Arms control
President Gerald R. Ford Soviet leader Leonid I. Brezhnev	Vladivostok, USSR	November 1974	Arms control
President Jimmy Carter Soviet leader Leonid I. Brezhnev	Vienna, Austria	June 1979	SALT II
President Ronald Reagan Soviet leader Mikhail S. Gorbachev	Geneva, Switzerland	November 1985	Arms control, U.S.-Soviet relations
President Ronald Reagan Soviet leader Mikhail S. Gorbachev	Reykjavik, Iceland	October 1986	Arms control
President Ronald Reagan Soviet leader Mikhail S. Gorbachev	Washington, D.C.	December 1987	Arms control
President Ronald Reagan Soviet leader Mikhail S. Gorbachev	Moscow, USSR	May-June 1988	Arms control, human rights
President Ronald Reagan Soviet leader Mikhail S. Gorbachev	New York, N.Y.	December 1988	Soviet troop cutbacks
President George Bush Soviet leader Mikhail S. Gorbachev	Malta	December 1989	Eastern Europe, trade
President George Bush Soviet leader Mikhail S. Gorbachev	Washington, D.C.	May-June 1990	Arms control, trade, reunification of Germany

the United States charged the Soviets with frequently violating the threshold.

In response to protocols signed in June 1990 that would enhance verification procedures, the Senate was scheduled to consider ratification of the treaties in the fall.

Carter: Continuing Dilemmas

Détente already had begun faltering before Jimmy Carter became president. Continued concern in the United States over the growth of Soviet and Warsaw Pact military capabilities prompted calls for more spending on defense.

Carter's first arms control dilemma was the neutron bomb, an enhanced radiation weapon designed to kill Soviet tank crews while limiting collateral destruction to cities and rural areas. Proponents of the weapon saw it as a means to counter the threat of a Soviet invasion of Western Europe. Armored vehicles were resistant to the blast and heat of a "regular" nuclear explosion, and Soviet vehicles, unlike their NATO counterparts, were equipped to shield their crews from radioactive fallout. The enhanced radiation warheads limited the radius of explosive blast, fire, and fallout. At the same time, they increased the fourth effect of a nuclear detonation: the momentary wave of neutron radiation that kills persons, even in a building or a tank, without harming the structures.

Critics of the neutron bomb in the United States and Europe, however, charged that limiting the destructive force of atomic weapons would increase the chances that NATO would resort to nuclear weapons early in a conflict, thus turning Europe into a nuclear battlefield. A Soviet propaganda campaign claimed that the neutron bomb was a despicable "capitalist weapon" because it killed people while leaving buildings and other property intact.

After protracted debate, Congress agreed to Carter's request to approve funding for production of the weapon. Criticism continued to mount at home and in Western European countries, however, and finally, on April 7, 1978, Carter decided to defer the bomb's production. "We will continue to move ahead with our allies to modernize and strengthen our military capabilities, both conventional and nuclear," he said, vowing to consult with NATO allies on the neutron decision and other arms control measures.

In late March 1977 Carter presented the Soviets with a comprehensive arms control plan and a plan to ratify the Vladivostok accord while leaving the cruise missile and Backfire bomber problems for later discussion. The Soviets, however, rejected both proposals. At the SALT talks in Geneva that May, negotiators developed a three-part blueprint to supersede the disputed Vladivostok agreement. The blueprint included a treaty placing ceilings on ballistic missiles until 1985, a three-year protocol covering cruise missiles and the Backfire, and a statement of general principles regarding the follow-up negotiations.

According to U.S. officials, the substance of the draft agreements, outlined in news reports in September, placed a ceiling of 2,250 on the total number of land- and sea-based missiles and long-range bombers, slightly less than a 10 percent reduction from the Vladivostok limits. In addition, three separate ceilings were placed on weapons armed with multiple warheads, including a limit of 1,320 for land- and sea-based missiles and for bombers equipped with cruise missiles. Finally, the number of large Soviet land-based missiles, the SS-18s, was restricted to 308. The three-year draft protocol placed a range restriction of 1,500 miles on cruise missiles launched by bombers and a range limit of 360 miles on the testing and deployment of new weapons for the period of the accord, including mobile ballistic missiles such as the proposed U.S. MX system. (The above figures are approximate and were the subject of continuing negotiation.)

The agreements involved concessions on both sides. The United States backed off from its insistence that the Backfire bomber be limited and allowed the Soviet Union to deploy twice as many SS-18 missiles as the administration originally desired. The United States also accepted temporary range restrictions on cruise missiles. The Soviet Union, for its part, agreed that the 1,200 ceiling on missiles equipped with multiple warheads would not cover aircraft armed with cruise missiles. Moscow also agreed to restrict the number of land-based missiles armed with multiple warheads to 800, a limit it had strongly resisted, and to refrain from increasing production of the Backfire bomber.

Between September 1977 and March 1978 congressional criticism of the proposed arms pact mounted, and some supporters expressed concern that a new agreement could not secure Senate ratification.

Senate opponents faulted the administration for leaving out the Backfire bomber and argued that no limits should be placed on bombers equipped with cruise missiles. Another concern was that the temporary restrictions in the draft protocol on cruise missiles would become permanent over time. They pointed to the importance that the United States' allies attached to the cruise missile for West European defense. The NATO allies themselves had voiced fears that the United States had conceded too much in the arms talks. Critics also contended that the limits on Soviet land-based missiles were too high, and they questioned whether key features of the agreement could be verified. The Soviets, they said, could make too many improvements in their missiles and could continue development of new weapons too easily.

The administration countered by saying the agreements contained significant Soviet concessions, were better than the Vladivostok accord, and would provide new sources of stability in the arms race. It argued that the Backfire's effectiveness had been exaggerated and that the proposed limits on U.S. bombers with cruise missiles were not unduly restrictive. Administration officials noted that the protocol would stop the testing and deployment of four new Soviet rockets then in the developmental stage. The administration also defended the verifiability of the proposals.

SALT II Agreement

Despite months of criticism, SALT negotiations continued through 1978. In May 1979 the two governments announced that a treaty would be ready to sign at the upcoming Vienna summit June 15-18. The treaty set basic numerical limits on intercontinental missiles and bombers through 1985:

● Of 2,250 weapons allowed each country (after 1982), no more than 1,320 could be missiles with multiple warheads (MIRVs) or bombers carrying long-range cruise missiles.

● Of those 1,320, no more than 1,200 could be missiles.

● Of those 1,200, no more than 820 could be land-based missiles (ICBMs).

Additional restrictions on mobile land-based missiles and cruise missiles launched from land or ships would run only until 1982.

Once home, Carter ran into significant trouble in trying to get SALT II ratified. A Soviet combat brigade was

Soviet foreign minister Eduard Shevardnadze, coarchitect of Mikhail S. Gorbachev's foreign policy, meets with Secretary of State George P. Shultz, September 15, 1987.

discovered in Cuba in 1979, and debates over its significance became daily events in Congress. Finally, in November 1979, the Senate Foreign Relations Committee voted to send the treaty to the full Senate. But after the Soviet Union invaded Afghanistan in December 1979, Carter, knowing the treaty had no chance of passing, asked the Senate to delay its consideration indefinitely. He pledged, however, to observe the unratified treaty as long as the Soviets observed it.

Reagan Takes Office

President Reagan came into office in 1981 publicly stating that the United States was strategically inferior to the Soviet Union and that the imbalance needed to be redressed. Administration officials asserted that past arms control agreements, such as the unratified but unofficially observed SALT II treaty, were hurting American national security interests, not serving them. The administration declared that unless the Soviet Union made some unilateral cuts in its nuclear forces, the United States would need to modernize its own forces before it would be ready to negotiate toward mutual reductions. The Soviet Union maintained that the nuclear arsenals of the two superpowers were roughly equal in strength.

Despite the administration's belief that it was not a propitious time for arms control, three important constituencies—the NATO allies, Congress, and the American public—wanted the United States to vigorously pursue an arms control agreement as soon as possible. Each constituency possessed leverage that disposed the Reagan administration to negotiate. West European governments could decide not to abide by a 1979 NATO decision to deploy American Pershing II intermediate-range missiles and GLCMs on their territory; Congress could limit funding for the administration's nuclear weapons modernization program; and many Americans might vote for the Democratic ticket in 1984. Some critics argued that the administration was not truly interested in arms control.

INF Negotiations

The INF negotiations were prompted by the Soviet deployment, during the late 1970s, of medium-range SS-20 missiles targeted on Western Europe. Helmut Schmidt, then chancellor of West Germany, sounded the alarm for American action. He feared the European allies were becoming "decoupled" from the U.S. nuclear deterrent and that the large Soviet advantage in intermediate-range nuclear weapons would leave the NATO allies vulnerable to an attack or to political blackmail. If the allies could not counter the Soviet missiles with comparable weapons deployed on their soil, the Kremlin might think it could strike, or credibly threaten to strike, Western Europe, without fearing retaliation from the United States. In December 1979, during the Carter presidency, NATO decided to adopt a "dual-track" approach. This meant preparing to deploy new intermediate-range nuclear weapons in Europe while simultaneously trying to negotiate with the Soviets to reduce such forces.

In November 1981 Reagan announced the "zero-option" proposal. Reagan offered to cancel the deployment of U.S. Pershing IIs and GLCMs in Europe if the Soviets would dismantle their SS-20s and their older intermediate-range SS-4 and SS-5 missiles. From the Soviet perspective, there were two major problems with this proposal. First, it did not take into account the French and British nuclear missiles targeted on the USSR. Second, the Soviets would be trading operational weapons for U.S. systems that were not yet deployed.

In December 1982 Yuri V. Andropov, Brezhnev's successor, offered to reduce the number of Soviet missiles aimed at Europe from 243 to 162 (the number deployed by France and Britain) if the United States would abandon its deployment plans. The Western allies rejected the proposal, but Reagan said that the United States would consider any Soviet proposal that would limit to equal numbers the U.S. and Soviet warheads deployed on land-based ballistic missiles in Europe.

In the summer of 1983, Andropov indicated some flexibility on INF, but on September 1 a Soviet pilot shot down a commercial Korean airliner that had strayed into Soviet airspace. All 269 people aboard were killed. The incident exacerbated U.S.-Soviet relations and undermined any chance for progress in arms control negotiations.

On November 23, 1983, after the West German Bundestag voted to accept the deployment of Pershing IIs on its soil, the Soviet INF negotiators walked out of Geneva without setting a date for the resumption of talks.

START Talks

After more than ten years of the SALT process, the Reagan administration decided to rename the main forum for arms control negotiations with the Soviet Union. To emphasize the new approach geared to "reductions" instead of "limitations," Reagan's team came up with the name Strategic Arms Reductions Talks, with the appealing acronym START.

In the START negotiations of 1981-1983, U.S. proposals primarily were designed to limit land-based ballistic missiles and throw-weight. Many of the officials who formulated START proposals contended that SALT II's equal limits and sublimits on strategic delivery vehicles—ICBMs, SLBMs, and bombers—did not prevent the Soviets from having an unacceptable advantage in ICBMs. Administration arms control advisers warned that Soviet "heavy" SS-19s and SS-18s, loaded with six and ten warheads, respectively, created a "window of vulnerability" in the U.S. nuclear deterrent. They maintained that the speed, accuracy, and potency of these missiles made them first-strike weapons capable of knocking out vulnerable U.S. land-based missiles. Conservative hard-liners posited a grim scenario wherein the Soviets would destroy a high percentage of the U.S. ICBM force in a first strike and then blackmail the American president into capitulation by threatening U.S. cities with a second strike if the president chose to retaliate with crippled forces. If the Soviets perceived the United States to be vulnerable, they might pursue their foreign policy goals more aggressively, resulting in super-power confrontations in which the United States might have to back down.

Based on this strategic assessment, the U.S. START proposal sought to limit the number of warheads deployed on ICBMs to 2,500. This would allow the United States to actually increase the number of warheads on its land-based missiles. However, because of the asymmetric nature of the respective nuclear force structures (the Soviets have emphasized land-based ICBMs, while the United States has emphasized submarine-launched missiles and bombers), the Soviet Union would have to cut the number of warheads on its ICBM forces by more than half. Another related U.S. proposal was to place an equal ceiling on aggregate missile throw-weight substantially below the existing Soviet level. The Soviets, with approximately a three-to-one advantage in total throw-weight, found these terms unacceptable. The Soviets proposed percentage reductions in strategic delivery systems based on SALT II limits and also a ban on long-range ground-launched and sea-launched cruise missiles, an area in which the United States had a decided advantage.

In January 1983 Reagan established the Commission on Strategic Forces, headed by retired lieutenant general Brent Scowcroft. The commission was charged with developing a basing plan for the MX missile. In April the Scow-

croft commission presented its report questioning the "window of vulnerability." The report argued that the U.S. strategic triad was not, for the immediate future, vulnerable to a disarming Soviet first strike. It also pointed out that making deep reductions in the number of launchers was not necessarily beneficial. The administration's original START proposal to cut ICBM and SLBM launchers to 850 would have increased the crucial warhead-to-launcher ratio. A MIRVed missile can eliminate several ICBM silos. Therefore, a reduced number of launchers would allow each country to allocate an increased number of warheads for striking each target. The land-based nuclear forces of both countries, thus, would become more vulnerable to a disarming first strike.

The Scowcroft commission recommended that the United States deploy one hundred MX missiles in existing ICBM silos, while developing a mobile single-warhead "Midgetman" ICBM. A mobile missile, it was argued, would strengthen deterrence because it would be harder to hit than a fixed one and thus more survivable. A single-warhead missile would be a less attractive target because at best the Soviets would be able to eliminate only one U.S. warhead for each Soviet warhead launched. It also was suggested that single warhead missiles were less threatening and therefore less likely to provoke a preemptive first strike.

The commission concluded that the controversial MX should be deployed in the interim because it would enhance deterrence, modernize the U.S. ICBM force, alleviate the strategic imbalance, and strengthen the U.S. bargaining position at Geneva. Reagan endorsed the commission's recommendation. Critics of the MX charged that it would be vulnerable sitting in fixed silos and that its ten warheads made it an attractive target. They argued that the MX therefore was a destabilizing first-strike weapon, better suited for launching an attack than deterring one.

As the vote to release funds for further MX development approached in May 1983, Sens. William Cohen, R-Maine, Sam Nunn, D-Ga., and Charles Percy, R-Ill., chairman of the Foreign Relations Committee, endorsed a new arms control approach called "build down." With this approach, both countries would dismantle a certain number of warheads for each new warhead deployed. The senators, who opposed the freeze, advocated build down because it allowed for reductions and modernization simultaneously.

They made it clear in a letter to President Reagan that their support for MX procurement was contingent on at least partial incorporation of the build-down approach into the administration's START proposals at Geneva as well as the inclusion of the Scowcroft recommendations for the Midgetman and de-MIRVing. Reagan approved the build-down concept in principle and indicated that he would modify his START proposal to include the Scowcroft commission's ideas. At the end of the month both the House and the Senate passed the resolution to release the MX funds.

In October, Reagan announced he would incorporate build down into the U.S. START proposal. Reportedly, the new position called for dismantling two old warheads for the deployment of each new MIRVed ICBM warhead, three old warheads for every two new SLBM warheads, and one old warhead for each new single-warhead ICBM. Such a formula encouraged a force structure emphasizing SLBMs over ICBMs and also provided an inducement for the deployment of single-warhead missiles as the Scowcroft commission had recommended. The proposed limit on ballistic missile launchers was raised from 850 to 1,250. This new offer would reduce the ratio of warheads to launchers relative to the result the earlier proposal would have achieved.

The USSR dismissed the offer as biased against ICBMs, which carried approximately 70 percent of Soviet strategic nuclear warheads compared with only about 20 percent of American strategic warheads. At the end of the year, when the United States began deploying the Euromissiles, Soviet START negotiators joined the Soviet INF negotiators in leaving the bargaining tables, saying that the strategic balance had been altered and would require a new assessment.

Debate on Reagan's SDI

On March 23, 1983, Reagan gave a speech challenging the scientific community to develop the technology for a space-based antiballistic missile defense that would someday make nuclear weapons "impotent and obsolete." During the first half of his second term, the issues surrounding arms control were dominated by the debate over SDI, commonly referred to as "Star Wars."

The initiative sparked tremendous controversy. Reagan stressed that the deployment of a strategic defense system was a moral imperative because, in contrast to offensive systems, it would destroy weapons instead of people. Supporters argued that SDI might eventually free the world from living under the "terror" of mutual assured destruction (MAD), the doctrine that both superpowers are deterred from starting a nuclear war by the threat of a devastating nuclear retaliatory strike.

Advocates of SDI also said strategic defense would be a stabilizing factor because it could enhance deterrence. They suggested that an ABM system protecting U.S. ICBM silos would so complicate calculations in Soviet strategic planning that a disarming first strike would be nearly impossible. The Soviets, SDI proponents contended, would never rationally launch a first strike knowing that relatively few ballistic missiles would penetrate the American defense. Supporters also argued that the United States needed a defensive system to protect itself from threats besides the Soviet Union. The United States, they pointed out, needed to protect itself from hostile Third World leaders, such as Libya's Muammar Qaddafi, who might one day gain access to nuclear weapons.

Critics argued that SDI's development would escalate the arms race because the Soviet Union would upgrade its offensive forces to maintain its ability to penetrate the American defense. They suggested Soviet countermeasures might draw both sides into an arms race in both offensive and defensive weapons that would be even more dangerous and expensive than the existing one.

Opponents also questioned SDI's cost and efficacy. It was projected to cost hundreds of billions of dollars in research and development, and many scientists believed that such a defensive system would never function effectively. In September 1985 the Office of Technology Assessment, a nonpartisan agency of Congress, said that a ballistic missile defense able to ensure the survival of the U.S. population did not appear to be technologically feasible unless the Soviet Union agreed to significant limits on its offensive nuclear weapons. The study suggested that a U.S. effort to develop such a system would probably provoke the Soviet Union to increase its offensive forces.

Skeptics of SDI, including Les Aspin, D-Wis., who became chairman of the House Armed Services Committee in January 1985, argued that the deployment of space-based ballistic missile defenses could undermine stability and increase the likelihood of a decision to launch a first strike. If both nations deployed somewhat imperfect systems, the argument ran, each side would have an incentive to launch a preemptive first strike. The side striking first would weaken the retaliatory forces of its adversary, making its own defense more viable and increasing its chances of survival.

Space-based antiballistic missile defense was challenged on the grounds that it could never be tested under realistic circumstances and that, even if it worked, it would not defend the United States against cruise missiles, bombers, and other contingencies such as terrorists or Soviet commandos smuggling in nuclear devices. Furthermore, some argued, a defensive system itself would not be survivable in space, if attacked by offensive space weapons.

The Soviet Union adamantly protested the U.S. development of strategic defense. The Soviets called it part of a U.S. first-strike strategy that would negate the Soviet Union's ability to maintain a credible nuclear deterrent. The Kremlin maintained that by deploying a strategic defense system the United States might be able to launch a successful surprise attack. U.S. strategic planners might expect that, after wiping out a high percentage of Soviet nuclear weapons, the American defense could repel the remainder of the depleted Soviet strategic forces. Moscow vowed to take countermeasures, if the United States proceeded with SDI development.

Reagan steadfastly supported SDI and declared that the research and development program would be nonnegotiable. During Reagan's second term, it was clear that hope for arms control between the superpowers rested on the resolution of the SDI issue.

Resumption of Talks

No formal arms control negotiations between the United States and the Soviet Union took place in 1984, but in January 1985 U.S. secretary of state George P. Shultz and Soviet foreign minister Andrei Gromyko met in Geneva to discuss possibilities for resuming talks. Following the meeting they announced that their respective countries would begin negotiations in Geneva on three types of weapons: intercontinental or "strategic" weapons; intermediate-range nuclear forces in Europe; and space weapons.

The March 12 opening of the Geneva talks coincided with a change at the top in the Kremlin. On March 10, Soviet leader Konstantin U. Chernenko died; Gorbachev was named general secretary the next day. On March 13, Reagan reversed his longstanding opposition to a get-acquainted summit meeting and offered to meet with Gorbachev. The two countries on July 3 formally announced a Reagan-Gorbachev meeting to be held in November.

There were two main reasons for the Soviet decision to return to the bargaining table. First, Moscow wanted to prevent, or at least slow down, the development of SDI. Second, by walking out of the arms control talks, the Soviets had made a costly public relations mistake in the contest for Western European public opinion. The Soviet Union not only failed to prevent the deployment of new American missiles in Western Europe, but it also appeared the more intransigent of the two superpowers when it came to pursuing arms control.

The growing perception that the new negotiations might lead to a beneficial treaty between the United States and the Soviet Union influenced some congressional leaders in their decisions on military spending and procurement of new nuclear weapons systems.

In late March, after intense lobbying by the administration, the House passed a bill to procure twenty-one more MX missiles for fiscal year 1985. To many, the most compelling argument in the new missile system's favor was that its deployment would indicate American resolve and improve the U.S. bargaining position at Geneva.

Summit Posturing

On April 7, 1985, the day Gorbachev tentatively accepted Reagan's proposal to hold a summit in 1985, the general secretary announced a moratorium on the deployment of intermediate-range nuclear missiles in Europe, with the hope that the United States would follow suit. Reagan dismissed the offer as a propaganda ploy that would lock in a Soviet advantage. Such exchanges set the tone for U.S.-Soviet dialogue for the next six months. The resumption of arms control talks and the preparation for the summit between the two leaders, which eventually was set for November 19-20, stimulated a propaganda war between the countries.

Following heated debate within the administration, Reagan announced June 10 his decision not to "undercut" the terms of the SALT II treaty. To stay under the SALT limit of 1,200 MIRVed ballistic missile launchers, the United States dismantled a Poseidon submarine before deploying a new Trident submarine. Reagan called this action an example of his willingness "to go the extra mile" to eventually achieve a meaningful arms control agreement. In this context, Reagan accused the Soviets of violating SALT II provisions and said that, if necessary, the United States would make "appropriate and proportional responses." Further decisions on adherence that would arise when new MIRVed missile launchers were deployed, such as the next Trident and the MX, would be made on a case-by-case basis in response to Soviet actions.

The Soviets dismissed Reagan's decision to continue adherence to the treaty, arguing that limits on defensive systems, such as those in the ABM treaty, are preconditions for limits on offensive systems. The Soviets claimed that development and testing of SDI, which they said would violate the ABM treaty, precluded stringent restraints on offensive weapons.

In July, Gorbachev declared a Soviet moratorium on the testing of nuclear weapons through the end of 1985, starting on August 6, the fortieth anniversary of the bombing of Hiroshima. The United States declined to stop testing, again accusing Gorbachev of a propaganda ploy. The administration said that the Soviets recently had tested their latest nuclear weapons and that a moratorium would hamper the progress of developing American programs needed to catch up. Furthermore, the United States said that such a testing moratorium would be unverifiable, given the Soviet refusal to allow on-site inspections. Instead of declaring a testing moratorium, the administration invited Soviet officials to monitor a U.S. underground nuclear test in Nevada. The Politburo turned down the offer.

The U.S. Air Force successfully tested an antisatellite (ASAT) weapon in September amidst great controversy. The Soviets, who had abstained from ASAT testing for two years, accused the United States of escalating the arms race in space and said that they no longer felt bound to their unilateral moratorium. The United States maintained that the test was necessary because the Soviets already had an operational system and an American counterpart could deter its use.

In October Gorbachev submitted a new arms control proposal to Reagan through his recently appointed foreign minister, Eduard Shevardnadze. The Soviets offered a 50 percent mutual reduction in strategic offensive weapons, if the United States would scrap its strategic defense program. The Reagan administration objected to many of the specifics of the plan, including its suggestion that SDI laboratory research should be prohibited as well as testing and deployment. The United States, even if it wanted to concur, believed that such a ban would be nearly impossible to verify.

The Soviets also proposed a freeze on the number of intermediate-range nuclear forces in Europe. The official offer would have banned U.S. Pershing IIs and GLCMs and reduced the number of Soviet SS-20s to 243, matching British and French force levels. The interim freeze proposal, however, offered hope to the United States for a potential INF agreement, as it implicitly acknowledged acceptance of the U.S. deployment of intermediate-range nuclear forces in Europe up to that time.

On October 6, 1985, Reagan's national security adviser, Robert C. McFarlane, announced that the administration had reexamined the 1972 ABM treaty and now interpreted it as allowing SDI development and testing. According to McFarlane, the 1972 agreement barred only deployment of a new ABM system. Gerard Smith, the U.S. chief negotiator for the ABM treaty, disputed the administration's findings.

The new interpretation created an uproar with the NATO allies. The ABM treaty was considered by many to be the cornerstone of arms control. To assuage NATO concerns, Secretary of State Shultz assured the West Europeans on October 14 that even though the new interpretation was correct the United States would continue to observe the older, more restrictive interpretation.

About three weeks before the summit Reagan's negotiators offered a counterproposal to Gorbachev's START plan. Reagan agreed to the concept of 50 percent cuts but wanted them made in ballistic warheads instead of in nuclear charges. The United States continued to stress that extremely accurate and potent ballistic missiles, which can hit their targets in less than thirty minutes, are the most dangerous nuclear weapons and should not be considered equal to slow-flying cruise missiles or bombs delivered by aircraft. The United States proposed a ceiling of 4,500 ballistic warheads, which was 500 fewer than its earlier proposal; and a sublimit on land-based warheads of 3,000, which was 500 more than its earlier proposal (and 600 fewer than the latest Soviet proposal).

The U.S. offer did not yield on Reagan's commitment to develop and test strategic defense. The proposal also sought a ban on mobile land-based missiles, repudiating the Scowcroft commission's recommendation and angering congressional leaders who had supported the MX in exchange for the administration's backing of Midgetman.

The administration defended its proposed ban on mobile ICBMs by pointing out that the Soviets would have to scrap their recently deployed SS-24 and SS-25 mobile missiles. It also noted that allowing mobile missile systems would create difficult verification problems and give an advantage to the Soviet Union, which has far more available land on which to deploy these systems. Further arguments against mobile systems included their cost and potentially negative impact on the environment.

The U.S. proposal also called for a limit on throw-weight, which would have forced the Soviets to reduce their existing throw-weight level from approximately 5.7 million kilograms to about 3 million kilograms. The existing U.S. throw-weight level was about 1.9 million kilograms. Another provision called for a ban on the modernization of heavy missiles, which would have denied the Soviets the option of upgrading their 308 SS-18s. Long-range bombers would have been limited to 350, and only 1,500 air-launched cruise missiles (ALCMs) could have been deployed.

For INF, the United States proposed a limit of 140 launchers for each country in Europe and also reductions in Soviet Asian-based SS-20s. This would have allowed the Soviets 140 3-warhead SS-20s, and the United States 36 single-warhead Pershing IIs and 104 GLCMs with 4 single-warhead missiles on each launcher, for 420 and 452 total warheads, respectively. The American offer did not count French and British forces. France and Great Britain were expected to MIRV their existing single-warhead missiles at the end of the 1980s, precluding any future deal to include French and British warheads in the balance.

About two weeks before the summit, Reagan granted an interview with four Soviet journalists and said, "We would not deploy [a strategic defense system] until we sit down with the other nations of the world, and those that have nuclear arsenals, and see if we cannot come to an agreement on which there will be deployment only if there is elimination of the [offensive] nuclear weapons.... We would want it [SDI] for everyone and the terms for getting it, and the terms for our own deployment would be the elimination of the offensive weapons." This indicated that Moscow might have the option to veto SDI deployment. Reagan's aides scrambled to qualify and modify his statement. They said that the president meant there would be a transitional period in which defensive systems were phased in and offensive systems were phased out.

Despite these corrections, the president's imprecision raised doubts about his grasp of arms control issues and the implications of his policies. Skeptics of Reagan's technology-sharing offer pointed out that by the time SDI reached fruition, if ever, Reagan would have long since left the presidency. The Soviets had no guarantee that future U.S. presidents would feel obligated to honor the offer.

The November 1985 summit meeting produced no surprise announcement of arms agreements. In a joint communiqué released November 21, Reagan and Gorbachev called their discussions "frank and useful," while acknowledging that "serious differences remain on a number of critical issues."

On arms control issues, the communiqué called for "early progress" on weapons reduction. Two areas were singled out: agreement on a 50 percent reduction in nuclear weapons of the two sides and a separate agreement on intermediate-range missiles in Europe.

The communiqué made no reference to Moscow's demands that an agreement to ban SDI and other space weapons accompany limits on intercontinental and intermediate-range nuclear missiles in Europe. But in a postsummit news conference, Gorbachev seemed to reaffirm the Soviet position that SDI limits would have to be part of any arms deal.

SALT II Compliance

Reagan made it clear following the summit that the United States would continue to abide by SALT II after it expired December 31, 1985, if the Soviets did the same. In a December 23 report to Congress, he officially confirmed U.S. intentions to continue complying with SALT II. But at the same time he accused the USSR of new arms control violations.

On May 27, 1986, however, Reagan announced that the United States no longer would observe the SALT II agreement, thus ending the six-year policy of informal SALT II compliance. Reagan said he was taking the step because the Soviets repeatedly had violated the terms of the treaty. The United States formally exceeded the numerical weapons limits in the treaty on November 28, 1986, when it put into service the 131st B-52 bomber equipped to carry long-range cruise missiles.

In 1987, however, the U.S. Congress approved binding SALT-compliance provisions attached to the fiscal 1988 defense authorization bill. The final version of the bill required the retirement of one missile-firing submarine, thus largely offsetting an increase in the number of missile-armed bombers scheduled to occur during the year. The bill set an informal cap on the number of U.S. weapons at a level slightly above one of the SALT II sublimits. In their report accompanying the compromise bill, House and Senate conferees declared their intention to continue retiring aging Poseidon subs as their turn for overhaul came due. Retiring these old ships when they required expensive overhaul could be justified as a budgetary measure, thus sparing the administration the need to accept a reduction of weapons for the sake of SALT II, which would have enraged conservative hard-liners.

Postsummit Developments

A December 5, 1985, letter to President Reagan from General Secretary Gorbachev (which was made public December 19) initiated an exchange of offers on nuclear weapons tests that built on the proposals of the previous summer. Gorbachev attempted to counter a primary Reagan administration objection to a mutual moratorium on nuclear testing by offering to allow U.S. inspections of some Soviet nuclear test facilities if the United States joined the USSR in an extended testing halt. Gorbachev's proposal for limited on-site verification broke with the usual Soviet pattern of refusing to consider such measures. Reagan welcomed Gorbachev's offer and proposed technical talks on improving verification of testing agreements. But the administration rejected Gorbachev's moratorium, saying the United States needed testing to maintain the reliability of its arsenal and that the Soviets could not be trusted to honor an extended moratorium. In January 1986 Gorbachev extended the five-month unilateral moratorium on nuclear tests until April, but the United States again refused to join the halt.

On January 15 Gorbachev caught the Reagan administration by surprise when he proposed a comprehensive ban on nuclear weapons to be achieved in stages by the year 2000. Gorbachev also called for a comprehensive ban on the production of chemical weapons, a resumption of talks on a comprehensive test ban, and progress on talks on conventional forces and confidence-building measures in Europe.

U.S. officials had said they did not expect a new Soviet proposal until after the Soviet Communist Party Congress ended in early March. Gorbachev's plan incorporated existing Soviet positions but introduced new ideas. His call for an initial 50 percent reduction in strategic arsenals with each side retaining no more than six thousand nuclear charges was basically the same offer made by the Soviets in Geneva before the summit. The plan also contained no easing of the Soviet demand that U.S. development of SDI and ASATs be discontinued before any reductions in nuclear weapons. However, with respect to intermediate-range missiles, the Reagan administration was encouraged by what it perceived as shifts in the Soviet position. Gorbachev called for the "complete liquidation" of all U.S. and Soviet intermediate-range missiles in Europe—a statement approaching the original zero-option proposal made by Reagan in 1981. The general secretary also said French and British nuclear weapons would not have to be included in an agreement so long as those countries pledged not to build up their arsenals.

These changes and Gorbachev's positive statements concerning Soviet willingness to cooperate on verification led U.S. officials to be optimistic about the chances for an INF agreement. This optimism was reinforced February 6 when Gorbachev told Sen. Edward M. Kennedy, D-Mass., in Moscow that the only conditions for an accord reducing intermediate-range missiles in Europe were a freeze on British and French nuclear arsenals and an agreement that the Western nuclear powers not move weapons to any other country. Gorbachev did not reiterate his January 15 statement that there would be no INF accord until the United States stopped development of space weapons.

The United States formally responded to Gorbachev's arms control plan February 24. In a letter to the general secretary, Reagan said the plan was "clearly not appropriate for consideration at this time." The president stated "the total elimination of nuclear weapons" could be accomplished only if the USSR fully complied with its treaty obligations, reduced its conventional forces in Europe, and cooperated in resolving regional conflicts. He asked that the two sides concentrate their efforts on phasing out intermediate-range nuclear weapons.

Reykjavik Summit

Arms control negotiations made little progress during the spring and summer of 1986. In the hope of advancing the arms talks and setting the agenda for a full summit to be held soon in the United States, Reagan and Gorbachev agreed to meet in Reykjavik, Iceland, October 11-12. At this "mini-summit," Reagan and Gorbachev discussed making sweeping reductions in their countries' nuclear arsenals. In addition to making progress on an INF agreement, the two apparently agreed on major elements of a START agreement, which included ceilings for each side of 1,600 "strategic delivery vehicles"—ICBMs, submarine-launched ballistic missiles, and long-range bombers; 6,000 warheads carried by those missiles and bombers; and 154 "heavy" ICBMs, carrying a total of no more than 1,540 warheads. The two sides also agreed that the total throw-weight of the remaining ICBMs and SLBMs would be roughly 50 percent of the current Soviet throw-weight.

The talks broke down, however, over Gorbachev's demand for a ten-year moratorium on field tests (all research done outside a laboratory) of SDI components. Reagan adamantly refused to agree to limit SDI efforts, even in return for major cuts in Soviet weapons levels. Gorbachev, in an October 14 televised address in Moscow, said that he

favored "reduction and then complete elimination of nuclear weapons" but that SDI amounted to a "new stage of the arms race." Nevertheless, Gorbachev indicated that Soviet concessions made in Iceland would remain on the table.

INF Treaty

During 1987 U.S.-Soviet arms control efforts focused on intermediate-range nuclear forces in Europe. Several Soviet concessions made conclusion of a treaty regarding these weapons possible. First, Moscow decoupled progress on an INF treaty from progress on limiting SDI. Second, the Soviets became more accepting of extremely intrusive verification procedures demanded by the United States. Finally, the Soviets agreed to terms that were close to Reagan's zero-option plan first proposed in November 1981. At that time, the plan was quickly rejected by the Soviets and widely dismissed as unrealistic by most defense analysts.

On December 8, 1987, Gorbachev and Reagan signed the INF treaty at a summit in Washington. The treaty would become the first U.S.-Soviet arms agreement ratified since 1972. It required the destruction within three years of all missiles with ranges of between 500 and 5,500 kilometers (roughly 300 to 3,400 miles), together with their associated launchers and support facilities. A total of 859 U.S. missiles and 1,836 Soviet missiles were to be destroyed.

In terms of the number of nuclear warheads that would be removed from service, the ratio was lopsided in the United States' favor, since a large proportion of the scrapped Soviet weapons were triple-warhead SS-20s. All of the U.S. missiles were single-warhead Pershing II and GLCMs.

To verify compliance, the pact established an unprecedented system for each country's inspectors to visit, on very short notice, facilities in the other country, where the banned missiles had been deployed, stored, or serviced.

The U.S. Senate approved the treaty on May 27, 1988, by a 93-5 vote. The documents of ratification for the treaty were exchanged by Reagan and Gorbachev at a summit in Moscow May 29-June 2. Actual destruction of INF missiles began on August 1 with the Soviets going first.

Moscow Summit

With the INF treaty completed, U.S. and Soviet leaders devoted more attention to making progress in START negotiations. At the Moscow summit, Gorbachev and Reagan agreed to order their negotiators to resume work on a treaty cutting arsenals of long-range nuclear weapons by 30 to 50 percent. But SDI remained the greatest obstacle. As in previous summits, Reagan and Gorbachev effectively agreed to disagree on the testing of SDI, thereby postponing tough decisions.

However, both sides reported "substantial additional common ground" on two of the START issues that probably were the easiest to resolve: verifying limits on mobile missiles and on long-range missiles launched from aircraft.

In lieu of a START pact, Secretary of State Shultz and Soviet foreign minister Shevardnadze signed two minor arms accords May 31:

● An agreement requiring each country to give the other at least twenty-four hours' advance notice of the test launching of any land-based or sea-based ICBM.

● An agreed-upon experiment for measuring underground nuclear tests in each country. The purpose of the experiment was to determine verification requirements for an unratified 1974 treaty establishing a limit of 150 kilotons on underground tests. The two sides also pledged to work on new agreements that would allow ratification of that treaty and a companion 1976 treaty establishing limits on peaceful nuclear explosions.

Gorbachev Troop Cuts

Six months after the Moscow summit, on December 7, Gorbachev delivered a wide-ranging and historic address to the UN General Assembly. In the speech he broke dramatically with traditional Soviet rhetoric, criticizing the role of military force and ideological struggle in world affairs. He announced Soviet plans to cut five hundred thousand of the country's nearly five million troops by 1991. Gorbachev also called for "consistent movement" toward a START agreement, "while preserving the ABM treaty."

Gorbachev's troop cut proposal prompted cautious optimism from Western officials. They noted that it seemed to meet NATO's insistence that any Soviet troop cut be tailored to hit in particular those Soviet forces in Eastern Europe that Western allies long had claimed were poised to mount a blitzkrieg against West Germany.

Although Gorbachev presented his arms cuts as unilateral, he subsequently told reporters that he hoped the United States and its European allies "will also take some steps." Reagan and Bush lauded the Soviet move. "If it is carried out speedily and in full," Reagan told a Washington audience later on December 7, "history will regard it as important—significant." But he warned against taking the Soviet reductions as a cue for similar U.S. cutbacks. "This still leaves them with superiority in the amount of conventional arms," the president said December 8 at a televised press conference. "We're still way below them." West European leaders echoed those thoughts.

The following March 6, the Conventional Forces in Europe (CFE) talks opened in Vienna. These negotiations replaced the Mutual and Balanced Force Reduction talks and included representatives of all NATO and Warsaw Pact countries. The CFE talks sought to reduce the alliances' inventories of conventional weapons such as tanks, aircraft, and artillery pieces, as well the number of military personnel deployed in Europe. The alliances traded proposals during the first weeks of negotiations. Then in late May President Bush outlined a comprehensive approach to limiting conventional forces at a NATO summit in Brussels. The central feature of his plan was that the United States and Soviet Union reduce their troop strength in Europe to 275,000 troops each.

At the NATO summit, Western leaders also agreed to link progress in the CFE talks to negotiations on limiting short-range nuclear weapons in Europe. The Soviets had stated their desire to eliminate these nuclear weapons, and the West German government, on whose soil most of the weapons were stationed, urged that negotiations be conducted toward this goal. Bush, however, maintained that short-range nuclear weapons were necessary as a deterrent against attack by superior numbers of Soviet conventional forces. After extensive negotiations, the Western leaders compromised on the issue. The summit communiqué stated: "Once implementation of such an agreement [on limiting conventional forces] is under way, the United States, in consultation with the allies concerned, is prepared to enter negotiations to achieve a partial reduction of American and Soviet land-based nuclear missile forces of shorter range to equal and verifiable levels."

Malta and Washington Summits

Bush and Gorbachev held a shipboard summit off the Mediterranean island of Malta, December 2-3, 1989. The meeting was held in a friendly, businesslike atmosphere, although bad weather forced the cancellation of one scheduled meeting. The astonishing events in Eastern Europe tended to upstage the Malta summit. The entire leadership of the East German Communist party resigned on December 3 as Bush and Gorbachev were winding up their talks. The next day, mass protests in Czechoslovakia forced concessions from that country's teetering Communist leadership.

Bush and Gorbachev agreed to speed up negotiations on arms control and economic issues—in effect keeping superpower relations on a par with the pace of political change in Eastern Europe. They agreed that Secretary of State James A. Baker and Foreign Minister Shevardnadze would meet in Moscow in January to work toward a START agreement that would cut each superpower's nuclear arsenal by about half. Bush and Gorbachev said they hoped a START treaty could be signed during 1990. The two sides also stated their intention to hasten their work on multilateral treaties limiting conventional forces in Europe and banning the use and possession of chemical and biological weapons.

Since Malta, U.S.-Soviet arms control efforts constantly have been in danger of being overtaken by events. Negotiations have moved forward slowly, while events on the world stage have moved forward with breathtaking speed.

Despite sincere U.S. and Soviet efforts, a START treaty was not ready to sign by the time Gorbachev was scheduled to come to Washington at the beginning of June 1990. The two leaders settled at the summit for signing statements outlining the major areas of agreement in the START treaty and setting goals for further reductions. Some negotiators have stated that the treaty is about 95 percent completed, and Bush has expressed optimism that it will be completed by the end of 1990, although many experts are skeptical and say that the middle of 1991 is more realistic.

The two sides have agreed on the overall total numbers of launchers and warheads to be permitted. Because of compromises in the counting rules, the actual cuts in warheads will be far below the 50 percent goal both sides had sought—probably about 30 percent. For example, because the number of ordinary nuclear bombs on a bomber cannot be easily verified, the sides agreed to count each bomber carrying such weapons as one warhead, though bombers can carry many more.

The United States has emphasized the limitation of land-based ICBMs because of Soviet advantages in these weapons and because they are the strategic weapons that are most accurate and vulnerable to attack. They would be the main element in any first-strike assault, because they are vulnerable, and a superpower may be tempted to launch them in a crisis situation because it feels it must "use them or lose them." The Soviets have sought to limit the number of submarine-based missiles because of significant American advantages in technology in this area.

Several other significant differences between the sides remain. The Soviets maintain that the Backfire bomber

U.S. and Soviet Strategic Forces under START

	As of July 1990		Under START	
	United States	Soviet Union	United States	Soviet Union
Warheads on intercontinental ballistic missiles	2,450	6,530	1,444	3,060
Warheads on submarine-launched ballistic missiles	5,024	3,642	3,456	1,840
Warheads on ballistic missiles	7,474	10,172	4,900[1]	4,900[1]
Air-launched cruise missiles	1,600	640	1,840	1,350
Other warheads carried by bombers	3,000	400	3,440	2,000
Sea-launched cruise missiles	350	0	880[2]	880[2]

[1] Submarine-launched ballistic missiles (SLBMs) that are being overhauled would be permitted beyond the 4,900 limit. The United States is overhauling 576 SLBMs; the Soviet Union is overhauling 528 SLBMs.

[2] The United States has declared that it plans to deploy a total of 758 sea-launched cruise missiles. Soviet sea-launched cruise missiles are under development.

Source: Arms Control Association

should not be considered a long-range weapon, while Americans continue to claim it has that capability. The United States wants to block scheduled modernization of the Soviets' SS-18 missile. The sides also must reach agreement on many verification issues.

The START provisions agreed upon would:

● Limit the number of warheads on ICBMs and SLBMs to 4,900 on each side.

● Limit the number of warheads on mobile ICBMs to 1,100.

● Eliminate half of the Soviets' 308 10-warhead SS-18 missiles.

● Permit 150 U.S. bombers carrying long-range cruise missiles and 210 Soviet bombers carrying fewer such missiles apiece.

● Bar each country through a separate agreement from deploying more than 880 sea-launched cruise missiles armed with nuclear warheads.

Bush and Gorbachev also signed a chemical weapons treaty at the Washington summit. It commits both sides to halt production of chemical weapons as soon as the pact is ratified. In 1992 it mandates that the superpowers begin destroying their stocks of chemical weapons so that by the year 2000 their arsenals will be half their present size. Two years later their chemical weapons stocks are to be just 20 percent of their current levels. Negotiators have yet to work out verification details.

In the first months of 1990, U.S.-Soviet disagreements on several issues slowed progress in the CFE talks. Warsaw

Pact and NATO negotiators agreed on limits of 20,000 tanks for each side and 195,000 foreign troops in Central Europe, along with other set numbers of armaments. However, negotiators have become bogged down in the complex nature of conventional arms control. Unlike strategic arms control, which deals with a few thousand weapons of just a few types, conventional arms control involves hundreds of thousands of pieces of equipment and millions of troops stationed at varying distances from the likely point of battle. Negotiators have been bogged down in mundane questions, such as the definition of a tank and determining principles of equivalence when weapons are of different power and quality. Verification also is complicated because of the small size of weapons.

While negotiators have been struggling with these questions, events in Europe have threatened to make the talks irrelevant. With the fall of communist governments in Eastern Europe, the Warsaw Pact no longer is a cohesive alliance system. The Soviets have signed bilateral agreements with Czechoslovakia and Hungary to withdraw all of their forces from those countries by July 1991. More important, Moscow has consented to a united Germany joining NATO and has agreed to pull all its troops out of Germany in three to four years. Because a large percentage of both alliances' troops, conventional weapons, and short-range nuclear weapons are deployed in Germany, German unification will profoundly change the rules under which negotiators have been operating. Meanwhile the U.S. Congress has begun planning deep unilateral cuts in U.S. forces.

Bush has called for a CFE treaty to be ready in 1991, but experts doubt that negotiators could resolve all the details by then. When completed, a CFE treaty may merely reflect unilateral cuts already taken.

Economic Relations

Economic relations between the United States and the Soviet Union have been affected by both political concerns and the myth of the great Soviet market—the idea that a vast, industrialized nation of nearly three hundred million people must be a tremendous untapped market for American exports. This idea has been around a long time. American business interests influenced Roosevelt's decision to finally recognize the Soviet regime in 1933. During the 1930s the Soviet Union was an important U.S. trading partner. The Soviets bought large amounts of U.S. metalworking and agricultural machinery needed for Joseph Stalin's collectivization and industrialization drives.

During the cold war, U.S. trade with Communist-bloc nations was substantially less than it was with the same nations before World War II. In 1963, for example, U.S. exports to the Communist bloc amounted to only 166.7 million dollars, which equaled just .7 percent of total U.S. exports of 20.2 billion dollars. In contrast, from 1926 to 1930, U.S. exports to the countries that would later make up the Communist bloc averaged 214 million dollars a year—4.7 percent of total exports. (This does not include exports to East Germany, for which separate figures were not then kept.) Because of U.S. restrictions on trade with the East bloc and the Soviet Union's failure to manufacture goods marketable in the West, trade between the superpowers in the postwar period never fulfilled its potential.

Some of these restrictions were coordinated with other Western nations. After the North Atlantic treaty was signed in 1949, the United States and its allies set up a Coordinating Committee (COCOM) to seek common policies on exports to communist nations. From the outset the allies agreed to bar shipments of arms to the East bloc, but they differed on what other items should be included in COCOM's list of embargoed goods. The United States consistently argued for a more extensive listing than did the Europeans. With the death of Stalin and the achievement of a truce in the Korean War in 1953, pressure mounted in Europe for reduced restrictions on trade with communist nations, and COCOM's list was cut sharply in 1954 and again in 1958. The United States, however, continued to maintain tighter restrictions on its own exports to the Soviet bloc.

Restrictions on trade with communist countries were relaxed with the passage of the Export Administration Act of 1969 (PL 91-184). The act, which replaced the expiring Export Control Act of 1949, contained a provision enabling U.S. companies to sell items to communist nations if the items were freely available from other areas or countries, such as Western Europe and Japan. The legislation also recognized that "the unwarranted restrictions of exports from the United States has a serious adverse effect on our balance of payments."

The Nixon administration asked for a simple four-year extension of the 1949 act. But supporters of eased restrictions argued that cold war hostilities had quieted and that the main effect of the controls in the old act was to deny U.S. exporters access to a growing East European market.

Trade under Détente

At the 1972 Moscow summit Nixon and Brezhnev agreed to improve and expand economic relations. The statement on basic principles released at the end of the summit noted that both sides viewed commercial ties "as an important and necessary element in the strengthening of their bilateral relations." In concrete terms, this meant the establishment of the Joint United States-USSR Commercial Commission on May 26, 1972, and the announcement July 8, 1972, that the United States had advanced to Moscow a 500 million dollar line of credit in return for a Soviet pledge to buy 750 million dollars' worth of U.S. grain over a three-year period. On July 5 the Soviets had contracted to buy more than 8.5 million tons of U.S. grain.

A major stumbling block to broader economic relations between the superpowers was settlement of the Soviet Union's World War II lend-lease debts to the United States. Administration officials insisted on settlement of the debts as part of any broad trade agreement. Negotiations culminated October 18 with the signing of a three-year trade pact and an agreement on repayment of the lend-lease debts.

Before the trade agreement could be implemented, Congress needed to approve most-favored-nation (MFN) status (nondiscrimination in customs matters) for Soviet products. If Congress refused to grant MFN status, the pact would not be implemented and the Soviet Union would not have to repay its 722 million dollars in lend-lease debt. According to the agreement, the Soviets would repay 48 million dollars by July 1975, but the remaining balance would be deferred until the United States granted MFN status.

Grain Sales

In 1972 the Nixon administration negotiated a grain sale to the Soviet Union that proved to be controversial. As described by the U.S. Agriculture Department, the bulk of the transaction was to consist of feed grains, such as corn, which would be used by the Soviets to bolster their poultry and livestock production. By late summer, however, it became apparent that Soviet interest had shifted to wheat. Agriculture Secretary Earl L. Butz said September 9 that Soviet purchases of wheat alone could reach four hundred million bushels in 1972—more than one-fourth the total U.S. crop. Butz added that total U.S. grain sales to the Soviets were approaching one billion dollars for the year, far more than the total value originally contemplated over the entire three-year life of the agreement.

In fact, the Soviets bought more than 700 million bushels of grain, including nearly 440 million bushels of wheat. As a result, the government paid more than 300 million dollars in export subsidies to U.S. grain traders. In addition, worldwide prices for grains rose steeply in the wake of the Soviet purchases, which, according to some critics of the sale, pushed up consumer costs in the United States.

There was speculation that the large grain traders were aware the Russians were planning to buy an unprecedented amount of grain—which would hike prices—but neglected to share this information with grain farmers before the farmers sold their goods. The Senate Government Operations Permanent Subcommittee on Investigations, in a report issued July 29, 1974, had harsh words for the Agriculture Department's handling of the 1972 grain sales. While the subcommittee lauded the Nixon administration's goals—easing tensions between the United States and Soviet Union, improving America's balance of payments deficit, and allowing U.S. farmers to profitably and usefully dispose of crop surpluses—it concluded that because of inept management and poor judgment in the Department of Agriculture the grain sale resulted in a domestic shortage of farm products, a snarled U.S. transportation system, waste of taxpayers' dollars, "unprecedented" rises in the cost of food, and added inflation.

Memories of the 1972 sale led to an informal administration embargo on grain sales to the Soviet Union in 1975 after Moscow again began buying large amounts of grain (9.8 million tons by late July). The embargo was lifted October 20 when a five-year Soviet-American grain agreement was signed in Moscow, pledging the Soviets to buy between six million and eight million tons of grain each year.

Trade Act of 1974

President Nixon followed up his commitment made to Kremlin leaders at the Moscow summit by submitting to Congress April 10, 1973, a bill empowering the president to extend MFN status to the Soviet Union.

When the General Agreement on Tariffs and Trade (GATT) was concluded in Geneva in 1947, the contracting parties agreed to extend MFN treatment to each other. This general rule required each party to accord equal treatment to the products of all other parties. In the president's trade bill, he requested authority to enter into bilateral commercial arrangements to extend MFN status to products of countries that did not receive such treatment. The president would be authorized to extend the treatment to countries that joined a multilateral trade agreement to which the United States was a party.

The authority to award MFN status was directed primarily at the Soviet Union. Implementation of the October 1972 trade agreement hinged on congressional approval of MFN treatment for Soviet products. If it was not granted, the pact would not enter into force, and the Soviets, in accordance with the other agreement signed in October, would not be obliged to repay the balance of their World War II lend-lease debt.

Anti-Soviet sentiment in Congress, however, had increased as a result of the Kremlin's backing of the Arab states in the 1973 Middle East war and its restrictions on Jewish emigration from the Soviet Union. As a result, many congressional leaders proposed to withhold MFN status from the Soviets. By the end of March 1973, 76 senators and 273 representatives joined in sponsoring an amendment that would bar MFN treatment and the extension of credits, credit guarantees, or investment credits to any nonmarket-economy country denying or taxing emigration. The amendment initiative was led in the Senate by Henry M. Jackson, D-Wash., and in the House by Charles A. Vanik, D-Ohio. Over administration opposition, the House December 11 passed the trade bill containing the restrictive Vanik amendment. The House-passed measure allowed the president to give MFN status to Soviet imports—but only if he certified to Congress that the Soviet government's restrictive emigration policies had been eased—and gave either the House or the Senate power to overrule the president's action. The Nixon administration protested that emigration from the Soviet Union by Jews and others would be facilitated not by confrontation, but

by an overall improvement in East-West relations.

House consideration of the bill was delayed three times in October and November 1973 at the request of President Nixon and Secretary of State Kissinger. With anti-Soviet, pro-Israeli congressional emotions aroused by the Arab-Israeli war in the Middle East, officials feared that House debate on the trade bill at that time could only increase U.S.-Soviet tensions.

The Senate did not act on the trade bill until late in 1974 as the controversy over Jewish emigration continued. Throughout the year, the Soviets took the position that emigration was an internal matter unrelated to U.S.-Soviet affairs. The administration was forced into negotiating with both the Kremlin and the Senate in an attempt to fashion a compromise that would not alienate the Soviets yet would satisfy Congress.

A compromise between the White House and Congress was announced October 18. An exchange of letters between Jackson and Kissinger released that day outlined the conditions the Soviets would have to meet in their emigration policies before the president would certify to Congress that their practices were leading substantially to a free emigration policy. Jackson said the agreement, based on assurances of Soviet leaders, assumed that the annual rate of emigration from the Soviet Union would rise from the 1973 level of about 35,000 and would in the future correspond to the number of applicants, which Jackson said exceeded 130,000. A benchmark of 60,000 annually would be considered a "minimum standard" of compliance, he said.

In testimony before the Senate Finance Committee on December 3, Kissinger said the compromise did not reflect "formal government commitments" between the two countries but was based on "clarifications of Soviet democratic practices from Soviet leaders." He cautioned the committee that any attempt "to nail down publicly" additional details or commitments was "likely to backfire." Kissinger said, "If I were to assert here that a formal agreement on emigration from the USSR exists between our governments, that statement would immediately be repudiated by the Soviet government." He added that no commitments had been made by Soviet leaders on specific numbers of emigrés.

The Soviet Union December 18 issued a statement denying it had given any specific assurances that emigration policies would be eased in return for American trade concessions and replying in particular to Jackson's claim that emigration would increase. It also released the text of an October 26 letter to Kissinger from Foreign Minister Gromyko, criticizing the Jackson-Kissinger letters as a "distorted picture of our position as well as of what we told the American side on that matter." Gromyko called the issue a wholly domestic one and said the Soviet Union expected a decrease, not an increase, in the number of persons wishing to emigrate.

Despite the confusion over what exactly had been worked out, Congress passed the bill—the Trade Act of 1974—December 20. Soviet reaction came quickly. Kissinger announced January 14, 1975, that the Kremlin had rejected the terms for trade contained in the Jackson-Vanik amendment and accordingly would not put into force the 1972 trade agreement.

U.S. Economic Sanctions

Commercial relations between the United States and the Soviet Union were damaged severely by the Soviet invasion of Afghanistan in December 1979 and the subsequent economic sanctions imposed on the USSR by the Carter administration. Among other measures, Carter imposed an embargo against the Soviet Union on sales of grain and items incorporating high technology. Carter later expanded export controls on high-technology exports to the USSR.

The embargo against Soviet grain sales affected all transactions above the eight million metric tons authorized under a 1975 U.S.-Soviet grain agreement, thus blocking a previously approved sale of 14.7 million metric tons of corn, wheat, and soybeans.

By the spring of 1981 farmers had become increasingly vocal in their opposition to the embargo. In part to placate farmers and in part to fulfill a campaign pledge, President Reagan lifted Carter's embargo on grain sales to the Soviet Union on April 24, 1981. "As a presidential candidate," he said, "I indicated my opposition to the curb on sales because American farmers had been unfairly singled out to bear the burden of this ineffective national policy." Reagan continued, "I decided [after entering office] that an immediate lifting of the sales limitation could be misinterpreted by the Soviet Union.... I have determined that our position now cannot be mistaken: The United States, along with the vast majority of nations, has condemned and remains opposed to the Soviet occupation of Afghanistan and other aggressive acts around the world. We will react strongly to acts of aggression wherever they take place. There will never be a weakening of this resolve." During the 1980s the superpowers signed several grain sale agreements, including a five-year purchasing arrangement in 1983.

Although Reagan lifted the grain embargo, he called for stricter controls on sales of high-technology items to the Soviet Union. After the Polish military imposed martial law in December 1981, Reagan announced new economic sanctions against Moscow. He suspended all validated export licenses for the Soviet Union and broadened the list of goods requiring licenses to equipment or technology needed for the transmission or refining of oil and natural gas. A principal goal of the sanctions was to prevent the Soviets from using U.S. technology to build a natural gas pipeline linking the vast natural gas reserves east of the Ural Mountains with markets in Western Europe. Reagan argued that the pipeline would make Western Europe overly dependent on the Soviet Union for energy supplies and would provide billions of dollars in hard currency to prop up the ailing Soviet economy.

The president raised the international stakes June 22, 1982, by also prohibiting foreign subsidiaries of U.S. firms from selling pipeline equipment and technology to the Soviets and prohibiting foreign companies from selling the Soviets those products under U.S. licenses. This move brought an angry reaction from Western European governments, which claimed that Reagan was attempting to use U.S. law to force non-American companies to break valid contracts. Great Britain, France, and Italy defied the ban and ordered their companies to fulfill their contractual obligations to the Soviet Union. In November Reagan relented and lifted the sanctions related to the pipeline.

East-West tension over Afghanistan, Poland, and the conflicts in Central America and the Middle East created a slump in U.S.-Soviet trade beginning in 1980, which had peaked in 1979 when American nonfarm exports to the USSR totaled 749 million dollars. A year later exports had fallen to just 363 million dollars.

Superpower Economic Ties under Gorbachev

Since Gorbachev has come to power, trade with the Soviet Union has grown but remains minuscule in comparison with U.S. trade with other industrialized nations. Soviet exports to the United States grew from 409 million dollars in 1986 to 703 million dollars in 1989. Imports from the United States have jumped from 2.4 billion dollars to 4.3 billion dollars in that same time period.

These figures, however, do not tell the whole story. Under Gorbachev, the Soviets have sought to use hard currency to purchase high technology and machine tools to modernize Soviet industry. But the bulk of imports from the United States have been grain shipments needed to make up for the failure of Soviet agriculture. Purchases of American grain rose from 1.7 billion dollars in 1985 to 3.3 billion dollars in 1989. The remainder of imports is mostly chemicals and machinery. The majority of Soviet exports to the United States consists of petroleum products, minerals, and chemicals, along with some vodka, caviar, and furs.

The role of Soviet manufactured goods in trade with Western nations is very small because the Soviet Union manufactures few items of a quality that can compete with Western goods. Manufactured goods represent only 2 percent of exports, while raw materials make up about 81 percent of trade with the West. This trading profile is very similar to that of a Third World country.

At the Malta summit Bush proposed that a trade agreement be signed between the superpowers, contingent on the Soviet Union codifying its new emigration policy in law. The agreement, which would give the Soviet Union MFN status, was signed when Gorbachev came to Washington at the end of May 1990. However, Bush stated that he would not send the treaty to Capitol Hill for ratification until the emigration rules are enacted in law. The Supreme Soviet is scheduled to consider emigration legislation in September 1990.

Most experts are doubtful the trade agreement will lead to dramatic expansion in U.S.-Soviet trade. Duties on Soviet goods will come down significantly, as much as 90 percent on some goods. Yet lower duties will not change the fact that the Soviet economy produces little that Americans seek to buy. Soviet vodka and some raw materials will be cheaper, but it still is unlikely that Soviet manufactured goods will find much of a market in the United States. Trade credits will become available to the Soviets, spurring some exports, but the Soviet Union already is significantly burdened with foreign debt from its trade imbalance.

Many Western companies are establishing operations in the Soviet Union under the new joint venture law. During his visit to the United States in June 1990, Gorbachev traveled to Minneapolis and San Francisco, where he urged American businesses to become involved in Soviet projects. American companies have not pursued opportunities for joint ventures in the Soviet Union as avidly as Japanese and German companies.

All Western companies are discovering that the Soviet Union still is a difficult place to do business and that their goals often differ significantly from those of their Soviet partners. The Soviets welcome foreign companies, hoping that they will set up manufacturing in the Soviet Union for products that can be exported. Foreign firms are attracted mainly by the untapped Soviet market, rather than by the chance to set up production in the Soviet Union. Thus they prefer to manufacture goods mainly for the Soviet market. Goods intended for the international market can be manufactured more easily, at a lower cost, and with better quality in the newly industrializing countries (for example, Thailand, South Korea, Singapore, Taiwan, and Brazil). In addition, Western companies complain that until serious reforms are implemented, doing business in the Soviet Union will be risky.

New Superpower Relationship

During the 1960s and 1970s the Soviet Union enjoyed a tranquil domestic situation that allowed it to concentrate on superpower relations and foreign affairs in general. During the 1980s and especially since Gorbachev came to power, the Soviet leadership has been forced to focus its attention inward as the USSR's economic and social problems have mounted. Under Gorbachev's new thinking, the primary foreign goals of the Soviet leaders ceased to be the accumulation of influence overseas and the ensuring of Soviet security through military strength. Instead, foreign policy was intended to create conditions that would benefit domestic reconstruction and improve the USSR's international standing. Thus the Soviets worked for a stable international environment, established more conciliatory relations with the United States and other Western nations, and became a more constructive member of international organizations. Soviet leaders hoped that these measures would lead to the integration of the Soviet Union into the world economy and allow them to transfer resources from defense production to the civilian economy.

As of 1990 Soviet foreign policy had not yielded benefits capable of turning the Soviet economy around. But Gorbachev had won the admiration of the U.S. public and the confidence of most U.S. policy makers by taking concrete steps to reduce the Soviet military threat and renounce the Soviet empire abroad. The most prominent of these steps have been the USSR's agreement to eliminate all intermediate-range nuclear missiles from Europe, its withdrawal from Afghanistan, its acceptance of the fall of communist governments in Eastern Europe, and its permitting a united Germany to be a member of NATO. These steps have proven to all but the most hard-line cold warriors in the United States that the Soviet leadership is sincere in its pursuit of a more cooperative superpower relationship.

Equally important to U.S. perceptions is the economic, political, and social change taking place in the Soviet Union. The Gorbachev regime has introduced democratic elections, de-emphasized Marxist-Leninist ideology, permitted freer Jewish emigration, and experimented with market reforms. These measures have held out the prospect of creating a radically altered Soviet state that would function as a partner of the United States in forging a stable, democratic-oriented, post-cold war international order.

Reacting to Soviet Reforms

How to react to Gorbachev's reforms has become a central question of U.S. foreign policy. Some conservatives have argued that because the conciliatory Soviet attitude may end if Gorbachev loses power, the United States should continue to modernize its armed forces and sustain its competitive pressure on Moscow. Other officials, also citing Gorbachev's domestic vulnerability, have advocated that the United States should quickly take advantage of the Soviet Union's economic needs by concluding far-reaching agreements on arms control and international co-operation as soon as possible, thereby codifying the new superpower relationship and making it difficult for any future Soviet leader to reverse. Still others have maintained that the United States must support Gorbachev and his reforms because he is the best hope for continued change that could transform the Soviet Union into a fully democratic nation.

The Bush administration's approach to the Soviet Union has evolved into an amalgamation of these three strategies. The president has resisted dramatic cuts in U.S. military spending, saying the threat from the Soviet Union has not disappeared. He also has aggressively pursued arms control treaties and other agreements with the Soviet Union. Finally, he has declared that the United States supports Gorbachev's domestic reform goals and has offered Moscow technical assistance and the prospect of expanded trade.

Bush's willingness to temper criticism of Soviet actions that might once have brought severe U.S. condemnation demonstrated his administration's hope that Gorbachev and his reform program would survive. During violent clashes between Armenians and Azerbaidzhanis in January 1990, the United States declared that Gorbachev's use of the army to restore order was a legitimate action intended to preserve domestic peace. Even more striking was the Bush administration's response to Moscow's pressure on the Baltic states not to secede. Since 1940 the United States has refused to recognize the incorporation of Latvia, Estonia, and Lithuania into the Soviet Union. Yet when Lithuania declared itself independent in March 1990, the administration declined to recognize Lithuania, despite pressure from many members of Congress to do so. Moreover when Moscow subsequently imposed an economic blockade against Lithuania to pressure it to renounce its declaration of independence, Bush reacted cautiously, urging a negotiated settlement of the crisis but declining to impose sanctions against Moscow. The administration believed that Lithuania's attempt to secede was giving Soviet conservatives opposed to Gorbachev ammunition to use against him, and thus was threatening Gorbachev and the entire reform movement. Some observers in the United States, including high-ranking administration officials, reasoned that Lithuania and other non-Russian republics would most likely be able to achieve a complete and secure independence if Gorbachev's reforms were allowed to proceed.

Bush has sought to help Gorbachev's reforms in other ways besides restraining U.S. rhetoric and sanctions. During late 1989, as communist regimes in Eastern Europe were falling in rapid succession, the Bush administration resisted the temptation to gloat about a victory in the cold war. Instead, Bush assured Gorbachev that the United States would not try to exploit the turmoil in Eastern Europe or encourage the rapid breakup of the Warsaw Pact. At the Malta summit that December, Bush pledged trade concessions and offered to help the Soviet Union enter the world economy.

The superpower accommodation reached new heights at the Washington summit in June 1990. There the United States and the Soviet Union signed a treaty providing for the destruction of the bulk of their chemical arsenals without first agreeing on the specifics of verification. Less than three years before, Reagan had made the phrase "trust but verify" a cornerstone of his administration's approach to

President Mikhail S. Gorbachev waves to onlookers during the spring 1990 summit in Washington, D.C.

the INF treaty. The Soviets' agreement to elaborate intrusive verification procedures had provided the breakthrough that made the INF treaty possible. Now it appeared that U.S. and Soviet policy makers trusted each other enough to move ahead with a major treaty before hammering out the details of verification. In addition, Bush signed a U.S.-Soviet trade pact even though the Lithuanian crisis remained unresolved and the Soviet Union had not yet formally passed a law providing for freer emigration. To satisfy congressional critics, Bush pledged not to submit the pact to Congress for approval until the Supreme Soviet had passed the emigration law.

The cooperation at the Washington summit was all the more significant given recent election results in the Soviet Union. The election of reformer Boris Yeltsin to the presidency of the Russian republic in May 1990, just before the summit, had changed how Gorbachev was perceived in the United States. Many U.S. policy makers had presumed that the alternative to a regime headed by Gorbachev would be one headed by a hard-line conservative or the military. Gorbachev had exploited his domestic weakness as a bargaining point, saying that the United States needed to support him to avoid having to deal with someone less conciliatory. Many observers in the United States agreed that it was important to do what was possible to help Gorbachev stay in power. Yeltsin's election as president of the largest republic in the USSR, however, signaled that Soviet liberals dedicated to radical reform might be more likely than conservatives to replace Gorbachev if he lost power. The poor showing by conservatives in government elections throughout the Soviet Union during 1989 and 1990 seemed to back up this view. Thus U.S. policies de-

signed to support Gorbachev's standing might slow inevitable social changes that would be in the interest of the United States.

The agreements signed at the Washington summit showed that superpower cooperation had become almost routine. Progress in the relationship was forthcoming regardless of calculations about Gorbachev's position.

After the Cold War

The superpowers are far from becoming allies. The present era of friendly relations begun in 1987 has not existed long enough to dispel seven decades of suspicion, competition, and hostility. Moreover, even if a START treaty is concluded in 1990, both sides will have thousands of nuclear warheads poised to destroy the other. The intelligence services of both sides still are oriented toward collection of intelligence related to their superpower rival, and the two countries continue to back opposing sides in several regional conflicts. Although the collapse of communist governments in Eastern Europe and elsewhere has made international ideological competition between capitalism and communism outmoded, the Soviet Union and the United States, as great powers, will continue to have conflicts of interest that must be managed. Consequently, the United States and the Soviet Union will remain the greatest threat to each other's security for the near future.

Yet the perceptions driving U.S.-Soviet relations have changed fundamentally. Many Soviet foreign policy actions have resulted in irreversible alterations in the international landscape that even the most reactionary Soviet leader would be unable to change. For example, the cohesion of the Warsaw pact alliance and the credibility of a conventional Soviet invasion of Western Europe are beyond restoration. In addition, as the world becomes increasingly multipolar, the Soviet Union and the United States will stop seeing each other as the only centers of geopolitical competition.

Regardless of Gorbachev's fate, the two superpowers will continue cooperating, not because of friendship developed between their leaders, but because it is in the mutual interest of the two nations to do so. The superpowers have accepted the unfamiliar and sometimes uncomfortable reality that their goals on many international issues have converged. Both sides seek to facilitate the reduction of their defense and military aid budgets by concluding arms control treaties and finding solutions to regional conflicts. The dangers presented by nuclear and chemical weapons proliferation and terrorism threaten the security of both nations and create opportunities for mutual action. Although the Soviet Union needs expanded trade relations more than the United States, American businesses will benefit from commercial opportunities in the Soviet Union. The complications created by the emergence of a united Germany also increase the superpowers' common interest in preserving European stability. Competition between the Soviet Union and United States will continue, but because these common interests will not diminish with the passage of time, a return to the cold war is highly unlikely.

Appendix

Biographies

At the Twenty-eighth Party Congress in July 1990, the composition of the Soviet leadership changed dramatically. Many Soviet officials who had played key roles during the late 1980s were retired or demoted. Others gave up their leadership positions in the Communist party as part of the movement to separate the party from government institutions.

Biographical information on Mikhail S. Gorbachev and six top government officials is given below. Following the biographies of these officials are shorter biographical sketches of forty-nine other current Soviet leaders. Finally, eighteen important figures in Soviet history are profiled.

Mikhail S. Gorbachev (1931-   )

On March 11, 1985, only four hours after the announcement of Konstantin U. Chernenko's death, Mikhail Sergeevich Gorbachev, fifty-four, became the youngest general secretary in the So-viet Union's history. He also became the first top Soviet leader from the generation that rose through the party ranks after Stalin's death. Gorbachev's accession to the leadership of the Communist Party of the Soviet Union (CPSU) marked the end of an era in Soviet politics dominated by aging leaders and bureaucratic inertia and the beginning of a period of change unprecedented in Soviet history, a period in which the truths that had been accepted since the revolution were being discarded one by one.

Gorbachev was born March 2, 1931, in the village of Privolnoye in the southern wheat-growing area of Stavropol in the Russian republic. His parents were peasants of modest means. Gorbachev has one brother, Aleksandr, who is seventeen years his junior. Their maternal grandfather was a committed Communist who headed a collective farm. As a teenager, Gorbachev did well in school and operated a combine during the summer. Compared with other Russian families, the Gorbachevs suffered little from collectivization and World War II, although the Stavropol area was

occupied by German forces for about six months.

Gorbachev entered the prestigious Moscow State University in 1950 at the age of nineteen. At twenty-one he became a member of the Communist party and three years later, in 1955, graduated with a degree in law. While in college, Gorbachev met his wife, Raisa. She has been the subject of much attention in the Western press because of her stylishness and public visibility compared with past Soviet leaders' wives. She studied philosophy at Moscow State, and she has lectured on that subject. The couple has a daughter, Irina, and a young granddaughter, Oksana. Irina and her husband are physicians.

Public Career. After graduating from Moscow State, Gorbachev returned to Stavropol, where he gained recognition as a leader in the Komsomol (Communist Youth League). He began full-time party work in 1962. He received a degree from the Stavropol Agricultural Institute in 1967. Under the tutelage of Fëdor Kulakov, first secretary of Stavropol *krai* (territory), he rose quickly through the local party ranks. In 1970, at the relatively young age of thirty-nine, he assumed his mentor's post after Kulakov had been promoted to a position in Moscow. Gorbachev's selection to full membership on the CPSU Central Committee in 1971 has been attributed by some to party ideologue Mikhail Suslov, who had strong ties to Stavropol.

In 1978 Kulakov died, and Gorbachev, then forty-seven, was called from Stavropol to take his place as the Central Committee secretary responsible for agriculture. Although a series of bad harvests followed, Gorbachev's career did not falter. He became a candidate member of the Politburo in 1979 and a full member in 1980. From 1979 until 1984 he chaired the Legislative Proposals Commission of the Council of the Union of the USSR Supreme Soviet.

Gorbachev continued his rise during the succession battles that followed Brezhnev's death in 1982. Under Yuri V. Andropov he was given oversight responsibility for the whole economy and lower-level party appointments. He developed a close working relationship with the ailing Andropov during the general secretary's confinement to a hospital apartment in late 1983 and early 1984.

After nominating Chernenko as party leader following Andropov's death, Gorbachev became de facto second secretary, although some tasks were shared with his rival Grigorii Romanov, the former Leningrad party first secretary who had been brought to the Secretariat by Andropov to supervise military industry. Gorbachev oversaw all aspects of the economy except for military-related industries and served as chairman of the Foreign Affairs Commission from early 1984 until July 1985. He shared supervision of state administrative organs with Romanov. After Chernenko's health began to fail, Gorbachev and Romanov alternated chairing Politburo meetings. Gorbachev's stature as a spokesman for Soviet interests abroad grew after he and his wife made a highly publicized trip to Great Britain in December 1984.

Despite Gorbachev's status as second in command, his rise was not guaranteed upon Chernenko's death. He was challenged by Romanov and Viktor Grishin, the conservative seventy-year-old Moscow party secretary. Gorbachev, however, overcame these challenges and was chosen general secretary.

On October 1, 1988, Gorbachev replaced Andrei Gromyko as chairman of the Presidium of the Supreme Soviet (president), thus combining the roles of head of the party and head of state. The Congress of People's Deputies (CPD) elected him to the revamped presidential office of chairman of the Supreme Soviet on May 25, 1989. He gave up this office in March 1990, when the CPD elected him to the new executive presidency for a five-year term. Gorbachev also was reelected general secretary of the Communist party at the Twenty-eighth Party Congress in July 1990.

Analysis. During his first year in office, Gorbachev gave little indication of being a radical reformer. Indeed, most Western observers expected him to be something of a younger and more telegenic Andropov, intent on jump-starting the economy by battling corruption and strengthening discipline at work.

Since then some scholars have spoken of "the education of Mikhail Gorbachev," during his tenure in office. At first he believed that the economy could be put back on its feet by using resources more efficiently, battling alcoholism, and introducing new technologies. He realized only gradually that more fundamental changes were necessary.

As a result of Gorbachev's "new thinking" in foreign policy, he has achieved great popularity in the West, particularly in Germany. He consistently ranks higher than Western leaders in Western polls measuring popularity. His popularity abroad also is significantly greater than his popularity at home. This is because Westerners have focused on the dramatically reduced Soviet military threat, the fall of Communist regimes in Eastern Europe, the improvement of human rights in the Soviet Union, and other dramatic changes that have resulted from Gorbachev's policies. Soviet citizens, however, are more concerned with the steadily declining Soviet economy. Thus, even as Gorbachev's reputation has soared in the West, his political support at home has weakened.

Gorbachev has repeatedly displayed keen political instincts that have allowed him to hold on to power despite his domestic troubles. He frequently has moved ahead of events. For example, after violent ethnic riots in Armenia and Azerbaidzhan in January 1990, Gorbachev came under strong criticism, and calls were made for his resignation. However, he was able to recapture the political spotlight by immediately proposing that the party give up its monopoly of power, a move so bold and unexpected that it threw all of his opponents off balance and allowed him to re-assert his own agenda.

Nevertheless, analysts have warned against assuming that Gorbachev is a Western-style politician with liberal democratic values. He has shown himself more willing to

tolerate criticism than past Soviet leaders, yet he has lashed out angrily at editors who have criticized him personally. He has been raised and educated in a socialist society and has worked his whole career under the Soviet system. While he has abandoned the most oppressive aspects of Soviet-style socialism, he does not seek to create a Soviet society modeled after the West.

Vladimir Kryuchkov (1924-   )

Vladimir Aleksandrovich Kryuchkov replaced Viktor Chebrikov as chairman of the Committee for State Security (KGB) in October 1988. Kryuchkov also was a full member of the Politburo from September 1989 until the July 1990 Twenty-eighth Party Congress, when he left the party leadership along with other top government officials. A career intelligence officer, Kryuchkov has been involved in a range of intelligence activities, including espionage in the United States.

Kryuchkov, an ethnic Russian, joined the Communist party in 1944 and spent his first years as a leader of various Komsomol (Communist Youth League) organizations. From 1946 to 1954 he worked in the Stalingrad (now Volgograd) city apparatus while earning degrees from the All Union Juridical Institute (1949) and the Foreign Ministry's Higher School for Diplomats (1954). Upon graduation, Kryuchkov's first diplomatic assignment was the Soviet embassy in Hungary, where he remained until 1959. In Budapest, he worked with Yuri V. Andropov, who was the Soviet ambassador at the time. As third secretary of the Soviet embassy, Kryuchkov was involved in the crushing of the Hungarian uprising of 1956.

Kryuchkov spent most of the 1960s working in the Central Committee apparatus before beginning his career in the KGB in 1967 under Andropov. Kryuchkov was appointed head of the KGB's First Chief Directorate in 1974, a post that gave him responsibility for, among other things, disinformation activities and the espionage operation against the United States. He became deputy chairman of the KGB in 1978. He holds the rank of general.

Under President Mikhail S. Gorbachev, the role of the KGB in Soviet society has been reexamined. Kryuchkov has encouraged more publicity about the KGB and has admitted that the KGB committed human rights violations in the past. He has allowed journalists to tour the infamous Moscow Lublyanka prison and has opened a KGB public affairs office. He insists that under his leadership the KGB's abuses have ended, and he has sought to portray the KGB as a modern law enforcement agency principally concerned with thwarting terrorism and catching drug smugglers.

The KGB's surveillance of Soviet society is not as pervasive or obvious as it once was, but under Kryuchkov the KGB has continued to keep watch over the activities of Soviet citizens. Opposition groups have complained about being monitored and harassed by the KGB. In addition, the KGB remains more a tool of the Communist party than of the new Soviet government institutions. Anatolii Sobchak, the head of the Leningrad city soviet, has complained that KGB intelligence reports on Leningrad are sent to the city party committee, but not to the city soviet.

Regarding the close association between the KGB and the party, Kryuchkov stated at the Twenty-eighth Party Congress that, in theory, as new parties become politically established they could share in the work of the KGB. Yet he simultaneously insisted that the security apparatus could never be entirely depoliticized, because its main job is "to protect the constitutional system and the political establishment of the Soviet state."

Anatolii Lukyanov (1930-   )

As chairman of the Supreme Soviet, Anatolii Ivanovich Lukyanov has been one of the driving forces behind the democratization measures and legal reforms that have been adopted by the Supreme So-  viet. Educated as a lawyer, he has helped shape the laws and constitutional amendments that established the new electoral system. As first vice chairman, and then chairman of the Supreme Soviet, Lukyanov has had the difficult job of chairing the frequently unruly meetings of the new Soviet legislature. He also is a member of the Commission for Further Study of Materials and Documents Related to the Repressions of the Stalin Years. This commission is responsible for reviewing sentences passed under Stalin and for rehabilitating thousands who were illegally tried and punished or expelled from the party without cause.

An ethnic Russian, Lukyanov was born in the city of Smolensk on May 7, 1930. He graduated with a law degree from Moscow State University in 1953 and then received a doctorate of juridical sciences in 1980. He became associated with Mikhail S. Gorbachev when they were both law students at Moscow State University. Lukyanov joined the party in 1955.

Lukyanov began his career as a senior consultant to the legal commission of the USSR Council of Ministers from 1956 to 1961. There he played an important role in developing some of Nikita S. Khrushchev's economic and legal reforms. From 1961 to 1976 Lukyanov was a senior researcher and then the deputy head of the Department of Soviet Activities of the Presidium of the USSR Supreme Soviet. After a year as a consultant to the Party Organizational Work Department of the Central Committee, he headed the Secretariat of the Supreme Soviet Presidium from 1977 to 1983. In 1983 he became deputy chairman and in 1985 chairman of the General Department of the Central Committee.

Lukyanov became first vice chairman of the Presidium of the Supreme Soviet in 1988. When Gorbachev assumed the new post of executive president in March 1990, Lukyanov took over his old position as chairman of the Presidium of the Supreme Soviet. Lukyanov also was a candidate member of the Politburo from September 1988 until the Twenty-eighth Party Congress in July 1990.

Lukyanov has been a strong supporter of Gorbachev's campaign to draw power away from the party to strengthen the soviets and other government institutions. He rose

through the party ranks as a protégé of Gorbachev and is considered very close to him politically. When rumors surfaced in January 1990 that Gorbachev was considering resigning as general secretary to concentrate on the presidency, some observers suggested that Gorbachev would arrange to have Lukyanov replace him.

Nikolai Ryzhkov (1929-   )

Nikolai Ivanovich Ryzhkov is the chairman of the Council of Ministers (premier) of the USSR and a member  of the Presidential Council. He has developed a reputation as a technocratic leader who is not swayed by ideology but is more concerned with figuring out what works. He has not been on the cutting edge of reform, but neither has he attempted to block change.

Ryzhkov is a Russian national born in the Ukraine September 28, 1929. He graduated from the Kramatorsk Machine Building School in the Ukraine in 1950 and received a degree in engineering from the Ural Polytechnic Institute in 1959. He joined the Communist party in 1956. Between 1950 and 1975 he worked at the Ural Heavy Machine Building Plant in Sverdlovsk, becoming plant director in 1970. From 1975 until 1979 he was a first deputy minister of heavy and transport machine building. In 1979 he became first deputy chairman of Gosplan, where he was responsible for the heavy industry and military sectors. There he developed a reputation as an efficient economic manager and caught the attention of Yuri V. Andropov.

Shortly after Andropov came to power in 1982, he appointed Ryzhkov as the Central Committee secretary for economic questions and also head of the Central Committee economics department. Ryzhkov was in the forefront of a new generation of well-educated and highly professional Soviet managers who came to power under Andropov and have continued to advance under Mikail S. Gorbachev. A few weeks after Gorbachev came to power in March 1985, Ryzhkov was appointed to full membership in the Politburo. The following September Ryzhkov was named premier. Shortly thereafter he relinquished his positions as Central Committee secretary and head of the economics department. In June 1989, he was reappointed premier and confirmed in this office by the newly elected Congress of People's Deputies. He was appointed to the Presidential Council in April 1990, and he left the Politburo at the Twenty-eighth Party Congress in July 1990 along with other top government officials.

Ryzhkov has occupied the middle ground in the leadership, proposing moderate changes while the debate on reform has moved to more radical proposals. For example, in May 1990 he proposed reducing food subsidies as a step in creating more rational prices—a necessary prerequisite for developing a market economy. The proposal led to panic buying, and Supreme Soviet deputies complained that the plan was not really an attempt to establish a market economy, but a means of squeezing consumers. Some deputies called for his resignation, and ultimately the Supreme Soviet rejected the price increases. Ryzhkov's proposal failed because it was a shy half-step, an attempt to modify the system without fundamentally changing it. Ryzhkov has become unpopular with more serious reformers, who dislike his cautious and evolutionary approach to the economy. Some observers have speculated that Gorbachev has been setting him up to take the blame for the declining Soviet economy, but as of mid-1990 Ryzhkov remained a key player in economic policy making.

Eduard Shevardnadze (1928-   )

Eduard Amvrosievich Shevardnadze rocketed to prominence on July 2, 1985, when he was named to replace Andrei Gromyko as minister of foreign affairs. Many Western observers speculated that the appointment of the seemingly inexperienced Shevardnadze was motivated by Mikhail S. Gorbachev's desire to control foreign affairs. Shevardnadze has since proven himself one of the most effective leaders of the Gorbachev generation.

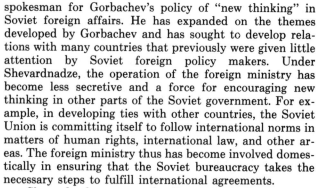

Shevardnadze was born in Mamati, Georgia, January 25, 1928. He joined the Communist party in 1948. Shevardnadze holds degrees from the Higher Party School of the Georgian Central Committee and from a pedagogical institute.

He became first secretary of the Georgian Komsomol (Communist Youth League) in 1957. The following year he became a full member of the Central Committee in Georgia. In 1961 he was elected to the bureau of the All-Union Komsomol, where he first forged a relationship with a young Mikhail Gorbachev. After serving in several low-level party posts in Georgia, Shevardnadze in 1964 was appointed first deputy minister of what is now the Georgian Ministry of Internal Affairs. From 1965 until 1972 he was minister of that body. As minister, Shevardnadze worked to expose corruption among Georgian party officials. His campaign eventually led to the political demise of Vasilii Mzhavanadze, the republic party chief, whom Shevardnadze succeeded in 1972. In 1976 Shevardnadze was rewarded with his election to the Central Committee.

As Georgian party boss from 1972 to 1985, Shevardnadze became known as an economic reformer. He improved the republic's economic performance and instituted agricultural production reforms that piqued the interest of then-Central Committee secretary for agriculture Gorbachev, who visited Georgia several times to praise Shevardnadze's reforms. These reforms included market- and profit-oriented experiments, as well as the use of public opinion polls.

Shevardnadze had visited only nine nations before his appointment as foreign minister. Since then he has become a familiar figure on the world scene, representing the Soviet Union during more than one hundred visits to approximately forty-five different countries. The affability and relaxed style of Shevardnadze are in stark contrast to the dour looks and stern rhetoric that marked Andrei Gromyko's tenure as foreign minister.

Shevardnadze's replacement of Gromyko also marked a dramatic shift in the substance of Soviet foreign policy. At home and abroad, Shevardnadze has been the primary spokesman for Gorbachev's policy of "new thinking" in Soviet foreign affairs. He has expanded on the themes developed by Gorbachev and has sought to develop relations with many countries that previously were given little attention by Soviet foreign policy makers. Under Shevardnadze, the operation of the foreign ministry has become less secretive and a force for encouraging new thinking in other parts of the Soviet government. For example, in developing ties with other countries, the Soviet Union is committing itself to follow international norms in matters of human rights, international law, and other areas. The foreign ministry thus has become involved domestically in ensuring that the Soviet bureaucracy takes the necessary steps to fulfill international agreements.

Shevardnadze came under fierce attacks from conservatives at the Twenty-eighth Party Congress for his policies and was forced to defend himself from charges of having a soft attitude toward Soviet security. Some senior military officers also have expressed unhappiness with the arms control agreements he has negotiated, charging that he has been too willing to make compromises in search of an agreement.

Aleksandr Yakovlev (1923-   )

Aleksandr Nikolaevich Yakovlev is a member of the Presidential Council and one of Mikhail S. Gorbachev's

closest political allies. He is a strong proponent of radical economic and political reform in the Soviet Union. Until the Twenty-eighth Party Congress, he was a Central Committee secretary, a member of the Politburo, and head of the Central Committee Commission on International Policy.

However, at the Congress, he declared that he was giving up his party posts to concentrate on his responsibilities as a member of the Presidential Council. This corresponded with his claim that government leaders who also hold positions in the party leadership have an inevitable conflict of interest.

Yakovlev, an ethnic Russian, was born September 2, 1923, in the Yaroslavl region of the Russian republic. He served in the army from 1941 to 1943 and received wounds that required him to spend almost a year in a hospital.

After the war he graduated from the Yaroslavl Pedagogical Institute. From 1946 to 1953 he worked in the Yaroslavl *oblast* (region) party organization. He then became deputy head of the Department of Science and Culture in Moscow. After attending the Academy of Social Sciences from 1956 to 1960, Yakovlev went to work for the Agitation and Propaganda Department (renamed the Propaganda Department in 1966). He rose through its ranks to become acting head in 1971. In late 1972 he published an article warning against the dangers of growing Russian nationalism in literature and social science. The article reportedly brought Yakovlev into disfavor with the party leadership, and in 1973 he was sent into political exile as the ambassador to Canada, where he would remain for a decade.

A month after Gorbachev's highly successful visit to

Canada in 1983, however, Yakovlev was brought back to Moscow to head the prestigious Institute of World Economics and International Relations of the USSR Academy of Sciences. In December 1984 Yakovlev accompanied Gorbachev on his trip to Great Britain. The following July Gorbachev named him head of the Central Committee's Propaganda Department, and in March 1986, Yakovlev was made Central Committee secretary in charge of propaganda and culture. In September 1988, his portfolio was changed to foreign affairs when he was made chairman of the new Central Committee Commission on International Policy. Since 1988 he also has been chairman of the Commission for Further Study of Materials and Documents Relating to the Repressions of the Stalin Years. In January 1987 he was appointed a candidate member of the Politburo. He was a full member of the Politburo from June 1987 until July 1990.

An expert on the United States, Yakovlev was an exchange student at Columbia University in New York in 1959. He eventually earned a doctor of historical sciences degree in the Soviet Union. Throughout most of his career Yakovlev has been a harsh critic of the United States, but as relations between the superpowers improved during the late 1980s, he tempered his criticism. He has written several monographs on U.S. foreign policy including *From Truman to Reagan: Doctrines and Reality of the Nuclear Age*, published in 1984.

Yakovlev has been among the most vocal advocates of reform within the Soviet leadership. As secretary in charge of propaganda and culture he fostered *glasnost* in the media, promoting liberal editors and encouraging daring reporting. For this he has been much criticized by conservatives. He has been active in Gorbachev's campaign to weaken the party stranglehold on society and to strengthen Soviet government institutions. At the Twenty-eighth Party Congress, the leaders of the Democratic Platform bloc called on Yakovlev to become party leader and declared that only if he was elected general secretary could the party undergo the renewal that they sought. When he declined, about fifty delegates followed Boris Yeltsin in turning in their party cards.

Dmitrii Yazov (1923-   )

Dmitrii Timofeyovich Yazov replaced Sergei Sokolov as minister of defense in May 1987. The change was part of a shake-up of the top military brass precipitated by an incident in which a young West German civilian pilot was able to avoid Soviet air defenses and land a small plane in Red Square. Yazov is a career military man who holds the rank of army general. He has been a member of the party since 1944. He served as a candidate member of the Politburo from June 1987 until the Twenty-eighth Party Congress in July 1990.

Yazov, a Russian, was born in the village of Yazov in the Omsk region on November 8, 1923. His father was a peasant who died during collectivization. Yazov graduated from the Frunze Military Academy in 1956 and the Military Academy of the General Staff of the Soviet Armed Forces in 1967. He saw action during World War II as a platoon commander and a deputy company commander and was severely wounded in 1942. After the war, he was stationed in the Leningrad military district until 1967, when he was promoted to major general and given command of a division in the Transbaikal military district. He continued to rise through the upper echelons of the military, becoming a colonel general and first deputy commander in chief of the Far Eastern military district in 1976 and the commander in chief of the Central Army Group in Czechoslovakia in 1979. In 1980 he was promoted to army general and given command of the Central Asian military district, where he was involved in war operations in Afghanistan. He became commander in chief of the Far Eastern military district in 1984 and deputy defense minister in January 1987.

The general is a strong advocate of military reform. As deputy defense minister for personnel he was charged with implementing *perestroika* in the armed forces. Yazov has supported Gorbachev's "new thinking" in defense policy. In his speech to the Twenty-eighth Party Congress, he reaffirmed the fundamentals of Gorbachev's defense policy: that Soviet security can be provided only by political means, that agreements with other countries involving national security must be mutually beneficial, and that Soviet security is best guaranteed by the lowest possible balanced level of strategic nuclear forces. He supports Gorbachev's drive for arms control.

Yazov has complained about journalistic attacks on the military. In his speech to the Twenty-eighth Party Congress, he described how the spring call-up of recruits had been blocked in some provinces, particularly in Armenia, and then noted bitterly that the mass media had supported such actions. Yazov also has rejected the proposal by radical reformers that the army ought to be depoliticized and that its party cells should be disbanded. At the party congress, he called this idea "flimsy in theory, and harmful in practice."

Other Notable Soviet Leaders

Leonid Abalkin (1930-   ). A deputy prime minister and chairman of the State Commission on Economic Reform, Abalkin is the chief architect of and point man for Mikhail S. Gorbachev's economic reforms. He is a strong supporter of the cooperative movement. Abalkin has written many articles in the Soviet press about the urgency of Gorbachev's economic reforms.

Yuri Afanaseyev. A dissident historian, Afanaseyev has become one of the leaders of the opposition Interregional Group in the Supreme Soviet. He has called for a comprehensive reevaluation of Soviet history and has fought for rehabilitation of Joseph Stalin's victims.

Abel Agenbegyan (1932-   ). An economist who helped develop Gorbachev's program of gradual economic reform, Agenbegyan has seen his influence wane as more radical proposals have taken center stage. He is the director of the Institute for Production Forces and National Resources and a member of the Presidium of the USSR Academy of Sciences. From 1967 to 1985 he worked in virtual academic exile at the Novosibirsk State University in Siberia. The ideas of Agenbegyan and other economists at Novosibirsk caught the attention of Gorbachev and formed much of the intellectual basis for his program.

Chingiz Aitmativ (1928-   ). Aitmativ is a liberal Kirgiz novelist who writes on sensitive topics such as religion, interethnic relations, drug abuse, and the Stalin period. In 1989 he caused a sensation in the Congress of People's Deputies when he held up the Western democracies as models for Soviet emulation. He is a member of the Presidential Council.

Nina Andreyeva (1938-   ). A chemistry teacher from Leningrad, Andreyeva had a lengthy letter published in *Sovetskaya Rossiya* (Soviet Russia) that gained national attention in March 1988. In the letter, she attacked Gorbachev's reform program as a complete rejection of socialism. She called for a return to discipline and central planning, which she claimed have been weakening since Stalin died in 1953. Her letter became a rallying point for Stalinists and Russian nationalists. Andreyeva also has ties to the Russian nationalist group *Pamiat* (Memory).

Georgii Arbatov (1923-   ). Arbatov has been head of the Institute for the Study of the USA and Canada since 1967. In this position he has been a top adviser to Kremlin officials on East-West relations. He has participated in numerous summits and has published articles in the Western press. Arbatov has been a member of the USSR Academy of Sciences since 1974 and was a member of the Central Committee from 1981 until 1990.

Vadim Bakatin (1937-   ). A close ally of Gorbachev, Bakatin is minister of internal affairs and a member of the Presidential Council. His career accelerated during the tenure of Yuri V. Andropov, when he gained a reputation as a reformer and capable administrator.

Aleksandr Bessmertnykh (1933-   ). A top Foreign Ministry expert on the United States and arms control, Bessmertnykh was appointed to replace Yuri Dubinin as ambassador to the United States in April 1990. Prior to that he was deputy minister of foreign affairs for USSR-USA relations. He is considered to be a close ally of Foreign Minister Eduard Shevardnadze. In July 1990 at the Twenty-eighth Party Congress, Bessmertnykh was appointed to the Central Committee.

Aleksandra Biriukova (1929-   ). Biriukova has been deputy chairman of the Council of Ministers for social questions since September 1988. She also was a candidate member of the Politburo from that time until she retired from the party leadership in July 1990. She had been a member of the Central Committee since 1976 and for a long time had been the only woman in the top party leadership. She is considered an expert on women's issues.

Oleg Bogomolov (1918-   ). Bogomolov is director of the Institute of the Economics of the World Socialist System. Under Bogomolov, the Institute has studied economic reforms implemented by other socialist countries and considered their applicability to the Soviet Union. Bogomolov has been influential in shaping the thinking of Soviet leaders about economic reform.

Valerii Boldin (1935-   ). A longtime adviser to Gorbachev, Boldin is the head of the General Department of the Central Committee. In this capacity, Boldin has served as Gorbachev's watchdog over the party.

Fëdor Burlatsky (1927-   ). A member of the Supreme Soviet and editor of *Literaturnaya Gazeta* (Literary Gazette), Burlatsky has developed a reputation as a reformer. During his long career as a political scientist and writer, his controversial ideas have cost him his job on several occasions. He was a member of the Central Committee staff under Nikita S. Khrushchev but was fired under Leonid I. Brezhnev. He later became influential as a protégé of Andropov. Since his election as a people's deputy, Burlatsky has focused on human rights issues.

Yuri Dubinin (1930-   ). A career foreign ministry bureaucrat, Dubinin served as ambassador to the United States from 1986 to 1990. American observers were puzzled by Dubinin's selection as the replacement of longtime ambassador to the United States Anatolii Dobrynin, in part because Dubinin did not speak fluent English. By most accounts, however, Dubinin performed well in the role, helping to facilitate the transition of superpower relations from confrontation to cooperation. Before his assignment to Washington, he was ambassador to Spain. In 1990 he was appointed ambassador to France.

Aleksandr Dzasokhov (1934-   ). Dzásokhov was appointed to the Politburo at the Twenty-eighth Party Congress in July 1990. He was elected to the Supreme Soviet in 1989, and since November of that year he has served as the chairman of the Supreme Soviet Committee for International Affairs. He is an advocate of arms control. From September 1986 to November 1988 he was Soviet ambassador to Syria. He then served as first secretary of the North-Osetian Autonomous Soviet Socialist Republic until his election to the Supreme Soviet.

Valentin Falin (1926-   ). Falin has been head of the International Department of the Central Committee since 1988. He has spent most of his career in the Foreign Ministry apparatus and is thought to have been a close associate of Andrei Gromyko. Falin is a leading expert on Western Europe and was ambassador to West Germany from 1971 to 1978.

Ivan Frolov (1929-   ). Frolov was appointed to the Politburo in July 1990 at the Twenty-eighth Party Congress. He has been chief editor of *Pravda* since he took over that post from conservative Viktor Afanaseyev in October 1989. Western observers expected that *Pravda* would follow a more liberal line under Frolov, but changes have been slow in coming. Frolov graduated from Moscow State University in 1953 and received his doctorate in philosophy in 1966. He had spent most of his career working for several journals, including *Kommunist*. Since 1987 he has been a personal adviser to Gorbachev on ideological questions.

Boris Gidaspov (1933-   ). Gidaspov was appointed Leningrad party leader after former leader Yuri Solovev failed to win a seat in the Congress of People's Deputies in the March 1989 elections. Gidaspov is considered a conservative and has worked most of his career in the military-industrial complex. He has developed a rivalry with the new mayor of Leningrad, radical reformer Anatolii Sobchak.

Vladimir Ivashko (1933-   ). A Ukrainian national, Ivashko was elected to the new post of deputy general secretary at the Twenty-eighth Party Congress in July 1990. At that time he resigned as president of the Ukraine, complaining that he had lost the confidence of Ukrainian legislators and could not implement reform there.

Ivashko began his career as a teacher at several institutions of higher education in Kharkov in 1957 but eventually became involved in party work. In 1986 he was chosen secretary of the Ukrainian Central Committee. In September 1989, he replaced conservative Vladimir Shcherbitskii as first secretary of the Ukraine. Ivashko then was appointed to the Politburo in December. In June 1990, he resigned as Ukrainian first secretary after he was elected president of the Ukraine. Ivashko is considered a moderate conservative. As deputy general secretary, he is responsible for running the day-to-day affairs of the party and trying to reconcile the party's liberal and conservative wings.

Albert Kauls (1938-   ). The Presidential Council member in charge of agriculture, Kauls is the head of the *kolkhoz* (collective farm) "Adazhi" in Latvia. He won fame as an agricultural reformer because of the economic success of his kolkhoz after he issued shares to the farmers.

Vitalii Korotich (1936-   ). Korotich is the outspoken, crusading editor of the popular weekly magazine *Ogonyok* (Flame). His magazine has focused public attention on numerous scandals and examples of economic mismanagement. Korotich is one of the chief targets of conservative critics of press excesses under *glasnost.*

Stanislav Kuniaev. Kuniaev was appointed chief editor of the Russian nationalist monthly *Nash Sovremennik* (Our Contemporary) in October 1989. Under Kuniaev, this journal has become known for anti-Semitism and vitriolic attacks on liberals and reformers. In 1989 Kuniaev campaigned for a seat in the Russian republic's congress of people's deputies as a part of the "patriotic bloc." He and most of the bloc's candidates were defeated.

Vytautas Landsbergis (1932-   ). A musician by profession, Landsbergis is head of the Lithuanian nationalist group *Sajudis* and chairman of the Lithuanian Parliament. An ardent nationalist, he pushed for the declaration of Lithuanian independence in March, which led to the Soviet economic blockade of Lithuania. Although he comes from a family with a history of Lithuanian nationalist activity, he cuts an unusual figure as a politician. The *New York Times* called him "a stooped introspective music professor, given to rumpled suits and sensible shoes."

Yegor Ligachev (1920-   ). Ligachev was forced into retirement in July 1990, when the Twenty-eighth Party Congress declined to nominate him for a spot on the Central Committee, thus relieving him of his membership in the Politburo and his post as party secretary for agriculture. Before his downfall, Ligachev had been the leading conservative on the Politburo and for a time had even seemed to be a threat to Gorbachev's position as general secretary.

Ligachev held several party posts in Novosibirsk before beginning work in the Central Committee apparatus in 1961. He became Central Committee secretary for ideology, cadres, and party administration in 1983, and a full Politburo member in April 1985. These positions gave him a rank in the party leadership second only to Gorbachev. He used his positions to argue against experimentation with market reforms or weakening of the Soviet military. In the first years of Gorbachev's tenure, Ligachev denied that he had differences with the general secretary. Over time, however, Ligachev became more willing to speak out against Gorbachev's policies. In September 1988, Gorbachev was able to change Ligachev's responsibilities on the Secretariat from ideology to agriculture, a less influential portfolio.

At the Twenty-eighth Party Congress, Ligachev ran against Vladimir Ivashko, Gorbachev's candidate, for the post of deputy general secretary. Ligachev was decisively rejected by the delegates, who feared that his election would provoke mass resignations by party members. Despite being forced out of the leadership, Ligachev still is popular with many party members and has strong ties to a number of senior military officers.

Vladimir Lysenko (1956-   ). A leader of the Democratic Platform bloc of the Communist party, Lysenko resigned from the party at the Twenty-eighth Party Congress and announced his intention to help create an organized opposition. He has claimed that as many as 40 percent of Soviet Communists support the Platform.

Yuri Maslyukov (1937-   ). In February 1988, Maslyukov replaced Nikolai Talyzin as chairman of Gosplan. Maslyukov was appointed to the Politburo in September 1989 but lost this position in July 1990 as part of Gorbachev's effort to separate top government officials from the party leadership. As head of Gosplan, Maslyukov is one of the key government officials responsible for implementing economic reforms.

Maslyukov received a degree in engineering from the Leningrad Institute for Mechanics in 1962. After joining the party four years later, he began a long career in the military-industrial complex, where he became a specialist in armament affairs. He became deputy minister of the defense industry in 1979 and was promoted to first deputy chairman of Gosplan in 1982. In the Politburo, Maslyukov was an ally of Nikolai Sliunkov and Nikolai Ryzhkov, the moderate reformers with whom he worked at Gosplan. Some Gorbachev allies have criticized Maslyukov for displaying too much caution toward economic reform.

Roy Medvedev (1926-   ). Historian Medvedev is one of the deans of Soviet dissent. He is a liberal Marxist-Leninist whose research has helped to document the atrocities of the Stalin era. He has estimated that more than forty million people were victims of Stalinist crimes. His best known work is *Let History Judge.* He is a people's deputy and was appointed to the Central Committee in July 1990 at the Twenty-eighth Party Congress.

Vadim Medvedev (1929-   ). Medvedev was retired from the party leadership at the Twenty-eighth Party Congress in July 1990. An academic specialist in science and technology, he was appointed to the Central Committee Secretariat in March 1986 and became a key figure in the leadership in September 1988, when he was given Yegor Ligachev's portfolio as chairman of the Ideology Commission. At that time Medvedev also was appointed a full member of the Politburo. A strong proponent of glasnost and economic reform, Medvedev became a close ally of Gorbachev, Aleksandr Yakovlev, and Eduard Shevardnadze on the Politburo. Conservatives criticized Medvedev at the Twenty-eighth Party Congress for "lack of imagination," and some observers believe that his retirement was a concession to the conservatives by Gorbachev.

Mikhail Moiseev (1939-   ). General Moiseev took over from Sergei Akhromeev as chief of the General Staff in 1988. He also is a first deputy minister of defense. A protégé of Defense Minister Dmitrii Yazov, Moiseev is part of a new generation of Soviet military leaders whose careers began after World War II. Moiseev is believed to be a supporter of Gorbachev, although he is not an ardent military reformer.

Yuri Osipyan (1931-   ). The only scientist on the Presidential Council, Osipyan is in charge of scientific and technical issues in that body. He is the director of the Solid State Physics Institute and since 1988 has been vice president of the USSR Academy of Sciences. Osipyan, an ethnic Armenian, has been described as an establishment scientist with moderate political views.

Ivan Polozkov (1935-   ). An outspoken conservative, Polozkov was elected to the position of first secretary of the new Russian branch of the Communist party in June 1990, after being beaten in May by Boris Yeltsin for the presidency of the Russian republic. At the Twenty-eighth Party Congress in July 1990 Polozkov was chosen to represent the Russian republic in the Politburo. He first became well known as a result of his vigorous crackdown on cooperatives as first party secretary in Krasnodar *krai* (territory) from 1985 to 1990. He has been a member of the Central Committee since 1986.

Polozkov is an unapologetic Leninist who has blamed the Gorbachev leadership for the economic and social problems afflicting the USSR. Polozkov is expected to become the leading voice of conservatives in the party leadership now that Yegor Ligachev has been retired. Polozkov's career has been spent in the party apparatus, mostly in the provinces.

Gavriil Popov (1937-   ). When the Democratic Russia bloc took over the Moscow city soviet, it selected Popov as the new mayor. A radical economist and chief editor of *Voprosy Ekonomiki* (Questions of Economics), Popov has been an outspoken member of the Congress of People's Deputies and a leader of the opposition Interregional Group. He has criticized the system of central planning and has called for a quick transition to a market economy. Popov was among a group of about fifty delegates to the Twenty-eighth Party Congress from the Democratic Platform bloc who followed Boris Yeltsin in resigning from the party and declaring their intention to establish a rival organization.

Yevgenii Primakov (1929-   ). A trained economist and an architect of the "new thinking" in Soviet foreign policy, Primakov has been director of the Institute for World Economy and International Relations since 1985. He is considered a liberal reformer and holds a seat on the Presidential Council. Before his appointment to that body, Primakov was chairman of the Council of Union of the Supreme Soviet. He served as a candidate member of the Politburo from September 1989 until July 1990.

Yuri Prokofiev (1939-   ). Prokofiev replaced Lev Zaikov as first party secretary of Moscow in November 1989 and was appointed to the Central Committee and the Politburo at the Twenty-eighth Party Congress in July 1990. He is a graduate of the Moscow Automobile Engineering Institute and the Moscow Higher Party School. He also holds a candidate's degree in economics. Prokofiev is a strong supporter of Gorbachev and of reform carried out by the party. In his speech to the Twenty-eighth Party Congress, he called for radically democratizing the party to "create it afresh as a political organism."

Boris Pugo (1937-   ). A native Latvian, Pugo is chairman of the Party Control Commission—the body that oversees party discipline and carries out expulsions. Pugo worked in the Committee for State Security (KGB) under Yuri Andropov and served as first secretary of Latvia from 1984 to 1988. He was a candidate member of the Politburo from September 1989 until July 1990.

Valentin Rasputin (1937-   ). A novelist and an extreme Russian nationalist, Rasputin is the only noncommunist to be appointed to the Presidential Council. He also is a people's deputy. Rasputin has deplored the extent of Western influences in Soviet society and has called for a spiritual regeneration. He is a strong supporter of the Russian Orthodox Church and has become well known for his outspoken anti-Semitic views.

Georgii Razumovskii (1936-   ). A close ally of Gorbachev, Razumovskii is the party secretary in charge of the Department of Party Development and Personnel. As party chief of Krasnodar krai in 1983-1985, he waged a vigorous struggle against corruption in the region. He is an agriculture specialist who worked closely with Gorbachev when the latter was Central Committee secretary for agri-

culture during the late 1970s and early 1980s. Razumovskii was a candidate member of the Politburo from February 1988 until July 1990.

Grigorii Revenko (1936-   ). Revenko is the only Ukrainian on the Presidential Council. He became first secretary of the Kiev *oblast* (region) in 1985, serving in that post until he was appointed to the Presidential Council in 1990. He is a member of the Central Committee Commission on Questions of International Politics.

Stanislav Shatalin (1934-   ). A radical economist and close adviser to Gorbachev, Shatalin was appointed to the Presidential Council for economic issues, a move that surprised some Western observers. He advocates private property, cuts in military spending, and a multi-party system. Shatalin has described himself as being on the party's "social-democratic" wing.

Ivan Silaev (1930-   ). In June 1990, Silaev was appointed the new prime minister of the Russian republic by Boris Yeltsin. Previously, Silaev had been deputy chairman of the USSR Council of Ministers. A protégé of Nikolai Ryzhkov, Silaev rose through the aviation industry to become minister of aviation. He has close ties to the Air Force and is considered a representative of the military-industrial complex.

Nikolai Sliunkov (1929-   ). Sliunkov was retired from the party leadership at the Twenty-eighth Party Congress in July 1990. He had been a full member of the Politburo since July 1987 and was the leadership's senior economic specialist as the Central Committee secretary for economic affairs. He was deputy chairman of Gosplan from 1974 until he was appointed head of the Belorussian party in 1983. At Gosplan he worked closely with Nikolai Ryzhkov. Sliunkov was considered a supporter of cautious economic reforms.

Anatolii Sobchak (1938-   ). A lawyer by profession, Sobchak was elected chairman of the Leningrad city soviet in May 1990, after a group of reformists came to power in that city. He also is one of the leaders of the Interregional Group in the Supreme Soviet. Sobchak is a radical reformer who has said he intends to make Leningrad a special economic zone in which free markets would be permitted. He has developed a rivalry with Leningrad party first secretary Boris Gidaspov over the future of the city. He was among a group of fifty delegates to the Twenty-eighth Party Congress from the Democratic Platform bloc who followed Boris Yeltsin in resigning from the party and declaring their intention to establish an opposition organization.

Viacheslav Starkov (1940-   ). Starkov gained prominence as the editor of *Argumenti i Facti* (Arguments and Facts), when he was verbally abused and pressured to resign by Gorbachev in October 1989 but refused to leave his job. The weekly newspaper had run a poll of the ten most popular people's deputies, and Gorbachev was furious about not being included on the final list. The newspaper has since become the weekly with the largest circulation in the Soviet Union (thirty-three million). Starkov is a member of the Russian republic's congress of people's deputies.

Yegor Stroev (1937-   ). Stroev has been Central Committee secretary for agriculture since late 1989. He was appointed a member of the Politburo at the Twenty-eighth Party Congress in July 1990 and also took over for the retired Yegor Ligachev as head of the agricultural commission of the Central Committee. Stroev is a graduate of the Michurin Fruit and Vegetable Institute (1960) and the Higher Party School (1969). He always has worked in the area of agriculture, beginning as an agronomist on a collective farm in his native Oryol region. He has become known as a moderate agricultural reformer for encouraging farm leasing.

Aleksandr Vlasov (1932-). Vlasov is chairman of the Council of Ministers of the Russian republic. In May 1990, he ran against Boris Yeltsin for the presidency of the Russian republic and was defeated despite vigorous campaigning on his behalf by Gorbachev. Vlasov opposed the resolution of Russian sovereignty, which subsequently was passed with Yeltsin's support. Vlasov was a candidate member of the Politburo from February 1988 until July 1990.

Vitalii Vorotnikov (1926-). Vorotnikov was retired from the party leadership at the Twenty-eighth Party Congress in July 1990. He had been a full member of the Politburo since December 1983. He also was chairman of the Presidium of the Russian republic's supreme soviet until he was replaced by Boris Yeltsin after free elections were held in May 1990. On the Politburo, Vorotnikov was considered a supporter of cautious reform.

Gennadii Yanaev (1937-). Yanaev is a representative of the trade unions in the Congress of People's Deputies and was appointed to the Politburo at the Twenty-eighth Party Congress in July 1990. Since April 1990 Yanaev has been the chairman of the All-Union Central Council of Trade Unions. He served on the government delegation in the negotiations with striking coal miners in the summer of 1989.

Veniamen Yarin (1940-). A metalworker from the Urals, Yarin is a spokesman for the conservative "Rossiya" group in the Congress of People's Deputies, a founder of the United Front of Russian Workers, and a member of the Presidential Council. He has worked to mobilize workers against the introduction of market reforms. He also is a vocal advocate of a strong defense posture.

Boris Yeltsin (1931-). In May 1990, Yeltsin was narrowly elected as the first president of the Russian republic despite strong opposition by Gorbachev. Yeltsin's populist message and his attacks against party privilege have made him one of the most popular politicians in the Soviet Union.

Gorbachev brought Yeltsin, an engineer and industrial specialist, to Moscow in April 1985 to head the Central Committee construction department. Before his promotion, Yeltsin had a typical career as a party functionary in Sverdlovsk. In December 1985, Yeltsin succeeded Viktor Grishin as head of the Moscow party organization. A week before the Twenty-seventh Party Congress in February 1986, Yeltsin became a candidate member of the Politburo. At the October 1987 Central Committee plenum, he attacked the party leadership and the slow pace of reform and charged that Gorbachev was developing a cult of personality. For this transgression against party discipline, he was expelled from the Politburo. Yeltsin continued to criticize the party leadership, however, building a reputation as a spokesman of the people. In March 1989 Yeltsin's political career rebounded when he was elected a people's deputy with 89 percent of the vote in his Moscow constituency.

At the Twenty-eighth Party Congress in July 1990 Yeltsin declared that "in view of my great responsibility toward the people of Russia and in connection with the move towards a multiparty system, I cannot fulfill only the instructions of the Communist party." Then with his flare for the theatrical, he announced his resignation from the party and walked out of the hall to shouts of "Shame!" A group of fifty delegates from the Democratic Platform bloc announced their intention to form an opposition party under his leadership.

Lev Zaikov (1923-). Zaikov was retired from the party leadership at the Twenty-eighth Party Congress in July 1990. He had been a full member of the Politburo since March 1986 and the Central Committee secretary responsible for the military-industrial complex since July 1985. He was a staunch advocate of scientific and technical progress but took a conservative approach to glasnost and political reform.

Past Soviet Leaders

Yuri V. Andropov (1914-1984)

Two days after the death of Leonid I. Brezhnev on November 10, 1982, Yuri Vladimirovich Andropov was named to succeed him as general secretary of the Communist party. On June 16, 1983, Andropov became chairman

of the Presidium of the Supreme Soviet (president), thus continuing a practice begun by Brezhnev of combining the role of head of state with that of party chief. An ailing sixty-eight-year-old when he took over, Andropov died February 10, 1984. Three days later the Central Committee chose Konstantin U. Chernenko as his successor.

Andropov was born the son of a railroad worker on June 15, 1914, in Nagutskaya, now in Stavropol territory. Andropov never received a college degree although he attended Petrozavodsk University. Between 1930 and 1932 he worked as a telegraph operator, an apprentice film mechanic, and a Volga boatman. Andropov began work in the Komsomol (Communist Youth League) in 1936. In 1938 he was promoted to regional first secretary of the Komsomol and the following year became a member of the Communist party.

Public Career. When Germany invaded the Soviet Union in 1941, Andropov was active in party politics in Karelia, near the Soviet border with Finland. For the next decade he worked alongside Otto Kuusinen, the top party leader in the Karelian autonomous republic.

With the backing of Kuusinen, Andropov was transferred to Moscow in 1951 to work for the Central Committee. In 1953, after Soviet leader Joseph Stalin died, Andropov suffered an apparent career setback when he was posted to the Soviet embassy in Budapest. The switch from inner party politics to diplomacy, however, did not stymie his career. In 1954 he was promoted from counselor to ambassador to Hungary, a post he held until 1957. Andropov played a leading role in suppressing the 1956 Hungarian revolt.

Between 1957 and 1967 he was back in Moscow serving as chief of the party's Department for Liaison with Communist and Workers' Parties of Socialist Countries, where he emphasized the importance of Soviet aid to socialist countries. During this period Andropov gathered around him a group of young, progressive advisers including Oleg Bogomolov, Aleksandr Bovin, and Fëdor Burlatsky, who later would become important reform intellectuals under Mikhail S. Gorbachev.

Andropov was made a candidate member of the Politburo in 1967, when he became chairman of the USSR Committee for State Security (KGB). He was promoted to full member of the Politburo in 1973 and thus became the first KGB head to have a vote on the Politburo since Lavrentii Beria was purged in 1953.

As head of the KGB, Andropov worked to destroy the dissident movement in the Soviet Union. Many prominent Soviet writers, scientists, and others agitating for greater liberalization were imprisoned or sent into exile under his authority.

In May 1982 Andropov resigned as KGB head and transferred to the Central Committee Secretariat, a better position from which to succeed Brezhnev. By that time he had already gained some important allies, including Foreign Minister Andrei Gromyko and Defense Minister Dmitri Ustinov, who would side with him in the struggle to succeed Brezhnev.

Analysis. Although Andropov's administration lasted only fifteen months, it brought significant changes to Soviet politics and society. During the last decade of Brezhnev's reign, few changes were made in the composition of the party leadership. But the complacency of the old guard was shaken by Andropov. He advanced Gorbachev and other younger leaders intent on instituting reforms, and he campaigned against corruption in the bureaucracy. Were it not for Andropov's domestic initiatives, many experts believe that Gorbachev would not have been able to consolidate his power so quickly. Consequently, Gorbachev and his reform program often have been seen as the legacy of Andropov.

Nevertheless, Andropov was not a radical reformer. Instead, he was an intelligent and loyal party leader who recognized his country's problems and tried to address them within the limits of the established system. Had he lived longer, he would not have pushed the reform process as far or as fast as Gorbachev.

Lavrentii Beria (1899-1953)

Lavrentii Pavlovich Beria, head of the secret police from 1938 to 1953, played an important role in maintaining the personal power of Joseph Stalin. The fear Beria engendered among his colleagues, however, led to his own arrest and execution after Stalin's death.

Beria was born on March 29, 1899, in Merkheuli, Georgia. His Georgian heritage endeared him to Stalin, another son of that republic. Beria was born into a peasant family and obtained a technical education in a Baku college. He joined the Bolshevik party in 1917 and began his career as a revolutionary worker in Georgia and Azerbaidzhan.

Public Career. Beria began working for the Transcaucasian Cheka in 1921. Later in the decade he continued his intelligence work in the Main Political Administration (GPU). Despite reports of abuses of power by Beria, Stalin promoted him to first secretary of the Transcaucasian Committee of the Communist party in 1931, a post that allowed Beria to exercise dictatorial power over the entire Transcaucasian region.

Stalin summoned Beria to Moscow in July 1938 and appointed him deputy to Nikolai Yezhov, head of the People's Commissariat of Internal Affairs (NKVD) and overseer of the purges. Yezhov was by this time marked by Stalin for execution, and his demise followed later in the year.

Beria took command of the secret police organization in December 1938. He investigated NKVD activities and is credited with rehabilitating certain victims of the purges and upgrading prison camp conditions. Beria's ability to magnify Stalin's suspicions of his colleagues and the dictator's great reliance on the secret police enabled Beria to consolidate quickly a powerful position. He became a candidate Politburo member in 1939.

World War II enhanced Beria's position. When the Germans invaded the Soviet Union in June 1941, Stalin appointed Beria to the State Defense Committee. His duties, in addition to supervising internal security and an international spy network, included the evacuation and resettlement of Soviet industry and later the production of ammunition. For his wartime service Beria was named a marshal of the Soviet Union in 1945. He became a full Politburo member in 1946.

Upon Stalin's death in 1953, Soviet leaders engaged in a power struggle. Beria was in contention for the top spot in the Soviet hierarchy, but initially a system of collective leadership was established. Georgii Malenkov became premier, Nikita S. Khrushchev served as party leader, and Beria continued to head up the secret police from his position as minister of internal affairs. Beria and the vast secret police network that he controlled were viewed by the other Politburo members as threats not only to their political aspirations but also to their lives. Determined that no one individual again would wield Stalin's power of life and death, the collective leadership led by Khrushchev and Malenkov engineered Beria's arrest in June 1953 on charges of "criminal antiparty and antistate activities." His alleged crimes included involvement with British intelligence and promotion of nationalistic sentiments. In December Beria was tried and executed.

Analysis. Beria's career often is described as that of an "evil genius" who ingratiated himself with Stalin by eliminating those whom Stalin perceived as enemies. He also is alleged to have approached his work with enthusiasm, personally torturing and killing many prisoners. Khrushchev maintained in his autobiography that Stalin, toward the end of his life, began to fear Beria.

In spite of Beria's lifetime association with Joseph Stalin, he proposed many modifications of the system after Stalin's death. In foreign policy Beria supported good relations with Western countries. He advocated restoring ties with Yugoslavia's Josip Broz Tito and opposed Russification of non-Russian regions of the Soviet Union.

Beria's execution marked a turning point in the way power was consolidated in the Soviet leadership. The leading members of the Communist party had suffered more at the hands of Stalin and the secret police apparatus during the purges than had any other group. After Beria's execution a tacit understanding developed among the Politburo members that enforced retirement would replace execution as a punishment for losing favor.

Leonid I. Brezhnev (1906-1982)

During the 1970s and early 1980s Leonid Ilich Brezhnev was the unrivaled leader of the Soviet Union. From 1977 until his death November 10, 1982, he was both general secretary of the Communist party and chairman of the

Presidium of the Supreme Soviet (president)—the first Soviet leader to hold both of these posts at the same time. Brezhnev's success as a politician was achieved through means different from earlier Soviet leaders. He did not have V. I. Lenin's visionary brilliance, Joseph Stalin's genius for terror, nor Nikita S. Khrushchev's overpowering personality. Instead he gained and held power because he worked hard and was adept at cultivating allies within the Soviet leadership, bureaucracy, and military.

Brezhnev, a Russian, was born December 19, 1906, into a steelworker's family in the Ukrainian town of Kamenskoe

(known since 1936 as Dneprodzerzhinsk). In 1915 he entered a school subsidized by the local steel plant where his father worked. When he graduated six years later, Brezhnev—who referred to himself as a "fifth-generation steelman"—went to work as a hired hand, stoker, and fitter in a metallurgical plant.

In 1923 Brezhnev enrolled in the Kursk School for Land Utilization and Reclamation. After graduating in 1927 he spent three years working as a land reclamation specialist in Stalin's collectivization program. He eventually became chief of a district land department and deputy chairman of the executive committee of a soviet, and later the first deputy chief of a regional land administration.

In 1930 Brezhnev spent a brief period at the Timiriazev Agricultural Academy in Moscow before returning to his hometown in 1931. He went to work once again as a fitter in the metallurgical plant and studied in the evenings at the F. E. Dzerzhinski Metallurgical Institute. Brezhnev, who had been a Komsomol (Communist Youth League) member (1923-1929) and had joined the Communist party in 1931, also served as secretary of the institute's Communist party committee and chairman of the plant's trade union committee.

Following his graduation from the institute in 1935, he worked as an engineer and briefly served in the Red Army as a political instructor. In 1937-1938 he was deputy chairman of the executive committee of the Dneprodzerzhinsk City Workers' Soviet and director of the city's metallurgical technical school.

Public Career. Brezhnev went to work full time for the Communist party in 1938. Although his switch to party politics came at the time of the Stalinist purges overseen in the Ukraine by Nikita Khrushchev, there is no evidence that Brezhnev took part.

Brezhnev's first position was as chief of a department of the Dnepropetrovsk regional party committee. In 1939 he became the committee's secretary for propaganda and the next year secretary for the defense industry. He remained in this post until 1941, when the German army overran the city.

During World War II Brezhnev rose from colonel to major general, serving with the political administration of the Southern and Ukrainian fronts and the Carpathian Military District. He fought in the Caucasus, on the Black Sea, in the Crimea, in the Ukraine, and in the liberation of Czechoslovakia.

In 1946 Brezhnev became party first secretary of Zaporozhe and, one year later, first secretary of Dnepropetrovsk,

both important industrial regions in the Ukraine. In 1950, after spending a few months in Moscow working in the Central Committee apparatus, he became first secretary of the Moldavian republic. He was elected a deputy of the Supreme Soviet the same year.

As part of Stalin's expansion of the top leadership in 1952, Brezhnev was named a full member of the Central Committee, one of its ten secretaries, and a candidate member of its Presidium. Following Stalin's death in March 1953, most of his 1952 additions to the Secretariat and Presidium—including Brezhnev—were dropped. Brezhnev then spent a year as first deputy chief of the Main Political Administration of the Soviet Army and Navy.

In 1954 Khrushchev, maneuvering for power after Stalin's death, staked his political future on his Virgin Lands program, which was aimed at increasing Soviet agricultural output by farming previously uncultivated lands. He chose Brezhnev to help carry out the venture. From 1954 to 1956 Brezhnev served as second secretary and later as first secretary of the party in the Central Asian republic of Kazakhstan, where many acres of virgin land were opened.

Having displayed his managerial and political skills in the agrarian program, Brezhnev returned in 1956 to Moscow to become once again a secretary of the party's Central Committee (for heavy industry and capital investment; after 1959, for defense and space exploration) and a candidate member of its Presidium. Brezhnev supported Khrushchev in his struggle with the "antiparty group" in early 1957, and Brezhnev was among the supporters Khrushchev chose that year to replace his discredited opponents on the Presidium.

In 1960 Brezhnev was named chairman of the Presidium of the Supreme Soviet (president). The ceremonial post of chief of state served Brezhnev well during his four-year tenure. He gained needed experience in the noncommunist world by traveling abroad as a spokesman for the Khrushchev regime's foreign policies.

A few months after his appointment as president, Brezhnev gave up his post as a secretary of the Central Committee. In 1963, however, Brezhnev was renamed to the Secretariat. He relinquished the chief of state post in July 1964. Then, as the unofficial second secretary, he turned his full attention to supervising daily party affairs. Three months later on October 14, 1964, Khrushchev was abruptly ousted from power. His protégé Brezhnev was one of the leaders of the mutiny. He was chosen as first secretary of the party, and Aleksei Kosygin was named head of the government. At the Twenty-third Party Congress in March 1966, Brezhnev's title reverted from "first secretary" to the Stalinist-era usage, "general secretary," and the party "Presidium" was renamed the "Politburo," symbolically concluding Khrushchev's de-Stalinization drive.

Initially, the collective leadership seemed to work. Brezhnev concerned himself with party affairs and relations within the international Communist movement, while Kosygin focused on the economy and ties with the noncommunist world. But by the early 1970s Brezhnev had eclipsed Kosygin. The party leader took over Kosygin's role as the Kremlin's spokesman in international affairs and its chief negotiator with foreign powers. By the time Kosygin resigned in 1980, his influence on economic issues had similarly declined.

In 1976 Brezhnev was named marshal of the Soviet Union, the nation's highest military rank, and his position as chairman of the USSR Defense Council—commander in chief of Soviet armed forces—was publicly acknowledged for the first time.

Brezhnev had another rival, Nikolai Podgornyi, dismissed in 1977 as chairman of the Presidium of the Supreme Soviet so that he could assume the post. Also in 1977 the Soviet Union adopted a new constitution, which was drafted under Brezhnev's supervision.

Analysis. In 1964, after Khrushchev's fall from power, some Western observers thought Brezhnev would be a transition figure, but he held power for eighteen years. Brezhnev was well prepared for the role of Soviet party leader. He brought a broad range of experience to the job that none of his rivals could match. He was experienced in agriculture and industry, had been a party leader in four different republics, had had seven years of political work in the military, and had gained experience in foreign affairs during his four years as chief of state.

Brezhnev's regime emphasized a "scientific approach" to decision making, implying a weighing of alternatives, an understanding of limitations, and a reliance on data. In internal politics Brezhnev displayed resourcefulness and an understanding of when to compromise and when to stand firm. He almost always managed to be on the winning side of major policy struggles.

Brezhnev pursued some apparently contradictory policies during his tenure as Soviet leader. He advanced a détente with the West that included significant arms control agreements, but he continued to challenge Western interests with a sustained arms buildup and Soviet backing of leftist revolutions in the Third World. Under his leadership the USSR launched an invasion of Afghanistan in 1979 and supported the imposition of martial law in Poland in 1981. These actions soured relations with the West and contributed to the Soviets' international isolation. Brezhnev also appeared willing to accept Western condemnation of his regime's treatment of dissidents rather than institute liberalizing reforms.

Under Mikhail S. Gorbachev, Brezhnev and his policies have been severely criticized. The former Soviet leader has been routinely ridiculed in the mass media and has become a symbol of unimaginative, stagnant, and corrupt leadership.

Nikolai Bukharin (1888-1938)

Nikolai Ivanovich Bukharin was a gifted thinker and one of the most popular Soviet revolutionary figures. In his final testament, V. I. Lenin called Bukharin "the Party's most eminent and valuable theoretician." Bukharin, however, became a victim of the Stalinist purges. He was executed in 1938.

Born in Moscow October 9, 1888, Bukharin was attracted to radical philosophies at a young age. In 1908 he joined the Moscow committee of the Bolshevik wing of the Russian Social Democratic Labor party. Two years later tsarist authorities broke up the Moscow organization, and Bukharin was arrested and exiled to Siberia. He subsequently escaped to Europe, where he began to write theoretical as well as political tracts. He first met Lenin in 1912 in Krakow. Bukharin was one of the few Russian revolutionaries to visit the United States. In 1916 and early 1917 he edited the Russian communist newspaper *Novy Mir* (New World) in New York City.

Public Career. After the March 1917 revolution Bukharin returned to Russia, where he was named a member of the Central Committee. He played an important role in Moscow during the Bolsheviks' seizure of power and became editor of the party newspaper *Pravda*. After the November revolution he opposed Lenin's positions on several issues, most notably on whether to continue the war with Germany. Bukharin argued for a continuation of the war, while Lenin oversaw the conclusion of the Brest-Litovsk peace treaty with Germany in 1918. Despite this disagreement, Bukharin remained influential in the party and with Lenin.

In 1919 Bukharin was elected to the Comintern (Communist International) at its formation. He joined the ruling Politburo in 1924 and enjoyed great popularity within the party. He was a strong supporter of Lenin's New Economic Policy (NEP), which allowed limited free market activity in an effort to help the nation recover from many years of revolution and war.

After Lenin's death, Bukharin sided with Stalin against the faction led by Leon Trotsky. But when Stalin began reversing NEP in the late 1920s, Bukharin and his fellow leaders of the "right opposition," Aleksei Rykov and Mikhail Tomskii, opposed Stalin. As a result of his challenge to Stalin, Bukharin was stripped of his Comintern and Politburo posts in November 1929. He submitted to "political self-criticism" and was allowed to continue party work until 1937. However, because he represented a potential source of opposition to Stalin, he fell victim to Stalin's purge. In March 1938 he took the witness stand as the main defendant of the third "show trial" in Moscow. The court found the former Politburo member guilty of counterrevolutionary activities, and he was executed immediately after the trial.

Analysis. Bukharin's writings are considered his most important legacy. They include *World Economy and Imperialism* (1918), *Program of the World Revolution* (1920), *The ABC of Communism* (1921), and *Historical Materialism* (1925). The evolution of Bukharin's political views charted his development from a revolutionary advocating the rapid extension of the Russian revolution to a proponent of the gradual spread of socialism. At first Bukharin believed that world upheaval would follow the Russian revolution. He lowered his expectations after the socialist revolution failed in Germany in 1923. He argued that Soviet Russia should build socialism internally. He complemented this notion with the theory that Russia would benefit economically if the assets of the wealthy peasants could be incorporated without force into the socialist system. Stalin's proposal for building "socialism in one country" was based on Bukharin's ideas, but Stalin deviated from them in launching a forcible collectivization of agriculture in 1928.

In 1988 the USSR Supreme Soviet officially rehabilitated Bukharin as part of the ongoing reevaluation of Soviet history. Bukharin's party membership was restored, many of his works were published, and he has been treated favorably in the media.

Konstantin U. Chernenko (1911-1985)

On February 13, 1984, Konstantin Ustinovich Chernenko, a party bureaucrat and longtime associate of Leonid I. Brezhnev, succeeded Yuri V. Andropov as general secretary of the Communist party. Two months later, on April 11, he became head of state when he was elected chairman of the Presidium of the USSR Supreme Soviet (president).

Chernenko, who was seventy-two years old when he took power, perpetuated the rule of old men in the Soviet Union. Weak from emphysema when he took office, Chernenko died a little more than a year later, on March 11, 1985. His death initiated an abrupt generational transition in Kremlin leadership as his successor, fifty-four-year-old Mikhail S. Gorbachev, rejuvenated the upper reaches of the party apparatus by promoting younger leaders.

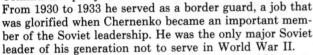

Chernenko was born into a peasant family on September 24, 1911, in Novoselovo, in the Siberian territory of Krasnoyarsk. He joined the Communist party in 1929. From 1930 to 1933 he served as a border guard, a job that was glorified when Chernenko became an important member of the Soviet leadership. He was the only major Soviet leader of his generation not to serve in World War II.

Public Career. Chernenko owed much of his party advancement to his association with Brezhnev. From 1948 to 1956 Chernenko served as chief of the Moldavian Central Committee's Propaganda and Agitation Department. For three of those years, 1950-1952, Brezhnev was first secretary of the Moldavian Central Committee. In 1956 Chernenko became chief of the Mass Agitation Work Sector of the USSR Central Committee.

When Brezhnev became chairman of the Presidium of the Supreme Soviet in 1960, Chernenko was appointed chief of the Supreme Soviet's secretariat. In 1965 he was named head of the USSR Central Committee's General Department, which coordinated the activities of the various departments and handled citizen complaints and classified documents.

Chernenko was made a secretary of the Central Committee in 1976 and also retained his responsibilities for managing the General Department. He was named a candidate member of the Politburo in 1977 and became a full member in 1978.

Analysis. Chernenko appeared to be a compromise choice for the post of general secretary. Brezhnev allies sought to slow the transfer of power to the younger generation, while Gorbachev's supporters did not yet have the power to challenge the authority of the senior members of the leadership. The selection of Chernenko gave something to both camps. His advanced age and poor health made it unlikely that he would significantly delay the advancement of the younger generation, while his loyalty to Brezhnev-era leaders ensured their positions a little longer.

As a result of the stalemate between Brezhnev-era bureaucrats wary of dramatic changes and reformist leaders, such as Gorbachev, intent on reconstructing both the Soviet economy and the Soviet image abroad, little happened during Chernenko's thirteen-month tenure. The progress of the limited political reforms begun by his more activist predecessor was slowed. He reversed one of Andropov's last decisions—to cut the bureaucracy by nearly 20 percent. Chernenko did not halt completely Andropov's domestic program of economic experimentation or his anticorruption campaign, but he lacked the health, will, and vision to spur modernization and reform. In foreign relations, Chernenko supported the status quo,

although he did promote the resumption of arms control talks with the United States.

Andrei Gromyko (1909-1989)

Andrei Andreevich Gromyko, a career diplomat, was elected chairman of the Presidium of the Supreme Soviet (president) on July 2, 1985. Gromyko became the highest official representative of the Soviet Union in its relations with foreign governments, although the presidency at that time was largely an honorific position. In 1988 Mikhail S. Gorbachev took Gromyko's place as president as part of the general secretary's effort to invigorate the Soviet leadership and reinforce his own power. Gromyko died at the age of seventy-nine, exactly four years after becoming president, on July 2, 1989, from an apparent stroke.

Gromyko, however, is best known as the Soviet foreign minister whose tenure spanned three decades (1957-1985). During his twenty-seven years in this post he became the most recognizable symbol of Soviet foreign policy. Near the end of Leonid I. Brezhnev's reign and through the regimes of Yuri V. Andropov and Konstantin U. Chernenko, Gromyko was not only the leading Soviet diplomatic representative, but also one of the prime architects of Soviet foreign policy.

Gromyko, an ethnic Russian, was born in Belorussia on July 18, 1909, and grew up on a farm near Minsk. He devoted much of his early adulthood to study and earned a candidate of economics degree in 1936. Gromyko became a doctor of economics in 1956.

Public Career. Gromyko taught at the Moscow Institute of Economics for three years before being recruited into the foreign service in 1939. Shortly afterward he was assigned to the Soviet embassy in Washington. In 1943 Joseph Stalin made the thirty-four-year-old diplomat ambassador to the United States, a post he held until 1946. Gromyko later became permanent representative to the United Nations (1946-1949) and ambassador to the United Kingdom (1952-1953). He served twice as first deputy minister of foreign affairs (1949-1952, 1953-1957). In 1957 he was appointed foreign minister under Nikita S. Khrushchev.

In tandem with his advancement within the government, Gromyko rose steadily in the Communist party. He joined the party in 1931 while still in school. He served as a deputy to the Council of the Union of the Supreme Soviet from 1946 to 1950. In 1952 he became a candidate member of the Central Committee and was promoted to full membership in 1956. He was made a full Politburo member in 1973, and ten years later he was appointed one of three first deputy prime ministers.

Analysis. As foreign minister, Gromyko traveled to more than forty countries and met most of the major world leaders of his era. He headed the Soviet delegation to every session of the UN General Assembly from 1962 until 1984 (except the 1983 opening following the Soviet downing of a Korean airliner) and participated in every U.S.-Soviet summit until the 1985 Geneva meeting between Gorbachev and President Ronald Reagan.

Gromyko was known for his refusal to make concessions but was respected for his intelligence and knowledge of the West. He was above all a loyal and pragmatic implementer of Politburo policy. As his experience and stature grew, so did his power. His 1973 selection to the Politburo signified his growing influence as a policy maker.

Gromyko also played a key role in Soviet internal politics in the 1980s. Together with Defense Minister Dmitri Ustinov, he was instrumental in Andropov's selection as general secretary over Chernenko in 1982. He also supported Gorbachev in his bid to succeed Chernenko in 1985 and delivered an eloquent speech nominating Gorbachev for general secretary. Gromyko's replacement as foreign minister in 1985 by Eduard Shevardnadze, a Georgian party boss with no diplomatic experience, caught Soviet and U.S. diplomats by surprise. Western observers suggested that Gromyko's appointment to the presidency was a reward for both his long service to the Soviet Union and his backing of Gorbachev during the succession process. But most experts also maintained that Gromyko's promotion was a graceful way for Gorbachev to retire Gromyko, thereby strengthening his own control over international affairs.

Perhaps because of his role in helping Gorbachev assume power, Gromyko has been spared the criticism heaped on many Brezhnev-era officials by Gorbachev and his allies. Upon Gromyko's death, Gorbachev spoke respectfully but offered little praise: "His entire life was connected with our history, with our achievements, with our problems, with everything that falls on the shoulders of a man who is in the thick of events for the course of decades."

Lev Kamenev (1883-1936)

Lev Borisovich Kamenev gained prominence as one of V. I. Lenin's closest associates. Born in Moscow on July 22,  1883, Kamenev was the son of Jewish parents named Rosenfeld who had taken part in the Russian revolutionary movement of the 1870s. Kamenev initially became involved with Marxist circles during his high school (gymnasium) years. His interest in revolutionary philosophy grew while he studied law at Moscow University, and in 1901 he joined the Russian Social Democratic Labor party. In 1908 he traveled to Europe and began working for *Iskra* (The Spark), the revolutionary journal founded by Lenin.

Kamenev continued his underground activity in Europe and later in Russia, staunchly upholding the Bolshevik line during the debates with the Menshevik faction of the Russian Social Democratic Labor party. Kamenev, along with Grigorii Zinoviev, became one of Lenin's closest literary and political collaborators.

In 1914 Kamenev went to St. Petersburg to oversee Bolshevik activities. He was arrested in 1915 and exiled to Siberia. After his release following the March 1917 revolution, he immmediately returned to St. Petersburg. There he served as a leading Bolshevik spokesman and backed the policy of supporting the Provisional Government.

When Lenin arrived in St. Petersburg in April he rejected cooperation with the government and began working toward a Bolshevik-led revolt and regime. Kamenev accepted the necessity of a further revolution but endorsed a seizure of power by a coalition government made up of all socialist parties. When the revolution actually took place in November 1917, however, Kamenev backed the Bolshevik cause. He was named a member of the first Politburo.

After Lenin's death in 1924, Kamenev joined with Zinoviev and Joseph Stalin against the leader of the "left opposition," Leon Trotsky. Kamenev and his ally, Zinoviev, reversed themselves in 1926, supporting Trotsky's ill-fated attempt to thwart Stalin's growing power. Despite later recantations of their alliance with Trotsky, both men lost their important party and government positions. Kamenev was expelled and readmitted to the Communist party three times between 1927 and 1934. In 1935 he was sentenced to five years in prison for "moral complicity" in the murder of the Leningrad party boss, Sergei Kirov. The following year, after being retried in the first "show trial" of Stalin's purge, he was sentenced to death and executed on August 24.

Aleksandr Kerensky (1881-1970)

Aleksandr Feodorovich Kerensky, a member of the Socialist Revolutionary party, headed the Russian Provisional Government on the eve of the Bolshevik Revolution in 1917 and later led an unsuccessful effort to overthrow the new communist regime.

Kerensky was born on April 22, 1881, in Simbirsk (now Ulyanovsk), in the Volga region of Russia where Lenin was born. Ironically, Kerensky's father was Lenin's high school principal. Kerensky became active in populist circles while a student in St. Petersburg. As a young socialist lawyer, he defended revolutionaries accused of political offenses. The failure of the promised reforms of the 1905 Russian revolution convinced Kerensky that the monarchy should be overthrown.

After the collapse of Tsar Nicholas II in March 1917, the Provisional Government assumed power. Kerensky was the only Social Revolutionary to accept a post in the new regime. He served as minister of justice under Prince Georgii Lvov, a liberal aristocrat who was prime minister. Later, Kerensky became minister of war. At the same time, he held a post in the Petrograd Soviet and functioned as an intermediary between the Soviet and the Provisional Government.

Kerensky replaced Lvov as prime minister in July 1917, at a time when the Bolsheviks gradually were gaining support and the mood of the people was becoming increasingly radical. Kerensky's government fell to the Bolsheviks in November 1917. He escaped from Petrograd and rallied loyal troops, but his attempts to overthrow the new regime failed. He emigrated and died in New York City at age eighty-eight on June 11, 1970.

Aleksei Kosygin (1904-1980)

Aleksei Nikolaevich Kosygin became premier when Nikita S. Khrushchev was ousted by his Politburo colleagues in October 1964. Initially he was coequal with Leonid I. Brezhnev in the collective post-Khrushchev leadership. But long before Kosygin resigned as premier sixteen years later, he had lost much of his authority to party leader Brezhnev.

Kosygin was born on February 20, 1904, in St. Petersburg (renamed Petrograd in 1914 and Leningrad in 1924). His father was a lathe operator. At the age of fifteen, Kosygin volunteered for service in the Red Army and fought in the Civil War until 1921. He graduated from the Leningrad Cooperative Technical School in 1924 and was sent to Siberia to help integrate that region's cooperative movement into the national economy.

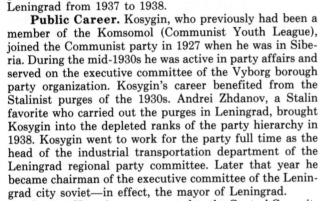

Kosygin returned home in 1929 to begin his studies at the Leningrad (later Kirov) Textile Institute. After graduating six years later as a textile engineer, he went to work first as a foreman and later as a shop superintendent at the Zhelyabov factory in Leningrad. He served as director of the Oktyabr spinning mill in Leningrad from 1937 to 1938.

Public Career. Kosygin, who previously had been a member of the Komsomol (Communist Youth League), joined the Communist party in 1927 when he was in Siberia. During the mid-1930s he was active in party affairs and served on the executive committee of the Vyborg borough party organization. Kosygin's career benefited from the Stalinist purges of the 1930s. Andrei Zhdanov, a Stalin favorite who carried out the purges in Leningrad, brought Kosygin into the depleted ranks of the party hierarchy in 1938. Kosygin went to work for the party full time as the head of the industrial transportation department of the Leningrad regional party committee. Later that year he became chairman of the executive committee of the Leningrad city soviet—in effect, the mayor of Leningrad.

In 1939 Kosygin was promoted to the Central Committee and received his first national government position, that of people's commissar for light industry. He was promoted one year later to the post of deputy chairman of the Council of People's Commissars (later renamed Council of Ministers), or deputy prime minister. He remained in that position until 1953.

In the early months of World War II Kosygin played an important role in increasing production in the Soviet defense industry. He also was in charge of the evacuation of five hundred thousand people from Leningrad in January 1942. After the war he served as USSR minister of finance until 1948 and then minister of light industry for the remainder of the Stalin period.

He continued his climb up the party ladder as well. After being elected a candidate member of the Politburo in 1946, Kosygin was made a full member in 1948. But Kosygin's fortunes soon changed. In 1948 Zhdanov died, and the following year Stalin began another round of executions and arrests, aimed primarily at the "Leningrad gang," many of whom were Kosygin's former associates.

Kosygin survived the purge but a shadow had been cast over his career. In 1952, when Stalin expanded the Politburo (which had been renamed the Presidium) from ten to twenty-five members, Kosygin was demoted to candidate status. He was the only full member to lose his seat. He did, however, retain his government positions in the Council of Ministers and Ministry of Light Industry.

Following Stalin's death in March 1953, Kosygin lost both his candidate membership in the Presidium and his government position as a deputy prime minister. He remained minister of food and light industry (later renamed the Ministry of Industrial Consumer Goods).

Late in 1953 Kosygin became a deputy prime minister once again and within a few months resigned from the consumer goods ministry to devote more time to the USSR Council of Ministers. In 1956 he was temporarily relieved of his post as a deputy prime minister and was named deputy chairman of Gosplan (the State Planning Committee).

In June 1957 Kosygin, as a member of the Central Committee, strongly supported Khrushchev in his confrontation with the "antiparty group," which sought Khrushchev's ouster. Khrushchev won the power struggle and rewarded Kosygin by granting him both candidate membership in the party Presidium and his old post of deputy prime minister.

In 1959 Kosygin was named chairman of Gosplan, thus becoming the country's chief economic planner with responsibility for the allocation of resources, production goals, and pricing. In 1960 he was elected a full member of the party Presidium and was appointed one of two first deputy prime ministers. As a deputy prime minister, Kosygin traveled frequently in Europe, Asia, and Latin America. In July 1964 he became the sole first deputy prime minister, ranking only behind Khrushchev in the government.

On October 14, 1964, a special session of the Central Committee suddenly removed Khrushchev from power. Kosygin was named to replace him as chairman of the USSR Council of Ministers, or prime minister. Brezhnev assumed Khrushchev's position as first secretary of the Communist party.

Initially, Kosygin was responsible for government affairs, including economic matters and foreign relations with nonsocialist countries, while Brezhnev was to handle party affairs and Soviet relations within the international communist movement. The division of labor seemed to work at first. While Brezhnev was busy consolidating his power within the party, Kosygin tackled the Soviet Union's economic problems. He also traveled abroad frequently. He was visiting Hanoi in early 1965 when U.S. president Lyndon B. Johnson ordered bombing raids on North Vietnam. The raids—and the entire U.S. policy in Southeast Asia—outraged Kosygin and blocked steps toward improved U.S.-Soviet relations for several years. But in 1967, during a visit to the United Nations, Kosygin met with Johnson in Glassboro, New Jersey. Although nothing substantive was resolved, the face-to-face meeting of the two leaders relieved superpower tensions.

Kosygin was actively involved in efforts to stem the tide of liberalization in Czechoslovakia in 1968. He favored negotiating and applying economic pressure to bring the Prague government back into line. Balancing Kosygin's moderate approach was the Soviet military, which favored armed intervention. Brezhnev, who was thought to have been in the middle, playing the role of mediator between the two positions, ultimately sided with the military. The Soviet decision-making process during the Czech crisis was instructive in that it showed the growing dominance of Brezhnev over Kosygin.

By the early 1970s there was no question as to who was running the Soviet Union. Brezhnev met with foreign leaders and conducted high-level summitry. Eventually he came to dominate the economic arena as well. Kosygin's failing health further accelerated his loss of authority. After he suffered a heart attack in 1976, many of his duties were taken over by Nikolai Tikhonov, an ally of Brezhnev who had been named a first deputy prime minister. Kosygin had another heart attack in 1979, and on October 23, 1980, he resigned as prime minister and gave up his seat in the Politburo.

Kosygin died December 18, 1980. His life and career were praised lavishly in the official obituary.

Analysis. Kosygin had two traits that probably accounted for much of his success in Soviet politics: he was a capable administrator and he seemed to have no aspirations to the top leadership position. He was extremely competent and posed little threat to incumbent political leaders.

These characteristics may explain, in part, Brezhnev's dominance of his one-time coequal. While Brezhnev consolidated his power, Kosygin was preoccupied with the troubled Soviet economy. He was said to have regarded revitalizing the economy as the major challenge of his career. It was a challenge he was unable to meet.

Nikita S. Khrushchev (1894-1971)

Nikita Sergeevich Khrushchev, one of Joseph Stalin's most loyal subordinates, won the struggle for power after Stalin's death. As party lead-

er and premier, however, Khrushchev initiated a campaign of de-Stalinization that denounced the late dictator's bloody methods and accumulation of power. Khrushchev's nine-year reign was marked by power struggles and contradictory policies in both domestic and foreign policy. He was ousted by his colleagues in 1964.

Born April 17, 1894, in the Kursk province of Russia near the Ukrainian border, Khrushchev came from a simple worker's background. Unlike many Communist leaders who joined the party as students in their late teens, Khrushchev did not join the Bolsheviks until 1918, when he was twenty-four. He spent the next three years fighting in the civil war. His first wife and two children perished during the famines of the 1920s. He subsequently married Nina Petrovna, who captured the interest of the American people when she accompanied him on a visit to the United States in 1959. The couple had three children.

After the civil war Khrushchev attended an adult technical school and engaged in party work in the Ukraine. He met Joseph Stalin in 1926 while serving as a delegate to a party congress. Transferred to Moscow in 1929, Khrushchev enrolled in the prestigious Industrial Academy where Nadezhda Alliluyeva, Stalin's second wife, was his classmate.

Public Career. Khrushchev's career gained momentum in the 1930s. An able and energetic administrator, he played a central role in the Moscow subway construction project. He was named to the party Central Committee in 1934 and became a candidate member of the Politburo and first secretary of the Ukrainian Communist party in 1938. The following year he was promoted to full Politburo status.

Khrushchev's exact role in the Stalinist purges is not known, but his participation probably was substantial. He supported Stalin against the protests of those in the party who were horrified by the executions and in doing so probably escaped being purged himself.

Before World War II, Khrushchev played an important role in the Soviet annexation of eastern Poland. After the outbreak of German-Soviet hostilities in 1941, he oversaw the war effort at various field commands. One of his duties was recommending military officers for promotion. These protégés later were instrumental in helping Khrushchev consolidate his own power. In 1944 Stalin sent Khrushchev back to the Ukraine to head the party. There he oversaw the republic's recovery from the devastation of the war and suppressed opposition to Soviet rule.

In December 1949 Khrushchev returned to Moscow to serve as a Central Committee secretary. After Stalin's death in 1953, Georgii Malenkov emerged as head of the government and party secretary, but Malenkov gave up his party post to Khrushchev who used the opportunity to augment his power base. Khrushchev initially upheld the Stalinist line and sided with those in the leadership who opposed Malenkov's bid for power and his more moderate course in domestic and foreign policy. Khrushchev also proposed a series of domestic reforms, including his Virgin Lands program to cultivate barren regions in Siberia and Central Asia. In 1955 Khrushchev orchestrated the demotion of Malenkov, thus securing his position as first among equals in the collective leadership. Later Khrushchev would adopt some of the policies Malenkov had endorsed, including a less hostile stance toward the West.

Khrushchev's "Secret Speech" to the delegates to the Twentieth Party Congress in February 1956 was a watershed for Soviet internal and foreign policies. In the speech Khrushchev revealed the extent of Stalin's tyranny and promised to rehabilitate the late dictator's victims. Earlier during the congress, he also proposed a policy of peaceful coexistence with the West, reversing the traditional Soviet claim that war between the capitalist and communist camps was inevitable. *(Excerpts from "Secret Speech," Appendix, p. 297)*

This first public denunciation of Stalin shocked the Communist community. East European leaders particularly were unnerved because their governments were built on Stalinist principles. Domestic upheavals occurred in Poland and Hungary. The Soviets invaded Hungary in 1956 to put down a liberalization movement that threatened communist rule. The People's Republic of China was outraged by Khrushchev's de-Stalinization campaign, which the Chinese termed a "revisionist" act by a leader whose stature could not compare with that of Stalin or of China's own leader, Mao Zedong. Despite these setbacks, Khrushchev's attack on Stalin had the desired effect—it separated him from his rivals for power in the Soviet Union by grouping them together as "Stalin's heirs," and it portrayed Khrushchev as a reformer who refused to follow Stalin's path.

Khrushchev faced formidable opposition within the Presidium (the name for the Politburo between 1952 and 1966). In mid-1957 a group of high party officials, including Malenkov, Viacheslav Molotov, Lazar Kaganovich, and Dmitri Shepilov, conspired to oust Khrushchev. He overcame the "antiparty group," as it was dubbed, by appealing to the Central Committee for support. Khrushchev's rivals were expelled from the Central Committee in mid-1957. By 1958 when Khrushchev took over the premiership, he had placed himself at the head of all party, government, and military organs and had begun developing his own "personality cult."

Khrushchev, in his conduct of foreign affairs, vacillated between threatening gestures toward the West and attempts to thaw out the cold war. Continuing disagreements with the West over the fate of Germany led to the erection of the Berlin Wall in 1961. In the fall of 1962 Khrushchev decided to install Soviet missiles in Cuba to improve the Soviet strategic position and to silence his hard-line critics in Beijing and Moscow. Instead, President John F. Kennedy's ultimatums forced Khrushchev to back down and remove the missiles from Cuba. Less than a year later the superpowers negotiated a treaty providing for a partial ban on nuclear testing.

By 1963 Khrushchev's colleagues were becoming increasingly unhappy with his domestic reforms. Neither his Virgin Lands program nor his ambitious economic plans came close to achieving their goals. A disastrous 1963 harvest intensified Soviet economic problems. Although Khrushchev tempered his drive to boost the supply of consumer goods in 1963, conservative Soviet leaders still feared that traditional investments in arms and heavy industry could be threatened. In addition, Khrushchev's bifurcation of the party and government structures into industrial and agricultural branches in 1962 displeased many leaders. These domestic factors, combined with the erosion of Khrushchev's prestige in Eastern Europe and China and the failure of his plan to put missiles in Cuba, led to his political demise. A conspiracy of the Soviet Union's highest officials removed him from power on October 14, 1964. He was replaced by Aleksei Kosygin as premier and by Leonid I. Brezhnev as party first secretary. Khrushchev lived in seclusion after his forced retirement and died September 11, 1971.

Analysis. Khrushchev had neither the theoretical brilliance and personal prestige of V. I. Lenin nor the secret police machine of Stalin. Instead, he relied on a reform program and his network of contacts in the party to secure his power and bring the Soviet Union out of its Stalinist past.

Khrushchev's ambition was to build the Soviet Union so that it would "overtake and outstrip" the West in technology, living standards, and international prestige. To this end he launched a variety of ambitious programs that he hoped would accelerate economic growth and make the Soviet Union a model for emulation. Many of his plans, however, ended in failure. His agricultural reforms proved disastrous, the Soviets were humiliated in the Cuban missile crisis, and relations with China grew increasingly bitter.

Despite these setbacks, during Khrushchev's tenure the Soviet Union broadened its efforts to gain influence in the Third World, expanded its nuclear arsenal, maintained domestic stability, and accomplished some impressive scientific feats. Most important, Khrushchev repudiated the terror and violence of the Stalin period. Although abuses of power continued under Khrushchev, for most Soviet citizens, the fear that had pervaded their daily lives was eliminated.

V. I. Lenin (1870-1924)

Vladimir Ilich Ulyanov was born in the Volga region of Russia on April 22, 1870. Later in life he would adopt a pseudonym, Lenin, to protect himself from tsarist police persecution. A brilliant theoretician, capable administrator, and inspiring leader, Lenin was principally responsible for bringing the Russian Revolution of 1917 to fruition.

The Ulyanov family enjoyed relatively high social status. Vladimir Ilich's father was educational administrator for the entire region of Simbirsk (now Ulyanovsk; the name of the region was changed in 1924 in honor of its most famous son). The first radical in the Ulyanov family was Vladimir's older brother, Aleksandr, who as a student took part in a populist revolutionary plot to assassinate Tsar Alexander III. He was arrested and executed when Vladimir was seventeen.

Lenin attended the University of Kazan in 1887 in the juridical program but soon was expelled for participating in a student demonstration.
While temporarily out of school, he spent his time reading revolutionary literature, educating himself, and developing his political views. Increasingly drawn to Marxism instead of the populist teaching his brother had adopted, Lenin particularly was impressed by two tracts: Karl Marx's *Das Kapital* and Georgii Plekhanov's *Our Disagreements*. After several years Lenin was readmitted to the university, where he completed studies for a law degree.

In the 1890s Lenin began working for the socialist cause in St. Petersburg. He traveled abroad in 1895 to meet the exiled leaders of Russian socialism, including Plekhanov. At the end of the year Lenin returned to Russia and was arrested for his work on an underground newspaper. He was sent to Siberia, but he continued writing and maintained contact with colleagues. He married Nadezhda Krupskaya, another revolutionary, who joined him in Siberia.

Public Career. While Lenin was in Siberia, the Russian Social Democratic Labor party (RSDLP) was formed in 1898 at an illegal congress in Minsk. After his release in 1900 Lenin emigrated to Europe and established himself as a leader among the Social Democrats. He founded a revolutionary journal *Iskra* (The Spark) with Plekhanov and other prominent revolutionaries. *Iskra*, secretly distributed throughout Russia, became the guiding force of the revolutionary movement for the next several years. Around this time, Lenin dropped his real name, Ulyanov, and began signing articles with his pseudonym.

While in Europe Lenin became increasingly concerned with the revolutionary program and tactics that the RSDLP was avowing. He set out his ideas in his pamphlet "What Is to Be Done?" published in 1902. Lenin favored a tightly knit, disciplined cadre of full-time revolutionaries who would lead the workers to overthrow the tsarist regime. To support these professionals, Lenin proposed a united and highly centralized party.

Members at the 1903 congress of the RSDLP split into two factions over the issue of revolutionary tactics. The group that won a slim majority on a vote concerning the composition of the editorial board of *Iskra*, the Bolsheviks (or "majoritarians"), rallied around Lenin's leadership and his avowal of armed insurrection. The Mensheviks (or "minoritarians") were led by Plekhanov. The Mensheviks, however, soon regained control of the journal, and Lenin resigned from the editorial board. After the party split, Lenin turned his attention toward underground activity in

Russia. He returned to Russia during the revolution of 1905, but the upheaval provided no opportunities to seize power, and, after a brief stay, Lenin was forced to emigrate to Europe a second time. There he continued his efforts to advance revolution in Russia, while dealing with constant quarrels within the socialist camp.

Following the establishment of the Provisional Government in 1917, Lenin secretly returned to Russia in a sealed train provided by the German government. After a tumultuous welcome at Finland Station in Petrograd, Lenin delivered two speeches before a joint session of Bolsheviks, Mensheviks, and other revolutionaries. These speeches, known as the April Theses, called on socialists to abandon collaboration with the Provisional Government and oppose Russia's efforts in World War I. He advocated "all land to the peasants" and "all power to the soviets"; that is, the transfer of government authority to the workers' councils organized in Petrograd, Moscow, and other Russian cities. The theses shocked traditional Marxists because they repudiated the Marxist dogma of revolutionary progression, a step-by-step process that ends with the seizure of power by the workers after the collapse of a highly developed capitalist system. Instead, Lenin proposed pressing forward with the revolution despite Russia's lack of capitalist development and the relative weakness of the Bolshevik party.

The year 1917 continued in a confusing pattern of unrest and uprisings. Lenin and most of the Bolshevik leaders were forced to flee Petrograd in July. From Finland Lenin attempted to foment the revolution, while much of the work on the scene was done by Leon Trotsky, who oversaw the rapid expansion of the Bolshevik party. Lenin returned to Petrograd on October 20, just a few weeks before the Bolshevik seizure of power in November. Other Bolshevik leaders, including Lev Kamenev and Grigorii Zinoviev, advocated a cautious approach to revolution until the party could be strengthened further, but Lenin urged his fellow party members to take over the government. Lenin's strategy prevailed, and the Bolsheviks overthrew the Provisional Government on November 7 and 8.

As head of the nascent government with the title "chairman of the Council of the People's Commissars," Lenin quickly consolidated the Bolsheviks' tenuous control. On the domestic front, civil war broke out between the Bolsheviks and opposition groups. In an attempt to keep industry operative, Lenin imposed "War Communism," a program that centralized the economy and abolished markets and money. In foreign policy, Lenin agreed to a peace with Germany. The March 1918 treaty at Brest-Litovsk was concluded over protests from members of his own government, including Trotsky. After the Bolsheviks had won the civil war, Lenin was forced to retreat from his harsh economic policies, and in 1921 he reinstituted a degree of free enterprise under the "New Economic Policy."

During the early 1920s Lenin began working at a slower pace. Heart disease and the effects of wounds he suffered in an assassination attempt in 1918 had weakened his health. He suffered a stroke in mid-1922, causing his health to deteriorate further. He had two more strokes before his death January 21, 1924.

Analysis. Lenin was not only an administrative and organizational genius, but he also was the party's leading theoretician. He adapted Marxist theory to conditions in early twentieth-century Russia. Like Marx, Lenin took as his goal the overthrow of capitalism and the establishment of socialism. Unlike Marx, he did not consider it necessary for capitalism to develop before a revolution took place. Another departure from Marxist theory was Lenin's reliance on a professional cadre of revolutionaries to lead the workers into action. Marx envisioned rule by the entire working class, but in Lenin's view the Russian proletariat was not ready for such a responsibility.

Lenin's idealism and desire to create a better Russia are unquestionable. After coming to power he lived a simple life and worked tirelessly until his failing health limited his activities. His belief that the Bolsheviks and Marxist philosophy held the keys to improving Russian society, however, led him to justify the use of any means (including violence and terror) to secure and consolidate power for the Bolshevik party. For example, he sanctioned the creation of a political police force (the Cheka) to control dissent and ordered grain to be forcibly requisitioned from the peasants during the civil war.

Despite Lenin's unrivaled position as Soviet leader, he was unable to engineer his own succession. Before his death, Lenin wrote a letter to party leaders advising them to remove Joseph Stalin from the post of general secretary. By the time the letter was read after Lenin's death, however, Stalin's position was secure enough for him to overcome this blow to his reputation.

Georgii Malenkov (1902-1988)

Georgii Maksimilianovich Malenkov succeeded Joseph Stalin as premier in 1953 but soon lost the title and his authority in a power struggle with Nikita S. Khrushchev.

Born in Orenburg, Russia, on January 8, 1902, Malenkov was a student during the Bolshevik Revolution. He joined the Red Army in 1919 and the Communist party in 1920. After the civil war he studied at the Moscow Higher Technical School, graduating in 1925. Soon after he went to work in the Central Committee bureaucracy and became a member of Stalin's personal secretariat. Between 1930 and 1934 Malenkov was in charge of the Moscow party's organization bureau. In 1934 he became a member of the organization bureau for the entire USSR. From this position, he played a particularly bloody role in the Stalinist purges of the 1930s. In 1939 he was elected to the Central Committee and the Secretariat. During World War II he oversaw aircraft production as a member of the State Defense Committee.

Stalin promoted Malenkov to full membership on the Politburo in 1946. Malenkov also served as second secretary of the Central Committee Secretariat and deputy prime minister. Because of his close association with Stalin and his official position as the second most powerful party member, Malenkov appeared to be in line to succeed him. Malenkov's position as heir apparent was reinforced in 1952, when Stalin requested that Malenkov deliver the general report in his place at the Nineteenth Party Congress in October 1952.

Following Stalin's death in 1953, Malenkov was for a short time both party first secretary and prime minister. However, within a few months Khrushchev replaced him as first secretary. Malenkov supported East-West coexistence and greater emphasis on the production of consumer goods. He also was instrumental in rehabilitating some citizens Stalin had accused of crimes.

Malenkov was challenged for supremacy by Khrushchev, who used his power base in the party to force him to resign as prime minister in 1955. Ironically, Khrushchev subsequently adopted many of Malenkov's policies, including peaceful coexistence with the West. Malenkov's final defeat came two years later, when Khrushchev attacked him and other opponents, dubbed the "antiparty group," who had conspired to unseat him. Malenkov was accused of participation in the crimes of Stalin's regime, as well as inept leadership during World War II. He subsequently was expelled from the Central Committee and demoted to the directorship of a power plant in Kazakhstan. He died February 1, 1988, at the age of eighty-six.

Viacheslav Molotov (1890-1986)

Viacheslav Mikhailovich Molotov became a familiar global figure during World War II as Soviet foreign minister, a post he held from 1939 to 1949 and from 1953 to 1956.

He represented the Soviet Union at wartime Allied conferences and was a vocal proponent of hard-line policies toward the West following the war.

Born on March 9, 1890, to shopkeeper parents named Skryabin in the Vyatka province of Russia, Molotov exhibited an early interest in Bolshevism. He worked in revolutionary organizations as a student and was arrested in 1909 and sent to Siberia. In 1912, after his exile had ended, Molotov sharpened his propaganda skills in St. Petersburg, where he edited and wrote for *Pravda*. Molotov participated in the 1917 Bolshevik revolution, although he did not play a leading role.

Molotov became a member of the Central Committee in 1921. He was an early supporter of Stalin, and as Stalin consolidated his power after Lenin's death, Molotov reaped the benefits of their association. He was appointed to full membership in the Politburo in 1925 and replaced Nikolai Bukharin as head of the Comintern in 1929. Molotov's pseudonym is derived from the Russian word for "hammer," which befitted his responsibilities as Stalin's strongman in the 1920s. He worked ruthlessly to strengthen Stalin's position against his opponents, and by the early 1930s Molotov was one of Stalin's closest associates.

Stalin replaced foreign affairs commissar Maksim Litvinov with Molotov in March 1939, a maneuver designed to facilitate negotiations with Nazi Germany. Molotov's diplomatic efforts led to the Nazi-Soviet Nonaggression pact (sometimes referred to as the Molotov-Ribbentrop pact) signed in August 1939. This agreement allowed the Nazis to invade Poland without fear of beginning a war with the Soviet Union. It also provided for the Soviet Union's domination of the Baltic states, eastern Poland, and Finland. As Stalin's foreign representative, Molotov undertook many other diplomatic missions during and after World War II. He attended the Tehran, Yalta, and Potsdam Allied conferences.

Molotov survived a purge of the Foreign Ministry officials in 1949. He resigned as foreign minister but retained his Politburo seat. During the next several years Stalin grew increasingly suspicious of Molotov, but the dictator died before taking action against him. Molotov became foreign minister again in 1953 after Stalin's death. Party leader Nikita S. Khrushchev engineered his removal from this post in 1956.

In 1957 Molotov was a leader of the "antiparty group," which tried to unseat Khrushchev. Khrushchev outmaneuvered his rivals and held on to power. Molotov's participation in the affair led to his demotion to the obscure post of ambassador to Mongolia. In 1961 he was named Soviet representative to the International Atomic Energy Agency, but in 1962 Molotov was expelled from the Communist party during another wave of de-Stalinization.

Molotov lived in obscurity until the Soviet Foreign Ministry announced on July 5, 1984, that he had been reinstated in the Communist party in honor of his ninety-fourth birthday March 9, 1984. Molotov died November 8, 1986.

Nikolai Podgornyi (1903-1983)

Nikolai Viktorovich Podgornyi had a lengthy and influential party and government career during the post-Stalin era. He served as chairman of the Presidium of the Supreme Soviet (president) from 1965 until 1977, when his rival, General Secretary Leonid I. Brezhnev, forced him into retirement and assumed the position for himself.

Born February 18, 1903, into the family of a foundry worker in the Ukrainian village of Karlovka, Podgornyi had a successful career as an engineer in sugar-beet refineries before he began his rise in the Communist party, which he joined when he was twenty-seven. Podgornyi's skill in engineering and administration led to his appointment in 1939 as deputy people's commissar of the food industry of the Ukrainian republic. During this time, he met Nikita S. Khrushchev, who then was chairman of the Ukrainian Communist party. Podgornyi later would become a Khrushchev protégé.

After serving as head of the Moscow Technological Institute of Food Industry during World War II, Podgornyi returned to his post in the Ukraine. In 1946 Khrushchev appointed him permanent representative of the Ukraine at the Soviet Council of Ministers.

From 1950 until 1953 he served as first secretary of the Kharkov province party committee. Between 1953 and 1957 he held a number of posts in the Ukrainian Communist party and then was appointed first secretary, a position he held until 1963. During this time, Podgornyi attained national prominence. In 1954 he was selected as a deputy to the Supreme Soviet; two years later he was elected to the Central Committee after being nominated by Khrushchev; and in May 1960 he was chosen as a member of the Presidium (later renamed Politburo). Three years later, he became a Central Committee secretary.

With the ouster of Khrushchev in 1964 Podgornyi was widely regarded as the third-ranking leader in the Kremlin behind First Secretary Brezhnev and Premier Aleksei Kosygin. Podgornyi assumed principal responsibility for party organization and instituted major reforms.

When Anastas Mikoian resigned as chairman of the Presidium of the Supreme Soviet in December 1965, Brezhnev nominated Podgornyi to the post. In that capacity he proclaimed all laws and decrees, represented the Soviet Union on official missions abroad, and received foreign dignitaries. Although the post was largely ceremonial, Podgornyi continued to hold powerful party positions.

Podgornyi's ouster from the Politburo in 1977 surprised Western analysts. His age (seventy-four) and health may have been factors, but it also is possible Brezhnev wanted to consolidate his power and assume the official title of head of state himself. Observers also pointed to policy differences between the two and Podgornyi's criticisms of the new constitution promoted by Brezhnev. Podgornyi's political career ended March 4, 1979, when he was excluded from the newly elected Supreme Soviet. He died January 12, 1983.

Joseph Stalin (1879-1953)

Joseph Stalin, one of the most powerful and feared leaders of the twentieth century, was the undisputed dictator of the Soviet Union from the late 1920s when he consolidated his power until his death in 1953. His rule was one of the bloodiest episodes in world history as tens of millions of Soviets died as a result of his policies and purges.

Born December 21, 1879, in Georgia, Stalin, unlike many revolutionary leaders, grew up in an impoverished and nonintellectual household. Georgia in the late 1890s was rife with nationalistic sentiment, a topic much discussed at the theological seminary in Tiflis, which Stalin entered in 1893 under his real name, Iosif Vissarionovich Dzhugashvili. While at the seminary Stalin became associated with Georgian nationalistic groups and began to study Marxism. His clandestine lectures on socialism resulted in his expulsion from the seminary in 1899 shortly before he was to graduate.

Stalin was drawn into propaganda and mass agitation activity for the Russian Social Democratic Labor party in Tiflis. His connection with the party led to his first arrest and deportation to Siberia in 1901. Before the 1917 revolution, Stalin's life was typical of young Russian revolutionaries of the time. Several times he was arrested and exiled to Siberia for his activities, but he always managed to return. Inspired by V. I. Lenin's writings, he had become a firm Bolshevik by 1904. Stalin gained a reputation as an efficient organizer during the revolution of 1905.

Public Career. When the Bolsheviks formed their own party in 1912, Lenin sponsored Stalin's membership on the Central Committee. Around this time he assumed the pseudonym he retained until the end of his life—Stalin, or the "man of steel." Stalin was arrested once more, in 1913, and remained in Siberia until he was released after the March revolution of 1917.

Stalin gained national prominence after the Bolshevik revolution in November. He served as commissar of nationalities (1917-1923) and helped draft the Soviet constitutions of 1918 and 1923. During the civil war Stalin served in military leadership posts, as did most of the Bolshevik leaders. His conduct during the war led to bitter disputes with Leon Trotsky, the commissar of war and organizer of the Red Army.

In April 1922 Stalin emerged as general secretary of the Communist party. After Lenin's death in 1924, he and Trotsky vied for power. Although a brilliant orator and theoretician, Trotsky was defeated by the triumvirate of party leaders—Stalin, Grigorii Zinoviev, and Lev Kamenev—who united against him. Stalin used anti-Trotsky

propaganda to weaken his rival's support until he was able to remove Trotsky from his government positions in 1925 and expel him from the Soviet Union four years later. Stalin then turned on Zinoviev and Kamenev, who in 1926 had briefly thrown their support behind Trotsky. Until his power was secure, Stalin forged an alliance with the party's right wing, led by Nikolai Bukharin.

Stalin defeated Trotsky partly by winning support for the concept of "socialism in one country." Unlike Trotsky, who promoted world revolution as the Soviet state's first priority, Stalin, along with Bukharin, advocated building Soviet socialism in isolation before spreading the revolution abroad.

His power unchallenged, Stalin next focused his attention on the USSR's economy. Beginning in 1928 Soviet peasants were brutally collectivized and Soviet industry underwent a program of rapid industrialization. Peasants who resisted were sent to Siberia or shot. The chaos created by collectivization led to famines that killed millions of Soviets.

As the industrialization campaign reached its peak in the mid-1930s, Stalin began a ruthless process of eliminating his perceived enemies. During the "Great Purge," most of the old Bolshevik leaders (including Stalin's former allies Kamenev, Zinoviev, and Bukharin), as well as a large percentage of the military and political elite, were tried and executed. Countless other Soviet citizens were arrested and sent to labor camps in Siberia. Historians generally agree that Stalin was in firm control of the Soviet Union long before he launched the Great Purge, and the killing of other prominent Soviet leaders was not necessary to maintain his hold on power.

Stalin's 1939 nonaggression pact with Adolf Hitler kept the USSR out of World War II for two years, but the German dictator abrogated the pact in June 1941, launching a massive invasion of the Soviet Union. Stalin allied the USSR to Great Britain and eventually the United States to fight the Nazi threat.

Under Stalin's leadership the Soviet Union survived severe human losses and property devastation until the tide of the war turned with the Soviet victory at Stalingrad in early 1943. Stalin proved to be a shrewd bargainer during the wartime allied conferences at Tehran, Yalta, and Potsdam as evidenced by his ability to secure Soviet dominance of Eastern Europe. The establishment of communist regimes there after the war contributed to the growing distrust and animosity between East and West.

By the end of the war, the "cult of Stalin" permeated every facet of life in the Soviet Union, making the dictator the authority in government, politics, art, learning, and science. Evidence suggests that Stalin was planning a second purge in the 1950s, but he died before it was implemented.

Stalin died of a cerebral hemorrhage on March 5, 1953. He was survived by his daughter, Svetlana Alliluyeva, who gained renown when she defected to the West in April 1967. She went back to the Soviet Union to live in 1984, but in 1986 she defected again and returned to the United States. Stalin's first wife, Ekaterina Svanidze, died around 1905, leaving a son, Yakov, who died in World War II after being taken prisoner by the Germans. Stalin's second wife, Nadezhda Alliluyeva, allegedly was driven to suicide in November 1932. She and Stalin had wed in 1918. They had two children, Svetlana and a son, Vasilii, an alleged alcoholic who, after a corrupt military career, died in 1962.

Analysis. Stalin was an organizer, a man of action,

rather than a theoretician or original thinker. Before and during the Russian Revolution, Stalin had been overshadowed by theoretically brilliant leaders with gifts for oratory such as Lenin and Trotsky. After the revolution, however, with Lenin's health declining, Stalin's ruthlessness and skills as an organizer enabled him to gradually take control of the party.

Stalin viewed his industrialization and collectivization drives of the late 1920s and 1930s as necessary to transform the Soviet Union from a backward nation into a world power. At great human cost, Stalin succeeded in making the Soviet Union into an industrial giant. Had he not launched the industrialization drive, the Soviet Union might not have survived the German invasion in 1941.

Stalin's main goal, however, was not strengthening the Soviet Union, but gathering supreme power for himself. His paranoid pursuit of absolute control led him to order the arrest and execution of many of his colleagues and contributed to the creation of a repressive system that continues to haunt the Soviet Union. Since Stalin's death, no Soviet leader has been allowed to become so powerful that he could safely disregard the interests and goals of his fellow leaders.

Mikhail Suslov (1902-1982)

At the time of his death in January 1982, Mikhail Andreevich Suslov—a member of both the Politburo and

Secretariat—was the Communist party's chief ideologist and one of the most powerful Kremlin leaders after Leonid I. Brezhnev.

Suslov came from a peasant background. He was born November 21, 1902, in the village of Shakhovskoe on the Volga in present-day Ulyanovsk *oblast* (province). In 1921 he joined the Communist party and went to Moscow to study. Following his graduation from a workers' school in 1924, he studied at the Plekhanov Institute of National Economy, graduating in 1928. He then attended the prestigious Economics Institute of Red Professors. From 1929 to 1931, while attending the institute, he taught at Moscow State University and the Stalin Academy of Industry. Among his students were Nikita S. Khrushchev and Nadezhda Alliluyeva, Joseph Stalin's second wife.

Public Career. In 1931 Suslov was named to the party's Central Control Commission and to the People's Commissariat of the Workers' and Peasants' Inspection, a combined watchdog group used by Stalin to root out those suspected of having unorthodox views. In 1933-1934 he was in charge of purges in the Ural and Chernigov regions.

From there Suslov moved on to hold various regional party posts. In 1937 he was sent to the Rostov region, where he served first as department chief and later as secretary of the regional party organization. In 1939 he became first secretary of the party in Stavropol territory in the North Caucasus, a post he held until 1944. As chairman of the party's Bureau for Lithuania from 1944 to 1946, Suslov directed the purge in that republic.

From 1941 to 1945, during World War II, he also was a member of the military council on the North Caucasian Front and chief of staff of the Stavropol territory partisan

forces. From 1939 to 1941 he was a member of the party's Central Auditing Commission, and in 1941 he became a full member of the Central Committee.

Suslov left his regional duties in 1946 and returned to Moscow to join the national party apparatus. From 1946 to 1952 he was a member of the Central Committee's Organization Bureau. In 1947 he became a secretary of the Central Committee in charge of the Propaganda and Agitation Department, which was concerned with domestic ideological control.

However, he soon began focusing on relations with other communist parties. He helped to establish the Cominform in 1947 and was a Soviet representative at the June 1948 Cominform meeting where Yugoslavia was expelled from the organization. Suslov became chairman of the Cominform in August 1948 and held that post until 1953. He was editor in chief of the newspaper *Pravda* in 1949-1950, a period during which he gave up his job as a Central Committee secretary.

In 1950 he became a member of the Presidium of the Supreme Soviet—his first high post in the government. He remained a member until 1954, the year he became chairman of the Supreme Soviet's Foreign Affairs Commission. In 1952 Suslov, with Stalin's backing, again became a secretary of the Central Committee and remained one until his death. In 1952, he also was made a member of the party's Presidium (renamed Politburo in 1966).

Following Stalin's death in 1953, the Presidium membership was reduced from twenty-five to ten, and Suslov was one of those dropped. However, in 1955 Khrushchev had Suslov promoted to full membership in the Presidium once again.

Following the ouster of Khrushchev in 1964—in which Suslov played a role—Suslov reportedly was considered for the position of party first secretary. However, Suslov preferred to take the role of second secretary, where he could concentrate on ideological matters and relations with other Communist countries. He remained in this position until his death in 1982.

Analysis. Suslov was considered to be a firm and unyielding Stalinist. Yet, he helped Khrushchev defeat the "antiparty group" of old Bolsheviks in 1957 and aided the de-Stalinization campaign under Khrushchev. By 1964, however, the conservative Suslov thought the campaign had gone too far, and he conspired with other Soviet leaders to oust Khrushchev for "adventurism" at home and abroad. He backed Brezhnev to succeed Khrushchev and was known to have exercised considerable influence over Brezhnev's policies.

From the closing years of the Stalin era until he died January 25, 1982, Suslov was the Soviet Union's spokesman in the international communist movement. He reportedly played a key role in the Kremlin decisions to suppress the Hungarian revolt in 1956, to end the liberalization in Czechoslovakia in 1968 (although some sources indicated he argued against military intervention), and to push Polish authorities to take a harsher line against the independent trade union Solidarity in 1981.

Leon Trotsky (1879-1940)

Leon Trotsky, one of the greatest theoreticians, orators, and military strategists of early Soviet history, was instrumental in planning, executing, and defending the 1917 Russian revolution. He later became Joseph Stalin's most bitter opponent.

Lev Davydovich Bronstein (Trotsky's given name) was born in the Ukraine on October 26, 1879, to a Jewish family. He studied briefly in Odessa and then moved to Nikolaev, where his radical activities led to his arrest and imprisonment in Siberia. During his four years in jail (1898-1902), Trotsky became acquainted with Marxism. After his escape from prison in 1902, he assumed the pseudonym Trotsky, which was the name of his jail warden, and traveled to Europe, where he collaborated with V. I. Lenin on the revolutionary journal *Iskra* (The Spark). When the Russian Social Democratic Labor party split into Bolshevik and Menshevik factions in 1903, Trotsky sided with the Mensheviks and became an outspoken opponent of Lenin.

Around 1904 Trotsky developed his "theory of permanent revolution," which looked beyond a revolution in Russia to a worldwide workers' struggle that would overthrow capitalism. For Trotsky, the class struggle was an international phenomenon. He would remain loyal to this theory throughout his life.

Public Career. Trotsky returned to Russia in 1905 and was a leader of the St. Petersburg Soviet during the 1905 Russian revolution. He was banished to Siberia in 1907, but he escaped to Europe, where he attempted to unify the badly fractured Social Democratic Labor party. He was expelled from France in 1916, spent a short time in the United States, and then returned to Russia in May 1917.

Back in Russia, Trotsky joined the Bolsheviks. Although a latecomer to the party, he was a guiding force behind the events leading to the Bolsheviks' seizure of power in the November revolution. While Lenin was in Finland hiding from the Provisional Government, Trotsky organized the Military Revolutionary Committee, which led the armed insurrection in Petrograd.

After the Bolshevik victory, Trotsky was entrusted with several positions in the new government, notably the commissariats for foreign and military/naval affairs. He established and organized the Red Army and engineered the Bolshevik victory in the civil war.

As Lenin approached death, Trotsky and Stalin emerged as rivals for leadership of the Communist party. After Lenin had died, Stalin denounced Trotsky's "theory of permanent revolution" as un-Leninist and gathered support for his own doctrine of "socialism in one country." Trotsky was stripped of his government positions in 1925, removed from the Politburo in 1927, and expelled from the Soviet Union in 1929. He spent the remainder of his life in exile in various countries, continuing to oppose Stalin through his writing.

During the purges of the 1930s, Trotsky was named as the main instigator of the alleged counterrevolutionary crimes against the Stalin regime. He was convicted and sentenced to death in absentia.

On August 21, 1940, Trotsky died in Mexico City from wounds inflicted the day before by an assassin reportedly sent to Mexico on Stalin's orders. Trotsky was survived by his second wife, Natasha, who left the Soviet Union with him and their two children in 1929. It is believed that Stalin arranged the deaths of the children, in 1933 and 1938. Stalin already had ordered the execution of Trotsky's first wife and their two children in the Soviet Union.

Of Trotsky's extensive works, many written after his exile from the Soviet Union, one of the best known is *The History of the Russian Revolution* (1932-1933). Unlike Nikolai Bukharin and other prominent victims of Stalin, as

of 1990 the Communist party had not rehabilitated Trotsky. There were signs, however, that an official rehabilitation might be forthcoming as part of the ongoing reassessment of Soviet history. In particular, excerpts from Trotsky's writings began appearing in the Soviet media for the first time in August 1989.

Analysis. Lenin called Leon Trotsky "personally perhaps the most capable" in the Central Committee, although he had doubts concerning Trotsky's "excessive liking for the administrative side of things." Trotsky had excellent organizational abilities and his skill for oratory was unmatched among his colleagues. However, his political fortunes were damaged by his early Menshevik loyalties and his proclivity for alienating his colleagues. Trotsky's concern for his political theories and their relation to world government put him in a vulnerable position against his chief opponent, Stalin, whose more immediate theory of socialism in one country was a powerfully persuasive tool.

Grigorii Zinoviev (1883-1936)

Grigorii Evseevich Zinoviev, one of the most prominent Bolsheviks during the Russian revolution, was born in the Ukraine to Jewish parents named Radomysl'skii in September 1883. Lacking any formal schooling, Zinoviev became involved with self-education circles, where he received his initial exposure to socialist theory. He joined the Russian Social Democratic Labor party in 1901, and that same year he fled to Europe to escape police persecution for his involvement in economic strikes. Zinoviev met V. I. Lenin in 1903 in Switzerland and supported his Bolshevik faction against the Mensheviks when the Social Democrats split later that year.

Zinoviev collaborated closely with Lenin in the years leading to the 1917 revolution. They returned together to Russia from Europe after the March 1917 revolution. Zinoviev, however, disagreed with Lenin's strategy of pursuing an exclusive Bolshevik seizure of power in Russia. In October Zinoviev and Lev Kamenev voted against the coup being organized by the party's Central Committee. After the revolution Zinoviev resigned from the party and demanded a coalition government composed of all socialist groups. He soon returned to the party, however, and was appointed to the Politburo. He also headed the powerful Petrograd Soviet. From his base in Petrograd, Zinoviev, according to Adam B. Ulam in *The Bolsheviks*, established "his little political kingdom from which he would not be dislodged by Stalin until 1925."

After Lenin's death in 1924, Zinoviev emerged as one of the top Soviet leaders along with Kamenev and Joseph Stalin. This triumvirate was challenged by the "left opposition" headed by Leon Trotsky. In the ongoing power struggle, Zinoviev and Kamenev became alarmed by Stalin's accumulation of power and belatedly joined Trotsky to oppose Stalin. The political struggle with the left opposition ultimately was won by Stalin with the help of Nikolai Bukharin and the "right opposition," which was then crushed in turn. Zinoviev's resistance to Stalin led to the loss of his leadership posts in 1926. In 1935 he was tried for "moral complicity" in the murder of Leningrad party leader Sergei Kirov and sentenced to ten years in jail.

A year later Zinoviev and fifteen others were tried in the first "show trial" of the Great Purge. He was convicted of a series of crimes related to allegedly treasonous and counterrevolutionary activities. Zinoviev was executed on August 25, 1936, immediately after the trial.

Major Events, 1900-1963

Following is a chronology of major events in Russian and Soviet history from the beginning of the twentieth century through 1963. A more detailed chronology of domestic and foreign events from 1964 to July 1990 is provided in the next section, which begins on p. 247.

1900. August, international military expedition, including Russian troops, occupies Beijing to put down the Boxer Rebellion in China. December, first issue of the revolutionary newspaper *Iskra* is published.

1901. Socialist Revolutionary party is established. Russian workers and university students begin using street demonstrations as a means of protest.

1902. January 30, Anglo-Japanese alliance is formed. Vladimir I. Lenin publishes his pamphlet entitled "What Is to Be Done?"

1903. July 30-August 23, Menshevik and Bolshevik factions split in the Russian Social Democratic Labor party during the Second Party Congress held in Brussels and London. (The First Party Congress was held March 13-15, 1898, in Minsk.)

1904. February 8, Japan attacks the Russian fleet at Port Arthur, beginning the Russo-Japanese War. May 27, Russian Baltic fleet is destroyed by the Japanese navy at the Battle of Tsushima Strait.

1905. January 22, "Bloody Sunday"—police fire at a peaceful demonstration of workers in St. Petersburg, killing more than a hundred. April 25-May 10, Third Russian Social Democratic Labor Party Congress is held in London. June, crew of the battleship *Potemkin* mutinies and sails to Romania. August 16, tsar's promise of an assembly elected by nobles, landed peasants, and the bourgeoisie fails to quell unrest. September 5, Treaty of Portsmouth (New Hampshire), mediated by President Theodore Roosevelt, ends the Russo-Japanese War. October 30, nationwide strikes begun earlier in the month force the tsar to issue the October Manifesto guaranteeing personal freedoms and establishing the first *Duma*.

1906. April 24, tsar publishes the Fundamental Laws. April 23-May 8, Fourth Russian Social Democratic Labor Party Congress is held in Stockholm. May 10, first Duma opens, but it is dissolved by the tsar July 21. November, Stolypin Land Reform program is launched.

1907. January 1, Russian government cancels peasant redemption payments. March 5, second Duma opens. June 16, tsar dissolves the Duma and changes the electoral laws

so that the next Duma will support him. May 13-June 1, Fifth Russian Social Democratic Labor Party Congress is held in London. June-October, Second Hague Peace Conference fails to make progress toward European disarmament. (First Hague Peace Conference was held in May 1899.) August 31, Russia signs an agreement with Great Britain demarcating spheres of influence in Afghanistan, Persia, and Pakistan; the pact resolves Anglo-Russian differences and results in the Triple Entente of France, Britain, and Russia, which is opposed to the Triple Alliance of Germany, Austria-Hungary, and Italy. November 1, third Duma opens (it serves a full five-year term).

1908. November, Leon Trotsky becomes editor of the recently founded newspaper *Pravda* in Vienna.

1909. February, Duma passes a law on the inviolability of person. October 24, Russia and Italy conclude a secret agreement on the Balkans.

1910. January, Russia and Japan reject an American proposal for an "open door" policy in Manchuria. January 15-February 5, prominent Mensheviks and Bolsheviks meet but fail to restore party unity.

1911. September 14, assassination of Russian prime minister Peter Stolypin.

1912. October 8, First Balkan War begins. November 28, fourth Duma opens (it remains in session until March 1917).

1913. May 30, Treaty of London ends the First Balkan War. June-August, Second Balkan War.

1914. June 28, Archduke Francis Ferdinand, heir to the Hapsburg throne, is assassinated in Sarajevo. July 30, tsar orders a general mobilization of Russian military capacity. August 1, Germany declares war on Russia; World War I begins. August 6, Austria-Hungary declares war against Russia. August 10, Austrians invade southern Poland, opening major fighting on the eastern front. November 1, Russia declares war against Turkey.

1915. September 5, tsar goes to the front to take personal command of his armies fighting the Germans. September, Lenin represents Bolsheviks at First International Socialist Conference and advocates transforming the World War into a civil war against imperialism.

1916. June, Russian forces win several battles, but the Germans and Austrians halt the Russian advance during July and August. December 30, Grigorii Rasputin is assassinated.

1917. March 11, tsar dissolves the Duma and orders

the suppression of demonstrations. March 12, Petrograd Soviet of Workers' and Soldiers' Deputies is established. March 15, Tsar Nicholas II abdicates; the United States is the first among the great powers to recognize the Provisional Government headed by Prince Georgii Lvov. April 16, Lenin arrives from Switzerland at Finland Station in Petrograd. April 20, *Pravda* publishes Lenin's April Theses. May 17, Trotsky reaches Petrograd from the United States. June 6-17, All-Russian Congress of Soviets meets. July 16-18, "July Days" mass demonstrations. July 20, Lvov resigns, and Aleksandr Kerensky takes over as prime minister. August 8-16, Sixth Russian Social Democratic Labor Party Congress is held in Petrograd. September 9-12, General Lavr Kornilov's counterrevolutionary plot fails. October 23, Bolshevik Central Committee advocates armed insurrection. November 7-8, Bolsheviks seize power. November 14, Kerensky's attempt to capture Petrograd fails. November 25, Constituent Assembly is elected. December 20, Cheka is established.

1918. January 8, President Woodrow Wilson issues "Fourteen Points" for a postwar settlement, which includes liberal treatment of Russia. January 19, Bolsheviks disband the Constituent Assembly. January 28, Bolshevik leaders order the organization of the Red Army. January 31, Russians adopt the Gregorian calendar. March 3, Russia signs the Treaty of Brest-Litovsk with Germany. March 6-8, Seventh Russian Social Democratic Labor Party (Bolshevik) Congress. March, Allied intervention in Russia begins. July 10, first Soviet Constitution is adopted, creating the Russian Soviet Federated Socialist Republic. July 16, tsar and his family are murdered by Bolsheviks near Ekaterinburg. August 30, Lenin is wounded in an assassination attempt by a Socialist Revolutionary. November 11, World War I ends. November 13, Bolsheviks repudiate the Treaty of Brest-Litovsk.

1919. March 2, Communist International (Comintern) is founded. March 18-23, Eighth Russian Communist Party (formerly Social Democratic Labor party, Bolshevik) Congress. June 28, Treaty of Versailles is signed. November-December, Red Army scores important victories over White armies.

1920. January, Allies lift the coastal blockade of the Soviet Union imposed in October 1919. March 29-April 5, Ninth Russian Communist Party Congress. April 25, Polish forces invade the Ukraine. July 8, United States imposes a trade embargo against the Soviet Union.

1921. March 2-18, Kronstadt rebellion. March 8-16, Tenth Russian Communist Party Congress. March 17, Lenin initiates the New Economic Policy. March 18, Russia and Poland sign the Treaty of Riga, giving Poland control of disputed territories and establishing the so-called Curzon Line.

1922. April 3, Joseph Stalin becomes general secretary of the Communist party. April 16, Soviet Union signs the Treaty of Rapallo with Germany. March 27-April 2, Eleventh Russian Communist Party Congress. May 26, Lenin suffers the first of three paralytic strokes. December 16, Lenin suffers his second stroke, which limits his public activities. December 24, Lenin writes his "Testament," which evaluates his potential successors. December 30, the Union of Soviet Socialist Republics is declared.

1923. January 4, in a postscript to his "Testament," Lenin advocates replacing Stalin as general secretary of the Communist party. March 9, Lenin suffers his third stroke. April 17-25, Twelfth Soviet Communist Party Congress accepts Stalin's plan to reorganize the party. October 15,

forty-six Communist party leaders present the Central Committee with the "Declaration of the Forty-Six," which criticizes the ruling regime.

1924. January 21, Lenin dies, causing the struggle for power between Stalin and Trotsky to intensify. January 27, Lenin's funeral. January 31, USSR Constitution is ratified. February 1, Great Britain recognizes the USSR, and within one year Italy, Norway, Austria, Sweden, Denmark, Mexico, France, and Japan also extend recognition. May 23-31, Thirteenth Soviet Communist Party Congress. November 6, Trotsky publishes *Lessons of October*, attacking Lev Kamenev and Grigorii Zinoviev.

1925. May 12, revised Soviet Constitution is ratified. December 18-31, Fourteenth Soviet Communist Party Congress.

1926. October 23, Trotsky and Kamenev are removed from the Politburo.

1927. April, USSR and the Chinese Kuomintang break diplomatic relations. November 12, Trotsky and Zinoviev are stripped of their party memberships. December, during the Fifteenth Soviet Communist Party Congress, Stalin and his followers score a decisive victory over the Trotskyites, dozens of whom are expelled from the party.

1928. August 27, United States, France, Germany, Great Britain, Italy, Belgium, Japan, Poland, and Czechoslovakia sign the Kellogg-Briand Peace Pact outlawing war. August 31, USSR announces its support of the pact. October 1, Stalin introduces the First Five-Year Plan.

1929. January 18, Trotsky is exiled from the USSR. November, Nikolai Bukharin, Aleksei Rykov, and Mikhail Tomskii, leaders of the "rightist" opposition, are expelled from the Politburo. December, Stalin advances the policy of eliminating the *kulaks* (wealthy peasants) as a class and launches a campaign to collectivize the peasantry.

1930. March 2, Stalin's "Dizziness with Success" article blames local party officials for abuses during the initial drive toward collectivization. June 26-July 13, Sixteenth Soviet Communist Party Congress.

1931. June, Stalin proposes a six-point program designed to spur industrialization.

1932. November 29, Soviets and French sign a non-aggression pact. December 31, Soviets declare that the First Five-Year Plan has been fulfilled early.

1933. November 16, USSR and the United States establish diplomatic relations.

1934. January 26-February 10, Seventeenth Soviet Communist Party Congress. September 18, Soviet Union joins the League of Nations. December 1, Sergei Kirov is murdered, setting off the Stalinist purges.

1935. May 2, Soviet-French mutual assistance treaty is signed. July 14, USSR and the United States sign a one-year reciprocal trade agreement.

1936. March 7, Hitler's armies occupy the Rhineland. July 18, Spanish Civil War begins; Soviet Union provides financial aid to the left-wing Loyalist side, which is fighting the Italian- and German-backed Nationalists. August 19-24, first "show trial" is held; Zinoviev and Kamenev are among the sixteen defendants, all of whom are found guilty and executed. November 25, Germany and Japan sign the Anti-Comintern Pact. December 6, new Soviet Constitution is adopted.

1937. January 23-30, second show trial is held; thirteen of seventeen defendants are sentenced to death, the other four are imprisoned.

1938. March 2-13, third and final show trial is held; eighteen of twenty-one defendants, including Nikolai Bukharin, are sentenced to death, the other three are imprisoned. March 12, Germany annexes Austria. September 29-30, Great Britain and France agree to Germany's annexation of Czechoslovakia's Sudetenland at the Munich conference.

1939. March 10-21, Eighteenth Soviet Communist Party Congress. March 28, Spanish Civil War ends in victory for the Nationalists. August 23, USSR and Nazi Germany sign a nonaggression pact. September 1, Germany invades Poland, triggering World War II; the Soviets subsequently invade eastern Poland. November 30, Soviet Union invades Finland. December 14, League of Nations expels the Soviet Union.

1940. March 12, Soviet-Finnish "Winter War" ends; Finland is forced to cede the Karelian Isthmus and other areas to the USSR. August 3-6, Lithuania, Latvia, and Estonia are incorporated into the Soviet Union. August 21, Trotsky is assassinated in Mexico City.

1941. April 13, USSR and Japan sign a neutrality treaty. June 22, Germany invades the Soviet Union. July 3, Stalin makes his first public statement on the German invasion. September 20, Germans capture Kiev. December, Soviets launch their first counteroffensive against the invading German forces. December 7, Japanese attack Pearl Harbor.

1942. January 1, Soviets sign the United Nations Declaration in Washington. June 11, USSR and the United States sign a lend-lease agreement providing for reciprocal defense aid. November 19, Soviets launch a successful counterattack at Stalingrad that traps nearly three hundred thousand German troops in and around the city.

1943. February 2, remnants of German Sixth Army surrender at Stalingrad. May 25, Stalin dissolves Comintern as concession to Western allies. November 28-December 1, U.S. president Franklin D. Roosevelt, British prime minister Winston Churchill, and Stalin meet in Tehran to discuss wartime strategy and postwar issues.

1944. January 11, Roosevelt denies that "secret treaties or financial commitments" were made at Tehran or other Allied negotiations. June 6, Western Allies land at Normandy, opening the western front. July 22, conference at Bretton Woods, New Hampshire, closes with the Soviet Union agreeing to subscribe $1.2 billion to the proposed International Bank for Reconstruction and Development. October 10-20, Churchill and Stalin meet in Moscow; they divide Europe into hypothetical spheres of influence.

1945. February 4-11, Roosevelt, Churchill, and Stalin meet at the Yalta conference in the Crimea. April 12, Roosevelt dies, Harry S. Truman becomes president. April 23, Russian forces fight their way into Berlin. April 25, Russian troops advancing from the east and American troops advancing from the west link at Torgau in Germany. May 7, German High Command surrenders at Reims. May 8, Allies proclaim victory in Europe. June 25, UN charter is approved in San Francisco. August 2, British prime minister Clement Atlee, Stalin, and Truman issue the Potsdam Declaration after their summit in Germany. August 6, United States drops an atomic bomb on Hiroshima. August 8, Soviet Union declares war on Japan. August 9, United States drops a second atomic bomb on Nagasaki. August 21, American lend-lease aid to the Soviet Union ends. September 2, Japan formally surrenders to the United States.

1946. January 10, first session of the United Nations opens. January 19, at the United Nations, Iran charges the Soviets with illegally occupying its Azerbaidzhan region.

January 29, Secretary of State James F. Byrnes confirms the existence of a secret Roosevelt-Churchill promise at Yalta to allow the Soviets to capture and control Sakhalin Island and the Kuril Islands in exchange for Soviet entry into the war against Japan. March 5, Churchill delivers his "Iron Curtain" speech at Fulton, Missouri. May, Soviets withdraw their troops from Iran. October 27, Communists assume power in Bulgaria.

1947. March 12, Truman asks Congress for $400 million in funds to aid the governments of Greece and Turkey in their fight against Communist rebels. June 5, Secretary of State George C. Marshall outlines a plan for European economic recovery (the Marshall Plan) at Harvard University's commencement. July, George Kennan publishes his article "by X" in *Foreign Affairs* outlining the strategy of containment. October 5, Cominform (the Communist Information Bureau, which succeeds the Comintern) is established. December, four-power conference on Germany in London breaks down.

1948. February 25, President Eduard Beneś of Czechoslovakia yields to a Soviet ultimatum to install a pro-Soviet cabinet and join the Communist bloc. June, Soviet Union begins the Berlin blockade. June 21, the United States and Great Britain launch a massive airlift of supplies to Berlin. June 28, Yugoslavia is expelled from the Cominform. August 3, Communist party member Arpad Szakasits becomes president of Hungary.

1949. January 25, Moscow announces the formation of a six-nation Council for Mutual Economic Assistance (CMEA) in Eastern Europe. April 4, North Atlantic Treaty is signed, establishing the North Atlantic Treaty Organization (NATO) alliance. May, Soviets lift the Berlin blockade. May 23, constitution of the Federal Republic of Germany (West Germany) is approved. September 21, Communist party leader Mao Zedong proclaims the People's Republic of China. September 23, Moscow announces a successful Soviet test of an atomic bomb. October 7, German Democratic Republic (East Germany) is established.

1950. February 14, Soviet Union and the People's Republic of China sign a treaty of alliance. June 25, North Korea invades South Korea. June 27, Truman orders U.S. forces under Gen. Douglas MacArthur to help repel the North Korean invasion. November 26, Chinese troops enter the war on the side of North Korea.

1951. July 10, Korean truce talks begin. November 23, Truman orders the withdrawal of all U.S. tariff concessions to the Soviet Union and Poland.

1952. October 5-14, Nineteenth Soviet Communist Party Congress. November 1, United States successfully tests a hydrogen bomb.

1953. January 13, arrest of nine Soviet doctors allegedly involved in the "Doctors' Plot" is disclosed. March 5, Stalin dies and is succeeded as premier and first secretary of the Communist party by Georgii Malenkov. March 14, Malenkov resigns as first secretary but retains the premiership. April 14, seven surviving doctors accused in the "Doctors' Plot" are exonerated. June 15, Soviet Union and Yugoslavia reestablish diplomatic relations. June 17, East Berlin riots. June 26, chief of secret police Lavrentii Beria is arrested. July 27, Korean War ends. August 8, Malenkov announces his proconsumer policy before the Supreme Soviet. August 12, Soviet Union explodes a hydrogen bomb. September 13, Nikita S. Khrushchev becomes first secretary of the Communist party. December 17, Beria is tried and found guilty; he is executed soon after.

1954. March, Malenkov asserts that war between imperialism and capitalism would mean "the destruction of world civilization." July 21, Vietnam is partitioned at the Geneva conference. October 23, West Germany is granted sovereignty and joins NATO.

1955. February 8, Malenkov resigns as prime minister and is replaced by Nikolai Bulganin. May 14, Warsaw Pact is established. May 15, Austrian state treaty is signed; Soviets subsequently withdraw their forces from the country. July 18-23, Geneva summit conference, attended by leaders of the United States, Britain, France, and the Soviet Union; Bulganin represents the USSR. September 9, USSR and West Germany establish diplomatic relations. September 27, Egypt announces that it will buy Soviet arms.

1956. February 14, Twentieth Soviet Communist Party Congress opens with a speech by Khrushchev in which he advocates "peaceful coexistence" with the West. February 24, Khrushchev denounces Stalin in his "Secret Speech" at the party congress, which ends the following day. April 18, Cominform is dissolved. June, Tito visits Moscow. June 4, State Department publishes text of the Secret Speech. June 28-30, strikes in Poland lead to a limited liberalization. July 26, Egypt nationalizes the Suez Canal. October 19, Soviet delegation meets with Polish leaders in Warsaw; they reach a compromise on Polish reforms. October 23, protests against communist rule in Hungary turn violent. October 29, Israel attacks Egypt in accordance with secret Israeli-French-British plan; British and French subsequently join the assault. October 30, Hungarian leader Imre Nagy calls for an end to one-party rule in Hungary and a Hungarian withdrawal from the Warsaw Pact. November 4, Soviet troops occupy Budapest and other major Hungarian cities, crushing the Hungarian revolution. November 7, under pressure from the United States, Great Britain and France agree to withdraw from the Sinai; Israel agrees to withdraw the following day.

1957. February, Andrei Gromyko becomes foreign minister succeeding Dmitri Shepilov. June, a coalition of Presidium members, including Malenkov, Viacheslav Molotov, and Lazar Kaganovich, demand Khrushchev's resignation; Khrushchev counters by convening the Central Committee, which supports him and removes the "antiparty group" from their government and party positions. August 26, Moscow announces the successful testing of an intercontinental ballistic missile. October 4, *Sputnik,* the first space satellite, is launched by the Soviet Union. October 15, Soviet Union and China sign a secret agreement pledging the Soviets to help the Chinese develop their own nuclear weapons. October, Khrushchev removes Marshal Georgii Zhukov from the Presidium and as defense minister.

1958. March 27, Khrushchev ousts Bulganin as prime minister and assumes the post himself; Khrushchev continues as first secretary. October-November, Quemoy-Matsu crisis. October 31, Geneva test-ban conference opens. November 10, Khrushchev sparks the Berlin crisis by calling for the withdrawal of Allied troops in West Berlin.

1959. January 1, Fidel Castro comes to power in Cuba. January 27-February 5, Twenty-first Soviet Communist Party Congress. June 20, Soviets rescind their nuclear weapons development agreement with China. July 24, "Kitchen Debate" between Vice President Richard Nixon and Khrushchev takes place at a U.S. exhibition in Moscow. September 14, Soviet rocket hits the moon. September 15-27, Khrushchev visits the United States. December 1, twelve countries, including the USSR and the United States, sign a treaty making Antarctica a scientific preserve free of military activities.

1960. January, Khrushchev announces defense budget cuts. February, Anastas Mikoian visits Cuba to establish diplomatic relations and sign an aid agreement. May 1, Soviets shoot down an American U-2 spy plane over the Soviet Union and capture its pilot, Francis Gary Powers. May 4, Aleksei Kosygin becomes a deputy prime minister. May 5, Soviets announce downing of U-2. May 7, Leonid I. Brezhnev becomes chairman of the Presidium of the Supreme Soviet. May 17, Paris summit conference, attended by President Dwight D. Eisenhower, Khrushchev, French president Charles de Gaulle, and British prime minister Harold Macmillan, breaks up after Khrushchev demands an apology for the U-2 flight. August, Soviet Union withdraws its technical experts from China. September 20-October 13, Khrushchev visits the United Nations.

1961. April 12, Soviet cosmonaut Yuri Gagarin becomes the first man in space. April 17, U.S.-supported "Bay of Pigs" invasion of Cuba is crushed by Castro. May 5, first American manned space flight. June 3-4, Khrushchev and President John F. Kennedy meet in Vienna but remain deadlocked on key issues. August 13, East Germany seals border between East and West Berlin and begins building Berlin Wall. September 1, Soviet Union resumes nuclear weapons testing, breaking an unofficial moratorium. October 17-31, Twenty-second Soviet Communist Party Congress; Khrushchev's party program is approved. October 30, party congress delegates vote unanimously to remove Stalin's remains from Lenin's Tomb and rebury them in a less honored spot near the Kremlin wall. December 10, Soviet Union breaks relations with Albania.

1962. February 10, USSR exchanges U-2 pilot Francis Gary Powers for Soviet spy Rudolph Abel, held by the United States. March 14, disarmament conference opens in Geneva; the conference recesses December 24. October 20-November 21, Sino-Indian border war. October 22-November 2, Cuban missile crisis, which ends when Kennedy announces Moscow's willingness to dismantle Soviet missile bases in Cuba. November, Khrushchev implements bifurcation of the agricultural and industrial branches of the Soviet party apparatus.

1963. February 12, Geneva disarmament conference resumes. June 4, Soviets announce abandonment of Seven-Year Plan. June 10, President Kennedy's American University speech. June 20, U.S.-Soviet "hot line" is established. July 21, talks in Moscow aimed at resolving Sino-Soviet ideological conflict end in failure. July 25, the United States, the Soviet Union, and Great Britain sign the Partial Nuclear Test Ban Treaty (Beijing denounces the pact). October 9, Kennedy approves the sale of wheat to the Soviet Union. November 22, Kennedy is assassinated; Lyndon B. Johnson becomes president.

Chronology of Events, 1964-1990

1964

January 2. *USSR Peace Message.* Soviet premier Nikita S. Khrushchev sends a personal message to all countries with which the USSR has relations, calling for the renunciation of war as a method of "settling diplomatic disputes." The plan calls for the United States to remove its military forces from West Germany, South Korea, and South Vietnam. American officials term the communiqué "disappointing."

January 29. *U.S. Plane Downed.* A U.S. training plane is shot down over East German airspace by a Soviet aircraft. Both the United States and the Soviet Union attempted to warn the plane during the event, in which three U.S. officers were killed. A similar incident occurs March 10 when an unarmed U.S. reconnaissance jet is downed over East Germany and its crew is held. Secretary of State Dean Rusk disclaims Soviet accusations of espionage. The three airmen are released March 27.

March 31-April 7. *Khrushchev on China.* While on a tour of Hungary, Premier Khrushchev denounces China several times for opposing his rejection of Stalinism and his policy of peaceful coexistence with the West. On April 5 he calls China's leaders "crazy."

April 20. *Joint Statement on Nuclear Cooperation.* President Lyndon B. Johnson and Premier Khrushchev declare their intention to reduce production of material used in nuclear weapons. The United States will cut back enriched uranium production, and the Soviet Union will not build several reactors designed to produce plutonium.

May 1. *Khrushchev's May Day Speech.* Premier Khrushchev denounces the United States for flying reconnaissance missions over Cuba. He maintains the alleged missions violate the understanding reached between himself and President John F. Kennedy in October 1962.

May 9. *Khrushchev in Egypt.* Large crowds give Premier Khrushchev a tumultuous welcome after he arrives in Egypt for a two-week visit. He attends nationwide celebrations, which begin May 15, of the completion of the first stage of the Aswan Dam.

June 1. *Consular Pact Signed.* Soviet and American representatives sign a pact in Moscow that outlines procedures for the establishment and operation of consulates.

June 12. *Soviet-East German Pact.* Premier Khrushchev and President Walter Ulbricht of East Germany sign a twenty-year friendship treaty that "asserts the legal existence of a Communist state in Eastern Germany." The pact is denounced by the United States, Great Britain, and France June 26 as an obstacle to bringing peace to divided Germany.

June 16-July 4. *Khrushchev in Scandinavia.* Premier Khrushchev tours Denmark, Sweden, and Norway and meets with their heads of state. He reports to the Soviet people July 1 that the trip was an exercise in peaceful coexistence that may reap possible trade benefits.

July 13. *Article on Sino-Soviet Split.* Two Chinese Communist party publications release the ninth and most vituperative article in a series on the Sino-Soviet split. Entitled "On Khrushchev's Phony Communism and Its Historical Lessons for the World," the article asserts that the Soviet premier heads a "privileged stratum" in his country that is attempting to restore capitalism while the "masses" are being exploited.

September 30. *Cyprus Receives Aid.* The Soviet Union and Cyprus sign an economic and military aid agreement. In August Cyprus had appealed for Soviet aid following Turkish air attacks. Cypriot officials declare that the accord contains "no strings or conditions."

October 14-15. *Khrushchev Ousted.* Nikita S. Khrushchev is forced to resign as premier of the Soviet government and first secretary of the Soviet Communist party. He is replaced as first secretary by Leonid I. Brezhnev and as premier by Aleksei Kosygin. Soviet ambassador to the United States Anatolii Dobrynin October 16 reassures President Johnson of the continuation of good U.S.-Soviet relations based on peaceful coexistence. Also October 16, China's leaders extend "warm greetings" to the new Soviet leaders. A *Pravda* editorial October 17 hints Khrushchev's "harebrained scheming" and "hasty decisions" contributed to his ouster.

October 16. *China Tests Atomic Device.* China explodes its first atomic device. The Chinese issue a statement saying, "China cannot remain idle and do nothing in the face of the ever-increasing threat posed by the United States."

October 26. *New Soviet Goals.* The Soviet government newspaper *Izvestiia* publishes an article entitled "A Commonwealth of Equals" in which the new regime outlines its goals for unity and equality in the communist movement. The Western media report October 30 that a document listing twenty-nine reasons why Khrushchev was removed had been circulated among Soviet Communist party officials. One of the main reasons cited was Khrushchev's poor handling of the Sino-Soviet rift.

November 6. *Brezhnev Speech.* Party head Leonid Brezhnev, in a speech during celebrations honoring the anniversary of the Bolshevik Revolution, declares that the new Soviet government will seek improved relations with capitalist nations. He urges greater unity within the communist world, more East-West trade, and "ever more democracy for Soviet people."

November 16. *Bifurcation Reversed.* The Central Committee officially reunites the industrial and agricultural bureaus of the party apparatus. The bureaucratic division had been engineered by Khrushchev two years before.

November 17. *Shifts in Presidium.* The Kremlin announces major personnel shifts in the Presidium and at the regional/district level of the party. Alexander Shelepin, thought to have had a key role in the Khrushchev ouster, and Petr Shelest are named full members of the Presidium.

1965

February 5. *Kosygin Abroad.* Premier Kosygin receives a cool reception in Beijing, where he stops on his way to Hanoi. On February 7 Kosygin assures a rally in Hanoi that his country will supply North Vietnam with "all necessary assistance if aggressors dare to encroach upon [its] independence and sovereignty."

February 9. *Demonstrations in Moscow.* Following American bombing raids in North Vietnam February 7, the U.S. embassy in Moscow is attacked by two thousand demonstrators, including many Chinese and Vietnamese students. The rioters throw rocks and bottles of ink at the embassy building, breaking many windows. The Soviet police guarding the embassy do not stop the attack, evoking protests from U.S. ambassador Foy D. Kohler. A similar demonstration by about two thousand Soviet, Asian, African, and Latin American students takes place at the U.S. embassy March 4. The students break through police barricades and storm the compound in protest against American air strikes on North Vietnam. The police, who number six hundred, are forced to call in five hundred army troops to quell the rioting.

March 26. *Moscow-Hanoi Agreement.* The Soviet Communist Party Central Committee ratifies a military aid agreement between the Soviet Union and North Vietnam aimed at "repelling aggression on the part of the United States imperialism." The Soviet Union, China, and North Vietnam April 10 reject an offer made by President Johnson April 7 for unconditional talks to end the Vietnam War in conjunction with a U.S.-financed Southeast Asian economic development program. Moscow and Hanoi issue a joint communiqué April 18 threatening to send Soviet troops to Vietnam if the United States "intensifies" its aggressive military action.

May 6. *U.S. Trade Study Findings.* A twelve-member committee appointed by President Johnson to assess the possibility of increased trade with the Soviet Union and Eastern Europe recommends easing existing trade restrictions.

May 7. *Soviet-Chinese Thrusts.* At a Moscow rally celebrating the anniversary of V-E Day, Premier Kosygin, referring to the Chinese Communists, states that "some people contend that only a new world war can bring about the unity and solidarity of the . . . international Communist movement." He adds: "We decisively reject such a position." On May 9 the Beijing *People's Daily* accuses Soviet leaders of "colluding with the United States aggressors and plotting to sell out the basic interests of the people of Vietnam and of all other countries, including the Soviet Union."

July 13. *Disarmament Talks to Reconvene.* President Johnson announces that the Soviet Union is once again willing to start disarmament talks in Geneva. The eighteen-nation UN Disarmament Committee is reconvened in Geneva July 27.

September 6. *India Invades Pakistan.* Indian troops invade West Pakistan, ostensibly to relieve pressure from Indian forces fighting Pakistani units on the border at Kashmir. In a September 7 Tass statement, the Soviet Union urges India and Pakistan to end the conflict and offers to mediate a peace settlement.

October 2. *Soviet Economic Changes.* The Supreme Soviet approves a series of domestic economic measures that centralize the administration of the economy. The moves are interpreted as an effort to revamp Khrushchev's system of regional economic councils.

December 6. *Kosygin Attacks U.S. "Militarism."* In a *New York Times* interview, Premier Kosygin accuses U.S. government officials of "trying to build up tensions, to create an atmosphere conducive to war." He maintains that American actions prevent the Soviet Union from reducing its military budget.

December 9. *Mikoian Steps Down.* Anastas Mikoian announces his resignation as president of the Presidium of the USSR Supreme Soviet. He is replaced by Nikolai Podgornyi. Health problems are cited as the reason for Mikoian's resignation.

1966

January 10. *Declaration of Tashkent.* Indian prime minister Lal Bahadur Shastri and Pakistani president Mohammed Ayub Khan sign the Declaration of Tashkent, ending the four-month border conflict between India and Pakistan. The negotiations, which began January 4, were mediated by Premier Kosygin. On January 11, while still in the Uzbekian Republic capital, Prime Minister Shastri dies of a heart attack.

March 19. *New Cultural Agreement.* U.S. and Soviet officials sign a new agreement on cultural, scientific, educational, and technical exchanges extending to 1967.

March 22. *Soviet Letter Attacks China.* A letter reportedly written by the Central Committee to the Communist parties of Eastern Europe is published by the West German newspaper *Die Welt.* An English translation appears two days later in the *New York Times.* The letter states there is "every reason to assert that it is one of the goals of the policy of the Chinese leadership on the Vietnam question to originate a military conflict between the USSR and the United States ... so that they may, as they say themselves, 'sit on the mountain and watch the fight of the tigers.' " The letter criticizes China for a wide range of transgressions, including provoking Sino-Soviet border conflicts.

March 23. *China Rejects Soviet Invitation.* China refuses to attend the Twenty-third Congress of the Communist Party of the Soviet Union. The Chinese announcement, referring to Moscow's anti-Chinese letter, states that "since you have gone so far, the Chinese Communist Party ... cannot send its delegation to attend this congress of yours."

March 29-April 8. *Soviet Party Congress.* The Twenty-third Congress of the Communist Party of the Soviet Union convenes in Moscow, the first under the leadership of party chief Leonid Brezhnev. Brezhnev calls for international communist unity despite the Sino-Soviet split. Brezhnev also announces that the Presidium will once again be called the "Politburo," and the title of the Communist party first secretary will revert to "general secretary." Nikolai Podgornyi is replaced on the Secretariat by Brezhnev's close associate Andrei Kirilenko. Premier Kosygin announces a new five-year plan. He outlines goals in Soviet economic development while enumerating advances made since 1928, the date of the First Five-Year Plan under Joseph Stalin. These developments were regarded in the West as a confirmation that the Soviet leadership had halted Khrushchev's de-Stalinization campaign.

April 27. *Gromyko Meets Pope Paul VI.* Soviet foreign minister Andrei Gromyko confers with Pope Paul VI in the Vatican, thereby becoming the highest-ranking Soviet official to have a papal audience. Gromyko also meets with Italian government leaders.

May 7. *Ceausescu on Foreign Policy.* Romanian general secretary Nicolae Ceausescu, speaking on the forty-fifth anniversary of the Romanian Communist party, asserts Romania's national sovereignty and foreign policy independence. Ceausescu declares his intention of improving relations with Western European countries. General Secretary Brezhnev visits Bucharest May 10-13, reportedly in response to the speech.

May 10-18. *Kosygin in Egypt.* Premier Kosygin travels to Cairo to confer with Egyptian president Gamal Abdel Nasser. The leaders issue a joint communiqué assailing U.S. policy in the Middle East, and Kosygin urges Nasser to improve ties with Syria.

June 20-July 1. *De Gaulle in USSR.* French president Charles de Gaulle visits the Soviet Union in an attempt to improve Franco-Soviet relations and to reduce postwar tension between East and West. De Gaulle, a highly honored Western leader in the Soviet Union, is allowed to stay at the Kremlin.

July 4-6. *Warsaw Pact Summit.* Leaders of the Warsaw Pact countries meet in Bucharest. Two statements are issued on the content of the meeting, the first outlines a promise to send "volunteers" to North Vietnam if so requested by Hanoi. The second calls for a general European conference on security in Europe and increased cooperation among nations.

August 29. *Anti-Soviet Rally.* Thousands of Red Guards march past the Soviet embassy in Beijing in an all-day demonstration against "revisionism." Although the parade is well disciplined, Chinese soldiers and police guard the building against possible attack.

October 7. *Johnson on Improved Relations.* President Johnson discusses ways to improve U.S.-Soviet relations. During a speech at the National Editorial Writers' Conference he suggests reducing the number of both U.S. and Soviet troops in Germany and increasing U.S. trade with Eastern Europe.

October 13. *Kosygin Accuses China.* Premier Kosygin, in a speech in Sverdlovsk, accuses China of blocking efforts by socialist countries to provide material assistance to North Vietnam.

November 4. *Commercial Aviation Pact.* Soviet and American officials sign an agreement providing direct air service between Moscow and New York.

November 21. *Sino-Soviet Border Tension.* The *New York Times* reports that Soviet diplomats openly discussed with American officials the growing concern of Moscow over a nuclear-armed China. According to the *Times,* a U.S. official described recent talks between Secretary of State Rusk and Foreign Minister Gromyko as the "most direct, honest, objective, and non-ideological in several years." The official added, "Mr. Gromyko made clear that the break with China is quite fundamental and that Russia is now more interested than ever in settling other outstanding issues."

December 1-9. *Kosygin in France.* Premier Kosygin visits France to improve Franco-Soviet cooperation. On December 6 he tells reporters in Lyons that he sees a "community of interests" between the United States and the Soviet Union, but he adds: "The United States is bombing defenseless people in Vietnam. We don't see any indication of the way the United States is going to end the war. If it were ended, relations would improve."

December 15. *Soviets Increase Defense Spending.* The Soviet Union announces it will increase its defense spending in 1967 by 8.2 percent because of "aggressive" U.S. policies, especially in Vietnam. American officials indicate, however, that the increases in Soviet military spending were prompted primarily by tensions between the Soviet Union and China.

1967

January 25. *Soviets, Chinese Clash in Moscow.* China protests to the Kremlin that Chinese students in Moscow were attacked "without provocation" by Soviet soldiers when they sought to place a wreath at the Lenin Mausoleum. The Soviet government accuses the students of provoking the "wild scene."

January 27. *Space Treaty Signed.* At simultaneous ceremonies in Washington, London, and Moscow, representatives from sixty countries sign a treaty banning the orbiting of nuclear or other mass-destruction weapons. The treaty takes effect October 10, 1967, upon ratification by the United States, the Soviet Union, Great Britain, and eight other countries.

January 28. *Anti-Soviet Demonstrations in Beijing.* Chinese soldiers take part in an enormous demonstration outside the Soviet embassy in Beijing. The troops wield rifles and bayonets in the third demonstration in as many days. The embassy's walls are plastered with posters reading "Shoot Brezhnev" and "Fry Kosygin." When the demonstrators return January 29, the Soviet government declares that it will take "necessary measures if the Chinese authorities fail to provide normal conditions for the activity of the Soviet representation." The demonstrations cease shortly afterward.

January 30. *Kennan on U.S.-Soviet Relations.* Former U.S. ambassador to the Soviet Union George F. Kennan tells the Senate Foreign Relations Committee that the irreparable disunity in the communist world presents the United States with an opportunity to take "greatly exciting" steps to improve U.S.-Soviet relations.

February 4. *Moscow Warns China.* In a formal note, Moscow demands that China stop vilifying the Soviet Union and humiliating Soviet citizens in Beijing. The Soviet note coincides with an evacuation of most of the Soviet diplomatic staff and their dependents from China. By February 7 it is reported that the remaining diplomats are virtual prisoners within their compound because of China's refusal to guarantee their safety outside the area.

February 11. *Consular Agreement Abrogated.* Beijing radio reports termination of the consular agreement between the Soviet Union and China. Travel without visas to and from the two countries will no longer be permitted.

March 2. *Soviets Willing on Arms.* President Johnson reveals a communiqué from Premier Kosygin stating Moscow's willingness to discuss arms limitations.

March 16. *U.S.-Soviet Treaty Approved.* The U.S. Senate ratifies, by a vote of 66-28, a consular treaty with the Soviet Union signed in 1964. The treaty specifies the conditions under which each country may set up and operate consulates in the other.

April 11. *Grechko Gains Post.* Tass announces that Marshal Andrei Grechko has been appointed Soviet defense minister. Grechko succeeds Marshal Rodion Malinovskii.

May 18. *Andropov to Head KGB.* Yuri V. Andropov replaces V. E. Semichastnyi as chairman of the Soviet Committee for State Security (KGB).

May 24-30. *Prelude to War.* Tension increases in the Middle East as Arab armies are massed along Israel's borders. The United Arab Republic threatens to blockade Israel's shipping in the Gulf of Aqaba. At a UN Security Council emergency session, the Soviet delegate supports the Arab position on the basis of Israel's "provocative" stance.

June 5. *Six-Day War.* Israeli warplanes and troops attack Arab forces in the Sinai Peninsula and Jerusalem. On June 7, with its forces in control of the Gaza strip, Jerusalem, and much of the Sinai, Israel announces that it will accept a UN cease-fire if the Arabs do the same. Jordan accepts immediately; Egypt accepts June 8. Fighting between Israel and Syria, however, continues until June 10, when the two nations sign a cease-fire agreement after Israeli forces capture the Golan Heights. During the fighting, the United States pledges to remain neutral while the USSR denounces Israel as the aggressor June 6. The Soviet Union breaks diplomatic ties with Israel June 10 and pledges assistance to Arab states if Israel refuses to withdraw from conquered territory. Israel announces June 12 that it will not withdraw. By June 13 Bulgaria, Czechoslovakia, Poland, Hungary, and Yugoslavia also sever ties with Israel.

June 14. *Soviet UN Resolution.* The UN Security Council rejects a Soviet resolution calling for denunciation of Israel and the withdrawal of its troops behind the 1949 armistice lines. On the same date Israeli sources report that Moscow has resumed sending military aid to Egypt and Syria, presumably to replace arms lost during the conflict with Israel.

June 17. *China Explodes Hydrogen Bomb.* Two years and eight months after its first test of a nuclear device, China announces detonation of the country's first hydrogen bomb.

June 19. *Johnson and Kosygin on the Middle East.* President Johnson in a nationally televised speech sets forth five points for peace in the Middle East: recognition of the right of each country's existence, just treatment of Arab refugees, freedom of innocent maritime passage, arms limitation, and guaranteed territorial integrity for each Middle East country. Meanwhile, at the United Nations, Premier Kosygin calls for the condemnation of Israel, the withdrawal of Israeli forces from occupied Arab lands, and Israeli reparations to Syria, Jordan, and Egypt.

June 23-25. *Glassboro Summit.* Premier Kosygin and President Johnson meet at Glassboro State College in New Jersey to discuss the Middle East, Vietnam, arms control, and nuclear proliferation. President Johnson suggested the meeting after Kosygin had arrived in New York June 17 to address a special session of the UN General Assembly. The site was chosen because of its location halfway between New York and Washington. The meeting is the first between the two leaders. After the talks Johnson states, "No agreement is readily in sight on the Middle Eastern crisis and our well-known differences over Vietnam continue." Kosygin, at a televised news conference in New York, emphasizes that Israel must withdraw to the 1949 armistice lines before progress toward peace in the Middle East can be achieved.

September 8. *Rusk on ABM.* Secretary of State Rusk states that the lack of U.S.-Soviet cooperation in limiting nuclear missiles may force the United States to build an antiballistic missile (ABM) defense system.

November 3-7. *Bolshevik Revolution Celebrated.* The Soviet Union engages in a series of festivities marking the fiftieth anniversary of the Bolshevik Revolution. In a four-and-a-half-hour speech November 3 General Secretary Brezhnev denounces China for disrupting the unity of the world socialist community. Brezhnev also castigates continued U.S. military involvement in Vietnam.

1968

January 5. *Dubcek Gains Power.* As demands for reform increase in Czechoslovakia, Alexander Dubcek succeeds Antonin Novotny as first secretary of the Czechoslovak Communist party.

January 23. *USS Pueblo Seized.* North Korean forces board the U.S. Navy intelligence ship *Pueblo* in the Sea of Japan and take the ship and its crew of eighty-three into a North Korean port. The Defense Department contends that the *Pueblo* was cruising in international waters, but the North Koreans claim the ship was on a spy mission in their territorial waters. The U.S. ambassador to the Soviet Union, Llewellyn E. Thompson, tries to enlist Soviet aid to win the release of the *Pueblo* but is rebuffed. The Soviet government newspaper *Izvestiia* January 26 accuses

President Johnson of manipulating the *Pueblo* incident to justify building up U.S. military forces in the area. Eleven months later, on December 23, the eighty-two surviving crew members are released.

March 23. *East European Summit.* The leaders of Warsaw Pact nations, excluding Romania, convene in Dresden to discuss the increasing liberalization in Czechoslovakia since the ouster of Czech Communist party head Antonin Novotny in January. Novotny's successor, Alexander Dubcek, is pressed to reverse the trends of democratization.

April 2-7. *Kosygin in Iran.* Premier Kosygin pays a state visit to Iran to promote bilateral economic cooperation.

June 4. *Johnson in Glassboro.* President Johnson delivers the commencement address at Glassboro State College in New Jersey, site of a June 1967 summit between himself and Premier Kosygin. The president appeals to Moscow to join in "the spirit of Glassboro" to work for world peace. Johnson focuses on the progress made in U.S.-Soviet relations. On June 12 an *Izvestiia* article belittles the "rosy picture" Johnson drew of U.S.-Soviet relations, contending instead that relations are "frozen" until the United States ceases all involvement in Vietnam.

June 13. *Consular Pact Ceremony.* The instruments of ratification of the U.S.-Soviet consular treaty are formally exchanged in a White House ceremony. The treaty, which is to take effect in thirty days, was ratified by the Presidium of the Supreme Soviet April 26 and by the U.S. Senate March 16, 1967.

July 1. *Non-Proliferation Treaty Signed.* Sixty-two nations, including the United States, the Soviet Union, and Great Britain, sign a treaty on the nonproliferation of nuclear weapons in ceremonies in the various capitals. The signing follows ratification of the treaty by the United Nations in June.

July 4-10. *Nasser in Moscow.* United Arab Republic president Gamal Abdel Nasser visits Moscow amid speculation that he is dissatisfied with the level of Soviet military assistance to the Arab world. On July 5 General Secretary Brezhnev promises at a Kremlin luncheon that the Soviet Union will "always side with the Arab nations for the withdrawal of Israeli troops from all the Arab land occupied as a result of the June [1967] aggression."

July 15. *Air Service Begins.* The first flights take place on the newly inaugurated Moscow to New York commercial airline service. Implementation of the updated agreement, signed November 4, 1966, had been delayed by technical problems and uncertain U.S.-Soviet relations during the interim.

July 14-23. *Czech Liberalization.* The continuing liberalization in Czechoslovakia overseen by Communist party first secretary Alexander Dubcek causes increasing tension between Moscow and Prague. The Soviet Union and its hard-line East European allies—East Germany, Hungary, Bulgaria, and Poland—draft a letter following a summit in Warsaw July 14-15, which calls the Czech liberalization "completely unacceptable." A July 22 *Pravda* article demands that Communist party control be firmly reinstated, in part by reimposing censorship and suppressing "anti-socialist and right-wing" forces. The Soviet Union July 23 announces massive military maneuvers in Czechoslovakia that will continue until August 10. The move is interpreted as an attempt to intimidate Czech authorities.

July 29. *Meeting in Cierna.* At Prague's request, the entire Politburo of the Soviet Communist party and the Presidium of the Czech Communist party meet under tight security in Cierna, Czechoslovakia, to discuss the Czech situation.

August 3. *Meeting in Bratislava.* As a ratification of the recent meeting in Cierna, the East European allies of Moscow, along with Soviet and Czech leaders, meet in Bratislava, Czechoslovakia, and accept the Soviet position that Prague be allowed to continue in its liberalization experiment within limits. Immediately preceding the Bratislava meeting the Czech Foreign Ministry announces that all Soviet troops on maneuvers have left the country. Reportedly, the Czech government made a few concessions to Moscow, including the establishment of an "advisory council" to diminish critical news reporting.

August 9-11 and 15-17. *Tito and Ceausescu in Prague.* Yugoslav president Josip Broz Tito and Romanian president Nicolae Ceausescu make separate visits to Czechoslovakia. Both leaders endorse the attempt by Czech Communist party leader Alexander Dubcek and his supporters to follow an independent socialist course.

August 20-21. *Warsaw Pact Invades Czechoslovakia.* Shortly before midnight Soviet tanks and troops supported by forces of East Germany, Poland, Hungary, and Bulgaria cross the Czech border. The Warsaw Pact force gains control of most of the country by morning. Leading members of the liberalization movement are seized and taken to Moscow for consultations. During the following week, the number of Warsaw Pact troops in Czechoslovakia increases from the initial invasion force of 200,000 to 650,000. The intervention, which encounters minimal armed resistance from the Czech population, ends Czechoslovakia's period of liberalization known as the "Prague Spring." President Johnson denounces the invasion August 21 but admits that there is no "safe" action the United States can take. The UN Security Council supports a resolution condemning the occupation and calling for the removal of Warsaw Pact forces. The resolution is vetoed by the Soviet Union. A secret congress of the Czech Communist party is held August 21-23, which elects a new leadership.

August 27. *Changes in Czechoslovakia.* The reversing of liberalization in Czechoslovakia begins with the return to Prague from Moscow of Czech president Ludvik Svoboda and first secretary Alexander Dubcek. The leaders announce an agreement with Moscow that results in several actions. A new Presidium of the Czech Communist party is elected September 1, superseding the secret congress results of August 23. On September 4 press censorship and disbanding of noncommunist organizations are implemented.

September 6. *Kuznetsov in Prague.* Soviet first deputy foreign minister Vasilii Kuznetsov visits Prague unexpectedly to mediate differences in the implementation of the Czech-Soviet agreement on restructuring the Communist government in Prague. A translation of the agreement is published September 8 in the West by the *New York Times.*

September 26. *Brezhnev Doctrine. Pravda* advances a new, ideological argument to justify the invasion of Czechoslovakia by the Warsaw Pact nations. The newspaper says, in effect, that the world socialist community has a right to intervene when socialism comes under attack in a fraternal socialist country. It denies that this in any way violates Czechoslovakia's "real sovereignty." The article asserts that "world Socialism is indivisible, and its defense is the common cause of all Communists." The article, written by the publication's ideological specialist, also states that "each Communist party is responsible not only to its own people, but also to all the Socialist countries, to the entire Communist movement." The doctrine of "limited sovereignty" soon receives elaboration from top Soviet officials and subsequently comes to be known as the "Brezhnev Doctrine."

October 16. *Kosygin in Prague.* Premier Kosygin flies to Prague to sign a treaty concluded in Moscow October 3-4, authorizing the stationing of Soviet troops in Czechoslovakia and abolishing all vestiges of the liberalization program.. The treaty is ratified by the Czech National Assembly October 18. Moscow continues its pressure on Czech officials October 19 by insisting that party membership be reduced by purging all liberal elements.

October 28. *Demonstrations in Prague.* Prague witnesses anti-Soviet demonstrations led by a youthful crowd on the fiftieth anniversary of the Republic of Czechoslovakia. Sporadic demonstrations continue into November, particularly on the anniversary of the Russian Revolution.

November 16. *NATO Warns Soviets.* After a three-day meeting, the North Atlantic Treaty Organization (NATO) Council of Ministers issues a sharp warning to Moscow that "any Soviet intervention ... in Europe or in the Mediterranean would create an international crisis with grave consequences." The message is seen as a sign of the Western alliance's increased solidarity in the wake of the Soviet intervention in Czechoslovakia.

1969

January 20. *U.S.-Soviet Overtures.* President Richard Nixon, who was elected November 5, 1968, calls for a new "era of negotiation" in his inaugural address. On the same day the Soviet Foreign Ministry reaffirms an interest in renewing arms reduction talks that had broken down when Warsaw Pact nations intervened in Czechoslovakia in August 1968.

February 26. *Nasser Interviewed.* President Gamal Abdel Nasser of Egypt states in a *New York Times* interview that he welcomes Soviet ships in Egyptian ports but his government has not provided naval bases to any country, including the Soviet Union. Nasser says there are fewer than one thousand Soviet advisers in Egypt but that "I am asking for more."

March 2. *Sino-Soviet Fighting.* Tensions on the Sino-Soviet border erupt into armed conflict when Chinese forces ambush a Soviet company making a routine patrol of Damanskii Island in the Ussuri River. During the rest of 1969 there would be more than four hundred skirmishes along the Sino-Soviet border.

April 17. *Dubcek Resignation.* Alexander Dubcek, the leading figure in the Czech liberalization program, resigns as Czechoslovak Communist party first secretary. His successor, Gustav Husak, states that the change in leadership is in the interest of Czech unity. Husak's appointment is welcomed by Moscow.

July 10. *Gromyko Stresses Improved Relations.* Soviet foreign minister Gromyko urges closer cooperation with the United States. In a speech to the Supreme Soviet

he suggests an exchange of delegations from the Supreme Soviet and the U.S. Congress. Gromyko characterizes Chinese policies toward the Soviet Union, on the other hand, as worse than those "of our most rabid enemies."

September 11. *Kosygin Visits China.* En route to Moscow after attending the funeral of North Vietnamese leader Ho Chi Minh, who died September 3, Premier Kosygin makes a surprise visit to China. His talks with Premier Chou En-lai reduce serious Sino-Soviet tensions caused by months of bloody border skirmishes between Soviet and Chinese troops.

September 18. *Nixon on Mideast Arms.* President Nixon in a speech to the UN General Assembly suggests a Middle East arms curb by the big powers. The Soviet Union rebuffs the suggestion.

October 7. *Seabed Pact.* The United States and the Soviet Union submit a joint draft to the UN conference of the Committee on Disarmament in Geneva. The pact bans nuclear and other destructive weapons outside a twelve-mile coastal limit as defined in the 1958 Geneva Convention on the Territorial Sea.

October 20. *China-USSR Negotiations.* Chinese and Soviet foreign ministers open negotiations in Beijing on Sino-Soviet border disputes.

November 17. *SALT Meeting.* The preliminary round of the Strategic Arms Limitation Talks (SALT) between the United States and Soviet Union opens in Helsinki. The U.S. delegation is led by Gerard Smith and the Soviet delegation is headed by Vladimir Semenov. The talks adjourn December 22.

November 24. *Nuclear Non-Proliferation Treaty.* Soviet president Nikolai Podgornyi and President Nixon sign the nuclear nonproliferation treaty during separate ceremonies in Washington and Moscow. The treaty had been approved by the U.S. Senate March 13.

December 7. *Soviet-West German Talks.* The Soviet Union accepts West German chancellor Willy Brandt's offer to begin negotiations on a bilateral treaty normalizing relations between the two countries. The Soviet Union states that conditions for approval of the treaty include recognition of East Germany and the exchange of diplomats.

1970

January 13. *Soviets Support U.S. Participation.* The Soviet Foreign Ministry announces that it favors U.S. participation at a proposed security conference of all European nations.

February 15. *Moscow Denies Planning Attack.* The Soviet newspaper *Pravda* criticizes Western press predictions of a Soviet attack on China. The article follows a statement by the Soviet news agency Tass describing such predictions as "insinuations" designed to "increase tension" between the Soviet Union and China.

March 19. *Soviet Troops in Egypt.* Diplomatic observers report that a large number of Soviet troops and antiaircraft missiles have arrived in Cairo.

April 17. *SALT Talks Resume in Vienna.* Strategic Arms Limitation Talks between the United States and the Soviet Union resume in Vienna. The talks had recessed December 22, 1969.

April 21. *Lenin's Centenary.* The communist world celebrates the centenary of Lenin's birth.

April 29. *Missions for Egypt.* The Israeli government says it has evidence to confirm accusations that Soviet pilots are flying missions for the Egyptian air force. Soviet sources deny the accusations.

April 30. *United States Invades Cambodia.* President Nixon announces in a televised address that U.S. troops have begun an "incursion" into Cambodia designed to disrupt North Vietnamese sanctuaries in that country. The operation draws sharp criticism at home and abroad. American forces are withdrawn from Cambodia June 29.

June 1. *Antiaircraft Missiles in Egypt.* A *Newsweek* magazine report alleges that the Soviets have installed twenty-two SAM-3 antiaircraft missile sites in Egypt. Other sites are under construction or planned. Foreign intelligence reports received in Washington June 24 indicate that Soviet pilots have taken over Egypt's air defenses.

June 26. *Dubcek Expelled.* Alexander Dubcek is expelled from the Czech Communist party. The action is regarded as further retaliation against the liberalization effort in Czechoslovakia.

July 10. *Soviets Call for Joint Action.* Soviet SALT negotiators reportedly propose that the United States and the Soviet Union agree to "joint retaliatory action" in response to any "provocative" acts or direct attacks by China. The proposal is not disclosed until 1973 and is denied by the Soviets at that time.

July 17. *Nasser in Moscow.* At the conclusion of a visit to Moscow by Egyptian president Gamal Abdel Nasser, a joint Soviet-Egyptian communiqué is issued calling for a political settlement of the Middle East crisis and accusing Israel of aggression.

August 12. *West German-Soviet Treaty.* Premier Kosygin and Chancellor Willy Brandt of West Germany sign a treaty in Moscow renouncing the use of force to settle disputes between their countries. The document includes recognition of the long-disputed Polish-East German border at the Oder-Neisse line.

September 25. *Soviet Activity in Cuba.* The Defense Department discloses the possible building of a Soviet strategic submarine base in Cuba. The suspicions of U.S. officials are aroused when heavy equipment is seen arriving from the Soviet Union. The United States warns Moscow against such a move, but construction efforts are denied in a September 30 *Pravda* commentary.

September 28. *Death of Nasser.* The president of Egypt, Gamal Abdel Nasser, dies in Cairo. Moscow issues a statement September 29 noting that Nasser's position on the Middle East conflict "will continue to enjoy our utmost support." Vice President Anwar Sadat becomes acting president.

September 30-October 2. *Nixon in Yugoslavia.* President Nixon becomes the first U.S. president to visit Yugoslavia, where he praises that country's nonaligned stance. Nixon's visit is the first stop of an eight-day, five-nation European tour.

October 8. *Solzhenitsyn Wins Nobel.* Soviet writer Alexander Solzhenitsyn wins the 1970 Nobel Prize for Literature. The Soviet writers' union October 9 calls the award decision "deplorable." Solzhenitsyn's works are banned in the Soviet Union.

October 25. *Ceausescu Visits Washington.* At the close of his two-week visit to the United States Romanian president Nicolae Ceausescu confers with President Nixon. The leaders reportedly discuss improving trade relations.

October 29. *U.S.-Soviet Space Pact.* Soviet and U.S. officials sign the first cooperative space effort agreement. The project involves a joint rendezvous and docking mission in space.

November 22. *Sino-Soviet Trade Pact.* The Soviet Union and China sign a trade agreement, the first since 1967. The agreement does not seem to be accompanied by a significant lessening of tension between the two countries.

December 15. *Polish Worker Unrest.* Demonstrations by Polish workers against increases in food prices lead to the resignation of Wladyslaw Gomulka as first secretary of the Polish Communist party. Edward Gierek replaces him. Polish troops are used to put down the unrest, which reportedly results in three hundred deaths.

1971

January 4. *Harassment of Diplomats.* Soviet diplomats protest harassment of Soviet officials at the United Nations by Americans and announce that the United States should "not expect" the Soviet government to ensure normal working conditions for U.S. diplomats in the Soviet Union. The protest is a response to an injury sustained by an employee of the Soviet mission to the United Nations during demonstrations in New York by members of the Jewish Defense League in late December 1970. In subsequent weeks numerous incidents of harassment of U.S. diplomats occur in Moscow. On July 8 a small bomb explodes outside the Soviet embassy in Washington, an incident for which the United States apologizes. The Jewish Defense League, which had announced January 10 a campaign "to follow, question, and harass" Soviet diplomats in New York, calls off its campaign January 19.

January 15. *Aswan Dam Dedicated.* Egyptian president Anwar Sadat and Soviet president Nikolai Podgornyi dedicate the completed Aswan Dam. Construction of the dam had begun in 1960.

February 25. *Nixon Doctrine.* President Nixon presents his annual State of the World report to Congress. The speech is construed as a formal enunciation of the "Nixon Doctrine"; namely, that the United States will honor all treaties with its allies, but they will be responsible for supplying their own troops to combat conventional aggression or subversion. Nixon describes U.S.-Soviet relations during his administration as "mixed." He cites positive developments such as advances in SALT talks, the ratification of the seabed and nuclear nonproliferation treaties, negotiations on the Berlin question, and beginnings of joint space cooperation. Obstacles remain over Soviet behavior in the Middle East and Cuba.

March 30-April 9. *Soviet Party Congress.* Speaking before the Twenty-fourth Congress of the Communist Party of the Soviet Union in Moscow, General Secretary Brezhnev reaffirms a desire for improved relations with the United States. Brezhnev also states that the Soviets oppose Chinese attempts to distort Marxism-Leninism and split the world communist movement. Four new full Politburo members are named—Fëdor Kulakov, Vladimir Shcherbitskii, Dinmukhamed Kunaev, and Viktor Grishin. Kulakov, a member of the Secretariat, had been promoted directly to full Politburo status, while the other three men had been candidate members of the Politburo.

April 6. *Ping-Pong Diplomacy.* The Chinese government makes a move toward better relations with the United States by inviting the U.S. table tennis team for a visit to begin April 10. A week later President Nixon announces a partial relaxation of the trade embargo with China.

May 7. *Ceylon Rebellion.* Soviets send a training mission to Ceylon to help the government quash an ultraleftist rebellion.

May 14. *Brezhnev Proposes Troop Cut Talks.* In a speech in Tiflis, General Secretary Brezhnev calls for talks aimed at reducing troop levels in Central Europe. American officials say they favor such talks as long as they have a reasonable chance of success. On June 4 NATO foreign ministers issue a communiqué saying they welcome such talks but are in need of "further clarification" from the Soviets about their nature.

May 20. *SALT Negotiators to Discuss ABM Issue.* The Soviet Union and the United States announce that representatives at the SALT talks in Vienna will begin negotiations on a pact to limit antiballistic missile (ABM) systems.

May 27. *Egyptian-Soviet Treaty.* Egypt and the Soviet Union sign a fifteen-year treaty of friendship and cooperation.

June 11. *Brezhnev Proposes Naval Talks.* General Secretary Brezhnev proposes talks aimed at limiting the naval operations of the superpowers.

July 4. *Egyptian-Soviet Joint Communiqué.* Egypt and the Soviet Union issue a joint communiqué declaring that the Suez Canal will be opened only after Israel withdraws all of its forces from Arab territory.

July 15. *Nixon to Visit China.* President Nixon accepts an invitation to visit the People's Republic of China in 1972. He emphasizes that the trip will in no way alter existing relations with any other country. A July 25 *Pravda* article warns the United States against using its contacts with Beijing to pressure the Soviet Union.

August 2. *Soviets Expelled from the Sudan.* Soviet officials are ordered out of the Sudan following a coup that almost topples Premier Mohammed Gaafar Nimeiry. The officials are accused of influencing the coup.

August 9. *Indian-Soviet Pact.* During a trip to New Delhi Soviet foreign minister Gromyko signs a twenty-year treaty of peace, friendship, and cooperation with India.

August 28. *Brezhnev on China.* Despite a recent escalation of verbal attacks against China in the Soviet press, General Secretary Brezhnev states that he does not blame China for the fact that the border talks are "going slowly" and promises the Soviets will "continue to display a constructive and patient approach."

September 11. *Khrushchev Dies.* The former head of the Soviet Union, Nikita S. Khrushchev, dies in Moscow at age seventy-seven. His death is ignored by the Soviet press except for one-sentence announcements in *Pravda* and *Izvestiia* two days later.

October 12. *Nixon to Visit USSR.* President Nixon announces a working summit in the Soviet Union planned for May 1972.

October 27-November 2. *Tito in United States.* Josip Broz Tito, president of Yugoslavia, visits the United States. Nixon strongly commends the Yugoslavian nonaligned stance in the world socialist movement.

December 3. *India Invades Pakistan.* Fortified by Soviet military aid and a new twenty-year treaty of friendship with the Soviet Union, India invades East Pakistan in support of the Bangladesh rebels who had been defeated by Pakistan in April. Beijing radio accuses Moscow of "supporting, encouraging and approving India's aggression against Pakistan." The United States expresses opposition to an increased Soviet naval presence in the area. Hostilities end December 16 with the surrender of Pakistani troops and the creation of the independent Bangladesh nation.

1972

January 28. *Gromyko on Nixon's China Trip.* Soviet foreign minister Gromyko, speaking at a news conference in Tokyo, tells reporters that the Soviet Union does not object to improved Sino-U.S. relations provided they do not "affect adversely the safety and interests of the Soviet Union."

February 21. *Nixon Arrives in China.* President Nixon arrives in China for a historic seven-day visit. It is the first time an American head of state has ever visited China, and the trip caps two years of negotiations. At the conclusion of talks in Shanghai February 27 between President Nixon and Premier Chou En-lai, the United States and China issue a joint communiqué that pledges both sides to work for a "normalization" of relations. *Pravda* expresses displeasure and contends that the United States is taking advantage of the Sino-Soviet rift.

April 11. *U.S.-Soviet Cooperation.* The United States offers to sell grain to the Soviet Union on three-year credit terms. The offer is extended by Secretary of Agriculture Earl Butz in Moscow. On the same day Soviet and U.S. officials sign an agreement extending and augmenting a fourteen-year-old cultural, educational, and scientific exchange program.

April 20-24. *Kissinger in Moscow.* Henry A. Kissinger, national security adviser to the president, visits Moscow to prepare for Nixon's forthcoming visit.

May 8. *United States Mines Haiphong.* President Nixon, faced with a worsening situation in South Vietnam, orders the mining of all North Vietnamese harbors. The move risks a direct confrontation with both China and the Soviet Union, whose ships are supplying Hanoi. No confrontation occurs, and Nixon's upcoming trip to Moscow is not jeopardized, despite indications of disagreement among Soviet leaders about whether to proceed with the summit.

May 22-30. *Summit in Moscow.* President Nixon travels to Moscow for a summit meeting with Soviet leaders. Among the many topics discussed are a European security conference and mutual balanced force reductions in Eastern Europe. Nixon and General Secretary Brezhnev sign the first Strategic Arms Limitation Treaty (SALT I) May 26. On the same day Brezhnev is reported to have assured Nixon that he would press Hanoi to settle the war in Vietnam. In a May 28 address on Soviet television, President Nixon says that as "great powers" the Soviet Union and the United States will "sometimes be competitors, but [we] need never be enemies." Nixon visits Kiev May 29 before flying to Iran May 30 for talks with the shah. He returns to the United States June 1 after a stop in Poland.

June 3. *Quadripartite Berlin Agreement.* The four countries that have responsibility for Berlin—the Soviet Union, the United States, France, and Great Britain—sign the "final protocol" of the Quadripartite Agreement on Berlin. The document, which is not a treaty, is expected to increase the frequency and efficiency of travel to and from West Berlin. The groundwork for the final protocol was laid in September 1971.

July 8. *U.S.-Soviet Grain Deal.* After months of negotiations, the Soviet Union and the United States agree on a three-year grain deal under which the Soviets will buy about $750 million worth of U.S. wheat, corn, and other grains. It is to date the largest commercial agreement between the two powers.

July 18. *Sadat Expels Soviet Advisers.* President Anwar Sadat orders all Soviet military advisers and experts out of Egypt and places all Soviet bases and equipment under Egyptian control. Sadat says in a four-hour speech July 24 that his decision was prompted by the Soviet Union's reticence in selling Egypt arms.

July 20-August 1. *U.S. Trade Officials in Moscow.* The U.S. government dispatches a thirty-member delegation, including Secretary of Commerce Peter G. Peterson, to Moscow to initiate discussion on U.S.-Soviet trade.

August 3. *Restrictions on Jewish Emigration.* The Soviet government announces an exit visa fee for Jewish citizens wishing to emigrate. According to Soviet officials, the fees are to reimburse the state for educational funds spent on its citizens. Fees range from $4,400 to $37,000, depending on the amount of education received.

September 5. *Soviet-Syrian Security Cooperation.* Syria and the Soviet Union agree to new security arrangements. The Soviet Union will improve naval facilities in two Syrian ports for Soviet use, and Syria will receive jet fighters and air defense missiles.

September 9. *Soviets Continue Asian Buildup.* Officials in Washington are quoted as saying the Soviets recently added several mechanized divisions to their troops on the Sino-Soviet border, increasing their strength in the area to nearly one-third of the Soviet army.

September 27. *Jackson on Exit Fees.* Sen. Henry M. Jackson, D-Wash., says he will introduce an amendment to the East-West trade relations act that would link trade concessions to the Soviet Union with "the freedom to emigrate without the payment of prohibitive taxes amounting to ransom." Administration officials maintain that "quiet diplomacy" is the best way to solve this problem.

October 2-3. *Nixon-Gromyko Talks.* In Washington President Nixon and Foreign Minister Gromyko discuss a wide range of topics. They sign documents implementing the SALT I arms accords concluded at the Moscow summit in May.

October 4. *Jackson-Vanik Amendment.* Sen. Henry M. Jackson, D-Wash., and seventy-five cosponsors introduce an amendment to the East-West trade bill, barring most-favored-nation status to nations that restrict emigration of their citizens. Rep. Charles A. Vanik, D-Ohio, introduces a similar measure in the House.

October 18. *U.S.-Soviet Trade Pact Signed.* Soviet and American officials sign a three-year trade relations agreement that includes a settlement of Soviet World War II lend-lease debt and a Nixon administration promise to push Congress to approve most-favored-nation status for the Soviet Union, despite congressional attempts to link trade concessions to a relaxation of Soviet restrictions on Jewish emigration. President Nixon promises to ask for credits for the Soviets from the Export-Import Bank as well. Trade between the United States and the Soviet Union in the next three years is projected to reach $1.5 billion.

November 7. *Nixon Reelected.* Richard Nixon easily defeats Democrat George McGovern to win another term as president.

November 21. *SALT II Negotiations Begin.* The second set of SALT negotiations begins in Geneva with the purpose of expanding the SALT I agreement.

December 18-30. *Bombing of North Vietnam.* American forces resume bombing North Vietnam above the twentieth parallel after peace negotiations in Paris are broken off. The massive air attacks against Hanoi and Haiphong cause many casualties and extensive damage. The White House announces December 30 that the bombings have been halted and that peace talks with North Vietnam will resume in Paris on January 8, 1973.

December 21-23. *Fiftieth Anniversary of USSR.* The fiftieth anniversary of the founding of the Soviet state is celebrated in Moscow. General Secretary Brezhnev delivers a lengthy speech in which he condemns the U.S. bombing in Vietnam. He also accuses China of "undisguised sabotage" of Soviet peace efforts and of attempts to "split" the world communist movement.

1973

January 27. *Peace Agreement Signed.* The United States, North Vietnam, South Vietnam, and the Viet Cong sign a peace agreement in Paris. Although the pact calls for a cease-fire in Vietnam, it does not end the fighting in Laos or Cambodia. On January 23 President Nixon had announced the completion of the agreement.

March 11-14. *Soviet-U.S. Trade Talks.* Secretary of the Treasury George P. Shultz discusses U.S.-Soviet trade with General Secretary Brezhnev in Moscow. On March 15, Sen. Henry M. Jackson, D-Wash., formally reintroduces his amendment to the East-West trade relations bill to "block trade concessions until free emigration [is] assured."

March 20. *Export-Import Loan Agreements.* The Soviet Union Foreign Trade Bank is granted its first loan from the Export-Import Bank. The Soviet Union receives $101.2 million in direct loans, while American banks promise another $101.2 million for the purchase of U.S. industrial equipment.

April 27. *Politburo Shake-up.* In a move viewed as bolstering General Secretary Brezhnev's authority, the Central Committee endorses the ouster from the Politburo of two of his conservative critics—Petr Shelest and Gennadii Voronov. The Central Committee simultaneously grants full Politburo membership to Andrei Grechko, defense minister; Andrei Gromyko, foreign minister; and Yuri Andropov, chairman of the KGB.

May 18-22. *Brezhnev in Bonn.* General Secretary Brezhnev visits West Germany and holds extensive talks with Chancellor Willy Brandt. They sign several accords May 19, including a ten-year economic cooperation agreement.

June 7. *Helsinki Preparatory Talks Close.* Six months of preparatory talks for the Conference on Security and Cooperation in Europe (CSCE) close in Helsinki after the agenda is finalized. The conference agenda includes European security and scientific cooperation. The United States receives reluctant agreement from the Soviet delegation for the inclusion of discussions on "freer exchange of people, ideas, and information."

June 16-25. *Summit in United States.* General Secretary Brezhnev arrives in Washington for talks with President Nixon. The two leaders sign agreements providing for cooperation on the development of atomic energy and for the exchange of information on agriculture, transportation, oceanography, and commerce. They also pledge to accelerate the SALT talks with the goal of completing a new treaty by the end of 1974.

July 3-7. *Opening of CSCE in Helsinki.* The first session of the Conference on Security and Cooperation in Europe (CSCE) opens in Helsinki. Thirty-three European nations plus the United States and Canada send representatives. Foreign Minister Gromyko represents the USSR.

August 21. *Sakharov Warnings.* In a discussion with Western media, Andrei Sakharov, a well-known Soviet dissident and physicist, warns of the dangers of accepting détente on Soviet terms. He says the Jackson-Vanik amendment to the East-West Trade Relations Act does not go far enough to pressure the Kremlin to improve its human rights policies.

September 9. *Reaction to Anti-Sakharov Letters.* In response to a Soviet press campaign against Andrei Sakharov, the U.S. National Academy of Sciences says that American scientists will not continue joint research projects with their Soviet counterparts unless the harassment is stopped. The Soviet campaign, which consists of a series of accusatory letters in Soviet publications, began August 29 with a letter written by thirty-nine academicians of the Soviet Academy of Sciences, of which Sakharov is a member. The letter accuses Sakharov of joining "the most reactionary imperialist circles."

September 29. *Nixon-Gromyko Talks.* President Nixon and Foreign Minister Gromyko meet in Washington. Nixon is believed to have assured Gromyko that he would continue to pressure Congress to grant the Soviet Union most-favored-nation status. They also discuss mutual balanced force reductions and SALT II.

October 1-3. *Shultz in Moscow.* Treasury Secretary Shultz notes at the conclusion of talks on bilateral trade in Moscow that expanded trade with the Soviet Union is held up by Congress's refusal to grant most-favored-nation status to the Soviet Union as well as by the Soviets' unwillingness to make further concessions on Jewish emigration.

October 6. *War in the Middle East.* On the Jewish holy day of Yom Kippur Egyptian forces attack Israeli units across the Suez Canal and Syria attacks the Golan Heights. Israeli forces counterattack on October 7. They push the Syrians back but are forced to retreat in the Sinai.

October 15. *Resupply Efforts.* The United States announces that it is resupplying Israel with military equipment to counterbalance a "massive airlift" to Egypt by the Soviet Union. Meanwhile, Israeli forces have recaptured lost territory in the Sinai and driven deep into Syrian territory.

October 17. *Sadat's Peace Proposal.* Egyptian President Anwar Sadat, in an open letter to President Nixon, proposes an immediate cease-fire with Israel on the condition that Israel withdraw to pre-1967 boundaries.

October 18. *Arab Oil Embargo.* After President Nixon asks Congress to appropriate $2.2 billion in emer-

gency military aid to Israel, Libya cuts off all oil shipments to the United States. On October 20 Saudi Arabia cuts off all oil exports to the United States. By October 21 all other Arab oil exporters join the boycott.

October 20. *Kissinger in Moscow.* Secretary of State Henry A. Kissinger arrives in Moscow for talks with Brezhnev on restoring peace to the Middle East.

October 21. *U.S.-Soviet Joint UN Resolution.* The United States and the Soviet Union present a joint resolution to the UN Security Council calling for a cease-fire in the Middle East and for implementation of a Security Council resolution calling for Israeli withdrawal from lands it has occupied since the 1967 war. The proposal, formulated during Secretary of State Kissinger's trip to Moscow, is adopted by the Security Council October 22.

October 22. *Cease-fire in the Middle East.* A cease-fire takes effect on the Egyptian-Israeli front, but sporadic fighting continues.

October 23. *Security Council Vote.* The UN Security Council votes to reaffirm the Middle East cease-fire, requests Egypt and Israel to return to the cease-fire line established the day before, and asks that UN observers be stationed along the Israeli-Egyptian cease-fire line.

October 24. *Sadat Appeal.* Egyptian president Anwar Sadat asks the United States and the Soviet Union to send troops for supervision of the cease-fire. The White House announces it will not send forces.

October 25. *Military Alert.* President Nixon orders a worldwide U.S. military alert as tension mounts over whether the Soviet Union will intervene in the Middle East crisis. Secretary of State Kissinger says in a news conference that the U.S. move is inspired by intelligence reports that the Soviet Union may attempt to airlift troops into Egypt, ostensibly as a peace-keeping force. To avert a U.S.-USSR confrontation in the Middle East, the UN Security Council votes to establish an emergency supervisory force to observe the cease-fire.

October 27. *Direct Negotiations.* The United States announces that Egypt and Israel have agreed to negotiate directly on implementing the cease-fire.

November 11. *Cease-fire Signed.* Israel and Egypt sign a cease-fire accord, drawn up by Secretary of State Kissinger and Egyptian president Anwar Sadat November 7 in Cairo.

December 11. *Trade Bill Passes.* The House passes the foreign trade bill, which includes the Jackson-Vanik amendment "barring most-favored-nation treatment for any nation that restricts emigration" for its citizens. The amendment is included over the objections of President Nixon, who had virtually assured the Soviet Union of most-favored-nation status. The Senate has yet to act on the bill.

December 21. *Mideast Peace Conference.* The first Arab-Israeli peace conference opens in Geneva, with Israel, Egypt, Jordan, the United States, and the Soviet Union taking part. Syria boycotts the conference.

1974

January 2. Gulag Archipelago *Condemned.* Tass responds with virulent criticism after Alexander Solzhenitsyn's book *The Gulag Archipelago, 1918-1956* is published in the West. In late December, the *New York Times* had published excerpts of the book, which describes the secret police and labor camp systems in the Soviet Union.

January 17. *Suez Disengagement Pact Signed.* Israel and Egypt sign accords on a disengagement of forces in the Suez. According to the agreement, the Egyptian and Israeli forces along the Suez Canal will be separated to specific disengagement zones. The pullback is to be completed in forty days, with a UN truce force acting as a buffer.

February 13. *Solzhenitsyn Deported.* Soviet author Alexander Solzhenitsyn is stripped of his Soviet citizenship and deported to West Germany following his arrest in Moscow. Soviet authorities take action after the widely publicized appearance of Solzhenitsyn's book *The Gulag Archipelago, 1918-1956* in the West.

March 11. *Credits to Soviet Union Halted.* A legal technicality causes a temporary cutoff of Export-Import Bank credits to the Soviet Union, Poland, Romania, and Yugoslavia. The action coincides with continuing controversy in the United States over whether to link favorable trade treatment for the Soviets with the Jewish emigration issue.

March 24-28. *Kissinger in Moscow.* Secretary of State Kissinger holds talks with Soviet leaders in Moscow in anticipation of President Nixon's upcoming visit to the Soviet Union. The talks reportedly fail to achieve Kissinger's aim of "concrete progress" on SALT II and East-West mutual troop reductions.

April 7. *Nixon Meets Podgornyi in Paris.* President Nixon and Soviet president Nikolai Podgornyi discuss the forthcoming Moscow summit and SALT II. Both are in Paris attending the funeral of French president Georges Pompidou.

April 12. *Gromyko in Washington.* After an appearance at the United Nations, Foreign Minister Gromyko visits Washington. His discussions with President Nixon and Secretary of State Kissinger focus on the Middle East and SALT II.

April 18. *Egyptian Arms.* President Anwar Sadat announces that Egypt no longer will rely solely on the Soviet Union for arms. Egypt had restored diplomatic relations with the United States February 28 after a seven-year break.

May 15. *Sino-Soviet Trade Agreement.* Despite an increase in the verbal hostility between the Soviet Union and China, the two nations sign a trade agreement that calls for a 12 percent increase in trade for 1974.

May 18. *India Nuclear Test.* After a successful detonation of a nuclear device, India denies any intention to use nuclear technology for military purposes. Prime Minister Indira Gandhi declares, "We are firmly committed only to the peaceful uses of atomic energy."

June 27-July 3. *Third Summit.* President Nixon and General Secretary Brezhnev sign a series of limited agreements on nuclear weapons in Moscow during their third summit meeting. They also issue a joint communiqué that states their commitment to negotiate a new interim strategic arms pact. In a Moscow press conference Secretary of State Kissinger blames the Watergate scandal for preventing substantial negotiations between the two leaders. He charges that Nixon's effectiveness as a leader is being impaired. Nixon returns to the United States July 3.

July 15. *Cyprus Crisis.* The Cypriot National Guard commanded by Greek officers overthrows the president of Cyprus, Archbishop Makarios. The new regime reaffirms a desire for an independent Cyprus, and there is no indica-

tion that a union of Cyprus with Greece will be attempted. Turkey, however, claims the coup threatens the well-being of the Turkish Cypriot minority. The Soviet Union supports the Turkish position. On July 20 Turkey invades Cyprus by sea and air. After Turkish forces gain control of part of the island, a UN cease-fire backed by Great Britain and the United States begins July 22.

August 8. *Nixon Resigns.* In a dramatic television address Richard Nixon announces his resignation from the presidency. Vice President Gerald R. Ford is sworn in as the thirty-eighth president the next day. Soviet reaction emphasizes that U.S.-Soviet relations will continue unchanged. Nixon is portrayed in an August 10 Moscow television program as a victim of political maneuvering and vicious media attacks.

October 23. *Kissinger in Moscow.* Secretary of State Kissinger visits Moscow as part of a three-week, worldwide diplomatic tour. Kissinger discusses arms limitation, trade, and the Middle East and reports some progress despite key differences. The Soviets are annoyed at U.S. publicity surrounding Soviet assurances to increase Jewish emigration. They also are resentful over the cancellation and only partial restoration of a recent grain deal with the United States. President Ford October 4 postponed a sales agreement for the shipment of 3.2 million tons of grain. On October 19 the Treasury Department announced a new agreement that allowed Moscow to purchase 2.2 million tons of U.S. grain through June 1975.

November 23-24. *Vladivostok Summit.* President Ford travels to the Soviet Union to sign a tentative agreement to limit the number of all U.S. and Soviet offensive nuclear weapons through 1985. The unexpected agreement provides guidelines to SALT negotiators who are to resume talks in January. Secretary of State Kissinger goes to China November 25 to brief Chinese leaders on the talks.

November 26. *Soviets Reject Chinese Offer.* Speaking at a rally in Ulan Bator, Mongolia, General Secretary Brezhnev rejects the Chinese offer to negotiate a resolution of the Sino-Soviet border dispute if the Soviets withdraw their troops from regions near the border.

December 20. *Foreign Trade Bill Clears.* Congress clears the foreign trade bill, which extends greater trade privileges to the Soviet Union in exchange for increased Jewish emigration. The bill clears despite a December 18 Tass statement denying any agreement by the Kremlin to allow freer emigration. The bill passed in the House December 11, 1973, and in the Senate December 13, 1974. President Ford signs the bill into law (PL 93-618) January 3, 1975.

December 30. *Brezhnev Cancels Mideast Trip.* General Secretary Brezhnev calls off a January visit to the Middle East. No official reason is given. Western speculation about the cause of the cancellation ranges from Brezhnev's health to diplomatic differences between Cairo and Moscow.

1975

January 14. *Soviets Cancel Trade Pact.* Secretary of State Kissinger announces the Soviet Union's cancellation of the 1972 trade agreement with the United States. The

Kremlin objects to recent U.S. legislation that limits credits to the Soviets and grants trade privileges only if the Soviet Union permits freer Jewish emigration. As a result, the Soviet Union will not pay its World War II lend-lease debts, and it will not receive most-favored-nation trade status or Export-Import Bank loans from the United States.

February 18. *Egypt Buys Soviet Arms.* Egypt confirms it is receiving Soviet arms for the first time since the 1973 Arab-Israeli war.

March 18. *Brezhnev Overture.* General Secretary Brezhnev reaffirms the Soviet desire for increased international détente. Speaking in Hungary, he emphasizes the need for a successful outcome of the upcoming Conference on Security and Cooperation in Europe (CSCE).

April 16. *Removal of Shelepin.* Alexander Shelepin, former head of the KGB, is removed from the Politburo. At one time considered a possible challenger to Brezhnev's authority, his influence had diminished since his demotion from the Secretariat in 1967.

April 30. *South Vietnam Surrenders.* The Vietnam War ends as the South Vietnamese government surrenders to Communist forces, and Viet Cong and North Vietnamese troops enter Saigon.

May 12-14. Mayaguez *Incident.* The Cambodian government May 12 seizes the American merchant ship *Mayaguez* in the Gulf of Siam. President Ford May 14 sends two hundred U.S. Marines to Cambodia, who rescue the ship and its crew. Tass describes the U.S. action as "a military intervention to rescue the spy ship *Mayaguez* seized earlier in Cambodian waters."

June 10. *Schlesinger on Soviet Military.* Secretary of Defense James R. Schlesinger at a Senate Armed Services Committee hearing accuses the Soviet Union of building naval facilities in the Somalian port of Berbera on the Gulf of Aden. It is thought the base will facilitate Soviet naval exercises in the Indian Ocean. Tass denies June 12 that the Soviets are building such a facility. On June 20 Schlesinger announces that, according to U.S. intelligence, the Soviet Union has recently deployed intercontinental ballistic missiles (ICBMs) armed for the first time with multiple independently targetable warheads.

June 30. *Solzhenitsyn in Washington.* In a speech to the AFL-CIO in Washington, Soviet author Alexander Solzhenitsyn warns of the dangers of détente and of making too many concessions to the Soviets. President Ford declines to meet with Solzhenitsyn July 2 because of a busy White House schedule. In a news conference July 16 Secretary of State Kissinger discloses that he and other White House aides believed the meeting would damage U.S.-Soviet relations.

July 10-11. *Kissinger-Gromyko Meeting.* Secretary of State Kissinger and Foreign Minister Gromyko meet in Geneva to discuss U.S.-Soviet relations, in particular the issues that have stalled SALT II negotiations.

July 17. *Apollo-Soyuz Mission.* The first joint Soviet-U.S. space exploration project (called the Apollo-Soyuz Test Project), which was initiated by President Nixon and General Secretary Brezhnev at the 1972 Moscow summit, is capped by the successful rendezvous in space of the Apollo and Soyuz spacecraft.

July 31-August 1. *Helsinki Summit.* The Conference on Security and Cooperation in Europe (CSCE) holds the largest summit conference in European history in Helsinki. Preparatory talks for the summit began in 1972. The conference culminates August 1 with the sign-ing of a hundred-page declaration (known as the Final Act) by leaders of the thirty-five participating nations. The Final Act's provisions express a desire for cooperation between nations, a permanent peace for Europe, and respect for the boundaries within the European continent. The Final Act is nonbinding and does not have treaty status. Both General Secretary Brezhnev and President Ford participate in the conference. The Helsinki meeting sparks controversy in the West, primarily because opponents consider the Final Act too conciliatory toward the Soviet Union.

August 14. *Superpowers on Portugal.* In a speech in Birmingham, Alabama, Secretary of State Kissinger objects to Soviet support of the Portuguese premier Vasco Goncalves and the Communist party, which are attempting to impose a Communist-led government. Kissinger states, "The Soviet Union should not assume it has the option, either directly or indirectly, to influence events contrary to the right of the Portuguese people to determine their own future." An August 19 *Pravda* article emphasizes "massive solidarity" with the Communist party in Portugal. On August 29, however, Goncalves is ousted, and a November coup attempt by Communist forces fails. A moderate Socialist, General Antonio Ramalho Eanes, is elected president in June 1976.

September 1. *Sinai Pact Signed.* In separate ceremonies in Jerusalem and Alexandria, Israeli and Egyptian leaders initial a new Sinai Pact, which provides for Israeli withdrawal from areas of the Sinai and the stationing of U.S. technicians in key locations to monitor the peace.

October 9. *Sakharov Wins Nobel.* Andrei Sakharov, a leading Soviet physicist and dissident, is awarded the Nobel Peace Prize. The action inspires press attacks on Sakharov in the Soviet Union. Moscow denies Sakharov a visa to attend the ceremonies in Oslo, Norway. Sakharov's wife, Yelena Bonner, participates in the Oslo ceremonies December 10 and accepts the Nobel Prize in his name.

October 20. *Soviets Purchase U.S. Grain.* A five-year agreement providing for the Soviet purchase of six million to eight million tons of American grain annually is announced by the White House. Four days later three U.S. grain corporations announce separate deals, bringing the total amount of grain sales to approximately 11.5 million tons in 1975.

November 12. *Soviets Deny Ideological Détente.* In an attempt to explain Soviet actions in Portugal and Angola, an article in the Soviet military newspaper *Krasnaya Zvezda* states that despite gains toward détente in the political/military sphere, ideological détente between the United States and the Soviet Union is not possible.

November 24. *United States on Angola.* Secretary of State Kissinger protests Soviet and Cuban military involvement in the ongoing Angolan civil war, claiming that Soviet actions have created "an increasingly skeptical administration view of the Soviet Union's sincerity in improving relations with the United States." President Ford adds December 16 that Soviet and Cuban military involvement in Angola is "not helpful" to détente. Kissinger states in a December 23 news conference that the Soviets have not directly responded to U.S. requests to end their involvement in Angola and that "there is no question that the United States will not accept Soviet military expansion of any kind." Kissinger expresses his support for continued U.S. aid to the anti-Soviet forces in Angola.

1976

January 21-23. *Kissinger in Moscow.* Secretary of State Kissinger cites "significant progress" on SALT II during his discussions with Soviet officials in Moscow. Kissinger says that he will return to the United States with new Soviet proposals. Kissinger also discusses the Angolan situation, but no agreements are achieved. Kissinger states in congressional testimony January 30 that the Ford administration will not ask Congress to reduce restrictions on U.S. trade with the Soviet Union until Moscow ends its involvement in Angola.

February 10. *U.S. Embassy Radiation Warning.* The State Department confirms that the U.S. embassy in Moscow has warned its employees about potentially dangerous radiation in the building caused by Soviet electronic eavesdropping devices. The State Department reports July 7 that the Soviets have reduced the level of radiation but not eliminated it entirely.

February 11. *MPLA Recognized.* The Popular Movement for the Liberation of Angola (MPLA), supported by thousands of Cuban troops, is judged by the Organization of African States to have established sufficient control over Angola and is recognized as its legitimate government. Many West European nations intend to recognize the MPLA by the end of the month.

February 24-March 5. *Soviet Party Congress.* The Twenty-fifth Congress of the Communist Party of the Soviet Union convenes in Moscow and, like the Twenty-fourth Congress, supports the program of General Secretary Brezhnev. Brezhnev reaffirms the Soviet commitment to détente as well as to an ideological struggle with the West. He states Soviet willingness to end the arms race and defends the Soviet role in Angola as one faithful to "our revolutionary conscience." Brezhnev also reproaches Chinese leaders for "frantic efforts to torpedo détente." Two leaders are appointed to full membership in the Politburo—Grigori Romanov, head of the Leningrad Communist Party Committee, and Dmitri Ustinov, Central Committee secretary responsible for the defense industry.

March 14. *Sadat Abrogates Treaty.* President Anwar Sadat proposes that Egypt abrogate its 1971 Treaty of Cooperation and Friendship with the Soviet Union. The Egyptian People's Assembly overwhelmingly approves the proposal March 15. Sadat cites Moscow's refusal to provide Egypt with arms or to reschedule Egypt's debts as reasons for his action.

April 2. *Soviet Concern Over Détente Slowdown.* Americanologist and director of the Soviet Union's Institute for the Study of the USA and Canada Georgii Arbatov warns in a Tass commentary that "deep-rooted enemies [in the United States] of the improvement in relations" could damage the political atmosphere between the two superpowers. He criticizes President Ford's recent usage of the phrase "peace through strength" instead of détente.

April 11. *SALT Deadlocked.* The *New York Times* reports that SALT II negotiations are at a stalemate. President Ford states April 29 that the "slowdown" in SALT negotiations is responsible for his decision to continue Minuteman III missile production, which originally was scheduled to end June 30.

April 29. *Ustinov Succeeds Grechko.* Dmitri Ustinov is appointed defense minister upon the death of his predecessor, Marshal Andrei Grechko.

May 28. *Nuclear Explosions Pact Signed.* In joint ceremonies in Washington and Moscow, President Ford and Soviet party chief Brezhnev sign the Peaceful Nuclear Explosions Treaty. The agreement prohibits nuclear blasts greater than 150 kilotons for excavation and other peaceful purposes.

June 2. *Philippines, USSR Establish Ties.* President Nikolai Podgornyi and Philippines president Ferdinand E. Marcos sign a document in Moscow establishing diplomatic ties between the two nations.

June 29-30. *European Communists Meet.* Twenty-nine West and East European Communist party leaders, including General Secretary Brezhnev, meet in East Berlin. On June 30 the conference issues a document that denies a dominant role for the Soviet Communist party in the international communist movement. Instead, the document says that each party may follow its own path to socialism.

September 9. *Mao Zedong Dies.* Chinese Communist party chairman Mao Zedong dies at age eighty-two. The Soviet Communist party sends a telegram to its Chinese counterpart—the first in more than a decade—expressing its "deep condolences." Beijing rejects the telegram September 14.

September 21. *SALT Talks Resume.* SALT negotiators return to the bargaining table in Geneva after a recess. The issue of how to deal with Soviet long-range bombers and U.S. cruise missiles remains troublesome. Despite an October 2 meeting between Foreign Minister Gromyko and President Ford, no progress on SALT is expected until after the U.S. presidential election.

October 6. *Ford-Carter Second Debate.* In the second of a series of debates between the two main U.S. presidential candidates, President Ford defends his record and the U.S.-Soviet relationship by stating that "there is no Soviet domination of Eastern Europe and there never will be under a Ford administration." Democratic challenger Jimmy Carter later calls the statement a "very serious blunder." Ford tries several times after the debate to clarify his statement but admits October 12 that he misspoke. Carter is elected November 2 by a small margin.

November 21. *U.S. Pact with Romania.* Secretary of Commerce Elliot L. Richardson signs a ten-year trade and economic cooperation pact with Romania in Bucharest. It is the most comprehensive agreement that the United States has negotiated with an East European nation.

November 28. *Sino-Soviet Border Talks Resume.* Leonid Ilyichev, Soviet deputy foreign minister, arrives in Beijing to resume the Sino-Soviet border talks that were suspended eighteen months before. Western experts, however, expect little progress.

November 30. *Brezhnev on SALT.* General Secretary Brezhnev tells U.S. businessmen attending the U.S.-USSR Trade and Economic Council in Moscow that SALT should be a top-priority concern of the new Carter administration. President-elect Carter, reportedly in response to Brezhnev's appeal, responds December 3 with a promise to move "aggressively" to conclude an agreement.

December 27. *Carter to Meet Brezhnev.* President-elect Carter announces that a summit meeting to discuss SALT with Brezhnev is a "likely prospect" before September 1977. Tass reports December 29 that Brezhnev also favors such a summit.

1977

January 25. *Sakharov Warned.* Soviet dissident Andrei Sakharov is warned by the Soviet deputy chief prosecutor to cease "hostile and slanderous" activities. The warning comes after Sakharov accuses the KGB of exploding a bomb in the Moscow subway to create a pretense for a crackdown on Soviet dissidents. The State Department issues a statement January 27 in defense of Sakharov. The action marks the first time the United States has publicly championed a Soviet dissident. On January 28 Sakharov writes President Carter, urging him to continue his efforts against human rights violations in the Soviet Union. Carter writes Sakharov February 17 to assure him that the United States is firm in its commitment to human rights.

February 8. *Carter on U.S.-Soviet Relations.* The main topic of President Carter's first news conference is an appeal to the Soviet Union to cooperate on SALT II and to discuss other arms issues. Carter states his intention to speak out against human rights violations but emphasizes that his administration will refrain from "linking" progress on SALT to human rights.

February 28. *Sino-Soviet Talks Break Off.* Soviet officials negotiating Sino-Soviet border talks depart for Moscow, marking the end of three months of negotiations. No progress is reported.

March 1. *Carter Receives Bukovsky.* At the White House President Carter receives exiled Soviet dissident Vladimir Bukovsky despite protests from Moscow.

March 15. *Shcharanskii Arrested.* Prominent Jewish dissident Anatolii Shcharanskii is arrested after being refused permission to emigrate. Soviet authorities accuse him of working for the CIA. Shcharanskii's arrest seems to be part of a Soviet campaign against dissidents begun in February. Alexander Ginzburg, an outspoken dissident, was arrested February 4; Ukrainian dissidents Mikola Rudenko and Olexy Tikhy were arrested February 7; and Yuri Orlov, leader of a group unofficially monitoring Soviet compliance with the Helsinki accords, was arrested February 10.

March 21. *Brezhnev Criticizes Carter.* In a speech in Moscow, General Secretary Brezhnev calls President Carter's recent support of Soviet dissidents "unwarranted interference in our internal affairs." The same day Carter asks Congress for twenty-eight additional radio transmitters to extend the range of the Voice of America and Radio Free Europe-Radio Liberty broadcasts.

March 31. *USSR-Mozambique Treaty Signed.* During a week-long tour of Africa, Soviet president Nikolai Podgornyi signs a Treaty of Friendship and Cooperation with the government of Mozambique. Podgornyi also visits Tanzania, Zambia, and Somalia.

May 16. *U.S.-Soviet Trade.* A report by the U.S. Commercial Office in London states that trade between the two superpowers is down 25 percent in early 1977.

May 18-21. *Vance-Gromyko Meeting.* Secretary of State Cyrus R. Vance and Foreign Minister Gromyko meet in Geneva to discuss SALT II. Vance states afterward that progress was made toward breaking the deadlock, but Gromyko cautions that "major, serious difficulties remain."

May 24. *Podgornyi Ousted.* Soviet president Nikolai Podgornyi is removed from the Politburo. Western experts speculate that he was forced out because he opposed Brezhnev on foreign policy issues and the new Soviet constitution.

June 1. *Shcharanskii Charged.* Soviet dissident Anatolii Shcharanskii is charged with treason. The White House expresses its concern June 2.

June 4. *New Soviet Constitution Published.* The draft of the new Soviet constitution is published. The new charter, the fourth in Soviet history, replaces the 1936 document promulgated under Joseph Stalin.

June 16. *Vance on Jackson-Vanik.* In a press conference Secretary of State Vance expresses the Carter administration's hope that Congress will repeal the Jackson-Vanik amendment. That amendment bars the granting of most-favored-nation trade status and Export-Import Bank credits to communist countries that do not permit freedom of emigration.

June 16. *Brezhnev Elected President.* The Supreme Soviet elects Leonid Brezhnev to the largely ceremonial post of president. He succeeds Nikolai Podgornyi, whose retirement is announced the same day. Brezhnev is the first Soviet leader to hold the positions of party general secretary and president at the same time.

June 23. *Computer Sale Canceled.* The Department of Commerce cancels a planned sale of Cyber 76 computers to the Soviet Union. The sale had been opposed earlier by sixty-five members of Congress because the Soviet Union could use the computers' advanced technology for military purposes.

July 4. *Toon Speech Canceled.* Malcolm Toon, U.S. ambassador to the Soviet Union, is not allowed to deliver his traditional Fourth of July speech on Soviet television because of a reference in the text to human rights. Toon protests the decision in a meeting with President Brezhnev the following day.

August 16. *Unrest in Ethiopia.* Following an escalation of fighting in the Ogaden region of Ethiopia, *Izvestiia* states that Ethiopia is the "victim of an armed invasion." Somali military units had invaded the region in July in support of ethnic Somali rebels living in the Ogaden who are fighting the Ethiopian government in an attempt to unite their region with Somalia. The Soviet Union supplies both sides with arms but supports Ethiopia in the current crisis. Western observers August 21 report the arrival of Soviet military aid in Ethiopia.

August 29. *Soviets on South Africa Bomb.* Tass says South Africa is close to testing a nuclear bomb and accuses NATO and Israel of helping Pretoria develop nuclear weapons. It is disclosed August 28 that President Brezhnev sent a letter to President Carter August 6 saying that the Soviet Union had reason to believe South Africa was preparing to test a nuclear weapon in the Kalahari Desert. Brezhnev requested Western action to stop the test.

September 23. *SALT I Extended.* The United States announces its intention to continue observing the 1972 SALT I agreement, which is scheduled to expire October 3. Responding September 25, the Soviet Union also promises to abide by the treaty.

October 1. *Joint U.S.-Soviet Statement.* The United States and the Soviet Union issue a joint declaration on a new Middle East peace conference in Geneva, suggesting that talks include discussion of "the legitimate rights of the Palestinian people." On October 2 Israel rejects the statement as "unacceptable." Israel and the United States October 5 announce agreement on procedures for reconvening the Geneva conference.

October 4. *Belgrade Meeting Opens.* Delegates from nations that signed the 1975 Helsinki accords meet in

Belgrade for the first formal conference to review the Helsinki Final Act.

November 2-7. *Bolshevik Revolution Anniversary.* President Brezhnev addresses the Central Committee and the Supreme Soviet as part of a week-long celebration of the sixtieth anniversary of the Bolshevik Revolution. Brezhnev stresses Soviet support for détente and the need for better economic performance at home.

November 13. *Moscow Loses African Ally.* The government of Somalia abrogates its 1974 treaty of friendship with the Soviet Union, breaks diplomatic relations with Moscow, bars Soviet ships from using the naval facility at Berbera, and orders all Soviet advisers to leave the country. The actions are a response to Soviet and Cuban military support of Ethiopia and Moscow's refusal to sell arms to Somalia.

November 29. *Soviets Attack Sadat.* Foreign Minister Gromyko announces that the USSR will not attend talks in Cairo to arrange a conference in Geneva on a Mideast settlement. Gromyko's statement follows the historic visit of President Anwar Sadat of Egypt to Israel November 19-21. During the visit Sadat had declared his intention to seek peace with Israel. Gromyko says Egypt has departed "from the common Arab front and sacrifices the interests of the Arab states as a whole." Sadat also had invited the United States and all Middle East countries, including Israel, to attend the meeting in Cairo.

December 5. *Egypt Severs Arab Ties.* Egypt severs diplomatic relations with Syria, Iraq, Libya, Algeria, and South Yemen, citing attempts by the hard-line Arab states to disrupt President Sadat's recent peace efforts. The action follows conclusion of a December 2 meeting in Tripoli, Libya, at which the Arab states declared a new "front for resistance and opposition" to thwart Egypt's peace initiatives. Egypt also closes several Soviet cultural centers and consulates in Cairo because of the Soviet Union's endorsement of the Tripoli Declaration.

December 14. *Cairo Conference Opens.* The Cairo conference to discuss procedures for reconvening the Geneva Middle East peace talks opens. Delegates from Egypt, Israel, and the United States participate; a UN representative attends as an observer.

1978

January 6. *Crown Returned to Hungary.* Secretary of State Vance visits Budapest and formally returns the crown of St. Stephen to Hungary. The crown, a Hungarian national treasure, had been in U.S. possession since 1945. The Carter administration returned the crown to symbolize the improvement of U.S.-Hungarian relations. The United States grants Hungary most-favored-nation trading status March 3.

January 11. *Syrian-Soviet Arms Deal.* Syria and the Soviet Union sign an arms deal under which Damascus will receive shipments of Soviet planes, tanks, and advanced air-defense missiles.

January 22. *Ethiopian Offensive.* Ethiopian forces, aided by Cuban troops and large amounts of Soviet arms, launch an offensive designed to clear Ethiopia's Ogaden region of invading Somali forces. Secretary of State Vance

announces February 10 that Moscow has assured the United States that Ethiopian troops would not cross the Somali border once the Ogaden region had been recaptured.

February 24. *ICBM Deployment Halt.* The United States announces an agreement with Moscow to halt all land-based ICBM deployments until September 1980. The agreement would be superseded by a SALT II agreement if one is concluded.

February 28. *USSR Compliance Satisfactory.* The State Department releases a Senate Foreign Relations Committee study that finds Soviet compliance with the 1972 SALT treaty satisfactory.

March 6-9. *Tito in United States.* Yugoslavian president Josip Broz Tito, on a good-will visit to the United States, requests U.S. arms.

March 9. *Somali Forces Begin Pullout.* President Carter announces that Somalia, under pressure from a Soviet-backed Ethiopian offensive, has begun a troop pullout from the Ogaden region of Ethiopia, raising hopes for the possible conclusion of the eight-month war.

March 9. *Belgrade Conference Ends.* The Belgrade Conference on Security and Cooperation in Europe (CSCE) ends with the adoption of summary documents and a pledge for a second review conference in Madrid in 1980. Western diplomats admit to being unable to obtain concrete improvements in human rights in the East Bloc.

March 17. *Carter at Wake Forest.* In a speech at Wake Forest University in North Carolina President Carter warns the Soviet Union about its arms buildup and its military involvement in regional disputes. He cites Soviet activity in the Horn of Africa as an example. Carter vows that the United States will not fall behind in military capabilities. Tass publishes a response the same day, scoring the United States for abandoning cooperative efforts and endorsing "a course of threats and a buildup of tension."

March 29. *U.S.-Soviet Trade Declines.* The U.S. embassy in Moscow reports that U.S.-Soviet trade declined 26.5 percent in 1977 (from $2.5 billion in 1976 to $1.9 billion in 1977). It is the first decline since the expansion of U.S.-Soviet trade in 1972.

April 7. *Neutron Bomb Deferred.* President Carter announces he has "decided to defer production" of the neutron bomb, stating that the issue's final outcome depends on Soviet restraint in arms production and deployment.

April 10. *Shevchenko Defects.* Arkady Shevchenko, UN under secretary general for political and Security Council affairs, defects to the United States. Shevchenko is considered the most important Soviet diplomat to defect to date.

April 20-22. *Vance in Moscow.* Secretary of State Vance meets in Moscow with Foreign Minister Gromyko and President Brezhnev to discuss SALT II. After the discussions both U.S. and Soviet officials report "some progress" in narrowing differences impeding agreement.

April 27. *Afghanistan Coup.* In a military coup in Afghanistan, President Muhammad Daoud, a neutralist, is killed. His government is replaced by a Marxist regime headed by Nur Muhammad Taraki.

May 28. *Brzezinski on Zaire.* U.S. national security adviser Zbigniew Brzezinski in a television interview accuses the Soviet Union, Cuba, and East Germany of involvement in Zaire's Shaba province, where secessionist rebels attacked Zairian troops on May 18. *Pravda* May 30 denies military participation in Zaire and calls Brzezinski an "enemy of détente."

June 7. *Carter in Annapolis.* President Carter, in a commencement address at the U.S. Naval Academy in Annapolis, Maryland, criticizes Soviet foreign and domestic policies. Carter is careful to point out progress in U.S.-Soviet relations on issues such as SALT II but states: "The Soviet Union can choose either confrontation or cooperation. The United States is adequately prepared to meet either choice."

June 8. *Solzhenitsyn's Harvard Address.* Nobel laureate and Soviet dissident Alexander Solzhenitsyn delivers a commencement address at Harvard on the "decline of courage" in the West.

June 29. *Vietnam Joins Comecon.* At an East bloc summit in Bucharest, Vietnam is admitted as the tenth full member of the Council for Mutual Economic Assistance (Comecon), the bloc's economic organization.

July 12-13. *Vance, Gromyko Discuss SALT.* Secretary of State Vance and Foreign Minister Gromyko meet in Geneva to discuss the remaining obstacles to a SALT II agreement: the Soviet Backfire bomber and the testing and deployment of missile systems.

July 13-14. *Ginzburg and Shcharanskii Sentenced.* Alexander Ginzburg is sentenced July 13 to eight years in a labor camp for "anti-Soviet agitation and propaganda." Fellow dissident Anatolii Shcharanskii is sentenced July 14 to three years in prison and ten years in a labor camp following his conviction for treason, espionage, and "anti-Soviet agitation." The trial, which began July 10 under heavy secrecy, focused on Shcharanskii's association with *Los Angeles Times* reporter Robert Toth, who was accused by the Soviet Union of being a spy. Shcharanskii defended himself after refusing a court-appointed lawyer. Congress adopts resolutions against the trials amid calls for suspending SALT, abrogating business deals, and moving the 1980 Olympic games from Moscow. On July 11, UN ambassador Andrew Young added to the furor by asserting that "there are hundreds, perhaps thousands of political prisoners in the United States." The White House protests the convictions July 18 by canceling the sale of sophisticated Sperry-Univac computers and further limiting the sale of oil technology to the Soviet Union.

August 12. *Sino-Japanese Treaty.* After three years of intermittent negotiations, China and Japan sign a treaty of peace and friendship in Tokyo. The Japanese previously had resisted signing a treaty with China that the Soviet Union might find offensive. Tass asserts August 12 that the treaty endangers Soviet-Japanese relations.

August 16. *Hua in Romania.* Chinese Communist party chairman Hua Guofeng arrives in Romania for an unofficial visit that draws worldwide attention and is generally seen as a challenge to Soviet claims of exclusive influence in Eastern Europe. After leaving Romania August 21, Hua flies to Yugoslavia for a nine-day visit. On August 24, *Pravda* attacks the Sino-Japanese peace treaty and Chairman Hua's visit to Eastern Europe.

September 5-17. *Camp David Summit.* Egyptian president Anwar Sadat, Israeli premier Menachem Begin, and President Carter meet in Camp David, Maryland, for a summit on the deadlocked Middle East peace negotiations. Tass denounces the summit September 6 as a "trick" to facilitate greater U.S. influence in the Middle East. After thirteen days of negotiations Carter announces the signing of two pacts that offer a framework for a "durable settlement" of Middle East problems. Brezhnev September 22

calls the agreements "a deal worked out behind the backs of the Arabs."

November 3. *Soviet Treaty with Vietnam.* The Soviet Union and Vietnam sign a twenty-five-year treaty of friendship and cooperation with Vietnam.

November 19. *Brezhnev on Iran.* In response to growing domestic unrest in Iran *Pravda* publishes a statement by President Brezhnev warning the United States not to interfere in Iranian affairs and reminding the United States that Iran borders the Soviet Union.

November 20. *Soviet-Ethiopian Agreement.* President Brezhnev and Ethiopian head of state Mengistu Haile Mariam sign a twenty-year friendship and cooperation pact in Moscow, climaxing a two-year improvement in relations that saw increased Soviet involvement in the Ethiopian war against Somalia and secessionist rebels in Eritrea and Ogaden. The pact promises military "consultation" instead of overt assistance.

December 5. *Soviet-Afghan Agreement.* President Brezhnev and Afghan premier Nur Muhammad Taraki sign a twenty-year treaty of friendship and cooperation in Moscow. The agreement provides for "mutual economic, military and technical assistance" and notes that the Soviet Union "respects the policy of non-alignment" of the Afghan government.

December 15. *United States Recognizes PRC.* The governments of the People's Republic of China (PRC) and the United States issue a joint communiqué announcing the establishment of diplomatic relations as of January 1, 1979. On December 19 Brezhnev sends President Carter a note that Carter describes as "very positive in tone." Tass December 21 disputes Carter's interpretation, disclosing that Moscow has deep reservations about normalization and particularly about the inclusion of a phrase in the December 15 communiqué condemning "hegemony," a word the Chinese often have used to criticize the Soviet Union.

December 21-23. *SALT II Agreement Nears.* Meeting in Geneva, Secretary of State Vance and Foreign Minister Gromyko announce agreement on "most issues," but a SALT treaty is not completed.

December 25. *Vietnam Invades Cambodia.* After months of border fighting, Vietnam launches a massive offensive into Cambodia. Western observers regard the Soviet-Vietnamese treaty signed in November as a measure taken by the Vietnamese to deter the Chinese from intervening on behalf of the pro-Beijing Khmer Rouge regime in Cambodia. Vietnamese forces capture Phnom Penh January 7.

1979

January 1. *China, United States Establish Ties.* The United States and China formally open full diplomatic relations.

January 6. *New Government in Iran.* Amidst growing domestic unrest the shah of Iran installs a new civilian government headed by Shahpur Bakhtiar. Shah Mohammed Reza Pahlavi leaves the country January 16 for a vacation that proves to be permanent exile.

January 8. *Khmer Rouge Ousted in Cambodia.* The Vietnamese-sponsored United Front for National Salvation announces the overthrow of the Khmer Rouge government and the formation of a People's Revolutionary Council. Heng Samrin becomes president of the new Cambodian government. On January 9 the Soviet Union sends a congratulatory telegram to Samrin.

January 15. *Soviet Veto.* The Soviet Union vetoes a UN Security Council resolution demanding the withdrawal of Vietnamese forces from Cambodia.

January 28. *Deng in United States.* Vice Premier Deng Xiaoping arrives in Washington for a nine-day visit, the first ever to the United States by a senior Chinese Communist leader. *Pravda* criticizes the U.S. government February 4 for allowing Deng to repeatedly denounce the Soviet Union during the visit. *Pravda* states that "the Soviet public cannot close its eyes to the fact" that Deng "was given a wide podium for slander on the USSR."

February 5. *Soviet Buildup Reported.* Japan reports that the Soviet Union is building bases and increasing its troop strength on the southernmost Kuril Island, adjacent to the northernmost Japanese island of Hokkaido. Both countries claim the Kuril Islands.

February 9-11. *Revolution in Iran.* Armed revolutionaries and army supporters of Ayatollah Ruhollah Khomeini overthrow the government of Shahpur Bakhtiar in Iran. Khomeini, who returned to Iran February 1 from exile in France, installs Mehdi Barzagan as premier of a provisional government. The Soviet Union recognizes the new government February 12.

February 17. *China Invades Vietnam.* In an action described by the Chinese as a "counterattack" brought on by repeated Vietnamese border incursions, Chinese troops invade Vietnam. Moscow vigorously protests and aids Vietnam with supplies and intelligence. However, the Kremlin does not offer armed support, and Soviet troops in Asian military districts are neither reinforced nor put on alert. On March 5 China begins withdrawing its forces after both sides suffer heavy casualties.

March 4. *Podgornyi Excluded.* The political career of Nikolai Podgornyi, former president of the Soviet Union (1965-1977), ends when he is not reelected to the Supreme Soviet.

March 26. *Egyptian-Israeli Peace Treaty.* Israeli prime minister Menachem Begin and Egyptian president Anwar Sadat sign a peace treaty that formally ends the state of war between their two countries. The ceremony, witnessed by President Carter, takes place on the White House lawn. Tass March 22 declares the treaty "a betrayal" of Arab interests.

April 27. *Soviet Dissidents Exchanged for Spies.* In the first exchange of its kind, five Soviet dissidents are flown to New York's Kennedy Airport and exchanged for two convicted Soviet spies. One of the dissidents released is Alexander Ginzburg, whose conviction in 1978 prompted worldwide protests. The other dissidents are Mark Dymshits and Eduard Kuznetsov, two Soviet Jews convicted of plotting to hijack a plane to Sweden; Valentin Moroz, a historian who advocates Ukrainian independence; and Georgi Vins, convicted for religious activities in the Ukraine.

May 9. *SALT II Draft Treaty Completed.* Secretary of State Vance announces the completion of a SALT II draft treaty with the Soviet Union, thereby clearing the path for a summit meeting between Presidents Brezhnev and Carter. On May 11 the White House announces that a summit will be held June 16-18 in Vienna.

June 2. *Pope Visits Poland.* Pope John Paul II makes a historic nine-day visit to his native Poland to mark the 900th anniversary of the martyrdom of St. Stanislaus, Poland's patron saint. It is the first time a Catholic pope has visited a communist country. A Soviet television broadcast states that "some circles in the Polish church are trying to use [the visit] for anti-state purposes."

June 16-18. *Vienna Summit.* Presidents Carter and Brezhnev meet for the first time at a U.S.-Soviet summit meeting in Vienna. The conference agenda includes five negotiating sessions and ends with the signing of the second strategic arms limitation treaty between the United States and the Soviet Union. Carter returns to the United States June 18 and asks a joint session of Congress to approve the SALT II treaty, which he says is "the most detailed, far-reaching, comprehensive treaty in the history of arms control."

June 25. *Gromyko Warns Senate.* Soviet foreign minister Gromyko warns the U.S. Senate against amending the SALT II treaty, stating that it "would be the end of negotiations . . . no matter what amendments would be made."

July 9. *SALT Hearings Begin.* The Senate Foreign Relations Committee opens three months of hearings on the SALT II treaty. Similar hearings in the Senate Armed Services Committee begin July 23.

July 17. *Somoza Resigns.* Nicaraguan president Anastasio Somoza resigns and flies to the United States. Two days later rebel Sandinista troops overcome disorganized national guard forces and take control of Managua.

August 31. *Soviet Troops in Cuba.* The State Department acknowledges the presence of a 2,000-3,000-man Soviet combat brigade in Cuba. President Carter claims the troops do not threaten U.S. security. Frank Church, D-Idaho, chairman of the Senate Foreign Relations Committee, states September 5 that he sees "no likelihood that the Senate would ratify the SALT II treaty as long as Soviet combat troops remain stationed in Cuba." In a nationally televised speech September 7, President Carter calls the presence of combat troops in Cuba "a very serious matter" but asks for "calm and a sense of proportion." On September 8 Carter says that Soviet troops in Cuba should not influence the Senate debate over ratification of SALT II, maintaining that the treaty should be judged "on its own merits."

September 10. *Moscow on Cuba.* In the first Soviet comments on the issue, a *Pravda* editorial denies the presence of Soviet combat troops in Cuba, while Tass states that there has been a training center in Cuba for seventeen years, and that its purpose (of training Cuban forces) has not changed.

September 16. *New Government in Afghanistan.* Premier Hafizullah Amin replaces Nur Muhammad Taraki as president of Afghanistan. Officially, Taraki is said to have resigned because of ill health, but it appears that he may have been killed during a government upheaval. Taraki's death is confirmed October 9, but the cause is given as "a severe and prolonged illness."

September 23. *Sino-Soviet Talks.* A Chinese negotiating team arrives in Moscow to begin talks aimed at easing Sino-Soviet tensions. It is the first Chinese diplomatic delegation to visit Moscow since 1964.

October 1. *Carter on Cuba.* In a nationally televised speech President Carter announces a comprehensive U.S. intelligence effort to survey Cuba and monitor military activity in the Caribbean. Carter stresses that "the brigade issue is certainly no reason for a return to the Cold War" and continues to press for SALT II ratification.

October 3. *Record Grain Sale Approved.* The largest

Soviet purchase of U.S. grain to date is approved by the Agriculture Department. The sale will involve up to twenty-five million metric tons of grain in the next year.

October 25. *South Yemen-USSR Pact.* Officials of the Soviet Union and South Yemen sign a twenty-year friendship pact in Moscow.

November 4. *Crisis in Iran.* Demanding the return of the shah, Iranian students seize the U.S. embassy in Tehran and take sixty-six Americans hostage. Thirteen are freed November 19-20.

November 9. *Committee Approves SALT.* The Senate Foreign Relations Committee votes 9-6 to recommend the SALT II treaty for ratification.

November 27. *Politburo Changes.* Deputy Prime Minister Nikolai Tikhonov is promoted to full membership in the Soviet Politburo. Mikhail S. Gorbachev is made a candidate (nonvoting) member, becoming the youngest participant at age forty-eight.

December 4. *United Nations Votes on Iran.* The UN Security Council votes to demand an immediate release of the remaining fifty-three American hostages in Iran. In a *Pravda* article December 5, Moscow supports the UN vote but, citing U.S. naval maneuvers in the Arabian Sea, accuses the United States of attempting to "blackmail Iran by massing forces on its borders" instead of returning the shah.

December 12. *NATO Dual-Track Policy.* NATO members agree to deploy 108 Pershing II and 464 land-based cruise missiles in Europe by 1983. The agreement calls for simultaneously engaging Moscow in arms control talks aimed at reducing nuclear weapons in Europe.

December 20. *Committee Rejects SALT.* The Senate Armed Services Committee votes 10-0 to recommend rejection of the SALT II treaty as "not in the national security interest of the United States."

December 24-27. *Soviets Invade Afghanistan.* The Soviet Union begins airlifting troops and supplies into Afghanistan under the guise of a military exercise. On December 27 about twenty thousand Soviet ground troops invade the country. That day Afghan president Hafizullah Amin is killed during fighting between Afghan units loyal to him and invading Soviet forces. He is succeeded as president by Babrak Karmal. By December 31 Soviet troops fan through the country to contain a rebellion by Moslem tribesmen who oppose Marxist rule. Moscow issues a series of statements December 28-30 supporting the new government and promising it aid. The first admission of the intervention comes December 30 in a *Pravda* article that states the troops will withdraw when they no longer are needed. By December 31 Soviet troops in Afghanistan reportedly number fifty thousand.

December 31. *Carter on Afghanistan.* In a televised interview President Carter states that the Soviet intervention in Afghanistan has changed his opinion of the Soviets more dramatically than any other event during his administration.

1980

January 3. *Carter Asks SALT Delay.* Senate Majority Leader Robert C. Byrd, D-W.Va., receives a letter from President Carter formally requesting the Senate to delay further consideration of the SALT II treaty in light of the Soviet invasion of Afghanistan.

January 4. *U.S. Response to Afghanistan.* In a nationally televised address, President Carter describes the Soviet intervention in Afghanistan as "an extremely serious threat to peace" and announces a series of retaliatory measures. These include: an embargo on the sale of grain and high technology items to the USSR, restraint of Soviet fishing privileges in U.S. waters, delayed construction of new Soviet and U.S. embassies, and a possible U.S. boycott of the Olympic games to be held in Moscow later in the year. Soviet sources January 5 call these responses a "flagrant violation" of détente and a return to cold war policies.

January 6. *Deng on Afghan Crisis.* Chinese vice premier Deng Xiaoping calls the Soviet invasion of Afghanistan "a grave step," repeats Beijing's "firm demand" that the troops be withdrawn, and declares that China will "work together with the Afghan people, and all countries and people ... to frustrate Soviet acts of aggression and expansion."

January 12. *Brezhnev on Afghanistan.* President Brezhnev makes his first official statement on the Afghanistan invasion, stating that "aggressive external forces of reaction" necessitated intervention.

January 13. *USSR Vetoes Iran Resolution.* A U.S.-proposed UN Security Council resolution urging economic sanctions against Iran for the taking of American hostages is vetoed by the Soviet Union. The Soviet Union justifies its decision on the grounds that sanctions would have "dealt a blow to the Iranian revolution."

January 14. *United States Offers Pakistan Military Aid.* The State Department announces that the United States plans to provide Pakistan with $400 million in economic and military aid because of the Soviet intervention in neighboring Afghanistan.

January 14. *United Nations on Afghanistan.* The UN General Assembly approves 104-18 a resolution condemning the Soviet intervention in Afghanistan and demanding a troop withdrawal.

January 20. *Carter Sees Danger.* Speaking on NBC's "Meet the Press," President Carter calls the Soviet invasion of Afghanistan the "most serious threat to peace since the Second World War."

January 22. *Sakharov Exiled.* Soviet authorities send Nobel prize winning scientist and human rights activist Andrei Sakharov and his wife into internal exile in the city of Gorkii. The Presidium of the Supreme Soviet strips Sakharov of his honors. Tass charges that Sakharov "has been conducting subversive activities against the Soviet Union for a number of years." The exiling apparently was prompted by Sakharov's protests against the Soviet invasion of Afghanistan and his support for a Western boycott of the Moscow Olympics.

January 23. *Carter Doctrine.* In what becomes known as the "Carter Doctrine," President Carter in his third State of the Union message declares that the United States will "use any means necessary, including force," to repel any attacks on the oil-producing Persian Gulf region.

January 29. *Senate on Olympics.* The Senate votes 88-4 to support a U.S. boycott of the Summer Olympics in Moscow. A similar resolution was adopted by the House January 24.

February 12. *IOC Reaffirms Moscow.* The International Olympic Committee (IOC) decides to retain Moscow as the site of the Summer Olympics despite pressure from the U.S. Olympic Committee to move the games.

February 22. *Brezhnev on Afghanistan.* President Brezhnev states that the need for Soviet involvement in Afghanistan would "cease to exist" if the governments of the United States, Pakistan, and China would end their alleged subversion of the Kabul government.

March 6. *Soviets on Poison Gas.* Moscow denies accusations made by Afghan refugees in Pakistan that Soviet troops are using poison gas on Afghan rebels.

April 24-25. *Failed Rescue Mission.* A U.S. commando mission to rescue American hostages in Iran is aborted in the Iranian desert because of equipment failures. Eight commandos are killed in a helicopter-airplane accident that occurs as the rescue team is about to take off. Tass comments April 25 that "the present master of the White House could not care less about his fellow citizens and is prepared to sacrifice their lives for his election interests."

May 4. *Tito Dies.* President Josip Broz Tito of Yugoslavia dies in Ljubljana after a long illness. Moscow, in response to Tito's death, makes no mention of the historically stormy relations between the two nations and does not dwell on Tito's expulsion from the international communist movement in 1948. Instead, the official statement praises Tito as "a leading figure of the international Communist and workers' movement."

May 9. *Carter on SALT II.* President Carter tells the World Affairs Council that he will seek the approval of SALT II "at the earliest opportune time" and that "we intend to abide by the treaty's terms as long as the Soviet Union, as observed by us, complies with those terms as well."

May 16. *Gromyko and Muskie in Vienna.* Secretary of State Edmund S. Muskie meets Foreign Minister Gromyko in Vienna in the first high-level U.S.-Soviet meeting since the Afghan invasion. The private meeting produces no conclusive agreements.

June 30-July 1. *Schmidt in Moscow.* West German chancellor Helmut Schmidt confers with President Brezhnev in Moscow. Schmidt proposes unconditional negotiations on medium-range missiles in Europe and appeals for the Soviet withdrawal of forces in Afghanistan. The two leaders conclude an economic agreement and make preliminary plans for a natural gas pipeline project from western Siberia to West Germany.

July 19. *Moscow Olympics.* The first Olympics held in a communist country open in Moscow. The games are boycotted by sixty-four countries. Of those, fifty-five reportedly refused to attend to protest the Afghanistan invasion.

August 5. *Presidential Directive 59.* The *New York Times* reports that the previous week President Carter signed Presidential Directive (PD) 59, detailing U.S. strategy against the Soviet Union in the event of a nuclear war. PD 59 emphasizes the destruction of the Soviet Union's strategic weapons and its command, control, and communications structure. The document also stresses the need for limited nuclear options and preparations for protracted nuclear war. Tass August 11 calls the document "insanity" developed by persons "who have lost all touch with reality and are prepared to push the world" into nuclear war.

August 14. *Workers Strike in Poland.* A labor crisis in Poland intensifies as seventeen thousand workers go on strike at the Lenin Shipyard in Gdansk. The strike spreads and by August 22 a strikers' committee representing 120,000 Polish workers from northern Poland delivers a request for political and economic reform to the Polish government. On August 21-22, the government arrests twenty-four leaders of the striking workers.

August 20. *Moscow Jams VOA.* The Soviet Union begins jamming Voice of America (VOA) broadcasts to the USSR, reportedly to prevent news of the labor crisis in Poland from reaching the Soviet population.

August 23. *Concessions to Workers.* The Polish government agrees to negotiate with representatives of the strikers. On August 24, Polish premier Edward Babiuch is ousted as part of a strike-inspired government shake-up. Despite a government promise of concessions, the strike reportedly swells to three hundred thousand workers.

August 27. *Moscow on Poland.* After strike leaders in Gdansk reject Polish government concessions, the Soviet Union, in its first direct response to the unrest in Poland, accuses "antisocialist forces" of attempting to disrupt Poland's socialist system.

September 3. *Polish Workers Return.* Most of the striking Polish workers return to their jobs by September 3 after the government announces an agreement allowing free trade unions and the right to strike. The agreement was concluded August 31. On August 21, coal miners in Silesia began their own strike, which lasted in most places until September 3.

September 6. *Gierek Replaced.* Polish Communist party secretary Edward Gierek, reportedly suffering from heart trouble, is replaced by Stanislaw Kania. The Kania government is expected to honor the concessions Gierek made to Polish workers.

September 20. *Outbreak of Iran-Iraq War.* A dispute between Iraq and Iran escalates into full-scale war. Both sides bomb oil fields; Iraqi forces invade Iran and threaten to block the strategic Strait of Hormuz. The United States and the Soviet Union September 23 pledge neutrality in the war.

September 24. *Solidarity Formed.* Poland's new independent trade unions register in a Warsaw court as a single nationwide organization called "Solidarity." Solidarity draft statutes are presented by the union's new leader, Lech Walesa.

October 8. *Soviet-Syrian Treaty.* President Brezhnev and Syrian president Hafez Assad sign a twenty-year friendship pact.

October 21. *Gorbachev Promoted.* Mikhail Gorbachev is promoted from candidate member of the Politburo to full member.

October 23. *Kosygin Resigns.* Aleksei Kosygin resigns as Soviet premier on grounds of ill health. Nikolai Tikhonov, an economic planner and Brezhnev protégé, becomes premier. Brezhnev tells the Supreme Soviet that Kosygin also wishes to be excused from his Politburo duties.

November 4. *Reagan Elected.* In a landslide election, Ronald Reagan defeats Jimmy Carter for the presidency. Premier Nikolai Tikhonov cautiously expresses Moscow's hopes that Reagan will assume "a constructive approach" in the area of U.S.-Soviet relations.

November 11. *CSCE Opens in Madrid.* The Conference on Security and Cooperation in Europe (CSCE) meets in Madrid to review the 1975 Helsinki accords. The Soviet Union and its East European allies protest discussion of the human rights issue, preferring more talk on a European disarmament conference. The first phase of the meeting closes December 19.

November 21. *Polish Shake-up.* In a major reorganization of the Polish Communist party and government, four cabinet ministers lose their jobs. The move ousts a conservative faction of the leadership that had resisted cooperation with the Polish trade union movement. East European allies of the Soviet Union attack Polish authorities for their inability to control Solidarity.

December 5. *Summit on Poland.* Leaders of the Soviet Union and East Europe attend an emergency summit in Moscow to discuss the crisis in Poland. Polish Communist party secretary Stanislaw Kania attends and proclaims Polish loyalty "to the Socialist commonwealth." Simultaneously, reports of Warsaw Pact troop movements increase Western fears that the Soviets will invade Poland.

December 17. *Kosygin Dies.* Former Soviet premier Aleksei Kosygin dies of cardiac arrest. His death is not disclosed by Tass until December 20, after the seventy-fourth birthday celebrations (December 19) for Leonid Brezhnev.

1981

January 20. *Iran Frees U.S. Hostages.* Iran releases the remaining fifty-two American hostages after U.S. and Iranian negotiators reach an agreement on the return of Iran's frozen assets in the United States. The hostages, who spent 444 days in captivity, fly out of Iran minutes after Ronald Reagan is inaugurated as the fortieth U.S. president.

January 29. *Reagan on Détente.* In his first news conference as president, Reagan maintains that "so far, détente's been a one-way street the Soviet Union has used to pursue its own aims," which the president describes as "the promotion of world revolution and a one-world ... Communist state." Reagan also says that in pursuit of their goals the Soviets reserve the "right to commit any crime, to lie, to cheat."

February 9. *Polish Government Shake-up.* Poland's defense minister, Gen. Wojciech Jaruzelski, is named premier following the dismissal of Josef Pinkowski. The government shuffle occurs amid continuing strikes in Poland.

February 14. *Moscow Denies Aid to El Salvador.* The Soviet Union denies U.S. allegations that it is supplying arms to Communist rebels in El Salvador but concedes that it has no restrictions on sending arms to Cuba or Ethiopia, two countries that allegedly provide the El Salvadorian rebels with arms. State Department sources February 23 claim "definite evidence" that Cuba and other communist countries have supplied the rebels with military equipment.

February 23-March 3. *Soviet Party Congress.* In an opening speech to the Twenty-sixth Congress of the Communist Party of the Soviet Union, President Brezhnev proposes a summit meeting with President Reagan. Secretary of State Alexander M. Haig, Jr., tells reporters that the United States is "very interested" in a summit, but that the idea should be considered "very, very carefully." Brezhnev announces at the end of the congress March 3 that the entire Politburo has been reelected, the first time a party congress has witnessed no change among the top leadership.

March 19. *Soyuz 81 Maneuvers.* Poland reports the beginning of Warsaw Pact maneuvers, code-named Soyuz 81, in Poland, the German Democratic Republic, the Soviet Union, and Czechoslovakia. The maneuvers are extended March 26 after Solidarity announces a warning strike for March 27, to be followed by a general strike. The general strike is subsequently canceled.

April 7. *Brezhnev on Poland.* Speaking in Prague, President Brezhnev states that it is not necessary for Moscow to solve Poland's problems. The Soyuz 81 Warsaw Pact maneuvers end the same day, but Western concern over Soviet intentions in Poland continues.

April 24. *Reagan Ends Grain Embargo.* President Reagan announces in a closed cabinet session that he will honor a campaign promise and lift the embargo on grain sales to the Soviet Union. President Carter imposed the embargo in January 1980 in response to the Soviet invasion of Afghanistan.

May 17. *Reagan at Notre Dame.* In a commencement speech at Notre Dame University in South Bend, Indiana, President Reagan declares that "The West will not contain Communism; it will transcend Communism. We will not bother to denounce it; we'll dismiss it as a sad, bizarre chapter in human history whose last pages are even now being written."

July 14-20. *Polish Emergency Congress.* Poland's Communist party convenes an emergency congress to discuss the political and economic crises buffeting the country. The congress is a watershed because it allows open criticism of party policies and voting by secret ballot. The Soviet Union protests the inclusion of democratic methods into congress procedures and sends a less important Politburo member, Viktor Grishin, as its representative. The meeting results in a large turnover of Polish Central Committee members and the reelection of Party boss Stanislaw Kania and Premier Wojciech Jaruzelski. Moscow gives the Polish congress perfunctory approval July 21, as Brezhnev sends a cool telegram asserting that the meeting has "set the task of stabilizing" the crisis in Poland. The message warns that internal and external subversive forces are "providing complications in Poland's relations with its true neighbors."

July 15. *Soviet-Brazilian Trade Accord.* Soviet and Brazilian officials sign a $6 billion trade accord in Moscow calling for the Soviet purchase of soybeans and the Brazilian purchase of Soviet oil.

September 5-October 7. *Solidarity Congress.* In an unprecedented action the Solidarity National Congress calls for free parliamentary elections in Poland. The Soviet Union immediately denounces the congress as an "anti-socialist, anti-Soviet orgy." The congress voted September 9 to urge other East European countries to encourage the development of independent trade unions. Lech Walesa is narrowly reelected as chairman. Polish authorities accuse the trade union September 16 of developing into an opposition movement that could push Poland into a "new national tragedy."

September 24. *Haig and Gromyko Meeting.* Secretary of State Haig and Foreign Minister Gromyko announce that negotiations on the limitation of medium-range nuclear weapons in Europe will begin November 30 in Geneva. The announcement comes on the second day of a two-day meeting in New York, the first high-level U.S.-Soviet contact of the Reagan administration.

October 6. *Sadat Assassinated.* President Anwar Sadat of Egypt is assassinated while reviewing a military parade. Vice President Hosni Mubarak is elected president October 13.

October 16. *Reagan on Nuclear War.* In a news conference President Reagan implies that it may be possible to use tactical nuclear weapons in a confrontation on European soil without igniting a full-scale nuclear war. Reagan's remarks cause a furor over apparent U.S. insensitivity to the fate of Western Europe. The statements cause a stir in Europe, where the antinuclear movement is gathering momentum.

October 18. *Kania Dismissed.* Polish Communist party head Stanislaw Kania is dismissed and replaced by Premier Wojciech Jaruzelski. Kania's removal comes amidst worsening economic conditions and increasing strikes. Kania was criticized for being too soft on Solidarity. Jaruzelski holds supreme power as first secretary of the party, commander of the armed forces, premier, and defense minister.

October 27. *CSCE Reconvenes.* The thirty-five-nation Conference on Security and Cooperation in Europe (CSCE) convenes in Madrid to review the 1975 Helsinki accords. The session opens with a tirade against the Soviet Union as European delegates repeat earlier accusations of accord violations in the human rights area and condemn Moscow for intervening in Afghanistan and conducting Warsaw Pact maneuvers around Poland. The session ends in a deadlock December 18.

November 2. *Brezhnev Interview.* President Brezhnev discusses the East-West balance of power, disarmament, and détente in an interview for the German publication *Der Spiegel.* The interview follows widespread demonstrations in Europe October 24-25 protesting NATO plans to deploy medium-range nuclear weapons in Europe. Brezhnev criticizes U.S. foreign policy as the main factor behind world tension.

November 16. *Brezhnev on Food Supply.* In his address to a Central Committee Plenum, President Brezhnev declares that the Soviet food supply is "economically and politically the central problem of the five-year plan." He pledges development of a new food program that will include more decentralized decision making in the agricultural economy, more incentives for local initiatives, and expanded use of private plots.

November 18. *Reagan's "Zero Option" Plan.* In a televised speech to the National Press Club, President Reagan announces that he will cancel plans for deployment of intermediate-range nuclear weapons in Europe if the Soviet Union will dismantle its intermediate-range missiles already in place. Tass calls the plan a "propaganda ploy designed to stalemate disarmament talks."

November 22-25. *Brezhnev in Bonn.* President Brezhnev visits West Germany and holds extensive talks with Chancellor Helmut Schmidt on economic and security issues.

November 30. *Arms Talks Begin.* Negotiations on the limitation of theater nuclear forces in Europe begin in Geneva. The negotiating teams headed by Paul H. Nitze for the United States and Yuli Kvitsinskii for the Soviet Union impose a news blackout. The United States bargaining position is Reagan's "zero option" plan forgoing deployment of medium-range missiles if the Soviets dismantle their comparable missiles already in place. The Soviet team proposes a freeze on medium-range missile deployment. The session recesses December 17.

December 10. *Sakharov Hunger Strike Ends.* Soviet officials confirm the end of a hunger strike by Soviet dissident Andrei Sakharov and his wife, Yelena Bonner. The Sakharovs began a fast November 22 to protest Moscow's

refusal to allow their daughter-in-law, Lisa Alekseyeva, to join her husband, Alexsei Semyonov, in the United States. *Izvestiia* announced December 4 that the Sakharovs had been hospitalized to prevent "complications in the state of their health." The Soviet Union made what is considered an unusual concession by allowing Alekseyeva to emigrate. She arrived in the United States December 20.

December 13. *Martial Law in Poland.* Premier Wojciech Jaruzelski declares a state of emergency in Poland and imposes martial law. The decree interrupts the operations of Solidarity and curtails the civil rights of Polish citizens. Jaruzelski's announcement follows a December 12 decision by Solidarity to call for a nationwide referendum to decide whether to maintain a communist system of government if Polish authorities do not agree to a new series of demands. Imposition of martial law includes a raid on Solidarity headquarters, detention of Lech Walesa and other Solidarity leaders, a news blackout, and the deployment of troops to ensure control. Tass December 14 calls events in Poland an "internal matter."

December 23. *U.S. Economic Sanctions.* President Reagan announces U.S. economic sanctions against Poland that include suspension of civil aviation and fishing rights and restriction of Export-Import Bank credits, high-technology exports, and exports of food products. Reagan places "a major share of the blame" on Moscow for the imposition of martial law. Despite Soviet denials of interference in Poland's internal affairs, the United States December 29 imposes economic sanctions against Moscow for the crackdown in Poland. These include the suspension of Aeroflot flights to the United States, a moratorium on renewals of scientific exchange agreements, and an increase in restrictions on the export of U.S. oil and natural gas equipment to the Soviet Union. The reaction of U.S. allies is mixed. West Germany in particular questions whether Moscow is indeed the prime mover behind the imposition of martial law in Poland.

1982

January 11. *NATO on Poland.* Foreign ministers of NATO countries meet in emergency session in Brussels and condemn the Soviet Union for its participation in "the system of repression in Poland." In contrast to the previous stance of West European leaders, the ministers call for Europe to join the United States in imposing economic sanctions against the Soviet Union. Great Britain on February 5 becomes the first NATO country to do so.

January 12. *Arms Talks Reconvene.* U.S. and Soviet negotiators return to Geneva to continue discussions on limiting medium-range missiles in Europe.

January 25. *Suslov Dies.* Influential Politburo member and chief Soviet ideologist Mikhail Suslov dies "after a brief illness."

January 26. *Gromyko and Haig in Geneva.* Secretary of State Haig and Foreign Minister Gromyko meet in Geneva. Haig calls the talks "beneficial" but says the Polish crisis casts "a long, dark shadow over all East-West issues."

March 8. *Chemical Warfare.* In testimony before the Senate Foreign Relations Committee, Deputy Secretary of

State Walter J. Stoessel, Jr., states that Soviet troops have been using extensive chemical warfare in Afghanistan.

March 16. *Brezhnev on SS-20s.* President Brezhnev announces that the Soviet Union will not deploy any new SS-20 intermediate-range missiles targeted on Europe. The ban is to stay in effect unless NATO begins its planned deployments of Pershing II and cruise missiles. The Reagan administration dismisses the move as part of Moscow's propaganda campaign against NATO's nuclear missile program.

March 24. *Brezhnev on China.* President Brezhnev delivers a conciliatory speech on Sino-Soviet relations in Tashkent, Uzbekistan. He calls for border negotiations and emphasizes Moscow's desire to normalize relations with Beijing.

April 2. *Falkland Islands Crisis.* Argentine troops seize control of Great Britain's Falkland Islands in the South Atlantic. British prime minister Margaret Thatcher orders a thirty-five-ship naval force to steam to the islands. Moscow declares its neutrality April 7, but subsequent Soviet statements support Argentina. British forces land on the islands May 21 and secure the surrender of the Argentine garrison June 14.

April 4-5. *Gromyko in Yugoslavia.* Soviet foreign minister Gromyko meets in Belgrade with Yugoslav officials. It is the first visit by a high-level Soviet official since President Tito's death two years before.

May 9. *Reagan's START Proposal.* President Reagan outlines a strategic arms reduction proposal in a speech at his alma mater, Eureka College, in Illinois. His plan calls for a one-third reduction in total warheads, with no more than half being deployed in ICBMs. He also proposes a total ceiling of 850 ICBMs and submarine-launched ballistic missiles (SLBMs) and limits on throw-weight. Reagan makes no mention of possible cuts in bombers and cruise missiles. President Brezhnev welcomes Reagan's interest in negotiations May 18 but rejects the specifics of his proposal as "one-sided."

May 10. *Soviet Aid to Nicaragua.* Following a visit to the Soviet Union by Nicaraguan president Daniel Ortega, the Soviets announce a five-year, $166.8 million, economic and technical aid package for Nicaragua.

May 24. *Brezhnev Presents Food Program.* In a widely publicized speech to the Central Committee, President Brezhnev outlines an expensive new food program designed to ensure reliable supplies of foodstuffs for the Soviet Union through the 1980s.

May 26. *Andropov Leaves KGB for Secretariat.* Following his promotion to the Secretariat May 24, Yuri Andropov resigns as head of the KGB. He is succeeded by Vitalii Fedorchuk.

June 2-11. *Reagan in Europe.* President Reagan travels to Europe for an economic summit in Versailles, France, June 4-6. The leaders of the seven major industrial democracies agree to "limit their government export credits" to the East bloc, with no specific credit ceiling agreed upon. Following the summit, Reagan visits Rome, Great Britain, Bonn, and Berlin. In separate speeches to the British and West German parliaments June 8 and 9, he criticizes Soviet aggression and suppression of democracy, but he expresses U.S. desires for arms control and East-West cooperation.

June 6. *Israel Invades Lebanon.* The Israeli army launches a major invasion into southern Lebanon, ostensibly to eliminate Palestine Liberation Organization (PLO) bases. By June 10 Israeli units are within a few miles of

Beirut and are engaging in sporadic battles with Syrian troops. On June 9 and 10 the Israeli air force effectively cripples Syria's air defenses by destroying its Soviet-supplied surface-to-air missile batteries and shooting down large numbers of Syrian fighters. Israel and Syria agree to a cease-fire June 11, but Israel and the PLO continue to fight. The Soviet Union June 14 demands that Israel withdraw from Lebanon and warns that developments in the Middle East "cannot help affecting the interests of the USSR."

June 15. *Gromyko Renounces First Use.* At the UN General Assembly's special session on disarmament, Foreign Minister Gromyko pledges that the Soviet Union will not be the first nation to use nuclear weapons. Two days later President Reagan addresses the special session but does not comment on Gromyko's speech. He emphasizes the U.S. commitment to arms control and accuses the Soviets of being insincere and pursuing a massive military buildup.

June 18. *United States Widens Pipeline Sanctions.* As a further response to martial law in Poland, President Reagan broadens sanctions aimed at delaying progress of the European-Siberian natural gas pipeline. The new measures prohibit foreign subsidiaries and licensees of U.S. companies from selling equipment for the pipeline. Previous sanctions enacted in December 1981 barred only the sale of American-made equipment. The European Economic Community unanimously opposes the U.S. move.

June 29. *START Talks Begin.* The opening round of the Strategic Arms Reduction Talks (START) begins in Geneva, with Edward L. Rowny heading the U.S. negotiating team and Victor Karpov heading the Soviet delegation.

July 16. *"Walk-in-the-Woods" Plan.* After weeks of unofficial conversations, U.S. arms negotiator Paul Nitze and his Soviet counterpart at the Geneva talks on intermediate nuclear forces (INF), Yuli Kvitsinskii, jointly develop a European arms control package for their respective governments to consider. The package, drawn up during a private walk in the Jura Mountains near Geneva, subsequently is rejected by both governments.

July 20. *United States Withdraws from Test Ban Talks.* President Reagan ends U.S. participation in talks on a comprehensive nuclear test ban until verification measures are improved. The three-way negotiations between Great Britain, the Soviet Union, and the United States had been suspended since November 1980. Great Britain and many members of the U.S. Congress oppose Reagan's decision. On July 21 Tass accuses Reagan of using verification problems as an excuse to sabotage the talks.

August 20. *U.S.-Soviet Grain Deal Extension.* The Soviet Union renews for another year the one-year grain sale agreement with the United States due to expire September 30. The extension follows a July 30 proposal by President Reagan to continue the current arrangement.

September 15. *Brezhnev's Middle East Peace Plan.* In a Kremlin speech President Brezhnev offers a six-point plan for achieving peace in the Middle East. It calls for an Israeli withdrawal to its pre-1967 borders and a UN-guaranteed settlement providing for the establishment of a Palestinian state. The plan is similar to one adopted by the Arab League September 9. Brezhnev attacks a September 1 peace proposal by President Reagan for its failure to advocate a completely independent Palestinian state and to recognize the Palestine Liberation Organization as the sole legitimate representative of the Palestinian people.

October 5. *Sino-Soviet Talks.* Formal "consultations" between Soviet and Chinese deputy foreign ministers begin in Beijing. It is the first official high-level meeting between the countries since China suspended talks in 1980 after the Soviet invasion of Afghanistan. The talks end October 21, but, as previously agreed, no official statement is released. The parties do agree to hold further meetings.

October 8. *Solidarity Banned.* The Polish Parliament votes to ban Solidarity and all other existing Polish labor organizations. President Reagan responds by announcing October 9 that he plans to end Poland's most-favored-nation trading status.

November 8. *Pope to Visit Poland.* Polish authorities announce that Pope John Paul II will visit Poland in June 1983. The trip previously had been scheduled for August 26, 1982, but was canceled by Polish leaders, who claimed a papal visit could disrupt national stability.

November 10. *Brezhnev Dies.* Soviet president and Communist party general secretary Leonid I. Brezhnev dies of a heart attack at age seventy-five. His death is not announced in the Soviet media until the following day. A four-day period of mourning is declared.

November 11. *Walesa Freed.* The Polish government announces the imminent release of Lech Walesa, leader of the banned Solidarity labor union. A government spokesman says Walesa would be free to "do whatever he wants." Walesa had been interned under martial law since December 1981. He arrives home in Gdansk November 14, where he says his future conduct "will be courageous but also prudent."

November 12. *Andropov Named General Secretary.* The Central Committee unanimously elects Yuri V. Andropov to succeed Leonid Brezhnev as general secretary. Andropov, a Politburo member and Central Committee secretary, is nominated by Brezhnev associate Konstantin Chernenko, himself considered a candidate for the top post. Andropov does not immediately assume the titular position of president, which Brezhnev also held.

November 13. *Reagan Lifts Pipeline Sanctions.* President Reagan ends sanctions designed to prevent U.S. and foreign companies from selling equipment to the Soviet Union for use in the construction of the European-Siberian natural gas pipeline. The sanctions (imposed December 1981 and widened June 1982) had caused considerable friction between the United States and its European allies. Reagan maintains the sanctions are no longer necessary because of the allies' new agreement concerning economic strategy toward the Soviet Union "that provides for stronger and more effective measures." However, French president François Mitterrand November 15 asserts France has not been a party to any such agreement.

November 15. *Brezhnev's Funeral.* Leonid Brezhnev is buried between the Lenin Mausoleum and the Kremlin wall following a nationally televised ceremony attended by many foreign dignitaries. Yuri Andropov delivers the first eulogy. After the funeral Andropov briefly meets with Vice President George Bush, the leader of the U.S. delegation. Bush describes the talks as "frank, cordial, and substantive." Andropov also meets with other world leaders in Moscow for Brezhnev's funeral, including Indian prime minister Indira Gandhi, Pakistani leader Zia ul-Haq, Cuban president Fidel Castro, and Afghan leader Babrak Karmal.

November 16. *Gromyko-Huang Discussions.* Soviet foreign minister Gromyko meets with Chinese foreign minister Huang Hua, who had attended Brezhnev's funeral the day before. It is the first time the countries' foreign ministers have met since the 1960s.

November 22. *Andropov Speech.* Yuri Andropov delivers his first policy speech as general secretary to the Central Committee. Andropov advocates more independence for manufacturing and agricultural enterprises and incentives to make workers more productive. He also expresses his support for détente with the West and improved relations with China.

December 6. *Ustinov on MX Deployment.* Soviet defense minister Dmitri Ustinov states the USSR will counter the MX missile with a new missile of its own, if the MX is deployed. On November 22 President Reagan had announced his support for an MX missile system deployed in a "dense pack" basing mode.

December 17. *Chebrikov to Head KGB.* Vitalii Fedorchuk moves from his post as head of the KGB to become minister of internal affairs. Fedorchuk replaces Nikolai Shchelokov, a Brezhnev ally who is demoted. Viktor Chebrikov replaces Fedorchuk as KGB head.

December 21. *Andropov Missile Proposal.* General Secretary Andropov proposes a reduction in the number of Soviet intermediate-range missiles targeted on Europe to 162, if NATO cancels its planned Pershing II and cruise missile deployments. The proposed figure is equal to the number of missiles deployed by Great Britain and France, which, along with the United States, immediately reject the offer.

1983

January 12. *Podgornyi Dies.* Nikolai Podgornyi, Soviet president from 1965 until 1977, dies in Moscow at the age of seventy-nine. Podgornyi had been retired since 1979.

January 17. *Soviet Missiles in Syria.* American intelligence officials report that Moscow has provided new surface-to-air missiles to Syria. The long-range SA-5 missiles are expected to significantly improve Syria's air defense capabilities, which were devastated by Israeli warplanes in June 1982.

February 23. *Andropov Urges Economic Reforms.* In an article in the party journal *Kommunist*, General Secretary Andropov says he plans to introduce wage incentives in an effort to increase productivity. He also advocates expanding the limits of local initiative.

March 6. *Kohl Wins Elections.* Chancellor Helmut Kohl and his Christian Democratic party are reelected in West Germany's national parliamentary elections. Their success is regarded as a victory for NATO's current "dual-track" approach to nuclear arms that advocates the deployment of Pershing II and cruise missiles in Europe if an arms control agreement is not reached with the USSR. Kohl supported the dual-track strategy, while his opponent, Social Democrat Hans-Jochen Vogel, criticized it.

March 8. *Reagan's "Evil Empire" Speech.* In a speech to a convention of Protestant evangelicals in Orlando, Florida, President Reagan denounces a nuclear freeze and urges the audience not to "ignore the facts of history and the aggressive impulses of an evil empire [the

Soviet Union]." Reagan also calls Soviet Communism "the focus of evil in the modern world." Tass comments March 9 that the speech shows the Reagan administration "can think only in terms of confrontation and bellicose, lunatic anticommunism."

March 23. *Reagan Calls for ABM Development.* In a nationally televised speech President Reagan warns of the Soviet military buildup and defends his record $280.5 billion defense budget request. He then calls on American scientists to develop an advanced antiballistic missile (ABM) defense system that would render nuclear ballistic missiles "impotent and obsolete." Reagan's speech leads to the establishment of the Strategic Defense Initiative (SDI), a long-term research and development program focusing on space-based ABM weapons. General Secretary Andropov claims March 26 that Reagan's ABM development plans threaten to fuel the arms race.

May 3. *Andropov Offers to Limit Warheads.* General Secretary Andropov proposes limiting the warheads, missiles, and bombers of the Warsaw Pact and NATO (including French and British forces) to equitable levels. American officials welcome the Soviets' new willingness to discuss limitations on warheads but object to Andropov's continued inclusion of French and British nuclear weapons as part of NATO's nuclear arsenal.

May 4. *Iran Disbands Communist Party.* The government of Iran bans the Iranian Communist Tudeh party after the party's head confesses to espionage and treason charges. The government also says Soviet embassy personnel interfered in Iran "by using and establishing links with mercenaries and traitors to the republic" and expels eighteen Soviet diplomats.

May 9. *Andropov Heads Defense Council.* Defense Minister Dmitri Ustinov discloses in a *Pravda* article that General Secretary Andropov functions as the chairman of the Defense Council.

May 16-23. *Gorbachev Visits Canada.* Politburo member and Central Committee secretary Mikhail Gorbachev travels across Canada as leader of a Soviet agricultural delegation. He meets with Prime Minister Pierre Trudeau in Ottawa May 18.

June 9. *British Conservatives Reelected.* The Conservative party, headed by Prime Minister Margaret Thatcher, is decisively returned to power in Great Britain's national parliamentary elections. The Conservative victory ensures that NATO's scheduled deployments of cruise missiles in Great Britain will occur.

June 16. *Andropov Elected President.* The Supreme Soviet formally elects General Secretary Andropov as president (chairman of the Presidium of the Supreme Soviet). Andropov becomes the only Soviet leader other than Leonid Brezhnev to be president and general secretary simultaneously.

June 16-23. *Pope Visits Poland.* Pope John Paul II travels to his native Poland for a visit that had been postponed by Polish leaders in 1982. In a brief televised speech the pope calls for social reform based on the August 1980 agreements that brought about the Solidarity union. The same day he meets for two hours with Wojciech Jaruzelski, the leader of the Polish regime. In subsequent speeches to huge crowds, the pope continues to emphasize Polish nationalism and social reform. He holds a private audience with Solidarity leader Lech Walesa June 23 before leaving for Rome.

June 26. *Pentecostals to Emigrate.* Seven Soviet Pentecostals who had been living in the U.S. embassy in Moscow since 1978 are granted permission to emigrate by Soviet authorities.

July 4-7. *Kohl Visits Soviet Union.* West German chancellor Helmut Kohl meets President Andropov in Moscow. Andropov reportedly tells Kohl that deployment of NATO missiles in West Germany would harm Soviet-West German relations. Kohl stops in Kiev July 7 before returning to Bonn.

July 21. *Poland Ends Martial Law.* Martial law is formally lifted in Poland after nineteen months. The government also extends amnesty to many political prisoners. However, the Polish Parliament enacts a series of laws that permits the government to tightly control Poland's economy and social programs.

July 26. *Experimental Economic Reforms.* The Soviet Union announces economic "experiments" designed to relax central bureaucratic controls. The plan gives factory managers in selected industries greater autonomy over budgets, investment, wages, and incentive bonuses. It is scheduled to begin January 1, 1984. President Andropov had publicly supported such reforms on several occasions.

August 18. *Andropov on ASAT Weapons.* At a Kremlin meeting with nine visiting U.S. Democratic senators, President Andropov declares a unilateral moratorium on the deployment of Soviet antisatellite (ASAT) weapons. He also asks the United States to agree to a treaty "on the elimination of the existing antisatellite systems and the prohibition of the development of new ones."

August 25. *U.S.-Soviet Grain Deal.* A five-year grain sale agreement is signed in Moscow by representatives of the United States and USSR. The pact obligates the Soviet Union to buy nine million tons of American grain during each of the next five years. The Soviets have the option to buy an additional three million tons annually without obtaining further U.S. government approval.

September 1. *Soviets Down Korean Airliner.* A Soviet warplane shoots down Korean Air Lines flight 007 over the Sea of Japan near Sakhalin Island. The Boeing 747, with 269 people on board, had strayed into Soviet airspace for unknown reasons. The Soviets do not admit until September 6 that they shot down the plane. Moscow claims the jetliner was spying for the United States and did not respond to warnings. Chief of the Soviet General Staff Marshal Nikolai Ogarkov tells foreign reporters September 9 that the order to shoot down the plane was "not an accident or an error." Many nations condemn the attack and temporarily restrict civil aviation with the USSR in protest. The Reagan administration suspends a U.S.-Soviet transportation agreement and talks on opening a U.S. consulate in Kiev.

September 15. *Soviet UN Delegation Blocked.* In response to the Soviet destruction of a Korean airliner, the governors of New Jersey and New York refuse to allow the Soviet delegation to the United Nations to land at New York area commercial airports. The governors also question whether they can ensure the Soviet delegation's security. The Reagan administration offers the Soviets the option of landing at a U.S. military airfield. Foreign Minister Gromyko cancels the Soviet visit September 17 and attacks the United States for failing to meet its host-country obligations.

September 26. *Reagan's UN Speech.* In a speech to the UN General Assembly, President Reagan calls on the USSR to accept global limits on intermediate-range missiles and offers to discuss limits on aircraft and a reduction in U.S. Pershing II deployments. Despite Reagan's tone of compromise concerning intermediate-range nuclear force talks, he attacks the USSR for human rights and arms control violations. President Andropov denounces Reagan's UN speech September 28 in a strongly worded Tass statement. He calls Reagan's arms control proposals "mere declarations" and accuses the United States of following "a militant course." Andropov also defends the downing of the Korean airliner and repeats Soviet accusations that the plane was on a spy mission.

October 5. *Walesa Awarded Peace Prize.* The head of the outlawed Polish Solidarity union, Lech Walesa, is awarded the Nobel Peace Prize. Walesa announces he will donate the prize money to a charity for Poland's farmers. The Polish government denounces the prize October 6. *Izvestiia,* the Soviet government newspaper, calls Walesa a "low-grade hustler" October 8 but does not mention his Nobel Peace Prize.

October 21. *Sino-Soviet Trade Agreement.* The Soviets and Chinese conclude an agreement to increase annual trade from $800 million to more than $1.6 billion. They also agree to increase cultural, sports, and student exchanges.

October 23. *Antinuclear Rallies.* Demonstrations in European cities against NATO's upcoming missile deployments collectively draw more than two million protesters.

October 25. *Grenada Invasion.* U.S. troops aided by forces from six Caribbean nations invade Grenada, an independently governed island near Venezuela. President Reagan says the United States was acting in response to a "formal request" by the Organization of Eastern Caribbean States to help restore order in Grenada. Reagan also cites concern for the safety of American citizens on the island. American troops overcome resistance by local militias and well-armed Cuban "construction workers." The pro-Cuban, hard-line Marxist regime is deposed. The United States declares an end to the fighting November 2. Many nations, including close U.S. allies, criticize the invasion. The Soviet Union condemns it as "direct, unprovoked aggression."

October 26. *Soviet INF Concessions.* In a *Pravda* interview Andropov announces that the USSR is willing to reduce the number of SS-20s aimed at Europe to "about 140" and to be more flexible in negotiating limits on medium-range bombers if NATO cancels its upcoming missile deployments. The Soviets previously had offered to reduce their SS-20 force to 162. Andropov also warns that the Soviets will leave the INF negotiations in Geneva if NATO begins deploying missiles. The State Department rejects Andropov's concessions as "vague" and says they were intended to influence Western European public opinion.

November 7. *Andropov Misses Parade.* President Andropov, who has not been seen in public since August 18, fails to appear at the annual parade in Moscow commemorating the Bolshevik Revolution. Kremlin spokesmen maintain Andropov has a "bad cold," but many Western analysts contend he would have attended the ceremonies were he not seriously ill.

November 14. *Missiles Arrive in Great Britain.* The first sixteen cruise missiles scheduled for deployment arrive at Greenham Common Air Base in England.

November 22. *West Germany Accepts NATO Missiles.* Following a stormy two-day debate, the West German Bundestag (Parliament) votes 286-226 to allow NATO missiles to be deployed in West Germany. The first nine Pershing II missiles arrive in the country the next day.

November 23. *Soviets Leave Talks.* At a brief, final meeting, Yuli Kvitsinskii, head of the Soviet delegation,

announces that the USSR is withdrawing indefinitely from the INF negotiations in Geneva to protest NATO's missile deployments. Kvitsinskii's American counterpart, Paul Nitze, says "the U.S. is prepared to continue the negotiations at any time."

November 24. *Soviet Countermeasures.* Andropov issues a statement condemning NATO missile deployments and announcing probable Soviet countermeasures. He says the USSR will end its moratorium on additional SS-20 missile deployments in Europe, accelerate the timetable for introducing new tactical nuclear missiles into Czechoslovakia and East Germany, and deploy submarines equipped with cruise missiles or depressed-trajectory ballistic missiles closer to U.S. shores.

December 7. *Wu on Sino-Soviet Talks.* Chinese Foreign Minister Wu Xueqian states that Sino-Soviet talks on normalizing relations are making no progress because of the Soviets' refusal to discuss their presence in Afghanistan, their support of Vietnam's aggression in Kampuchea, and their military maneuvers on the Chinese border.

December 8. *START Talks End.* The Soviet delegation to the START negotiations in Geneva refuses to set a date for further talks. The Soviets say they must reexamine their positions in the wake of NATO's intermediate-range missile deployments. The Warsaw Pact also refuses to set a date for resumption of the Mutual and Balanced Force Reduction (MBFR) talks before these negotiations adjourn in Vienna December 15.

December 26. *Kremlin Leadership Changes.* A Central Committee plenum approves promotions of candidate Politburo members Vitalii Vorotnikov and Mikhail Solomentsev to full membership. Although Andropov does not attend the plenum and has not been seen in public since August, many Western observers regard the promotions as evidence that Andropov is still in control. The plenum also approves the appointments of Yegor Ligachev to the Central Committee Secretariat and KGB head Viktor Chebrikov to candidate member status on the Politburo.

1984

January 10. *Chemical Weapons Talks Proposed.* The USSR proposes that NATO and the Warsaw Pact hold negotiations on banning chemical weapons in Europe. Western officials welcome the offer but express doubts that Moscow would agree to adequate verification measures.

January 12. *Negotiators Trade Accusations.* In a *New York Times* article, Yuli Kvitsinskii, chief Soviet negotiator at the INF talks, blames the United States and Paul Nitze, chief U.S. negotiator, for the failure of the talks. Nitze in a January 19 *New York Times* article disputes Kvitsinskii's version of events, including the "walk-in-the-woods" negotiating session of July 1982. Nitze says for Kvitsinskii "the truth or falsity of any statement is only of secondary interest."

January 16. *Reagan on East-West Relations.* President Reagan calls for a resumption of arms negotiations in an address notable for its conciliatory tone. He says the principles of "realism, strength, and dialogue" should determine U.S. policy toward the Soviet Union.

January 17. *Stockholm Conference Opens.* The thirty-five-nation Conference on Confidence and Security-Building Measures and Disarmament in Europe opens in Stockholm. Secretary of State George P. Shultz proposes a six-point NATO plan to reduce the chances of military confrontation. He attacks the Soviet Union's human rights record and its imposition of "an artificial barrier" dividing Europe. In a harshly worded speech January 18, Foreign Minister Gromyko says "the aggressive foreign policy of the United States is the main threat to peace." Shultz and Gromyko meet the same day, but Shultz says January 19 that they made no progress toward resumption of arms control talks.

January 22. *MBFR Talks to Resume.* Secretary of State Shultz announces that the United States has accepted a Soviet proposal to reopen the Mutual and Balanced Force Reduction (MBFR) talks in Vienna March 16.

January 23. *Soviet Arms Violations.* President Reagan sends a classified report to Congress describing alleged Soviet arms control violations. The infractions described in an unclassified synopsis include Soviet use of chemical weapons in Afghanistan; construction of an illegally positioned phased-array radar near Krasnoyarsk, Siberia; and development of a second new ICBM prohibited by the unratified SALT II treaty. A January 29 Soviet statement dismisses the accusations and charges the United States with violations of its own.

January 24. *Andropov on East-West Relations.* In a *Pravda* interview carried in advance by Tass, President Andropov responds to President Reagan's January 16 speech. Andropov criticizes Reagan for insisting on negotiating from a position of strength instead of on "an equal footing." Andropov calls on the United States to take "concrete steps" to improve relations. The interview's tone, however, is moderate compared with recent anti-American rhetoric. Western speculation is that the interview was actually a Politburo policy statement issued in the name of Andropov, who is rumored to be seriously ill.

February 9. *Andropov Dies.* Soviet leader Yuri V. Andropov dies at age sixty-nine in Moscow of complications caused by acute kidney problems. A bulletin issued February 10 announces Andropov's death and states that he had been receiving kidney dialysis therapy for the last year. Since August 18, 1983, when Andropov was last seen in public, Soviet officials had insisted that he was not ill.

February 13. *Chernenko Chosen General Secretary.* Konstantin U. Chernenko, a close ally of Leonid Brezhnev, is unanimously elected general secretary by the Communist Party Central Committee. The seventy-two-year-old Chernenko is the oldest man to become general secretary. Chernenko tells the Central Committee that recent economic reforms should continue. He also calls for "peaceful coexistence of states with different social systems" but warns the West against trying to upset the current military balance. No successor is named to fill the post of president, which Andropov also occupied.

February 14. *Andropov's Funeral.* Yuri Andropov is buried behind the Lenin Mausoleum following a televised ceremony in Red Square. General Secretary Chernenko, Defense Minister Ustinov, and Foreign Minister Gromyko deliver eulogies. Numerous foreign leaders attend the funeral, including Vice President George Bush, who meets with Chernenko for thirty minutes.

February 23. *Chernenko Heads Defense Council.* Western military attachés say Marshal Nikolai Ogarkov, chief of the Soviet general staff, referred to General Secre-

tary Chernenko as head of the Defense Council at a Soviet Armed Forces Day reception. Andropov also led the small body, which is believed to direct defense policy.

March 2. *Chernenko Address.* Prior to the upcoming Supreme Soviet elections, Chernenko delivers his first policy address as general secretary. He endorses Andropov's economic and anticorruption programs, expresses Soviet desires to normalize relations with China, and calls for improved East-West relations backed up by new arms control agreements. However, Chernenko seemed to indicate that intermediate-range nuclear force and strategic arms reduction talks would not resume unless NATO reversed its decision to deploy intermediate-range missiles.

March 21. *Collision at Sea.* While surfacing in the Sea of Japan, a Soviet nuclear-powered submarine strikes the U.S. aircraft carrier *Kitty Hawk.* The submarine had been routinely trailing the carrier. The Defense Department accuses the submarine of violating several international navigation laws.

April 11. *Chernenko Elected President.* The Supreme Soviet names Chernenko president (chairman of the Presidium of the Supreme Soviet). The titular post had been vacant since Andropov's death. Politburo member Mikhail Gorbachev formally nominates Chernenko.

April 26-May 1. *Reagan Visits China.* Chinese leaders cordially receive President Reagan during his six-day visit to the People's Republic of China. Several protocols are signed, including a peaceful nuclear cooperation agreement. Reagan is allowed to appear on Chinese television twice, but his implied criticism of the Soviet Union is deleted. During the visit the Soviet press attacked China for its cooperation with the United States.

May 2. *Sakharov Hunger Strike.* Soviet dissident Andrei Sakharov begins a hunger strike to pressure the government to allow his wife, Yelena Bonner, to receive medical treatment in the West. Bonner reports that Sakharov had been taken to an unknown location by authorities May 7. The Sakharovs' treatment brings widespread condemnation from the West.

May 7. *Soviets Withdraw from Olympics.* The Soviet National Olympic Committee announces that the Soviet team will not attend the summer games in Los Angeles because of "inadequate security." The statement says "chauvinistic sentiments and anti-Soviet hysteria are being whipped up" in the United States. All Soviet-bloc nations but Romania also pull out of the games.

June 21. *Naval Base Explosion.* American intelligence sources say a huge explosion occurred in mid-May at the Soviet northern fleet naval base at Severomorsk. The blast reportedly killed more than two hundred people and destroyed large stocks of ammunition and conventional missiles. The following day the Kremlin denies knowledge of the explosion.

June 29. *Space Weapons Talks Proposed.* The Soviet government sends a formal note to the United States proposing U.S.-Soviet negotiations on banning weapons in space. The United States responds the same day by offering to engage in talks on space weapons if they are linked to negotiations on limiting strategic and intermediate-range nuclear weapons. The Soviets reject the U.S. proposal July 1 but repeat their call for talks on space weapons.

July 5. *Molotov Reinstated.* Ninety-four-year-old Viacheslav Molotov is readmitted to the Soviet Communist party. Molotov, who had served as prime minister and foreign minister under Joseph Stalin, was removed from power in 1957 by Nikita Khrushchev.

July 11. *Kuwait Buys Soviet Weapons.* Kuwait announces it will buy $327 million in weapons from the Soviet Union. The sale includes surface-to-air missiles intended to protect Persian Gulf shipping from attacks related to the Iran-Iraq war. The deal follows a U.S. refusal to sell Kuwait Stinger antiaircraft missiles.

July 17. *Hot Line Improved.* Soviet and U.S. officials sign an agreement to modernize the crisis hot line between Washington and Moscow. The new hot line will transmit words three times faster than the current sixty-four-words-per-minute teleprinters.

July 21. *Poland Frees Political Prisoners.* The Polish government announces that 652 political prisoners will be released as part of a larger amnesty for criminals serving short sentences. On August 3 the United States lifts some of the sanctions imposed against Poland in 1981.

August 11. *Reagan Joke.* During a "voice check" before his regular weekly radio broadcast, President Reagan says, "My fellow Americans, I'm pleased to tell you today that I've signed legislation that will outlaw Russia forever. We begin bombing in five minutes." Although the remark is made off the record as a joke, it prompts a wave of criticism from U.S. allies and Reagan's political opponents. Moscow sharply condemns Reagan's statement as "unprecedentedly hostile toward the USSR and dangerous to the cause of peace."

August 18. *Friendship '84 Games Begin.* The Soviet Union's sports festival for nations that had pulled out of the Summer Olympics opens in Moscow.

September 4. *Honecker Visit Postponed.* East German Communist party leader Erich Honecker indefinitely postpones his scheduled visit to West Germany, which would have been the first visit to that country by an East German leader. The Soviet Union, which recently had intensified its verbal attacks against the West German government and the growing détente between the two Germanys, appeared to have pressured Honecker into the postponement.

September 6. *Ogarkov Removed.* Marshal Nikolai Ogarkov is removed as chief of the Soviet general staff and reassigned to unspecified duties. He is succeeded by Marshal Sergei Akhromeev, his deputy. Tass in announcing the move gives no reason for Ogarkov's apparent demotion.

September 21-22. *Gromyko-Wu Talks.* The foreign ministers of the Soviet Union and China, Andrei Gromyko and Wu Xueqian, meet while in New York for the opening of the UN General Assembly. The talks are described by both sides as positive.

September 24. *Reagan's UN Speech.* President Reagan omits direct criticism of the Soviet Union from his address to the UN General Assembly. He calls for an overall improvement in U.S.-Soviet relations and negotiations on arms control, regional conflicts, and the militarization of space.

September 26-28. *Gromyko Meetings.* Foreign Minister Gromyko and Secretary of State Shultz talk for three hours in New York September 26. In an address to the United Nations September 27, Gromyko attacks U.S. foreign policy and accuses the Reagan administration of deliberately undermining arms control negotiations. On September 28 Gromyko travels to Washington for a three-and-a-half-hour meeting with President Reagan. It is the first time the president has met with a Soviet leader. No concrete results are reported.

November 6. *Reagan Reelected.* Ronald Reagan overwhelmingly defeats Democratic candidate Walter Mondale to win a second term as president.

November 14. *Dobrynin on Arms Talks.* Anatolii Dobrynin, the Soviet ambassador to the United States, tells reporters his government is interested in an American proposal made months before to begin talks that would address every aspect of the nuclear arms race.

November 22. *Arms Talks Announced.* The Soviet Union and the United States announce that Secretary of State Shultz and Foreign Minister Gromyko will meet in Geneva January 7-8, 1985, to lay the groundwork for future arms control negotiations.

December 15-21. *Gorbachev in Great Britain.* Politburo member Mikhail Gorbachev and his wife, Raisa, make a highly publicized trip to Great Britain. Gorbachev meets with Prime Minister Margaret Thatcher, who says December 17, "I like Mr. Gorbachev—we can do business together." Gorbachev criticizes the Reagan administration's Strategic Defense Initiative (SDI)—an effort to develop a space-based antiballistic missile system—but speaks positively about the prospects for arms control. He returns to Moscow December 21, a day earlier than planned, after personally announcing to the West that Defense Minister Dmitri Ustinov had died.

December 20. *Ustinov Dies.* Soviet defense minister and Politburo member Dmitri Ustinov dies at age seventy-six. Many Western observers expected Ustinov to be succeeded by Politburo member and Central Committee secretary Grigori Romanov, but Marshal Sergei Sokolov is appointed defense minister. President Chernenko is absent from Ustinov's December 24 funeral.

December 21-29. *Arkhipov in Beijing.* First Deputy Premier Ivan Arkhipov travels to Beijing for an official visit that had been postponed since May. Arkhipov and Chinese leaders sign accords on economic, scientific, and technological cooperation. They also agree to begin talks on a trade pact covering the period from 1986 to 1990. China calls the accords "the most substantial agreements since relations between our two countries were strained in the 1960s."

December 27. *Chernenko Appears.* President Chernenko, who had missed Dmitri Ustinov's funeral and was believed to be ill, awards several Soviet authors medals for literature. The Soviet media give the ceremony unusually prominent coverage.

1985

January 7-8. *Gromyko and Shultz in Geneva.* Foreign Minister Gromyko and Secretary of State Shultz meet in Geneva to discuss the resumption of arms control negotiations. They agree to hold umbrella talks divided into three subgroups: strategic nuclear weapons, intermediate-range nuclear weapons, and weapons in space. The date and site are to be determined later.

January 13. *Gromyko Interview.* In a Soviet television interview, Foreign Minister Gromyko asserts that the Strategic Defense Initiative could be used to "blackmail and pressure" the Soviet Union. He says that without movement toward preventing the militarization of space no progress can be made on limiting strategic weapons.

January 24. *Soviet Economic Statistics.* The Soviet

government reports that the economy grew by 2.6 percent in 1984. Although the West considers Soviet economic statistics to be inflated, the announcement is viewed as significant since the increase is the lowest reported since World War II. The Soviets indicate that the poor performance of the agricultural sector held down overall growth.

January 26. *Arms Talks Set.* The Soviet Union and the United States announce that arms negotiations will begin March 12 in Geneva. The Soviet Foreign Ministry also says Viktor Karpov, Yuli Kvitsinskii, and Aleksei Obukhov will be the chief Soviet negotiators. The United States had announced its negotiators—Max Kampelman, John Tower, and Maynard Glitman—January 18. Karpov and Kampelman will lead the delegations.

February 11-14. *Papandreou in Moscow.* Greek premier Andreas Papandreou is warmly received during a four-day visit to the Soviet Union. He and Soviet leaders sign several economic accords. Papandreou's scheduled February 12 meeting with President Chernenko is canceled, fueling speculation that Chernenko is ill.

February 20. *Thatcher Endorses SDI.* During a three-day visit to the United States, Prime Minister Margaret Thatcher of Great Britain endorses President Reagan's SDI in a speech before a joint session of Congress. Her support is preceded by West German chancellor Helmut Kohl's qualified endorsement February 9.

February 21. *Soviets Allow Inspections.* The USSR signs a nuclear safeguards accord with the International Atomic Energy Agency, which provides for the opening of some Soviet civilian nuclear power plants to international inspection. Western officials praise Moscow's action.

February 24. *Chernenko Appears.* A frail President Chernenko, supported by an aide, appears briefly before television cameras to cast a ballot at a Moscow polling place. It is the first time Chernenko has been seen in public in more than eight weeks. Meanwhile, Politburo member Mikhail Gorbachev arrives at another polling place accompanied by his family. He jokes with reporters in front of Western cameras.

February 25-March 1. *Gromyko Trip.* Foreign Minister Gromyko repeatedly attacks SDI during state visits to Italy and Spain. In Rome February 27, Gromyko holds his first meeting with Pope John Paul II since 1979.

March 7-10. *Shcherbitskii in United States.* Politburo member and Ukrainian Communist party leader Vladimir Shcherbitskii visits the United States as head of a parliamentary delegation. Shcherbitskii is the first Soviet Politburo member other than Foreign Minister Gromyko to visit the United States since 1973. Shcherbitskii returns early to the USSR March 10, apparently after receiving word of Chernenko's death.

March 10. *Chernenko Dies.* President Konstantin U. Chernenko dies in Moscow of heart failure at age seventy-three. He had been weakened by a variety of ailments including emphysema, hepatitis, and cirrhosis of the liver. His death is not announced until March 11.

March 11. *Gorbachev Chosen General Secretary.* The Central Committee elects fifty-four-year-old Mikhail S. Gorbachev to replace Konstantin Chernenko as general secretary of the Communist party within hours of the announcement of Chernenko's death. Western observers regard the unusual speed of the succession as evidence that Soviet leaders had agreed to Gorbachev's selection before Chernenko died. In his acceptance speech, Gorbachev promises to continue the policies of the two previous general secretaries, Chernenko and Andropov, and says economic improvement is his most important goal.

March 12. *Arms Talks Begin.* Despite Chernenko's death, the Geneva arms negotiations begin on schedule. Chief Soviet negotiator Viktor Karpov tells reporters that General Secretary Gorbachev "presided over the Politburo meeting that approved the instructions" for the Soviet negotiating team. Both sides agree to keep the substance of their talks confidential.

March 13. *Chernenko's Funeral.* Konstantin Chernenko is buried near the Kremlin wall following a Red Square ceremony. General Secretary Gorbachev eulogizes Chernenko as a "steadfast fighter for noble communist ideals." Against the advice of several aides, President Reagan does not go to Moscow but instead sends Vice President Bush. However, Reagan does invite Gorbachev to the United States in a letter presented to him by Bush. Gorbachev also meets with many other foreign dignitaries, including Chinese vice premier Li Peng.

March 20. *Belgium Accepts Missiles.* The Belgian Parliament approves the deployment of NATO cruise missiles in Belgium by a 116-93 vote.

March 24. *American Officer Killed.* U.S. Army Maj. Arthur Nicholson, Jr., is shot by a Soviet guard while observing a Soviet military installation in East Germany. Soviet officials claim Nicholson was in a restricted area and failed to heed a warning shot. The United States says he was conducting routine, sanctioned observations in a nonrestricted area in accordance with a 1947 agreement allowing such observations. President Reagan condemns the shooting as an "unwarranted act of violence."

March 28. *MX Funds Appropriated.* Following an intense White House lobbying effort, the House of Representatives appropriates $1.5 billion for the production of twenty-one MX missiles by a 217-210 vote. The Senate had approved the funding earlier in the month, 55-45. The administration had argued that the Soviet Union would be unlikely to agree to equitable arms cuts if Congress did not support the MX.

April 7. *Soviet Missile Moratorium.* General Secretary Gorbachev announces Moscow has suspended deployment of intermediate-range missiles in Europe until November and asks NATO to halt its missile deployments. Gorbachev also states he is agreeable to a summit with President Reagan in the near future. The Reagan administration says that Gorbachev's freeze would not affect the scheduled deployments.

April 23. *Politburo Promotions.* Central Committee secretaries Nikolai Ryzhkov and Yegor Ligachev are promoted to full Politburo status along with KGB head Viktor Chebrikov. The Ryzhkov and Ligachev promotions represent dramatic advancements, since they bypassed the traditional step of candidate Politburo membership. Defense Minister Sergei Sokolov is elevated to candidate Politburo status. Viktor Nikonov is named to the Central Committee Secretariat with responsibility for agriculture.

April 25-26. *Warsaw Pact Summit.* Leaders of the seven Warsaw Pact nations meet in Warsaw and approve a twenty-year extension of the treaty April 26. Gorbachev attends the summit, making his first foreign trip since becoming general secretary. He stays in Warsaw April 27 for talks with Polish leader Wojciech Jaruzelski.

April 28-29. *Ortega in Moscow.* Nicaraguan president Daniel Ortega visits Moscow to discuss Soviet economic assistance. He meets with General Secretary Gorbachev April 29. Although no specific aid is announced, Tass quotes Gorbachev as having promised to continue economic, political, and diplomatic support of Nicaragua.

May 1. *U.S. Embargo.* President Reagan places an embargo on trade with Nicaragua and bans Nicaraguan shipping and air traffic from the United States. In a letter to Congress he says the growing Nicaraguan threat to Central American and U.S. security prompted his action.

May 1. *Reagan in Europe.* President Reagan arrives in Europe for a ten-day visit that includes an economic summit in Bonn May 2-4 and a controversial May 5 stop at a military cemetery in Bitburg, West Germany, where a number of Nazi SS troops are buried. General Secretary Gorbachev and Reagan deliver speeches May 8, the fortieth anniversary of the surrender of Nazi Germany. In Moscow, Gorbachev condemns U.S. "state terrorism" against Nicaragua and aid to Afghan rebels. He also criticizes Reagan's visit to Bitburg Cemetery, saying there were political figures at the recent Western summit who were "ready to forget or even justify the SS cutthroats and, moreover, pay homage to them." Despite the attacks, Gorbachev calls for a return to détente. Reagan, speaking before the European Parliament in Strasbourg, France, accuses the Soviets of "undermining stability and the basis for nuclear deterrence" by proceeding with plans to deploy a new mobile intercontinental ballistic missile.

May 16. *Anti-alcoholism Program.* The Soviet government announces new measures designed to combat drunkenness and alcoholism. Beginning June 1 the legal drinking age will be raised from eighteen to twenty-one, liquor store hours will be shortened, and alcohol production will be gradually reduced.

May 20. *Walker Arrested.* The FBI arrests John Walker, Jr., a retired U.S. Navy warrant officer, on charges of selling military secrets to the Soviet Union. The case widens during the following two weeks as three other people, including Walker's son and brother, are arrested for spying.

May 22. *Indo-Soviet Economic Pacts.* Prime Minister Rajiv Gandhi of India and General Secretary Gorbachev sign an agreement that provides for $1.2 billion in Soviet credits for construction of industrial and energy projects in India. They also agree to a new fifteen-year economic and technological cooperation agreement.

June 10. *United States to Abide by SALT II.* President Reagan says that the United States will stay within restrictions established by the unratified SALT II treaty. He says that when the next Trident submarine is deployed the Navy will dismantle an older Poseidon submarine to stay within the treaty's 1,200 multiple warhead missile limit.

June 11. *Gorbachev Calls for Reforms.* Speaking before top Soviet officials, General Secretary Gorbachev criticizes the draft of the 1986-1990 five-year plan and several government ministers. He calls for increased production of quality consumer goods, enhancement of the role of local factory managers, curtailment of central planning in day-to-day factory affairs, and greater emphasis on market forces.

July 1-2. *Soviet Leadership Shuffle.* The Central Committee announces that Grigorii Romanov, who had been a rival to Gorbachev for the general secretary post, has resigned from the Politburo for health reasons. Western analysts generally agree Romanov was ousted. The Central Committee also promotes Georgian Communist party leader Eduard Shevardnadze to full Politburo status. On July 2 Shevardnadze is named foreign minister, replacing Andrei Gromyko, who is elected to the vacant ceremonial office of president (chairman of the Presidium of the Supreme Soviet).

July 2. *Summit Announced.* American officials say the Soviets have agreed to a summit conference between President Reagan and General Secretary Gorbachev in Geneva November 19-20.

July 10. *Sino-Soviet Trade Pact.* Chinese and Soviet representatives sign an agreement that will sharply increase bilateral trade to $14 billion over the five-year period from 1986 to 1990. Annual trade between the countries is expected to rise to $3.5 billion by 1990, compared with a projected $1.8 billion in 1985.

July 17. *Ogarkov Reappointed.* Reports emerge that Nikolai Ogarkov, who was removed as military chief of staff in September 1984, has been appointed commander in chief of Warsaw Pact forces.

July 29. *Nuclear Test Proposals.* General Secretary Gorbachev declares a unilateral Soviet moratorium on nuclear tests to begin August 6. The moratorium is to continue until the end of the year and will be indefinitely extended if the United States also stops its nuclear tests. U.S. officials quickly reject the proposal, citing a recent spurt of Soviet testing. President Reagan instead invites Soviet experts to observe a U.S. nuclear test explosion. The Soviets decline but say they will proceed with their unilateral moratorium.

July 30-August 1. *Helsinki Accords Anniversary.* The representatives of thirty-five nations meet in Helsinki to mark the tenth anniversary of the Helsinki accords. In speeches July 30, Secretary of State Shultz criticizes the Soviet Union's human rights record, while Foreign Minister Shevardnadze asserts that the USSR, unlike Western countries, protects its people from poverty, unemployment, and discrimination. The two leaders meet July 31 to discuss the upcoming Reagan-Gorbachev summit.

August 21. *Tracking Dust Allegation.* The United States accuses the Soviet Union of using a chemical dust thought to be carcinogenic to track American diplomats in Moscow. The Soviets deny the allegation as "absurd" August 22.

August 26. *Gorbachev Interview.* In an interview published in *Time* magazine September 9, General Secretary Gorbachev says he regrets that U.S.-Soviet relations are not improving. He criticizes the Reagan administration for downplaying the upcoming summit and portraying Moscow's arms control proposals as propaganda.

September 10. *Gorbachev on Chemical Arms.* General Secretary Gorbachev proposes establishing a chemical weapons-free zone in central Europe. The Reagan administration immediately rejects the proposal, saying it wants a "comprehensive verifiable ban" on chemical weapons.

September 12. *Defection Prompts Expulsions.* Great Britain announces that the top KGB agent in Britain, Oleg Gordievskii, has defected. He had been a political counselor at the Soviet embassy in London. Great Britain expels twenty-five Soviets, including diplomats, journalists, and trade representatives, whom Gordievskii is said to have named as spies. The Soviet Union retaliates by expelling twenty-five British citizens September 14. London expels six additional Soviets September 16; Moscow responds by expelling six Britons September 18.

September 13. *ASAT Test.* An American F-15 fighter plane launches an antisatellite weapon that destroys a U.S. satellite orbiting 290 miles above Earth. The missile test had been announced August 20. On September 4 Tass had warned that if the test took place the Soviet

Union would "consider itself free of its unilateral commitment" not to deploy ASATs in space.

September 17. *Reagan on SDI.* President Reagan says in a press conference that he would not negotiate limits on the development and testing of SDI to achieve an arms control agreement with the Soviets.

September 23-24. *UN Speeches.* Secretary of State Shultz and Foreign Minister Shevardnadze speak on arms control at the opening of the UN General Assembly. Shultz accuses the USSR September 23 of pursuing "the world's most active military space program," while simultaneously objecting to U.S. research on space weapons. On September 24 Shevardnadze portrays SDI as a U.S. attempt to gain military superiority and says the USSR is ready to negotiate an arms control agreement that would bring "truly radical reductions" in nuclear arms. After his UN visit Shevardnadze meets with President Reagan in Washington September 27 and delivers a new Soviet arms control proposal.

September 26. *KGB Agent Defects.* U.S. officials confirm that Vitalii Yurchenko, a high-ranking KGB agent, has defected. Yurchenko, a counselor with the Soviet Foreign Ministry in Rome, had been taken to Washington for debriefing following his defection. He reportedly provided information about Soviet double agents.

September 27. *Ryzhkov Replaces Tikhonov.* Nikolai Tikhonov retires as premier, citing health reasons. He is succeeded by Nikolai Ryzhkov, who had been appointed to the Politburo in April. Ryzhkov resigns October 15 from his post as a Central Committee secretary.

September 30. *Soviet Arms Proposal.* The Soviets formally present a plan at the Geneva arms control talks to substantially cut the nuclear arsenals of both superpowers. Foreign Minister Shevardnadze had outlined the offer during his September 27 meeting with President Reagan. The plan's main feature is a 50 percent reduction in the strategic weapons of both sides. Reagan said September 28 that he welcomed the Soviet offer and hoped it would provide a basis for discussion. However, senior U.S. administration officials express dissatisfaction with many aspects of the plan.

September 30. *Soviets Kidnapped.* In two coordinated incidents four Soviet diplomats are kidnapped in West Beirut. The Islamic Liberation Organization (ILO) issues photographs of the Soviet hostages October 1 and threatens to kill them unless the USSR pressures Syria to halt an offensive by Syrian-backed leftist militias against Moslem fundamentalists in Tripoli, Lebanon. One of the hostages is found dead October 2. The Soviet Union evacuates families and nonessential personnel from its West Beirut embassy October 4. In response to Soviet requests for help in resolving the crisis, Syria negotiates a truce between the warring factions in Tripoli. Syrian troops enter the city October 6 to enforce a cease-fire. The ILO releases the remaining three Soviet hostages unharmed October 30.

October 2-5. *Gorbachev in France.* Gorbachev travels to France for his first visit to the West since becoming general secretary. He proposes October 3 that France and Great Britain join the Soviet Union in talks on nuclear weapons in Europe, separate from the Geneva negotiations. France and Great Britain decline the invitation October 4. Gorbachev says his discussions with President François Mitterand were "fruitful and constructive." Western observers point out, however, that the visit did not produce a joint Soviet-French communiqué denouncing SDI, as Gorbachev may have hoped.

October 15. *Gorbachev Presents Programs.* General Secretary Gorbachev presents drafts of new economic and political programs to the Central Committee. The economic program calls for a 150 percent increase in labor productivity and 100 percent increases in national income and industrial output by the year 2000.

October 22. *Weinberger on Soviet Missile.* Defense Secretary Caspar W. Weinberger says the Soviet Union has begun deploying the SS-25, a new mobile ICBM. He claims its deployment violates the SALT II treaty because the Soviets also have tested the new SS-24 ICBM. The treaty allows each side to develop only one new type of ICBM. Moscow maintains the new missiles are merely permissible modifications of older missile types.

October 24. *Reagan, Shevardnadze Speak.* At the United Nations' fortieth anniversary celebration, President Reagan calls for a "fresh start" in U.S.-Soviet relations and asks the Soviets to join the United States in finding ways to end regional conflicts in Afghanistan, Cambodia, Ethiopia, Angola, and Nicaragua. Foreign Minister Shevardnadze says the arms race must be stopped "from spreading to space."

October 31. *Reagan Interview.* Four Soviet journalists interview President Reagan in Washington. The interview, which focuses on superpower relations and the U.S. role in world affairs, is published November 4 in *Izvestiia*. Several of Reagan's responses are censored, however, and the interview is accompanied by a rebuttal.

November 1. *Netherlands Accepts Missiles.* Dutch prime minister Ruud Lubbers, citing increases in the Soviet SS-20 arsenal, announces that the Netherlands will accept forty-eight U.S. cruise missiles in 1988. In June 1984 the Dutch government said it would accept the missiles November 1, 1985, unless the Soviets had reduced the number of SS-20s.

November 4. *Yurchenko Reversal.* Vitalii Yurchenko, whose defection to the West was announced September 26, declares in a press conference at the Soviet embassy in Washington that he had been kidnapped in Rome by American agents and held in the United States until his recent escape. U.S. officials say Yurchenko defected voluntarily. Yurchenko November 5 meets with State Department officials, who determine he freely decided to return to the USSR. Yurchenko reportedly left a Washington restaurant, where he was dining with a CIA agent, and went to the Soviet embassy.

November 16. *Weinberger Letter.* The *New York Times* and *Washington Post* report that Defense Secretary Weinberger gave President Reagan a letter November 13 advising him not to make an agreement at the Geneva summit affirming a restrictive interpretation of the ABM treaty or committing the United States to adhere to the SALT II treaty. The letter is attached to a Pentagon report on Soviet arms control violations.

November 19-21. *Geneva Summit.* President Reagan and General Secretary Gorbachev meet in Geneva for the first summit between U.S. and Soviet leaders since 1979. They achieve no breakthroughs on major issues such as arms control, human rights, or regional conflicts, but both men indicate the meeting was useful. In addition to negotiating sessions with aides present, they spend about five hours in private conversation, accompanied only by their interpreters. They sign bilateral agreements November 21 that provide for the establishment of consuls in New York and Kiev, resumption of civil aviation ties, improved air safety over the northern Pacific, and cultural and scien-

1986

tific exchanges. At the end of the summit they issue a joint communiqué stating their intention to accelerate the arms control process. The statement also says both sides favor a 50 percent reduction in nuclear weapons and an interim agreement on intermediate-range nuclear weapons. Reagan and Gorbachev announce they plan to meet again, beginning with a tentative trip to the United States by Gorbachev in 1986. Before leaving Geneva November 21 the general secretary attacks Reagan's inflexibility on SDI and says the USSR would counter a U.S. space-based ABM system.

December 2. *Bonner Travels to West.* Yelena Bonner, wife of Soviet dissident Andrei Sakharov, leaves the Soviet Union on a three-month exit visa for medical treatment in the West. She promised Soviet authorities she would not make public statements during her trip. Bonner officially received permission to go abroad October 24. She arrives in the United States December 7, after seeing doctors in Rome.

December 10. *Rights Vigil Broken Up.* An American television camera crew and Soviet citizens are assaulted and twelve are arrested by Soviet police as they gather in Moscow's Pushkin Square in a silent vigil commemorating UN Human Rights Day.

December 13. *Foreign Minister Exchange.* Soviet officials in Beijing announce that Chinese foreign minister Wu Xueqian will visit Moscow in May 1986 and Soviet foreign minister Shevardnadze will go to Beijing later that year. It will be the first time in twenty years that the countries have exchanged foreign ministers.

December 15-16. *Shultz in East Europe.* During a tour of six European nations, Secretary of State Shultz stops in Romania and Hungary. Shultz warns Romanian president Nicolae Ceausescu December 15 that the United States might revoke Romania's most-favored-nation trading status if he fails to improve its human rights record. In Hungary December 16 Shultz speaks optimistically about the development of U.S.-Hungarian relations.

December 19. *Soviet Inspections Offer.* The Reagan administration discloses that General Secretary Gorbachev December 5 offered in a letter to allow U.S. technicians to inspect some Soviet nuclear test facilities if the United States joined the USSR in an extended moratorium on nuclear tests. The White House rejects Gorbachev's call for a moratorium but says December 23 that Reagan sent a message to Gorbachev welcoming his inspection offer.

December 20. *Libyan Missiles.* The State Department discloses that the USSR has sold Libya long-range, surface-to-air SA-5 missiles that could threaten aircraft over the Mediterranean. The Egyptian newspaper *Al Ahram* reports December 31 that about two thousand Soviet advisers arrived in Libya in late December.

December 23. *Reagan on SALT II.* President Reagan reports to Congress that the United States will continue to observe the unratified SALT II treaty despite a "continuing pattern of Soviet noncompliance" with arms control agreements.

December 24. *Grishin Removed.* Viktor Grishin is replaced as first secretary of the Moscow City party committee by Central Committee secretary Boris Yeltsin. Western analysts regard the move as part of General Secretary Gorbachev's drive to retire older officials who might obstruct his reforms. Grishin loses his seat on the Politburo January 10, 1986.

January 1. *Gorbachev, Reagan Messages.* General Secretary Gorbachev and President Reagan deliver five-minute speeches shown on television in each other's country. Both men express their hopes for peace and say the Geneva summit began a movement toward better superpower relations. The United States had proposed the exchange before the summit; Moscow accepted the idea December 20, 1985.

January 13. *Civil War in South Yemen.* An attempt by President Ali Nasser Muhammad to have rival South Yemen Politburo members assassinated precipitates a coup against his rule, which leads to civil war. Thousands of foreigners are evacuated by British and Soviet ships. Western sources report as many as ten thousand killed. Both sides declare their allegiance to Moscow. Radical Marxist opponents of the president gain the upper hand after almost two weeks of fighting. Prime Minister Haider Abu Bakr al-Attas, who was in New Delhi when the fighting erupted, returns to Aden January 25 and is named provisional president in a Marxist coalition government. Ali Nasser Muhammad reportedly flees the country.

January 15. *Gorbachev Arms Plan.* Mikhail Gorbachev proposes a comprehensive global ban on nuclear weapons to be achieved in stages by the year 2000. He says the United States must stop development of ASATs (antisatellite weapons) and SDI (the Strategic Defense Initiative) before the plan can be implemented. President Reagan says the United States will study the proposal. Other U.S. officials say that much of Gorbachev's offer is not new, but they praise Gorbachev's willingness to cooperate on verification. Gorbachev also calls for a ban on the production of chemical weapons and announces a three-month extension of the Soviet nuclear test moratorium.

January 15-19. *Shevardnadze in Tokyo.* Eduard Shevardnadze becomes the first Soviet foreign minister to visit Japan since 1976. He signs several cultural and trade accords and presses the Japanese not to participate in SDI research. Shevardnadze says that he discussed the issue of Soviet control of the Japanese-claimed Kuril Islands with Japanese leaders, but neither side reports progress.

January 28. *Challenger Explodes.* The U.S. space shuttle *Challenger* explodes in flight after takeoff, killing all seven crew members. General Secretary Gorbachev sends a warm message of condolence to President Reagan that is printed on the front page of *Pravda*. Subsequent articles in the Soviet press, however, cite the disaster as an example of the risks of militarizing space.

February 2-4. *Soviet-Iranian Talks.* Soviet first deputy premier Georgii Kornienko travels to Tehran for a three-day visit, which both sides call successful. Kornienko invites the Iranian foreign minister to Moscow and signs an agreement to resume Aeroflot flights to Tehran.

February 3. *France Expels Soviets.* The French government expels four Soviet diplomats after accusing them of being Soviet military intelligence agents. Moscow retaliates by expelling four French diplomats.

February 6. *Gorbachev Arms Shift.* In Moscow, General Secretary Gorbachev tells visiting U.S. senator Edward M. Kennedy, D-Mass., that the only preconditions for reducing intermediate-range nuclear forces (INF) in Europe are a freeze on the expansion of British and French nuclear forces and a pledge by the United States not to transfer nuclear weapons to other nations. Gorbachev surprises U.S. officials by not mentioning progress in talks on strategic and space weapons as a requirement for an INF accord.

February 11. *Chemical Arms Plan Rejected.* The United States dismisses a Soviet proposal for a multilateral agreement that would ban the spread of chemical weapons. General Secretary Gorbachev offered the proposal in his January 15 arms control speech as an interim step toward the elimination of chemical weapons. The Gorbachev plan would bar the transfer of chemical arms between states and their deployment on the soil of other states. U.S. officials say guarantees that chemical weapons production will be stopped and existing stockpiles destroyed are needed before an agreement can be reached.

February 15. *Sakharov Letter Revealed.* A letter dated October 15, 1984, from Soviet dissident Andrei Sakharov to Anatolii Aleksandrov, president of the Soviet Academy of Sciences, is made public in the West after being smuggled out of the Soviet Union. It details the forced feeding and other mental and physical abuses that KGB agents inflicted on Sakharov during his four-month incarceration in a Gorkii hospital in 1984. Sakharov's relatives and friends in the United States say the letter is authentic. A London newspaper, the *Observer,* publishes the letter February 16.

February 24. *Reagan Arms Response.* President Reagan formally responds to General Secretary Gorbachev's January 15 nuclear arms control proposal by offering two optional three-year timetables for the removal of U.S. and Soviet intermediate-range missiles from Europe and Asia. He says Gorbachev's plan to eliminate all nuclear weapons by the end of the century is "clearly not appropriate for consideration at this time."

February 25-March 6. *Soviet Party Congress.* More than five thousand Soviet delegates attend the Twenty-seventh Congress of the Communist Party of the Soviet Union in Moscow. General Secretary Gorbachev delivers a five-and-a-half-hour televised keynote address February 25. He indirectly criticizes the policies of the Brezhnev era and calls for numerous economic reforms, including increased autonomy for local managers, revision of the pricing system, and new incentives to increase agricultural production. Gorbachev also advocates a peaceful coexistence policy with the West but denounces President Reagan's February 24 arms control proposal. On March 5 the party congress ratifies the fifteen-year economic and political programs written under Gorbachev's guidance. Many leadership changes are announced, including the promotions of Central Committee secretary Lev Zaikov to full Politburo membership and longtime ambassador to the United States Anatolii Dobrynin to the Central Committee Secretariat.

March 6. *Soviet Probes Study Comet.* The unmanned Soviet spacecraft *Vega 1* takes pictures and gathers data as it passes near Halley's comet. A second Soviet craft, *Vega 2,* flies even closer to the comet March 9. The *Vega* probes carry equipment designed by scientists of other nations, and the Soviets participated extensively in the international effort to study Halley's comet.

March 7. *Soviet UN Staff Cuts.* The White House orders the Soviet Union to reduce the combined staffs of the Soviet, Belorussian, and Ukrainian missions to the United Nations from 275 to 170 officials. Under a 1945 agreement, the Soviet Union gained UN representation for the Belorussian and Ukrainian republics. The White House says the large number of Soviet staff members engaged in espionage increases the security threat to the United States. The USSR March 11 protests the action as "unlawful." Reductions in Soviet personnel begin in October 1986.

March 13. *Gorbachev on Nuclear Testing.* General Secretary Gorbachev announces that the USSR will extend indefinitely its seven-month nuclear testing moratorium set to expire March 31, if the United States joins the halt. The White House rejects the offer and indicates that a nuclear test scheduled for March 22 in Nevada will be conducted on schedule.

March 13. Mir *Space Mission.* Two Soviet cosmonauts blast off in a *Soyuz* spacecraft that carries them to a mission aboard *Mir,* the orbiting Soviet space station launched February 20. The liftoff is broadcast live on Soviet television—a departure from Moscow's past practice of televising only space missions in which astronauts of other nations are participating.

March 14. *Reagan Verification Proposals.* President Reagan announces proposals aimed at enhancing verification of nuclear testing limitations. Reagan asks for talks on improving verification methods, invites Soviet scientists to witness a nuclear test in the United States in April, and offers the Soviets advanced monitoring technology. The same day the White House outlines an ambitious plan for verifying any future treaties limiting intermediate-range missiles. The proposal includes an exchange of inspectors who would count weapons and monitor their production. Tass denounces the verification proposals March 15 as "a political maneuver."

March 20. *Reagan Declines Bonner Meeting.* President Reagan decides not to meet with Yelena Bonner, wife of Soviet dissident Andrei Sakharov. Bonner's visa, which had been set to expire in early March, had been extended by the Soviet government until June. White House officials say the president was concerned that a meeting could jeopardize Bonner's reentry into the Soviet Union and the future release of Soviet citizens seeking to emigrate.

March 24-25. *U.S.-Libyan Clash.* U.S. ships and warplanes retaliate against Libyan targets after Libya launches Soviet-made missiles at elements of the Sixth Fleet conducting maneuvers in the Gulf of Sidra. American missiles damage or destroy several Libyan ships and a surface-to-air missile radar site near the Libyan coast. General Secretary Gorbachev denounces the U.S. actions as "provocative and threatening" and proposes the withdrawal of all Soviet and U.S. military ships from the Mediterranean. Washington rejects the proposal.

March 29. *Test Ban Summit Proposal.* General Secretary Gorbachev offers to meet President Reagan in Europe to discuss a nuclear test ban. In spite of the United States' March 22 nuclear test, Gorbachev says the Soviet Union would continue its halt of nuclear testing until the United States conducted another test. President Reagan rejects Gorbachev's summit proposal, saying a meeting should "deal with the entire range" of U.S.-Soviet relations. Moscow says April 1 that a test ban summit would not necessarily replace a more comprehensive meeting.

April 8. *Dobrynin Farewell Meeting.* Departing Soviet ambassador to the United States Anatolii Dobrynin and President Reagan discuss a possible 1986 summit. Following the discussions Secretary of State Shultz says he and Foreign Minister Shevardnadze will hold talks in mid-May to prepare for a summit meeting.

April 11. *Soviets to End Test Halt.* In response to a

U.S. nuclear test conducted April 10, Moscow says it will end its eight-month moratorium on nuclear testing.

April 14. *United States Bombs Libya.* U.S. Sixth Fleet naval aircraft and bombers based in England launch a massive coordinated air strike against Libya. President Reagan says the bombing was in retaliation for Col. Muammar Qaddafi's involvement in recent terrorist activities. In response to the attack, Moscow April 15 cancels the summit planning meeting scheduled for May 14-16 between Foreign Minister Shevardnadze and Secretary of State Shultz. The Soviet action renders a summer 1986 summit unlikely.

April 16. *Alliluyeva Returns to United States.* Joseph Stalin's daughter, Svetlana Alliluyeva, returns to the United States and renounces her Soviet citizenship. She defected to the United States in 1967 but returned to the USSR in 1984. She says Mikhail Gorbachev aided her efforts to leave.

April 16-22. *Gorbachev in East Germany.* General Secretary Gorbachev attends the East German Communist Party Congress in East Berlin. In an address April 18 he offers to negotiate troop and arms reductions in Europe.

April 26. *Chernobyl Nuclear Accident.* Just after 1:00 a.m. a fire starts in the Soviet nuclear power station at Chernobyl, eighty miles north of Kiev. Complications from the fire quickly cause a meltdown to begin in the reactor's core. Hydrogen gas forms in the overheated reactor and explodes, blowing a hole in the reinforced concrete roof. Huge quantities of radiation escape into the atmosphere. The Soviets delay disclosure of the accident. Not until the next afternoon do they evacuate nearly fifty thousand people from a 6.2-mile radius around the plant.

April 28. *Nuclear Accident Revealed.* Abnormally high levels of radiation are detected in Sweden. Stockholm demands an explanation from Soviet officials after atmospheric analysis reveals the radiation is coming from the USSR. Tass announces several hours later that a nuclear accident had taken place but says only that "measures are being taken to eliminate the consequences of the accident. Aid is being given to those affected."

April 29-May 29. *Nuclear Disaster Unfolds.* Radioactivity levels rise throughout much of Europe as Soviet workers attempt to contain the effects of the nuclear meltdown. The Soviets say April 29 that two people were killed at Chernobyl. Some early Western estimates of the dead go as high as two thousand, but later these are proved wrong. By May 29 Moscow reports twenty-one people had died. Dr. Robert Gale, a U.S. physician, performs bone marrow transplants in Moscow on victims and predicts the death toll will continue to rise. Premier Nikolai Ryzhkov, Central Committee secretary Yegor Ligachev, and Ukrainian party leader Vladimir Shcherbitskii visit the disaster area May 3. The next day the evacuation zone is widened to eighteen miles around the reactor. Numerous countries criticize the Soviets for not announcing the disaster immediately. Eventually Moscow releases films and pictures of the reactor and agrees to provide the International Atomic Energy Agency with more information. Many East and West European governments warn of health hazards from food and rainwater affected by the Chernobyl radiation. The European Community May 10 temporarily bans all fresh food imports from the Soviet Union and six East European countries.

May 4. *Karmal Replaced.* Najibullah becomes general secretary of the Afghanistan Communist party when Babrak Karmal resigns citing poor health. Najibullah formerly headed the Afghan secret police.

May 13. *Shcharanskii Meets Reagan.* Recently freed Soviet Jewish dissident Anatolii Shcharanskii meets with President Reagan in Washington. White House spokesmen say the president will continue to use quiet diplomacy to advance human rights in the USSR.

May 14. *Gorbachev on Chernobyl.* General Secretary Gorbachev gives a televised address on the Chernobyl nuclear disaster. He says 9 people have died and 299 are hospitalized, but "the worst has passed." He attacks the West for using the accident for anti-Soviet propaganda purposes and denies the USSR withheld timely information on the disaster. Gorbachev renews his offer to meet President Reagan to discuss a nuclear test ban and extends the Soviet moratorium on nuclear testing until August 6.

May 20. *Dubinin Named Ambassador.* Tass reports that Yuri Dubinin will become the next Soviet ambassador to the United States. The fifty-five-year-old diplomat had served as the Soviet envoy to the United Nations since March 1986. Dubinin had been ambassador to Spain for seven years before his UN assignment. A European specialist, he speaks little English and had never been to the United States before 1986. Dubinin's selection surprises Western observers, who expected an American specialist to fill the post.

May 24. *Bonner Leaves for Soviet Union.* Yelena Bonner leaves the United States to return home after a six-month trip to the West for medical treatment.

May 27. *SALT II Limits to Be Observed.* President Reagan announces that the United States will dismantle two nuclear missile submarines to stay within the SALT II treaty's limits on multiple warhead launchers. He warns, however, that in the future the Soviet military buildup may force the United States to abandon observation of the treaty. At the Geneva arms talks May 29, the Soviets offer to cut their offensive nuclear arsenal if the United States agrees to negotiate more precise definitions of the activities prohibited by the ABM treaty and pledges not to withdraw from the treaty for fifteen to twenty years. On June 11 Soviet negotiators at the START talks in Geneva expand on the proposal, offering to drop their previous demand that U.S. forward-based bombers and sea-launched cruise missiles be eliminated.

June 19. *Reagan Delivers Conciliatory Speech.* Speaking at a high school graduation in Glassboro, New Jersey, where a 1967 U.S.-Soviet summit was held, President Reagan says the Soviet Union is making a "serious effort" to negotiate on arms control.

June 30. *Gorbachev Attacks U.S. Policies.* In a speech to the Polish Communist Party Congress, General Secretary Gorbachev says Washington is obstructing progress on arms control and undermining the SALT II treaty.

July 28. *Gorbachev Announces Troop Withdrawals.* During a speech on Soviet relations with Asia delivered in Vladivostok, General Secretary Gorbachev announces the impending withdrawal of six Soviet regiments from Afghanistan. Gorbachev also calls for closer Sino-Soviet ties and says the withdrawal of some Soviet troops from Mongolia is being examined.

August 18. *Test Moratorium Extended.* General Secretary Gorbachev announces that the Soviet Union again will extend its unilateral nuclear test moratorium, this time until January 1, 1987.

August 18. *Soviet-Israeli Talks.* Soviet and Israeli diplomats meet in Helsinki to discuss the establishment of consulates. The talks are the first formal diplomatic contact between the two countries in nineteen years. The Soviets say the move does not signify any basic change in policy toward Israel.

August 21. *Chernobyl Report.* The Soviets release a 382-page report on the Chernobyl nuclear disaster. The report blames the accident primarily on human error and estimates that 5,300 will die from direct exposure over the next seventy years.

August 23. *Zakharov Arrested.* Gennadii Zakharov, a Soviet physicist who is employed by the United Nations, is arrested in New York after he pays undercover agents for three classified documents.

August 30. *Daniloff Affair.* Soviet authorities arrest Nicholas Daniloff, a correspondent for *U.S. News and World Report,* on charges of espionage. Daniloff was arrested after being handed a package containing top secret maps by an acquaintance in a Moscow park. The United States charges that Daniloff was framed to provide the Soviets with a pawn to gain the release of Gennadii Zakharov, a Soviet arrested in New York for spying a week before. On September 5, President Reagan sends a letter to General Secretary Gorbachev giving him his personal assurance that Daniloff is not a spy. Daniloff is formally charged September 7 with espionage; Zakharov is indicted on three counts of espionage two days later. Zakharov and Daniloff are released to the custody of their respective embassies in Washington and Moscow September 12 pending their trials. On September 18, Gorbachev calls Daniloff a "spy who was caught red handed." The same day, Foreign Minister Shevardnadze arrives in Washington for talks with Secretary of State Shultz on plans for a superpower summit. The Daniloff case dominates their discussions, and Shevardnadze also meets with Reagan. The Soviets release Daniloff and drop all charges against him September 29. Zakharov is released one day later after pleading no contest to charges of spying. As part of the arrangement, Moscow also allows dissident Yuri Orlov and his wife, Irina Valitova, to emigrate to the United States.

September 1. *Soviet Ships Collide.* The 17,053-ton Soviet passenger ship *Admiral Nakhimov* and the Soviet freighter *Pyotr Vasov* collide in the Black Sea, eight miles from the port of Novorossisk. The *Admiral Nakhimov* sinks, resulting in the deaths of 398 people. Details of the accident are swiftly announced by the Soviet government.

September 17. *Soviets Expelled.* The Reagan administration expels twenty-five members of the Soviet delegation to the United Nations for alleged espionage activities. The White House denies the expulsions are linked to the Daniloff affair. All twenty-five leave by October 14.

September 22. *New Security Pact.* The Conference on Confidence- and Security-Building Measures in Europe approves a new European security pact designed to reduce the risk of accidental war. The agreement provides for prior notification and verification of troop movements by the NATO and Warsaw Pact alliances. It takes effect January 1, 1987.

September 30. *Iceland Summit Announced.* President Reagan announces that he and General Secretary Gorbachev will meet in Iceland in October.

October 3. *Soviet Nuclear Sub Sinks.* An explosion and fire aboard a Soviet Yankee-class nuclear missile submarine patrolling in the Atlantic kills three Soviet sailors. The disabled sub sinks while in tow about six hundred miles from Bermuda.

October 11-12. *Iceland Summit.* President Reagan and General Secretary Gorbachev meet in Reykjavik, Iceland, for talks intended to set the agenda for a full summit in early 1987. Initially, the two leaders and their aides make substantial progress toward an arms control agreement. They agree to limit the number of warheads on their intermediate-range missiles to one hundred and ban these weapons from being deployed in Europe. They also agree on a 50 percent reduction in strategic weapons. In a major concession, Gorbachev agrees to exclude sea-launched cruise missiles from the warhead count. However, Gorbachev refuses to approve these arms control measures unless the United States agrees to adhere to a strict interpretation of the 1972 ABM treaty for ten years. Reagan rejects Gorbachev's position because it would prohibit testing of SDI outside the laboratory. The talks break down amid mutual recriminations. No date is set for a future summit. On October 17, Secretary of State Shultz releases the texts of Reagan's main arms control proposals to dispel claims that Reagan had agreed in principle to eliminate all nuclear forces. But on October 22, Gorbachev insists on Soviet television that Reagan had expressed support for his proposal to seek the elimination of all nuclear arms within ten years.

October 19-22. *Diplomats Expelled.* The Soviet Union expels five U.S. diplomats for engaging in "impermissible activities," in retaliation for Washington's expulsion of twenty-five Soviet UN personnel in September. The United States expels fifty-five more Soviet diplomats October 21. The Soviets expel five more American diplomats the following day and announce that the United States will lose the services of the 260 Soviet employees working at the U.S. Moscow embassy and Leningrad consulate.

November 8. *Molotov Dies.* Viacheslav Molotov, who served as foreign minister under Joseph Stalin, dies in Moscow at the age of ninety-six.

November 19. *Private Enterprise Legislation.* The Supreme Soviet passes a law that sanctions some types of small-scale private enterprise. The law takes effect May 1987.

November 28. *SALT II Limits Exceeded.* The United States exceeds the limitations of the unratified SALT II treaty by deploying its 131st B-52 bomber capable of carrying cruise missiles. The Soviet Union announces December 5 that it will continue to comply with the treaty but no longer considers itself obligated to do so. Reagan administration officials accuse the Soviets of hypocrisy, saying the Soviets have been violating the treaty for years.

December 16. *Kunaev Loses Position.* Politburo member Dinmukhamed Kunaev, an ethnic Kazakh, is replaced as party leader of Kazakhstan by Gennadii Kolbin, who is an ethnic Russian. The next day riots erupt in Alma-Alta, the capital of Kazakhstan, in response to the move.

December 18. *Soviets End Test Moratorium.* The Soviet government announces that it will end its unilateral moratorium on nuclear weapons testing when the United States conducts its first nuclear test in 1987.

December 19. *Sakharov and Bonner Freed.* Physicist and Nobel Peace Prize winner Andrei Sakharov's banishment to the city of Gorkii is lifted by the Soviet government. Sakharov's wife, Yelena Bonner, receives a pardon the same day. Sakharov reveals that General Secretary Gorbachev had personally phoned him to inform him of his release.

1987

January 10. *Marine Guard Scandal.* The Marine Corps announces the detention of Sgt. Clayton Lonetree, a former guard at the U.S. embassy in Moscow who confessed to supplying the KGB with secret information after being seduced by a female agent. Lonetree is formally charged on January 31. A second former embassy guard, Cpl. Arnold Bracey, is arrested on March 24 on similar charges, but they are dropped June 12. Lonetree is convicted on thirteen counts of espionage August 21 and is sentenced to thirty years in prison.

January 15. *Export Ban Lifted.* The Commerce Department lifts a nine-year ban on the export of oil-drilling equipment to the Soviet Union.

January 27. *Central Committee Plenum.* General Secretary Gorbachev opens a Central Committee plenum with a speech calling for major political reforms. He outlines new procedures to elect party officials that include secret balloting and a choice of candidates for voters in general elections. Dinmukhamed Kunaev is removed from the Politburo, while Aleksandr Yakovlev is appointed a candidate member of the body. Anatolii Lukyanov and Nikolai Sliunkov are appointed to the Secretariat.

February 10. *Political Prisoners Released.* The Soviet Foreign Ministry announces that 140 persons convicted of subversive activities have been pardoned. The release of 150 more dissidents is announced February 17. Three days later, the Soviets also release prominent Jewish dissident Joseph Begun.

February 14. *Peace and Disarmament Forum.* The Soviet Union hosts an international peace and disarmament forum that is attended by more than seven hundred artists, scientists, business leaders, and officials from around the world. Dissident Andrei Sakharov speaks at the gathering and calls for democratic reform. In an address to the forum, General Secretary Gorbachev says the Soviet Union desires international stability so that it can pursue domestic reform.

February 19. *Reagan Lifts Polish Sanctions.* President Reagan removes all remaining U.S. economic sanctions against Poland, saying the move was a response to Polish governmental reform.

February 26. *Test Moratorium Ends.* The USSR ends an eighteen-month unilateral moratorium on nuclear testing by conducting an underground nuclear test in Kazakhstan.

February 28. *Gorbachev Separates SDI and INF.* General Secretary Gorbachev announces that he is willing to sign an agreement eliminating U.S. and Soviet intermediate-range nuclear forces in Europe without regard to progress on limiting space-based ABM weapons.

March 28. *Thatcher Visits Moscow.* British prime minister Margaret Thatcher meets with General Secretary Gorbachev in Moscow. They discuss arms control and Soviet human rights policies. The leaders sign four bilateral protocols on March 31 providing for diplomatic, scientific, cultural, and educational cooperation.

April 2. *France Expels Soviets.* France expels three Soviet diplomats after learning of Soviet participation in a spy ring designed to obtain secrets concerning the European space program. The Soviets April 4 expel two French businessmen in retaliation.

April 6. *New U.S. Embassy in Moscow Bugged.* Rep. Olympia J. Snowe, R-Maine, and Rep. Daniel A. Mica, D-Fla., tour the Moscow embassy building and pronounce it "fully compromised" by electronic listening devices. The president and the State Department order separate studies of the situation the following day.

April 9. *Gorbachev Visits Prague.* Czechoslovak president Gustav Husak and General Secretary Gorbachev meet in Prague. In a speech April 10, Gorbachev says the USSR does not demand that Czechoslovakia and other Eastern European countries adopt Soviet-style reforms, but he claims the restructuring of the Soviet Union is "in accordance with the very essence of socialism."

April 13. *Shultz in Moscow.* Secretary of State Shultz visits Moscow for extensive talks with Foreign Minister Shevardnadze on arms control, human rights, and Soviet espionage at the U.S. embassy in Moscow. On April 14, Shultz meets with General Secretary Gorbachev, who proposes the elimination from Europe of nuclear weapons having an approximate range of three hundred to six hundred miles.

April 23. *Honecker Rejects Reform.* Speaking before a trade union congress, East German leader Erich Honecker says that reforms initiated in the Soviet Union should not be implemented in East Germany.

April 30. *Wheat Sale.* Agriculture Secretary Richard Lyng announces that the Soviet Union will buy four million metric tons of subsidized American wheat to be delivered by the end of September.

May 8. *Draft START Treaty Unveiled.* The United States offers a draft treaty that would cut U.S. and Soviet strategic nuclear arsenals by 50 percent over seven years. Under the plan, both sides would be left with 1,600 delivery vehicles and 6,000 warheads. The Soviets criticize the plan for failing to curtail the development of space weapons.

May 19. *Asian Missile Offer.* In a speech in Moscow, General Secretary Gorbachev says the Soviet Union would be willing to eliminate its intermediate-range missiles based in Asia if the United States withdrew its nuclear weapons from Japan, South Korea, and the Philippines and withdrew its naval forces in the Pacific "behind agreed lines."

May 23. *Voice of America Jamming Stopped.* For the first time since 1980, the Soviet Union stops jamming Voice of America radio broadcasts, although it continues to jam other Western radio networks.

May 25. *Gorbachev in Romania.* General Secretary Gorbachev begins a three-day visit to Romania, where he receives a polite but cool reception. In a speech before a meeting of five thousand Communist party officials, he outlines his reform program to an unreceptive audience.

May 29. *Teen Pilot Lands in Red Square.* Mathias Rust, a West German teenager, flies a small plane from Helsinki to Moscow, landing in Red Square. The incident leads to the removal of Soviet defense minister Sergei Sokolov and commander of Soviet air defenses Aleksandr Koldunov May 30. Dmitrii Yazov replaces Sokolov as defense minister.

June 8. *Schlesinger Embassy Report.* James R. Schlesinger, head of a special State Department panel studying the Moscow embassy, holds a news conference in the embassy at the end of his committee's ten-day investigation. He confirms reports that the nearly completed Moscow embassy is riddled with electronic listening devices and recommends that the building be partly dismantled and rebuilt by American laborers using U.S.-made components. Schlesinger also suggests that an adjacent annex be built to house the embassy's most secret activities.

June 8-14. *Pope Visits Poland.* Pope John Paul II makes his third visit to his native Poland as pope. During his visit he meets with both Lech Walesa, leader of the Solidarity labor union, and President Wojciech Jaruzelski.

June 12. *Reagan in West Berlin.* In a speech in West Berlin at the Brandenburg Gate during celebrations of the 750th anniversary of the city, President Reagan challenges Gorbachev to "tear down" the Berlin Wall.

June 16. *INF Proposal.* The United States formally proposes a global ban on all intermediate-range nuclear missiles with ranges between 500 and 3,400 miles.

June 25. *Gorbachev on Economic Reform.* At a Central Committee plenum, General Secretary Gorbachev calls for economic reforms that would further decentralize the Soviet economy. He proposed, among other measures, that state-owned enterprises become self-financing and that central control over prices and distribution decrease. The Central Committee approves the plan June 26. Aleksandr Yakovlev, Nikolai Sliunkov, and Viktor Nikonov each are promoted to full membership in the Politburo, while Defense Minister Yazov is given candidate status.

July 15. *Ukrainian Party Shake-up.* Aleksandr Lyashko retires as Ukrainian premier amid a party shake-up involving at least eight other top officials. Vitalii Masol is named to replace Lyashko. Politburo member Vladimir Shcherbitskii remains first secretary of the Ukrainian Communist party.

July 22. *Gorbachev Accepts Global INF Ban.* In an interview in an Indonesian newspaper, General Secretary Gorbachev says the Soviets would be willing to accept the global elimination of all intermediate-range nuclear missiles. Gorbachev thus dropped the earlier Soviet demand that the USSR be allowed to keep some intermediate-range missiles in Asia. Soviet negotiators at the INF talks in Geneva adopt this position July 23.

July 27. *NATO Calls for New Talks.* NATO proposes to replace the Mutual and Balanced Force Reduction talks with a new forum on conventional force reductions to be conducted within the framework of the Conference on Security and Cooperation in Europe. The new talks would not include representatives of neutral nations.

July 31. *Soviet Draft Treaty.* Soviet negotiators at Geneva present a draft treaty for a START agreement that links 50 percent cuts in strategic weapons to an agreement to limit development of space-based ABM weapons.

August 11. *Soviets Deploy SS-24s.* The Soviet Union confirms that it has begun deployment of the SS-24 intercontinental ballistic missile.

August 26. *Bonn Offers to Scrap Missiles.* The West German government announces that it would dismantle its seventy-two Pershing IA missiles if the superpowers concluded a treaty banning intermediate-range nuclear missiles. The United States controls the nuclear warheads for the missiles.

September 1. *Honecker Visits West Germany.* East German leader Erich Honecker holds talks with West German chancellor Helmut Kohl in Bonn. Honecker is the first East German head of state ever to visit West Germany. The two leaders announce agreements on a range of issues.

September 18. *Tentative Agreement on INF Treaty.* After three days of talks between Foreign Minister Shevardnadze and Secretary of State Shultz in Washington, President Reagan announces that a tentative agree-

ment has been reached on a treaty eliminating intermediate-range nuclear missiles. Reagan says the two sides were in the process of arranging a summit meeting for late 1987 at which the treaty would be signed.

October 15. *Soviets to Pay UN Debts.* The Soviet government announces that it will pay all its outstanding debts (about $245 million) to the United Nations.

October 21. *Aliev Removed from Politburo.* The Central Committee removes Geidar Aliev as a full member of the Politburo.

October 22-30. *Summit Dispute.* Secretary of State Shultz travels to the Soviet Union for talks intended to finalize the INF treaty and prepare for a summit. He meets October 23 with General Secretary Gorbachev, who unexpectedly refuses to set a summit date because of Soviet objections to SDI. Shultz leaves Moscow October 24. The Soviets reverse their position October 27, requesting consultations on arranging a summit meeting. Foreign Minister Shevardnadze arrives in Washington October 29, where he meets with Shultz and President Reagan. The next day Reagan announces that Gorbachev will come to Washington for a summit in December.

November 2. *Gorbachev Speech.* In a speech beginning the celebration of the seventieth anniversary of the Bolshevik Revolution, General Secretary Gorbachev revives the reputations of Nikita Khrushchev and Nikolai Bukharin and says Joseph Stalin was guilty of "enormous and unforgivable" crimes. Gorbachev also defends perestroika and asserts that the era of conflict between communism and capitalism was giving way to a new spirit of cooperation.

November 9. *New Geneva Talks Begin.* The superpowers begin talks in Geneva on banning underground nuclear tests.

November 11. *Yeltsin Dismissed.* Boris Yeltsin is removed as Moscow party chief. At a Central Committee meeting October 21, he had denounced the slow pace of reform. He is named deputy director of the State Committee for Construction November 18.

November 22. *Shultz and Shevardnadze in Geneva.* Secretary of State Shultz and Foreign Minister Shevardnadze meet in Geneva to resolve remaining disagreements over the INF treaty. They also develop an agenda for the Washington summit.

November 29. *Polish Reforms Defeated.* A referendum on political and economic reform is defeated in Poland. The Solidarity movement opposed the government's reform plan and had asked Poles to boycott the referendum, which asked citizens if they were willing to accept hardships in pursuit of radical economic reform and if they supported a "profound democratization of political life." Because of a low voter turnout, neither question received the support of 50 percent of eligible voters—the amount required for passage.

November 30. *Gorbachev Interview.* Tom Brokaw of NBC News interviews General Secretary Gorbachev for one hour on national television. Gorbachev calls for a 50 percent mutual reduction in strategic nuclear arms and indicates that the USSR is prepared to counter any U.S. deployment of SDI with a similar system of its own.

December 7-10. *Washington Summit.* General Secretary Gorbachev and President Reagan hold a summit meeting in Washington, D.C. On December 8, they sign the INF treaty, which provides for the elimination of U.S. and Soviet intermediate-range nuclear missiles. The treaty is accompanied by a thirteen-year verification agreement that includes on-site inspections. Gorbachev meets with members of Congress at the Soviet embassy December 9. Later in the day Reagan and Gorbachev discuss Afghanistan and proposals to reduce strategic nuclear weapons. Gorbachev insists that any strategic arms treaty be accompanied by limits on SDI research. Gorbachev holds meetings with Vice President Bush and Reagan December 10 before leaving the United States. The same day NATO foreign ministers call on the U.S. Senate to ratify the INF treaty.

December 17. *Husak Resigns.* Gustav Husak resigns as Czechoslovak Communist party leader. He is replaced by Milos Jakes.

1988

January 6. *Shevardnadze on Afghanistan.* Foreign Minister Shevardnadze says in an interview in Kabul that the USSR hopes to withdraw all its forces from Afghanistan by the end of 1988. He maintains that withdrawal of Soviet troops does not depend on a friendly government remaining in power in Afghanistan.

February 1. *Poles Protest Price Increases.* The Polish government implements an economic reform plan that increases the price of basic foods, alcoholic beverages, and other items by more than 40 percent. The price increases are accompanied by a 16 percent devaluation in the nation's currency. The Solidarity labor movement denounces the price increases but urges restraint on the part of the population. Nevertheless, thousands of Poles demonstrate against the price increases.

February 6. *Talyzin Replaced as Gosplan Chief.* Nikolai Talyzin, head of the State Planning Committee (Gosplan), is replaced by his first deputy chairman, Yuri Maslyukov. General Secretary Gorbachev had criticized Talyzin for failing to implement economic reforms.

February 8. *Gorbachev Troop Withdrawal Proposal.* In a statement broadcast on Soviet television, General Secretary Gorbachev says that if a settlement of the Afghanistan conflict can be reached in March at UN-sponsored peace talks in Geneva, the Soviet Union would begin withdrawing troops from Afghanistan by May 15. He asserts that the withdrawal could be completed within ten months.

February 11. *Armenians Demonstrate.* Thousands of Armenians living in the predominantly Armenian Nagorno-Karabakh autonomous region of the Azerbaidzhani republic hold demonstrations to demand reunification with the Armenian republic. Rallies attended by tens of thousands of protesters begin February 20 in Armenia in support of the Armenians in Nagorno-Karabakh. On February 26, General Secretary Gorbachev calls for a restoration of order. Armenian leaders agree to a temporary suspension of the demonstrations the following day.

February 18. *Yeltsin Removed.* Former Moscow party chief Boris Yeltsin is removed from candidate status in the Politburo at a Central Committee plenum. Georgii Razumovskii and Yuri Maslyukov are named candidate members of the Politburo.

February 26. *Romania Loses MFN Status.* The United States announces that it is withdrawing Romania's most-favored-nation (MFN) trading status because of human rights violations by the Romanian government.

February 28. *Ethnic Riots in Sumgait.* Riots in the Azerbaidzhan city of Sumgait reportedly result in the deaths of at least thirty-two people. Soviet troops are sent to the city to enforce a dusk-to-dawn curfew. During the following weeks reports in the Soviet press suggest that the violence may have been more serious. Several Soviet journalists and officials maintain that the riots were pogroms against the Armenian minority in Sumgait that left hundreds dead.

March 6. *Soviet Embassy in Tehran Attacked.* An Iranian mob, angered by Soviet sales of missiles to Iraq, attacks the Soviet embassy in Tehran with rocks and Molotov cocktails. No Soviet personnel are killed, but the incident damages Soviet-Iranian relations.

March 13. *Gorbachev Criticized in Soviet Press.* The newspaper *Sovietskaya Rossiya* publishes a letter by Leningrad schoolteacher Nina Andreyeva critical of General Secretary Gorbachev's "leftist-liberal" policies. She calls for a return to the more disciplined line followed by Joseph Stalin. Authority for publishing the letter is traced to second-ranking Kremlin figure Yegor Ligachev.

April 14. *Afghan Agreements Signed.* The governments of Afghanistan and Pakistan sign accords in Geneva mandating the withdrawal of Soviet forces from Afghanistan, the neutrality of the Afghan state, and the repatriation of Afghan refugees. The Soviet Union and United States sign a separate accord that commits them to guarantee the Afghan agreements.

April 19. *Politburo Rift.* The Politburo reportedly orders Yegor Ligachev to take a two-month vacation after he clashes with General Secretary Gorbachev over policy.

April 25. *Labor Upheaval in Poland.* Hundreds of transportation workers in Bydgoszcz go on strike and are granted a pay increase the following day. During the next few days, workers strike at a steel mill in Nowa Huta and at shipyards in Gdansk, demanding higher wages and recognition of the Solidarity labor movement. Demonstrators and police clash on May 3 in Warsaw, Krakow, Lublin, and Lodz. Police crack down on the strikers May 5, when the government and workers fail to negotiate an agreement. On May 10, 2,500 workers who had been sealed inside a Gdansk shipyard give up their protest.

May 7-9. *Soviet Opposition Drafts Charter.* More than one hundred Soviet opposition leaders meet in Moscow, where they draft the charter of the Democratic Union, an independent political party. Five members of the group, including Sergei Grigoryants, editor of the journal *Glasnost*, are arrested May 9 and ordered to leave Moscow.

May 15. *Soviets Begin Afghanistan Withdrawal.* The Soviet Union begins to withdraw its 115,000 troops from Afghanistan. The withdrawal is scheduled to be completed February 15, 1989. On May 25 the Soviet Union for the first time releases Soviet casualty figures related to the fighting in Afghanistan. According to the Ministry of Defense, 13,310 Soviet troops had been killed as of May 1 and 35,478 had been wounded.

May 22. *Kadar Removed in Hungary.* Janos Kadar is replaced as general secretary of the Hungarian Communist party by Karoly Grosz.

May 27. *INF Treaty Ratified.* The Senate ratifies the INF treaty by a vote of 93-5.

May 27. *Private Cooperatives Approved.* The Supreme Soviet passes a law legalizing private cooperatives. More than twenty thousand cooperatives already have been formed by Soviet citizens, in anticipation of the law's passage.

May 29-June 2. *Moscow Summit.* President Reagan travels to Moscow to meet with General Secretary Gorbachev. Although no major arms control breakthroughs are achieved, meetings between the two leaders are held in a jovial atmosphere, and they sign nine bilateral agreements. During the visit, Reagan raises the issue of human rights in public speeches, in meetings with refuseniks, and in his talks with Gorbachev. The Soviets retaliate by sponsoring a Moscow press conference for American Indians who claim they are discriminated against by the Reagan administration. On June 1 Reagan and Gorbachev exchange the formal documents of ratification of the INF treaty.

June 5-12. *Millennium Celebrated.* With the support of the Soviet government, the Russian Orthodox Church observes the one thousandth anniversary of the establishment of Christianity in Russia.

June 6. *Lenin Criticized.* Soviet founding father V. I. Lenin, long considered beyond reproach in Soviet political and journalistic circles, is criticized in the monthly magazine *Novy Mir.* The author of the article, historian Vasilii Selyunin, faults Lenin for having initiated the systematic use of terror to intimidate enemies of the Bolshevik party and eliminate "potential opponents."

June 15. *Armenia Requests Nagorno-Karabakh.* The Armenian Supreme Soviet officially asks that Nagorno-Karabakh, the Armenian enclave within the borders of neighboring Azerbaidzhan, be reunited with Armenia.

June 21. *Canada Announces Expulsions.* Canadian prime minister Brian Mulroney reveals that eight Soviet diplomats had been expelled June 14 for attempting to obtain defense technology secrets. He also says that nine diplomats currently outside Canada would be denied reentry. The Soviets retaliate by expelling five Canadian diplomats June 22, and Canada responds with two more expulsions.

June 27. *Hungarians Protest Romanian Program.* Tens of thousands of Hungarians protest in Budapest against a Romanian plan to "systematize" seven thousand Romanian villages, mainly in the ethnically Hungarian region of Transylvania, by replacing them with five hundred agro-industrial complexes.

June 28-July 1. *Nineteenth Party Conference.* In his opening speech to the first all-union party conference since 1941, General Secretary Gorbachev calls for restructuring the Soviet government. He proposes creating a more democratic national legislature—the Congress of People's Deputies (CPD). The 2,250-seat body would consist of 1,500 deputies elected in multi-candidate elections and 750 appointed by various organizations. Under the proposal, the CPD, which would meet semi-annually, would select a standing Supreme Soviet of about 450 members and a strong president. Gorbachev also calls for more authority for local soviets, multi-candidate elections, and a ban on interference in the economy by local party organizations. The conference July 1 adopts resolutions supporting Gorbachev's government reorganization plan, legal reform, and greater independence for national regions.

July 9. *Bukharin Rehabilitated.* Soviet revolutionary figure Nikolai Bukharin, who was executed by the regime of Joseph Stalin in 1937, is posthumously reinstated to membership in the Communist party.

July 11-16. *Gorbachev in Poland.* In a speech to the parliament at the beginning of a six-day visit to Poland, General Secretary Gorbachev denounces Joseph Stalin's deportation of thousands of Poles to the Soviet Union after World War II. Warsaw Pact leaders convene in Warsaw on July 15-16 and call for a moratorium on nuclear weapons testing and chemical weapons production and separate talks with NATO on tactical nuclear arms.

August 15. *Polish Unrest.* Coal miners strike in Jastrzebie following a clash between Polish police and pro-Solidarity protesters in Gdansk the previous day. The strikes quickly spread across Poland. The government August 23 rejects Solidarity's call for direct negotiations. Many of the strikes collapse by August 25.

August 17. *Joint Nuclear Test.* The United States and the Soviet Union conduct a joint nuclear test in Nevada. The test is intended to advance verification of test ban agreements by comparing U.S. and Soviet methods of measuring a nuclear detonation.

August 21. *Prague Demonstration.* An estimated ten thousand people demonstrate in Prague to commemorate the twentieth anniversary of the Soviet invasion of Czechoslovakia. Riot police use tear gas to disperse the gathering.

August 31. *Kiszczak Meets with Walesa.* Interior Minister Czeslaw Kiszczak meets with Solidarity leader Lech Walesa to discuss Poland's labor unrest. It is the first official meeting between the government and Solidarity since 1982. The two sides announce progress toward an agreement on holding round-table discussions. The government says it would be willing to discuss the legalization of Solidarity. After the meeting, Walesa calls for an end to strikes.

September 16. *Gorbachev on Radar.* During a visit to Krasnoyarsk, Siberia, General Secretary Gorbachev offers to turn the controversial Krasnoyarsk radar station into a space research facility and place it under international control. The Reagan administration says the radar must be dismantled unconditionally. Gorbachev also offers to close the Soviet Cam Rahn Bay naval base in Vietnam if the United States abandons its bases in the Philippines.

September 19. *Polish Leadership Resigns.* Premier Zbigniew Messner and his cabinet resign in response to parliamentary criticism of their economic policy. Messner is succeeded by Mieczyslaw Rakowski September 27.

September 30. *Leadership Shake-up at Plenum.* At a Central Committee plenum, Yegor Ligachev, leader of the conservative wing of the Politburo, is transferred from his position as party secretary for ideology to the less important post of secretary for agriculture. He retains his seat on the Politburo. Vadim Medvedev, a close associate of General Secretary Gorbachev, is given responsibility for ideology as well as propaganda. Aleksandr Yakovlev replaces Anatolii Dobrynin as secretary for foreign affairs. Mikhail Solomentsev is retired from the Politburo and from the chairmanship of the Party Control Committee. The following day, at a meeting of the Supreme Soviet, President Andrei Gromyko is retired, and Gorbachev is confirmed as the new president (chairman of the presidium of the Supreme Soviet). Viktor Chebrikov, who was named secretary in charge of legal affairs the previous day, is replaced as head of the KGB by Vladimir Kryuchkov, a career KGB officer. Anatolii Lukyanov is confirmed as Soviet vice president.

October 24-27. *Kohl Visits Moscow.* West German chancellor Helmut Kohl meets with Soviet president Gorbachev in Moscow. Kohl asserts October 26 that the Kremlin had promised to release all political prisoners by the end of 1988. The Soviet Foreign Ministry refuses to confirm the report.

October 27. *Soviets Admit Budget Deficit.* Finance Minister Boris Gostev says that in the past Moscow has hidden Soviet budget deficits. He estimates that the budget deficit for 1988 will be about $58 billion.

October 31. *Lenin Shipyard Controversy.* The Polish government announces its intention to close Gdansk's Lenin Shipyard, where the Solidarity labor movement was founded in 1980. The action is to occur in stages beginning December 1. The government maintains the shipyard must be closed because it is losing money. Solidarity leader Lech Walesa November 6 threatens to call a strike if the decision is not reversed. After shipyard officials assure Solidarity representatives November 7 that the shutdown will be spread over two or three years and shipyard workers will be guaranteed jobs in the Gdansk area, Walesa withdraws the threat of an immediate strike. He vows, however, to fight in the coming year to keep the shipyard open.

November 15. *Soviets Launch Space Shuttle.* The first flight of a Soviet space shuttle is successful. The unmanned *Buran* spacecraft completes two orbits before returning to earth.

November 16. *Estonian Constitutional Conflict.* The Estonian Supreme Soviet passes an amendment to its constitution that allows Estonian officials to give precedence to Estonian laws that conflict with USSR laws. The Presidium of the Soviet Union declares the Estonian amendment unconstitutional November 26.

November 18-20. *Gorbachev in India.* President Gorbachev visits India, where he meets with Prime Minister Rajiv Gandhi. Gorbachev discusses the Soviet withdrawal from Afghanistan with Indian officials and assures them that recent efforts by Moscow to improve relations with China will not affect Soviet-Indian relations.

November 22. *Violence in Azerbaidzhan.* Anti-Armenian riots in Baku and several other Azerbaidzhani cities leave eight dead and more than one hundred injured.

December 1. *Supreme Soviet Amends Constitution.* The Supreme Soviet amends the Soviet Constitution, adopting the recommendations of the Nineteenth Party Conference for a revamped legislature and presidency.

December 1. *School Bus Hijacking.* Four Soviets hijack a school bus in the Caucasus Mountains. Soviet officials give the hijackers money and a cargo plane. The hijackers order the plane's crew to fly to Tel Aviv. After landing, the hijackers, who are neither Jews nor dissidents, are arrested by Israeli authorities and returned to the Soviet Union.

December 2. *Sino-Soviet Summit Announced.* Officials in Moscow and Beijing announce that President Gorbachev will meet with Chinese leader Deng Xiaoping during the first half of 1989.

December 6-8. *Gorbachev in United States.* President Gorbachev arrives in New York to address the United Nations and meet with President Reagan and President-elect Bush. In his historic speech to the UN General Assembly December 7, Gorbachev announces a unilateral military cut of five hundred thousand troops. He also says 50,000 troops will be withdrawn from Eastern Europe during the next two years, along with 10,000 tanks, 8,500 artillery pieces, and 800 combat aircraft. He asserts that the Soviet military will operate under a defensive military doctrine. After his speech, Gorbachev meets Reagan and Bush. Gorbachev cancels the rest of his trip and returns to the Soviet Union December 8 in response to a severe earthquake in Armenia the previous day.

December 7. *Armenian Earthquake.* An earthquake registering 6.9 on the Richter scale devastates Armenia. At least twenty-five thousand people are killed. The town of Spitak is completely leveled, and the larger cities of Leninakan and Kirovakan sustain severe damage. President Gorbachev tours the area December 10-11.

December 7. *Akhromeev Retires.* Soviet chief of staff and deputy defense minister Marshal Sergei Akhromeev retires amid unconfirmed rumors that he had opposed President Gorbachev's military reforms and troop cuts.

December 13. *Soviets to Dismantle Radar Sites.* The Soviet Union announces that it will dismantle a radar site near Moscow and one near Gomel that the United States maintains are in violation of the ABM treaty.

1989

January 5. *Soviet-Iran Thaw.* Soviet officials receive an Iranian diplomatic delegation in Moscow. In a letter delivered to Mikhail Gorbachev, the Ayatollah Khomeini asks the Soviet leader to abandon communism and study Islam.

January 8. *Shevardnadze on Chemical Arms.* Foreign Minister Shevardnadze announces at a 149-nation conference in Paris on chemical weapons that the Soviet Union will begin reducing its stocks of chemical arms unilaterally.

January 15. *Helsinki Accords Enhanced.* The thirty-five countries of the Conference on Security and Cooperation in Europe agree in Vienna on an enhancement of the 1975 Helsinki Final Act. The new accord specified freedoms that should be protected and outlined measures for assuring human rights.

January 15. *Protest in Czechoslovakia.* An estimated two thousand protesters demonstrate in Prague to commemorate the twentieth anniversary of a suicide committed by a Czechoslovak student in protest of the 1968 Soviet invasion. Police break up the demonstration. Dissident playwright Vaclav Havel is arrested the following day and charged with inciting the riots. Havel is released from prison on May 17, after serving nearly half of his nine-month sentence.

January 27. *Round-table Talks Announced.* Solidarity, the Polish government, and the Catholic Church announce they will hold round-table talks to discuss Poland's political and economic future. The talks open February 6.

February 11. *Multiple Parties in Hungary.* The Central Committee of the Hungarian Communist party sanctions the establishment of independent political parties.

February 15. *Afghan Pullout Completed.* The final Soviet troops remaining in Afghanistan cross the border into the Soviet Union, thereby completing the nine-month Soviet withdrawal on schedule.

February 18-27. *Shevardnadze Tours Middle East.* Foreign Minister Shevardnadze visits Syria, Jordan, Egypt, Iraq, and Iran during a ten-day visit to the Middle East. At separate meetings in Cairo February 22, he confers with Israeli foreign minister Moshe Arens and PLO leader Yasir Arafat. Shevardnadze's trip is seen as an effort by Moscow to improve relations with Middle Eastern states following completion of the Soviet troop withdrawal from Afghanistan. During the trip Shevardnadze reiterates Soviet support for a UN-sponsored Middle East peace conference.

March 6. *CFE Talks Open.* The Conventional Forces in Europe (CFE) talks open in Vienna. They replace the Mutual and Balanced Force Reduction talks, which close permanently in Vienna by mutual agreement March 2. The CFE talks are attended by the members of the NATO and Warsaw Pact alliances and are intended to achieve cuts in conventional weapons in Europe.

March 5. *Yeltsin Supporters Demonstrate.* Five thousand supporters of Boris Yeltsin's candidacy for the Congress of People's Deputies demonstrate in Moscow. On March 19, ten thousand people march on the Moscow city hall to protest a Central Committee investigation of whether Yeltsin broke party discipline by calling for open parliamentary elections.

March 16. *Farm Plan Backed.* The Central Committee endorses President Gorbachev's plan to invigorate Soviet agriculture. Among other features, the plan sanctions the leasing of land from collective farms, abolishes the government's central agriculture agency (Gosagroprom), and allocates more resources to improve rural life.

March 26. *Nationwide Elections Held.* Multi-candidate elections are held for 1,500 seats in the 2,250-seat Congress of People's Deputies. The Communist party's candidates win a large majority of the seats, as expected, but a surprisingly large number of party officials are defeated by reformists and nationalist figures. Yuri Solovev, the first secretary of Leningrad, is rejected when he fails to receive 50 percent of the vote, despite running unopposed. Boris Yeltsin is elected to the Moscow at-large seat with 89 percent of the vote. Nationalists win a majority of the seats in the Baltic republics. Final results of the elections are made public March 31.

March 29. *Gorbachev on Intervention.* After a two-day visit with President Gorbachev in Moscow, Hungarian leader Karoly Grosz tells the Central Committee of the Hungarian Communist party that Gorbachev had denounced Soviet intervention in the affairs of Eastern European nations.

April 2-7. *Gorbachev Trip.* President Gorbachev travels to Cuba and Great Britain. He canceled visits to these countries in December 1988, when the earthquake in Armenia forced him to remain home. Despite Cuba's resistance to Soviet-style reform, Gorbachev is received warmly in Havana April 2. Gorbachev arrives in London April 5. He and British prime minister Thatcher discuss Soviet economic reform, arms control, and regional conflicts. On April 7 Gorbachev delivers a speech at London's Guildhall and meets with Queen Elizabeth II, whom he invites to the Soviet Union.

April 5. *Polish Reform Agreement.* Negotiations between Solidarity and government officials result in agreement on major political and economic reforms. The two sides agree to replace the present unicameral legislature with a bicameral system consisting of a 460-seat lower house and 100-seat upper house. The Communists and their allies are to be guaranteed 65 percent of the seats in the lower house. All seats in the upper house and the remaining seats in the lower house are to be popularly elected. The two also agree to strengthen the presidency, legalize Solidarity, and lift price controls on privately grown farm produce.

April 7. *Soviet Nuclear Sub Sinks.* A Soviet nuclear-powered submarine catches fire and sinks near Norway. The Soviets report the following day that the submarine's reactors had been shut down before it sank. Forty-two of the crew's sixty-nine members are killed.

April 9. *Soldiers Clash with Georgian Protesters.* In Tbilisi, Soviet soldiers attack a crowd of more than ten thousand Georgian protesters, who had been calling for annexation of the autonomous republic of Abkhazia into Georgia. The Soviet government says twenty demonstrators were killed. Georgian party leader Dzhumber Patiashvili resigns. A Georgian newspaper subsequently charges that the Soviet army used poison gas against the crowd. The Politburo authorizes an investigation of the incident April 21. New Georgian Communist party leader Givi Gumbaraidze says April 24 that poison gas was responsible for the deaths of some protesters. Politburo member Vadim Medvedev says April 25 that the authority to break up the protest came from Georgian party leaders, not the Kremlin.

April 25. *Central Committee Purge.* President Gorbachev engineers a purge of the Central Committee. Seventy-four full members and twenty-four candidate members of the Central Committee and twelve members of the Central Oversight Commission are forcibly retired. Most are former high-ranking officials from the Brezhnev era. Andrei Gromyko, Geidar Aliev, Mikhail Solomentsev, Sergei Sokolov, and Boris Ponomarev all lose their Central Committee seats.

April 25. *Conventional Reductions Begin.* The Soviet Union withdraws one thousand tanks from Hungary, the first step in the unilateral conventional force reductions in Eastern Europe announced by President Gorbachev in December 1988.

May 2. *Hungary Ruptures Iron Curtain.* The Hungarian government begins dismantling the barbed wire fence separating it from Austria. Because Hungarians already can travel to Western Europe, no flood of Hungarian refugees is expected. The government says border patrols will continue to discourage citizens of other Eastern European countries visiting Hungary from crossing the border into Austria. East Germany, Hungary, and Romania protest the removal of the fence.

May 10-11. *Baker Visits Moscow.* James A. Baker makes his first trip to Moscow as secretary of state. He and Foreign Minister Shevardnadze agree to resume the START talks, which have been suspended since November 1988. He meets May 11 with President Gorbachev, who announces that the Soviet Union will unilaterally withdraw five hundred nuclear warheads from Europe. Gorbachev also presents Baker with a proposal to cut conventional forces in Europe that would equalize the two sides' forces by 1997. In a commencement address May 12 at Texas A & M University, President Bush says it is "time to move beyond containment" in dealings with the Soviet Union.

May 15-18. *Sino-Soviet Summit.* President Mikhail Gorbachev makes the first trip to China by a Soviet leader since 1959. On May 16 he meets with Deng Xiaoping, and they formally announce the normalization of relations between their two countries. Gorbachev reportedly proposes easing the confrontational military posture along the Sino-Soviet border. His visit is upstaged by massive pro-democracy protests in Beijing's Tiananmen Square that swell to one million people May 17. The Chinese government announces martial law May 20 in an attempt to end the protests. The Chinese army violently crushes the pro-democracy movement June 3-4.

May 16. *Soviets Halt Arms Shipments.* The White House announces that President Gorbachev has informed the Bush administration that the Soviet Union has cut off arms shipments to Nicaragua.

May 25. *Congress Convenes in Moscow.* The new Congress of People's Deputies convenes in Moscow. The congress elects a 542-seat Supreme Soviet dominated by conservatives. Mikhail Gorbachev is elected to the strengthened position of chairman of the Supreme Soviet (president) with 95.6 percent of the deputies' votes. Moscow liberal Boris Yeltsin narrowly misses being elected to the Supreme Soviet. In response to protests in Moscow over Yeltsin's exclusion, Gorbachev says that Yeltsin may have a Supreme Soviet seat if someone else gives one up. A member yields his seat to Yeltsin May 29. The same day Anatolii Lukyanov is elected vice president after being nominated for the post by Gorbachev. The congress' shockingly candid debates on previously taboo subjects are followed closely on television by the Soviet population. Debate topics include the role of the KGB, the recent ethnic unrest in the Caucasus, and defense spending.

May 29. *Bush Conventional Forces Proposal.* At a NATO summit in Brussels, President Bush attempts to seize the arms control initiative from Moscow by outlining a detailed plan for reducing conventional forces in Europe. His plan calls for ceilings on tanks, armored personnel carriers, artillery pieces, helicopters, and fighter aircraft. It also proposes that the Soviet Union and United States reduce their troop strength in Europe to 275,000 soldiers each.

June 3. *Train Wreck Kills Hundreds.* Two passenger trains in the Ural Mountains are destroyed when a gas pipeline explodes near the tracks on which they are traveling. An estimated four hundred persons are killed in the disaster.

June 3-15. *Rioting in Uzbekistan.* Ethnic rioting between Uzbeks and Meskhetians in Uzbekistan leaves nearly one hundred dead. Soviet troops are sent to the region June 4.

June 4. *Polish Elections Held.* Elections are held in Poland for the new legislature. Solidarity dominates the voting, winning virtually every contested seat. Although Communist candidates run unopposed for 299 of the 460 seats in the Sejm (assembly), only five candidates receive the requisite 50 percent of the vote. President Jaruzelski June 6 asks Solidarity to form a coalition government with the communists and their allies, but he is rejected. After runoff elections June 18, Solidarity holds 99 of 100 Senate seats and all 161 opposition seats in the Sejm. Communist party candidates fill the other 294 Sejm seats only after a rule change allows unopposed candidates to win a seat with less than 50 percent of the vote. Jaruzelski announces June 30 that he will not run for president, even though his election to that office had been part of the agreement between the government and Solidarity. The Polish parliament convenes July 4.

June 12-14. *Gorbachev in West Germany.* President Gorbachev travels to Bonn for meetings with Chancellor Kohl. The two leaders sign a joint declaration supporting national self-determination, arms reductions, and the development of a "common European home."

June 16. *Nagy Reburied.* Imre Nagy, who served as prime minister of Hungary and was executed in 1958 for his role in the 1956 Hungarian uprising, is reburied as a national hero amidst a great outpouring of Hungarian nationalist sentiment.

June 19. *Geneva Talks Resume.* Negotiations on strategic arms reductions and space weapons resume in Geneva.

June 27. *Ministerial Nominations Rejected.* For the first time ever, the USSR Supreme Soviet rejects ministerial nominations. Six of Prime Minister Nikolai Ryzhkov's 57 nominees for the Council of Ministers are rejected, forcing him to withdraw the nominations.

July 1. *Gorbachev on Ethnic Violence.* In a nationally televised speech, President Gorbachev warns Soviet citizens that ethnic violence and nationalism threaten his reform program and the Soviet Union as a whole.

July 6. *Gorbachev Speech to Council of Europe.* In a July 6 speech before the Council of Europe in Strasbourg, Gorbachev indicates that he is willing to reduce the Soviet arsenal of short-range missiles and withdraw all Soviet forces from Warsaw Pact territory if the United States will respond with similar measures. Gorbachev also says the Soviet Union will not interfere with the reform movements in Poland and Hungary.

July 6. *Janos Kadar Dies.* Former Hungarian general secretary Janos Kadar, who led the country from 1956 to 1988, dies. He is buried on July 14.

July 7. *Warsaw Pact Summit.* Leaders of the members of the Warsaw Pact nations meet in Bucharest. President Gorbachev calls for "independent solutions of national problems."

July 9-13. *Bush Visits Eastern Europe.* President Bush travels to Poland and Hungary. On July 10 he addresses the Polish parliament and outlines the U.S. aid program for Poland. He meets with Lech Walesa in Gdansk July 11. Walesa presents Bush with a plan calling for $10 billion in U.S. aid (compared with Bush's proposal of $115 million). Bush goes to Budapest July 12, where he meets with Hungarian leaders.

July 10. *Soviet Coal Miners Strike.* Miners in the western Siberian town of Mezhdurechensk strike to protest low wages, poor working and living conditions, shortages of basic products, and environmental destruction. The strike quickly spreads to mining towns throughout the Kuznetsky Basin and threatens the entire Soviet economy. Negotiations between strikers and government officials begin July 17. The same day miners at eight coal mines in the Ukraine's Donetsk Basin go on strike, touching off a widespread walkout in that region. Siberian miners agree July 19 to return to work after the government promises them higher wages, improved living and working conditions, and greater control over mine operations. Strikes in the Ukraine dissipate by July 26, after the government makes similar promises to miners there.

July 18. *Gorbachev Threatens a Purge.* In a speech to the Central Committee, President Gorbachev expresses concern over the people's loss of faith in Communist party leadership. He threatens to purge officials who attempt to block his reform program.

July 19. *Jaruzelski Elected President.* The Polish parliament elects Gen. Wojciech Jaruzelski president. He runs unopposed but receives only the minimum number of votes necessary for election. Jaruzelski, who had previously said he would not run, announced his candidacy the day before the vote.

July 30. *Inter-Regional Group Formed.* About three hundred members of the Congress of People's Deputies form the Inter-Regional Group, an opposition bloc within the congress.

August 7. *East Germans in West German Missions.* The East German government protests Bonn's refusal to expel 130 East Germans who sought refuge in its Berlin mission. Another 180 East Germans take refuge at the

West German embassy in Budapest. On August 24, the Budapest refugees are flown to West Germany. During August growing numbers of East Germans cross the border from Hungary to Austria.

August 18. *Nazi-Soviet Protocols Revealed.* Politburo member Aleksandr Yakovlev admits that the Soviet Union signed secret protocols to the 1939 Nazi-Soviet Nonaggression Pact, which called for the partition of Poland and allowed the Soviet Union to dominate the Baltic states. On August 22, the Lithuanian Supreme Soviet declares the 1940 Soviet annexation of Lithuania illegal.

August 24. *Mazowiecki Becomes Premier.* The Polish Sejm confirms Solidarity member Tadeusz Mazowiecki as premier. The Polish Communist party had been unable to form a government. President Jaruzelski agreed August 17 to allow Solidarity to put together a ruling coalition under the condition that communists head the ministries of defense and interior. President Gorbachev had encouraged the Polish Communists to join the ruling coalition in an August 22 phone call to party leader Mieczyslaw Rakowski.

September 4. *Hungary on Refugees.* The Hungarian government says that East German refugees will not be allowed to cross into Austria until East and West Germany conclude an agreement on their status. Thousands of East German tourists, hoping to flee to Austria, have been piling up in Hungary, creating a crisis for the Hungarian government, trapped between the competing demands of East and West Germany.

September 9. *Yeltsin Visits the United States.* Boris Yeltsin arrives in New York for an eight-day speaking tour that includes stops in Washington, Baltimore, and Chicago. He meets briefly with President Bush at the White House September 12. On September 14, an Italian newspaper accuses Yeltsin of drunken behavior while in the United States. *Pravda* reprints the report September 18.

September 10. *Hungary Opens Border.* The Hungarian government opens the border to Austria to unrestricted emigration by East Germans. Within two days more than ten thousand East Germans cross into Austria on their way to West Germany. In response, East Germany sharply restricts travel to Hungary.

September 12. *Polish Cabinet Formed.* A twenty-three-member cabinet is nominated by Premier Mazowiecki and approved by vote of the Sejm the same day. Eleven Solidarity members, four Communists, and eight representatives of smaller parties make up the cabinet. The Communists are assigned the ministries of defense and interior, as promised, as well as the transportation and foreign trade ministries.

September 19-20. *Politburo Purge.* At a Central Committee plenum, Vladimir Shcherbitskii, Viktor Chebrikov, and Viktor Nikonov are ousted from the Politburo. The plenum promotes KGB head Vladimir Kryuchkov and Gosplan chairman Yuri Maslyukov to full Politburo status. Shcherbitskii is replaced as first secretary of the Ukrainian party September 28 by Vladimir Ivashko.

September 21. *Shevardnadze in United States.* Foreign Minister Shevardnadze visits Washington and delivers a letter to President Bush from President Gorbachev. In the letter, Gorbachev agrees to destroy the Krasnoyarsk radar station, which the United States claims violates the ABM treaty. Shevardnadze and Secretary of State Baker meet September 22 in Jackson Hole, Wyoming. They agree to tentative plans for a 1990 summit meeting. The following day, Baker and Shevardnadze sign agreements concerning prior notification of nuclear tests and exchange of information on nuclear and chemical weapons stockpiles.

September 30. *East German Refugee Agreement.* The East German government agrees to transport 5,500 East Germans to West Germany who have taken refuge in the West German embassy in Prague. After the announcement another five thousand East Germans enter the Prague embassy. Responding to a flood of East Germans into Czechoslovakia, the East German government October 3 restricts travel to that country. On October 4, eleven thousand East Germans board trains in Prague bound for West Germany. Thousands of East Germans jam the tracks along the trains' route through East Germany, hoping to climb on board the refugee trains.

October 1. *Yazov Visits the United States.* Soviet defense minister Dmitrii Yazov begins a six-day tour of the United States. On October 6, he meets with Defense Secretary Richard Cheney at the Pentagon.

October 4. *Additional Aid for Poland.* The White House announces that President Bush will ask for an additional $200 million in economic aid for Poland. The additional assistance would be conditional on the Polish government concluding an agreement with the International Monetary Fund on economic restructuring.

October 6. *Fortieth Anniversary of East Germany.* In a speech in East Berlin on the occasion of the German Democratic Republic's fortieth anniversary, President Gorbachev says that East Germany should adopt Soviet reforms. Large demonstrations break out in several East German cities October 7-9.

October 7. *Hungarian Party Reorganizes.* The Hungarian Socialist Workers (Communist) party changes its name to the Hungarian Socialist party and adopts a social-democratic platform.

October 9. *Law on Strikes Passed.* The Supreme Soviet passes a law legalizing strikes under limited conditions. Strikes by workers in the transportation, communication, defense, and power industries continue to be forbidden.

October 12. *Polish Economic Reform.* The Polish Solidarity-led government announces an economic program designed to combat inflation. Among other measures, state subsidies are cut and the indexing of wages to inflation is limited.

October 18. *Krenz Replaces Honecker.* Egon Krenz replaces Erich Honecker as leader of the East German Communist party and head of state. Honecker reportedly is forced out by his colleagues, who regard his hard-line approach to upheaval in Eastern Europe as impractical. On October 16, one hundred thousand people demonstrated in Leipzig for reforms. Demonstrations continue during the following weeks, including a rally by as many as three hundred thousand protesters in Leipzig October 23.

October 18. *Hungary Amends Constitution.* The Hungarian National Assembly changes the name of the country from "People's Republic of Hungary" to "Republic of Hungary." It also amends the constitution to allow for the establishment of political parties and the strengthening of civil rights guarantees.

October 23. *Shevardnadze Speech.* In a speech to the Supreme Soviet, Foreign Minister Shevardnadze concedes that the Krasnoyarsk radar station violates the ABM treaty. He also says the 1979 Soviet invasion of Afghanistan was an illegal act.

October 25-27. *Gorbachev in Finland.* President Gorbachev visits Helsinki, where he meets with Finnish president Mauno Koivisto. The two leaders sign a joint declaration advocating noninterference in the internal affairs of other countries.

October 28. *Protests in Prague.* On the seventy-first anniversary of the founding of the Czechoslovak Republic, about ten thousand people gather in Prague's Wenceslas Square. Police charge the crowd, beating and arresting hundreds of protesters.

October 31. *Krenz Visits Moscow.* Egon Krenz meets with President Gorbachev in Moscow. On his return to East Germany November 1, Krenz declares his complete support for the policy of perestroika.

October 31. *Malta Summit Announced.* President Bush announces that he and President Gorbachev will meet on ships off the coast of Malta December 2-3.

November 1. *Upheaval in East Germany.* In response to continuing protests, the East German government opens its border with Czechoslovakia, precipitating a flood of refugees into that country who are hoping to reach the West. Five East German Politburo members are removed November 3, and six more are ousted November 8. Half a million people demonstrate in East Berlin for political reforms November 4. Huge crowds also gather in Dresden, Leipzig, and other East German cities. Prime Minister Willi Stoph and the entire cabinet resign November 7. The following day Hans Modrow, reformer from Dresden, is named premier.

November 4. *Kryuchkov Admits KGB Mistakes.* In a televised speech, KGB head Vladimir Kryuchkov says that the KGB once served as a tool of Stalinist repression. He promises that the KGB will never serve such a function again.

November 9. *East Germany Opens Borders.* The East German government announces that East Germans will be free to travel to West Germany or West Berlin without receiving special permission. The order effectively throws open the nation's borders to unrestricted travel and emigration. Thousands of jubilant East and West Berliners hold a spontaneous celebration at the Berlin Wall that lasts for two days.

November 11. *Protest Held in Bulgaria.* Amidst growing protests in Bulgaria, General Secretary Todor Zhivkov unexpectedly resigns and is replaced by Foreign Minister Petar Mladenov.

November 14. *Gorbachev Warning.* In a commentary published in *Pravda*, President Gorbachev warns the West not to interfere in Eastern Europe.

November 15. *Walesa Asks for Marshall Plan.* During a visit to the United States, Polish Solidarity leader Lech Walesa addresses a joint session of Congress and exhorts U.S. policy makers to embark on a new Marshall Plan that would rebuild the economies of Eastern Europe. President Bush awarded Walesa the Medal of Freedom at the White House November 13.

November 17. *Uprising in Czechoslovakia.* A rally in Prague commemorating an anti-Nazi protest held fifty years ago draws twenty thousand people and turns into an antigovernment demonstration. Police break up the demonstration, arresting more than a hundred protesters. One student is rumored to have been killed. The next day two thousand people gather in Prague to protest the student's death. On November 19, Vaclav Havel and other dissidents form the opposition Civic Forum. A peaceful crowd of two hundred thousand demands the resignation of party leader Milos Jakes November 20. Alexander Dubcek, a symbol of the 1968 reform movement, addresses a crowd of two hun-

dred thousand in Prague November 24. The same day, Jakes and the entire Politburo submit their resignations. Karel Urbanek is appointed the new general secretary. Havel warns a massive crowd in Prague estimated at eight hundred thousand not to be fooled by the leadership shuffle, because many hard-liners remain in power. On November 25, Prime Minister Ladislav Adamec announces his resignation but stays on as caretaker. Millions of Czechoslovaks stage a two-hour nationwide strike to demand further liberal changes from the government. Adamec opens negotiations with the Civic Forum on November 28.

November 17. *Modrow Names Cabinet.* East German premier Hans Modrow names a new cabinet. Eleven of twenty-seven members are noncommunists. He also promises to reform the feared Stasis security police force.

November 20. *Ceausescu Reelected.* Nicolae Ceausescu is reelected by the Communist party to another five-year term as general secretary.

November 30. *Gorbachev on Common European Home.* While in Rome on his way to the Malta summit, President Gorbachev delivers a speech in which he outlines his vision of a common European home, where all nations are independent and cooperate economically. He meets with Pope John Paul II December 1, and they agree to work toward establishing diplomatic relations.

December 2-3. *Malta Summit.* President Bush and President Gorbachev travel to Malta for a shipboard summit that is held in a cordial atmosphere despite bad weather that forces changes in the summit agenda. The two leaders discuss the changes in Eastern Europe and agree to accelerate negotiations on chemical weapons and strategic nuclear forces with the intention of concluding arms control treaties sometime in 1990. They also agree to begin talks on a new trade pact that will be contingent on Soviet emigration policy. The summit concludes December 3 with a joint news conference.

December 2. *East German Corruption.* A special parliamentary committee finds that Erich Honecker and other East German leaders engaged in embezzlement, bribe-taking, and currency speculation. On December 3, Honecker and eleven other Communist party leaders are expelled from the party. All members of the Politburo, including General Secretary Egon Krenz and Premier Hans Modrow, resign their party positions. Honecker and the other implicated officials are placed under house arrest December 5. Krenz resigns as president December 6 and is replaced by Manfred Gerlach, head of the Liberal Democratic party, which is allied with the Communists.

December 6. *Lithuanian Communist Monopoly Ended.* The Lithuanian Supreme Soviet votes to end the Communist party's monopoly on political power. The following day, a similar vote legalizes opposition groups.

December 7. *East Germans Set Election Date.* Talks between the Communist party and other political groups set May 6, 1990, as the date for free elections. A Communist party congress December 9 appoints Gregor Gysi the new general secretary and rejects German reunification. Two hundred thousand East Germans demonstrate in Leipzig for reunification December 11.

December 8. Pravda *on Article 6.* A commentary in *Pravda* hints that Article 6 of the USSR Constitution, which guarantees the leading role of the party in Soviet society, could eventually be revoked. President Gorbachev tells the Congress of People's Deputies, which opens on December 12, that it is too soon to discuss Article 6. The Congress votes to delay consideration of the matter.

December 10. *New Czechoslovak Government.* President Gustav Husak resigns after swearing in a new cabinet. Negotiations between outgoing prime minister Ladislav Adamec and the opposition Civic Forum had resulted in agreement on the composition of a new government. Communist reformer Marian Calfa becomes premier. He heads a twenty-one-member cabinet consisting of ten Communists and eleven noncommunists. Parliament is to select an interim president in the near future, and the new government will serve until free parliamentary elections are held. Millions of Czechoslovaks join in a nationwide celebration of the new government December 11.

December 13. *East European Aid Discussed.* The foreign ministers of twenty-four Western nations meet in Brussels to discuss emergency funding for East Europe. The group approves a $1 billion emergency stabilization fund for Poland and a $1 billion loan to Hungary.

December 14. *Sakharov Dies.* Soviet physicist and leading opposition figure Andrei Sakharov suffers a heart attack and dies in Moscow.

December 15-25. *Revolution in Romania.* Crowds in Timisoara prevent Romanian police from arresting Reverend Laszlo Tokes, who had been active in promoting the rights of ethnic Hungarians. Gatherings to protect Tokes turn into pro-democracy demonstrations December 16. Army and security police (Securitate) forces attack demonstrators in Timisoara December 17. At least several hundred and perhaps thousands of citizens are killed and wounded in the assault. On December 20, fifty thousand people in Timisoara rally in protest, causing President Nicolae Ceausescu to return from a state visit to Iran. On December 21, Ceausescu is shouted down as he delivers a speech from the balcony of his Bucharest palace. Violence erupts between crowds of demonstrators in Bucharest and the Securitate forces. The Securitate is unable to control the rebellion, and the army joins the population December 22. A virtual civil war rages in the capital throughout the day. By evening the anti-Ceausescu forces have captured the Royal Palace and most strategic locations in Bucharest. Radio Bucharest announces that a coalition of dissidents, intellectuals, military officers, and former Communists had formed the National Salvation Front to take control of the country. Fighting continues for more than a week between the army and remnants of the Securitate. Ceausescu and his wife, who had disappeared when the fighting began, are captured by the army and executed after a swift military trial on December 25. The Soviet government December 22 hails the overthrow of the Ceausescu regime. The United States moves to recognize the new government on December 25.

December 17. *Polish Economic Measures.* The Polish government announces an austerity program designed to combat inflation. Both houses of parliament subsequently approve the plan, which includes wage ceilings.

December 18. *Soviet-European Agreement.* The Soviet Union and the European Community conclude a ten-year commercial agreement that ends European quotas on most Soviet products.

December 19. *Czechoslovak Elections Scheduled.* The Czechoslovak parliament schedules elections for June 1990 and votes to reconstruct the country's social and economic systems. Premier Calfa meets with President Gorbachev in Moscow on December 20. They agree to open negotiations on the withdrawal of Soviet troops from Czechoslovakia.

December 20. *Lithuanian Communist Declaration.*

The Lithuanian Communist party declares itself independent of the Communist Party of the Soviet Union. Lithuanian party leader Algirdas Brazauskas announces that his party supports the creation of "an independent democratic Lithuanian state." President Gorbachev condemns the action.

December 24. *Nazi-Soviet Pact Condemned.* The Congress of People's Deputies declares that the Soviet Union illegally conspired in 1939 with Nazi Germany to occupy independent nations, including those of the Baltic region. The congress asserts that the Nazi-Soviet non-aggression pact was "invalid."

December 28. *Dubcek, Havel Elected.* The Czechoslovak parliament unanimously elects Alexander Dubcek as its chairman. The next day, the parliament unanimously elects playwright Vaclav Havel interim president.

1990

January 7. *Troops Sent to Georgia.* The Soviet government announces that troops have been sent to Georgia to prevent fighting between Georgian nationalists and members of the Ossetian ethnic group.

January 9. *Ryzhkov Proposal to CMEA.* Prime Minister Ryzhkov formally proposes to the members of the Council for Mutual Economic Assistance (CMEA) that the organization begin basing trade on hard currency and market prices in 1991.

January 11-13. *Gorbachev in Lithuania.* Gorbachev makes a three-day visit to Lithuania in an effort to persuade Communist party officials there to rescind their break with Moscow. Gorbachev is received politely, but Lithuanian leaders and citizens convey their intention to continue seeking independence.

January 15. *State of Emergency in Azerbaidzhan.* Widespread fighting between Armenians and Azerbaidzhanis prompts the Presidium of the Supreme Soviet to decree a state of emergency in parts of Azerbaidzhan. President Gorbachev dispatches eleven thousand Soviet troops to the region January 16. They raise the total Soviet troop strength in Azerbaidzhan to sixteen thousand. Azerbaidzhanis in Baku carried out a pogrom January 13-14 against Armenians in the city that resulted in the deaths of about thirty people. Both sides had responded to the killings by forming volunteer militias. Prime Minister Ryzhkov, in a radio interview, says that the Kremlin had to intervene with armed force to prevent a civil war between Armenia and Azerbaidzhan. The Bush administration gives its support to the Soviet action, characterizing it is as a necessary step to maintain order and protect citizens, not as a move to suppress dissent. The Soviet government reveals January 18 that it is calling up reservists from Slavic republics to support troops in the Caucasus. Widespread protests against the move, however, cause the government to abandon the call-up order December 19.

January 20-21. *Soviet Troops Occupy Baku.* Soviet troops break past barricades and enter Baku during a coordinated nighttime attack. President Gorbachev claims the raid, which was spearheaded by tanks, was necessary as a means of stopping a threatened coup by the Azerbaidzhani Popular Front and restoring order in Baku.

The Azerbaidzhani legislature condemns the Soviet occupation January 22 and threatens to call for a national referendum on secession from the USSR unless all Soviet troops are withdrawn within forty-eight hours. The same day Soviet troops seal the border with Iran to cut off the flow of weapons into Soviet Azerbaidzhan.

January 31. *Bush Troop Proposal.* In his State of the Union address, President Bush proposes that the Soviet Union and the United States cut their forces in Europe to just 195,000 each.

February 2. *Armenian-Azerbaidzhani Peace Talks.* Representatives of Armenia and Azerbaidzhan meet in Riga, Latvia, for peace talks. The two groups will discuss humanitarian issues raised by the conflict in the Caucasus, but they will not address the key issue of control over Nagorno-Karabakh. At the outset, the two groups agree to condemn Moscow's use of troops in the region.

February 4. *Moscow Rally Backs Democratization.* More than a hundred thousand people participate in a pro-democracy rally in Moscow. It is the largest unofficial demonstration since the Bolshevik Revolution. A reformist member of the Supreme Soviet maintains February 5 that President Gorbachev was behind the rally, which he hoped would strengthen his position on the eve of a Central Committee plenum.

February 6. *Monetary Unification Plan.* The West German government proposes unifying the currencies of the two Germanys as a step toward reunification. West German chancellor Helmut Kohl and East German premier Hans Modrow agree February 13 to begin talks on monetary unification.

February 6-11. *Baker in Eastern Europe.* Secretary of State Baker embarks on a five-day tour of Eastern Europe. On February 6, he meets with Czechoslovak president Vaclav Havel. They discuss a U.S. assistance package for Czechoslovakia. Baker arrives in Moscow February 7 for a series of meetings with Soviet officials. He meets with President Gorbachev February 9, and they report progress on arms control issues. On February 10, Baker becomes the first U.S. official to testify before a Soviet parliamentary committee, fielding questions from members of the International Affairs Committee of the Supreme Soviet. Baker flies to Sofia that evening and meets with Bulgarian president Petar Mladenov. He then travels to Bucharest February 11, where he promises Romanian leaders $93.5 million in U.S. emergency food aid.

February 7. *Party Renounces Power Monopoly.* After three days of contentious debate, the Central Committee approves a platform renouncing the Communist party's monopoly on power encoded in Article 6 of the USSR Constitution. The plenum also endorses Gorbachev's proposal to create a Western-style executive presidency.

February 8. *Soviet Arms to Afghanistan.* Gen. H. Norman Schwarzkopf of the U.S. Army tells the Senate Armed Services Committee that the Soviet Union is "pouring" arms and equipment into Afghanistan at a higher rate than when the Soviets were still occupying the country.

February 9. *Soviets Announce Czech Withdrawal.* The Soviet government announces that it will begin to withdraw its troops from Czechoslovakia within the month and will have withdrawn the "fundamental part" of the Soviet combat force by the end of May. The Czechoslovak government had demanded a substantial Soviet withdrawal before elections scheduled for June.

February 10. *Kohl Visits Moscow.* West German chancellor Helmut Kohl meets with President Gorbachev in Moscow. Kohl says after the meeting that Gorbachev had agreed that reunification was a matter for Germans to decide. During the meeting, Gorbachev emphasizes the security interests of Germany's European neighbors.

February 12. *Violence in Tadzhikistan.* Soviet Interior Ministry troops move into the city of Dushanbe in an attempt to quell three days of anti-Armenian rioting in the Central Asian republic of Tadzhikistan. Rioting in the city left 37 dead and 108 wounded.

February 12. *U.S.-Soviet Trade Talks.* Representatives of the United States and the Soviet Union open talks on normalizing trade relations. The talks are designed to produce an agreement that could be signed by President Bush and President Gorbachev at the summit being planned for June in the United States.

February 16. *Shcherbitskii Dies.* Former Ukrainian party chief and Politburo member Vladimir Shcherbitskii dies after a long illness.

February 21. *Poles Request Soviet Military Force.* Polish prime minister Tadeusz Mazowiecki says that Soviet troops should remain in Poland until ambiguities concerning the border between a reunified German state and Poland are resolved.

February 24. *Lithuanian Elections.* The Communist party is soundly defeated in Lithuanian elections, capturing only seven of the ninety republic supreme soviet seats contested. The Sajudis nationalist movement wins an overwhelming majority of the seats.

February 26. *Soviet Troop Withdrawal.* President Gorbachev and Czechoslovak president Havel sign an agreement on removing Soviet troops from Czechoslovakia. The withdrawal is to begin immediately and be completed in stages by July 1, 1991.

March 4. *Elections in Slavic Republics.* Reformist and nationalist candidates dominate voting in elections to republic legislatures and other local offices in Russia, Belorussia, and the Ukraine.

March 11. *Lithuania Declares Independence.* The Supreme Soviet of Lithuania votes 124-0 (with six abstentions) to declare the republic an independent nation. The body elects Vytautas Landsbergis president. Conservative Politburo member Yegor Ligachev says March 12 that force will not be used against Lithuania. President Gorbachev March 13 calls the Lithuanian declaration "illegitimate and invalid" and rules out negotiations.

March 13-15. *Congress Revamps Presidency.* The Congress of People's Deputies votes to strengthen the USSR presidency in accordance with a plan put forward at the February 1990 Central Committee plenum. The same day the congress repeals Article 6 of the USSR Constitution, which guarantees the Communist party's monopoly on power. On March 14, the congress votes to elect the first executive president itself for the first five-year term, then have the president chosen by popular vote beginning in 1995. The following day Mikhail Gorbachev runs unopposed for the new presidency and is elected by a 1,329-495 vote in a secret ballot. Almost four hundred deputies abstain. The new presidential office gives Gorbachev broad executive powers. Many deputies had criticized the restructured presidency as concentrating too much power in one person. The president will have the power to veto legislation, declare war "in case of attack," command the armed forces and the KGB, negotiate all international treaties, issue executive orders, declare martial law, and dissolve the legislature.

March 18. *East German Elections.* A coalition of

parties allied with West German chancellor Helmut Kohl's conservative Christian Democratic party scores a clear victory in East German elections. The coalition favors a rapid reunification with West Germany.

March 18. *Moscow Pressures Lithuania.* Soviet forces begin large-scale maneuvers in Lithuania as part of a campaign to pressure Lithuanian leaders into revoking their declaration of independence. President Gorbachev issues a decree March 21 prohibiting the sale of guns in Lithuania and ordering the KGB to tighten security around Lithuania's borders.

March 24-26. *Presidential Council Appointed.* President Gorbachev appoints a sixteen-member Presidential Council in accordance with legislation passed earlier in the month by the Congress of People's Deputies. The council will advise the president and formulate national policy.

March 25. *Communist Headquarters Seized.* Despite denials by Moscow that it will use military force in Lithuania, Soviet troops occupy the headquarters of the Lithuanian Communist party in Vilnius. Troops also raid a psychiatric hospital in Vilnius March 27 and remove twenty-three Lithuanian military deserters given refuge there.

March 31. *Gorbachev Warning.* President Gorbachev warns Lithuanian leaders to renounce their independence declaration or face "grave consequences." Lithuanian president Landsbergis says April 2 that the republic's move to independence was intended to be gradual and its timing could be negotiated. He repeats an earlier call for negotiations with Moscow on the crisis.

April 5. *Summit Announced.* During talks in Washington, Secretary of State Baker and Foreign Minister Shevardnadze announce agreement on holding a U.S.-Soviet summit in the United States from May 30 to June 3. The two men also discuss the situation in Lithuania. Baker reportedly emphasized that superpower relations would be damaged if Moscow used force against Lithuania.

April 18. *Oil Shipments to Lithuania Stopped.* The Soviet leadership orders that Lithuania's oil supply be cut off to force the republic's leaders to rescind their declaration of independence. Natural gas pipelines supplying Lithuania are closed the following day. On April 13 President Gorbachev had threatened an economic embargo against Lithuania if it did not rescind its independence declaration.

April 24. *Bush Avoids Imposing Sanctions.* President Bush April 24 delays consideration of sanctions against the Soviet Union for its conduct toward Lithuania. He says U.S. sanctions could hurt Lithuania's cause and the progress of reform in the Soviet Union. Lithuanian president Vytautas Landsbergis denounces Bush's decision.

May 1. *May Day Protest.* President Gorbachev and other Soviet leaders are jeered by protesters at the yearly May Day parade in Moscow. Traditionally the parade in Red Square had been a well-orchestrated affair supporting the Kremlin's political line, but the Soviet leadership had decided that for the first time unofficial marchers would be allowed to participate. After the organized parade passes through the square, thousands of demonstrators march in, shouting slogans and holding banners that denounce Gorbachev, the Communist party, and Marxist-Leninist ideology. Gorbachev and the leadership watch the display from the top of Lenin's Mausoleum for about twenty-five minutes before leaving.

May 2. *West German President Affirms Border.* During a visit to Warsaw, West German president Richard von Weizsaecker declares that current Polish borders are "inviolable." The East and West German parliaments approve a resolution guaranteeing Poland's borders June 21.

May 3. *Bush Meets Lithuanian Prime Minister.* Prime Minister Kazimiera Prunskiene of Lithuania meets with President Bush at the White House. Bush rejects her suggestion that the United States could mediate the dispute between Lithuania and Moscow.

May 4. *Latvia Moves for Independence.* Defying warnings from Moscow, the Latvian parliament announces the beginning of a transition period leading to the republic's independence. Mindful of Moscow's economic blockade against Lithuania, the Latvians proceed more cautiously, declaring that the USSR Constitution and most Soviet laws would be applicable in the republic until independence, which would come only after negotiations with Moscow.

May 5. *German Reunification Talks Open.* Talks on German reunification between the four victorious powers from World War II and the two Germanys open in Bonn. Foreign Minister Shevardnadze states that the Soviet Union will accept a united Germany but will not allow it to be a member of NATO.

May 12. *Baltics Agree to Coordination.* The presidents of the three Baltic republics meet and agree to coordinate their domestic and foreign policies in an effort to regain their independence from the Soviet Union.

May 16. *USSR Granted GATT Observer Status.* At the urging of the Bush administration, the Soviet Union is granted observer status in GATT (General Agreement on Tariffs and Trade). At the Malta summit, Bush had promised to remove American obstacles to Soviet participation.

May 17. *Gorbachev Meets with Prunskiene.* President Gorbachev meets with Prime Minister Kazimiera Prunskiene of Lithuania in the Kremlin. It is Gorbachev's first face-to-face meeting with a representative of the new Lithuanian government. The day before, the Lithuanian parliament had agreed to suspend all laws implementing its declaration of independence, although not the act itself. However, Gorbachev continues to insist that suspension of the declaration is a precondition to beginning formal negotiations.

May 18. *Baker Negotiates Arms Pact in Moscow.* Secretary of State Baker announces that after four days of intensive negotiations in Moscow, major differences on cruise missiles have been resolved, so that a general statement of principles on the strategic arms reduction treaty can be signed at the upcoming Washington summit. Progress also is made on a chemical weapons agreement.

May 21. *Ruling Front Wins in Romania.* Romanians go against the anticommunist electoral tide in Eastern Europe by giving the ruling National Salvation Front, which is dominated by former Communists, 73 percent of the vote, and electing Ion Iliescu as president with 89 percent of the vote. Foreign observers noted that, despite some local irregularities, the elections were generally free and fair.

May 21. *Law on Presidential Insult Passed.* The Supreme Soviet passes a law making insulting the Soviet president a crime punishable by a prison term, but only if the insults are expressed "in an indecent way."

May 24. *Ryzhkov Economic Plan.* Prime Minister Ryzhkov introduces a plan in the Supreme Soviet to double food prices as a first step in economic reform. The price increases would be subject to a public referendum. Ryzhkov sets a "regulated market economy" as his goal.

The announcement triggers panic buying in Moscow stores, and sales of certain items are restricted to legal residents of Moscow. Ryzhkov's plan is harshly criticized by legislators.

May 29. *Yeltsin Elected Russian President.* Maverick populist Boris Yeltsin is elected president of the Russian republic, defeating Gorbachev's ally, Aleksandr Vlasov.

May 31-June 3. *Washington Summit.* At a summit in Washington, President Bush and President Gorbachev sign an agreement outlining mutual reductions in their countries' strategic nuclear arsenals. The agreement is to serve as a basis for a formal treaty that the leaders indicate could be concluded by the end of the year. They also sign a treaty providing for major reductions in chemical weapons. Bush unexpectedly signs a trade treaty with the Soviet Union, even though a Soviet law formally codifying the removal of restrictions on emigration has not yet been passed. Congress had declared passage of the law to be a precondition to normal U.S.-Soviet trade. To avoid a confrontation with Congress, Bush says he will not submit the treaty for congressional approval until the Soviets pass the law. After leaving Washington, Gorbachev visits Minnesota June 3 and San Francisco June 4, where he meets with South Korean leader Roh Tae Woo.

June 8. *Russian Republic Declares Sovereignty.* The Russian supreme soviet declares that its laws take precedence over Soviet laws. The move is considered a victory for new Russian president Boris Yeltsin, even though the vote falls short of the two-thirds majority needed to amend the Russian constitution.

June 8. *Elections in Czechoslovakia.* President Vaclav Havel's Civic Forum and its Slovak counterpart, Public Against Violence, win a broad majority in the national parliament, reflecting popular enthusiasm for Havel's management of the government.

June 10. *Soviets Intervene in Kirgizia Violence.* Soviet troops intervene to break up violence between Kirgiz and Uzbeks after the death toll rises to at least 107.

June 12. *Supreme Soviet Passes Press Law.* A law on freedom of the press is approved, forbidding government censorship and allowing any citizen eighteen years or older to open a newspaper. Supporters hail the law as a major step in expanding glasnost but complain that the government still is able to control the nation's publishing through its power to allocate the limited supplies of newsprint.

June 12. *Gorbachev Concession on Germany.* In a speech to the Supreme Soviet, Gorbachev hints that German membership in NATO might be acceptable if Germany retained "associate membership" in the Warsaw Pact. This formulation is considered a concession to the Western position that a united Germany must be a member of NATO. West Germany welcomes the shift as positive but insists that it does not want dual membership.

June 14. *Government Economic Plan Rejected.* Responding to popular concern, the Supreme Soviet rejects the government's proposal to increase food prices by a vote of 319 to 33. The Supreme Soviet approves a plan to develop joint stock companies and a commercial banking system.

June 18. *Bulgarian Communists' Electoral Victory.* Election results are released showing that Bulgaria's former Communist party (renamed the Socialist party) has won a majority of the seats in the country's new parliament, based on runoffs in the first free multi-party elections in Bulgaria in forty-five years. Although charges of intimidation and fraud were raised after the first round, international observers called the elections generally free and fair.

June 19-23. *Russian Party Congress.* The newly formed Russian wing of the Communist party holds its first congress. The meeting is dominated by conservatives who criticize President Gorbachev and his program. Gorbachev defends his record, saying the hard-liners had "lost touch with reality long ago." Angered by the criticism, he hints that he might resign his post as general secretary at the upcoming Twenty-eighth Party Congress. Conservative Ivan Polozkov, a doctrinaire Leninist and critic of Gorbachev, is elected Russian party leader.

June 21. *Two Germanys Approve Economic Union.* The parliaments of the two Germanys approve a treaty on economic and monetary union. According to the treaty, the two economies will be merged on July 1.

June 29. *Lithuania Delays Independence.* The Lithuanian parliament agrees to suspend its declaration of independence for a hundred days in exchange for negotiations with Moscow and the lifting of economic sanctions. Moscow reopens the oil pipeline to Lithuania June 30. The end of the embargo is formally announced in a brief telephone call to the Lithuanian government from the Ministry of Petroleum and Gas Industry.

July 1. *East and West German Economies Merge.* The East and West Germany economic systems are united. East Germans trade their currency for deutschemarks. East German shops are immediately stocked with Western goods. Fears of inflation fueled by massive East German spending prove unwarranted, and the deutschemark remains steady on international currency markets.

July 2-14. *Soviet Party Congress.* The Twenty-eighth Congress of the Communist Party of the Soviet Union opens in Moscow with a speech by President Gorbachev defending his policies and pleading for party unity. Later July 2 the congress rejects a demand by a conservative delegate for the entire leadership to resign. On July 7, Gorbachev is able to reverse a decision by the delegates to subject each member of the leadership to an individual vote of confidence. The same day, the Ukrainian supreme soviet calls home deputies who are members of the body to discuss a proposal for Ukrainian sovereignty. Gorbachev responds to critics of his reform program in a blunt speech delivered July 10. After the address he is overwhelmingly reelected general secretary. On July 12, the congress elects Gorbachev's candidate, Vladimir Ivashko, to the post of deputy general secretary. Ivashko defeats leading conservative Politburo member Yegor Ligachev. Later that day, Russian president Boris Yeltsin announces that he is resigning from the party. During the next two days dozens of other liberal delegates follow his example and resign. On July 14 the congress selects members for a reorganized and expanded Politburo that includes only Gorbachev and Ivashko from the old Politburo. The new Politburo contains twenty-four members, including the first secretaries of all fifteen republics. Western observers say the expansion of the Politburo will reduce its influence and facilitate the ongoing transfer of power from party to government institutions.

July 5. *Havel Reelected President.* Vaclav Havel is elected president of Czechoslovakia by a 234-50 vote of the parliament, for an initial two-year term. He had been elected president for an interim period, which began December 29, 1989.

July 5-6. *NATO Leaders Meet.* In a historic meeting, NATO leaders gather in London and declare that the cold war is over. They announce a new defensive doctrine that would use nuclear forces as "weapons of last resort" and propose that NATO, the Warsaw Pact, and other European states join in a "commitment to nonaggression." Gorbachev is invited to address the NATO leaders in Brussels. The language of the declaration is clearly intended to bolster Gorbachev by addressing his concerns about NATO.

July 15-16. *Gorbachev Accepts Germany in NATO.* On the second day of talks between President Gorbachev and Chancellor Helmut Kohl, the two sides announce agreement on all major issues relating to German unification. The Soviet Union will renounce all restrictions on German sovereignty. These include allowing Germany to join any alliance it chooses. West German leaders have stated their intention to make a united Germany a full member of NATO. In exchange for Soviet approval of German unification on German terms, Kohl promises to negotiate a treaty with the Soviet Union covering political, economic, military, scientific, and cultural relations. The Soviet Union agrees to withdraw its approximately 380,000 troops from East Germany within three or four years. West Germany will help pay the costs of their maintenance and withdrawal. In addition the agreement limits the size of the united Germany's military to 370,000 troops. Currently, the German armies combined have 667,000 troops.

July 16. *Ukrainians Declare Sovereignty.* The Communist-controlled Ukrainian parliament passes a motion of sovereignty, 355-4, but stops short of declaring full independence. The Ukraine is the tenth republic to pass some type of sovereignty declaration. The measure asserts that the Ukraine has the right to mint its own currency, organize its own military, and establish citizenship requirements.

Selected Documents

Following are texts of selected documents, speeches, and letters that have figured prominently in Soviet affairs since the end of World War II. The texts are arranged in chronological order.

WINSTON CHURCHILL'S 'IRON CURTAIN' SPEECH

Following are excerpts from Winston Churchill's "Iron Curtain" speech, delivered March 5, 1946, at Westminster College, Fulton, Missouri. The text is excerpted from The Sinews of Peace: Post-war Speeches by Winston S. Churchill, *ed. Randolph S. Churchill (Boston: Houghton Mifflin Co., 1949).*

. . . The United States stands at this time at the pinnacle of world power. It is a solemn moment for the American Democracy. For with primacy in power is also joined an awe-inspiring accountability to the future. If you look around you, you must feel not only the sense of duty done but also you must feel anxiety lest you fall below the level of achievement. Opportunity is here now, clear and shining for both our countries. To reject it or ignore it or fritter it away will bring upon us all the long reproaches of the after-time. It is necessary that constancy of mind, persistency of purpose, and the grand simplicity of decision shall guide and rule the conduct of the English-speaking peoples in peace as they did in war. . . .

When American military men approach some serious situation they are wont to write at the head of their directive the words "over-all strategic concept". There is wisdom in this, as it leads to clarity of thought. What then is the over-all strategic concept which we should inscribe today? It is nothing less than the safety and welfare, the freedom and progress, of all the homes and families of all the men and women in all the lands. . . . To give security to these countless homes, they must be shielded from the two giant marauders, war and tyranny. . . . The awful ruin of Europe, with all its vanished glories, and of large parts of Asia glares us in the eyes. . . . When I stand here, this quiet afternoon I shudder to visualise what is actually happening to millions now and what is going to happen in this period when famine stalks the earth. None can compute what has been called "the unestimated sum of human pain". Our supreme task and duty is to guard the homes of the common people from the horrors and miseries of another war. We are all agreed on that.

Our American military colleagues, after having proclaimed their "over-all strategic concept" and computed available resources, always proceed to the next step — namely, the method. Here again there is widespread agreement. A world organisation has already been erected for the prime purpose of preventing war. UNO [United Nations Organization], the successor of the League of Nations, with the decisive addition of the United States and all that that means, is already at work. We must make sure that its work is fruitful, that it is a reality and not a sham, that it is a force for action, and not merely a frothing of words, that it is a true temple of peace in which the shields of many nations can some day be hung up, and not merely a cockpit in a Tower of Babel. Before we cast away the solid assurances of national armaments for self-preservation we must be certain that our temple is built, not upon shifting sands or quagmires, but upon the rock. Anyone can see with his eyes open that our path will be difficult and also long, but if we persevere together as we did in the two world wars — though not, alas, in the interval between them — I cannot doubt that we shall achieve our common purpose in the end.

I have, however, a definite and practical proposal to make for action. Courts and magistrates may be set up but they cannot function without sheriffs and constables. The United Nations Organisation must immediately begin to be equipped with an international armed force. . . . I propose that each of the Powers and States should be invited to delegate a certain number of air squadrons to the service of the world organisation. These squadrons would be trained and prepared in their own countries, but would move around in rotation from one country to another. They would wear the uniform of their own countries but with different badges. They would not be required to act against their own nation, but in other respects they would be directed by the world organisation. This might be started on a modest scale and would grow as confidence grew. I wished to see this done after the first world war, and I devoutly trust it may be done forthwith.

It would nevertheless be wrong and imprudent to entrust the secret knowledge or experience of the atomic bomb, which the United States, Great Britain, and Canada now share, to the world organisation, while it is still in its infancy. It would be criminal madness to cast it adrift in this still agitated and un-united world. No one in any country has slept less well in their beds because this knowledge, and the method and the raw materials to apply it, are at present largely retained in American hands. I do not believe we should all have slept so soundly had the position been reversed and if some Communist or neo-Fascist State monopolised for the time being these dread agencies. The fear of them alone might easily have been used to enforce totalitarian systems upon the free democratic world, with consequences appalling to human imagination. God has willed that this shall not be and we have at least a breathing space to set our house in order before this peril has to be encountered: and even then, if no effort is spared, we should still possess so formidable a superiority as to impose effective deterrents upon its employment, or threat of employment, by others.

Ultimately, when the essential brotherhood of man is truly embodied and expressed in a world organisation with all the necessary practical safeguards to make it effective, these powers would naturally be confided to that world organisation.

Now I come to the second danger of these two marauders which threatens the cottage, the home, and the ordinary people — namely, tyranny. We cannot be blind to the fact that the liberties enjoyed by individual citizens throughout the British Empire are not valid in a considerable number of countries, some of which are very powerful. In these States control is enforced upon the common people by various kinds of all-embracing police governments. The power of the State is exercised without restraint, either by dictators or by compact oligarchies operating through a privileged party and a political police. It is not our duty at this time when difficulties are so numerous to interfere forcibly in the internal affairs of countries which we have not conquered in war. But we must never cease to proclaim in fearless tones the great principles of freedom and the rights of man which are the joint inheritance of the English-speaking world and which through Magna Carta, the Bill of Rights, the Habeas Corpus, trial by jury, and the English common law find their most famous expression in the American Declaration of Independence.

'Title Deeds of Freedom'

... Here are the title deeds of freedom which should lie in every cottage home. Here is the message of the British and American peoples to mankind. Let us preach what we practise — let us practise what we preach.

I have now stated the two great dangers which menace the homes of the people: War and Tyranny. I have not yet spoken of poverty and privation which are in many cases the prevailing anxiety. But if the dangers of war and tyranny are removed, there is no doubt that science and co-operation can bring in the next few years to the world, certainly in the next few decades newly taught in the sharpening school of war, an expansion of material well-being beyond anything that has yet occurred in human experience. Now, at this sad and breathless moment, we are plunged in the hunger and distress which are the aftermath of our stupendous struggle; but this will pass and may pass quickly, and there is no reason except human folly or sub-human crime which should deny to all the nations the inauguration and enjoyment of an age of plenty. ...

Now, while still pursuing the method of realising our overall strategic concept, I come to the crux of what I have travelled here to say. Neither the sure prevention of war, nor the continuous rise of world organisation, will be gained without what I have called the fraternal association of the English-speaking peoples. This means a special relationship between the British Commonwealth and Empire and the United States. ... Fraternal association requires not only the growing friendship and mutual understanding between our two vast but kindred systems of society, but the continuance of the intimate relationship between our military advisers, leading to common study of potential dangers. ... The United States has already a Permanent Defence Agreement with the Dominion of Canada, which is so devotedly attached to the British Commonwealth and Empire. This Agreement is more effective than many of those which have often been made under formal alliances. This principle should be extended to all British Commonwealths with full reciprocity. Thus, whatever happens, and thus only, shall we be secure ourselves and able to work together for the high and simple causes that are dear to us and bode no ill to any. Eventually there may come — I feel eventually there will come — the principle of common citizenship, but that we may be content to leave to destiny, whose outstretched arm many of us can already clearly see. ...

A shadow has fallen upon the scenes so lately lighted by the Allied victory. Nobody knows what Soviet Russia and its Communist international organisation intends to do in the immediate future, or what are the limits, if any, to their expansive and proselytising tendencies. I have a strong admiration and regard for the valiant Russian people and for my wartime comrade, Marshal Stalin. There is deep sympathy and goodwill in Britain — and I doubt not here also — towards the peoples of all the Russias and a resolve to persevere through many differences and rebuffs in establishing lasting friendships. We understand the Russian need to be secure on her western frontiers by the removal of all possibility of German aggression. We welcome Russia to her rightful place among the leading nations of the world. We welcome her flag upon the seas. Above all, we welcome constant, frequent and growing contacts between the Russian people and our own people on both sides of the Atlantic. It is my duty however, for I am sure you would wish me to state the facts as I see them to you, to place before you certain facts about the present position in Europe.

'An Iron Curtain Has Descended'

From Stettin in the Baltic to Trieste in the Adriatic, an iron curtain has descended across the Continent. Behind that line lie all the capitals of the ancient states of Central and Eastern Europe. Warsaw, Berlin, Prague, Vienna, Budapest, Belgrade, Bucharest and Sofia, all these famous cities and the populations around them lie in what I must call the Soviet sphere, and all are subject in one form or another, not only to Soviet influence but to a very high and, in many cases, increasing measure of control from Moscow. Athens alone — Greece with its immortal glories — is free to decide its future at an election under British, American and French observation. The Russian-dominated Polish Government has been encouraged to make enormous and wrongful inroads upon Germany, and mass expulsions of millions of Germans on a scale grievous and undreamed of are now taking place. The Communist parties, which were very small in all these Eastern States of Europe, have been raised to pre-eminence and power far beyond their numbers and are seeking everywhere to obtain totalitarian control. Police governments are prevailing in nearly every case, and so far, except in Czechoslovakia, there is no true democracy.

Turkey and Persia are both profoundly alarmed and disturbed at the claims which are being made upon them and at the pressure being exerted by the Moscow Government. An attempt is being made by the Russians in Berlin to build up a quasi-Communist party in their zone of Occupied Germany by showing special favours to groups of left-wing German leaders. At the end of the fighting last June, the American and British Armies withdrew westwards, in accordance with an earlier agreement, to a depth at some points of 150 miles upon a front of nearly four hundred miles, in order to allow our Russian allies to occupy this vast expanse of territory which the Western Democracies had conquered.

If now the Soviet Government tries, by separate action, to build up a pro-Communist Germany in their areas, this will cause new serious difficulties in the British and American zones, and will give the defeated Germans the power of putting themselves up to auction between the Soviets and the Western Democracies. Whatever conclusions may be drawn from these facts — and facts they are — this is certainly not the Liberated Europe we fought to build up. Nor is it one which contains the essentials of permanent peace.

The safety of the world requires a new unity in Europe, from which no nation should be permanently outcast. It is from the quarrels of the strong parent races in Europe that the world wars we have witnessed, or which occurred in former times, have sprung. Twice in our own lifetime we have seen the United States, against their wishes and their traditions, against arguments, the force of which it is impossible not to comprehend, drawn by irresistible forces, into these wars in time to secure the victory of the good cause, but only after frightful slaughter and devastation had occurred. Twice the United States has had to send several millions of its young men across the Atlantic to find the war; but now war can find any nation, wherever it may dwell between dusk and dawn. Surely we should work with conscious purpose for a grand pacification of Europe, within the structure of the United Nations and in accordance with its Charter. That I feel is an open cause of policy of very great importance.

'Other Causes for Anxiety'

In front of the iron curtain which lies across Europe are other causes for anxiety. In Italy the Communist Party is seriously hampered by having to support the Communist-trained Marshal Tito's claims to former Italian territory at the head of the Adriatic. Nevertheless the future of Italy hangs in the balance. Again one cannot imagine a regenerated Europe without a strong France. All my public life I have worked for a strong France and I never lost faith in her destiny, even in the darkest hours. I will not lose faith now. However, in a great number of countries, far from the Russian frontiers and throughout the world, Communist fifth columns are established and work in complete unity and absolute obedience to the directions they receive from the Communist centre. Except in the British Commonwealth and in the United States where Communism is in its infancy, the Communist parties or fifth columns constitute a growing challenge and peril to Christian civilisation. These are sombre facts for anyone to have to recite on the morrow of a victory gained by so much splendid comradeship in arms and in the cause of freedom and democracy; but we should be most unwise not to face them squarely while time remains.

The outlook is also anxious in the Far East and especially in Manchuria. The Agreement which was made at Yalta, to which I was a party, was extremely favourable to Soviet Russia, but it was made at a time when no one could say that the German war might not extend all through the summer and autumn of 1945 and when the Japanese war was expected to last for a further 18 months from the end of the German war. In this country you are all so well-informed about the Far East, and such devoted friends of China, that I do not need to expatiate on the situation there....

In those days [of the Versailles Treaty] there were high hopes and unbounded confidence that the wars were over, and that the League of Nations would become all-powerful. I do not see or feel that same confidence or even the same hopes in the haggard world at the present time.

On the other hand I repulse the idea that a new war is inevitable; still more that it is imminent. It is because I am sure that our fortunes are still in our own hands and that we hold the power to save the future, that I feel the duty to speak out now that I have the occasion and the opportunity to do so. I do not believe that Soviet Russia desires war. What they desire is the fruits of war and the indefinite expansion of their power and doctrines. But what we have to consider here to-day while time remains, is the permanent prevention of war and the establishment of conditions of freedom and democracy as rapidly as possible in all countries. Our difficulties and dangers will not be removed by closing our eyes to them. They will not be removed by mere waiting to see what happens; nor will they be removed by a policy of appeasement. What is needed is a settlement, and the longer this is delayed, the more difficult it will be and the greater our dangers will become.

From what I have seen of our Russian friends and Allies during the war, I am convinced that there is nothing they admire so much as strength, and there is nothing for which they have less respect than for weakness, especially military weakness. For that reason the old doctrine of a balance of power is unsound. We cannot afford, if we can help it, to work on narrow margins, offering temptations to a trial of strength. If the Western Democracies stand together in strict adherence to the principles of the United Nations Charter, their influence for furthering those principles will be immense and no one is likely to molest them. If however they become divided or falter in their duty and if these all-important years are allowed to slip away then indeed catastrophe may overwhelm us all.

'The Sinews of Peace'

... There never was a war in all history easier to prevent by timely action than the one which has just desolated such great areas of the globe. It could have been prevented in my belief without the firing of a single shot, and Germany might be powerful, prosperous and honoured to-day; but no one would listen and one by one we were all sucked into the awful whirlpool. We surely must not let that happen again. This can only be achieved by reaching now, in 1946, a good understanding on all points with Russia under the general authority of the United Nations Organisation and by the maintenance of that good understanding through many peaceful years, by the world instrument, supported by the whole strength of the English-speaking world and all its connections. There is the solution which I respectfully offer to you in this Address to which I have given the title "The Sinews of Peace".

Let no man underrate the abiding power of the British Empire and Commonwealth.... If the population of the English-speaking Commonwealths be added to that of the United States with all that such co-operation implies in the air, on the sea, all over the globe and in science and in industry, and in moral force, there will be no quivering, precarious balance of power to offer its temptation to ambition or adventure. On the contrary, there will be an overwhelming assurance of security. If we adhere faithfully to the Charter of the United Nations and walk forward in sedate and sober strength seeking no one's land or treasure, seeking to lay no arbitrary control upon the thoughts of men; if all British moral and material forces and convictions are joined with your own in fraternal association, the highroads of the future will be clear, not only for us but for all, not only for our time, but for a century to come.

THE 'SECRET SPEECH' OF NIKITA KHRUSHCHEV

Following are excerpts from the "Secret Speech" delivered by Nikita S. Khrushchev February 24, 1956, at the Twentieth Soviet Communist Party Congress, text as supplied by the U.S. Department of State. (Note: Remarks in parentheses describe audience reaction. Explanations and identifying notes in brackets were added by Congressional Quarterly.)

Comrades! In the report of the Central Committee of the party at the 20th Congress, in a number of speeches by delegates to the congress, as also formerly during the plenary CC/CPSU [Central Committee/Communist Party of the Soviet Union] sessions, quite a lot has been said about the cult of the individual and about its harmful consequences.

After Stalin's death the Central Committee of the party began to implement a policy of explaining concisely and consistently that it is impermissible and foreign to the spirit of Marxism-Leninism to elevate one person, to transform him into a superman possessing supernatural characteristics akin to those of a god. Such a man supposedly knows everything, sees everything, thinks for everyone, can do anything, is infallible in his behavior.

Such a belief about a man, and specifically about Stalin, was cultivated among us for many years....

The great modesty of the genius of the revolution, Vladimir Ilyich Lenin, is known. Lenin had always stressed the role of the people as the creator of history, the directing and organizational role of the party as a living and creative organism, and also the role of the Central Committee.

Marxism does not negate the role of the leaders of the workers' class in directing the revolutionary liberation movement.

While ascribing great importance to the role of the leaders and organizers of the masses, Lenin at the same time mercilessly stigmatized every manifestation of the cult of the individual, inexorably combated the foreign-to-Marxism views about a "hero" and a "crowd" and countered all efforts to oppose a "hero" to the masses and to the people.

Lenin taught that the party's strength depends on its indissoluble unity with the masses, on the fact that behind the party follow the people — workers, peasants and intelligentsia. "Only he will win and retain the power," said Lenin, "who believes in the people, who submerges himself in the fountain of the living creativeness of the people."...

During Lenin's life the Central Committee of the party was a real expression of collective leadership of the party and of the nation. Being a militant Marxist-revolutionist, always unyielding in matters of principle, Lenin never imposed by force his views upon his co-workers. He tried to convince; he patiently explained his opinions to others. Lenin always diligently observed that the norms of party life were realized, that the party statute was enforced, that the party congresses and the plenary sessions of the Central Committee took place at the proper intervals.

In addition to the great accomplishments of V. I. Lenin for the victory of the working class and of the working peasants, for the victory of our party and for the application of the ideas of scientific communism to life, his acute mind expressed itself also in this, that he detected in Stalin in time those negative characteristics which resulted later in grave consequences. Fearing for the future fate of the party and of the Soviet nation, V. I. Lenin made a completely correct characterization of Stalin, pointing out that it was necessary to consider the question of transferring Stalin from the position of the secretary general because of the fact that Stalin is excessively rude, that he does not have a proper attitude toward his comrades, that he is capricious and abuses his power.

In December 1922 in a letter to the Party Congress Vladimir Ilyich wrote: "After taking over the position of secretary general Comrade Stalin accumulated in his hands immeasurable power and I am not certain whether he will be always able to use this power with the required care."

This letter — a political document of tremendous importance, known in the party history as Lenin's "testament" — was distributed among the delegates to the 20th Party Congress. You have read it, and will undoubtedly read it again more than once. You might reflect on Lenin's plain words, in which expression is given to Vladimir Ilyich's anxiety concerning the party, the people, the state, and the future direction of party policy....

This document of Lenin's was made known to the delegates at the 13th Party Congress [May 1924], who discussed the question of transferring Stalin from the position of secretary general. The delegates declared themselves in favor of retaining Stalin in this post, hoping that he would heed the critical remarks of Vladimir Ilyich and would be able to overcome the defects which caused Lenin serious anxiety.

Comrades! The Party Congress should become acquainted with two new documents, which confirm Stalin's character as already outlined by Vladimir Ilyich Lenin in his "testament." These documents are a letter from Nadezhda Konstantinovna Krupskaya [Lenin's wife] to [Lev B.] Kamenev, who was at that time head of the Political Bureau, and a personal letter from Vladimir Ilyich Lenin to Stalin.

I will now read these documents:

"Lev Borisovich!

"Because of a short letter which I had written in words dictated to me by Vladimir Ilyich by permission of the doctors, Stalin allowed himself yesterday an unusually rude outburst directed at me. This is not my first day in the party. During all these thirty years I have never heard from any comrade one word of rudeness. The business of the party and of Ilyich are not less dear to me than to Stalin. I need at present the maximum of self-control. What one can and what one cannot discuss with Ilyich — I know better than any doctor, because I know what makes him nervous and what does not, in any case I know better than Stalin. I am turning to you and to Grigory [Zinoviev] as to much closer comrades of V. I. and I beg you to protect me from rude interference with my private life and from vile invectives and threats. I have no doubt as to what will be the unanimous decision of the Control Commission, with which Stalin sees fit to threaten me; however, I have neither the strength nor the time to waste on this foolish quarrel. And I am a living person and my nerves are strained to the utmost.

"N. Krupskaya"

Nadezhda Konstantinovna wrote this letter on December 23, 1922. After two and a half months, in March 1923, Vladimir Ilyich Lenin sent Stalin the following letter:

"To Comrade Stalin:

"Copies for: Kamenev and Zinoviev.

"Dear Comrade Stalin!

"You permitted yourself a rude summons of my wife to the telephone and a rude reprimand of her. Despite the fact that she told you that she agreed to forget what was said, nevertheless Zinoviev and Kamenev heard about it from her. I have no intention to forget so easily that which is being done against me, and I need not stress here that I consider as directed against me that which is being done against my wife. I ask you, therefore, that you weigh carefully whether you are agreeable to retracting your words and apologizing or whether you prefer the severance of relations between us.

"Sincerely:
"Lenin

"March 5, 1923"

(Commotion in the hall)

Comrades! I will not comment on these documents. They speak eloquently for themselves. Since Stalin could behave in this manner during Lenin's life, could thus behave toward Nadezhda Konstantinovna Krupskaya, whom the party knows well and values highly as a loyal friend of Lenin and as an active fighter for the cause of the party since its creation — we can easily imagine how Stalin treated other people. These negative characteristics of his developed steadily and during the last years acquired an absolutely insufferable character.

As later events have proven, Lenin's anxiety was justified: in the first period after Lenin's death Stalin still paid attention to his [Lenin's] advice, but later he began to disregard the serious admonitions of Vladimir Ilyich.

'Grave Abuse of Power by Stalin'

When we analyze the practice of Stalin in regard to the direction of the party and of the country, when we pause to consider everything which Stalin perpetrated, we must be convinced that Lenin's fears were justified. The negative characteristics of Stalin, which, in Lenin's time, were only incipient, transformed themselves during the last years into a grave abuse of power by Stalin, which caused untold harm to our party.

We have to consider seriously and analyze correctly this matter in order that we may preclude any possibility of a repetition in any form whatever of what took place during the life of Stalin, who absolutely did not tolerate collegiality in leadership and in work, and who practiced brutal violence, not only toward everything which opposed him, but also toward that which seemed to his capricious and despotic character contrary to his concepts.

Stalin acted not through persuasion, explanation, and patient cooperation with people, but by imposing his concepts and demanding absolute submission to his opinion. Whoever opposed this concept or tried to prove his viewpoint, and the correctness of his position, was doomed to removal from the leading collective and to subsequent moral and physical annihilation. This was especially true during the period following the 17th Party Congress [January-February 1934], when many prominent party leaders and rank-and-file party workers, honest and dedicated to the cause of communism, fell victim to Stalin's despotism.

We must affirm that the party had fought a serious fight against the Trotskyites, rightists and bourgeois nationalists, and that it disarmed ideologically all the enemies of Leninism. This ideological fight was carried on successfully, as a result of which the party became strengthened and tempered. Here Stalin played a positive role.

The party led a great political ideological struggle against those in its own ranks who proposed anti-Leninist theses, who represented a political line hostile to the party and to the cause of socialism.... Let us consider for a moment what would have happened if in 1928-1929 the political line of right deviation had prevailed among us, or orientation toward "cotton-dress industrialization," or toward the kulak [wealthy peasants], etc. We would not now have a powerful heavy industry, we would not have the *kolkhozes* [collective farms], we would find ourselves disarmed and weak in a capitalist encirclement....

Worth noting is the fact that even during the progress of the furious ideological fight against the Trotskyites, the Zinovievites, the Bukharinites and others, extreme repressive measures were not used against them. The fight was on ideological grounds. But some years later when socialism in our country was fundamentally constructed, . . . when the ideological opponents of the party were long since defeated politically — then the repression directed against them began.

It was precisely during this period (1935-1937-1938) that the practice of mass repression through the government apparatus was born, first against the enemies of Leninism — Trotskyites, Zinovievites, Bukharinites, long since politically defeated by the party, and subsequently also against many honest communists, against those party cadres who had borne the heavy load of the civil war and the first and most difficult years of industrialization and collectivization, who actively fought against the Trotskyites and the rightists for the Leninist party line.

Stalin originated the concept "enemy of the people." This term automatically rendered it unnecessary that the ideological errors of a man or men engaged in a controversy be proven; this term made possible the usage of the most cruel repression, violating all norms of revolutionary legality, against anyone who in any way disagreed with Stalin, against those who were only suspected of hostile intent, against those who had bad reputations. This concept, "enemy of the people," actually eliminated the possibility of any kind of ideological fight or the making of one's views known on this or that issue, even those of a practical character. In the main, and in actuality, the only proof of guilt used, against all norms of current legal science, was the "confession" of the accused himself; and, as subsequent probing proved, "confessions" were acquired through physical pressures against the accused. This led to glaring violations of revolutionary legality, and to the fact that many entirely innocent persons, who in the past had defended the party line, became victims.

We must assert that in regard to those persons who in their time had opposed the party line, there were often no sufficiently serious reasons for their physical annihilation. The formula, "enemy of the people," was specifically introduced for the purpose of physically annihilating such individuals.

It is a fact that many persons, who were later annihilated as enemies of the party and people, had worked with Lenin during his life. Some of these persons had made errors during Lenin's life, but, despite this, Lenin benefited by their work, he corrected them and he did everything possible to retain them in the ranks of the party; he induced them to follow him. . . .

'Violence, Mass Repressions, and Terror'

An entirely different relationship with people characterized Stalin. Lenin's traits — patient work with people; stubborn and painstaking education of them; the ability to induce people to follow him without using compulsion, but rather through the ideological influence on them of the whole collective — were entirely foreign to Stalin. He discarded the Leninist method of convincing and educating; he abandoned the method of ideological struggle for that of administrative violence, mass repressions, and terror. He acted on an increasingly larger scale and more stubbornly through punitive organs, at the same time often violating all existing norms of morality and of Soviet laws. . . .

Let us recall some historical facts.

In the days before the October Revolution two members of the Central Committee of the Bolshevik Party — Kamenev and Zinoviev — declared themselves against Lenin's plan for an armed uprising. In addition, on October 18 [1917], they published in the Menshevik newspaper, *Novaya Zhizn,* a statement declaring that the Bolsheviks were making preparations for an uprising and that they considered it adventuristic. Kamenev and Zinoviev thus disclosed to the enemy the decision of the Central Committee to stage the uprising, and that the uprising had been organized to take place within the very near future.

This was treason against the party and against the revolution. In this connection, V. I. Lenin wrote: "Kamenev and Zinoviev revealed the decision of the Central Committee of their party on the armed uprising to [*Duma* president Mikhail] Rodzyanko and [Aleksandr F.] Kerensky [head of the provisional government from July to October 1917]. . . ." He put before the Central Committee

the question of Zinoviev's and Kamenev's expulsion from the party.

However, after the Great Socialist October Revolution, as is known, Zinoviev and Kamenev were given leading positions. Lenin put them in positions in which they carried out most responsible party tasks and participated actively in the work of the leading party and Soviet organs. It is known that Zinoviev and Kamenev committed a number of other serious errors during Lenin's life. In his "testament" Lenin warned that "Zinoviev's and Kamenev's October episode was of course not an accident." But Lenin did not pose the question of their arrest and certainly not their shooting.

Or, let us take the example of the Trotskyites. At present, after a sufficiently long historical period, we can speak about the fight with the Trotskyites with complete calm and can analyze this matter with sufficient objectivity. After all, around Trotsky were people whose origin cannot by any means be traced to bourgeois society. Part of them belonged to the party intelligentsia and a certain part were recruited from among the workers. We can name many individuals who in their time joined the Trotskyites; however, these same individuals took an active part in the workers' movement before the revolution, during the Socialist October Revolution itself, and also in the consolidation of the victory of this greatest of revolutions. Many of them broke with Trotskyism and returned to Leninist positions. Was it necessary to annihilate such people? We are deeply convinced that had Lenin lived such an extreme method would not have been used against many of them.

Such are only a few historical facts. But can it be said that Lenin did not decide to use even the most severe means against enemies of the revolution when this was actually necessary? No, no one can say this. Vladimir Ilyich demanded uncompromising dealings with the enemies of the revolution and of the working class and when necessary resorted ruthlessly to such methods. You will recall only V. I. Lenin's fight with the Socialist Revolutionary organizers of the anti-Soviet uprising, with the counter-revolutionary kulaks in 1918 and with others, when Lenin without hesitation used the most extreme methods against the enemies. Lenin used such methods, however, only against actual class enemies and not against those who blunder, who err, and whom it was possible to lead through ideological influence, and even retain in the leadership. . . .

Stalin, on the other hand, used extreme methods and mass repressions at a time when the revolution was already victorious, when the Soviet state was strengthened, when the exploiting classes were already liquidated and socialist relations were rooted solidly in all phases of national economy, when our party was politically consolidated and had strengthened itself both numerically and ideologically.

It is clear that here Stalin showed in a whole series of cases his intolerance, his brutality and his abuse of power. Instead of proving his political correctness and mobilizing the masses, he often chose the path of repression and physical annihilation, not only against actual enemies, but also against individuals who had not committed any crimes against the party and the Soviet government. Here we see no wisdom but only a demonstration of the brutal force which had once so alarmed V. I. Lenin.

'A Very Ugly Picture'

Lately, especially after the unmasking of the [Lavrentii] Beria gang, the Central Committee has looked into a series of matters fabricated by this gang. This revealed a very ugly picture of brutal willfulness connected with the incorrect behavior of Stalin. As facts prove, Stalin, using his unlimited power, allowed himself many abuses, acting in the name of the Central Committee, not asking for the opinion of the committee members nor even of the members of the Central Committee's Political Bureau; often he did not inform them about his personal decisions concerning very important party and government matters.

Considering the question of the cult of an individual we must first of all show everyone what harm this caused to the interests of our party. . . .

Collegiality of leadership flows from the very nature of our party, a party built on the principles of democratic centralism. "This means," said Lenin, "that all party matters are accomplished by all party members — directly or through representatives — who without any exceptions are subject to the same rules; in addition, all administrative members, all directing collegia, all holders of party positions are elective, they must account for their activities and are recallable.". . .

During Lenin's life Party Congresses were convened regularly; always, when a radical turn in the development of the party and the country took place, Lenin considered it absolutely necessary that the party discuss at length all the basic matters pertaining to internal and foreign policy and to questions bearing on the development of party and government. . . .

Were our party's holy Leninist principles observed after the death of Vladimir Ilyich?

Whereas during the first few years after Lenin's death Party Congresses and Central Committee plenums took place more or less regularly, later, when Stalin began increasingly to abuse his power, these principles were brutally violated. This was especially evident during the last 15 years of his life. Was it a normal situation when over 13 years elapsed between the 18th [March 1939] and 19th [October 1952] Party Congresses, years during which our party and our country had experienced so many important events? These events demanded categorically that the party should have passed resolutions pertaining to the country's defense during the Patriotic War [World War II] and to peacetime construction after the war. Even after the end of the war a Congress was not convened for over seven years. Central Committee plenums were hardly ever called. It should be sufficient to mention that during all the years of the Patriotic War not a single Central Committee plenum took place. It is true that there was an attempt to call a Central Committee plenum in October 1941, when Central Committee members from the whole country were called to Moscow. They waited two days for the opening of the plenum, but in vain. Stalin did not even want to meet and to talk to the Central Committee members. This fact shows how demoralized Stalin was in the first months of the war and how haughtily and disdainfully he treated the Central Committee members.

In practice Stalin ignored the norms of party life and trampled on the Leninist principle of collective party leadership. . . .

Having at its disposal numerous data showing brutal willfulness toward party cadres, the Central Committee has created a party commission under the control of the Central Committee Presidium; it was charged with investigating what made possible the mass repressions against the majority of the Central Committee members and candidates elected at the 17th Congress of the All-Union Communist Party (Bolsheviks).

The commission has become acquainted with a large quantity of materials in the NKVD [People's Commissariat of Internal Affairs, the name of the secret police from 1934 to 1943] archives and with other documents and has established many facts pertaining to the fabrication of cases against communists, to false accusations, to glaring abuses of socialist legality — which resulted in the death of innocent people. It became apparent that many party, Soviet and economic activists who were branded in 1937-1938 as "enemies" were actually never enemies, spies, wreckers, etc., but were always honest communists; they were only so stigmatized, and often, no longer able to bear barbaric tortures, they charged themselves (at the order of the investigative judges — falsifiers) with all kinds of grave and unlikely crimes. . . .

'98 Persons . . . Arrested and Shot'

It was determined that of the 139 members and candidates of the party's Central Committee who were elected at the 17th Congress, 98 persons, i.e., 70 percent, were arrested and shot (mostly in 1937-1938). (Indignation in the hall.)

The same fate met not only the Central Committee members but also the majority of the delegates to the 17th Party Congress. Of 1,966 delegates with either voting or advisory rights, 1,108 persons were arrested on charges of anti-revolutionary crimes, i.e., decidedly more than a majority. This very fact shows how absurd, wild and contrary to common sense were the charges of counter-revolutionary crimes made out, as we now see, against a majority of participants at the 17th Party Congress. (Indignation in the hall.). . .

We should recall that the 17th Party Congress is historically known as the Congress of Victors. Delegates to the Congress were active participants in the building of our socialist state; many of them suffered and fought for party interests during the pre-Revolutionary years in the conspiracy and at the civil war fronts; they fought their enemies valiantly and often nervelessly looked into the face of death.

How then can we believe that such people could prove to be "two-faced" and had joined the camps of the enemies of socialism during the era after the political liquidation of Zinovievites, Trotskyites and rightists and after the great accomplishments of socialist construction? This was the result of the abuse of power by Stalin, who began to use mass terror against the party cadres. . . .

After the criminal murder of S. M. Kirov [Leningrad party boss assassinated December 1, 1934], mass repressions and brutal acts of violation of socialist legality began. On the evening of December 1, 1934, on Stalin's initiative (without the approval of the Political Bureau — which was passed two days later, casually) the Secretary of the Presidium of the Central Executive Committee, [Abel Sofronovich] Yenukidze, signed the following directive:

"1. Investigative agencies are directed to speed up the cases of those accused of the preparation or execution of acts of terror.

"2. Judicial organs are directed not to hold up the execution of death sentences pertaining to crimes of this category in order to consider the possibility of pardon, because the Presidium of the Central Executive Committee [of the] USSR does not consider as possible the receiving of petitions of this sort.

"3. The organs of the Commissariat of Internal Affairs [NKVD] are directed to execute death sentences against criminals of the above-mentioned category immediately after the passage of sentences."

This directive became the basis for mass acts of abuse against socialist legality. During many of the fabricated court cases the accused were charged with "the preparation" of terroristic acts; this deprived them of any possibility that their cases might be re-examined, even when they stated before the court that their "confessions" were secured by force, and when, in a convincing manner, they disproved the accusations against them. . . .

It must be asserted that to this day the circumstances surrounding Kirov's murder hide many things which are inexplicable and mysterious and demand a most careful examination. There are reasons for the suspicion that the killer of Kirov, [Leonid V.] Nikolayev, was assisted by someone from among the people whose duty it was to protect the person of Kirov.

A month and a half before the killing, Nikolayev was arrested on the grounds of suspicious behavior, but he was released and not even searched. It is an unusually suspicious circumstance that when the Chekist [secret police agent] assigned to protect Kirov was being brought for an interrogation, on December 2, 1934, he was killed in a car "accident" in which no other occupants of the car were harmed. After the murder of Kirov, top functionaries of the Leningrad NKVD were given very light sentences, but in 1937 they were shot. We can assume that they were shot in order to cover the traces of the organizers of Kirov's killing. (Movement in the hall.)

Mass repressions grew tremendously from the end of 1936 after a telegram from Stalin and [Stalin supporter Andrei] Zhdanov, dated from Sochi on September 25, 1936, was addressed to [Lazar] Kaganovich, [Viacheslav] Molotov and other members of the Political Bureau. The content of the telegram was as follows:

"We deem it absolutely necessary and urgent that Comrade [Nikolai] Yezhov be nominated to the post of People's Commissar for Internal Affairs. [Secret police head Genrikh] Yagoda has definitely proved himself to be incapable of unmasking the Trotskyite-Zinovievite bloc. The OGPU [Unified State Political Administration, the name of the secret police from 1922 until 1934] is four years behind in this matter. This is noted by all party workers and by the majority of the representatives of the NKVD."

Strictly speaking we should stress that Stalin did not meet with and therefore could not know the opinion of party workers.

This Stalinist formulation that the "NKVD is four years behind" in applying mass repression and that there is a necessity for "catching up" with the neglected work directly pushed the NKVD workers on the path of mass arrests and executions....

Stalin's report at the February-March Central Committee Plenum in 1937, "Deficiencies of party work and methods for the liquidation of the Trotskyites and of other two-facers," contained an attempt at theoretical justification of the mass terror policy under the pretext that as we march forward toward socialism, class war must allegedly sharpen. Stalin asserted that both history and Lenin taught him this.

Actually Lenin taught that the application of revolutionary violence is necessitated by the resistance of the exploiting classes, and this referred to the era when the exploiting classes existed and were powerful. As soon as the nation's political situation had improved, when in January 1920 the Red Army took Rostov and thus won a most important victory over [White Russian forces led by General Anton] Deniken, Lenin instructed [Felix] Dzerzhinsky [first head of the secret police] to stop mass terror and to abolish the death penalty....

Stalin deviated from these clear and plain precepts of Lenin. Stalin put the party and the NKVD up to the use of mass terror when the exploiting classes had been liquidated in our country and when there were no serious reasons for the use of extraordinary mass terror....

Mass arrests of party, Soviet, economic and military workers caused tremendous harm to our country and to the cause of socialist advancement....

Only because our party has at its disposal such great moral-political strength was it possible for it to survive the difficult events in 1937-1938 and to educate new cadres. There is, however, no doubt that our march forward toward socialism and toward the preparation of the country's defense would have been much more successful were it not for the tremendous loss in the cadres suffered as a result of the baseless and false mass repressions in 1937-1938. We are justly accusing [NKVD chief Nikolai] Yezhov for the degenerate practices of 1937. But we have to answer these questions:

Could Yezhov have arrested Kossior, for instance, without the knowledge of Stalin? Was there an exchange of opinions or a Political Bureau decision concerning this?

No, there was not, as there was none regarding other cases of this type.

Could Yezhov have decided such important matters as the fate of such eminent party figures?

No, it would be a display of naivete to consider this the work of Yezhov alone. It is clear that these matters were decided by Stalin, and that without his orders and his sanction Yezhov could not have done this....

'Stalin Was ... Sickly Suspicious'

Facts prove that many abuses were made on Stalin's orders without reckoning with any norms of party and Soviet legality. Stalin was a very distrustful man, sickly suspicious; we knew this from our work with him. He could look at a man and say: "Why are your eyes so shifty today" or "Why are you turning so much today and avoiding to look me directly in the eyes?" The sickly suspicion created in him a general distrust even toward eminent party workers whom he had known for years. Everywhere and in everything he saw "enemies," "two-facers" and "spies.".…

When Stalin said that one or another should be arrested, it was necessary to accept on faith that he was an "enemy of the people." Meanwhile, Beria's gang, which ran the organs of state security, outdid itself in proving the guilt of the arrested and the truth of materials which it falsified. And what proofs were offered? The confessions of the arrested, and the investigative judges accepted these "confessions." And how is it possible that a person confesses to crimes which he has not committed? Only in one way — because of application of physical methods of pressuring him, tortures, bringing him to a state of unconsciousness, deprivation of his judgment, taking away of his human dignity. In this manner were "confessions" acquired....

The power accumulated in the hands of one person, Stalin, led to serious consequences during the Great Patriotic War [World War II].

When we look at many of our novels, films and historical "scientific studies," the role of Stalin in the Patriotic War appears to be entirely improbable. Stalin had foreseen everything. The Soviet Army, on the basis of a strategic plan prepared by Stalin long before, used the tactics of so-called "active defense," i.e., tactics which, we know, allowed the Germans to come up to Moscow and Stalingrad. Using such tactics the Soviet Army, supposedly thanks only to Stalin's genius, turned to the offensive and subdued the enemy. The epic victory gained through the armed might of the land of the Soviets, through our heroic people, is ascribed in this type of novel, film and "scientific study" as being completely due to the strategic genius of Stalin....

During the war and after the war Stalin put forward the thesis that the tragedy which our nation experienced in the first part of the war was the result of the "unexpected" attack of the Germans against the Soviet Union. But, Comrades, this is completely untrue. As soon as Hitler came to power in Germany he assigned to himself the task of liquidating Communism. The fascists were saying this openly; they did not hide their plans....

Documents which have now been published show that by April 3, 1941, Churchill, through his ambassador to the USSR, [Sir Stafford] Cripps, personally warned Stalin that the Germans had begun regrouping their armed units with the intent of attacking the Soviet Union....

However, Stalin took no heed of these warnings. What is more, Stalin ordered that no credence be given to information of this sort, in order not to provoke the initiation of military operations.

We must assert that information of this sort concerning the threat of German armed invasion of Soviet territory was coming in also from our own military and diplomatic sources; however, because the leadership was conditioned against such information, such data was dispatched with fear and assessed with reservation.

Thus, for instance, information sent from Berlin on May 6, 1941, by the Soviet military attaché ... stated: "Soviet citizen Bozer ... communicated to the deputy naval attaché that according to a statement of a certain German officer from Hitler's Headquarters, Germany is preparing to invade the USSR on May 14 through Finland, the Baltic countries and Latvia. At the same time Moscow and Leningrad will be heavily raided and paratroopers landed in border cities...."

In his report of May 22, 1941, the deputy military attaché in Berlin ... communicated that "... the attack of the German army is reportedly scheduled for June 15, but it is possible that it may begin in the first days of June...."

A cable from our London Embassy dated June 18, 1941, stated: "As of now Cripps is deeply convinced of the inevitability of armed conflict between Germany and the USSR which will begin not later than the middle of June. According to Cripps, the Germans have presently concentrated 147 divisions (including air force and service units) along the Soviet borders...."

Despite these particularly grave warnings, the necessary steps were not taken to prepare the country properly for defense and to prevent it from being caught unawares.

Did we have time and the capabilities for such preparations? Yes, we had the time and the capabilities....

Had our industry been mobilized properly and in time to supply the army with the necessary matériel, our wartime losses would have been decidedly smaller. Such mobilization had not been, however, started in time. And already in the first days of the war it became evident that our army was badly armed, that we did not have enough artillery, tanks and planes to throw the enemy back....

In this connection we cannot forget, for instance, the following fact: Shortly before the invasion of the Soviet Union by the Hitlerite army, ... [the] Chief of the Kiev Special Military District (he was later killed at the front) wrote to Stalin that the German armies were at the Bug River, were preparing for an attack and in the very near future would probably start their offensive. In this connection ... [he] proposed that a strong defense be organized, that 300,000 people be evacuated from the border areas and that several strong points be organized there: antitank ditches, trenches for the soldiers, etc.

Moscow answered this proposition with the assertion that this would be a provocation, that no preparatory defensive work should be undertaken at the borders, that the Germans were not to be given any pretext for the initiation of military action against us. Thus, our borders were insufficiently prepared to repel the enemy....

And what were the results of this carefree attitude, this disregard of clear facts? The result was that already in the first hours and days the enemy had destroyed in our border regions a large part of our air force, artillery and other military equipment; he annihilated large numbers of our military cadres and disorganized our military leadership; consequently we could not prevent the enemy from marching deep into the country.

Very grievous consequences, especially in reference to the beginning of the war, followed Stalin's annihilation of many military commanders and political workers during 1937-1941 because of his suspiciousness and through slanderous accusations. During these years repressions were instituted against certain parts of military cadres beginning literally at the company and battalion commander level and extending to the higher military centers; during this time the cadre of leaders who had gained military experience in Spain and in the Far East was almost completely liquidated.

The policy of large-scale repression against the military cadres led also to undermined military discipline, because for several years officers of all ranks and even soldiers in the party and Komsomol cells were taught to "unmask" their superiors as hidden enemies. (Movement in the hall.) It is natural that this caused a negative influence on the state of military discipline in the first war period.... All this brought about the situation which existed at the beginning of the war and which was the great threat to our Fatherland.

'This Was the End'

It would be incorrect to forget that after the first severe disaster and defeats at the front, Stalin thought that this was the end. In one of his speeches in those days he said: "All that which Lenin created we have lost forever."

After this Stalin for a long time actually did not direct the military operations and ceased to do anything whatever. He returned to active leadership only when some members of the Political Bureau visited him and told him that it was necessary to take certain steps immediately in order to improve the situation at the front.

Therefore, the threatening danger which hung over our Fatherland in the first period of the war was largely due to the faulty methods of directing the nation and the party by Stalin himself.

However, we speak not only about the moment when the war began, which led to serious disorganization of our army and brought us severe losses. Even after the war began, the nervousness and hysteria which Stalin demonstrated, interfering with actual military operations, caused our army serious damage.

Stalin was very far from an understanding of the real situation which was developing at the front. This was natural because during the whole Patriotic War he never visited any section of the front or any liberated city except for one short ride on the Mozhaisk Highway during a stabilized situation at the front. To this incident were dedicated many literary works full of fantasies of all sorts and so many paintings. Simultaneously, Stalin was interfering with operations and issuing orders which did not take into consideration the real situation at a given section of the front and which could not help but result in huge personnel losses.

I will allow myself in this connection to bring out one characteristic fact which illustrates how Stalin directed operations at the fronts. There is present at this Congress Marshal [Ivan] Bagramyan who was once the chief of operations in the headquarters of the southwestern front and who can corroborate what I tell you.

When there developed an exceptionally serious situation for our Army in 1942 in the Kharkov region, we had correctly decided to drop an operation whose objective was to encircle Kharkov, because the real situation at that time would have threatened our Army with fatal consequences if this operation were continued....

Contrary to common sense, Stalin rejected our suggestion and issued the order to continue the operation aimed at the encirclement of Kharkov, despite the fact that at this time many Army concentrations were themselves actually threatened with encirclement and liquidation....

And what was the result of this? The worst that we had expected. The Germans surrounded our Army concentrations and consequently we lost hundreds of thousands of our soldiers. This is Stalin's military "genius"; this is what it cost us. (Movement in the hall.)...

The tactics on which Stalin insisted without knowing the essence of the conduct of battle operations cost us much blood until we succeeded in stopping the opponent and going over to the offensive.

The military know that already by the end of 1941 instead of great operational maneuvers flanking the opponent and penetrating behind his back, Stalin demanded incessant frontal attacks and the capture of one village after another.

Because of this we paid with great losses — until our generals, on whose shoulders rested the whole weight of conducting the war, succeeded in changing the situation and shifting to flexible-maneuver operations, which immediately brought serious changes at the front favorable to us.

All the more shameful was the fact that after our great victory over the enemy which cost us so much, Stalin began to downgrade many of the commanders who contributed so much to the victory over the enemy, because Stalin excluded every possibility that services rendered at the front should be credited to anyone but himself....

In the same vein, let us take, for instance, our historical and military films and some literary creations; they make us feel sick. Their true objective is the propagation of the theme of praising Stalin as a military genius. Let us recall the film, *The Fall of Berlin.* Here only Stalin acts; he issues orders in the hall in which there are many empty chairs and only one man approaches him and reports something to him — that is [A. N.] Poskrebyshev [Stalin's secretary and trusted aide], his loyal shield-bearer. (Laughter in the hall.)

And where is the military command? Where is the Political Bureau? Where is the Government? What are they doing and with what are they engaged? There is nothing about them in the film. Stalin acts for everybody; he does not reckon with anyone; he asks no one for advice. Everything is shown to the nation in this false light. Why? In order to surround Stalin with glory, contrary to the facts and contrary to historical truth.

The question arises: And where are the military on whose shoulders rested the burden of the war? They are not in the film; with Stalin in, no room was left for them.

Not Stalin, but the party as a whole, the Soviet government, our heroic Army, its talented leaders and brave soldiers, the whole Soviet nation — these are the ones who assured the victory in the Great Patriotic War. (Tempestuous and prolonged applause.)...

The main role and the main credit for the victorious ending of the war belongs to our Communist Party, to the armed forces of the Soviet Union, and to the tens of millions of Soviet people raised by the party. (Thunderous and prolonged applause.)

Comrades, let us reach for some other facts. The Soviet Union is justly considered as a model of a multinational state because we have in practice assured the equality and friendship of all nations which live in our great Fatherland.

'Mass Deportations'

All the more monstrous are the acts whose initiator was Stalin and which are rude violations of the basic Leninist principles of the nationality policy of the Soviet state. We refer to the mass deportations from their native places of whole nations, together with all Communists and Komsomols without any exception; this deportation action was not dictated by any military considerations.

Thus, already at the end of 1943, when there occurred a permanent breakthrough at the fronts of the Great Patriotic War benefiting the Soviet Union, a decision was taken and executed concerning the deportation of all the Karachai from the lands on which they lived.

In the same period, at the end of December 1943, the same lot befell the whole population of the Autonomous Kalmyk Republic. In March 1944 all the Chechen and Ingush peoples were deported and the Chechen-Ingush Autonomous Republic was liquidated. In April 1944, all Balkars were deported to faraway places from the territory of the Kabardino-Balkar Autonomous Republic and the Republic itself was renamed the Autonomous Kabardin Republic.

The Ukrainians avoided meeting this fate only because there were too many of them and there was no place to which to deport them. Otherwise, he would have deported them also. (Laughter and animation in the hall.)...

After the conclusion of the Patriotic War, the Soviet nation stressed with pride the magnificent victories gained through great sacrifices and tremendous efforts. The country experienced a period of political enthusiasm. The party came out of the war even more united; in the fire of the war party cadres were tempered and hardened. Under such conditions nobody could have even thought of the possibility of some plot in the party.

And it was precisely at this time that the so-called "Leningrad affair" was born. As we have now proven, this case was fabricated. Those who innocently lost their lives included Comrades [Nikolai A.] Voznesensky, [A. A.] Kuznetsov, [Mikhail I.] Rodinov, [Pyotr S.] Popkov, and others.

As is known, Voznesensky and Kuznetsov were talented and eminent leaders. Once they stood very close to Stalin. It is sufficient to mention that Stalin made Voznesensky first deputy to the chairman of the Council of Ministers and Kuznetsov was elected Secretary of the Central Committee. The very fact that Stalin entrusted Kuznetsov with the supervision of the state security organs shows the trust which he enjoyed.

How did it happen that these persons were branded as enemies of the people and liquidated?

Facts prove that the "Leningrad affair" is also the result of willfulness which Stalin exercised against party cadres. Had a normal situation existed in the party's Central Committee and in the Central Committee Political Bureau, affairs of this nature would have been examined there in accordance with party practice, and all pertinent facts assessed; as a result such an affair as well as others would not have happened.

We must state that after the war the situation became even more complicated. Stalin became even more capricious, irritable and brutal; in particular his suspicion grew. His persecution mania reached unbelievable dimensions. Many workers were becoming enemies before his very eyes. After the war Stalin separated himself from the collective even more. Everything was decided by him alone without any consideration for anyone or anything.

This unbelievable suspicion was cleverly taken advantage of by the abject provocateur and vile enemy, Beria, who had murdered thousands of Communists and loyal Soviet people. The elevation of Voznesensky and Kuznetsov alarmed Beria. As we have now proven, it had been precisely Beria who had "suggested" to Stalin the fabrication by him and by his confidants of materials in the form of declarations and anonymous letters, and in the form of various rumors and talks.

The party's Central Committee has examined this so-called "Leningrad affair"; persons who innocently suffered are now rehabilitated and honor has been restored to the glorious Leningrad party organization. [Victor S.] Abakumov [minister of state security, 1947-1951] and others who had fabricated this affair were brought before a court; their trial took place in Leningrad and they received what they deserved.

The question arises: Why is it that we see the truth of this affair only now, and why did we not do something earlier, during Stalin's life, in order to prevent the loss of innocent lives? It was because Stalin personally supervised the "Leningrad affair," and the majority of the Political Bureau members did not, at that time, know all of the circumstances in these matters, and could not therefore intervene....

The willfulness of Stalin showed itself not only in decisions concerning the internal life of the country but also in the international relations of the Soviet Union.

The July plenum of the Central Committee studied in detail the reasons for the development of conflict with Yugoslavia. It was a shameful role which Stalin played here. The "Yugoslav affair" contained no problems which could not have been solved through party discussions among comrades. There was no significant basis for the development of this "affair"; it was completely possible to have prevented the rupture of relations with that country. This does not mean, however, that the Yugoslav leaders did not make mistakes or did not have shortcomings. But these mistakes and shortcomings were magnified in a monstrous manner by Stalin, which resulted in a break of relations with a friendly country....

You see to what Stalin's mania for greatness led. He had completely lost consciousness of reality; he demonstrated his suspicion and haughtiness not only in relation to individuals in the USSR, but in relation to whole parties and nations.

We have carefully examined the case of Yugoslavia and have found a proper solution which is approved by the peoples of the Soviet Union and of Yugoslavia as well as by the working masses of all the people's democracies and by all progressive humanity. The liquidation of the abnormal relationship with Yugoslavia was done in the interest of the whole camp of socialism, in the interest of strengthening peace in the whole world.

'Affair of the Doctor-Plotters'

Let us also recall the "affair of the doctor-plotters." (Animation in the hall.) Actually there was no "Affair" outside of the declaration of the woman doctor, [Lydia] Timashuk, who was probably influenced or ordered by someone (after all, she was an unofficial collaborator of the organs of state security) to write Stalin a letter in which she declared that doctors were applying supposedly improper methods of medical treatment.

Such a letter was sufficient for Stalin to reach an immediate conclusion that there were doctor-plotters in the Soviet Union. He issued orders to arrest a group of eminent Soviet medical specialists. He personally issued advice on the conduct of the investigation and the method of interrogation of the arrested persons. He said that the academician [A. I.] Vinogradov should be put in chains, another one should be beaten. Present at this Congress as a delegate is the former Minister of State Security, Comrade [S. D.] Ignatiev. Stalin told him curtly, "If you do not obtain confessions from the doctors we will shorten you by a head." (Tumult in the hall.)

Stalin personally called the investigative judge, gave him instructions, advised him on which investigative methods should be used; these methods were simple — beat, beat and, once again, beat.

Shortly after the doctors were arrested we members of the Political Bureau received protocols with the doctors' confessions of guilt. After distributing these protocols Stalin told us, "You are blind like young kittens; what will happen without me? The country will perish because you do not know how to recognize enemies."

The case was so presented that no one could verify the facts on which the investigation was based. There was no possibility of trying to verify facts by contacting those who had made the confessions of guilt.

We felt, however, that the case of the arrested doctors was questionable. We knew some of these people personally because they had once treated us. When we examined this "case" after Stalin's death, we found it to be fabricated from beginning to end.

This ignominious "case" was set up by Stalin; he did not, however, have the time in which to bring it to an end (as he conceived that end), and for this reason the doctors are still alive. Now all have been rehabilitated; they are working in the same places they were working before; they treat top individuals, not excluding members of the government; they have our full confidence; and they execute their duties honestly, as they did before....

'The Cult of the Individual'

Comrades: The cult of the individual acquired such monstrous size chiefly because Stalin himself, using all conceivable methods, supported the glorification of his own person. This is supported by numerous facts. One of the most characteristic examples of Stalin's self-glorification and his lack of even elementary modesty is the edition of his *Short Biography,* which was published in 1948....

We need not give here examples of the loathsome adulation filling this book. All we need to add is that they all were approved and edited by Stalin personally and some of them were added in his own handwriting to the draft text of the book.

What did Stalin consider essential to write into this book? Did he want to cool the ardor of his flatterers who were composing his *Short Biography?* No! He marked the very places where he thought that the praise of his services was insufficient.

Here are some examples characterizing Stalin's activity, added in Stalin's own hand:

"In this fight against the skeptics and capitulators, the Trotskyites, Zinovievites, Bukharinites and Kamenevites, there was definitely welded together, after Lenin's death, that leading core of the Party ... that upheld the great manner of Lenin, rallied the Party behind Lenin's behests, and brought the Soviet people into the broad road of industrializing the country and collectivizing the rural economy. The leader of this core and the guiding force of the Party and the State was Comrade Stalin."

Thus writes Stalin himself! Then he adds:

"Although he performed his task of leader of the Party and the people with consummate skill and enjoyed the unreserved support of the entire Soviet people, Stalin never allowed his work to be marred by the slightest hint of vanity, conceit or self-adulation."

Where and when could a leader so praise himself? Is this worthy of a leader of the Marxist-Leninist type? No. Precisely against this did Marx and Engels take such a strong position. This also was always sharply condemned by Vladimir Ilyich Lenin....

Stalin recognized as the best a text of the national anthem of the Soviet Union which contains not a word about the Communist Party; it contains, however, the following unprecedented praise of Stalin: *"Stalin brought us up in loyalty to the people. He inspired us to great toil and acts."*

In these lines of the anthem is the whole educational, directional and inspirational activity of the great Leninist party ascribed to Stalin. This is, of course, a clear deviation from Marxism-Leninism, a clear debasing and belittling of the role of the party. We should add for your information that the Presidium of the Central Committee has already passed a resolution concerning the composition of a new text of the anthem, which will reflect the role of the people, and the role of the party. (Loud, prolonged applause.)

And was it without Stalin's knowledge that many of the largest enterprises and towns were named after him? Was it without his knowledge that Stalin monuments were erected in the whole country — these "memorials to the living"? It is a fact that Stalin himself had signed on July 2, 1951, a resolution of the USSR Council of Ministers concerning the erection on the Volga-Don Canal of an impressive monument to Stalin; on September 4 of the same year he issued an order making 33 tons of copper available for the construction of this impressive monument. Anyone who has visited the Stalingrad area must have seen the huge statue which is being built there, and that on a site which hardly any people frequent. Huge sums were spent to build it at a time when people of this area had lived since the war in huts. Consider yourself, was Stalin right when he wrote in his biography that "... he did not allow in himself ... even a shadow of conceit, pride, or self-adoration"?

At the same time Stalin gave proofs of his lack of respect for Lenin's memory. It is not a coincidence that, despite the decision taken over 30 years ago to build a Palace of Soviets as a monument to Vladimir Ilyich, this palace was not built, its construction was always postponed, and the project allowed to lapse.

We cannot forget to recall the Soviet Government resolution of August 14, 1925, concerning "the founding of Lenin prizes for educational work." This resolution was published in the press, but until this day there are no Lenin prizes. This, too, should be corrected. (Tumultuous, prolonged applause.)

During Stalin's life, thanks to known methods which I have mentioned, and quoting facts, for instance, from the *Short Biography* of Stalin — all events were explained as if Lenin played only a secondary role, even during the October Socialist Revolution. In many films and in many literary works, the figure of Lenin was incorrectly presented and inadmissibly depreciated.

Stalin loved to see the film *The Unforgettable Year of 1919,* in which he was shown on the steps of an armored train and where he was practically vanquishing the foe with his own saber. Let Kliment Yefremovich [Voroshilov, chairman of the Presidium of the Supreme Soviet, 1953-1960], our dear friend, find the necessary courage and write the truth about Stalin; after all, he knows how Stalin had fought. It will be difficult for Comrade Voroshilov to undertake this, but it would be good if he did it. Everyone will approve of it, both the people and the party. Even his grandsons will thank him. (Prolonged applause.)

In speaking about the events of the October Revolution and about the civil war, the impression was created that Stalin always played the main role, as if everywhere and always Stalin had suggested to Lenin what to do and how to do it. However, this is slander of Lenin. (Prolonged applause.)

I will probably not sin against the truth when I say that 99 percent of the persons present here heard and knew very little about Stalin before the year 1924, while Lenin was known to all; he was known to the whole party, to the whole nation, from the children up to the graybeards. (Tumultuous, prolonged applause.)

All this has to be thoroughly revised, so that history, literature, and the fine arts properly reflect V. I. Lenin's role and the great deeds of our Communist Party and of the Soviet people — the creative people. (Applause.)

Comrades! The cult of the individual has caused the employment of faulty principles in party work and in economic activity; it brought about rude violation of internal party and Soviet democracy, sterile administration, deviations of all sorts, covering up of shortcomings and varnishing of reality. Our nation gave birth to many flatterers and specialists in false optimism and deceit.

We should also not forget that due to the numerous arrests of party, Soviet and economic leaders, many workers began to work uncertainly, showed over-cautiousness, feared all which was new, feared their own shadows and began to show less initiative in their work....

Stalin's reluctance to consider life's realities and the fact that he was not aware of the real state of affairs in the provinces can be illustrated by his direction of agriculture.

All those who interested themselves even a little in the national situation saw the difficult situation in agriculture, but Stalin never even noted it. Did we tell Stalin about this? Yes, we told him, but he did not support us. Why? Because Stalin never traveled anywhere, did not meet city and *kolkhoz* workers; he did not know the actual situation in the provinces.

He knew the country and agriculture only from films. And these films had dressed up and beautified the existing situation in agriculture....

Vladimir Ilyich Lenin looked at life differently; he was always close to the people; he used to receive peasant delegates, and often spoke at factory gatherings; he used to visit villages and talk with the peasants.

Stalin separated himself from the people and never went anywhere. This lasted tens of years. The last time he visited a village was in January 1928 when he visited Siberia in connection with grain deliveries. How then could he have known the situation in the provinces? ...

Comrades! If we sharply criticize today the cult of the individual which was so widespread during Stalin's life and if we speak about the many negative phenomena generated by this cult which is so alien to the spirit of Marxism-Leninism, various persons may ask: How could it be? Stalin headed the party and the country for 30 years and many victories were gained during his lifetime. Can we deny this? In my opinion, the question can be asked in this manner only by those who are blinded and hopelessly hypnotized by the cult of the individual, only by those who do not understand the essence of the revolution and of the Soviet state, only by those who do not understand, in a Leninist manner, the role of the party and of the nation in the development of the Soviet society.

The Socialist Revolution was attained by the working class and by the poor peasantry with the partial support of middle-class peasants. It was attained by the people under the leadership of the Bolshevik Party. Lenin's great service consisted of the fact that he created a militant party of the working class, but he was armed with Marxist understanding of the laws of social development and with the science of proletarian victory in the fight with capitalism, and he steeled this party in the crucible of revolutionary struggle of the masses of the people.

During this fight the party consistently defended the interests of the people, became its experienced leader, and led the working masses to power, to the creation of the first socialist state....

Our historical victories were attained thanks to the organizational work of the party, to the many provincial organizations, and to the self-sacrificing work of our great nation. These victories are the result of the great drive and activity of the nation and of the party as a whole; they are not at all the fruit of the leadership of Stalin, as the situation was pictured during the period of the cult of the individual....

In the last years, when we managed to free ourselves of the harmful practice of the cult of the individual and took several proper steps in the sphere of internal and external policies, everyone saw how activity grew before their very eyes, how the creative activity of the broad working masses developed, how favorably all this acted upon the development of economy and of culture. (Applause.)

Where Was the Political Bureau?

Some comrades may ask us: Where were the members of the Political Bureau of the Central Committee? Why did they not assert themselves against the cult of the individual in time? And why is this being done only now?

First of all we have to consider the fact that the members of the Political Bureau viewed these matters in a different way at different times. Initially, many of them backed Stalin actively because Stalin was one of the strongest Marxists and his logic, his strength and his will greatly influenced the cadres and party work.

It is known that Stalin, after Lenin's death, especially during the first years, actively fought for Leninism against the enemies of Leninist theory and against those who deviated. Beginning with Leninist theory, the party, with its Central Committee at the head, started on a great scale the work of socialist industrialization of the country, agricultural collectivization and the cultural revolution.

At that time Stalin gained great popularity, sympathy and support. The party had to fight those who attempted to lead the country away from the correct Leninist path; it had to fight Trotskyites, Zinovievites and rightists, and the bourgeois nationalists. This fight was indispensable.

Later, however, Stalin, abusing his power more and more, began to fight eminent party and government leaders and to use terroristic methods against honest Soviet people....

It is clear that such conditions put every member of the Political Bureau in a very difficult situation. And when we also consider the fact that in the last years the Central Committee plenary sessions were not convened and that the sessions of the Political Bureau occurred only occasionally, from time to time, then we will understand how difficult it was for any member of the Political Bureau to take a stand against one or another unjust or improper procedure, against serious errors and shortcomings in the practices of leadership....

Let us consider the first Central Committee Plenum after the 19th Party Congress when Stalin, in his talk at the Plenum, characterized Vyacheslav Mikhailovich Molotov and Anastas Ivanovich Mikoyan and suggested that these old workers of our party were guilty of some baseless charges. It is not excluded that had Stalin remained at the helm for another several months,

Comrades Molotov and Mikoyan would probably have not delivered any speeches at this Congress.

Stalin evidently had plans to finish off the old members of the Political Bureau. He often stated that Political Bureau members should be replaced by new ones.

His proposal, after the 19th Congress, concerning the selection of 25 persons to the Central Committee Presidium, was aimed at the removal of the old Political Bureau members and the bringing in of less experienced persons so that these would extol him in all sorts of ways.

We can assume that this was also a design for the future annihilation of the old Political Bureau members and in this way a cover for all shameful acts of Stalin, acts which we are now considering.

Comrades! In order not to repeat errors of the past, the Central Committee has declared itself resolutely against the cult of the individual. We consider that Stalin was excessively extolled. However, in the past Stalin doubtless performed great services to the party, to the working class, and to the international workers' movement.

This question is complicated by the fact that all this which we have just discussed was done during Stalin's life under his leadership and with his concurrence; here Stalin was convinced that this was necessary for the defense of the interests of the working classes against the plotting of the enemies and against the attack of the imperialist camp.

He saw this from the position of the interest of the working class, of the interest of the laboring people, of the interest of the victory of socialism and communism. We cannot say that these were the deeds of a giddy despot. He considered that this should be done in the interest of the party; of the working masses, in the name of the defense of the revolution's gains. In this lies the whole tragedy!...

We should in all seriousness consider the question of the cult of the individual. We cannot let this matter get out of the party, especially not to the press. It is for this reason that we are considering it here at a closed Congress session. We should know the limits; we should not give ammunition to the enemy; we should not wash our dirty linen before their eyes. I think that the delegates to the Congress will understand and assess properly all these proposals. (Tumultuous applause.)

Comrades: We must abolish the cult of the individual decisively, once and for all; we must draw the proper conclusions concerning both ideological-theoretical and practical work. It is necessary for this purpose:

First, in a Bolshevik manner to condemn and to eradicate the cult of the individual as alien to Marxism-Leninism and not consonant with the principles of party leadership and the norms of party life, and to fight inexorably all attempts at bringing back this practice in one form or another.

To return to and actually practice in all our ideological work the most important theses of Marxist-Leninist science about the people as the creator of history and as the creator of all material and spiritual good of humanity, about the decisive role of the Marxist party in the revolutionary fight for the transformation of society, about the victory of communism.

In this connection we will be forced to do much work in order to examine critically from the Marxist-Leninist viewpoint and to correct the widely spread erroneous views connected with the cult of the individual in the sphere of history, philosophy, economy and of other sciences, as well as in literature and the fine arts. It is especially necessary that in the immediate future we compile a serious textbook of the history of our party which will be edited in accordance with scientific Marxist objectivism, a textbook of the history of Soviet society, a book pertaining to the events of the civil war and the Great Patriotic War.

Secondly, to continue systematically and consistently the work done by the party's Central Committee during the last years, a work characterized by minute observation in all party organizations, from the bottom to the top, of the Leninist principles of party leadership, characterized, above all, by the main principle of collective leadership, characterized by the observation of the norms of party life described in the statutes of our party, and finally, characterized by the wide practice of criticism and self-criticism.

Thirdly, to restore completely the Leninist principles of Soviet socialist democracy, expressed in the Constitution of the Soviet Union, to fight willfulness of individuals abusing their power. The evil caused by acts violating revolutionary socialist legality which have accumulated during a long time as a result of the negative influence of the cult of the individual has to be completely corrected.

Comrades! The 20th Congress of the Communist Party of the Soviet Union has manifested with a new strength the unshakable unity of our party, its cohesiveness around the Central Committee, its resolute will to accomplish the great task of building communism. (Tumultuous applause.)

And the fact that we present in all their ramifications the basic problems of overcoming the cult of the individual which is alien to Marxism-Leninism, as well as the problem of liquidating its burdensome consequences, is an evidence of the great moral and political strength of our party. (Prolonged applause.)

We are absolutely certain that our party, armed with the historical resolutions of the 20th Congress, will lead the Soviet people along the Leninist path to new successes, to new victories. (Tumultuous, prolonged applause.)

Long live the victorious banner of our party — Leninism! (Tumultuous, prolonged applause ending in ovation. All rise.)

'KITCHEN DEBATE' OF NIXON AND KHRUSHCHEV

Following are excerpts from an exchange between Vice President Richard Nixon and Soviet premier Nikita S. Khrushchev at a U.S. trade exhibition in Moscow, July 24, 1959, as published in The Challenges We Face, *edited and compiled from the speeches and papers of Richard Nixon (New York: McGraw-Hill, 1980).*

Khrushchev: "Americans have lost their ability to trade. Now you have grown older and you don't trade the way you used to. You need to be invigorated."

Nixon: "You need to have goods to trade."

Nixon: "There must be a free exchange of ideas. . . ."

Khrushchev: "We want to live in peace and friendship with Americans because we are the two most powerful countries, and if we live in friendship, then other countries will also live in friendship. But if there is a country that is too war-minded we could pull its ears a little and say, 'Don't you dare; fighting is not allowed now.' This is a period of atomic armament; some foolish one could start a war and then even a wise one couldn't finish the war. Therefore, we are governed by this idea in our policy, internal and foreign. How long has America existed? Three hundred years?"

Nixon: "More than one hundred and fifty years."

Khrushchev: "More than one hundred and fifty years? Well, then, we will say America has been in existence for 150 years and this is the level she has reached. We have existed not quite forty-two years and in another seven years we will be on the same level as America.

"When we catch you up, in passing you by, we will wave to you. Then if you wish we can stop and say: Please follow up. Plainly speaking, if you want capitalism you can live that way. That is your own affair and doesn't concern us. We can still feel sorry for you, but since you don't understand us, live as you do understand.

"We are all glad to be here at the Exhibition with Vice President Nixon. I personally, and on behalf of my colleagues, express my thanks for the President's message. I have not as yet read it but I know beforehand that it contains good wishes. I think

you will be satisfied with your visit and if — I cannot go on without saying it — if you would not take such a position [captive nations resolution passed by Congress July 17] which has not been thought out thoroughly, as was approved by Congress, your trip would be excellent. But you have churned the water yourselves — why this was necessary God only knows.

"What happened? What black cat crossed your path and confused you? But that is your affair; we do not interfere with your problems." (Wrapping his arms about a Soviet workman.) "Does this man look like a slave laborer?" (Waving at others.) "With men with such spirit how can we lose?"

Nixon (pointing to American workmen): "With men like that we are strong. But these men, Soviet and American, work together well for peace, even as they have worked together in building this Exhibition. This is the way it should be.

"Your remarks are in the tradition of what we have come to expect — sweeping and extemporaneous. Later on we will both have an opportunity to speak, and consequently I will not comment on the various points that you raised, except to say this — this color television is one of the most advanced developments in communication that we have.

"I can say that if this competition in which you plan to outstrip us is to do the best for both of our peoples and for peoples everywhere, there must be a free exchange of ideas. After all, you don't know everything. . . ."

Khrushchev: "If I don't know everything, you don't know anything about communism except fear of it."

Nixon: "There are some instances where you may be ahead of us; for example, in the development of the thrust of your rockets for the investigation of outer space; there may be some instances in which we are ahead of you — in color television, for instance."

'We Have Bested You'

Khrushchev: "No, we are up with you on this too. We have bested you in one technique and also in the other."

Nixon: "You see, you never concede anything."

Khrushchev: "I do not give up."

Nixon: "Wait till you see the picture. Let's have far more communication and exchange in this very area that we speak of. We should hear you more on our television. You should hear us more on yours."

Khrushchev: "That's a good idea. Let's do it like this. You appear before our people. We will appear before your people. People will see and appreciate this."

Nixon: "There is not a day in the United States when we cannot read what you say. When [Soviet first deputy premier Frol R.] Kozlov was speaking in California about peace, you were talking here in somewhat different terms. This was reported extensively in the American press. Never make a statement here if you don't want it to be read in the United States. I can promise you every word you say will be translated into English."

Khrushchev: "I doubt it. I want you to give your word that this speech of mine will be heard by the American people."

Nixon (shaking hands on it): "By the same token, everything I say will be translated and heard all over the Soviet Union?"

Khrushchev: "That's agreed."

Nixon: "You must not be afraid of ideas."

Khrushchev: "We are telling you not to be afraid of ideas. We have no reason to be afraid. We have already broken free from such a situation."

Nixon: "Well, then, let's have more exchange of them. We are all agreed on that. All right? All right?"

Khrushchev: "Fine." (Aside.) "Agreed to what? All right, I am in agreement. But I want to stress what I am in agreement with. I know that I am dealing with a very good lawyer. I also want to uphold my own miner's flag so that the coal miners can say, 'Our man does not concede.' "

Nixon: "No question about that."

Khrushchev: "You are a lawyer for capitalism and I am a lawyer for communism. Let's compete."

Nixon: "The way you dominate the conversation you would make a good lawyer yourself. If you were in the United States

Senate you would be accused of filibustering."

Khrushchev: "If your reporters will check on the time, they will see who has talked more."

'You Do All the Talking'

Nixon: "You do all the talking and do not let anyone else talk."

Khrushchev (referring to American model home): "You think the Russian people will be dumbfounded to see this? But I tell you all our modern homes have equipment of this sort, and to get a flat you have only to be a Soviet visitor, not a citizen."

Nixon: "We do not claim to astonish the Russian people. We hope to show our diversity and our right to choose. We do not wish to have decisions made at the top by government officials who say that all homes should be built in the same way. Would it not be better to compete in the relative merits of washing machines than in the strength of rockets? Is this the kind of competition you want?"

Khrushchev: "Yes, that's the kind of competition we want, but your generals say we must compete in rockets. Your generals say they are so powerful they can destroy us. We can also show you something so that you will know the Russian spirit. We are strong; we can beat you. But in this respect we can also show you something."

Nixon: "To me you are strong and we are strong. In some ways, you are stronger than we are. In others, we are stronger, but to me it seems that in this day and age to argue who is the stronger completely misses the point. We are both strong, not only from the standpoint of weapons but also from the standpoint of will and spirit.

"No one should ever use his strength to put another in the position where he in effect has an ultimatum. For us to argue who is the stronger misses the point. If war comes we both lose."

Khrushchev: "For the fourth time I have to say I cannot recognize my friend Mr. Nixon. If all Americans agree with you, then who don't we agree [with]? This is what we want."

Nixon: "Anyone who believes the American government does not reflect the people is not an accurate observer of the American scene. I hope the Prime Minister understands all the implications of what I have just said. When you place either one of the powerful nations or any other nations in a position so that they have no choice but to accept dictation or fight, then you are playing with the most destructive thing in the world.

"This is very important in the present world context. It is very dangerous. When we sit down at a conference table it cannot all be one way. One side cannot put an ultimatum to another. It is impossible. But I shall talk to you about this later."

Khrushchev: "Who is raising an ultimatum?"

Nixon: "We will discuss that later."

Khrushchev: "If you have raised the question, why not go on with it now while the people are listening? We know something about politics, too. Let your correspondents compare watches and see who is filibustering. You put great emphasis on *diktat* [dictation]. Our country has never been guided by *diktat. Diktat* is a foolish policy."

Nixon: "I am talking about it in the international sense."

No Threats

Khrushchev: "It sounds to me like a threat. We, too, are giants. You want to threaten — we will answer threats with threats."

Nixon: "That's not my point. We will never engage in threats."

Khrushchev: "You wanted indirectly to threaten me. But we have the means to threaten too."

Nixon: "Who wants to threaten?"

Khrushchev: "You are talking about implications. I have not been. We have the means at our disposal. Ours are better than yours. It is you who want to compete. *Da, da, da.*"

Nixon: "We are well aware that you have the means. To me who is best is not material."

Khrushchev: "You raised the point. We want peace and friendship with all nations, especially with America."

Nixon: "We want peace, too, and I believe that you do also."

Khrushchev: "Yes, I believe that."

Nixon: "I see that you want to build a good life. But I don't think that the cause of peace is helped by reminders that you have greater strength than we do, because this is a threat, too."

Khrushchev: "I was answering your words. You challenged me. Let's argue fairly."

Nixon: "My point was that in today's world it is immaterial which of the two great countries at any particular moment has the advantage. In war, these advantages are illusory. Can we agree on that?"

Khrushchev: "Not quite. Let's not beat around the bush."

Nixon: "I like the way he talks."

Khrushchev: "We want to liquidate all bases from foreign lands. Until that happens we will speak different languages. One who is for putting an end to bases on foreign lands is for peace. One who is against it is for war. We have liquidated our bases, reduced our forces, and offered to make a peace treaty and eliminate the point of friction in Berlin. Until we settle that question, we will talk different languages."

Nixon: "Do you think it can be settled at Geneva?"

Khrushchev: "If we considered it otherwise, we would not have incurred the expense of sending our Foreign Minister to Geneva. [Andrei] Gromyko is not an idler. He is a very good man."

Nixon: "We have great respect for Mr. Gromyko. Some people say he looks like me. I think he is better-looking. I hope it [the Geneva Conference] will be successful."

Khrushchev: "It does not depend on us."

Nixon: "It takes two to make an agreement. You cannot have it all your own way."

Khrushchev: "These are questions that have the same aim. To put an end to the vestiges of war, to make a peace treaty with Germany — that is what we want. It is very bad that we quarrel over the question of war and peace."

Nixon: "There is no question but that your people and you want the government of the United States to be for peace — anyone who thinks that our government is not for peace is not an accurate observer of America. In order to have peace, Mr. Prime Minister, even in an argument between friends, there must be sitting-down around a table. There must be discussion. Each side must find areas where it looks at the other's point of view. The world looks to you today with regard to Geneva. I believe it would be a grave mistake and a blow to peace if it were allowed to fail."

Khrushchev: "This is our understanding as well."

Nixon: "So this is something. The present position is stalemate. Ways must be found to discuss it."

Khrushchev: "The two sides must seek ways of agreement."

KENNEDY, KHRUSHCHEV ON CUBAN MISSILE CRISIS

Following are the texts of President Kennedy's October 22, 1962, television address about Soviet offensive missiles in Cuba and Kennedy's October 27 message to Soviet premier Nikita S. Khrushchev, and excerpts from Khrushchev's October 27 and October 28 messages to Kennedy and Kennedy's October 28 reply.

Kennedy Speech October 22

Good evening, my fellow citizens:

This Government, as promised, has maintained the closest surveillance of the Soviet military buildup on the island of Cuba.

Within the past week, unmistakable evidence has established the fact that a series of offensive missile sites is now in preparation on that imprisoned island. The purpose of these bases can be none other than to provide a nuclear strike capability against the Western Hemisphere.

Upon receiving the first preliminary hard information of this nature last Tuesday morning at 9 a.m., I directed that our surveillance be stepped up. And having now confirmed and completed our evaluation of the evidence and our decision on a course of action, this Government feels obliged to report this new crisis to you in fullest detail.

The characteristics of these new missile sites indicate two distinct types of installations. Several of them include medium range ballistic missiles, capable of carrying a nuclear warhead for a distance of more than 1,000 nautical miles. Each of these missiles, in short, is capable of striking Washington, D.C., the Panama Canal, Cape Canaveral, Mexico City, or any other city in the southeastern part of the United States, in Central America, or in the Caribbean area.

Additional sites not yet completed appear to be designed for intermediate range ballistic missiles — capable of traveling more than twice as far — and thus capable of striking most of the major cities in the Western Hemisphere, ranging as far north as Hudson Bay, Canada, and as far south as Lima, Peru. In addition, jet bombers, capable of carrying nuclear weapons, are now being uncrated and assembled in Cuba, while the necessary air bases are being prepared.

This urgent transformation of Cuba into an important strategic base — by the presence of these large, long-range, and clearly offensive weapons of sudden mass destruction — constitutes an explicit threat to the peace and security of all the Americas, in flagrant and deliberate defiance of the Rio Pact of 1947, the traditions of this Nation and hemisphere, the joint resolution of the 87th Congress, the Charter of the United Nations, and my own public warnings to the Soviets on September 4 and 13. This action also contradicts the repeated assurances of Soviet spokesmen, both publicly and privately delivered, that the arms buildup in Cuba would retain its original defensive character, and that the Soviet Union had no need or desire to station strategic missiles on the territory of any other nation.

The size of this undertaking makes clear that it has been planned for some months. Yet only last month, after I had made clear the distinction between any introduction of ground-to-ground missiles and the existence of defensive antiaircraft missiles, the Soviet Government publicly stated on September 11 that, and I quote, "the armaments and military equipment sent to Cuba are designed exclusively for defensive purposes," that, and I quote the Soviet Government, "there is no need for the Soviet Government to shift its weapons . . . for a retaliatory blow to any other country, for instance Cuba," and that, and I quote their government, "the Soviet Union has so powerful rockets to carry these nuclear warheads that there is no need to search for sites for them beyond the boundaries of the Soviet Union." That statement was false.

Only last Thursday, as evidence of this rapid offensive buildup was already in my hand, Soviet Foreign Minister Gromyko told me in my office that he was instructed to make it clear once again, as he said his government had already done, that Soviet assistance to Cuba, and I quote, "pursued solely the purpose of contributing to the defense capabilities of Cuba," that, and I quote him, "training by Soviet specialists of Cuban nationals in handling defensive armaments was by no means offensive, and if it were otherwise," Mr. Gromyko went on, "the Soviet Government would never become involved in rendering such assistance." That statement also was false.

Neither the United States of America nor the world community of nations can tolerate deliberate deception and offensive threats on the part of any nation, large or small. We no longer live in a world where only the actual firing of weapons represents a sufficient challenge to a nation's security to constitute maximum peril. Nuclear weapons are so destructive and ballistic missiles are so swift, that any substantially increased possibility of their use or any sudden change in their deployment may well be regarded as a definite threat to peace.

For many years, both the Soviet Union and the United States, recognizing this fact, have deployed strategic nuclear weapons with great care, never upsetting the precarious status quo which insured that these weapons would not be used in the absence of some vital challenge. Our own strategic missiles have never been transferred to the territory of any other nation under a cloak of secrecy and deception; and our history — unlike that of the Soviets since the end of World War II — demonstrates that we have no desire to dominate or conquer any other nation or impose our system upon its people. Nevertheless, American citizens have become adjusted to living daily on the bull's-eye of Soviet missiles located inside the U.S.S.R. or in submarines.

In that sense, missiles in Cuba add to an already clear and present danger — although it should be noted the nations of Latin America have never previously been subjected to a potential nuclear threat.

But this secret, swift, and extraordinary buildup of Communist missiles — in an area well known to have a special and historical relationship to the United States and the nations of the Western Hemisphere, in violation of Soviet assurances, and in defiance of American and hemispheric policy — this sudden, clandestine decision to station strategic weapons for the first time outside of Soviet soil — is a deliberately provocative and unjustified change in the status quo which cannot be accepted by this country, if our courage and our commitments are ever to be trusted again by either friend or foe.

The 1930's taught us a clear lesson: aggressive conduct, if allowed to go unchecked and unchallenged, ultimately leads to war. This nation is opposed to war. We are also true to our word. Our unswerving objective, therefore, must be to prevent the use of these missiles against this or any other country, and to secure their withdrawal or elimination from the Western Hemisphere.

Our policy has been one of patience and restraint, as befits a peaceful and powerful nation, which leads a worldwide alliance. We have been determined not to be diverted from our central concerns by mere irritants and fanatics. But now further action is required — and it is under way; and these actions may only be the beginning. We will not prematurely or unnecessarily risk the costs of worldwide nuclear war in which even the fruits of victory would be ashes in our mouth — but neither will we shrink from that risk at any time it must be faced.

Acting, therefore, in the defense of our own security and of the entire Western Hemisphere, and under the authority entrusted to me by the Constitution as endorsed by the resolution of the Congress, I have directed that the following *initial* steps be taken immediately:

First: To halt this offensive buildup, a strict quarantine on all offensive military equipment under shipment to Cuba is being initiated. All ships of any kind bound for Cuba from whatever nation or port will, if found to contain cargoes of offensive weapons, be turned back. This quarantine will be extended, if needed, to other types of cargo and carriers. We are not at this time, however, denying the necessities of life as the Soviets attempted to do in their Berlin blockade of 1948.

Second: I have directed the continued and increased close surveillance of Cuba and its military buildup. The foreign ministers of the OAS [Organization of American States], in their communique of October 6, rejected secrecy on such matters in this hemisphere. Should these offensive military preparations continue, thus increasing the threat to the hemisphere, further action will be justified. I have directed the Armed Forces to prepare for any eventualities; and I trust that in the interest of both the Cuban people and the Soviet technicians at the sites, the hazards to all concerned of continuing this threat will be recognized.

Third: It shall be the policy of this Nation to regard any nuclear missile launched from Cuba against any nation in the Western Hemisphere as an attack by the Soviet Union on the United States, requiring a full retaliatory response upon the Soviet Union.

Fourth: As a necessary military precaution, I have reinforced our base at Guantanamo, evacuated today the dependents of our personnel there, and ordered additional military units to be on a standby alert basis.

Fifth: We are calling tonight for an immediate meeting of the Organ of Consultation under the Organization of American States, to consider this threat to hemispheric security and to invoke articles 6 and 8 of the Rio Treaty in support of all necessary action. The United Nations Charter allows for regional security arrangements — and the nations of this hemisphere decided long ago against the military presence of outside powers. Our other allies around the world have also been alerted.

Sixth: Under the Charter of the United Nations, we are asking tonight that an emergency meeting of the Security Council be convoked without delay to take action against this latest Soviet threat to world peace. Our resolution will call for prompt dismantling and withdrawal of all offensive weapons in Cuba, under the supervision of U.N. observers, before the quarantine can be lifted.

Seventh and finally: I call upon Chairman Khrushchev to halt and eliminate this clandestine, reckless, and provocative threat to world peace and to stable relations between our two nations. I call upon him further to abandon this course of world domination, and to join in an historic effort to end the perilous arms race and to transform the history of man. He has an opportunity now to move the world back from the abyss of destruction — by returning to his government's own words that it had no need to station missiles outside its own territory, and withdrawing these weapons from Cuba — by refraining from any action which will widen or deepen the present crisis — and then by participating in a search for peaceful and permanent solutions.

This Nation is prepared to present its case against the Soviet threat to peace, and our own proposals for a peaceful world, at any time and in any forum — in the OAS, in the United Nations, or in any other meeting that could be useful — without limiting our freedom of action. We have in the past made strenuous efforts to limit the spread of nuclear weapons. We have proposed the elimination of all arms and military bases in a fair and effective disarmament treaty. We are prepared to discuss new proposals for the removal of tensions on both sides — including the possibilities of a genuinely independent Cuba, free to determine its own destiny. We have no wish to war with the Soviet Union — for we are a peaceful people who desire to live in peace with all other peoples.

'An Atmosphere of Intimidation'

But it is difficult to settle or even discuss these problems in an atmosphere of intimidation. That is why this latest Soviet threat — or any other threat which is made either independently or in response to our actions this week — must and will be met with determination. Any hostile move anywhere in the world against the safety and freedom of peoples to whom we are committed — including in particular the brave people of West Berlin — will be met by whatever action is needed.

Finally, I want to say a few words to the captive people of Cuba, to whom this speech is being directly carried by special radio facilities. I speak to you as a friend, as one who knows of your deep attachment to your fatherland, as one who shares your aspirations for liberty and justice for all. And I have watched and the American people have watched with deep sorrow how your nationalist revolution was betrayed — and how your fatherland fell under foreign domination. Now your leaders are no longer Cuban leaders inspired by Cuban ideals. They are puppets and agents of an international conspiracy which has turned Cuba against your friends and neighbors in the Americas — and turned it into the first Latin American country to become a target for nuclear war — the first Latin American country to have these weapons on its soil.

These new weapons are not in your interest. They contribute nothing to your peace and well-being. They can only undermine it. But this country has no wish to cause you to suffer or to impose any system upon you. We know that your lives and land are being used as pawns by those who deny your freedom.

Many times in the past, the Cuban people have risen to throw out tyrants who destroyed their liberty. And I have no doubt that most Cubans today look forward to the time when they will be truly free — free from foreign domination, free to choose their own leaders, free to select their own system, free to own their own land, free to speak and write and worship without fear or degradation.

And then shall Cuba be welcomed back to the society of free nations and to the associations of this hemisphere.

My fellow citizens: let no one doubt that this is a difficult and dangerous effort on which we have set out. No one can foresee precisely what course it will take or what costs or casualties will be incurred. Many months of sacrifice and self-discipline lie ahead — months in which both our patience and our will will be tested — months in which many threats and denunciations will keep us aware of our dangers. But the greatest danger of all would be to do nothing.

The path we have chosen for the present is full of hazards, as all paths are — but it is the one most consistent with our character and courage as a nation and our commitments around the world. The cost of freedom is always high — but Americans have always paid it. And one path we shall never choose, and that is the path of surrender or submission.

Our goal is not the victory of might, but the vindication of right — not peace at the expense of freedom, but both peace *and* freedom, here in this hemisphere, and, we hope, around the world. God willing, that goal will be achieved.

Thank you and good night.

Khrushchev's October 27 Message

...I understand your concern for the security of the United States, Mr. President, because this is the first duty of the president. However, these questions are also uppermost in our minds. The same duties rest with me as chairman of the USSR Council of Ministers. You have been worried over our assisting Cuba with arms designed to strengthen its defensive potential — precisely defensive potential — because Cuba, no matter what weapons it had, could not compare with you since these are different dimensions, the more so given up-to-date means of extermination.

Our purpose has been and is to help Cuba, and no one can challenge the humanity of our motives aimed at allowing Cuba to live peacefully and develop as its people desire. You want to relieve your country from danger and this is understandable. However, Cuba also wants this. All countries want to relieve themselves from danger. But how can we, the Soviet Union and our government, assess your actions which, in effect, mean that you have surrounded the Soviet Union with military bases, surrounded our allies with military bases, set up military bases literally around our country, and stationed your rocket weapons at them? This is no secret. High-placed American officials demonstratively declare this. Your rockets are stationed in Britain and in Italy and pointed at us. Your rockets are stationed in Turkey.

You are worried over Cuba. You say that it worries you because it lies at a distance of 90 miles across the sea from the shores of the United States. However, Turkey lies next to us. Our sentinels are pacing up and down and watching each other. Do you believe that you have the right to demand security for your country and the removal of such weapons that you qualify as offensive, while not recognizing this right for us?

You have stationed devastating rocket weapons, which you call offensive, in Turkey literally right next to us. How then does recognition of our equal military possibilities tally with such unequal relations between our great states? This does not tally at all.

It is good, Mr. President, that you agreed for our representatives to meet and begin talks, apparently with the participation of U.N. Acting Secretary General U Thant. Consequently, to some extent, he assumes the role of intermediary, and we believe that he can cope with the responsible mission if, of course, every side that is drawn into this conflict shows good will.

I think that one could rapidly eliminate the conflict and normalize the situation. Then people would heave a sigh of relief, considering that the statesmen who bear the responsibility have sober minds, an awareness of their responsibility, and an ability to solve complicated problems and not allow matters to slide to the disaster of war.

This is why I make this proposal: We agree to remove those weapons from Cuba which you regard as offensive weapons. We agree to do this and to state this commitment to the United

Nations. Your representatives will make a statement to the effect that the United States, on its part, bearing in mind the anxiety and concern of the Soviet state, will evacuate its analogous weapons from Turkey. Let us reach an understanding on what time you and we need to put this into effect.

After this, representatives of the U.N. Security Council could control on-the-spot the fulfillment of these commitments. Of course, it is necessary that the Governments of Cuba and Turkey would allow these representatives to come to their countries and check fulfillment of this commitment, which each side undertakes. Apparently, it would be better if these representatives enjoyed the trust of the Security Council and ours — the United States and the Soviet Union — as well as of Turkey and Cuba. I think that it will not be difficult to find such people who enjoy the trust and respect of all interested sides.

We, having assumed this commitment in order to give satisfaction and hope to the peoples of Cuba and Turkey and to increase their confidence in their security, will make a statement in the Security Council to the effect that the Soviet Government gives a solemn pledge to respect the integrity of the frontiers and the sovereignty of Turkey, not to intervene in its domestic affairs, not to invade Turkey, not to make available its territory as a place d'armes for such invasion, and also will restrain those who would think of launching an aggression against Turkey either from Soviet territory or from the territory of other states bordering on Turkey.

The U.S. Government will make the same statement in the Security Council with regard to Cuba. It will declare that the United States will respect the integrity of the frontiers of Cuba, its sovereignty, undertakes not to intervene in its domestic affairs, not to invade and not to make its territory available as place d'armes for the invasion of Cuba, and also will restrain those who would think of launching an aggression against Cuba either from U.S. territory or from the territory of other places bordering on Cuba.

Of course, for this we would have to reach agreement with you and to arrange for some deadline. Let us agree to give some time, but not to delay, two or three weeks, not more than a month.

The weapons on Cuba, that you have mentioned and which, as you say, alarm you, are in the hands of Soviet officers. Therefore any accidental use of them whatsoever to the detriment of the United States of America is excluded. These means are stationed in Cuba at the request of the Cuban Government and only in defensive aims. Therefore, if there is no invasion of Cuba, or an attack on the Soviet Union, or other of our allies then, of course, these means do not threaten anyone and will not threaten. For they do not pursue offensive aims.

If you accept my proposal, Mr. President, we would send our representatives to New York, to the United Nations, and would give them exhaustive instructions in order to come to terms sooner. If you would also appoint your men and give them appropriate instructions, this problem could be solved soon.

Why would I like to achieve this? Because the entire world is now agitated and expects reasonable actions from us. The greatest pleasure for all the peoples would be an announcement on our agreement, on nipping in the bud the conflict that has arisen. I attach a great importance to such understanding because it might be a good beginning and, specifically, facilitate a nuclear test ban agreement. The problem of tests could be solved simultaneously, not linking one with the other, because they are different problems. However, it is important to reach an understanding to both these problems in order to make a good gift to the people, to let them rejoice in the news that a nuclear test ban agreement has also been reached and thus there will be no further contamination of the atmosphere. Your and our positions on this issue are very close.

All this, possibly, would serve as a good impetus to searching for mutually acceptable agreements on other disputed issues, too, on which there is an exchange of opinion between us. These problems have not yet been solved but they wait for an urgent solution which would clear the international atmosphere. We are ready for this.

These are my proposals, Mr. President.

Respectfully yours,

Nikita Khrushchev
October 27, 1962

Kennedy's October 27 Response

Dear Mr. Chairman:

I have read your letter of October 26th [not made public] with great care and welcomed the statement of your desire to seek a prompt solution to the problem. The first thing that needs to be done, however, is for work to cease on offensive missile bases in Cuba and for all weapons systems in Cuba capable of offensive use to be rendered inoperable, under effective United Nations arrangements.

Assuming this is done promptly, I have given my representatives in New York instructions that will permit them to work out this weekend — in cooperation with the Acting Secretary General and your representative — an arrangement for a permanent solution to the Cuban problem along the lines suggested in your letter of October 26th. As I read your letter, the key elements of your proposals — which seem generally acceptable as I understand them — are as follows:

1. You would agree to remove these weapons systems from Cuba under appropriate United Nations observation and supervision; and undertake, with suitable safeguards, to halt the further introduction of such weapons systems into Cuba.

2. We, on our part, would agree — upon the establishment of adequate arrangements through the United Nations to ensure the carrying out and continuation of these commitments — (a) to remove promptly the quarantine measures now in effect and (b) to give assurances against an invasion of Cuba. I am confident that other nations of the Western Hemisphere would be prepared to do likewise.

If you will give your representative similar instructions, there is no reason why we should not be able to complete these arrangements and announce them to the world within a couple of days. The effect of such a settlement on easing world tensions would enable us to work toward a more general arrangement regarding "other armaments," as proposed in your second letter which you made public. I would like to say again that the United States is very much interested in reducing tensions and halting the arms race; and if your letter signifies that you are prepared to discuss a detente affecting NATO and the Warsaw Pact, we are quite prepared to consider with our allies any useful proposals.

But the first ingredient, let me emphasize, is the cessation of work on missile sites in Cuba and measures to render such weapons inoperable, under effective international guarantees. The continuation of this threat, or a prolonging of this discussion concerning Cuba by linking these problems to the broader questions of European and world security, would surely lead to an intensification of the Cuban crisis and a grave risk to the peace of the world. For this reason I hope we can quickly agree along the lines outlined in this letter and in your letter of October 26th.

John F. Kennedy

Khrushchev's October 28 Message

Dear Mr. President: I have received your message of 27 October. I express my satisfaction and thank you for the sense of proportion you have displayed and for realization of the responsibility which now devolves on you for the preservation of the peace of the world....

In order to eliminate as rapidly as possible the conflict which endangers the cause of peace, to give an assurance to all people who crave peace, and to reassure the American people, who, I am certain, also want peace, as do the people of the Soviet Union, the Soviet Government, in addition to earlier instructions on the discontinuation of further work on weapons construction sites, has given a new order to dismantle the arms which you described as offensive, and to crate and return them to the Soviet Union.

Mr. President, I should like to repeat what I had already written to you in my earlier messages — that the Soviet Government has given economic assistance to the Republic of Cuba, as well as arms, because Cuba and the Cuban people were constantly under the continuous threat of an invasion of Cuba....

The Cuban people want to build their life in their own interests without external interference. This is their right, and they cannot be blamed for wanting to be masters of their own country and disposing of the fruits of their own labor. The threat of invasion of Cuba and all other schemes for creating tension over China are designed to strike the Cuban people with a sense of insecurity, intimidate them, and prevent them from peacefully building their new life.

Mr. President, I should like to say clearly once more that we could not remain indifferent to this. The Soviet Government decided to render assistance to Cuba with means of defense against aggression — only with means for defense purposes. We have supplied the defense means which you describe as offensive means. We have supplied them to prevent an attack on Cuba — to prevent rash acts.

I regard with respect and trust the statement you made in your message of 27 October 1962 that there would be no attack, no invasion of Cuba, and not only on the part of the United States, but also on the part of other nations of the Western Hemisphere, as you said in your same message. Then the motives which induced us to render assistance of such a kind to Cuba disappear.

It is for this reason that we instructed our officers — these means as I had already informed you earlier are in the hands of the Soviet officers — to take appropriate measures to discontinue construction of the aforementioned facilities, to dismantle them, and to return them to the Soviet Union. As I had informed you in the letter of 27 October, we are prepared to reach agreement to enable U.N. representatives to verify the dismantling of these means. Thus in view of the assurances you have given and our instructions on dismantling, there is every condition for eliminating the present conflict....

In conclusion, I should like to say something about a detente between NATO and the Warsaw Treaty countries that you have mentioned. We have spoken about this long since and are prepared to continue to exchange views on this question with you and to find a reasonable solution.

We should like to continue the exchange of views on the prohibition of atomic and thermonuclear weapons, general disarmament, and other problems relating to the relaxation of international tension....

We are confident that the people of all countries, like you, Mr. President, will understand me correctly. We are not threatening. We want nothing but peace. Our country is now on the upsurge. Our people are enjoying the fruits of their peaceful labor. They have achieved tremendous successes since the October Revolution, and created the greatest material, spiritual, and cultural values. Our people are enjoying these values; they want to continue developing their achievements and insure their further development on the way of peace and social progress by their persistent labor.

I should like to remind you, Mr. President, that military reconnaissance planes have violated the borders of the Soviet Union....

[O]n 28 October, ... one of your reconnaissance planes intruded over Soviet borders in the Chukotka Peninsula area in the north and flew over our territory. The question is, Mr. President: How should we regard this? What is this, a provocation? One of your planes violates our frontier during this anxious time we are both experiencing, when everything has been put into combat readiness. Is it not a fact that an intruding American plane could be easily taken for a nuclear bomber, which might push us to a fateful step; and all the more so since the U.S. Government and Pentagon long ago declared that you are maintaining a continuous nuclear bomber patrol?

Therefore, you can imagine the responsibility you are assuming; especially now, when we are living through such anxious times.

I should also like to express the following wish; it concerns the Cuban people. You do not have diplomatic relations. But through my officers in Cuba, I have reports that American planes are making flights over Cuba.

We are interested that there should be no war in the world, and that the Cuban people should live in peace. And besides, Mr. President, it is no secret that we have our people on Cuba. Under a treaty with the Cuban Government we have sent there officers, instructors, mostly plain people: specialists, agronomists, zootechnicians, irrigators, land reclamation specialists, plain workers, tractor drivers, and others. We are concerned about them.

I should like you to consider, Mr. President, that violation of Cuban airspace by American planes could also lead to dangerous consequences. And if you do not want this to happen, it would be better if no cause is given for a dangerous situation to arise. We must be careful now and refrain from any steps which would not be useful to the defense of the states involved in the conflict, which could only cause irritation and even serve as a provocation for a fateful step. Therefore, we must display sanity, reason, and refrain from such steps.

We value peace perhaps even more than other peoples because we went through a terrible war with Hitler. But our people will not falter in the face of any test. Our people trust their government, and we assure our people and world public opinion that the Soviet Government will not allow itself to be provoked. But if the provocateurs unleash a war, they will not evade responsibility and the grave consequences a war would bring upon them. But we are confident that reason will triumph, that war will not be unleashed, and peace and the security of the peoples will be insured....

N. Khrushchev
28 October 1962

Kennedy's October 28 Reply

... I consider my letter to you of October twenty-seventh and your reply of today as firm undertakings on the part of both our governments which should be promptly carried out. I hope that the necessary measures can at once be taken through the United Nations, as your message says, so that the United States in turn will be able to remove the quarantine measures now in effect. I have already made arrangements to report all these matters to the Organization of American States, whose members share a deep interest in a genuine peace in the Caribbean area.

You referred in your letter to a violation of your frontier by an American aircraft in the area of the Chukotskiy Peninsula. I have learned that this plane, without arms or photographic equipment, was engaged in an air sampling mission in connection with your nuclear tests.... I regret this incident and will see to it that every precaution is taken to prevent recurrence.

Mr. Chairman, both of our countries have great unfinished tasks and I know that your people as well as those of the United States can ask for nothing better than to pursue them free from the fear of war. Modern science and technology have given us the possibility of making labor fruitful beyond anything that could have been dreamed of a few decades ago.

I agree with you that we must devote urgent attention to the problem of disarmament, as it relates to the whole world and also to critical areas. Perhaps now, as we step back from danger, we can together make real progress in this vital field. I think we should give priority to questions relating to the proliferation of nuclear weapons, on earth and in outer space, and to the great effort for a nuclear test ban. But we should also work hard to see if wider measures of disarmament can be agreed and put into operation at an early date. The United States Government will be prepared to discuss these questions urgently, and in a constructive spirit, at Geneva or elsewhere.

John F. Kennedy

CHINESE REJECTION OF INVITATION TO MOSCOW

Following are excerpts from a March 23, 1966, letter sent to Moscow by the Chinese declining an invitation to attend the Twenty-third Party Congress. The Chinese rejection was a formal acknowledgment of the serious rift that had developed between the two former allies.

In normal circumstances it would be considered an indication of friendship for one party to invite another fraternal party to send a delegation to its Congress. But around the time you sent this invitation, you distributed an anti-Chinese document in the Soviet Union, both inside and outside the party, and organized a whole series of anti-Chinese reports from top to bottom, right down to the basic units, whipping up hysteria against China.

Moreover, you sent an anti-Chinese letter to other parties, instigating them to join you in opposing China. You wantonly vilified the Communist Chinese party as being "bellicose" and "pseudo-revolutionary," as "refusing to oppose imperialism" and "encouraging United States imperialist aggression," and as being guilty of "adventurism," "splitism," "Trotskyism," "nationalism," "great power chauvinism," "dogmatism," and so on and so forth.

You have also been spreading rumors alleging that China "is obstructing aid to Vietnam" and that "China has been encroaching on Soviet territory." You have gone so far as to state that "China is not a Socialist country.". . . In these circumstances, how can the Chinese Communist party, which you look upon as an enemy, be expected to attend your Congress?

The Chinese Communist party has attended many of the Congresses of the CPSU. Also, we sent delegations to your 20th, 21st and 22nd Congresses, after the Khrushchev revisionist group usurped the leadership of the CPSU. But at the 20th Congress of the CPSU you suddenly lashed out at Stalin. Stalin was a great Marxist-Leninist.

In attacking Stalin, you were attacking Marxism-Leninism, the Soviet Union, Communist parties, China, the people and all the Marxist-Leninists of the world. At the 22nd Party Congress you adopted an out-and-out revisionist program, made a wild public attack on Albania and reproached the Chinese Communist party, so that the head of our delegation had to leave for home while the Congress was only half way through. . . .

Over the last years, we have made a series of efforts in the hope that you would return to the path of Marxism-Leninism. Since Khrushchev's downfall, we have advised the new leaders of the CPSU on a number of occasions to make a fresh start. We have done everything we could, but you have not shown the slightest repentance.

Since coming to power, the new leaders of the CPSU have gone farther and farther down the road of revisionism, splitism and great power chauvinism. . . .

Despite the tricks you have been playing to deceive people, you are pursuing United States-Soviet collaboration for the domination of the world with your heart and soul. In mouthing a few words against United States imperialism and making a show of supporting anti-imperialist struggles, you are conducting only minor attacks on United States imperialism while rendering it major help.

. . . Your clamor for "united action," especially on the Vietnam question, is nothing but a trap for the purpose of deceiving the Soviet people and the revolutionary people of the world. You have all along been acting in coordination with the United States in its plot for peace talks, vainly attempting to sell out the struggle of the Vietnamese people against United States aggression and for national salvation and to drag the Vietnam question into the orbit of Soviet-United States collaboration.

You have worked hand in glove with the United States in a whole series of dirty deals inside and outside the United Nations. In close coordination with the counter-revolutionary "global strategy" of United States imperialism, you are now actively trying to build a ring of encirclement around socialist China. Not only have you excluded yourself from the international united front of all peoples against United States imperialism and its lackeys, you have even aligned yourselves with United States imperialism, the main enemy of the people of the world, and established a holy alliance against China, against the movement and against the Marxist-Leninists. . . .

We are confident that in all parts of the world, including the Soviet Union, the masses of the people, who constitute more than 90 percent of the population, are for revolution and against imperialism and its lackeys. In the ranks of the international Communist movement, including the Communist party of the Soviet Union, more than 90 percent of the Communists and cadres will eventually march along the path of Marxism-Leninism.

. . . The Soviet people may rest assured that once the Soviet Union meets with imperialist aggression and puts up resolute resistance, China will definitely stand side by side with the Soviet Union and fight against the common enemy.

With fraternal greetings.

BREZHNEV DOCTRINE OF LIMITED SOVEREIGNTY

Following are excerpts from Soviet leader Leonid I. Brezhnev's November 13, 1968, speech to the Fifth Congress of the Polish United Workers' Party and his October 28, 1969, address to visiting Czech officials.

Speech to Poles

. . . The experience of struggle and realistic stocktaking of the situation obtaining in the world with utmost clarity shows that it is vitally necessary for the Communists of the socialist countries to carry high the banner of socialist internationalism, constantly to strengthen the cohesion and solidarity of the countries of socialism. Therein lies one of the main conditions for the successful construction of socialism and communism in each of our countries and the successful struggle of the world system of socialism against imperialism.

The interests of the defence of each socialist country, the interests of its economic, scientific and cultural advance, all this calls for broadest cooperation between the fraternal countries, the all-round development of various contacts between them, genuine internationalism. . . .

The socialist states stand for strict respect for the sovereignty of all countries. We emphatically oppose interference into the affairs of any states, violations of their sovereignty.

At the same time the establishment and defence of the sovereignty of states which have embarked upon the road of building socialism is of particular significance for us, Communists. The forces of imperialism and reaction seek to deprive the people now of . . . their sovereign right . . . to ensure the prosperity of their country, the well-being and happiness of the broad mass of the working people through building a society free from any oppression and exploitation. . . .

It is common knowledge that the Soviet Union has done much for the real strengthening of the sovereignty and independence of the socialist countries. The CPSU [Communist Party of the Soviet Union] has always advocated that each socialist country determine the specific forms of its development along the road of socialism with consideration of its specific national conditions. However, it is known, Comrades, that there are also common laws governing socialist construction a deviation from which might lead to a deviation from socialism as such.

And when the internal and external forces hostile to socialism seek to revert the development of any socialist country towards the restoration of the capitalist order, when a threat to the cause of socialism in that country, a threat to the security of the socialist community as a whole emerges, this is no longer only a problem of the people of that country but also a common problem, concern of all socialist countries.

It goes without saying that such an action as military aid to a fraternal country to cut short the threat to the socialist order is an extraordinary, enforced step, it can be sparked off only by direct actions of the enemies of socialism inside the country and beyond its boundaries, actions creating a threat to the common interests of the camp of socialism. . . .

Let all those who are inclined to forget the lessons of history and who would like to engage again in recarving the map of Europe know that the frontiers of Poland, the German Democratic Republic, Czechoslovakia, just as any other member-country of the Warsaw Treaty, are immutable and inviolable. These frontiers are defended by the entire armed might of the socialist community. We advise all who like to encroach upon other peoples' frontiers to remember this well! . . .

Speech to Czechs

. . . Comrades! For almost a year and a half now, the thoughts and feelings of Soviet Communists and all Soviet people, as well as those of people in other socialist countries, have been focused on the events in Czechoslovakia. We had to experience a great deal in this period — anxiety for the destiny of socialism in a fraternal country subjected to the onslaught of the joint forces of internal and external reaction, sentiments of combat solidarity with the principled and staunch Marxists-Leninists in the Communist Party of Czechoslovakia who courageously rose to struggle for the cause of socialism and, last but not least, pride in the successes scored by Czechoslovakia's Communists in this hard struggle. . . .

Hardly can anyone deny now that the forces of socialism have stood this test — test by practice, test by struggle — with honor. The principled stand of Communists, the unity of socialist countries and their international solidarity proved to be stronger than those who wanted to reverse the history of Czechoslovak society and to wrest state power from the hands of the working class, and from the hands of working people. . . .

The CPSU [Communist Party of the Soviet Union] and our entire people had faith that this would be so. We, the allies of Czechoslovakia, did our internationalist duty. . . .

[T]he struggle against the anti-socialist, counter-revolutionary forces in Czechoslovakia raised in all sharpness the question of international responsibility of the Communists for the fate of socialism. There can be only one reply to the attempts of external and internal reaction to weaken the positions of socialism, to impair the socialist community, and that reply is still greater cohesion of the fraternal countries on the basis of socialist internationalism, and mutual support in the struggle against the intrigues of imperialism and for the consolidation of the socialist system.

Our common stand on this issue is clearly expressed in the well-known Bratislava Statement of the fraternal Parties of six socialist countries [issued after an August 3, 1968, meeting of Eastern-bloc nations]. It says there, that the support, strengthening and defence of the gains of socialism "are the common international duty of all the socialist countries." And the summing-up document of the recent International Conference of Communist Parties says: "The defence of socialism is the international duty of the Communists." Our invincible strength lies in the close solidarity of the fraternal socialist countries, in the unity of the national detachments of Communists. . . .

NIXON-BREZHNEV 1972 SUMMIT STATEMENTS

Following are the texts of the declaration of basic principles of relations between the United States and the Soviet Union signed May 29, 1972, by President Richard Nixon and Communist party leader Leonid I. Brezhnev

and a joint communiqué issued by Nixon and Soviet leaders on May 29. The Moscow summit, which produced the documents, was the result of efforts by the Nixon administration and the Kremlin to establish a détente between the superpowers. Earlier in the summit Nixon and Brezhnev had signed the SALT I Treaty, providing for limits on the strategic nuclear arsenals of both countries.

Declaration of Principles

The United States of America and the Union of Soviet Socialist Republics,

Guided by their obligations under the Charter of the United Nations and by a desire to strengthen peaceful relations with each other and to place these relations on the firmest possible basis,

Aware of the need to make every effort to remove the threat of war and to create conditions which promote the reduction of tensions in the world and the strengthening of universal security and international cooperation,

Believing that the improvement of US-Soviet relations and their mutually advantageous development in such areas as economics, science and culture, will meet these objectives and contribute to better mutual understanding and business-like cooperation, without in any way prejudicing the interests of third countries,

Conscious that these objectives reflect the interests of the peoples of both countries.

Have agreed as follows:

First. They will proceed from the common determination that in the nuclear age there is no alternative to conducting their mutual relations on the basis of peaceful coexistence. Differences in ideology and in the social systems of the USA and the USSR are not obstacles to the bilateral development of normal relations based on the principles of sovereignty, equality, non-interference in internal affairs and mutual advantage.

Second. The USA and the USSR attach major importance to preventing the development of situations capable of causing a dangerous exacerbation of their relations. Therefore, they will do their utmost to avoid military confrontations and to prevent the outbreak of nuclear war. They will always exercise restraint in their mutual relations, and will be prepared to negotiate and settle differences by peaceful means. Discussions and negotiations on outstanding issues will be conducted in a spirit of reciprocity, mutual accommodations and mutual benefit.

Both sides recognize that efforts to obtain unilateral advantage at the expense of the other, directly or indirectly, are inconsistent with these objectives. The prerequisites for maintaining and strengthening peaceful relations between the USA and the USSR are the recognition of the security interests of the Parties based on the principle of equality and the renunciation of the use or threat of force.

Third. The USA and the USSR have a special responsibility, as do other countries which are permanent members of the United Nations Security Council, to do everything in their power so that conflicts or situations will not arise which would serve to increase international tensions. Accordingly, they will seek to promote conditions in which all countries will live in peace and security and will not be subject to outside interference in their internal affairs.

Fourth. The USA and the USSR intend to widen the juridical basis of their mutual relations and to exert the necessary efforts so that bilateral agreements which they have concluded and multilateral treaties and agreements to which they are jointly parties are faithfully implemented.

Fifth. The USA and the USSR reaffirm their readiness to continue the practice of exchanging views on problems of mutual interest and, when necessary, to conduct such exchanges at the highest level, including meetings between leaders of the two countries.

The two governments welcome and will facilitate an increase in productive contacts between representatives of the legislative bodies of the two countries.

Sixth. The Parties will continue their efforts to limit armaments on a bilateral as well as on a multilateral basis. They will continue to make special efforts to limit strategic armaments. Whenever possible, they will conclude concrete agreements aimed at achieving these purposes.

The USA and the USSR regard as the ultimate objective of their efforts the achievement of general and complete disarmament and the establishment of an effective system of international security in accordance with the purposes and principles of the United Nations.

Seventh. The USA and the USSR regard commercial and economic ties as an important and necessary element in the strengthening of their bilateral relations and thus will actively promote the growth of such ties. They will facilitate cooperation between the relevant organizations and enterprises of the two countries and the conclusion of appropriate agreements and contracts, including long-term ones.

The two countries will contribute to the improvement of maritime and air communications between them.

Eighth. The two sides consider it timely and useful to develop mutual contacts and cooperation in the fields of science and technology. Where suitable, the USA and the USSR will conclude appropriate agreements dealing with concrete cooperation in these fields.

Ninth. The two sides reaffirm their intention to deepen cultural ties with one another and to encourage fuller familiarization with each other's cultural values. They will promote improved conditions for cultural exchanges and tourism.

Tenth. The USA and the USSR will seek to ensure that their ties and cooperation in all the above-mentioned fields and in any others in their mutual interest are built on a firm and long-term basis. To give a permanent character to these efforts, they will establish in all fields where this is feasible joint commissions or other joint bodies.

Eleventh. The USA and the USSR make no claim for themselves and would not recognize the claims of anyone else to any special rights or advantages in world affairs. They recognize the sovereign equality of all states.

The Development of US-Soviet relations is not directed against third countries and their interests.

Twelfth. The basic principles set forth in this document do not affect any obligations with respect to other countries earlier assumed by the USA and the USSR.

Moscow, May 29, 1972

For the United States of America	For the Union of Soviet Socialist Republics
RICHARD NIXON President of the United States of America	LEONID I. BREZHNEV General Secretary of the Central Committee, CPSU

USA-USSR Joint Communiqué

By mutual agreement between the United States of America and the Union of Soviet Socialist Republics, the President of the United States and Mrs. Richard Nixon paid an official visit to the Soviet Union from May 22 to May 30, 1972. The President was accompanied by Secretary of State William P. Rogers, assistant to the President Dr. H. A. Kissinger, and other American officials. During his stay in the U.S.S.R. President Nixon visited, in addition to Moscow, the cities of Leningrad and Kiev.

President Nixon and L. I. Brezhnev, general secretary of the Central Committee of the Communist Party of the Soviet Union, N. Podgorny, chairman of the Supreme Soviet of the U.S.S.R., and A. N. Kosygin, chairman of the Council of Ministers of the U.S.S.R., conducted talks on fundamental problems of American-Soviet relations and the current international situation.

Also taking part in the conversations were:

On the American side: William P. Rogers, secretary of state, Jacob D. Beam, American ambassador to the U.S.S.R., Dr. Henry A. Kissinger, assistant to the President for national security affairs, Peter M. Flanigan, assistant to the President, and Martin J.

Hillenbrand, assistant secretary of state for European affairs.

On the Soviet side: A. A. Gromyko, minister of foreign affairs of the U.S.S.R., N. S. Patolichev, minister of foreign trade, V. V. Kuznetsov, deputy minister of foreign affairs of the U.S.S.R., A. F. Dobrynin, Soviet ambassador to the U.S.A., A. M. Aleksandrov, assistant to the general secretary of the Central Committee, C.P.S.U., G. M. Korniyenko, member of the collegium of the Ministry of Foreign Affairs of the U.S.S.R.

The discussions covered a wide range of questions of mutual interest and were frank and thorough. They defined more precisely those areas where there are prospects for developing greater cooperation between the two countries, as well as those areas where the positions of the two sides are different.

I. Bilateral Relations

Guided by the desire to place U.S.-Soviet relations on a more stable and constructive foundation, and mindful of their responsibilities for maintaining world peace and for facilitating the relaxation of international tension, the two sides adopted a document entitled: "Basic Principles of Mutual Relations Between the United States of America and the Union of Soviet Socialist Republics," signed on behalf of the U.S. by President Nixon and on behalf of the U.S.S.R. by General Secretary Brezhnev.

Both sides are convinced that the provisions of that document open new possibilities for the development of peaceful relations and mutually beneficial cooperation between the U.S.A. and the U.S.S.R.

Having considered various areas of bilateral U.S.-Soviet relations, the two sides agreed that an improvement of relations is possible and desirable. They expressed their firm intention to act in accordance with the provisions set forth in the above-mentioned document.

As a result of progress made in negotiations which preceded the summit meeting, and in the course of the meeting itself, a number of significant agreements were reached. This will intensify bilateral cooperation in areas of common concern as well as in areas relevant to the cause of peace and international cooperation.

Limitation of Strategic Armaments

The two sides gave primary attention to the problem of reducing the danger of nuclear war. They believe that curbing the competition in strategic arms will make a significant and tangible contribution to this cause.

The two sides attach great importance to the treaty on the limitation of anti-ballistic missile systems and the interim agreement on certain measures with respect to the limitation of strategic offensive arms concluded between them.

These agreements, which were concluded as a result of the negotiations in Moscow, constitute a major step towards curbing and ultimately ending the arms race.

They are a concrete expression of the intention of the two sides to contribute to the relaxation of international tension and the strengthening of confidence between states as well as to carry out the obligations assumed by them in the Treaty on the Non-proliferation of Nuclear Weapons Article VI. Both sides are convinced that the achievement of the above agreements is a practical step toward saving mankind from the threat of the outbreak of nuclear war. Accordingly, it corresponds to the vital interests of the American and Soviet peoples as well as to the vital interests of all other peoples.

The two sides intend to continue active negotiations for the limitation of strategic offensive arms and to conduct them in a spirit of good will, respect for each other's legitimate interests and observance of the principle of equal security.

Both sides are also convinced that the agreement on measures to reduce the risk of outbreak of nuclear war between the U.S.A. and the U.S.S.R. signed in Washington Sept. 30, 1971, serves the interest not only of the Soviet and American peoples, but of all mankind.

Commercial and Economic Relations

Both sides agreed on measures designed to establish more favorable conditions for developing commercial and other economic ties between the U.S.A. and the U.S.S.R. They agree that realistic conditions exist for increasing economic ties. These ties should develop on the basis of mutual benefit and in accordance with generally accepted international practice.

Believing that these aims would be served by conclusion of a trade agreement between the U.S.A. and the U.S.S.R., the two sides decided to complete in the near future the work necessary to conclude such an agreement. They agreed on the desirability of credit arrangements to develop mutual trade and of early efforts to resolve other financial and economic issues. It was agreed that a lend-lease settlement will be negotiated concurrently with a trade agreement.

In the interests of broadening and facilitating commercial ties between the two countries, and to work out specific arrangements, the two sides decided to create a U.S.-Soviet joint commercial commission. Its first meeting will be held in Moscow in the summer of 1972.

Each side will promote the establishment of effective working arrangements between organizations and firms of both countries and encouraging the conclusion of long-term contracts.

Maritime Matters, Incidents at Sea

The two sides agreed to continue the negotiations aimed at reaching an agreement on maritime and related matters. They believe that such an agreement would mark a positive step in facilitating the expansion of commerce between the United States and the Soviet Union.

An agreement was concluded between the two sides on measures to prevent incidents at sea and in air space over it between vessels and aircraft of the U.S. and Soviet navies. By providing agreed procedures for ships and aircraft of the two navies operating in close proximity, this agreement will diminish the chances of dangerous accidents.

Cooperation in Science and Technology

It was recognized that the cooperation now under way in areas such as atomic energy research, space research, health and other fields benefits both nations and has contributed positively to their over-all relations. It was agreed that increased scientific and technical cooperation on the basis of mutual benefit and shared effort for common goals is in the interest of both nations and would contribute to a further improvement in their bilateral relations. For these purposes the two sides signed an agreement for cooperation in the fields of science and technology. A U.S.-Soviet joint commission on scientific and technical cooperation will be created for identifying and establishing cooperative programs.

Cooperation in Space

Having in mind the role played by the U.S. and the U.S.S.R. in the peaceful exploration of outer space, both sides emphasized the importance of further bilateral cooperation in this sphere. In order to increase the safety of man's flights in outer space and the future prospects of joint scientific experiments, the two sides agreed to make suitable arrangements to permit the docking of American and Soviet spacecraft and stations. The first joint docking experiment of the two countries' piloted spacecraft, with visits by astronauts and cosmonauts to each other's spacecraft, is contemplated for 1975. The planning and implementation of this flight will be carried out by the U.S. National Aeronautics and Space Administration and the U.S.S.R. Academy of Sciences, according to principles and procedures developed through mutual consultations.

Cooperation in the Field of Health

The two sides concluded an agreement on health cooperation which marks a fruitful beginning of sharing knowledge about, and

collaborative attacks on, the common enemies, disease and disability. The initial research efforts of the program will concentrate on health problems important to the whole world — cancer, heart diseases, and the environmental health sciences.

This cooperation subsequently will be broadened to include other health problems of mutual interest. The two sides pledged their full support for the health cooperation program and agreed to continue the active participation of the two governments in the work of international organizations in the health field.

Environmental Cooperation

The two sides agreed to initiate a program of cooperation in the protection and enhancement of man's environment. Through joint research and joint measures, the United States and the U.S.S.R. hope to contribute to the preservation of a healthful environment in their countries and throughout the world. Under the new agreement on environmental cooperation there will be consultations in the near future in Moscow on specific cooperative projects.

Exchanges in the Fields of Science, Technology, Education and Culture

Both sides note the importance of the agreement on exchanges and cooperation in scientific, technical, educational, cultural, and other fields in 1972-1973, signed in Moscow on April 11, 1972. Continuation and expansion of bilateral exchanges in these fields will lead to better understanding and help improve the general state of relations between the two countries. Within the broad framework provided by this agreement the two sides have agreed to expand the areas of cooperation, as reflected in new agreements concerning space, health, the environment and science and technology.

The U.S. side, noting the existence of an extensive program of English-language instruction in the Soviet Union, indicated its intention to encourage Russian-language programs in the United States.

II. International Issues

Europe

In the course of the discussions on the international situation, both sides took note of favorable developments in the relaxation of tensions in Europe.

Recognizing the importance to world peace of developments in Europe, where both world wars originated, and mindful of the responsibilities and commitments which they share with other powers under appropriate agreements, the U.S.A. and the U.S.S.R. intend to make further efforts to ensure a peaceful future for Europe, free of tensions, crises and conflicts.

They agree that the territorial integrity of all states in Europe should be respected.

Both sides view the Sept. 3, 1971, quadripartite agreement relating to the western sectors of Berlin as a good example of fruitful cooperation between the states concerned, including the U.S.A. and the U.S.S.R. The two sides believe that the implementation of that agreement in the near future, along with other steps, will further improve the European situation and contribute to the necessary trust among states.

Both sides welcomed the treaty between the U.S.S.R. and the Federal Republic of Germany signed on Aug. 12, 1970. They noted the significance of the provisions of this treaty as well as of other recent agreements in contributing to confidence and cooperation among the European states.

The U.S.A. and the U.S.S.R. are prepared to make appropriate contributions to the positive trends on the European continent toward a genuine detente and the development of relations of peaceful cooperation among states in Europe on the basis of the principles of territorial integrity and inviolability of frontiers, non-interference in internal affairs, sovereign equality in independence and renunciation of the use or threat of force.

The U.S. and U.S.S.R. are in accord that multilateral consultations looking toward a conference on security and cooperation in Europe could begin after the signature of the final quadripartite protocol of the agreement of Sept. 3, 1971. The two governments agree that the conference should be carefully prepared in order that it may concretely consider specific problems of security and cooperation and thus contribute to the progressive reduction of the underlying causes of tension in Europe. This conference should be convened at a time to be agreed by the countries concerned, but without undue delay.

Both sides believe that the goal of ensuring stability and security in Europe would be served by a reciprocal reduction of armed forces and armaments, first of all in central Europe. Any agreement on this question should not diminish the security of any of the sides. Appropriate agreement should be reached as soon as practicable between the states concerned on the procedures for negotiations on this subject in a special forum.

The Middle East

The two sides set out their positions on this question. They reaffirm their support for a peaceful settlement in the Middle East in accordance with Security Council Resolution 242.

Noting the significance of constructive cooperation of the parties concerned with the special representative of the U.N. secretary general, Ambassador Jarring, the U.S. and the U.S.S.R. confirm their desire to contribute to his mission's success and also declare their readiness to play their part in bringing about a peaceful settlement in the Middle East. In the view of the U.S. and the U.S.S.R., the achievement of such a settlement would open prospects for the normalization of the Middle East situation and would permit, in particular, consideration of further steps to bring about a military relaxation in that area.

Indochina

Each side set forth its respective standpoint with regard to the continuing war in Vietnam and the situation in the area of Indochina as a whole.

The U.S. side emphasized the need to bring an end to the military conflict as soon as possible and reaffirmed its commitment to the principle that the political future of South Vietnam should be left for the South Vietnamese people to decide for themselves, free from outside interference.

The U.S. side explained its view that the quickest and most effective way to attain the above-mentioned objectives is through negotiations leading to the return of all Americans held captive in the region, the implementation of an internationally supervised, Indochina-wide cease-fire and the subsequent withdrawal of all American forces stationed in South Vietnam within four months, leaving the political questions to be resolved by the Indochinese peoples themselves.

The United States reiterated its willingness to enter into serious negotiations with the North Vietnamese side to settle the war in Indochina on a basis just to all.

The Soviet side stressed its solidarity with the just struggle of the peoples of Vietnam, Laos and Cambodia for their freedom, independence and social progress. Firmly supporting the proposals of the DRV (North Vietnam) and the Provisional Revolutionary Government of the Republic of South Vietnam, which provide a realistic and constructive basis for settling the Vietnam problem, the Soviet Union stands for a cessation of bombings of the DRV, for a complete and unequivocal withdrawal of the troops of the U.S.A. and its allies from South Vietnam, so that the people of Indochina would have the possibility to determine for themselves their fate without any outside interference.

Disarmament Issues

The two sides note that in recent years their joint and parallel actions have facilitated the working out and conclusion of treaties which curb the arms race or ban some of the most dangerous types of weapons. They note further that these treaties were welcomed by a large majority of the states in the world, which became parties to them.

Both sides regard the convention on the prohibition of the development, production and stockpiling of bacteriological, biological and toxic weapons and on their destruction, as an essential disarmament measure. Along with Great Britain, they are the depositories for the convention which was recently opened for signature by all states. The U.S.A. and U.S.S.R. will continue their efforts to reach an international agreement regarding chemical weapons.

The U.S.A. and the U.S.S.R., proceeding from the need to take into account the security interests of both countries on the basis of the principle of equality, and without prejudice to the security interests of third countries, will actively participate in negotiations aimed at working out new measures designed to curb and end the arms race. The ultimate purpose is general and complete disarmament, including nuclear disarmament, under strict international control. A world disarmament conference could play a role in this process at an appropriate time.

Strengthening the United Nations

Both sides will strive to strengthen the effectiveness of the United Nations on the basis of strict observance of the U.N. charter.

They regard the United Nations as an instrument for maintaining world peace and security, discouraging conflicts, and developing international cooperation. Accordingly, they will do their best to support United Nations efforts in the interests of international peace.

Both sides emphasized that agreements and understandings reached in the negotiations in Moscow, as well as the contents and nature of these negotiations, are not in any way directed against any other country. Both sides proceed from the recognition of the role, the responsibility and the prerogatives of other interested states, existing international obligations and agreements, and the principles and purposes of the U.N. charter.

Both sides believe that positive results were accomplished in the course of the talks at the highest level. These results indicate that despite the differences between the U.S.A. and the U.S.S.R. in social systems, ideologies, and policy principles, it is possible to develop mutually advantageous cooperation between the peoples of both countries, in the interests of strengthening peace and international security.

Both sides expressed the desire to continue close contact on a number of issues that were under discussion. They agreed that regular consultations on questions of mutual interest, including meetings at the highest level, would be useful.

In expressing his appreciation for the hospitality accorded him in the Soviet Union, President Nixon invited General Secretary L. I. Brezhnev, Chairman N. V. Podgorny and Chairman A. N. Kosygin to visit the United States at a mutually convenient time. This invitation was accepted.

1977 SOVIET CONSTITUTION

Following are excerpts from the constitution ratified by the Supreme Soviet October 7, 1977.

Constitution of the Soviet Union

The Soviet people, guided by the ideas of scientific communism and remaining true to their revolutionary traditions, resting on the great social, economic and political achievements of socialism, striving to further develop socialist democracy, taking into account the international position of the USSR as part of the world socialist system and conscious of their international responsibility, preserving the continuity of the ideas and principles of the 1918 Constitution of the RSFSR, the 1924 Constitution of the USSR and the 1936 Constitution of the USSR, proclaim the aims and principles, define the foundations of the organization of the socialist state of the whole people, and formalize them in this Constitution. . . .

The Political System

Article 1. The Union of Soviet Socialist Republics is a socialist state of the whole people, expressing the will and interests of the working class, the peasantry and the intelligentsia, of all the nations and nationalities in the country.

Article 2. All power in the USSR shall be vested in the people.

The people shall exercise state power through the Soviets of People's Deputies, which constitute the political foundation of the USSR.

All other organs of state shall be under the control of and accountable to the Soviets.

Article 3. The Soviet state shall be organized and shall function in accordance with the principle of democratic centralism: electivity of all organs of state power from top to bottom, their accountability to the people, and mandatory fulfillment of the decisions of higher organs by lower organs. Democratic centralism shall combine single leadership with local initiative and creative activity, with the responsibility of each state organ and each official for the work at hand.

Article 4. The Soviet state, in all its organs, shall function on the basis of socialist legality and ensure the protection of law and order, the interests of society and the rights of citizens. State institutions, public organizations and officials shall observe the Constitution of the USSR and Soviet laws. . . .

Article 6. The Communist Party of the Soviet Union is the leading and guiding force of Soviet society and the nucleus of its political system, of all state and public organizations. The CPSU exists for the people and serves the people.

Armed with the Marxist-Leninist (body of) teaching, the Communist Party shall determine the general perspective of society's development and the guidelines for the internal and external policy of the USSR, give guidance to the great creative endeavor of the Soviet people, and place their struggle for the triumph of communism on a planned, scientific basis. . . .

The Economic System

Article 9. Socialist ownership of the means of production shall be the foundation of the economic system of the USSR. Socialist ownership shall comprise: state property (belonging to the whole people), property of collective farms and other cooperative organizations (collective farm-cooperative property), and property of trade unions and other public organizations.

The state shall protect socialist property and create the conditions for augmenting it.

No one shall have the right to use socialist property for personal gain.

Article 10. State property, i.e., property belonging to the whole people, shall be the principal form of socialist ownership.

The land, its minerals, waters and forests shall be the exclusive property of the state. The state shall be in possession of the basic means of production: industrial, building and agricultural enterprises, means of transport and communication, and also the banks, distributive enterprises and community services and the bulk of urban housing. . . .

Article 13. The free labor of Soviet people shall be the basis of the growth of social wealth and the welfare of the people, of every Soviet citizen.

The state shall control the measure of labor and consumption in accordance with the principle: "From each according to his ability, to each according to his work." It shall determine the rates

of the income tax and establish the level of wages exempted from taxes.

Socially useful work and its results shall determine a citizen's status in society. By combining material and moral incentives the state shall help turn labor into the prime need in the life of every Soviet citizen. . . .

Article 15. The economy of the USSR shall be an integral economic complex embracing all the elements of social production, distribution and exchange on the territory of the USSR.

The economy shall be managed on the basis of state plans for economic, social and cultural development with due account taken of the branch and territorial principles, and combining centralized leadership with the economic independence and initiative of enterprises, associations and other organizations. Here active use shall be made of cost accounting, profit and production costs. . . .

Social Development and Culture

Article 19. The Soviet state shall create the conditions for enhancing society's social homogeneity, erasing the essential distinctions between town and countryside and between mental and manual labor, and further developing and drawing together all the nations and nationalities of the USSR.

Article 20. In accordance with the communist ideal, "the free development of each is the condition for the free development of all," the Soviet state shall pursue the aim of expanding the actual possibilities for citizens to develop and apply their creative strength, abilities and talents, for the all-around development of the individual. . . .

Foreign Policy

Article 28. The Soviet state shall consistently pursue the Leninist policy of peace and stand for the consolidation of the security of peoples and broad international cooperation.

The foreign policy of the USSR shall be aimed at ensuring favorable international conditions for the building of communism in the USSR, at strengthening the positions of world socialism, supporting the struggle of peoples for national liberation and social progress, preventing wars of aggression, and consistently implementing the principle of peaceful coexistence of states with different social systems.

In the USSR war propaganda shall be prohibited by law.

Article 29. The relations of the USSR with other states shall be based on the observance of the principle of mutual renunciation of the use or threats of force, and of the principles of sovereign equality, inviolability of frontiers, territorial integrity of states, peaceful settlement of disputes, non-interference in internal affairs, respect for human rights and basic freedoms, equality and the right of peoples to decide their own destiny, cooperation between states, scrupulous fulfillment of commitments emanating from universally recognized principles and norms of international law, and the international treaties signed by the USSR.

Article 30. As part of the world socialist system, of the socialist community, the Soviet Union shall promote and strengthen friendship, cooperation and comradely mutual assistance with the other socialist countries on the basis of socialist internationalism, and shall actively participate in economic integration and in the international socialist division of labor. . . .

The State and the Individual

Article 33. Soviet citizenship shall be uniform for the whole Union of Soviet Socialist Republics. Every citizen of a Union Republic shall be a citizen of the USSR.

The grounds and procedure of acquiring or losing Soviet citizenship shall be established by the law of the USSR.

Citizens of the USSR living abroad shall have the protection and guardianship of the Soviet state.

Article 34. Citizens of the USSR shall be equal before the law, irrespective of origin, social and property status, nationality or race, sex, education, language, attitude to religion, type or character of occupation, domicile, or other particulars.

Equality of rights of citizens of the USSR shall be ensured in all fields of economic, political, social, and cultural life.

Article 35. In the USSR women shall have equal rights with men.

Exercise of these rights shall be ensured by according to women equal opportunities (with men) for education and professional training, for employment, remuneration and promotion, for social, political and cultural activity, and likewise by special measures for the protection of the labor and health of women; by legal protection, material and moral support of mother and child, including paid leaves and other benefits to mothers and expectant mothers, and state aid to unmarried mothers.

Article 36. Soviet citizens of different nationalities and races shall have equal rights.

The exercise of these rights shall be ensured by the policy of all-around development and drawing together of all nations and nationalities of the USSR, education of citizens in the spirit of Soviet patriotism and socialist internationalism, and the opportunity for using their mother tongue as well as the languages of the other peoples of the USSR.

Any and all direct or indirect restrictions of the rights of, or the establishment of direct or indirect privileges for, citizens on grounds of race or nationality, and likewise any advocacy of racial or national exclusiveness, hostility or contempt, shall be punishable by law.

Article 37. In the USSR citizens of other countries and stateless persons shall be guaranteed the rights and freedoms provided for by law, including the right of instituting proceedings in law courts and other state organs in protection of personal, proprietary, family and other rights accorded to them by law.

On the territory of the USSR, citizens of other countries and stateless persons shall be obliged to respect the Constitution of the USSR and to observe Soviet laws.

Article 38. The USSR shall afford the right of asylum to foreign nationals persecuted for upholding the interests of the working people and the cause of peace, or for participating in a revolutionary or national liberation movement, or for progressive social, political, scientific or other creative activity.

Rights, Freedoms and Duties

Article 39. Citizens of the USSR shall enjoy in their entirety the social, economic, political and personal rights and freedoms proclaimed and guaranteed by the Constitution of the USSR and Soviet laws. The socialist system shall ensure extension of rights and freedoms and unintermittent improvement of the conditions of life of citizens relative to the fulfillment of programs of social, economic and cultural development.

Exercise by citizens of rights and freedoms must not injure the interests of society and the state, or the rights of other citizens.

Article 40. Citizens of the USSR shall have the right to work, that is, to guaranteed employment and remuneration for their work in accordance with its quantity and quality, including the right to choice of profession, type of occupation and employment, in accordance with their vocation, abilities, training, education, and with due account taken of the needs of society....

Article 41. Citizens of the USSR shall have the right to rest and leisure....

Article 42. Citizens of the USSR shall have the right to health protection....

Article 43. Citizens of the USSR shall have the right to maintenance in old age, in the event of sickness, and likewise in the event of complete or partial disability or loss of breadwinner....

Article 44. Citizens of the USSR shall have the right to housing. This right shall be ensured by the development and protection of state and public housing, assistance to co-operative and individual house-building, fair distribution under public control of housing, allotted with reference to the implementation of the housing program, and likewise by low rent.

Article 45. Citizens of the USSR shall have the right to education....

Article 46. Citizens of the USSR shall have the right to make use of the achievements of culture....

Article 48. Citizens of the USSR shall have the right to take part in the administration of state and public affairs....

Article 49. Every citizen of the USSR shall have the right to submit to state organs and public organizations proposals for improving their activity, to criticize shortcomings in their work. Officials shall be bound, within terms established by law, to examine proposals and requests made by citizens, reply to them and take due action.

Persecution for criticism shall be prohibited.

Article 50. In conformity with the interests of the working people and for the purpose of strengthening the socialist system, citizens of the USSR shall be guaranteed freedom of speech, press, assembly, meetings, street processions and demonstrations. Exercise of these political freedoms shall be ensured by putting at the disposal of the working people and their organizations public buildings, streets and squares, by broad dissemination of information, and by the opportunity to use the press, television and radio....

Article 52. Freedom of conscience, that is, the right to profess any religion and perform religious rites, or not to profess any religion and to conduct atheistic propaganda, shall be recognized for all citizens of the USSR. Incitement of hostility and hatred on religious grounds shall be prohibited.

The church in the USSR shall be separated from the state, and the school from the church.

Article 53. The family shall be under the protection of the state.

Marriage shall be entered into with the free consent of the intending spouses; spouses shall be completely equal in their matrimonial relations....

Article 54. Citizens of the USSR shall be guaranteed inviolability of the person. No person shall be subjected to arrest other than by decision of a court of law, or with the sanction of a prosecutor.

Article 55. Citizens of the USSR shall be guaranteed inviolability of the home. No person shall without lawful grounds enter a home against the will of the persons residing in it.

Article 56. The privacy of citizens, of correspondence, telephone conversations and telegraphic messages shall be protected by law.

Article 57. Respect for the individual and protection of the rights and freedoms of Soviet citizens shall be the duty of all state organs, public organizations and officials....

Article 58. Citizens of the USSR shall have the right to lodge complaints against actions of officials in state organs and public organizations. These complaints shall be examined in the manner and within the terms defined by law....

Citizens of the USSR shall have the right to compensation for damage inflicted by unlawful actions of state institutions and public organizations, and likewise by officials in the performance of their duties, in the manner and within the limits defined by law.

Article 59. Exercise of rights and freedoms shall be inseparable from the performance by citizens of their duties....

Article 62. The citizens of the USSR shall be obliged to safeguard the interests of the Soviet state, to contribute to the strengthening of its might and prestige.

Defense of the socialist motherland shall be the sacred duty of every citizen of the USSR.

High treason shall be the gravest crime against the people....

Article 64. It shall be the duty of every citizen of the USSR to respect the national dignity of other citizens, to strengthen the friendship of the nations and nationalities of the Soviet multinational state....

Article 67. Citizens of the USSR shall be obligated to protect nature, to safeguard its wealth.

Concern for the preservation of historical monuments and other cultural values shall be the duty of citizens of the USSR.

Article 68. It shall be the internationalist duty of citizens of the USSR to further the development of friendship and cooperation with the peoples of other countries and the maintenance and consolidation of world peace....

The USSR—A Federal State

Article 69. The Union of Soviet Socialist Republics is an integral federal multinational state formed on the basis of the free self-determination of nations and the voluntary union of equal Soviet Socialist Republics.

The USSR embodies the state unity of the Soviet people and brings all the nations and nationalities together for the joint building of communism....

Article 71. Every Union Republic shall retain the right freely to secede from the USSR....

The Soviets of People's Deputies

Article 88. The Soviets of People's Deputies — the Supreme Soviet of the USSR, the Supreme Soviets of the Union Republics, the Supreme Soviets of the Autonomous Republics, the Territorial and Regional Soviets of People's Deputies, the Soviets of People's Deputies of Autonomous Regions and Autonomous Areas, and the city, district, city district, township and village Soviets of People's Deputies — shall comprise an integral system of organs of state power....

Article 101. Deputies shall be authorized representatives of the people in the Soviets of People's Deputies.

By participating in the work of the Soviets, deputies shall resolve matters related to state, economic, social and cultural development, organize the execution of the decisions of the Soviets, and exercise control over the work of state organs, enterprises, institutions and organizations....

Article 103. A deputy shall have the right to address an inquiry to the appropriate state organs and officials, who shall be obliged to reply to the inquiry at a session of the Soviet.

Deputies shall have the right to address an inquiry to any state or public organ, enterprise, institution or organization on questions within their terms of reference as deputies and to take part in considering the questions thus raised. The heads of the respective state or public organs, enterprises, institutions or organizations shall be obliged to receive deputies without delay and consider their recommendations within the period established by law.

Article 104. Deputies shall be assured conditions for the unobstructed and effective exercise of their rights and duties.

The immunity of deputies, as well as other guarantees of their functions as deputies, shall be defined in the Law on the Status of Deputies and other legislation of the USSR and of the Union and Autonomous Republics....

The Supreme Soviet

Article 106. The Supreme Soviet of the USSR shall be the highest organ of state power in the USSR.

The Supreme Soviet of the USSR shall be empowered to deal with all matters placed within the jurisdiction of the Union of Soviet Socialist Republics by the present Constitution.

The adoption of the Constitution of the USSR and amendments to it, the admission of new Republics to the USSR, approval of the formation of new Autonomous Republics and Autonomous Regions, endorsement of state plans of economic, social and cultural development and of the State Budget of the USSR, and of reports on their execution, and the formation of organs of the USSR accountable to it shall be the exclusive competence of the Supreme Soviet of the USSR.

Laws of the USSR shall be enacted solely by the Supreme Soviet of the USSR.

Article 107. The Supreme Soviet of the USSR shall consist of two chambers: the Soviet of the Union and the Soviet of Nationalities.

The two chambers of the Supreme Soviet of the USSR shall have equal rights.

Article 108. The Soviet of the Union and the Soviet of Nationalities shall have an equal number of deputies.

The Soviet of the Union shall be elected by constituencies with equal populations.

The Soviet of Nationalities shall be elected on the basis of the following quotas: 32 deputies from each Union Republic, 11 deputies from each Autonomous Republic, 5 deputies from each Autonomous Region, and one deputy from each Autonomous Area.

Upon representation by the credentials commissions elected by them, the Soviet of the Union and the Soviet of Nationalities shall recognize the credentials of deputies, and in cases where the election law has been violated, declare the election of individual deputies invalid....

Article 111. The right to initiate legislation in the Supreme Soviet of the USSR shall be exercised by the Soviet of the Union and the Soviet of Nationalities, the Presidium of the Supreme Soviet of the USSR, the Council of Ministers of the USSR, the Union Republics represented by their higher organs of state power, the commissions of the Supreme Soviet of the USSR and the Standing commissions of its chambers, deputies of the Supreme Soviet of the USSR, the Supreme Court of the USSR, and the Prosecutor-General of the USSR.

The right to initiate legislation shall be enjoyed also by mass public organizations represented by their all-Union organs....

Article 117. The Supreme Soviet of the USSR at a joint sitting of the two chambers shall elect the Presidium of the Supreme Soviet of the USSR, the continuously functioning organs of the Supreme Soviet of the USSR accountable to it in all its activities.

Article 118. The Presidium of the Supreme Soviet of the USSR shall be elected from among deputies and shall consist of a President, a First Vice-President, 15 Vice Presidents, i.e., one from each Union Republic, a Secretary of the Presidium, and 21 members of the Presidium of the Supreme Soviet of the USSR....

The Council of Ministers of the USSR

Article 127. The Council of Ministers of the USSR — the Government of the USSR — shall be the highest executive and administrative organ of state power in the USSR.

Article 128. The Council of Ministers of the USSR shall be formed by the Supreme Soviet of the USSR at a joint sitting of the Soviet of the Union and the Soviet of Nationalities and consist of: the Chairman of the Council of Ministers of the USSR, First Vice-Chairmen and Vice-Chairmen of the Council of Ministers of the USSR, the Ministers of the USSR, the Chairmen of state committees of the USSR.

The Council of Ministers of the USSR shall include, by virtue of their office, the Chairmen of the Councils of Ministers of Union Republics.

Upon submission by the Chairman of the Council of Ministers of the USSR, the Supreme Soviet of the USSR may include in the Government of the USSR leaders of other organs and organizations of the USSR.

Article 129. The Council of Ministers of the USSR shall be responsible and accountable to the Supreme Soviet of the USSR, and between sessions of the Supreme Soviet of the USSR to the Presidium of the Supreme Soviet of the USSR, to which it shall be accountable.

The Council of Ministers of the USSR shall regularly report on its work to the Supreme Soviet of the USSR....

Article 131. The Presidium of the Council of Ministers of the USSR, consisting of the Chairman of the Council of Ministers of the USSR and the First Vice-Chairmen and Vice-Chairmen of the Council of Ministers of the USSR, shall function as a permanent organ of the Council of Ministers of the USSR for the purpose of dealing with matters related to the administration of the economy and to other questions of state administration....

Courts of Law and Arbitration

Article 150. In the USSR justice shall be administered exclusively by courts of law.

In the USSR the court system shall consist of the following: the Supreme Court of the USSR, Supreme Courts of Union Republics, Supreme Courts of Autonomous Republics, territorial, regional and city courts, courts of Autonomous Regions, courts of

Autonomous Areas, district (city) people's courts, and military tribunals in the Armed Forces.

Article 151. All courts in the USSR shall be formed on the principle of electivity of judges and people's assessors. . . .

The Prosecutor's Office

Article 163. Supreme supervisory power over the precise and uniform execution of laws by all ministries, state committees and departments, enterprises, institutions and organizations, executive and administrative organs of local Soviets of People's Deputies, collective farms, cooperative and other public organizations, officials and citizens, shall be exercised by the Prosecutor General of the USSR and prosecutors subordinate to him.

Article 164. The Prosecutor General of the USSR shall be appointed by the Supreme Soviet of the USSR and shall be responsible and accountable to it, or between sessions of the Supreme Soviet to the Presidium of the Supreme Soviet of the USSR, to which he is accountable. . . .

Amendment of the Constitution of the USSR

Article 172. The Constitution of the USSR shall have supreme legal force. All laws and other acts of state organs shall be issued on the basis of, and in conformity with, the Constitution of the USSR.

The Constitution of the USSR shall be effective from the time of its adoption.

Article 173. Amendment of the Constitution of the USSR shall be by decision of the Supreme Soviet of the USSR, adopted by a majority of not less than two-thirds of the total number of deputies of each of its chambers.

GORBACHEV UN SPEECH

Following are excerpts from Soviet leader Mikhail S. Gorbachev's December 7, 1988, speech to the UN General Assembly.

Esteemed Mr. President,
Esteemed Mr. Secretary-General,
Distinguished delegates,

We have come here to show our respect for the United Nations, which increasingly has been manifesting its ability to act as a unique international center in the service of peace and security.

We have come here to show our respect for the dignity of this organization which is capable of accumulating the collective wisdom and will of mankind.

Recent events have been making it increasingly clear that the world needs such an organization, and that the organization itself needs the active involvement of all of its members, their support for its initiatives and actions and their potential and original contributions that enrich its activity. . . .

The role played by the Soviet Union in world affairs is well-known and, in view of the revolutionary perestroika under way in our country, which contains a tremendous potential for peace and international cooperation, we are now particularly interested in being properly understood.

That is why we have come here to address this most authoritative world body and to share our thoughts with it. We want it to be the first to learn of our new important decisions.

I

What will mankind be like when it enters the twenty-first century? People are already fascinated by this not too distant future. We are looking ahead to it with hopes for the best and yet with a feeling of concern.

The world in which we live today is radically different from what it was at the beginning or even in the middle of this century. And it continues to change as do all its components.

The advent of nuclear weapons was just another tragic reminder of the fundamental nature of that change. A material symbol and expression of absolute military power, nuclear weapons at the same time revealed the absolute limits of that power.

The problem of mankind's survival and self-preservation came to the fore. . . .

Today the preservation of any kind of "closed" societies is hardly possible. This calls for a radical review of approaches to the totality of the problems of international cooperation as a major element of universal security.

The world economy is becoming a single organism, and no state, whatever its social system or economic status, can normally develop outside it. . . .

Today, further world progress is only possible through a search for universal human consensus as we move forward to a new world order.

We have come to a point when the disorderly play of elemental forces leads into an impasse. The international community must learn how it can shape and guide developments in such a way as to preserve our civilization, to make it safe for all and more conducive to normal life. . . .

Efforts to solve global problems require a new scope and quality of interaction of states and sociopolitical currents, regardless of ideological or other differences.

Of course, radical changes and revolutionary transformations will continue to occur within individual countries and social structures. This is how it was and how it will be.

But here too, our time marks a change. Internal transformations no longer can advance their national goals if they develop just along "parallel courses" with others, without making use of the achievements of the outside world and of the potential inherent in equitable cooperation.

In these circumstances, any interference in those internal developments, designed to redirect them to someone's liking, would have all the more destructive consequences for establishing a peaceful order. . . .

It is obvious, for instance, that the use or threat of force no longer can or must be an instrument of foreign policy. This applies above all to nuclear arms, but that is not the only thing that matters. All of us, and primarily the stronger of us, must exercise self-restraint and totally rule out any outward-oriented use of force. . . .

After all, it is now quite clear that building up military power makes no country omnipotent. What is more, one-sided reliance on military power ultimately weakens other components of national security.

It is also quite clear to us that the principle of freedom of choice is mandatory. Its nonrecognition is fraught with extremely grave consequences for world peace. . . .

This objective fact calls for respect for the views and positions of others, tolerance, a willingness to perceive something different as not necessarily bad or hostile, and an ability to learn to live side-by-side with others while remaining different and not always agreeing with each other. . . .

What we are talking about, therefore, is unity in diversity. If we assert this politically, if we reaffirm our adherence to freedom of choice, then there is no room for the view that some live on earth by virtue of divine will while others are here quite by chance. . . .

The new phase also requires de-ideologizing relations among states. We are not abandoning our convictions, our philosophy or traditions, nor do we urge anyone to abandon theirs.

But neither do we have any intention to be hemmed in by our values. That would result in intellectual impoverishment, for it would mean rejecting a powerful source of development—the exchange of everything original that each nation has independently created.

In the course of such exchange, let everyone show the advantages of their social system, way of life or values—and not just by words or propaganda, but by real deeds.

That would be a fair rivalry of ideologies. But it should not be extended to relations among states. Otherwise, we would simply be unable to solve any of the world's problems, such as:
- Developing wide-ranging, mutually beneficial and equitable cooperation among nations;
- Making efficient use of the achievement of scientific and technological revolution;
- Restructuring the world economy and protecting the environment;
- Overcoming backwardness, eliminating hunger, disease, illiteracy and other global scourges.

Nor, of course, shall we then be able to eliminate the nuclear threat and militarism....

In short, the understanding of the need for a period of peace is gaining ground and beginning to prevail. This has made it possible to take the first real steps in creating a healthier international environment and in disarmament....

I am referring to the process of negotiations on nuclear arms, conventional weapons and chemical weapons, and to the search for political approaches to ending regional conflicts.

Of course, I am referring above all to political dialogue—a more intense and open dialogue pointed at the very heart of the problems instead of confrontation, at an exchange of constructive ideas instead of recriminations. Without political dialogue the process of negotiations cannot advance.

We regard prospects for the near and more distant future quite optimistically.

Just look at the changes in our relations with the United States. Little by little, mutual understanding has started to develop and elements of trust have emerged, without which it is very hard to make headway in politics.

In Europe, these elements are even more numerous. The Helsinki process is a great process. I believe that it remains fully valid. Its philosophical, political, practical and other dimensions must all be preserved and enhanced, while taking into account new circumstances.

Current realities make it imperative that the dialogue that ensures normal and constructive evolution of international affairs involve, on a continuous and active basis, all countries and regions of the world, including such major powers as India, China, Japan and Brazil and other countries—big, medium and small....

II

In this specific historical situation, we face the question of a new role for the United Nations....

The recent reinvigoration of its peace-making role has again demonstrated the United Nations' ability to assist its members in coping with the daunting challenges of our time and working to humanize their relations.

Regrettably, shortly after it was established, the organization went through the onslaught of the cold war. For many years, it was the scene of propaganda battles and continuous political confrontation.

Let historians argue who is more and who is less to blame for it. What political leaders today need to do is to draw lessons from that chapter in the history of the United Nations which turned out to be at odds with the very meaning and objectives of our organization.

One of the most bitter and important lessons lies in the long list of missed opportunities. As a result, at a certain point the authority of the United Nations diminished and many of its attempts to act failed.

It is highly significant that the reinvigoration of the role of the United Nations is linked to an improvement in the international climate....

What is needed here is joining the efforts and taking into account the interests of all groups of countries, something that only this organization, the United Nations, can accomplish....

I would like to join the voice of my country in the expressions of high appreciation for the significance of the universal declaration of human rights adopted forty years ago on December 19, 1948.

Today, this document retains its significance. It, too, reflects the universal nature of the goals and objectives of the United Nations.

The most fitting way for a state to observe this anniversary of the declaration is to improve its domestic conditions for respecting and protecting the rights of its own citizens.

Before I inform you on what specifically we have undertaken recently in this respect, I would like to say the following.

Our country is going through a period of truly revolutionary uplifting.

The process of perestroika is gaining momentum. We began with the formulation of the theoretical concept of perestroika. We had to evaluate the nature and the magnitude of problems, to understand the lessons of the past and express that in the form of political conclusions and programs. This was done....

For our society to participate in efforts to implement the plans of perestroika, it had to be democratized in practice. Under the sign of democratization, perestroika has now spread to politics, the economy, intellectual life, and ideology.

We have initiated a radical economic reform. We have gained experience. At the start of next year the entire national economy will be redirected to new forms and methods of operation. This also means profoundly reorganizing relations of production and releasing the tremendous potential inherent in socialist property.

Undertaking such bold revolutionary transformations, we realized that there would be mistakes and also opposition, that new approaches would generate new problems. We also foresaw the possibility of slowdowns....

But the guarantee that the overall process of perestroika will steadily move forward and gain strength lies in a profound democratic reform of the entire system of power and administration.

With the recent decisions by the USSR Supreme Soviet on amendments to the Constitution and the adoption of the law on elections we have completed the first stage of the process of political reform.

Without pausing, we have begun the second stage of this process with the main task of improving the relationship between the center and the republics, harmonizing inter-ethnic relations on the principles of Leninist internationalism that we inherited from the great revolution, and at the same time reorganizing the local system of Soviet power....

We have become deeply involved in building a socialist state based on the rule of law. Work on a series of new laws has been completed or is nearing completion.

Many of them will enter into force as early as 1989, and we expect them to meet the highest standards from the standpoint of ensuring the rights of the individual.

Soviet democracy will be placed on a solid normative base. I am referring, in particular, to laws on the freedom of conscience, glasnost, public associations and organizations, and many others.

In places of confinement there are no persons convicted for their political or religious beliefs.

Additional guarantees are to be included in the new draft laws that rule out any form of persecution on those grounds.

Naturally, this does not apply to those who committed actual criminal offenses or state crimes such as espionage, sabotage, terrorism, etc., whatever their political or ideological beliefs....

The problem of exit from and entry to our country, including the question of leaving it for family reunification, is being dealt with in a humane spirit.

As you know, one of the reasons for refusal to leave is a person's knowledge of secrets. Strictly warranted time limitations on the secrecy rule will now be applied. Every person seeking employment at certain agencies or enterprises will be informed of this rule. In case of disputes there is a right of appeal under the law.

This removes from the agenda the problem of the so-called "refuseniks."

We intend to expand the Soviet Union's participation in the United Nations and CSCE [Conference on Security and Cooperation in Europe] human rights monitoring arrangements. We believe that the jurisdiction of the International Court of Justice at the Hague as regards the interpretation and implementation of agreements on human rights should be binding on all states.

We regard as part of the Helsinki process the cessation of jamming of all foreign radio broadcasts beamed at the Soviet Union....

III

Now let me turn to the main issue—disarmament, without which none of the problems of the coming century can be solved....

Tomorrow marks the first anniversary of the signing of the INF Treaty [for the reduction of intermediate-range nuclear weapons in Europe]. I am therefore particularly pleased to note that the implementation of the treaty—the elimination of missiles—is proceeding normally, in an atmosphere of trust and businesslike work....

The Soviet leadership has decided to demonstrate once again its readiness to reinforce this healthy process not only by words but also by deeds.

Today, I can report to you that the Soviet Union has taken a decision to reduce its armed forces.

Within the next two years their numerical strength will be reduced by 500,000 men. The numbers of conventional armaments will also be substantially reduced. This will be done unilaterally, without relation to the talks on the mandate of the Vienna meeting.

By agreement with our Warsaw Treaty allies, we have decided to withdraw by 1991 six tank divisions from the German Democratic Republic, Czechoslovakia and Hungary, and to disband them.

Assault landing troops and several other formations and units, including assault crossing units with their weapons and combat equipment, will also be withdrawn from the groups of Soviet forces stationed in those countries.

Soviet forces stationed in those countries will be reduced by 50,000 men and their armaments, by 5,000 tanks.

All Soviet divisions remaining, for the time being, in the territory of our allies are being reorganized. Their structure will be different from what it is now; after a major cutback of their tanks it will become clearly defensive.

At the same time, we shall reduce the numerical strength of the armed forces and the numbers of armaments stationed in the European part of the USSR.

In total, Soviet armed forces in this part of our country and in the territories of our European allies will be reduced by 10,000 tanks, 8,500 artillery systems and 800 combat aircraft.

Over these two years we intend to reduce significantly our armed forces in the Asian part of our country, too. By agreement with the government of the Mongolian People's Republic a major portion of Soviet troops temporarily stationed there will return home.

In taking this fundamental decision the Soviet leadership expresses the will of the people, who have undertaken a profound renewal of their entire socialist society.

We shall maintain our country's defense capability at a level of reasonable and reliable sufficiency so that no one might be tempted to encroach on the security of the USSR and our allies.

By this action, and by all our activities in favor of demilitarizing international relations, we wish to draw the attention of the international community to yet another pressing problem—the problem of transition from the economy of armaments to an economy of disarmament.

Is conversion of military production a realistic idea? I have already had occasion to speak about this. We think that, indeed, it is realistic.

For its part, the Soviet Union is prepared:

• In the framework of our economic reform we are ready to draw up and make public our internal plan of conversion; in the course of 1989 to draw up, as an experiment, conversion plans for two or three defense plants;

• To make public our experience in providing employment for specialists from military industry and in using its equipment, buildings and structures in civilian production.

It is desirable that all states, in the first place major military powers, should submit to the United Nations their national conversion plans.

It would also be useful to set up a group of scientists to undertake a thorough analysis of the problem of conversion as a whole and as applied to individual countries and regions and report to the Secretary-General of the United Nations and, subsequently, to have this matter considered at a session of the General Assembly.

IV

And finally, since I am here on American soil, and also for other obvious reasons, I have to turn to the subject of our relations with this great country. I had a chance to appreciate the full measure of its hospitality during my memorable visit to Washington exactly a year ago....

[I]n the last few years the entire world could breath a sigh of relief thanks to the changes for the better in the substance and the atmosphere of the relationship between Moscow and Washington....

The USSR and the United States have built the largest nuclear and missile arsenals. But it is those two countries that, having become specifically aware of their responsibility, were the first to conclude a treaty on the reduction and physical elimination of a portion of these armaments which posed a threat to both of them and to all others.

Both countries possess the greatest and the most sophisticated military secrets. But it is those two countries that have laid a basis for and are further developing a system of mutual verification both of the elimination of armaments and of the reduction and prohibition of their production.

It is those two countries that are accumulating the experience for future bilateral and multilateral agreements.

We value this. We acknowledge and appreciate the contribution made by President Ronald Reagan and by the members of his administration, particularly Mr. George Shultz.

All this is our joint investment in a venture of historic importance. We must not lose this investment, or leave it idle.

The next U.S. Administration headed by President-elect George Bush will find in us a partner who is ready—without long pauses or backtracking—to continue the dialogue in a spirit of realism, openness and goodwill, with a willingness to achieve concrete results working on the agenda which covers the main issues of Soviet-U.S. relations and world politics.

I have in mind, above all:

• Consistent movement toward a treaty on 50 percent reductions in strategic offensive arms while preserving the ABM Treaty;

• Working out a convention on the elimination of chemical weapons—here, as we see it, prerequisites exist to make 1989 a decisive year;

• And negotiations on the reduction of conventional arms and armed forces in Europe.

We also have in mind economic, environmental and humanistic problems in their broadest sense....

I am concluding my first address to the United Nations with the same feeling that I had when I began it—a feeling of responsibility to my own people and to the world community.

We are meeting at the end of a year which has meant so much for the United Nations and on the eve of a year from which we all expect so much.

I would like to believe that our hopes will be matched by our joint effort to put an end to an era of wars, confrontation and regional conflicts, to aggressions against nature, to the terror of hunger and poverty as well as to political terrorism.

This is our common goal and we can only reach it together. Thank you.

PARTY RENUNCIATION OF MONOPOLY ON POWER

Following are excerpts from the Communist Party Central Committee Platform published February 13, 1990, in Pravda. *The platform was adopted February 7 at the end of a Central Committee plenum. In addition to outlining party positions on many issues, the document renounced the Communist party's monopoly on power codified in Article 6 of the USSR Constitution.*

At this sharp turning point, the party will be able to retain its vanguard positions and to pursue the cause which it has launched and which enjoys the people's support provided it radically restructures itself.

The authoritarian regime had an extremely negative effect on the party, its role in society, and its work methods. In practice a party-state structure of power developed. In terms of internal party life, relations between primary organizations and leadership organs were deformed, communists were isolated from the shaping of party policy and had hardly any influence on the activity of higher-ranking party committees. Great harm was done by supercentralization, the stifling of free thought, and the repressions. The party's prestige suffered tremendous damage as a result of cases of ideological and moral degeneration.

Nontheless, the broad party masses retained a commitment to Lenin's ideals, selflessness, and self-sacrifice in serving the people. The CPSU [Communist Party of the Soviet Union] always had active living forces, and this is precisely why it managed to overcome the inertia of Stalinism and stagnation, headed the revolutionary turnabout, and thus proved again its ability to play a vanguard role.

The scale and newness of the tasks which emerged urgently raised the question of the need to fundamentally change the CPSU's position in society, to abandon the claims to infallibility and political monopolism. Moreover, the dynamics of changes in society dictate the fast pace of the party's transformation—otherwise it runs the risk of being forced onto the sidelines of political life. The party masses are acutely aware of this situation: The question of reforming the party and profoundly restructuring it is being raised with growing persistence.

The CPSU is a self-managing sociopolitical organization, a voluntary union of like-mined communists. We conceive the renewed CPSU as a party of socialist choice which expresses the interests of the working class and all working people and builds its policy on the basis of scientific analysis of new realities, creatively developing the legacy of Marx, Engels, and Lenin in the context of all social thought and historical experience of the 20th century.

In its theory and practice, the CPSU relies on the democratic and humanist traditions of all peoples in the Soviet Union. Organically combining national and international principles, the party is implacable toward chauvinism, nationalism, and racism and toward any other manifestations of reactionary ideology and obscurantism. It is cleansing its ranks of those who reject its ideopolitical and organizational foundations and those who participate in antisocialist, nationalist, and anti-Soviet organizations and actions.

The CPSU's position and role in a society undergoing renewal. The CPSU will pursue its policy and will struggle to retain the position of a ruling party within the framework of the democratic process, gaining in elections the voters' votes so as to obtain the people's mandate for shaping leadership organs at the center, in the republics, and at local level.

The CPSU, just like other sociopolitical organizations and mass movements, participates in the management of state and social affairs and nominates its representatives for soviets of people's deputies and other state organs. The party does not take on any powers of state authority. Its role is to be the democratically recognized political leader, acting through communists without claiming an advantage or the enshrining of its special status in the USSR Constitution. In this context, the party deems it necessary to exercise the right of legislative initiative and to submit to the Congress of USSR People's Deputies an appropriate proposal concerning Article 6 of the country's Fundamental Law.

The CPSU, based on the principles of Marxism-Leninism, engages in ideopolitical work among the masses to propagandize its policy and program objectives, to disseminate the humanist values of socialism, and to agitate for the achievement of perestroika's goals.

By casting off duties that are alien to its nature, the CPSU will be able to concentrate its efforts on the elaboration of theory and action programs, on organizational and educational work, on the implementation of the party's cadre policy, and on the resolution of the tasks of society's consolidation along the paths of its revolutionary renewal. Therein lies the main essence of its vanguard role. This will dominate its new relations with all sociopolitical organizations operating within the framework of the USSR Constitution—relations of dialogue, debate, cooperation, and partnership....

The party initiated the affirmation of glasnost in the country. It will continue to do everything to ensure that glasnost becomes the natural environment for shaping public opinion, a powerful means of the people's direct influence on policy and of citizens' participation in all affairs of state and society, a factor of perestroika's irreversibility and dynamization. Taking into account the mass media's important role in society's life, primarily in the implementation of glasnost, the party will assist their activity by all possible means and will exercise its ideological influence on them on a democratic basis. The CPSU will struggle against disinformation, against the mass media being used to promote selfish personal and group interests, to fan interethnic dissension, or to propagandize ideas which are alien to humane and democratic socialism.

This is how we perceive the party's new role in society. This does not mean that everything in the future is clear. The unfolding of reforms will make it possible to amplify the answers to numerous specific questions.

GORBACHEV SPEECH AT 28TH PARTY CONGRESS

Following are excerpts from the text of President Mikhail S. Gorbachev's July 10, 1990, speech to the Twenty-eighth Party Congress of the Communist Party of the Soviet Union. In the address, Gorbachev responded candidly to the contentious debates among the delegates that occurred during the congress' first week. Later in the day Gorbachev was overwhelmingly reelected as general secretary of the Communist party.

The debate is only just developing, there is still a lot to come. It has gone on both here in this hall, and in the sections, and in the commissions with congress delegates actively participating in their work. Add to this the debates which have also taken place at our meetings with delegates—workers and peasants, secretaries of party organizations and of rayon and city party committees, and with agrarian workers, then the congress has, so to speak, brought a great deal to the surface. On the one hand, these debates have confirmed what we knew about the processes taking place in the country. But the congress has also added a lot, especially from the viewpoint of appraising the possible consequences if various tendencies were to develop in our society....

The first point which should be emphasized is that, with few exceptions, the political policy of perestroika, of renewal of the whole of our society within the framework of socialist choice is not being placed in doubt, it is supported by the congress. The majority of delegates understand that it was dictated by life and, being transformed into a policy along all avenues, from the economy to the spiritual sphere, it has already brought about colossal changes within society and continues to exert a huge influence on our entire development. My position—you must have full clarity in relation to this—is as follows. Despite the mistakes, miscalculations and delays—which delegates here correctly mentioned and criticized, seeing that all this has inflicted major losses on society and the party—and despite the dramatic nature of the current situation in the country, I consider the overall result of the changes which have taken place to be significant and progressive.

Opinions clashed at the congress on the question of what perestroika has given to the country. There were attempts to quantify it using a pharmacist's scales and the four arithmetical functions. This is a joke, comrades. A phenomenon like perestroika and the revolutionary transformation of society must be judged by new criteria, criteria on an historic scale.

Those who truly understand that perestroika is necessary, that it is a revolution and not, so to say, simply a repainting of the facade, also understand that we still have a lot to overcome. Accepting the criticism—with all its harshness—against the initiators of perestroika, and despite the critical appraisal of the accountability report, I do not go back on anything that was said in the report because everything was thought out and weighed up.

The main positive aspect of what has been achieved is that society has gained freedom. This has unleashed the energy of the people, given a green light to ideas and concerns about the fate of the country and the fate of socialism that were squeezed in the pincers of dogmas and old schemes, it has made it possible to bring millions of people into politics and to start the transformations which had become vitally urgent. Had there been no freedom, there would not have been either this congress or the atmosphere it is being held in.

Not everything that had accumulated in the stifling and repressive atmosphere of Stalinshchina and stagnation, and which has now burst onto the surface, has turned out to be pleasant and constructive. But we have to take this into account—this is the purpose of revolution, its primary function is always to give the people freedom. And perestroika, with its democratization and glasnost, has already fulfilled this paramount task.

Spiritual rebirth is as essential to society as oxygen. It is taking place before our very eyes and, despite all the costs of this process, it has already exerted a huge influence. Society has become different, and we all have become different. It is a different matter that neither the party, nor the country as a whole, nor the old nor the newly formed organizations and movements, nor our new power—all of us, comrades—have yet learned to use the freedom that we have gained.

For that reason the most urgent task is to learn this faster and better.

We have advanced quite far in political reform, we have created new structures of power from top to bottom on the basis of the democratic expression of the people's will. They are still being improved, but they have already begun to function, filling our democracy and the concept of a rule-of-law state with specific content. In their work—and a great deal has been said on this during these days—there are many weaknesses, there is still a lack of experience, procedures and mechanisms have not been finely tuned, at times there is a lack of political culture, competence, and specialized knowledge. The process of forming a corps of cadres for the soviets is still incomplete. Nonetheless, the new soviets have started doing their work, and people's deputies are becoming more responsible and more eager to tackle as quickly as possible specific problems and people's need.

It is a gratifying fact that real soviet power is thus being restored, it is one of the most important gains of perestroika, in which communists and party organizations have taken part and are still taking part. And yet one can sense in places a certain gulf, I would say a coolness, between the soviets and the party. Here communists have to be very careful, and primarily have to look at themselves. It is always necessary to start with one's own self. Is

this alienation not connected with the fact that we are quite unable to renounce the former methods of contacts with soviets, the methods inherited from the administrative edict system? The new organs of power, for their part are also responding painfully to such complaints.

I said in the report, and I would like to repeat once again, that the strengthening of legality, the imposition of order, and the setting up of a mechanism with whose help resolutions and decisions will be implemented, are now directly linked with soviets at all levels acquiring full power and rights as quickly as possible. And it is the sacred obligation of the party, of party organizations and committees, and of communists working in the soviets and in production collectives to help in this. I would simultaneously urge the deputies of all soviets to work constructively, within the framework of the Constitution and the law. I address them primarily in my capacity as president. Bluntly speaking, a confrontational stance is beginning to take shape among some deputies, and this does not bode well. It is bad if communists do not understand what renewed soviets are today, and that they have to play their part for the normalization of the situation in the interests of the people. It is bad if the soviets, too, do not understand the need for collaboration with party organizations.

Speaking of the debate's second lesson, I would like to share the assessments by delegates who, supporting the perestroika line, voiced many sharp critical remarks in connection with the fact that this line has not always been consistently pursued. Many important decisions and laws which should have directed social processes and forestalled the emergence of negative phenomena, were not implemented. All this has to be interpreted and conclusions for the future must be drawn.

It so happened that, endeavoring to react as speedily as possible to the demands of life and to elaborate the necessary laws and decisions, we devoted very little attention to their fulfillment and, in essence, we failed to create a proper mechanism. Hence it became obvious that presidential power was needed, that it was necessary to more speedily implement the political reform and set up new soviets, because without them all these laws would be suspended, as it were, in mid-air.

This must to a significant extent be regarded as being on the conscience of the center. But I also want to speak of the responsibility of comrades who work at republic and local level. There is no need to shift blame either from the center to the local level or from the local level to the center, it is necessary to cooperate, to act by pooling our efforts, without seeking others to blame.

Much can probably be explained also by the fact that comrades in the republics and at local level, to say nothing of the center, have simply become confused and have found themselves in a state of shock. An old illness has made itself felt here: Lack of initiative and independent approach, inability to act in an unorthodox manner in the conditions of democracy and in a situation that is out of the ordinary.

Here is the reason why I want to speak of this. All the difficulties of perestroika, the fact that the new organs are entering life and gathering their momentum slowly and with difficulty, cannot be attributed only to resistance by those who reject perestroika. Of course such people exist, and I spoke of them in the report, at the meetings with workers and with party organization secretaries. However, many people have yet simply to comprehend this present situation.

Here we are, talking about the crisis of the party. It is in fact rooted in the inability, and in many cases the unwillingness, to fully understand that we are already living and working in a new society now, an unprecedentedly politicized society, a society with broad and virtually unlimited glasnost, a society of a freedom unseen throughout history. But many party organizations and communists continue to act using the habitual methods inherited from the past, which are pulling us back by our coattails. And if any delegates—and, judging from the speeches, there are such among us—have come to the congress in the hope of returning the party to the previous conditions of edicts and orders then, I have to say, they are deliberately and profoundly mistaken. We have to devote every hour to the advancement of perestroika, the adaptation of our work to the new conditions.

The party will be the vanguard of society and will be able to act successfully only if it recognizes fully its new role and completes its reform along the paths of democratization on a very short timescale and learns as soon as possible to work with the masses in a new way. It is essential to overcome that alienation from the people that is rooted in the times long past. Primarily by renewing the activity of primary party organizations, by renewing cadres and enhancing their prestige.

... We are not changing our line or our choice, we are committed to socialist values. But do believe me that the party's success depends on the party understanding that society is already different. Otherwise the party will be squeezed out by other forces and we will lose our positions. Whereas at the moment we have enormous potential, and the entire point is to realize the main thing: Without renewal, without democratization, without strengthening our living bond with the people and our vigorous work amongst the masses, we will not advance very far....

The next lesson from the debate that took place is on how to act in future along the main avenues of perestroika. The party and state leadership has been criticized mercilessly for the economic situation, the state of the market, and the supply of goods to the population.

The key tasks here are the solution of the food question—I put that to the fore because if we reduce the urgency of that matter the urgency of the situation in the social sphere will drop by 70 or 80 percent—and the transition to a regulated market and the housing question.

In this context, I am not going to conceal the fact that I was disturbed when the congress decided, by three-fourths of votes, to alter the name of the Economic Reform Commission, leaving out the word "market". So, there remains a lack of understanding of the sharp about-turn to making radical changes in the situation in the national economy, which society has been offered.

Has our entire history, comrades, really failed to demonstrate the futility of attempts to get away from the plight in which the state and citizens have found themselves by means of darning and patching the command management system? We have already borne huge losses by stubbornly hanging on to it for decades, and even now still hanging on to it and thereby holding up renewal and our arrival at new forms of economic life in the country. And if we proceed like this further, then, I will say it bluntly, we will lead the country to bankruptcy. I am voicing my point of view quite definitely.

The advantages of the market economy have been proven on a worldwide scale, and the question now is only whether it is possible in the conditions of the market to ensure the high level of social protection characteristic of our socialist system, the system of working people. The answer is this: It is not only possible, but it is precisely the regulated market economy which will allow public wealth to increase in such a way that as a result everybody's standards of living will rise. And, of course, we have in our hands the state power which is capable of having such laws, and such decisions which will "form dykes" for the process of transition to market relations.

Of course, before the advantages of the market produce their full effect, the period of its establishment must take place. And the most complex task in this period is to elaborate and implement a package of special measures for social protection, especially for citizens on low incomes. It was already said in the report: The way the intention to switch to the market economy was announced, scared the people. Their vision of the market presented not well-stocked store shelves but high prices. I did say that starting with prices was not the right way. But, having launched the reform, it must be borne in mind: There can be no transition to the market without reform of price formation....

I have expressed my attitude: We here at the congress have to take a political stance regarding the peasantry and the countryside, and not just regarding the food question. It is only a part of the problem. If the countryside feels strong, if our peasantry is confident and lives well, and if it receives opportunities for its enterprising work, this means that the food question will be resolved more quickly. (Applause)

... From this platform I repeat once again to the congress, the party, and the whole country: Our position is that it is necessary to, first, give total freedom to all types of economic management in the countryside on the basis of total freedom of choice. Second, to establish a reasonable exchange between town and countryside, between industry and agriculture, which would promote the revival of the countryside in the shortest possible historical timespan. Third, the state has to promote to the maximum degree the resolution of the urgent problems of the rural sector, primarily the creation of decent living conditions for our peasantry. It is on these three pillars that the countryside can be regenerated, and the country be supplied with food. And not a single element can be removed from this triad, otherwise the entire system will collapse. (Applause)

... Two other subjects were sharply raised, and it was not easy to listen to all that since they touch on people's lives, and have already resulted in serious consequences. First, there is the ecology—one of today's most acute problems, and we must not put off its solution. We realized it late but, comrades, a lot can be put right. This can be seen from foreign experience. About three decades ago dozens of cities in the United States were ecological disaster areas, rivers were literally dead, the Great Lakes were on the verge of death, but large investments and the implementation of special programs made it possible to improve the situation sharply. The same is being done in Europe, which is full of industry and chemical enterprises. This is why, no matter how hard it might be for us now, we have to embark on large-scale investments of money in the nature protection area, regarding it as being on an absolutely equal level with such vitally important tasks as supplying people with food and housing. Man needs pure air and water as much as he needs bread, comrades. And, of course, I think there will be a need for state programs, both on ecology as a whole, and on major ecological problems.

We all are painfully affected by the consequences of the Chernobyl accident. I ask the comrades from Belorussia, the Ukraine, and Bryansk oblast to understand that we are sharing their misfortune....

Delegates are legitimately worried by what is happening in the spiritual sphere, the sphere of culture, science, and education. I have received dozens of collective letters from representatives of the intelligentsia, and it is not just a matter of the material base having fallen behind, even though this must be borne in mind. I hope that the congress will express the firm position that we need to support the development and rise of all of our culture, science, education, art, and literature.

I fully share the alarm expressed by teachers who spoke here about the fact that the real revival of our schools is a decisive precondition for the future of our country. There is a direct dependence here—we will never be able to create a flourishing economy, raise our science and technology to a world level, or wage a successful struggle against alcoholism, drug addiction, and the decline of morals, unless we elevate educational work to an appropriate height, unless we elevate the role of teachers....

We have inherited from Marx, Engels, and Lenin a high class of methodology in thinking, a dialectical form of ideas, on which we will continue to depend in theory and in politics. But we will not allow everything created by the classics to be turned into another short course, something that evidently some people regret, judging from some speeches. This will not happen, it would mean ruin for perestroika and for society. (Applause)

I have been struck by the fact that no sooner had a speaker come up to the rostrum and tried to philosophically raise questions of our times, and in this context to consider all our work, than apathy set in the hall and people began to clap. How accustomed we have become to simple and clear formulas: "To be or not to be," "Down with or not down with." (Applause) Let us reflect, after all we are a party, claiming to be the vanguard of society.

... Delegates have brought to the 28th congress all their anxiety concerning the instability in society. So, at the meeting with workers, one worker could not bear it: "Mikhail Sergeyevich, Nikolay Ivanovich, answer two questions: When will there be order in the country, and when will there be no speculators?" (Applause) They seem simple questions demanding a simple answer, but there is no simple answer. This is how I would put it: The quicker we saturate the market, and the quicker we get the economy working more efficiently, the quicker we will defeat the speculators and the shadow economy.

A rayon party committee secretary said: "Can you do what Andropov did?" I answered that question, and I can repeat here at the congress: 80 percent of the struggle against speculation is an economic matter. (Applause) If the economy is not developed, speculators will flourish! It is on shortages that these shadowy dealers and corrupt elements thrive as parasites.

Does this mean, however, that until we have solved these issues, everyone should sit idle? No, of course not! You are right to demand of us to strengthen order, and I would like to demand something of you—let us activate the entire system of soviets that we have been shaping for a whole year while speculators and criminals got on with their own business. Now that it has been shaped, let us pool our efforts and deal them a real blow! (Applause) It is precisely with this, with the work of soviet, economic, the party organs, that the process of stabilization in society will now be connected.

The fact that we have overlooked a great deal in interethnic relations is a lesson for us all, we lost time and when we spotted this we took action too late. I am not going to justify myself now, the one thing I really dislike is justifying myself. What's done is done. Yet how many Politburo sittings there were, how many meetings—with first secretaries and in commissions, how many trips. But evidently, all of this was not enough. The main point is that we did not detect the danger soon enough, we all—go on, admit it honestly—believed that all of this had been happily resolved and for the most part we were drinking toasts to the friendship of peoples. That's what our work in the area of nationalities policy amounted to. And suddenly we saw the problems that faced us. But we did not react immediately, we did not immediately reach a correct assessment. The platform on whose basis we are now working emerged only later. Now we have to act without wasting time. We have political evaluations, we have a party platform, and many decisions have been adopted by the Supreme Soviet. The Council of the Federation has at last started work, and the process of the preparation and elaboration of a new Union treaty is under way. I propose that the congress, on behalf of communists, appeal to all peoples of the country: Let us halt, let us cease testing fate, and let us get down to imparting new breath to our Union on the basis of these documents and approaches, which are already clear to us all. This is the main point now. I think that everyone will heed us and will respond to this appeal, but this presupposes active work by us. (Applause)

Both at the congress of the Communist Party of the Russian Federation and at this congress, especially in the commissions, we again heard sharp criticism and direct objections to our new foreign policy. We will, of course, take any competent opinions on specific questions into account. But I reject any attempt to raise doubts about our policy as totally unacceptable and dictated by some people's selfish interests.

Our new foreign policy has affected the economy, the Army, and defense. We are moving toward reforms along all these avenues, including a state program for the social protection of servicemen. We must do this to ensure that the Army senses the people's support.

It is also necessary to help our collectives in the defense industry, where the best cadres and scientific forces are pooled, where there are good assets for restructuring production within a short time and embarking on the manufacture of high-quality output which the country very badly needs. The whole country will gain from this, primarily as regards the retooling of sectors manufacturing consumer goods.

There are, of course, difficulties but they are temporary. The problems existing here must be solved more quickly. But surely this is not a reason for closing one's eyes to everything that our foreign policy has given the country and the world as a whole. I reject all attempts to raise doubts about all this. One of the secretaries even advised me not to travel outside the country. But why do we go there? In order to prevent war, to carry out perestroika in normal conditions and, finally, to release resources and channel them toward the country's needs.

It is impossible to be under the thumb of people who are incompetent, in politics, this will be a disaster. A party claiming to be the vanguard ought to lead, rather than play to sundry moods. (Applause) After all, look at the questions being asked: Have we been correct in taking the path of disarmament and reduction of excessive military spending which is unnecessary to guarantee security? The answer suggests itself directly from the question. Have we been correct in not intervening in questions that have arisen in East Europe? What, tanks again, once more teaching people how to live? I think that the whole world is listening to us when we pursue the cause of perestroika and wish to show that our society is capable of being progressive, disposed toward all peoples with friendship, and that it offers cooperation. This is how we influence the world. (Applause)

Think of it, there are still people who ask this question: Were we correct in withdrawing from Afghanistan? Well, in this case I simply do not know who we are dealing with!

And something else. Were we correct in establishing good relations with dozens in all continents? Yes, we were correct, and they did respond, not just the rulers but the peoples as well. You must be blind not to see this. Common sense, if it is not befogged by selfishly departmental considerations, says that all this was correctly done, that all this is in keeping with the vital interests of our people and the norms of morality. To say nothing of the fact that, without a new foreign policy, we would have been in no position to transform our own country....

Now about the party and its future. The question which brought us here is one of the main questions. For me it is a question of the my entire life and my human position. What is the lesson of the congress here? Comrades have expressed their acute alarm because the party is losing its prestige and its positions are weakening. It is being squeezed out by other political forces and in some places communists have been forced to go into opposition. The blame for this has been laid against the leadership of the CPSU [Communist Party of the Soviet Union] and especially some of its members. I will say right away that this criticism is, comrades, largely justified in essence. I am only against its form. There should not be two extremes here at our congress: talking down to anyone or loutishness. That's all, but all the rest must be bluntly said. (Applause)

I conclude from this that the impulses that went out from the Central Committee along all these avenues were insufficient. At the same time, party committees at all levels bear their share of guilt. The time has gone for ever, comrades, when you could get a kind of mandate from the Central Committee to administer a rayon, a city, an oblast, or a republic, and sit in that place until your dying day, regardless of how you conducted affairs or what people thought of you. We must state that here at the top, it was like that at republic level, it was like that at all levels. We must state this. But that time has passed, and it has passed never to return. I am convinced of that. We cannot bring back yesterday in any way. No dictatorship—in case such a delirious idea might be fermenting in someone's brain—will solve anything....

I am in complete agreement with congress delegates, with workers who spoke saying that it is necessary to promote to top jobs considerably more front-ranking and intelligent workers who are enthusiastic supporters of perestroika. The kind of people that perestroika has revealed! Even the meeting which was attended by those representing the working class at this congress as invitees and as delegates revealed them as people capable of reflection, of political analysis. They are not just babblers, striving to have their "worker-like poignant say" or beating their chests saying that they have come right "from where it counts."

This "from where it counts" of course means having come from the machine tools, from the shop floor, and so on, where our might is being forged and the foundation on which we stand is being laid.

Here we are, arguing, electing, shaping the system. But what does the country stand on? On the workers, the peasants, and the intelligentsia who hold the national economy together. (Applause)

To continue. The ossified ideological cliches by which people are guided not only in debates but also in practical affairs, must be renounced. As before, there are frequent cases where it is not the demands of life that are put above all else, not the results of work, but the extent to which someone's behavior corresponds to entrenched dogma. Commitment to dogmas is especially hampering the establishment of new forms of economic management, of people's initiative. If we are are going to act in that way, then we shall certainly discredit the socialist choice, and the people will turn away from us.

What is more, the party will not be able to restructure itself until we all realize that the end of the CPSU's monopoly on power and government has come. Even if we manage to win a majority at elections—and we can and must act so as to win this majority and preserve our position as the ruling party—even in these cases, it makes sense to opt for cooperation with nonparty deputies, with representatives of other political streams recognized under the law and sincerely concerned about the country's destiny. To put an end to sectarian sentiments and to this monopoly for ever, to eradicate it from the minds of party workers and all communists.

We must cooperate! I share the point of view expressed here by Comrade Luchinskiy. The Central Committee's accountability report raised the question of the desirability, under present-day conditions, of entering into a coalition of all democratic and socialist forces. Only by putting aside party-political and national differences will we be able to concentrate all our efforts on extricating the country from the present grave situation and implement far-reaching reforms along all avenues of society's life.

I am convinced that it is precisely this, consolidation of the party itself and of all sensible political forces that genuinely care for prosperity of the people, that is expected of us by millions of communists and the overwhelming majority of Soviet people. I speak of this confidently, because this very call is repeated in many of the letters sent to me and the telegrams addressed to the congress. Comrades, let us heed this voice of the people, the voice of the times!

I have picked up a subtext in many of the speeches: It is perestroika which is allegedly to blame for all our troubles. In some there was even a hint of longing for old times, for the old ways of working.

. . . I have to say that if perestroika is to blame for anything, then it is for the fact that it has not been carried out with sufficient consistency and determination. And this, incidentally, comes up against the standpoint of cadres, both in the center and at local level. So, let us change this standpoint and get the perestroika process moving forward. Then the changes will proceed more quickly and we will more rapidly achieve results that our whole people will feel. I do not see any other path than the continuation of perestroika, resolute and purposeful, of all that we have been doing to transform the economy, the social sphere, the political system, and our multinational state.

Let us get to work, comrades, we have entered the most crucial phase of perestroika and major reforms lie ahead. (Applause)

Bibliography

CHAPTER 1
Imperial Russia and the Revolution

Books

Bain, Robert N. *First Romanovs, 1613-1725.* New York: Russell & Russell, 1967.

Ball, Alan M. *Russia's Last Capitalists: The Nepmen, 1921-1929.* Berkeley: University of California Press, 1987.

Bashkina, Nina N., ed. *The United States and Russia: The Beginning of Relations, 1765-1815.* Washington, D.C.: Government Printing Office, 1980.

Berlin, Isaiah. *Karl Marx: His Life and Environment.* New York: Oxford University Press, 1959.

Billington, James H. *The Icon and the Axe.* New York: Random House, 1970.

Browder, Robert P., and Alexander F. Kerensky, eds. *The Russian Provisional Government Documents.* 3 vols. Stanford, Calif.: Stanford University Press, 1961.

Budurowycz, Bohdan B. *Polish-Soviet Relations, 1917-1921.* Cambridge, Mass.: Harvard University Press, 1969.

Carr, Edward H. *A History of Soviet Russia.* 3 vols. New York: Macmillan, 1953.

Chernov, Victor M. *The Great Russian Revolution.* Translated and abridged by Philip E. Moseley. New Haven, Conn.: Yale University Press, 1936.

Clarkson, Jesse D. *History of Russia.* New York: Random House, 1969.

Crankshaw, Edward. *The Shadow of the Winter Palace: The Drift to Revolution, 1825-1917.* New York: Penguin Books, 1976.

Curtiss, John S. *Russian Army under Nicholas I.* Durham, N.C.: Duke University Press, 1965.

Deutscher, Isaac. *The Prophet Armed: Trotsky, 1879-1921.* New York: Oxford University Press, 1954.

Dukes, P. *Catherine the Great and the Russian Nobility.* New York: Cambridge University Press, 1968.

Fedyshyn, Oleh S. *Germany's Drive to the East and the Ukrainian Revolution, 1917-1918.* New Brunswick, N.J.: Rutgers University Press, 1971.

Field, Daniel. *Rebels in the Name of the Tsar.* Boston: Houghton Mifflin, 1976.

Freeze, Gregory L. *From Supplication to Revolution: A Documentary Social History of Imperial Russia.* New York: Oxford University Press, 1988.

Graham, Stephen. *Tsar of Freedom: The Life and Reign of Alexander II.* Hamden, Conn.: Shoe String Press, 1968.

Hingley, Ronald. *Tsars: From Ivan the Terrible to Nicholas II, 1533-1917.* Urbana: University of Illinois Press, 1968.

Johnson, Robert E. *Peasant and Proletarian: The Working Class of Moscow at the End of the 19th Century.* New Brunswick,

N.J.: Rutgers University Press, 1979.

Kahan, Arcadius. *Russian Economic History: The Nineteenth Century.* Chicago: University of Chicago Press, 1989.

Kenez, Peter. *Civil War in South Russia, 1919-1920: The Defeat of the Whites.* Berkeley: University of California Press, 1977.

Kerensky, Alexander. *The Catastrophe.* New York: Appleton-Century-Crofts, 1929.

Kettle, Michael. *Road to Intervention: March-November 1918.* New York: Routledge, 1988.

Kochan, Miriam L. *The Last Days of Imperial Russia: 1910-1917.* New York: Macmillan, 1976.

———. *Life in Russia under Catherine the Great.* New York: Putnam, 1969.

Koenker, Diane, William G. Rosenberg, and Ronald Grigor Suny, eds. *Party, State and Society in the Russian Civil War: Explorations in Social History.* Bloomington: Indiana University Press, 1989.

Lane, David. *The Roots of Russian Communism: A Social and Historical Study of Russian Social Democracy, 1898-1907.* University Park: Pennsylvania State University Press, 1975.

Lawrence, John. *A History of Russia.* New York: New American Library, 1978.

Leggett, George. *The Cheka: Lenin's Secret Police.* New York: Oxford University Press, 1981.

Lenin, V. I. *Selected Works.* 12 vols. New York: International Publishers, 1938.

Lewin, Moshe. *Lenin's Last Struggle.* New York: Monthly Review Press, 1978.

Lyons, Marvin. *Nicholas II: The Last Tsar.* New York: St. Martin's Press, 1975.

Massie, Robert P. *Nicholas and Alexandra.* New York: Atheneum, 1967.

———. *Peter the Great.* New York: Random House, 1981.

McCauley, Martin, and Peter Waldron. *The Emergence of the Modern Russian State, 1855-1881.* Basingstoke: Macmillan Press, 1988.

Medvedev, Roy A. *The October Revolution.* New York: Columbia University Press, 1979.

Mosse, Werner E. *Alexander the Second and the Modernization of Russia.* New York: Macmillan, 1962.

Offord, Derek. *The Russian Revolutionary Movement in the 1880's.* New York: Cambridge University Press, 1986.

Pares, Sir Bernard. *The Fall of the Russian Monarchy: A Study of the Evidence.* New York: Knopf, 1939.

———. *A History of Russia.* New York: Knopf, 1953.

Pipes, Richard, ed. *Revolutionary Russia.* Cambridge, Mass.: Harvard University Press, 1968.

Presniakov, Alexander E. *Emperor Nicholas the First of Russia: The Apogee of Autocracy, 1825-1855.* Gulf Breeze, Fla.: Academic International, 1974.

Riasanovsky, Nicholas V. *A History of Russia.* 3d ed. New York:

Oxford University Press, 1977.

Rywkin, Michael, ed. *Russian Colonial Expansion to 1917*. New York: Mansell, 1988.

Saul, Norman E. *Sailors in Revolt: The Russian Baltic Fleet in 1917*. Lawrence: University of Kansas Press, 1978.

Seton-Watson, Hugh. *The Decline of Imperial Russia, 1855-1914*. New York: Praeger Publishers, 1952.

―――. *Russian Empire, 1801-1917*. New York: Oxford University Press, 1967.

Shanin, Teodor. *Russia, 1905-1907: Revolution as a Moment of Truth*. New Haven: Yale University Press, 1986.

Smith, Edward E. *The Young Stalin: The Early Years of an Elusive Revolutionary*. New York: Farrar, Strauss & Giroux, 1967.

Sokol, Edward D. *The Revolt of 1916 in Russian Central Asia*. New York: AMS Press, 1978.

Szamuely, Tibor. *The Russian Tradition*. New York: McGraw-Hill, 1975.

Thomas, Benjamin P. *Russo-American Relations, 1815-1867*. New York: AMS Press, 1978.

Troyat, Henri. *Catherine the Great*. New York: E. P. Dutton, 1980.

Tucker, Robert C., ed. *The Lenin Anthology*. New York: W. W. Norton, 1975.

Ulam, Adam B. *The Bolsheviks*. New York: Collier Books, 1968.

Vernadsky, George. *A History of Russia*. 6th ed. New Haven, Conn.: Yale University Press, 1969.

Von Laue, Theodore H. *Why Lenin? Why Stalin? A Reappraisal of the Russian Revolution*. New York: Harper & Row, 1971.

Wolfe, Bertram D. *Three Who Made a Revolution*. New York: Dial Press, 1964.

Yanov, Alexander. *The Origins of Autocracy: Ivan the Terrible in Russian History*. Berkeley: University of California Press, 1981.

CHAPTER 2
Stalin Era

Books

Antonov-Ovseyenko, Anton. *The Time of Stalin: Portrait of a Tyranny*. New York: Harper & Row, 1982.

Bialer, Seweryn, ed. *Stalin and His Generals: Soviet Military Memoirs of World War II*. New York: Pegasus, 1969.

Brzezinski, Zbigniew. *The Permanent Purge: Politics of Soviet Totalitarianism*. Cambridge, Mass.: Harvard University Press, 1956.

Clark, Alan. *Barbarossa: The Russian-German Conflict, 1941-45*. New York: William Morrow, 1965.

Clemens, Diane Shaver. *Yalta*. New York: Oxford University Press, 1970.

Conquest, Robert. *The Great Terror: Stalin's Purge of the Thirties*. New York: Macmillan, 1968.

―――. Conquest, Robert. *The Great Terror: A Reassessment*. New York: Oxford University Press, 1990.

Dallin, David J. *Soviet Russia's Foreign Policy: 1939-1942*. New Haven, Conn.: Yale University Press, 1942.

Davis, Lynn E. *The Cold War Begins*. Princeton, N.J.: Princeton University Press, 1974.

Deane, John R. *The Strange Alliance: The Story of Our Efforts at Wartime Cooperation with Russia*. New York: Viking, 1947.

Dedjer, Vladimir. *The Battle Stalin Lost: Memoirs of Yugoslavia, 1948-1953*. New York: Viking, 1971.

Deutscher, Isaac. *Stalin: A Political Biography*. 2d ed. New York: Oxford University Press, 1966.

Djilas, Milovan. *Conversations with Stalin*. Translated by Michael B. Petrovich. New York: Harcourt, Brace & World, 1962.

Druks, Herbert. *Harry S. Truman and the Russians, 1945-1953*. New York: Speller & Sons, 1967.

Feis, Herbert. *Churchill, Roosevelt, Stalin: The War They Waged and the Peace They Sought*. Princeton, N.J.: Princeton Uni-

versity Press, 1957.

Fischer, George. *Soviet Opposition to Stalin: A Case Study in World War II*. Cambridge, Mass.: Harvard University Press, 1952.

Fleming, D. F. *The Cold War and Its Origins: 1917-1960*. 2 vols. Garden City, N.Y.: Doubleday, 1961.

Gaddis, John Lewis. *The United States and the Origins of the Cold War, 1941-1947*. New York: Columbia University Press, 1972.

Gormly, James L. *Collapse of the Grand Alliance, 1945-1948*. Baton Rouge: Louisiana State University Press, 1987.

Hahn, Werner G. *Postwar Soviet Politics: The Fall of Zhdanov and the Defeat of Moderation*. Ithaca, N.Y.: Cornell University Press, 1982.

Kennan, George F. *Soviet Foreign Policy, 1917-1941*. New York: Van Nostrand, 1960.

Levytsky, Borys. *The Stalinist Terror in the Thirties*. Stanford, Calif.: Hoover Institution Press, 1974.

McNeal, Robert Hatch. *Stalin: Man and Ruler*. New York: New York University Press, 1988.

Medvedev, Roy A. *All Stalin's Men: Six Who Carried Out the Bloody Policies*. Garden City, N.Y.: Anchor Books, 1985.

―――. *Let History Judge*. Rev. ed. New York: Columbia University Press, 1989.

Neumann, William L. *After Victory: Churchill, Roosevelt, Stalin and the Making of the Peace*. New York: Harper & Row, 1967.

Resis, Albert. *Stalin, the Politburo, and the Onset of the Cold War*. Pittsburgh: University of Pittsburgh Press, 1988.

Salisbury, Harrison E. *Moscow Journal: The End of Stalin*. Chicago: University of Chicago Press, 1961.

―――. *900 Days: The Siege of Leningrad*. New York: Harper & Row, 1969.

Seabury, Paul. *The Rise and Decline of the Cold War*. New York: Basic Books, 1967.

Solzhenitsyn, Alexander. *The Gulag Archipelago, 1918-1956: An Experiment in Literary Investigation*. 2 vols. New York: Harper & Row, 1974.

Sontag, Raymond J., and James S. Beddie, eds. *Nazi-Soviet Relations, 1939-1941: Documents from Archives of German Foreign Office*. Westport, Conn.: Greenwood Press, 1976.

Stalin, J. V. *On the Great Patriotic War of the Soviet Union*. Moscow: Foreign Languages Publishing House, 1945.

Stettinius, Edward R., Jr. *Roosevelt and the Russians: The Yalta Conference*. Garden City, N.Y.: Doubleday, 1949.

Taubman, William. *Stalin's American Policy: From Entente to Détente to Cold War*. New York: W. W. Norton, 1982.

Trotsky, Leon. *Trotsky's Diary in Exile, 1935*. Cambridge, Mass.: Harvard University Press, 1959.

Tucker, Robert C. *Stalin as Revolutionary, 1879-1929: A Study in History and Personality*. New York: W. W. Norton, 1973.

Ulam, Adam B. *Stalin: The Man and His Era*. New York: Viking Press, 1973.

Voznesensky, Nicholas. *Economy of the USSR during World War II*. Washington, D.C.: Public Affairs Press, 1948.

Wittlin, Thaddeus. *Commissar: The Life and Death of Lavrenty Pavlovich Beria*. New York: Macmillan, 1972.

Wolin, Simon, and Robert M. Slusser, eds. *The Soviet Secret Police*. New York: Praeger Publishers, 1957.

CHAPTER 3
Khrushchev Era

Books

Allison, Graham T. *Essence of Decision: Explaining the Cuban Missile Crisis*. Boston: Little, Brown, 1971.

Armstrong, John A. *The Politics of Totalitarianism*. New York: Random House, 1961.

Bialer, Seweryn. *Stalin's Successors: Leadership, Stability, and Change in the Soviet Union*. New York: Cambridge University Press, 1980.

Breslauer, George W. *Khrushchev and Brezhnev as Leaders: Building Authority in Soviet Politics*. Winchester, Mass.: Allen & Unwin, 1982.

Brzezinski, Zbigniew, and Samuel P. Huntington. *Political Power: USA/USSR*. New York: Viking Press, 1964.

Crankshaw, Edward. *Khrushchev: A Career*. New York: Penguin, 1966.

Dallin, Alexander, ed. *Soviet Conduct in World Affairs*. New York: Columbia University Press, 1960.

Dinerstein, Herbert S. *The Making of a Missile Crisis: October 1962*. Baltimore: Johns Hopkins University Press, 1976.

Dornberg, John. *The New Tsars: Russia under Stalin's Heirs*. Garden City, N.Y.: Doubleday, 1972.

Garthoff, Raymond L. *Soviet Strategy in the Nuclear Age*. New York: Praeger Publishers, 1958.

Gehlen, Michael P. *The Politics of Coexistence: Soviet Methods and Motives*. Bloomington: Indiana University Press, 1967.

Goldman, Eric. *The Crucial Decade and After, 1945-1960*. New York: Vintage Books, 1960.

Horelick, Arnold L., and Myron Rush. *Strategic Power and Soviet Foreign Policy*. Chicago: University of Chicago Press, 1965.

Hyland, William, and Richard W. Shryock. *The Fall of Khrushchev*. New York: Funk & Wagnalls, 1968.

Jones, Goronwy J. *From Stalin to Khrushchev*. London: Linden Press, 1960.

Kennedy, Robert F. *Thirteen Days: A Memoir of the Cuban Missile Crisis*. New York: W. W. Norton, 1971.

Linden, Carl A. *Khrushchev and the Soviet Leadership, 1957-1964*. Baltimore: Johns Hopkins University Press, 1966.

McClosky, Herbert, and John E. Turner. *The Soviet Dictatorship*. New York: McGraw-Hill, 1960.

Overstreet, Harry A., and Bonaro Overstreet. *War Called Peace: Khrushchev's Communism*. New York: W. W. Norton, 1961.

Smolansky, Oles. *The Soviet Union and the Arab East under Khrushchev*. Lewisburg, Pa.: Bucknell University Press, 1974.

Talbott, Strobe, ed. *Khrushchev Remembers*. Boston: Little, Brown, 1970.

———. *The Last Testament*. Boston: Little, Brown, 1974.

CHAPTER 4
Brezhnev Era

Books

Amalrik, Andrei. *Will the Soviet Union Survive until 1984?* New York: Harper & Row, 1970.

Dallin, Alexander, and Thomas H. Larson, eds. *Soviet Politics since Khrushchev*. Englewood Cliffs, N.J.: Prentice-Hall, 1968.

Dawisha, Karen. *Kremlin and the Prague Spring*. Berkeley: University of California Press, 1984.

Dornberg, John. *Brezhnev: The Masks of Power*. New York: Basic Books, 1974.

Dzirkals, Lilita, Thane Gustafson, and A. Ross Johnson. *The Media and Intra-Elite Communication in the USSR*. Santa Monica, Calif.: The Rand Corporation, 1982.

Edmonds, Robin. *Soviet Foreign Policy 1962-1973: The Parody of Super Power*. New York: Oxford University Press, 1975.

Eidlin, Fred. *The Logic of Normalization: The Soviet Intervention in Czechoslovakia of 21 August 1968 and the Czechoslovakia Response*. New York: Columbia University Press, 1980.

Gelman, Harry. *The Brezhnev Politburo and the Decline of Détente*. Ithaca, N.Y.: Cornell University Press, 1984.

Hough, Jerry F. *Soviet Leadership in Transition*. Washington, D.C.: Brookings Institution, 1977.

———. *The Soviet Prefects*. Cambridge, Mass.: Harvard University Press, 1969.

Kelley, Donald R., ed. *Soviet Politics in the Brezhnev Era*. New York: Praeger Publishers, 1980.

Levesque, Jacques. *The USSR and the Cuban Revolution: Soviet Ideological and Strategical Perspectives, 1959-77*. New York: Praeger Publishers, 1981.

London, Kurt, ed. *The Soviet Union in World Politics*. Boulder, Colo.: Westview Press, 1980.

Nixon, Richard. *RN: The Memoirs of Richard Nixon*. New York: Grosset & Dunlap, 1978.

Pipes, Richard. *U.S.-Soviet Relations in the Era of Détente*. Boulder, Colo.: Westview Press, 1981.

Simes, Dimitri K. *Détente and Conflict: Soviet Foreign Policy, 1972-1977*. Beverly Hills, Calif.: Sage Publications, 1977.

Simon, Jeffrey. *Ruling Communist Parties and Détente: A Documentary History*. Washington, D.C.: American Enterprise Institute for Public Policy Research, 1975.

Stoessinger, John G. *Nations in Darkness: China, Russia and America*. New York: Random House, 1981.

Strong, John W. *Soviet Union under Brezhnev and Kosygin: The Transition Years*. New York: Van Nostrand Reinhold, 1971.

Tatu, Michel. *Power in the Kremlin from Khrushchev to Kosygin*. New York: Macmillan, 1969.

Ulam, Adam B. *Dangerous Relations: The Soviet Union in World Politics, 1970-1982*. New York: Oxford University Press, 1983.

Valenta, Jiri. *Soviet Intervention in Czechoslovakia, 1968*. Baltimore: Johns Hopkins University Press, 1979.

Yanov, Alexander. *Détente after Brezhnev: The Domestic Roots of Soviet Foreign Policy*. Berkeley: Institute of International Studies, University of California, 1977.

Zeman, Z. A. B. *Prague Spring: A Report on Czechoslovakia*. Baltimore: Penguin Books, 1969.

Articles

Arbatov, Georgii. "The Great Lie of the Opponents of Détente." *Pravda*, February 5, 1977.

Aspaturian, Vernon V. "The Aftermath of the Czech Invasion." *Current History* (November 1968): 263-267.

Blumenfeld, Yorick. "Russia's Diplomatic Offensive." *Editorial Research Reports*, April 5, 1972, 253-270.

Borisov, A. "A Chronicle of Soviet Foreign Policy." *Internation[al] Affairs* (January 1981): 88-92.

Campbell, John C. "Soviet-American Relati[ons ...] operation." *Current History* (Octo[ber ...])

Cohen, Stephen F. "The Friends and F[...] and Conservatism in the Soviet Union." *Slavic Review* (June 1979): 197-202.

Conquest, Robert. "The Limits of Détente." *Foreign Affairs* (Summer 1968): 733-742.

———. "A New Russia? A New World?" *Foreign Affairs* (Spring 1975): 482-497.

Costello, Mary. "Russia after Détente." *Editorial Research Reports*, February 6, 1981, 83-104.

Deans, Ralph C. "Trends in U.S.-Soviet Relations." *Editorial Research Reports*, May 25, 1973, 399-416.

Freedman, Robert O. "The Soviet Image of the Carter Administration's Policy toward the USSR: From the Inauguration to the Invasion of Afghanistan." *Korea and World Affairs* 4, no. 2 (Summer 1980): 224-267.

Gilison, Jerome M. "New Factors of Stability in Soviet Collective Leadership." *World Politics* (July 1967): 563-581.

Gitelman, Zvi. "The Politics of Socialist Restoration in Hungary and Czechoslovakia." *Comparative Politics* (January 1981): 187-210.

Gray, Colin. "The Most Dangerous Decade: Historic Mission, Legitimacy, and Dynamics of the Soviet Empire in the 1980s." *Orbis* (Spring 1981): 13-28.

Hopkins, Mark. "The Legacy of Leonid Brezhnev." *New Leader*, February 23, 1981, 5-8.

Hough, Jerry. "The Soviet Elite: In Whose Hands the Future?" *Problems of Communism* (March/April 1967): 18-25.

Laqueur, Walter. "Reagan and the Russians." *Commentary* (January 1982): 19-26.

Legvold, Robert. "The Nature of Soviet Power." *Foreign Affairs* (Fall 1977): 49-71.

Leonhard, Wolfgang. "The Domestic Politics of the New Soviet Foreign Policy." *Foreign Affairs* (Fall 1973): 59-74.

Liska, George. "Russia and the West: The Next to the Last Phase." *SAIS Review* (Summer 1981): 141-153.

Meissner, Boris. "The Soviet Union under Brezhnev and Kosygin." *Modern Age* (Winter 1966/1967): 7-23.

Nitze, Paul H. "Strategy in the Decade of the 1980s." *Foreign Affairs* (Fall 1980): 82-101.

Pennar, Jaan. "The Arabs, Marxism and Moscow: A Historical Survey." *Middle East Journal* (September 1968): 433-447.

Pick, Otto. "Reacting to Reagan: Soviet Fears and Opportunities." *World Today* (July/August 1981): 262-291.

Ploss, Sidney. "Politics in the Kremlin." *Problems of Communism* (May-June 1970): 1-14.

Salisbury, Harrison E. "Russia vs. China: Global Conflict?" *Antioch Review* (Winter 1967/1968): 425-439.

Schapiro, Leonard. "The CPSU International Department." *International Journal* (Winter 1966-1967): 41-55.

Shulman, Marshall D. "Toward a Western Philosophy of Coexistence." *Foreign Affairs* (Fall 1973): 35-58.

Sorensen, Theodore C. "Most-Favored-Nation and Less Favorite Nations." *Foreign Affairs* (Winter 1973-1974): 273-286.

Spechler, Dina Rome. "The USSR and Third World Conflicts: Domestic Debate and Soviet Policy in the Middle East, 1967-1973." *World Politics* (April 1986): 435-461.

Tucker, Robert C. "Swollen State, Spent Society: Stalin's Legacy to Brezhnev's Russia." *Foreign Affairs* (Winter 1981-1982): 414-435.

CHAPTER 5
Gorbachev Gains Power

Books

Beichman, Arnold, and M. S. Bernstam. *Andropov: New Challenge to the West.* New York: Stein & Day, 1983.

⸺, ⸺eryn. *The Soviet Paradox: External* ⸺⸺⸺⸺*ial* ⸺ York: A⸺⸺

⸺⸺⸺ons: Conflict and Co-⸺⸺ber 1967): 193-202.

⸺oes of Change: Reformism ⸺⸺⸺

Byrnes, R⸺⸺⸺⸺ *After Br⸺⸺⸺ ⸺ces of Soviet Conduct in the 1980s.* Bloomington: Indiana University Press and Georgetown University Center for Strategic and International Studies, 1983.

Dallin, Alexander, and CondoLeezza Rice, eds. *The Gorbachev Era.* Stanford, Calif.: Stanford University Press, 1986.

Doder, Dusko. *Shadows and Whispers: Power Politics inside the Kremlin from Brezhnev to Gorbachev.* New York: Random House, 1986.

Ebon, Martin. *The Andropov File.* New York: McGraw-Hill, 1983.

Gorbachev, Mikhail. *A Time for Peace.* New York: Richardson & Steirman, 1986.

Gunlicks, Arthur B., and John D. Treadway, eds. *Soviet Union under Gorbachev: Assessing the First Year.* New York: Praeger, 1987.

Hazan, Barukh. *From Brezhnev to Gorbachev: Infighting in the Kremlin.* Boulder, Colo.: Westview Press, 1987.

McCauley, Martin, ed. *The Soviet Union under Gorbachev.* New York: St. Martin's Press, 1987.

Medvedev, Zhores A. *Andropov.* New York: W. W. Norton, 1983.

⸺. *Gorbachev.* New York: W. W. Norton, 1986.

Solovyov, Vladimir, and Elena Klepikova. *Yuri Andropov: A Secret Passage into the Kremlin.* New York: Macmillan, 1983.

Zemtsov, Ilya. *Chernenko: The Last Bolshevik: The Soviet Union on the Eve of Perestroika.* New Brunswick, N.J.: Transaction, 1989.

Articles

Bialer, Seweryn, and Joan Afferica. "Gorbachev's World." *Foreign Affairs* (America and the World 1985): 605-644.

Bilinsky, Yaroslav. "Shcherbytskiy, Ukraine, and Kremlin Politics." *Problems of Communism* (July-August 1983): 1-20.

Brown, Archie. "Andropov: Discipline *and* Reform." *Problems of Communism* (January-February 1983): 18-31.

Caldwell, Lawrence, and Robert Legvold. "Reagan through Soviet Eyes." *Foreign Policy* (Fall 1983): 3-21.

Cooper, Mary H. "Gorbachev's Challenge." *Editorial Research Reports,* February 14, 1986, 107-124.

Epstein, Edward Jay. "The Andropov File." *New Republic,* February 7, 1983, 18-21.

Gati, Charles. "Soviet Empire: Alive But Not Well." *Problems of Communism* (March-April 1985): 73-86.

Gelb, Leslie H. "What We Really Know about Russia." *New York Times Magazine,* December 28, 1984, 22-25.

Griffiths, Franklyn. "The Sources of American Conduct: Soviet Perspectives and Their Policy Implications." *International Security* (Fall 1984): 3-50.

Gustafson, Thane, and Dawn Mann. "Gorbachev's First Year: Building Power and Authority." *Problems of Communism* (May-June 1986): 1-19.

Ploss, Sidney I. "A New Soviet Era?" *Foreign Policy* (Spring 1986): 46-60.

Rumor, Boris. "The Consequences of Chernobyl." *Problems of Communism* (November-December 1986): 1-58.

Simes, Dimitri. "America's New Edge." *Foreign Policy* (Fall 1984): 24-43.

⸺. "National Security under Andropov." *Problems of Communism* (January-February 1983): 32-39.

⸺. "The New Soviet Challenge." *Foreign Policy* (Summer 1984): 113-131.

Zagoria, Donald. "The Moscow-Beijing Détente." *Foreign Affairs* (Spring 1983): 853-873.

Zelnick, Robert C. "The Foundering Soviets." *Foreign Policy* (Winter 1984-1985): 92-107.

Zlotnik, Marc D. "Chernenko Succeeds." *Problems of Communism* (March-April 1984): 17-31.

CHAPTER 6
Land and State

Books

Baradat, Leon. *Soviet Political Society.* Englewood Cliffs, N.J.: Prentice Hall, 1989.

Black, Cyril. *Understanding Soviet Politics.* Boulder, Colo.: Westview Press, 1986.

Brown, Archie, ed. *Political Leadership in the Soviet Union.* Bloomington: Indiana University Press, 1990.

Conquest, Robert. *The Soviet Political System.* New York: Praeger Publishers, 1968.

Cracraft, James, ed. *The Soviet Union Today: An Interpretive Guide.* Chicago: University of Chicago Press, 1988.

Hazard, John N. *The Soviet System of Government.* Chicago: University of Chicago Press, 1968.

Hough, Jerry F., and Merle Fainsod. *How the Soviet Union Is Governed.* Cambridge, Mass.: Harvard University Press, 1979.

Hunt, R. N. Carew. *The Theory and Practice of Communism.* New York: Macmillan, 1957.

Miller, Wright. *Who Are the Russians? A History of the Russian People.* New York: Taplinger, 1973.

Potichnyj, Peter, ed. *The Soviet Union: Party and Society.* New York: Cambridge University Press, 1988.

Ra'anan, Uri, and Charles M. Perry, eds. *The USSR Today and Tomorrow.* Lexington, Mass.: Lexington Books, 1987.

Raymond, Ellsworth. *The Soviet State.* New York: Collier-Macmillan, 1968.

Salisbury, Harrison E., ed. *The Soviet Union: The Fifty Years.* New York: Harcourt, Brace & World, 1967.

Schapiro, Leonard. *The Communist Party of the Soviet Union.* Rev. ed. New York: Vintage Books, 1971.

Voslensky, Michael. *Nomenklatura.* New York: Doubleday, 1985.

Articles

Goldman, Stuart. "The New Soviet Legislative Branch." *CRS Review* (March-April 1990): 20-22.

Hahn, Jeffrey W. "Power to the Soviets?" *Problems of Communism* (January-February 1989): 34-46.

Levi, Arrigo. "The Evolution of the Soviet System." *Problems of Communism* (July/August 1967): 24-29.

Mote, Max E. "Electing the USSR Congress of People's Deputies." *Problems of Communism* (November-December 1989): 51-56.

CHAPTER 7
Reforming the Soviet System

Books

Clark, Susan L. *Gorbachev's Agenda.* Boulder, Colo.: Westview Press, 1989.

Colton, Timothy J. *The Dilemma of Reform in the Soviet Union.* New York: Council of Foreign Relations, 1986.

Davies, Robert Will. *Soviet History in the Gorbachev Revolution.* Basingstoke: Macmillan, 1989.

Desai, Padma. *Perestroika in Perspective: The Design and Dilemmas of Soviet Reform.* Princeton, N.J.: Princeton University Press, 1989.

Dizard, Wilson, and S. Blake Swensrud. *Gorbachev's Information Revolution: Controlling Glasnost in a New Electronic Age.* Boulder, Colo.: Westview Press, 1987.

Doder, Dusko, and Louise Branson. *Gorbachev: Heretic in the Kremlin.* New York: Viking Press, 1990.

Dyker, David A., ed. *The Soviet Union under Gorbachev: The Real Prospects for Reform.* London: Croom Helm, 1987.

Eklof, Ben. *Soviet Briefing: Gorbachev and the Reform Period.* Boulder, Colo.: Westview Press, 1989.

Goldman, Marshall I. *Gorbachev's Challenge: Economic Reform in the Age of High Technology.* New York: W. W. Norton, 1987.

Gorbachev, Mikhail S. *Perestroika: New Thinking for Our Country and the World.* New York: Harper & Row, 1987.

Hough, Jerry F. *Russia and the West: Gorbachev and the Politics of Reform.* New York: Simon and Schuster, 1988.

Kerblay, Basile H. *Gorbachev's Russia.* New York: Pantheon Books, 1989.

Laqueur, Walter. *The Long Road to Freedom: Russia and Glasnost.* London: Unwin Hyman, 1989.

Lerner, Lawrence, and Donald Treadgold, eds. *Gorbachev and the Soviet Future.* Boulder, Colo.: Westview Press, 1988.

Linz, Susan, and William Moskoff, eds. *Reorganization and Reform in the Soviet Economy.* Armonk: M. E. Sharpe, 1988.

Miller, Robert F., John H. Miller, and Thomas H. Rigby, eds. *Gorbachev at the Helm: A New Era in Soviet Politics?* London: Croom Helm, 1987.

Miller, William Green, ed. *Toward a More Civil Society?: The USSR under Mikhail Sergeyevich Gorbachev.* New York: Harper & Row, 1989.

Niiseki, Kinya, ed. *The Soviet Union in Transition.* Boulder, Colo.: Westview Press, 1987.

Novak, Michael. *Taking Glasnost Seriously: Toward an Open Soviet Union.* Washington, D.C.: American Enterprise Institute for Public Policy Research, 1988.

Shlapentokh, Vladimir. *Soviet Ideologies in the Period of Glasnost: Responses to Brezhnev's Stagnation.* New York: Praeger, 1988.

Smith, Gordon B. *Soviet Politics: Continuity and Contradiction.* New York: St. Martin's Press, 1988.

Tarasulo, Isaac J., ed. *Gorbachev and Glasnost: Viewpoints from the Soviet Press.* Wilmington, Del.: Scholarly Resources, 1989.

Taubman, William, and Jane Taubman. *Moscow Spring.* New York: Summit Books, 1989.

Woodby, Sylvia. *Gorbachev and the Decline of Ideology.* Boulder, Colo.: Westview Press, 1989.

Zemstov, Ilya, and John Farrar. *Gorbachev: The Man and the System.* New Brunswick, N.J.: Transaction, 1989.

Articles

Bialer, Seweryn. "Gorbachev's Move." *Foreign Policy* (Fall 1987): 59-87.

Brown, Archie. "Change in the Soviet Union." *Foreign Affairs* (Summer 1986): 1048-1065.

Brudny, Yitzhak M. "The Heralds of Opposition to Perestroyka." *Soviet Economy* (April-June 1989): 162.

Connor, Walter D. "Social Policy under Gorbachev." *Problems of Communism* (July-August 1986): 31-46.

Green, William C. "Are There 'Hawks' and 'Doves' in the Soviet Leadership?" *Strategic Review* (Winter 1987): 31-42.

Hahn, Werner. "Electoral Choice in the Soviet Bloc." *Problems of Communism* (March-April 1987): 29-39.

Houslohner, Peter. "Gorbachev's Social Contract." *Soviet Economy* (January-March 1987): 54-89.

Katsenelinboigen, Aron. "Will Glasnost Bring the Reactionaries to Power?" *Orbis* (Spring 1987): 217-230.

Latey, Maurice. "The General Crisis of Socialism." *World Today* (August-September 1989): 131-134.

Lih, Lars T. "Gorbachev and the Reform Movement." *Current History* (October 1987): 309-312.

Lyne, Roderic. "Making Waves: Mr. Gorbachev's Public Policy, 1985-1986." *International Affairs* (Spring 1987): 205-224.

Powell, David E. "Soviet Glasnost: Definitions and Dimensions." *Current History* (October 1988): 321-324.

Ruble, Blair A. "The Social Dimensions of Perestroyka." *Soviet Economy* (April-June 1987): 171-183.

Sherlock, Thomas. "Politics and History under Gorbachev." *Problems of Communism* (May-August 1988): 16-42.

Tatu, Michael. "Nineteenth Party Conference." *Problems of Communism* (May-August 1988): 1-15.

Thornburgh, Richard. "The Soviet Union and the Rule of Law." *Foreign Affairs* (Spring 1990): 13-27.

CHAPTER 8
The Soviet Economy

Books

Aslund, Anders. *Gorbachev's Struggle for Economic Reform: The Soviet Reform Process.* Ithaca, N.Y.: Cornell University Press, 1989.

Becker, Abraham Samuel. *Soviet Central Decision Making and Economic Growth.* Santa Monica, Calif.: The Rand Corporation, 1986.

———. *Gorbachev's Program for Economic Modernization and Reform.* Santa Monica, Calif.: The Rand Corporation, 1987.

Berliner, Joseph. *Soviet Industry from Stalin to Gorbachev.* Ithaca, N.Y.: Cornell University Press, 1988.

Bornstein, Morris. *The Soviet Economy: Continuity and Change.* Boulder, Colo.: Westview Press, 1981.

Caldwell, Lawrence T., and William Diebold. *Soviet-American Relations in the 1980s: Superpower Politics and East-West Trade.* New York: McGraw-Hill, 1981.

Chadwick, Margaret. *Soviet Oil Exports.* Oxford, England: Oxford University Press, 1987.

Davies, Robert W. *The Soviet Economy in Turmoil.* Cambridge, Mass.: Harvard University Press, 1989.

Desai, Padma. *The Soviet Economy: Problems and Prospects.* Oxford, England: Blackwell, 1987.

Dienes, Leslie. *Soviet Asia, Economic Development and National Policy Choices.* Boulder, Colo.: Westview Press, 1987.

Guidelines for the Economic and Social Development of the USSR for 1986-1990 and for the Period Ending in 2000. Moscow: Novosti Press Agency, 1985.

Hahn, Werner G. *The Politics of Soviet Agriculture, 1960-1970.* Baltimore: Johns Hopkins University Press, 1972.

Hewett, Ed A. *Energy, Economics, and Foreign Policy in the*

Soviet Union. Washington, D.C.: Brookings Institution, 1984.
———. *Reforming the Soviet Economy.* Washington, D.C.: Brookings Institution, 1988.

Hough, Jerry F. *Opening Up the Soviet Economy.* Washington, D.C.: Brookings Institution, 1988.

Ioffe, Olimpiad. *Gorbachev's Economic Dilemma: An Insider's View.* St. Paul: Merrill/Mangus, 1989.

Johnson, D. Gale, and Karen McConnell Brooks. *Prospects for Soviet Agriculture in the 1980s.* Bloomington: Indiana University Press, 1983.

Kanet, Roger, and Donna Bahry, eds. *Soviet Economic and Political Relations with the Developing World.* New York: Praeger Publishers, 1975.

Liebowitz, Ronald D., ed. *Gorbachev's New Thinking: Prospects for Joint Ventures.* Cambridge, Mass.: Ballinger Publishers, 1988.

Parrott, Bruce, ed. *Trade, Technology and Soviet-American Relations.* Bloomington: Indiana University Press and Georgetown University Center for Strategic and International Studies, 1985.

Sokoloff, Georges. *The Economy of Détente.* New York: St. Martin's Press, 1987.

Articles

Aganbegyan, Abel G. "Basic Directions of Perestroyka." *Soviet Economy* (October-December 1987): 277-297.

Aslund, Anders. "Gorbachev's Economic Advisors." *Soviet Economy* (July-September 1987): 246-269.

Bond, Daniel. "Impact on Soviet Trade of a Sharp Decline in Oil Prices." Vol. 5, no. 79-80. Washington, D.C.: Wharton Econometrics Centrally Planned Economies Current Analysis, October 29, 1985.

Chapman, Janet G. "Gorbachev's Wage Reform." *Soviet Economy* (October-December 1988): 338-365.

Colton, Timothy J. "Approaches to the Politics of Systematic Reform in the Soviet Union." *Soviet Economy* (April-June 1987): 145-170.

Cooper, Mary H. "Communist Reformers Look West." *Editorial Research Reports,* March 4, 1988, 110-123.

Costello, Mary. "Soviet Economic Dilemma." *Editorial Research Reports,* February 19, 1982, 127-146.

Goldman, Marshall I. "Gorbachev the Economist." *Foreign Affairs* (Spring 1990): 28-44.

——— and Merle Goldman. "Soviet and Chinese Economic Reform." *Foreign Affairs,* no. 3 (1988): 551-573.

Gregory, Paul R., and Irwin L. Collier, Jr. "Unemployment in the Soviet Union: Evidence from the Soviet Interview Project." *American Economic Review* (September 1988): 613-632.

Hewett, Ed A. "Perestroyka and the Congress of People's Deputies." *Soviet Economy* (January-March 1989): 47-69.

Hough, Jerry F. "The Politics of Successful Economic Reform." *Soviet Economy* (January-March 1989): 3-46.

Kaser, Michael. "One Economy, Two Systems: Parallels Between Soviet and Chinese Reform." *International Affairs* (Summer 1987): 395-412.

Kostakov, Vladimir G. "Labor Problems in Light of Perestroyka." *Soviet Economy* (January-March 1988): 95-101.

Lavoie, Louis. "The Limits of Soviet Technology." *Technology Review* (November-December 1985): 69-75.

Nove, Alec. "A Review of Soviet Economic Progress." *National Institute Economic Review* (November 1959): 37-47.

Ofer, Gur. "Budget Deficit, Market Disequilibrium and Soviet Economic Reforms." *Soviet Economy* (April-June 1989): 107-161.

Roucek, Libor. "Private Enterprise in Soviet Political Debates." *Soviet Studies* (January 1988): 46-63.

Rumor, Boris. "Realities of Gorbachev's Economic Program." *Problems of Communism* (May-June 1986): 20-31.

Schroeder, Gertrude E. "Soviet Economic Reforms: A Study in Contradictions." *Soviet Studies* (July 1988): 1-21.

Schwartz, Charles A. "Economic Crime in the USSR: A Comparison of the Khrushchev and Brezhnev Eras." *International Comparative Law Quarterly* (April 1981): 281-296.

Staar, Richard F. "The High-Tech Transfer Offensive of the Soviet Union." *Strategic Review* (Spring 1989): 32-39.

Toumanoff, Peter. "Economic Reform and Industrial Performance in the Soviet Union: 1954-1984." *Comparative Economic Studies* (Winter 1987): 128-149.

Treml, Vladimir G. "Perestroyka and Soviet Statistics." *Soviet Economy* (January-March 1988): 65-94.

U.S. Department of Commerce. "Foreign Economic Trends and Their Implications for the United States." International Marketing Information Series, USSR. Washington, D.C.: Government Printing Office, December 1985.

CHAPTER 9
Ethnicity and Society

Books

Alexeyeva, Ludmilla. *Soviet Dissent.* Middletown, Conn.: Wesleyan University Press, 1985.

Alliluyeva, Svetlana. *Only One Year.* New York: Harper & Row, 1969.

———. *Twenty Letters to a Friend.* New York: Harper & Row, 1967.

Allworth, Edward, ed. *Central Asia: 120 Years of Russian Rule.* Durham, N.C.: Duke University Press, 1989.

Amalrik, Andrei. *Will the Soviet Union Survive until 1984?* New York: Harper & Row, 1970.

Bialer, Seweryn, ed. *Politics, Society and Nationality inside Gorbachev's Russia.* Boulder, Colo.: Westview Press, 1989.

Brown, Clarence, ed. *The Portable Twentieth-Century Russian Reader.* New York: Viking/Penguin, 1985.

Churchward, L. G. *The Soviet Intelligentsia: An Essay on the Social Structure and Roles of Soviet Intellectuals during the 1960s.* Boston: Routledge & Kegan Paul, 1973.

Conquest, Robert, ed. *The Last Empire: Nationality and the Soviet Future.* Stanford, Calif.: Hoover Institution Press, 1986.

Hubbs, Joanna. *Mother Russia: The Feminine Myth in Russian Culture.* Bloomington: Indiana University Press, 1988.

Kaiser, Robert G. *Russia: The People and Power.* New York: Washington Square Press, 1984.

Karklins, Rasma. *Ethnic Relations in the USSR: The Perspective from Below.* Boston: Allen & Unwin, 1986.

Kozlov, Viktor I. *The Peoples of the Soviet Union.* Bloomington: Indiana University Press, 1988.

Lebov, Oleg, and John Crowfoot, eds. *The Soviet Empire: Its Nations Speak Out.* New York: Harwood, 1989.

Lowe, David. *Russian Writing since 1953: A Critical Survey.* New York: Ungar, 1987.

Medvedev, Zhores A. *Ten Years after Ivan Denisovich.* New York: Vintage, 1974.

Motyl, Alexander J. *Will the Non-Russians Rebel?* Ithaca, N.Y.: Cornell University Press, 1987.

Newberg, Paula R., ed. *The Politics of Human Rights.* New York: New York University Press, 1980.

Pankhurst, Jerry G., and Michael Paul Sacks. *Contemporary Soviet Society: Sociological Perspectives.* New York: Praeger Publishers, 1980.

Pushkarev, Sergei, Vladimir Rusak, and Gleb Yakunin. *Christianity and Government in Russia and the Soviet Union.* Boulder, Colo.: Westview Press, 1989.

Riordan, Jim, ed. *Soviet Youth Culture.* Bloomington: Indiana University Press, 1989.

Rumer, Boris Z. *Soviet Central Asia: "A Tragic Experiment."* Boston: Unwin Hyman, 1989.

Sacks, Michael Paul, and Jerry G. Pankhurst, eds. *Understanding Soviet Society.* Boston: Allen & Unwin, 1988.

Sakharov, Andrei. *Memoirs.* Translated by Richard Lourie. New York: A. A. Knopf, 1990.

Shlapentokh, Vladimir. *Public and Private Life of the Soviet People: Changing Values in Post-Stalin Russia.* New York:

Oxford University Press, 1989.

Simis, Konstantin M. *USSR: The Corrupt Society (The Secret World of Soviet Capitalism)*. New York: Simon and Schuster, 1982.

Steeves, Paul. *Keeping the Faiths: Religion and Ideology in the Soviet Union*. New York: Holmes and Meier, 1989.

Swearingen, Rodger, ed. *Siberia and the Soviet Far East*. Stanford, Calif.: Hoover Institution Press, 1987.

Taheri, Amir. *Crescent in a Red Sky: The Future of Islam in the Soviet Union*. London: Hutchinson, 1989.

Thompson, Terry L., and R. Sheldon, eds. *Soviet Society and Culture: Essays in Honor of Vera S. Dunham*. Boulder, Colo.: Westview Press, 1988.

Tökes, Rudolph L., ed. *Dissent in the USSR: Politics, Ideology and People*. Baltimore: Johns Hopkins University Press, 1975.

Vucinich, Alexander. *Science in Russian Culture, 1867-1917*. Stanford, Calif.: Stanford University Press, 1970.

Westwood, J. N. *Endurance and Endeavor: Russian History 1812-1980*. New York: Oxford University Press, 1981.

Willis, David K. *Klass: How Russians Really Live*. New York: St. Martin's Press, 1985.

Articles

Bilinsky, Yaroslav. "Nationality Policy in Gorbachev's First Year." *Orbis* (Summer 1986): 331-342.

Blumenfeld, Yorick. "Dissent in Russia." *Editorial Research Reports*, June 28, 1972, 481-498.

Brzezinski, Zbigniew. "Post-Communist Nationalism." *Foreign Affairs* (Winter 1989-1990): 1-25.

Cockburn, Patrick. "Dateline USSR: Ethnic Tremors." *Foreign Policy* (Spring 1989): 168-184.

Cullen, Robert B. "Soviet Jewry." *Foreign Affairs* (Winter 1986-1987): 252-266.

Dunlop, John B. "Soviet Cultural Politics." *Problems of Communism* (November-December 1987): 34-56.

Gitelman, Zvi. "Moscow and the Soviet Jews: A Parting of the Ways." *Problems of Communism* (January-February 1980): 18-34.

Hajda, Lubomyr. "The Nationalities Problem in the Soviet Union." *Current History* (October 1988): 325-328.

Hochman, Jiri. "The Soviet Historical Debate." *Orbis* (Summer 1988): 369-384.

Kramer, John M. "Drug Abuse in the Soviet Union." *Problems of Communism* (March-April 1988): 28-40.

Lapidus, Gail W. "Gorbachev's Nationalities Problem." *Foreign Affairs* (Fall 1989): 92-108.

Szporluk, Roman. "Dilemmas of Russian Nationalism." *Problems of Communism* (July-August 1989): 15-35.

Vardys, V. Stanley. "Lithuanian National Politics." *Problems of Communism* (July-August 1989): 53-76.

Wall, Josephine. "Glasnost and Soviet Culture." *Problems of Communism* (November-December 1989): 40-50.

CHAPTER 10
Soviet Foreign Policy

Books

Bradsher, Henry S. *Afghanistan and the Soviet Union*. 2d ed. Durham, N.C.: Duke University Press, 1983.

Breslauer, George W. *Soviet Strategy in the Middle East*. Boston: Unwin Hyman, 1990.

Campbell, Kurk M., and S. Neil Macfarlane. *Gorbachev's Third World Dilemmas*. New York: Routledge, 1989.

Clark, Susan L., ed. *Gorbachev's Agenda: Changes in Soviet Domestic and Foreign Policy*. Boulder, Colo.: Westview Press, 1989.

Clemens, Walter C. *Can Russia Change? The USSR Confronts Global Interdependence*. Boston: Unwin Hyman, 1990.

Congressional Research Service. *The Soviet Union in the Third World, 1980-1985: An Imperial Burden or Political Asset?* Report prepared for the Committee on Foreign Affairs of the U.S. House of Representatives, September 23, 1985.

Connor, Walter D. *Socialism's Dilemmas: State and Society in the Soviet Bloc*. New York: Columbia University Press, 1988.

Dawisha, Adeed, and Karen Dawisha. *The Soviet Union in the Middle East: Perspectives and Policies*. New York: Holmes & Meier, 1982.

Donaldson, Robert, ed. *The Soviet Union in the Third World*. Boulder, Colo.: Westview Press, 1981.

Duncan, Raymond W., ed. *Soviet Policy in the Third World*. Elmsford, N.Y.: Pergamon, 1980.

Edmonds, Robin. *Soviet Foreign Policy: The Brezhnev Years*. New York: Oxford University Press, 1983.

Eusebio, Mujal-Leon. *The USSR and Latin America: A Developing Relationship*. Boston: Unwin Hyman, 1989.

Freedman, Robert O. *Soviet Policy toward the Middle East since 1970*. 3d ed. New York: Praeger Publishers, 1982.

Fukuyama, Francis. *The Tenth Period of Soviet Third World Activity*. Santa Monica, Calif.: The Rand Corporation, 1987.

Gelman, Harry. *Gorbachev's Policies toward Western Europe: A Balance Sheet*. Santa Monica, Calif.: The Rand Corporation, 1987.

Golan, Galia. *The Soviet Union and the National Liberation Movements in the Third World*. Boston: Allen & Unwin, 1988.

Hammond, Thomas T. *Red Flag over Afghanistan: The Communist Coup, the Soviet Invasion, and the Consequences*. Boulder, Colo.: Westview Press, 1984.

Haslam, Jonathan. *The Soviet Union and the Politics of Nuclear Weapons in Europe, 1969-1987*. Basingstoke: Macmillan, 1989.

Hoffman, Fred, Albert Wohlstetter, and David Yost. *Swords and Sheilds*. Lexington, Mass.: Lexington Books, 1987.

Hoffmann, Erik P., and Frederick Fleron, eds. *The Conduct of Soviet Foreign Policy*. Hawthorne, N.Y.: Aldine, 1980.

Holden, Gerard. *The Warsaw Pact: Soviet Security Policy and Bloc Politics*. New York: Blackwell, 1989.

Horak, Stephan. *Russia, the USSR, and Eastern Europe*. Littleton: Libraries Unlimited, 1987.

Hough, Jerry. *The Struggle for the Third World: Soviet Debates and American Options*. Washington, D.C.: Brookings Institution, 1985.

Jacobsen, Carl G., ed. *Soviet Foreign Policy: New Dynamics, New Themes*. New York: St. Martin's Press, 1989.

Johnson, A. Ross. *The Impact of Eastern Europe on Soviet Policy toward Western Europe*. Santa Monica, Calif.: The Rand Corporation, 1986.

Klinghoffer, Arthur J. *The Angolan War: A Study in Soviet Foreign Policy in the Third World*. Boulder, Colo.: Westview Press, 1980.

Kolodziej, Edward A., and Roger E. Kanet, eds. *Limits of Soviet Power in the Developing World*. Baltimore: Johns Hopkins University Press, 1989.

Korbonski, Andrzej, and Francis Fukuyama, eds. *The Soviet Union and the Third World: The Last Three Decades*. Ithaca, N.Y.: Cornell University Press, 1987.

Laird, Robbin F., and Susan L. Clark. *The USSR and the Western Alliance*. Boston: Unwin Hyman, 1990.

Leiken, Robert, ed., *Central America: Anatomy of Conflict*. Elmsford, N.Y.: Pergamon, 1984.

Low, Alfred D. *The Sino-Soviet Confrontation since Mao Zedong*. Boulder, Colo.: Westview Press, 1987.

Lynch, Allen. *Gorbachev's International Outlook*. Boulder, Colo.: Westview Press, 1989.

Menon, Rajan, and Daniel N. Nelson. *Limits to Soviet Power*. Lexington, Mass.: Lexington Books, 1989.

Miller, Nicola. *Soviet Relations with Latin America, 1959-1987*. New York: Cambridge University Press, 1989

Nogee, Joseph L., and Robert H. Donaldson. *Soviet Foreign Policy since World War II*. 2d ed. Elmsford, N.Y.: Pergamon, 1984.

Porter, Bruce D. *The USSR in Third World Conflicts*. New York: Cambridge University Press, 1984.

Robertson, Myles. *Soviet Policy toward Japan*. New York: Cambridge University Press, 1988.

Rotberg, Robert I., Henry S. Bienen, Robert Legvold, and Gavin G. Maasdorp. *South Africa and Its Neighbors.* Lexington, Mass.: Lexington Books, 1985.

Robertson, Myles. *Soviet Policy toward Japan.* New York: Cambridge University Press, 1988.

Rubinstein, Alvin Z. *Moscow's Third World Strategy.* Princeton, N.J.: Princeton University Press, 1988.

Saivetz, Carol R., ed. *The Soviet Union in the Third World.* Boulder, Colo.: Westview Press, 1989.

Staar, Richard F. *USSR Foreign Policies after Détente.* Stanford, Calif.: Hoover Institution Press, 1987.

Thambipillai, Pushpa, and Daniel T. Matuszewski, eds. *The Soviet Union and the Asia Pacific Region.* New York: Praeger, 1989.

Timmermann, Heinz. *The Decline of the World Communist Movement.* Boulder, Colo.: Westview Press, 1987.

Ulam, Adam B. *Expansion and Coexistence: Soviet Foreign Policy, 1917-73.* 2d ed. New York: Praeger Publishers, 1974.

Zacec, Jane Shapiro, ed. *The Gorbachev Generation: Issues in Soviet Foreign Policy.* New York: Paragon House, 1988.

Zagoria, Donald S., ed. *Soviet Policy in East Asia.* New Haven, Conn.: Yale University Press, 1982.

Articles

Acharya, Amitav. "The Asia Pacific Region: Cockpit for Superpower Rivalry." *World Today* (August-September 1987): 155-158.

Anderson, Richard D., Jr. "Soviet Decisionmaking and Poland." *Problems of Communism* (March-April 1982): 22-36.

Banjaree, Jyotirmoy. "Moscow's Indian Alliance." *Problems of Communism* (January-February 1987): 1-12.

Clement, Peter. "Moscow and Southern Africa." *Problems of Communism* (March-April 1985): 29-50.

Dawisha, Karen, and Jonathan Valdez. "Socialist Internationalism in Eastern Europe." *Problems of Communism* (March-April 1987): 1-14.

Fukuyama, Francis. "Gorbachev and the Third World." *Foreign Affairs* (Spring 1986): 715-731.

Gati, Charles. "Gorbachev and Eastern Europe." *Foreign Affairs* (Summer 1987): 958-975.

Gawad, Atef A. "Moscow's Arms-for-Oil Diplomacy." *Foreign Policy* (Summer 1986): 147-168.

Golan, Galia. "Moscow and the Third World National Liberation Movements: The Soviet Role." *Journal of International Affairs* (Spring 1987): 303-323.

Goldstein, Steven M. "Diplomacy amid Protest: The Sino-Soviet Summit." *Problems of Communism* (September-October 1989): 49-71.

Goodman, Melvin A., and Carolyn McGiffert Ekedahl. "Gorbachev's 'New Directions' in the Middle East." *Middle East Journal* (Autumn 1988): 571-586.

Hamilton, Daniel. "Dateline East Germany: The Wall Behind the Wall." *Foreign Policy* (Fall 1989): 176-197.

Haslam, Jonathan. "The UN and the Soviet Union: New Thinking." *International Affairs* (Autumn 1989): 677-684.

Hauner, Milan. "Soviet Eurasian Empire and the Indo-Persian Corridor." *Problems of Communism* (January-February 1987): 25-35.

Howe, Sir Geoffrey. "Soviet Foreign Policy under Gorbachev." *World Today* (March 1989): 40-45.

Keegan, John. "The Ordeal of Afghanistan." *Atlantic Monthly,* November 1985, 94-105.

Kramer, Mark N. "Soviet Arms Transfers to the Third World." *Problems of Communism* (September-October 1987): 52-68.

Kull, Steven. "Burying Lenin." *Foreign Policy* (Spring 1990): 172-191.

Legvold, Robert. "The Super Rivals: Conflict in the Third World." *Foreign Affairs* 57 (Spring 1979): 755-778.

Leiken, Robert. "Fantasies and Facts: The Soviet Union and Nicaragua." *Current History* 83 (October 1984): 314-317+.

Luard, Evan. "Superpowers and Regional Conflicts." *Foreign Af-*

fairs (Summer 1986): 1006-1025.

Macfarlane, S. Neil. "The Soviet Union and Southern African Security." *Problems of Communism* (March-June 1989): 71-89.

Menon, Rajan. "New Thinking and Northeast Asian Security." *Problems of Communism* (March-June 1989): 1-29.

———. "Soviet Arms Transfers to the Third World: Characteristics and Consequences." *Journal of International Affairs* (Summer 1986): 59-76.

Schopflin, George. "Why Communism Collapsed." *International Affairs* (January 1990): 3-16.

Schroeder, Richard C. "Soviets' Latin Influence." *Editorial Research Reports,* March 6, 1987, 102-111.

Segal, Gerald. "Sino-Soviet Détente: How Far, How Fast?" *World Today* (May 1987): 87-91.

———. "Sino-Soviet Relations: The New Agenda." *World Today* (June 1988): 95-99.

Sestanovich, Stephen. "Gorbachev's Foreign Policy: A Diplomacy of Decline." *Problems of Communism* (January-February 1988): 1-15.

Strmecki, Marin. "Gorbachev's New Strategy in Afghanistan." *Strategic Review* (Summer 1987): 31-42.

Szaikowski, Bogdan. "Ethiopia: A Weakening Soviet Connection?" *World Today* (August-September 1989): 153-156

Szayna, Thomas S. "Addressing 'Blank Spots' in Polish-Soviet Relations." *Problems of Communism* (November-December 1988): 37-61.

Valenta, Jiri. "From Prague to Kabul: The Soviet Style of Invasion." *International Security* (Fall 1980): 114-141.

Wettig, Gerhard. "New Thinking on Security and East-West Relations." *Problems of Communism* (March-April 1988): 1-14.

CHAPTER 11
The Role of the Military

Books

Alexis, Alexander R., and S. Enders Wimbush, eds. *Ethnic Minorities in the Red Army: Asset or Liability?* Boulder, Colo.: Westview Press, 1988.

Azrael, Jeremy. *The Soviet Civilian Leadership and the Military High Command, 1976-1986.* Santa Monica, Calif.: The Rand Corporation, 1987.

Bertram, Christopher. *Prospects of Soviet Power in the 1980s.* Hamden, Conn.: Archon Books, 1980.

Burt, Richard, ed. *Arms Control and Defense Postures in the 1980s.* Boulder, Colo.: Westview Press, 1981.

Cockburn, Andrew. *The Threat: Inside the Soviet Military Machine.* New York: Random House, 1983.

Colton, Timothy J. *Commissars, Commanders, and Civilian Authority: Structure of Soviet Military Politics.* Cambridge, Mass.: Harvard University Press, 1979.

Cooper, Leo. *The Political Economy of Soviet Military Power.* Basingstoke: Macmillan, 1989.

Erikson, John, Lynn Hansen, and William Schneider. *Soviet Ground Forces: An Operational Assessment.* London: Croom Helm, 1986.

Garthoff, Raymond L. *Soviet Military Policy: A Historical Analysis.* New York: Praeger Publishers, 1966.

Gelman, Harry. *The Soviet Far East Buildup and Soviet Risk-Taking against China.* Santa Monica, Calif.: The Rand Corporation, 1982.

Hansen, James H. *Correlation of Forces: Four Decades of Soviet Military Development.* New York: Praeger, 1987.

Jones, Ellen. *Red Army and Society: A Sociology of the Soviet Military.* Winchester, Mass.: Allen & Unwin, 1985.

Kaplan, Stephen S. *Diplomacy of Power: Soviet Armed Forces as a Political Instrument.* 2d ed. Washington, D.C.: Brookings Institution, 1985.

Katz, Mark N. *Gorbachev's Military Policy in the Third World.* New York: Praeger, 1989.

Leebaert, Derek, ed. *Soviet Military Thinking*. London: Allen & Unwin, 1981.

Lynn-Jones, Sean M., Steven E. Miller, and Stephen Van Evra, eds. *Soviet Military Policy: An International Security Reader*. Cambridge, Mass.: Massachusetts Institute of Technology Press, 1989.

Parrott, Bruce. *The Soviet Union and Ballistic Missile Defense*. Boulder, Colo.: Westview Press, 1987.

Record, Jeffrey. *Sizing Up the Russian Army*. Washington, D.C.: Brookings Institution, 1975.

Richelson, Jeffrey T. *Sword and Shield: Soviet Intelligence and Security Apparatus*. Cambridge, Mass.: Ballinger, 1986.

Scott, Harriet Fast, and William F. Scott. *The Armed Forces of the USSR*. 3d ed. Boulder, Colo.: Westview Press, 1984.

Suvorov, Victor. *Spetsnaz: The Story behind the Soviet SAS*. London: Hamish Hamilton, 1987.

U.S. Department of Defense. *Soviet Military Power 1989*. Washington, D.C.: Government Printing Office, 1989.

Valenta, Jiri, and William C. Potter, eds. *Soviet Decisionmaking for National Security*. London: Allen & Unwin, 1985.

Warner, Edward, Josephine Bonan, and Erma Packman. *Key Personnel and Organizations of the Soviet Military High Command*. Santa Monica, Calif.: The Rand Corporation, 1987.

Zamascikov, Sergei. *Gorbachev and the Soviet Military*. Santa Monica, Calif.: The Rand Corporation, 1988.

Articles

Campbell, Kurt M. "The Soldiers' Summit." *Foreign Policy* (Summer 1989): 76-91.

Checinski, Michael. "Warsaw Pact-CMEA Military Economic Trends." *Problems of Communism* (March-April 1987): 15-28.

Dean, Jonathan. "Military Security in Europe." *Foreign Affairs* (Fall 1987): 22-40.

Garthoff, Raymond L. "Estimating Soviet Military Force Levels: Some Light from the Past." *International Security* (Spring 1990): 93-116.

Goure, Daniel. "A New Soviet National Security Policy for the Twenty-first Century." *Strategic Review* (Fall 1989): 36-46.

Kaufman, Richard F. "Causes of the Slowdown in Soviet Defense." *Soviet Economy* (January-March 1985): 9-41.

Kolkowicz, Roman. "U.S. and Soviet Approaches to Military Strategy: Theory vs. Experience." *Orbis* (Summer 1981): 307-329.

Larrabee, F. Stephen. "Gorbachev and the Soviet Military." *Foreign Affairs* (Summer 1986): 1002-1026.

McConnell, James M. "SDI, the Soviet Investment Debate and Soviet Military Policy." *Strategic Review* (Winter 1988): 47-62.

Parrott, Bruce. "Soviet National Security under Gorbachev." *Problems of Communism* (November-December 1988): 1-36.

Soll, Richard S. "The Soviet Union and Protracted Nuclear War." *Strategic Review* (Fall 1980): 15-28.

Suvorov, Viktor. "Spetsnaz: The Soviet Union's Special Forces." *Military Review* (March 1984): 30-46.

Weickhardt, George G. "The Soviet Military Industrial Complex and Economic Reform." *Soviet Economy* (July-September 1986): 193-227.

CHAPTER 12
U.S.-Soviet Relations

Books

Allison, Graham T., William L. Ury, and Bruce Allyn, eds. *Windows of Opportunity*. Cambridge, Mass.: Ballinger Publishing Company, 1989.

Barkenbus, Jack N. *U.S.-Soviet Relations: An Agenda for the Future*. Baltimore: Johns Hopkins University Press, 1988.

Barnet, Richard J. *The Giants: Russia and America*. New York: Simon and Schuster, 1977.

Bialer, Seweryn, and Michael Mandelbaum. *Global Rivals*. New York: A. A. Knopf, 1988.

——, eds. *Gorbachev's Russia and American Foreign Policy*. Boulder, Colo.: Westview Press, 1988.

Blacker, Coit D. *Reluctant Warriors: The U.S. and the Soviet Union and Arms Control*. New York: W. H. Freeman, 1987.

Browder, Robert P. *The Origins of the Soviet-American Diplomacy*. Princeton, N.J.: Princeton University Press, 1953.

Brzezinski, Zbigniew. *Game Plan: The Geostrategic Framework for the Conduct of the U.S.-Soviet Contest*. Boston: Atlantic Monthly Press, 1986.

Carvounis, Chris, and Brinda Z. Carvounis. *U.S. Commercial Opportunities in the Soviet Union*. New York: Quorum Books, 1989.

Freedman, Robert Owen. *The Soviet Union and the Carter Administration*. Pittsburgh: University of Pittsburgh Press, 1989.

Gaddis, John Lewis. *Long Peace: Inquiries into the History of the Cold War*. New York: Oxford University Press, 1987.

Galbraith, John Kenneth, and Stanislav Menshikov. *Capitalism, Communism, and Coexistence: From the Bitter Past to the Better Prospect*. Boston: Houghton Mifflin, 1988.

Garthoff, Raymond. *Détente and Confrontation: American-Soviet Relations from Nixon to Reagan*. Washington, D.C.: Brookings Institution, 1985.

George, Alexander L., Philip Farley, and Alexander Dallin, eds. *U.S.-Soviet Security Cooperation*. New York: Oxford University Press, 1988.

Gordon, Lincoln. *Integrating Economic and Security Factors in East-West Relations*. Washington, D.C.: Atlantic Council, 1988.

Greenwald, G. Jonathan, and Leonard Sullivan. *The Western Stake in the Future of the Soviet Economy*. Washington, D.C.: Atlantic Council, 1987.

Griffith, William E. *The Super Powers and Regional Tensions: The USSR and the U.S. and Europe*. Lexington, Mass.: Lexington Books, 1981.

Harriman, William Averell. *America and Russia in a Changing World: A Half Century of Personal Observation*. Garden City, N.Y.: Doubleday, 1971.

Horelick, Arnold Lawrence. *U.S.-Soviet Relations: The Next Phase*. Ithaca, N.Y.: Cornell University Press, 1986.

Hyland, William G. *Mortal Rivals: Superpower Relations from Nixon to Reagan*. New York: Random House, 1987.

Kalb, Marvin, and Bernard Kalb. *Kissinger*. Boston: Little, Brown, 1974.

Kissinger, Henry. *White House Years*. Boston: Little, Brown, 1979.

Legvold, Robert. *Gorbachev's Foreign Policy: How Should The U.S. Respond?* New York: Foreign Policy Association, 1988.

Libbey, James K. *American-Russian Economic Relations*. Claremont, Calif.: Regina Books, 1989.

Litwak, Robert, and Samuel Wells, eds. *Superpower Competition and Security in the Third World*. Cambridge, Mass.: Ballinger Publishing Company, 1988.

Mandelbaum, Michael, and Strobe Talbott. *Reagan and Gorbachev*. New York: Vintage Books, 1987.

McNamara, Robert S. *Out of the Cold*. New York: Simon and Schuster, 1989.

Payne, Samuel B. *The Soviet Union and SALT*. Cambridge, Mass.: MIT Press, 1980.

Potter, William C., ed. *Verification and SALT: The Challenge of Strategic Deception*. Boulder, Colo.: Westview Press, 1980.

Seaborg, Glenn T., et al. *Kennedy, Khrushchev and the Test Ban*. Berkeley: University of California Press, 1981.

Sherr, Alan B. *The Other Side of Arms Control: Soviet Objectives in the Gorbachev Era*. Boston: Unwin Hyman, 1988.

Sherr, James. *Soviet Power: The Continuing Challenge*. Basingstoke: Macmillan, 1987.

Sivachev, Nikolai, and Nikolai Yakovlev. *Russia and the United States*. Chicago: The University of Chicago Press, 1979.

Smith, Gerard. *Doubletalk: The Story of the First Strategic Arms*

Limitation Talks. Garden City, N.Y.: Doubleday, 1980.

Smith, Raymond F. *Negotiating with the Soviets.* Bloomington: Indiana University Press, 1989.

Talbott, Strobe. *Deadly Gambits.* New York: Random House, 1984.

———. *Endgame: The Inside Story of SALT II.* New York: Harper & Row, 1980.

Ulam, Adam B. *The Rivals: America and Russia since World War II.* New York: Viking Press, 1971.

Vance, Cyrus. *Hard Choices: Critical Years in America's Foreign Policy.* New York: Simon and Schuster, 1983.

Wolfe, Thomas W. *The SALT Experience.* Cambridge, Mass.: Ballinger, 1979.

Articles

Azrael, Jeremy R., and Stephen Sestanovich. "Superpower Balancing Acts." *Foreign Affairs* (Fall 1986): 479-498.

Bertram, Christoph. "The German Question." *Foreign Affairs* (Spring 1990): 45-62.

Blight, James G., et al. "The Cuban Missile Crisis Revisited." *Foreign Affairs* (Fall 1987): 170-188.

Brzezinski, Zbigniew. "The U.S.-Soviet Relationship: Paradoxes and Prospects." *Strategic Review* (Spring 1987): 11-18.

Bundy, McGeorge. "From Cold War toward Trusting Peace." *Foreign Affairs* (America and the World 1989-1990): 51-69.

Chase, James. "A New Grand Strategy." *Foreign Policy* (Spring 1988): 3-25.

Cooper, Mary H. "Soviet Trade: In America's Best Interest?" *Editorial Research Reports,* February 10, 1989, 74-87.

Gaddis, John Lewis. "The Long Peace: Elements of Stability in the Postwar International System." *International Security* (Spring 1986): 99-142.

Haley, P. Edward. "You Could Have Said Yes: Lessons from Reykjavik." *Orbis* (Spring 1987): 75-98.

Horelick, Arnold L. "U.S.-Soviet Relations: The Threshold of a New Era." *Foreign Affairs* (America and the World 1989-1990): 51-69.

Husband, William B. "Soviet Perspectives of U.S. 'Positions-of-Strength' Diplomacy in the 1970s." *World Politics* (July 1979): 495-517.

Hyland, William G. "U.S.-Soviet Relations: The Long Road Back." *Foreign Affairs* (America and the World 1981): 525-550.

Kennan, George F. "Containment Then and Now." *Foreign Affairs* (Spring 1987): 885-890.

Larrabee, F. Stephen, and Allen Lynch. "Gorbachev: The Road to Reykjavik." *Foreign Policy* (Winter 1986-1987): 3-28.

Marantz, Paul. "Soviet 'New Thinking' and East-West Relations." *Current History* (October 1988): 309-312.

May, Michael, et al. "Strategic Arsenals after START: The Implications of Deep Cuts." *International Security* (Summer 1988): 90-133.

Rogov, Sergey M. "Detente Is Not Enough." *Foreign Policy* (Spring 1989): 86-102.

Rose, Francois de. "NATO and Nuclear Weapons." *Strategic Review* (Fall 1987): 27-35.

Schlesinger, Arthur M., Jr. "Origins of the Cold War." *Foreign Affairs* (Fall 1967): 22-52.

Seabury, Paul, and Brian Thomas. "Cold War Origins." *Journal of Contemporary History* (January 1968): 169-198.

Sempa, Francis P. "Geopolitics and American Strategy: A Reassessment." *Strategic Review* (Spring 1987): 27-38.

Sharp, Jane M. O. "After Reykjavik: Arms Control and the Allies." *International Affairs* (Spring 1987): 239-257.

Slater, Jerome. "The Eleventh Hour of the Cuban Missile Crisis." *International Security* (Winter 1987-1988): 5-92.

General Readings

Bialer, Seweryn. *The Soviet Paradox: External Expansion, Internal Decline.* New York: A. A. Knopf, 1986.

Black, Cyril Edwin. *Understanding Soviet Politics: The Perspective of Russian History.* Boulder, Colo.: Westview Press, 1986.

Current Digest of the Soviet Press. Weekly compilation of translated Soviet articles; since 1949.

Dmytryshyn, Basil. *USSR: A Concise History.* 4th ed. New York: Charles Scribner's Sons, 1984.

Foreign Broadcast Information Service. *Daily Report: Soviet Union.*

Haupt, Georges, and Jean-Jaques Marie. *Makers of the Russian Revolution: Biographies of Soviet Leaders.* Ithaca, N.Y.: Cornell University Press, 1974.

Hoffmann, Erik P., ed. *The Soviet Union in the 1980s.* New York: The Academy of Political Science, 1984.

Kanet, Roger E., ed. *The Behavioral Revolution and Communist Studies.* New York: Free Press, 1971.

Medish, Vadim. *The Soviet Union.* 2d ed. Englewood Cliffs, N.J.: Prentice-Hall, 1985.

Rahr, Alexander G. *A Biographic Directory of 100 Leading Soviet Officials.* 4th ed. Washington, D.C.: Radio Free Europe/Radio Liberty, 1989.

Scholar's Guide for Washington, D.C., Russian/Soviet Studies. 2d rev. ed. Washington, D.C.: Smithsonian Institution Press, 1983.

Thompson, John M. *Russia and the Soviet Union: An Historical Introduction.* New York: Charles Scribner's Sons, 1986.

Ulam, Adam B. *A History of Soviet Russia.* New York: Praeger Publishers, 1976.

Utechin, S. V. *A Concise Encyclopaedia of Russia.* New York: E. P. Dutton & Co., 1964.

Index

352   Index